A COMPLETE HISTORY OF
WORLD CUP
CRICKET
1975–1999

A COMPLETE HISTORY OF
WORLD CUP CRICKET
1975–1999

Mark Browning

Kangaroo Press

In memory of Douglas James Browning

Acknowledgements

I would like to acknowledge the assistance of the following people in the compilation of this book. I am grateful to Bob Simpson for kindly providing an apt and entertaining foreword and his assistance in answering my inquiries about the 1987, 1992 and 1996 World Cup campaigns. My thanks also to Rick McCosker, Doug Walters, Bob Taylor, Mike Veletta and Asanka Gurusinha for their recollections of World Cup Finals. Ken Piesse, Kersi Meher-Homji, Rick Smith and Roger Page also provided some crucial assistance.

I am especially grateful to Ben Browning for his efforts in compiling the statistical section and Carl Harrison-Ford for encouragement and vigilance in examination and correction of the manuscript.

A COMPLETE HISTORY OF WORLD CUP CRICKET

First published in Australia in 1999 by Kangaroo Press
an imprint of Simon & Schuster (Australia) Pty Limited
20 Barcoo Street, East Roseville NSW 2069

A Viacom Company
Sydney New York London Toronto Tokyo Singapore

© Mark Browning, 1999

National Library of Australia
Cataloguing-in-Publication data

Browning, Mark, 1957– .
  A complete history of World Cup cricket

  Bibliography.
  Includes index.
  ISBN 0 7318 0833 9.

  1. World Cup (Cricket)—History. 2. Cricket—Tournaments
  —History. I. Title

796.35865

Cover design by Anna Soo
Typeset by Midland Typesetters, Maryborough, Victoria
Set in 10/12 pt Times
Printed by Australian Print Group, Maryborough, Victoria
10 9 8 7 6 5 4 3 2

Foreword

In the late 1950s I was honoured to be invited to go on tour with the Rothman's Cavaliers. The late Ron Roberts, a respected freelance English journalist, had come up with the concept of using recently retired 'greats' and linking them with promising youngsters to tour cricketing countries that were not receiving many international tours at the time. The tours were great fun and we visited South Africa, the then Rhodesia, Kenya, Hong Kong, New Zealand, India, Pakistan, Singapore and the West Indies.

The Cavaliers' tours were also enormously popular, as they should have been with the personnel involved. On my first trip I had Denis Compton, Godfrey Evans, Fred Trueman, Colin Ingleby-Mackenzie, Frank Tyson, Richie Benaud, Norm O'Neill and Gary Sobers as some of my team-mates. I still remember the first words spoken to me by Denis Compton: 'Remember, young Simpson, your job is to score runs on this tour and my job is to teach you how to enjoy touring.'

After a couple of years Roberts and Bagenal Harvey, at the time one of the first player-managers, got together to try and reproduce a similar format in England and came up with a concept for BBC 2. The fledgling TV channel was keen to telecast two hours of cricket on Sunday afternoons and wanted the cricket to produce a result while they were on the air.

The concept that was sold to them was that the Cavaliers would stage games for county players who were enjoying a benefit year, and they would play on a limited-overs basis. The games were to be 40 overs per side and would take two hours per innings. In those days teams easily got through 20 overs per hour. How things have changed.

The second innings was televised and one-day cricket was born. It became immediately successful, with crowds of up to 20,000 in attendance. The matches had the blessing of the Marylebone Criket Club (MCC) for the first few years, but when they became too successful the MCC decided to begin a Sunday limited-over county competition of their own. They didn't ban the Cavaliers, but they wouldn't allow any of their county players to compete in other televised games!

From this single competition one-day cricket was introduced to the world and finally a World Cup was instigated.

The early World Cups were dominated by the great West Indian teams of the '70s. The limited-overs game was played with a little more urgency, but very few other differences from the longer form of the game. It wasn't until India surprised the West Indies in the final of the 1983 World Cup, with their well-controlled swing bowlers who changed their pace brilliantly to deceive the hard-hitting West Indian batsmen and won the final, that anything different was tried.

Four years later Australia stunned the cricketing world, but not themselves, by comfortably winning the fourth World Cup with a well-planned and professional approach to the game. New tactics were introduced with the guile of Simon O'Donnell and Steve Waugh who confounded all the batsmen with their mixture of fast-medium and change-of-pace leg spinners.

Australia were a busy and controlled batting team. They rarely missed an extra run between wickets, kept their wickets in hand for a final onslaught and were seldom panicked. Their fielding was superb and they brought a new intensity and standard of physical fitness to the one-day game.

The first-ever World Cup on the subcontinent

also saw spinners come into their own in limited-overs cricket. Previously they were generally restricted to bowling fast darts, designed to restrict the batsmen rather than get them out. Australia's innovative approach and desire always to bowl the opposition out and not just restrict them set the pattern for the future.

Pakistan's bowlers, brilliantly led by Imran Khan and Wasim Akram, were too good for the opposition in the semi-final and final of the 1992 World Cup in Australasia and Sri Lanka's innovative batting on the subcontinent in 1996 changed the one-day scene again. Then, after nearly four years of trying to copy the Sri Lankan batting frenzy approach without success,

Australia returned to the style that had gained them so much success in the late '80s and into the '90s and won a resounding victory in the 1999 final at Lord's.

One-day cricket has gone from the poor relation to Test cricket until it is now the most important factor in the game. It brings people to the cricket and provides the money to support and promote the game on a worldwide basis.

It is fitting that Mark Browning should honour the pinnacle of the one-day game and his excellent book will fill a void in the history and appreciation of this exciting form of cricket.

Bob Simpson

Contents

1

Something Had To Be Done

When Frank Woolley dismissed the last Australian batsman at The Oval on 22 August 1912, everyone breathed a collective sigh of relief. Even Woolley, who had a brilliant match, taking 10–49 with his left-arm spinners, would have been grateful that the sodden, ill-fated Triangular Tournament had finally been laid to rest. The sinking of the *Titanic* was the greatest disaster of 1912, but this bad-tempered, poorly attended first attempt at a cricket world cup came a close second.

Even today the suggestion by the Imperial Cricket Conference of 1909 that Test matches should be regulated by a regular program of tours, including a four-yearly triangular tournament between Australia, England and South Africa, seems meritorious. The prospect of a World Test Championship is growing by the day and although it is still at the embryonic stage it is generating plenty of passionate discussion at official and unofficial levels. However, everything conspired against that first brave attempt and instead of an epoch-making occasion it is remembered as one of cricket's greatest failures.

When the idea was conceived Australia and South Africa were both worthy adversaries of the English team. The idea of three Test teams doing battle in one English summer had first been mooted by Sir Abe Bailey, who by his encouragement and money had already done a great deal to get South Africa up and running as a competitive Test nation. By 1912, though, their playing strength had, temporarily at least, waned badly.

The Australians were more doubtful of the worth of the enterprise. They knocked back the original proposal for the tournament to be held in 1909 on the grounds that a traditional Ashes tour of England would be more profitable to all

concerned, particularly the Australians. This upset the English counties, who favoured the concept, and put the tour by Monty Noble's Australians at risk. It took a letter to *The Times* by F.S. (later Sir Stanley) Jackson to placate everybody.

Eventually the Australians had a successful tour in 1909, but three years later Australian cricket was plagued by internal strife. The players demanded that they be allowed to choose their manager for the trip as they had in the past. The board, unhappy with the players' man, Frank Laver, wanted to make their own choice. Their appointment of G.S. Crouch meant that six of Australia's best players—Clem Hill, Warwick Armstrong, Hanson Carter, Vernon Ransford, Albert Cotter and, saddest of all, Victor Trumper—did not make the trip to England. A number of their replacements were hardly great ambassadors. There were reports of 'unpleasantness' and the tourists behaved so badly that they were 'socially ostracised'. Despite the latter-day efforts of the likes of Rod Marsh, Doug Walters and David Boon, Syd Gregory's side still probably holds the record for alcoholic consumption on an Australian tour of England.

Perhaps they were overwhelmed by the English team that confronted them. It contained the bulk of the side that had just returned from a triumphant tour of Australia. In addition to the all-round skills of Woolley, the hosts boasted names like Jack Hobbs, Wilfred Rhodes, Charles Fry, Frank Foster and Syd Barnes.

It rained and rained in 1912. Australia vs South Africa without a lot of stars was already a doubtful attraction. Most Mancunians found it an even more unappetising prospect when Old Trafford remained cold, grey and damp throughout late May. Forty-four thousand attended the four days of the Oval Test, the third of the series between England and Australia and, being the decider, the first to be scheduled to be played to a finish, but overall lots of money was lost that terrible summer. *Wisden* said, 'Such a combination of adverse conditions could not be imagined'. A second triangular tournament was originally scheduled for 1916. However, the failure of the first one and an intrusive event called the Great War ensured that it did not occur. There was no thought of another cricket world cup for 60 years.

Former English captain Ted Dexter has always been considered something of a semi-eccentric character. He is full of ideas. Some have had merit; others could often be dismissed as fanciful. His early 1969 prediction that 'one-day Test matches' were 'just around the corner' seemed to fit into the latter category, but within two years his crystal-ball gazing proved to be accurate. At the MCG on 5 January 1971, as a substitute for the abandoned Third Test between Australia and England, 46,000 spectators watched an International match restricted to 40 eight-ball overs per side.

In an instant Test cricket, the pride of the Commonwealth's summer game, had a fresh-faced, exciting and very marketable competitor. The sun shone warmly that day and the crowd loved the energetic approach of the players. They in turn relished the opportunity for some exercise after they had been cooped up inside a damp dressing-room watching the rain fall for several days. In addition, the happy patrons saw a result, and it was the one most of them wanted; a win to Australia.

Although Dexter's one-day Test call had been dismissed by traditionalists as extremist rubbish, it had as its basis the fact that at that time first-class and Test cricket was at a low ebb as a sporting attraction. Following the postwar boom period of the late 1940s and early 1950s, crowds at first-class and Test matches in both England and Australia had begun to decrease alarmingly. Many economic and social factors contributed to this, but the game did not help itself in either country when the Ashes contests, for so long the showpiece of world cricket, turned into series after series of grinding attritional matches relished by the devotee, but hardly anyone else.

As the money coming in each season dwindled, the game's authorities started to look for ways to regain the lost ground. From committees were formed subcommittees, which discussed and researched this and that and forwarded proposals. These proposals were further debated back at full committee level and usually, whatever their merits, thrown out at some stage or so watered down as to be rendered useless by the notoriously conservative cricket establishment in both Australia and England. So the problem of falling attendances continued.

As early as 1944 there had been a recommendation by an MCC Committee headed by the famous Yorkshireman and former England captain, Sir Stanley Jackson, that upon the resumption of postwar cricket, a county knockout competition be established along the lines of the fabulously successful Football Association (FA) Cup. Much of the cricket played during the Second World War was by necessity of the one-day variety, although the proposal put forward by Jackson's committee was for a tournament of three-day matches. Their suggestion was temporarily shelved because of the talk of a possible government ban on mid-week sport to help lift the country's industrial productivity.

By 1956, attendances at English county matches were half those of 1947. They continued to decline. Another committee, led by the respected Harry Altham, again recommended a county knockout cup. This time it was suggested the games be in a one-day format. In 1961, when hardly anybody was watching county championship cricket, the concept was finally accepted. A sponsored cup competition was to be fitted into a reduced first-class program. The number of overs per side was to be restricted to 65 per innings.

So in 1963 the Gillette Cup began. It was an immediate success. Sussex, who had never won the County Championship, took the first title. Their captain was Ted Dexter. Lord's filled for the final and has done so on each succeeding year. The matches also created a lot of interest through the various knockout rounds. Once the

Gillette Cup was established as a moneymaker the amount of one-day county cricket was quickly expanded. The John Player Sunday League started in 1969 and another tournament, the zonal-based Benson and Hedges Cup, increased the chances of sides winning some sort of silverware even further in 1972.

In Australia by the end of the 1960s there had been limited-overs matches at club level. The prospects for a financially productive summer in 1969–70 were not good. The Test team was away on what proved to be a near impossible twin tour assignment in India and South Africa. Attendances during the visits by India in 1967–68 and in 1968–69 by the West Indies had been modest. A knockout cup, to include all the Sheffield Shield playing states plus Tasmania and New Zealand, was inaugurated. Vehicle and General were the sponsors and each innings was to be restricted to 40 eight-ball overs per innings. Richie Benaud was the public relations director. New Zealand, to the relief of a nation with Test match status, won a lacklustre first final. The competition, without New Zealand and under the latest of several different sponsors, continues to this day.

South Africa, soon to be totally ostracised from official international cricket, also began their domestic limited-overs competition in 1969–70. It was another Gillette Cup and was restricted to 60 six-ball overs per innings. Gillette in England eventually dropped their sponsorship in 1980 because their name was becoming publicly associated more with a limited-over cricket final than with shaving. The razor blade company handed out sponsorship cash again when the West Indies started their inter-island limited-over competition in 1976. This immediately went to a 50 over per side format. Indian spectators got their first taste of limited-overs cricket in 1973. The Deodhar Trophy was a 60 overs per side zonal competition. The Wills Trophy got under way in Pakistan in 1980–81, nine years later than New Zealand who even before they had pulled out of the Australian competition had started their own inter-provincial tournament in 1971–72.

Limited-Over Internationals were well estab-

lished before one-day cricket was embraced domestically in Pakistan and the West Indies. However, cricket administrators around the world were still reluctant to undermine the authority of first-class cricket with the shortened game. They have long been criticised for this and in some ways, mostly for economic reasons and player treatment, this is justified. By the same token Test and first-class cricket is still seen by the cricket purist and the majority of the players both at club and first-class level as the superior form of the game. In most respects they are right. It will never be abandoned casually.

Despite the apparent success of the fill-in match now recognised as the first Limited-Overs International in Melbourne in January 1971, the next recognised Limited-Over International was not played until August 1972. That match at the MCG was not a totally isolated event, though. When England were making short work of India and South Africa in 1959 and 1960, players were made to fill in the rest of the day after an early finish with a limited-overs exhibition match. No-one enjoyed these empty contests and it was during one such exhibition game that Sid Buller no-balled South African Geoff Griffin out of cricket for throwing.

The Australian authorities were not totally blind to the success of the one-off game against England. When the South African tour of 1971–72 was replaced by a Rest of the World side they sprinkled the program with one-day games. A few were originally scheduled, others were fitted in to fill days in the same way they had been in England a decade before. One limited-overs match in Melbourne was finished so quickly a second 15 overs per side slog was scheduled on the same afternoon!

The Prudential Assurance Company sponsored the little festival of games at the conclusion of the Test series in England in 1972, 1973 and 1974. It was the women cricketers who first revived the idea of a world cup, however. The most significant female innovation to the game since the introduction of round-arm bowling was largely funded by the players themselves. Teams from Trinidad and Tobago and Jamaica received government assistance and a benefactor named

Jack Hayward put in some money, but then as now, the women proved to be wonderfully resourceful.

The tournament was played all over England in June and July 1973. Australia and England dominated and then contested the final at Edgbaston on 28 July. A fine century by Enid Bakewell led the home side to a comfortable 92-run victory. To date the English men have never been able to emulate the success of their female counterparts.

Two days before the women's final, the International Cricket Conference at their annual meeting at Lord's approved a plan put forward by the Test and County Cricket Board that a 60 overs a side tournament involving all current Test playing sides be played in England in 1975. The competition was to be organised around a round robin between two sets of four sides, followed by two semi-finals and a final at Lord's. Unlike the women, there was never any doubt the men would be able to play their first World Cup final at the home of cricket.

The tournament would cost £100,000 to run over a two-week period. A sponsor was sought to cover the expenses. Prudential again came forward. The ICC and certain renowned scribes like E.W. Swanton did not want the tournament to be called the World Cup. This was a fall back to the status of the one-day game against Test matches. In the 1976 *Wisden* it was called The

Prudential Cup. But everywhere else it was accepted in common parlance as, indeed, the World Cup. South Africa were scheduled to tour England that year, but in 1975 the government of that country remained intransigent in its policy of apartheid and there was never a chance they would be allowed to visit. With no South African tour, English cricket officials were unsure of the likely public support of their program. So as an added insurance Australia were invited to stay on after the World Cup to play a four-Test Ashes series.

South Africa's exclusion meant two extra teams had to be found to raise the number of competitors to eight. Sri Lanka, soon to be the eighth Test-playing nation, were an obvious choice, while East Africa literally and figuratively made up the numbers. England and Australia were placed in separate groups. This was another indication of the uncertainty surrounding the venture. A semi-final or even final clash between the traditional rivals would be likely from such a draw. That might be needed to compensate for the lack of interest in games like East Africa vs India and Pakistan vs Sri Lanka. Three days were to be set aside for each game. That was wise. They would be played in England in June and nobody wanted a repeat of the fiasco of 1912. Another failed World Cup might have seen the concept disappear forever.

2

The First Prudential World Cup:
The Glory of 1975

If the 1912 Triangular Tournament was doomed from the outset, the 1975 Prudential Cup was equally blessed. When the authorities set aside three days for each of the 60 overs per side matches they were not being overly pessimistic. May and June of 1972 had been diabolically wet; 1973 cold, grey and damp; and in 1974 everyone got soaked. Days before the tournament got under way there was frost, snow and washouts. Yet every one of the games in the 1975 World Cup was completed in a day and they were all, for the most part, played in the most glorious sunshine imaginable.

The winners of the Prudential Cup would split £9000 between them. The runners-up £2000 and the semi-finalists would pocket £1000 each. In addition, each game would have a Man of the Match award, the winner to receive £50 in the first-round games, £100 in the semi-finals and £200 for the Man of the Match in the final. Radio and newspaper commentator Henry Blofeld, having witnessed the recent Ashes Test series, imagined the pace bowling of Lillee and Thomson would be irresistible and made Australia outright favourites. Former England spinner and esteemed television commentator Jim Laker believed England would win every one of their matches, including the final. John Arlott was far less confident. Betting agency Ladbrokes had the West Indies at 9–4 official favourites, with England second at 11–4. Pakistan were third and Australia fourth. A punter could get 1500–1 on East Africa winning the tournament. There is no evidence that Rod Marsh or Dennis Lillee wagered any money on the team whose manager is alleged to have said that his

side were in England, 'To enjoy our cricket and drink plenty of booze'.

Although there was fear of the unknown, the cricketing prospects were really quite tantalising. England were not long returned from Australia where they received a hiding from Ian Chappell's aggressive, slightly rough-edged but immensely talented side. The cornerstone of their success was the fast-bowling duo of Dennis Lillee and Jeff Thomson. Bristling with intimidating intent, they had cut a bruising swathe through the touring Englishmen. They were trumped up as long-haired anti-heroes. Cricketers for the new era, they arrived in England to a media response befitting pop stars.

Their experience of local conditions, the draw, and all the limited-overs cricket played in the three county competitions seemed likely to be to the advantage of the English side. Most of the West Indians also played county cricket so they were similarly advantaged. Indeed their captain Clive Lloyd had already made one-day Lord's finals something of his speciality, his 126 for Lancashire against Warwickshire in the 1972 Gillette Cup final being a typically thrilling knock.

Lloyd brought a West Indian side to the World Cup that was just coming out of a period of transition. The majority of the old guard from the successful teams of the 1960s were gone. Garry Sobers had originally been selected in the squad of 14. Sadly, the 38-year-old champion all-rounder had to withdraw with a groin injury. The first World Cup might have been a fitting swan-song to a fantastic career. But Sobers had played his last international match. Lloyd had taken over the captaincy from Rohan Kanhai for the tour of India, Sri Lanka and Pakistan from November 1974 to March 1975. Included in that party were several newcomers. Among them were Gordon Greenidge, Viv Richards and Andy Roberts.

In Roberts, Lloyd had a fast bowler fit to challenge Lillee and Thomson for speed and aggression. He was another West Indian figure familiar to English cricket followers. In the 1974 County Championship he had taken 111 wickets for Hampshire at an outstanding average of 13.45. Roberts gained a reputation as a cold, unsmiling assassin. At Basingstoke he had felled 41-year-old Colin Cowdrey with a vicious bouncer. Soon after, despite the fact that his arm was always ramrod straight, accusations were made in the English tabloid press that Roberts threw. They soon died a natural death.

Equally exciting was the West Indian batting line-up. Their array of strokeplayers, three of them left-handers, as much as anything made them favourites with the punters. Roy Fredericks and Gordon Greenidge formed a powerful opening partnership. Alvin Kallicharran at the time was rated not far short of being the best batsman in the world, his Test average being 57. Sobers' replacement, another veteran from the previous era, Kanhai, had lost none of his steely wristed timing and Lloyd himself had a fantastic tour of the subcontinent, gorging himself on the local spinners with his long reach and awesomely heavy bat. At number six in the order came the young Viv Richards, oozing still largely untapped potential.

With a large expatriate West Indian contingent in the country they would prove to be almost as big a drawcard as England. Indeed the match between the West Indies and Australia, scheduled for The Oval on Saturday 14 June was sold out prior to the commencement of the tournament.

England's greatest advantage, after their one-day county experiences, was seen to be the support of the crowds. That had helped the soccer team of 1966 secure their famous victory at Wembley. It was believed the cricketers might also benefit. A similar thought has pervaded the thinking before each succeeding World Cup. As yet, however, the home side has never taken out the trophy.

The pressure on the captaincy of Mike Denness had been intense since his appointment at the end of 1973. But he was not blamed for the hammering England had received in Australia and had scored 188, 181 and 59 not out in his last three Test innings, allowing him to cling onto the job. Early in the season classy Yorkshire opening batsman Geoff Boycott announced he would continue his controversial self-imposed exile from the England team. He preferred to score his runs for 'his' Yorkshire and Barnsley. At the time it was suggested Boycott might be trying to avoid having to face the extreme pace of the likes of Lillee, Thomson and Roberts. That was in fact not the case. Rather, he was dissatisfied with playing under a captain he did not consider worthy of a Test place. However, the other English problem child, veteran fast bowler John Snow, was set to return. Denness had wanted him in his side all along, but had not been able to sway the selectors. Despite being 34, Snow was still considered the best fast bowler in the country.

England's squad had a solid look, and it was expected that the likes of Keith Fletcher and Dennis Amiss would find runs easier to come by in the one-day environment than they had in the boiling cauldrons of the Australian Test match grounds. In the tall South African, Tony Greig, the home side had an all-rounder the equal of any in the world, while their seamers like Geoff Arnold and Chris Old could be a handful in cloudy conditions on green wickets.

Bushy haired, moustachioed and brash, the Australians almost had a pre-punk image in their disdain of certain conventions. They arrived having re-established their position at the top of the Test match tree. Ian Chappell led a side that had restored the popularity of cricket in Australia. In addition to Lillee and Thomson, they had a fine batting side led by the fighting capabilities of the captain, the stylish authority of his brother Greg, and the enigmatic brilliance of Doug Walters.

It was believed big strong inswing bowler Max Walker would relish the wickets in England, while the belligerent left-handed batting of wicketkeeper Rod Marsh in the middle order could be a key to the chances of Australian success. However, Australia missed the stability of Ian Redpath's solid technique at the top of the order. Like Boycott, he had withdrawn his services. One of the least outspoken players in the game's history, no-one questioned his right to stay at home in Geelong to ensure the success of his antique shop.

Ian Chappell said that the main objective of his side was to retain the recently hard won Ashes later in the summer, but that they would fight all the way to win the Cup.

Pakistan, as ever, were the wild card of the tournament. They had been unbeaten on their 1974 tour of England and had made short work of the home side in two Limited-Over Internationals. But they were in the hard side of the draw and had to overcome Australia and the West Indies to reach the semi-finals. Laden with quality batting and valuable all-rounders, their temperament at crucial times might be called into question if things got tight.

Nevertheless, their team boasted a fine array of talent. The strokeplay of Asif Iqbal, Zaheer Abbas, Majid Khan and the Mohammad brothers, Sadiq and Mushtaq, was the equal of any. Their bowling attack was less impressive, but in Imran Khan and Javed Miandad Pakistan could point to some unparalleled junior talent. Asif Iqbal had just replaced Intikhab Alam as captain, but his fitness did not see him through the tournament. Majid took over the reins. Both those players were stood aside and Mushtaq was the new man in charge by the time New Zealand arrived in Pakistan in October the following year. Some things in cricket never change.

Despite their Test match status, neither India nor New Zealand was thought to have the depth of ability to go all the way and win the Prudential Cup. India had bowed to the philosophy that spinners made little impact in the shortened game and filled their team with medium pacers who could bat a bit. Eknath Solkar, Abid Ali, Mohinder Amarnath, Madan Lal and Karsan Ghavri were thought unlikely to keep the best sides to a losing score. Gundappa Viswanath,

Farokh Engineer and Sunil Gavaskar led the batting capably, but India's batting was notably unreliable and in contrast to Pakistan they had been annihilated in England the previous year.

New Zealand's batting was built around their prolific opener and captain Glenn Turner. Another player with extensive experience in English county cricket, Turner had been turned from a strokeless wonder into a stylish shot maker by the need to adapt his game to the more urgent demands of limited-overs cricket. He had reliable run-making support in Brian Hastings, John Morrison and Worcestershire team-mate, John Parker. Dayle Hadlee, Richard Collinge and Hedley Howarth were all to be respected rather than feared. Dayle's younger brother, Richard, was raw, but it was thought he might make a reasonable bowler of international standard at some stage, too. The unavailability of the likes of Mark Burgess, Vic Pollard, Bevan Congdon and Bruce Taylor told against a team already struggling to find enough quality players from their small population base.

Outside the Indian subcontinent, little was known about the Sri Lankan side. The country had only had its new name for three years. The majority of the names of the players had a fairly new ring to them, too. But some like Sunil Wettimuny, young Duleep Mendis and leg-spinner Somachandra de Silva would eventually be able to look back at the 1975 World Cup as the moment when their country launched them onto the road of full international recognition. That recognition reached fruition when they and their nation made their simultaneous Test debut in February 1982.

If little was known of the Sri Lankans, virtually none of the players from Kenya, Zambia, Tanzania and Uganda had been heard of in the wider cricketing community. The only players from the region with first-class experience, Basharat Hassan of Nottinghamshire and John Solanky of Glamorgan, were left out in favour of locally based players. Don Pringle, a landscape consultant from Kenya and already 42 years old, was father of future England Test cricketer, Derek, but that was hardly a cause for renown in 1975. Like Hassan and Solanky, he had at one point been offered the chance to play county cricket. Wicketkeeper Hamish McLeod, a Slazenger representative from Zambia, stood out on the team sheet because he did not have a very East African name. That was almost the extent of it. They played mostly one-day cricket but were still lambs to the slaughter.

One thing that would help them was an ICC ruling that any bouncer that passed over the head of the batsman would be called a wide and that non-recognised batsmen were not to be submitted to facing such deliveries. Lillee and Thomson were not impressed. Andy Roberts called the ruling 'Ridiculous'.

The sides did not arrive en masse at Heathrow. A number of New Zealanders, Pakistanis and West Indians were already involved with county cricket. The 10 remaining Kiwis touched down on 27 May, the Australians two days later following a short stopover in Canada where they suffered a surprising defeat. The following day the three West Indians not on county contracts landed.

All teams tried to acclimatise with practice matches against various county sides and amongst themselves. Such was the interest in the Australians that 15,000 attended one such game against Middlesex at Lord's, much to the delight of the club's beneficiary, stalwart wicketkeeper John Murray.

On Friday 6 June all eight sides met the Queen at Buckingham Palace. They were also greeted by Prince Philip, Prince Charles and Sir Alec Douglas-Home. Then it was down Park Lane and Baker Street, past Hyde Park and Sherlock Holmes and Madame Tussaud's territory, along Park Road, left into St John's Wood Road to the Grace Gates of Lord's cricket ground. There, the players mingled with each other, numerous cricket officials and Prince Philip, who had followed them. A sense of excitement, nervousness and anticipation prevailed during the luncheon. Ties were loosened, the sun was out and the weather was warm. Lord's under blue skies is at its grandest and Saturday 7 June was D-Day for the 112 cricketers playing in the first World Cup.

SATURDAY 7 JUNE 1975
THE PRUDENTIAL CUP: ROUND ONE
GROUP A: ENGLAND VS INDIA
LORD'S: ENGLAND WON BY 202 RUNS

The best and worst features of limited-overs cricket were evident in this showcase game on the first day of the Prudential Cup. After England, led by Dennis Amiss, had pulverised India's array of tame medium pacers to the tune of 4–334 in their 60 overs India admitted immediate defeat and crawled their way to 3–132 in reply, also off 60 overs. A cursory glance at the scoreboard would suggest interference from rain. Instead, as Tony Lewis called it, India's batting was a display of 'senseless perversity'. Richie Benaud's critique amounted to 'One of the most astonishing games of limited-overs cricket I've ever seen'.

The 16,274 spectators who paid £19,000, basked in the early-afternoon warmth of English batsmen scoring at will against inadequate bowling. It was far closer to their cricketing ideal than watching them dodging the firepower of Lillee and Thomson. Amiss relished the downgrading of the physical threat more than anyone as he unleashed his fluent array of off-side strokes. He raced to his 50 in 66 balls, promptly hit Mohinder Amarnath for three fours in three balls between third man and cover point, then went on to his century in 112 deliveries.

He lost his opening partner, the recalled John Jameson, when the score was 54 but then added 176 for the second wicket with Keith Fletcher. At the time such things meant nothing, but 24 years later this stand remains the best for the second wicket in the World Cup. Amiss was 98 out of 1–150 at lunch and by the time he was bowled for 137, slogging at Madan Lal in the 51st over with the total on 245, he had hit 18 sumptuous boundaries.

Fletcher had already been dismissed for 68 in the same way and Tony Greig went cheaply, giving Abid Ali's figures a modicum of respectability. But that only unleashed the batting mayhem of a Chris Old—Mike Denness partnership which yielded 89 runs in 10 overs, including 63 in the last five. Old, picked for his bowling, belted 51 in 28 balls. A couple of his best smites went for six, one over the short Mound Stand boundary, the other straight to the Nursery End sightscreen. Fletcher, accelerating as his innings progressed, and Denness had also made good use of that inviting short boundary, depositing the ball once each among the spectators.

Feast was followed by famine and the chief culprit was Sunil Gavaskar, who carried his bat throughout the innings for 36. He faced 174 balls and kept everyone out on the ground until 7.30 pm. No-one was really sure why. Tony Lewis suggested it might have been a protest at the omission of Bishen Bedi from the team. The actions, or in this case inactions, of Gavaskar himself invited plenty of protests. Demonstrators continually ran on to the ground imploring their countrymen to play some shots. One Indian supporter became so irate he punched two policemen and was sentenced to six months gaol.

Those who weren't protesting were either drinking themselves into a stupor or quietly dozing off in the afternoon sunshine.

Neither the Indian manager, Gulabrai Ramchand, nor his captain, Srinivas Venkataraghavan could offer a reason for Gavaskar's approach. It probably did not make any difference to the result of this match, but it massacred India's run rate which meant that on the first day of competition they had severely reduced their chances of reaching the semi-finals.

The man who went on to become the game's greatest century maker in Test cricket later said he was just completely and utterly out of form. He couldn't even get out when he tried and considered standing aside and letting a straight ball bowl him. In his defence, he was dropped a couple of times. Also, Gavaskar in 1975 was not yet the confident and complete player he would later become. Since his astonishing debut series in the Caribbean in 1971 the 26-year-old opener had made just one more Test hundred in 13 Tests. Nevertheless, this was a bizarre performance. Ramchand admitted to being disappointed but he said it would not lead to disciplinary action against Gavaskar.

ENGLAND

J.A. Jameson c Venkat b Amarnath	21
D.L. Amiss b Madan Lal	137
K.W.R. Fletcher b Abid Ali	68
A.W. Greig lbw Abid Ali	4
M.H. Denness (capt) not out	37
C.M. Old not out	51
Extras (lb 12, w 2, nb 2).	16
(60 overs)	4–334

Did not bat: B. Wood, A.P.E. Knott (wk), J.A. Snow, P. Lever, G.G. Arnold

1/54 2/230 3/237 4/245

Bowling: Madan Lal 12-1-64-1; Amarnath 12-2-60-1; Abid Ali 12-0-58-2; Ghavri 11-1-83-0; Venkataraghavan 12-0-41-0; Solkar 1-0-12-0

INDIA

S.M. Gavaskar not out	36
E.D. Solkar c Lever b Arnold	8
A.D. Gaekwad c Knott b Lever	22
G. Viswanath c Fletcher b Old	37
B.P. Patel not out	16
Extras (lb 3, w 1, nb 9)	13
(60 overs)	3–132

Did not bat: M. Amarnath, F.M. Engineer (wk), S. Abid Ali, Madan Lal, S. Venkataraghavan (capt), K. Ghavri

1/21 2/50 3/108

Bowling: Snow 12-2-24-0; Old 12-4-26-1; Greig 9-1-26-0; Lever 10-0-16-1; Jameson 2-1-3-0; Arnold 10-2-20-1; Wood 5-2-4-0

Umpires: D.J. Constant, J.G. Langridge.

Toss: England. Points: England 4, India 0

GROUP A: NEW ZEALAND vs EAST AFRICA
EDGBASTON: NEW ZEALAND WON BY 181 RUNS

The scoreboards of the first two Group A matches look remarkably similar. There was little

surprise, however, at the turn of events at Edgbaston. As most people had suspected, East

Africa were totally out of their depth against New Zealand. If Amiss' century showed up the inadequacy of the Indian bowling, Glenn Turner was clinical in his destruction of the hopes of the East African combine. He won the toss, batted and then occupied the crease for the duration of the 60 overs, scoring 171 runs in the meantime.

The Edgbaston wicket was on the slow side and it required a period of adjustment from the Kiwi batsman. Turner offered sharp chances at 16 and 27, one to left-arm spinner P.G. Nana who impressed with his control, and another to a slow-moving mid-off fieldsman. New Zealand was 2–145 from 40 overs at lunch and the match remained competitive until John Parker joined his captain and Worcestershire team-mate in a 149-run partnership for the third wicket in 23 overs. They continually pierced the field with strong drives, lifting the run rate almost at will.

Parker was dismissed at 252 but Turner by this time had reached his hundred and was starting to belt the forlorn bowlers to all parts. Two sixes sailed over the mid-wicket boundary in one over. Normally very correct, the New

Zealand opener had struck 16 fours including a series of hoicks and swipes, by the time the innings closed on 5–309. The final 20 overs, had seen the addition of 164 runs.

For the 4000 faithful patrons in the ground the fun was now over. East Africa never challenged the New Zealand total. Their openers looked solid enough and Frasat Ali lasted 39 overs for his 45. He even managed a big straight six off left-arm spinner Hedley Howarth. But Howarth soon had his revenge, young Brian McKechnie, later to face the infamous grubber on the MCG in 1981, scored a direct-hit run-out; and Dayle Hadlee picked up three cheap victims. Mehmood Quraishy and Zulfiqar Ali ensured that the total reached three figures and that the humiliation of not batting out the overs was avoided. Zulfiqar hit a rare boundary and two young boys ran out on to the ground to congratulate him. Unfortunately they went up to Quraishy instead and were then escorted away by the police. In the end East Africa was 20 runs closer to victory than India had been. I don't know if that was any consolation to them.

NEW ZEALAND	
G.M. Turner (capt) not out	171
J.F.M. Morrison c & b Nana	14
G.P. Howarth b Quraishy	20
J.M. Parker c Zulfiqar b Sethi	66
B.F. Hastings c Sethi b Zulfiqar	8
K.J. Wadsworth (wk) b Nagenda	10
R.J. Hadlee not out	6
Extras (b 1, lb 8, w 5)	14
(60 overs)	5–309

Did not bat: B.J. McKechnie, D.R. Hadlee, H.J. Howarth, R.O. Collinge

1/51 2/103 3/252 4/278 5/292

Bowling: Nagenda 9-1-50-1; Nana 12-2-34-1; Zulfiqar 12-0-71-1; Frasat 9-0-50-0; Sethi 10-1-51-1; Quraishy 8-0-39-1

EAST AFRICA	
Frasat Ali st Wadsworth b H.J. Howarth	45
Sam Walusimba b D.R. Hadlee	15
Ramesh Sethi run out	1
Shiraz Sumar b D.R. Hadlee	4
Jawahir Shah c & b H.J. Howarth	5
Harilal, R. Shah (capt) lbw, H.J. Howarth	0
Mehmood Quraishy not out	16
Zulfiqar Ali b D.R. Hadlee	30
H. McLeod (wk) b Collinge	5
P.G. Nana not out	1
Extras (lb 5, nb 1)	6
(60 overs)	8–128

Did not bat: John Nagenda

1/30 2/32 3/36 4/59 5/59 6/84 7/121 8/126

Bowling: Collinge 12-5-23-1; McKechnie 12-2-39-0; H.J. Howarth 12-3-29-3; R.J. Hadlee 12-6-10-0; D.R. Hadlee 12-1-21-3

Umpires: H.D. Bird, A.E. Fagg.

Toss: New Zealand. Points: New Zealand 4, East Africa 0

GROUP B: WEST INDIES vs SRI LANKA
OLD TRAFFORD: WEST INDIES WON BY 9 WICKETS

When the West Indies toured the Indian subcontinent early in 1975, they had played a few

games in Sri Lanka between their Test commitments in India and Pakistan. Then, the locals had given a fairly decent account of themselves. They held Clive Lloyd's side to draws in two three-day representative games, taking a big first-innings lead in the second match. On the neutral territory of Old Trafford in Manchester, though, their resistance against the tournament favourites lasted until just 3.30 in the afternoon.

Sent in to bat by Clive Lloyd on a sunny morning in front of 5000 fans, the Indian batsmen were badly found out by the West Indian pace attack, even though the pitch offered no real assistance. Left-arm swing bowler Bernard Julien began the demolition in the fourth over. Opener/wicketkeeper Edwards Fernando was caught behind and then in the biggest blow of all, captain Anura Tennekoon, who had scored a century against this attack in Colombo, was also dismissed by the Murray/Julien combination with the score still on five. After fewer than 40 overs it was the West Indies' turn to bat. Even the final Sri Lankan total of 86 was only boosted by a last-wicket partnership of 28 between Soma-chandra de Silva and Lalith Kaluperuma. It was fortunate that the last three wickets had doubled the score or the match might have been embar-rassingly completed before lunch. Sri Lanka had

lost three wickets moving from 41 to 42 and had been 9–58 at the break. Sri Lanka's total was the first under 100 in Limited-Over Internationals.

As in the England vs India game, the pitch was occasionally disrupted by demonstrators during the Sri Lankan innings. This time the protests were politically motivated. The pitch invaders might have added to their 'Racist' placards something about the fact that the Sri Lankan batting perform-ance was a setback to their country's plan to receive full recognition by the ICC. Julien and Keith Boyce did the bulk of the damage, but the Sri Lankans showed a lack of technique against all four West Indian fast bowlers. Only from aging off spinner Lance Gibbs were they able to score a few worthwhile runs.

Leg spinner de Silva opened the bowling and claimed the only wicket to fall in the 21 overs the West Indies needed to score the 87 runs they required for victory. He had Roy Fredericks caught at point before Alvin Kallicharran and wicketkeeper Deryck Murray, promoted to opener, completed the formalities. For anyone who wanted to stay, an exhibition match filled in an extra couple of hours following the abbrevi-ated main event.

SRI LANKA

E.R. Fernando (wk) c Murray b Julien	4
B. Warnapura c Murray b Boyce	8
A. Tennekoon (capt) c Murray b Julien	0
P.D. Heyn c Lloyd b Roberts	2
M. Tissera c Kallicharran b Julien	14
D. Mendis c Murray b Boyce	8
A. Ranasinghe b Boyce	0
H.S.M. Peris c Lloyd b Julien	3
M. Opatha b Roberts	11
S. de Silva c Lloyd b Holder	21
L. Kaluperuma not out	6
Extras (b 3, lb 3, nb 3)	9
(37.2 overs)	86

1/5 2/5 3/16 4/21 5/41 6/41 7/42 8/48 9/58

Bowling: Roberts 12–5–16–2; Boyce 8–1–22–3; Holder 1.2–0–2–1; Julien 12–3–20–4; Gibbs 4–0–17–0

WEST INDIES

R.C. Fredericks c Warnapura b de Silva	33
D.L. Murray (wk) not out	30
A.I. Kallicharran not out	19
Extras (b 2, lb 1, w 1, nb 1)	5
(20.4 overs)	1–87

Did not bat: R.B. Kanhai, C.H. Lloyd (capt), I.V.A. Richards, B.D. Julien, K.D. Boyce, V.A. Holder, A.M.E. Roberts, L.R. Gibbs

1/52

Bowling: Opatha 4–0–19–0; de Silva 8–0–33–1; Peris 2–0–13–0; Kaluperuma 6.4–1–17–0

Umpires: W.L. Budd, A. Jepson.

Toss: West Indies. Points: West Indies 4, Sri Lanka 0

GROUP B: AUSTRALIA vs PAKISTAN
HEADINGLEY: AUSTRALIA WON BY 73 RUNS

This game justified its Match of the Day status by the fact that it was a contest between two evenly matched teams. And like a quality Aussie

Rules match it was tight all day until the last quarter, when a champion took the game by the scruff of the neck and carried his side to what, on paper, looked like a comfortable victory.

Headingley was full to capacity when Ian Chappell won the toss and elected to bat. There was some early new-ball movement for Sarfraz Nawaz, Naseer Malik and Asif Masood, but Alan Turner and Rick McCosker, both from New South Wales and both new to English conditions, rode their luck well. Turner, who was surprised at his inclusion ahead of Bruce Laird, in particular hit aggressively to the onside and the pair had put on 63 by the 15th over. The large crowd, mainly made up of local Pakistani immigrants and Yorkshiremen, probably keen to see Australia get beaten, had been relatively restrained until then.

Asif Iqbal, once his country's leading paceman, now just a change bowler, then had Turner caught at square leg. This led to a period of dominance by the Pakistanis and Australia slipped to 4–124. McCosker was becalmed until being caught behind from the last ball before lunch, Ian Chappell was caught deep on the leg side after a couple of fine shots, and Doug Walters' appalling record in England was continued when he was caught at slip for two.

Greg Chappell was also struggling for timing and it took some fine positive batting by Ross Edwards to restore Australia's momentum. The West Australian added 60 with Greg Chappell until the younger Chappell brother was caught trying to hit the ball over cover from the 22-year-old all-rounder Imran Khan. Edwards put on 48 with Max Walker and then 35 with Jeff Thomson. Walker had batted brilliantly in the recent Ashes series in Australia and he used his long reach to good effect again in this innings. Thomson's style was one more normally associated with tail enders. He trusted his eye and hit the ball powerfully to unguarded areas of the outfield.

Edwards, having survived an early lbw scare against Asif Masood, ran brilliantly between wickets and remained unbeaten on 80. Seventy-nine runs were added in the final 10 overs. 7–278 was a lot more than had seemed likely at 6–195.

Scoring 20 not out was just about the highlight of Jeff Thomson's day. In his first over in international cricket in England the new terror of the cricketing world sprayed the ball, his limbs and his invective all over the place. As Umpire Tom Spencer continued to call no-ball after no-ball and once also, wide, the crowd roared as loudly as they had done all day. Thomson rewarded their 'encouragement' with a two-fingered salute at the end of his 11-ball over. He eventually overstepped 12 times during his eight-over spell, giving the local scribes plenty to write about.

The whole crowd appreciated the batting of Majid Khan, who carried on against the world's fastest bowlers in his usual unhurried fashion as if they were mere trundlers. He lost Sadiq and Zaheer early, the latter to a mishook off Thomson. Majid reached 65 out of 104 before being fourth out to a faint leg-side tickle from the bowling of off spinner Ashley Mallett. Ian Chappell had introduced Mallett and the medium pace of Doug Walters as first and second change, holding the extra paceman, Max Walker, in reserve.

The captain, Asif Iqbal, and Wasim Raja rallied the Pakistanis to 4–181. Asif, hands apart on the bat handle, nudging and improvising while Wasim, left-handed and flamboyant, took risks and got away with them. At the 40 over mark they were actually 24 runs ahead of what Australia's total had been. The enthusiastic waving of flags and banners by their supporters added to the atmosphere as the game seemed to be building towards a thrilling climax. Just under 100 runs in more than 15 overs with six wickets in hand looked gettable, but the return of Lillee in the 43rd over changed the course of the match again, this time irrevocably. He removed Asif's off-stump as clean as a whistle and, well supported by Walker, promptly cleaned up the tail. The Australians, still slightly suspicious of limited-overs cricket, had maintained their recent dominance over Pakistani teams. For Asif Iqbal's team the loss meant they were already unlikely to reach the semi-finals.

AUSTRALIA

A. Turner c Mushtaq b Asif Iqbal		46
R.B. McCosker c Wasim Bari b Malik		25
I.M. Chappell (capt) c Wasim Raja b Sarfraz Nawaz		28
G.S. Chappell c Asif Iqbal b Imran Khan		45
K.D. Walters c Sarfraz Nawaz b Malik		2
R. Edwards not out		80
R.W. Marsh (wk) c Wasim Bari b Imran Khan		1
M.H.N. Walker b Asif Masood		18
J.R. Thomson not out		20
Extras (lb 7, nb 6)		13
(60 overs)		7-278

Did not bat: A.A. Mallett, D.K. Lillee

1/63 2/99 3/110 4/124 5/184 6/195 7/243

Bowling: Malik 12-2-37-2; Sarfraz 12-0-63-1; Imran Khan 10-0-44-2; Asif Masood 12-0-50-1; Asif Iqbal 12-0-58-1; Wasim Raja 2-0-13-0

PAKISTAN

Sadiq Mohammad b Lillee		4
Majid Khan c Marsh b Mallett		65
Zaheer Abbas c Turner b Thomson		8
Mushtaq Mohammad c G. Chappell b Walters		8
Asif Iqbal (capt) b Lillee		53
Wasim Raja c Thomson b Walker		31
Imran Khan c Turner b Walker		9
Sarfraz Nawaz c Marsh b Lillee		0
Wasim Bari (wk) c Marsh b Lillee		2
Asif Masood c Walker b Lillee		6
Naseer Malik not out		0
Extras (lb 4, w 3, nb 12)		19
(53 overs)		205

1/15 2/27 3/68 4/104 5/181 6/189 7/189 8/195 9/203

Bowling: Lillee 12-2-34-5; Thomson 8-2-25-1; Mallett 12-1-49-1; Walters 6-0-29-1; Walker 12-3-32-2; G.S. Chappell 3-0-17-0

Umpires: T.W. Spencer, W.E. Alley.

Toss: Australia. Points: Australia 4, Pakistan 0

WEDNESDAY 11 JUNE 1975
THE PRUDENTIAL CUP: ROUND TWO
GROUP A: ENGLAND vs NEW ZEALAND
TRENT BRIDGE: ENGLAND WON BY 80 RUNS

Sunny Saturday turned into blazing Wednesday as the Prudential Cup began to take real shape under perfect, clear blue skies. It was a cutthroat day during which most of the semi-final positions in both groups would be determined.

Lancastrian fast bowler Peter Lever took just one wicket in the game in Nottingham, yet in most people's minds it won the match for England. New Zealand's main hope of scoring the 267 runs they needed to defeat Mike Denness' side was for Glenn Turner to build another major innings like the one he had on the Saturday. When Lever bowled him for 12 in the 10th over with the score on 30 the Kiwis were in very big trouble.

England still had to work a bit harder for their points than they had against India. They left out John Snow and Barry Wood for the spin of Derek Underwood and for another batsman, Frank Hayes. Turner won the toss and sent England in, hoping to take advantage of the heavy, misty atmosphere. His big left-arm seamer Richard Collinge responded well, bowling Dennis Amiss with an in-swinger and

then having John Jameson caught behind in his next over to leave England 2–28. However the sun beat down, the shirts came off in the crowd and the conditions soon settled. So did Frank Hayes and Keith Fletcher, who added 83 for the third wicket before Hayes badly misjudged a pull shot in the 32nd over.

The loss of a third wicket on 111 may have been a bad omen for England, but Fletcher was now well entrenched and Denness, at his stylish and aggressive best, put on another 66 in 16 overs with him. The run rate was steady rather than spectacular until Denness on-drove Hedley Howarth for six, then swept him for four next ball. The English captain soon perished, caught in the deep at mid wicket, and Tony Greig, wearing silly batting gloves, was bowled swinging across the line.

England still had wickets and Fletcher in hand. The Essex 'gnome' stepped away and clipped Collinge through point for three to bring up his century in the 55th over. Chris Old again chimed in with a very handy 20, once smacking young Richard Hadlee out of the ground over mid wicket. Fifty-three runs had been scored in the final five overs.

When Fletcher was run-out going for a second suicidal run off the last ball of the innings, New Zealand knew they had their work cut out for them. Despite the loss of Turner they got to 1–83, but the run rate became an increasing problem as the innings progressed. Barry Hadlee, the third Hadlee brother in the New Zealand side playing the second of his two Limited-Over Internationals, supported John Morrison who went on to complete a solid half century before being caught at square leg off Underwood. Tony Greig, bowling his mixture of off-cutters and seamers, did most damage as the Kiwi challenge subsided. Chris Old came as close as is humanly possible to claiming a hat-trick without actually getting one. He had Brian Hastings caught by Derek Underwood, bowled Richard Hadlee next ball and then brushed Dayle Hadlee's stumps without removing a bail on the hat-trick ball. Dayle Hadlee and Brian McKechnie then added 48 but the match was over as a contest. In such situations the interest of all concerned quickly subsides. The last wicket did not fall until the final ball of the innings, Underwood bowling Richard Collinge perhaps looking for a way to score the 81 runs required for victory.

ENGLAND

D.L. Amiss b Collinge	16
J.A. Jameson c Wadsworth b Collinge	11
K.W.R. Fletcher run-out	131
F.C. Hayes lbw, R.J. Hadlee	34
M.H. Denness (capt) c Morrison b D.R. Hadlee	37
A.W. Greig b D.R. Hadlee	9
C.M. Old not out	20
Extras (lb 6, w 1, nb 1)	8
(60 overs)	6–266

Did not bat: A.P.E. Knott (wk), D.L. Underwood, G.G. Arnold, P. Lever

1/27 2/28 3/111 4/177 5/200 6/266

Bowling: Collinge 12–2–43–2; R.J. Hadlee 12–2–66–1; D.R. Hadlee 12–1–55–2; McKechnie 12–2–38–0; Howarth 12–2–56–0

NEW ZEALAND

J.F.M. Morrison c Old b Underwood	55
G.M. Turner (capt) b Lever	12
B.G. Hadlee c Old b Greig	19
J.M. Parker b Greig	1
B.F. Hastings c Underwood b Old	10
K.J. Wadsworth (wk) b Arnold	25
R.J. Hadlee b Old	0
B.J. McKechnie c Underwood b Greig	27
D.R. Hadlee c Arnold b Greig	20
H.J. Howarth not out	1
R.O. Collinge b Underwood	6
Extras (b 1, lb 4, w 1, nb 4)	10
(60 overs)	186

1/30 2/83 3/91 4/95 5/129 6/129 7/129 8/177 9/180

Bowling: Arnold 12–3–35–1; Lever 12–0–37–1; Old 12–2–29–2; Underwood 12–2–30–2; Greig 12–0–45–4

Umpires: W.E. Alley, T.W. Spencer.

Toss: New Zealand. Points: England 4, New Zealand 0

GROUP A: INDIA vs EAST AFRICA
HEADINGLEY: INDIA WON BY 10 WICKETS

The official attendance figure said 6000, but only 720 people actually paid to see this second East African mismatch at Leeds. Harilal Shah won the toss and his side batted and lasted 55.3 overs, but even so they could only muster 120 runs against a similar attack to the one that had conceded 334 to England on the Saturday.

There was one change to the Indian bowling line-up. Sikh left-arm spinner Bishen Bedi returned for young Karsan Ghavri. He claimed only one wicket, but otherwise mesmerised the hapless East Africans with his beautifully concealed variations, conceding just six runs in his 12 over spell. The score stumbled along to 5–56 in the 39th over. The captain was caught behind for his second first-ball duck and his side were looking at an embarrassingly low total. Jawahir Shah and Ramesh Sethi then added 42 to, temporarily at least, slow the progress of the Indians. Shah put a few nice shots through the covers and Sethi completed a couple of effective leg-side hits.

It kept the paying Headingley 720 a bit longer in their warm sunny seats and allowed Sunil

Gavaskar and Farokh Engineer enough scope to each pass the half-century mark in the 179 balls it took them to pass their target of 120. Madan Lal had polished off the East African tail to finish with the best bowling figures, but it was Engineer who received the Man of the Match award from former Yorkshire and England wicketkeeper, Jimmy Binks. Gavaskar had actually outscored Engineer at the batting crease, but Binks may have wanted to reward a fellow member of the wicketkeepers' union. Or perhaps he felt it inappropriate for Gavaskar to be recognised in such a way just a couple of days after his debacle against England at Lord's. Engineer's was quite a brave effort—the veteran was playing with a torn hamstring and he had to walk most of his runs. He was, however, rarely stretched by the East African bowlers or their fieldsmen.

EAST AFRICA

Frasat Ali b Abid Ali	12
Sam Walusimba lbw Abid Ali	16
Praful Mehta (wk) run-out	12
Yunus Badat b Bedi	1
Jawahir Shah b Amarnath	37
Harilal, R. Shah (capt) c Engineer b Amarnath	0
Ramesh Sethi c Gaekwad b Madan Lal	23
Mehmood Quraishy run out	6
Zulfiqar Ali not out	2
P.G. Nana lbw Madan Lal	0
D. Pringle b Madan Lal	2
Extras (lb 8, nb 1)	9
(55.3 overs)	120

1/27 2/36 3/37 4/56 5/56 6/98 7/116 8/116 9/116

Bowling: Abid Ali 12-5-22-2; Madan Lal 9.3-2-15-3; Bedi 12-8-6-1; Venkataraghavan 12-4-29-0; Amarnath 10-0-39-2

INDIA

S.M. Gavaskar not out	65
F.M. Engineer (wk) not out	54
Extras (b 4)	4
(29.5 overs)	0-123

Did not bat: A.D. Gaekwad, G.R. Viswanath, B.P. Patel, E.D. Solkar, S. Abid Ali, Madan Lal, M. Amarnath, S. Venkataraghavan (capt), B.S. Bedi

Bowling: Frasat Ali 6-1-17-0; Pringle 3-1-14-0; Zulfiqar 11-3-32-0; Nana 4.5-0-36-0; Sethi 5-0-20-0

Umpires: H.D. Bird, A. Jepson.

Toss: East Africa. Points: India 4, East Africa 0

GROUP B: AUSTRALIA vs SRI LANKA
THE OVAL: AUSTRALIA WON BY 52 RUNS

His friends and colleagues are quick to point out that Jeff Thomson was and is basically a fairly placid fellow with no cross to bear and a love of the outdoor life. This is despite the infamous article that bore his name in 1974 claiming that he enjoyed seeing batsmen screaming in pain on the pitch after being struck by him. He was probably pining very much for some quiet outdoor Australian activity after just a couple of weeks and two games of cricket in England.

After his no-ball problems at Leeds and the negative press reactions, Thomson had to bear close scrutiny at the nets at Lord's in preparation for the match against Sri Lanka. When the cameras were lined up with the bowling crease his team-mates encouraged Thomson to deliberately overstep. His captain, Ian Chappell said, 'He's had a gutful of this business'.

History has shown that an angry fast bowler can be a dangerous fast bowler and there is no doubt the Sri Lankan batsmen who faced the wrath of Jeff Thomson at The Oval on 12 June 1975 wish that he had been left alone. Thomson's figures from the match seem modestly respectable. He claimed 1–22 from 12 overs. Sri Lanka's 4–276 looks a case of bat dominating ball. Bat did dominate ball, too, except when it was in Thomson's hands. Then it was a case of ball dominating body.

In addition to taking one wicket Thomson put two Sri Lankan batsmen into St Thomas's Hospital, Lambeth. He bowled a wide at the start of his second spell which raised his ire. Duleep Mendis was concussed after being hit on the side of the head by a bouncer. He stayed for a little longer, but a second deflected blow to his forehead finished him. 'I'm going boss, I'm going,' he replied to his captain's inquiry as to his intentions. Sunil Wettimuny compiled a brave half century. However, he was beaten about the body by Thomson's phenomenally quick bowling, and retired after chopping the ball into the same battered foot for the second time.

Many in the 6000 strong crowd at The Oval started jeering, especially when Thomson threw down the stumps and appealed for a run-out with Wettimuny still hopping around. If the Queenslander was hoping to avoid attention he was going the wrong way about it. The initial reaction of the Sri Lankan manager, Mr Pereira, was that bouncers were not allowed at unrecognised batsmen and that all Sri Lankans fell into that category. The next day, having had time to reflect, he revised that opinion. As Fred Bennett the Australian manager pointed out, 'What do you expect Thomson to do . . . bowl underarm?'

All of which detracted from a game that featured a feast of run making. Over the day 604 runs were scored for the loss of nine wickets.

Alan Turner and Rick McCosker got Australia away to a flyer after Tennekoon won the toss and invited Ian Chappell's side to bat. The decision seemed to be based as much on wanting to give the spectators close to a full day's cricket as on gaining any special tactical advantage. The pair of New South Welshmen had put on 178 in 34 overs by lunch. Turner had already completed his century, the first by an Australian in any Limited-Over Internationals. 'I don't think I've hit the ball better, and you certainly didn't have to worry about life and limb with those guys,' he said.

He hit one big six over long-on, a mighty stroke on the large playing field of The Oval. But immediately after the interval leg spinner Somachandra de Silva struck twice and three wickets fell for nine runs in 11 balls. Greg Chappell and Doug Walters responded to the collapse by adding 117 runs in 19 overs, leaving the Sri Lankans an awesome chase.

They didn't get there and there was no feature innings, but their consistency and determination frustrated the Australians and gained them great admiration and plenty of sympathy from neutrals. They really got stuck into Ashley Mallett's off spin and Greg Chappell's and Doug Walters' medium pace. Wettimuny passed 50, so did Michael Tissera. The bruises became badges of courage. *Wisden* said Australia did not gain many admirers. Even the Australian players believed they had been a bit lucky.

AUSTRALIA

R.B. McCosker b de Silva	73
A. Turner c Mendis b de Silva	101
I.M. Chappell (capt) b Kaluperuma	4
G.S. Chappell c Opatha b Pieris	50
K.D. Walters c Tennekoon b Pieris	59
J.R. Thomson not out	9
R.W. Marsh (wk) not out	9
Extras (lb 20, b 1, w 1, nb 1)	23
(60 overs)	5-328

Did not bat: R. Edwards, M.H.N. Walker, D.K. Lillee, A.A. Mallett

1/182 2/187 3/191 4/308 5/308

Bowling: Opatha 9-0-32-0; Pieris 11-0-68-2; Warnapura 9-0-40-0; Ranasinghe 7-0-55-0; de Silva 12-3-60-2; Kaluperuma 12-0-50-1

SRI LANKA

S.R. de S. Wettimuny retired hurt	53
R. Fernando (wk) b Thomson	22
B. Warnapura st Marsh b Mallett	31
D. Mendis retired hurt	32
A. Tennekoon (capt) b I.M. Chappell	48
M. Tissera c Turner b I.M. Chappell	52
A. Ranasinghe not out	14
H.S.M. Pieris not out	0
Extras (b 6, lb 8, w 8, nb 2)	24
(60 overs)	4-276

Did not bat: T. Opatha, D.S. de Silva, L. Kaluperuma

1/30 2/84 3/246 4/268

Bowling: Lillee 10-0-42-0; Thomson 12-2-22-1; Mallett 12-0-72-1; Walters 6-0-33-0; Walker 12-1-44-0; G.S. Chappell 4-0-25-0; I.M. Chappell 4-0-14-2

Umpires: W.L. Budd, A.E. Fagg.

Toss: Sri Lanka. Points: Australia 4, Sri Lanka 0

GROUP B: PAKISTAN vs WEST INDIES
EDGBASTON: WEST INDIES WON BY 1 WICKET

The superiority of the World Cup and the significance of the games ahead of all other Limited-Over Internationals could not be better emphasised than by this encounter at Edgbaston which remains an all-time classic.

Clive Lloyd has gone so far as to suggest the match signalled the start of the West Indies self-belief that they had the talent to win the tournament and to then emerge as the best team in the world. Whether that was the case, this was a great game of cricket. The result seemed for most of the day to be going one way only for the plot to have a late and unpredictable twist, like the very best drama. If there was a down side it was that the result condemned the talented Pakistanis to an early finish in the tournament. They made all the running, but lacked enough killer instinct to finish off the West Indies.

In one way the quality and closeness of the game should not have been a total surprise. Over the years the West Indies and Pakistan have been remarkably evenly matched, even through the West Indies halcyon years in the 1980s.

Not that the Pakistanis were at full strength. Their captain, Asif Iqbal, was in a hospital in Birmingham having a haemorrhoid operation and Imran Khan was also unavailable due to examination commitments at Oxford University. Despite missing both players and the early loss of Sadiq to Bernard Julien, they got away to an excellent start after acting captain Majid Khan won the toss and elected to bat in front of a healthy mix of Pakistani and West Indian expatriates and a few English locals.

The crowd of 16,000 saw a typically graceful half century from Majid. Under a sunhat that was darker than the colour of his bat he hit the ball with exquisite timing before being caught behind off his opposite number. Zaheer chipped in with a solid 31 before future captain, Mushtaq Mohammad, and Wasim Raja added an important 62 runs for the fourth wicket. Mushtaq barely scored in front of square, twirling his bat and flicking the ball on both sides of the wicket with incredible effectiveness. Wasim, who seemed to relish West Indian bowling, benefited from some sloppy fielding, after earlier brilliance from the likes of Keith Boyce. Boyce also revealed the West Indians' sense of growing frustration when he bowled a 'beamer' at Mushtaq for daring to charge and slice him for four over covers.

Pakistan's 7–266 was healthy rather than insurmountable on a flat track in beautiful weather. Clive Lloyd said his side were confident of reaching their target. Sarfraz Nawaz had other ideas. Perhaps he was annoyed by the strange, coloured towelling hats worn by the West Indian top order. Whatever the motivation the big, lumbering medium pacer made short work of Greenidge, Fredericks and Kallicharran. Each was beaten on merit as the West Indies tumbled to 3–36. Sarfraz by then had 3–10 in 3.4 overs. Lloyd made a half century, being upset when given out caught behind off 17-year-old Javed Miandad. The West Indies kept up with the required run rate, but regularly lost wickets. On 8–166 they seemed destined to lose. BBC Television commentator Richie Benaud confirmed the feeling when, after Boyce played on, he said, 'The West Indies surely cannot win'.

However the Pakistan bowling ranks were thinning and the West Indies batted right down to number 11. Wicketkeeper Deryck Murray, an experienced and fighting campaigner, gave his team a glimmer of hope. Vanburn Holder, choking down low on the bat handle stayed just long enough for the 200 to be passed. When last man Andy Roberts walked to the crease 64 were required for the last wicket in 14 overs.

Clive Lloyd's accountant put £150 on the West Indies to win at 66–1. Lloyd himself started drinking a crate of pale ale and told Gordon Andrews he was very unwise with his money. He was still stewing over the decision that had gone against him.

As the overs passed the stack of pale ale empties grew, as did the tension inside the West Indies dressing-room. Murray hit sweet boundaries through mid wicket and the covers. Roberts clubbed the full-pitched deliveries off the back foot straight and to the cover boundary. Sarfraz finished his overs. A win was possible. The target was reduced to 29 runs off six overs, then 16 off four. Parvez Mir bowled a critical maiden. But someone had miscalculated and Wasim Raja, normally a fastish leg-spinner, was called on to bowl medium pace for the 60th over. He had five runs to play with. Roberts and Murray scrambled a tight leg bye, but Pakistan saw their great

victory chance slipping away and instead of a run-out there was an overthrow. The Hollies Stand vibrated with the excitement of the West Indian supporters. A quiet little push to mid wicket off the fourth ball and it was all over. The ground was invaded, Murray was swamped.

Clive Lloyd, drunk, ecstatic but still smarting charged out of the dressing-room and yelled into the members' enclosure, 'That will teach you . . . you cheats!' It had been a wonderful, pressure-packed occasion.

PAKISTAN

Majid Khan (capt) c Murray b Lloyd	60
Sadiq Mohammad c Kanhai b Julien	7
Zaheer Abbas lbw Richards	31
Mushtaq Mohammad b Boyce	55
Wasim Raja b Roberts	58
Javed Miandad run out	24
Parvez Mir run out	4
Wasim Bari (wk) not out	1
Sarfraz Nawaz not out	0
Extras (b 1, lb 15, w 4, nb 6)	26
(60 overs)	7–266

Did not bat: Asif Masood, Naseer Malik

1/21 2/83 3/140 4/202 5/249 6/263 7/265

Bowling: Roberts 12–1–47–1; Boyce 12–2–44–1; Richards 4–0–21–1; Julien 12–1–41–1; Holder 12–3–56–0; Lloyd 8–1–31–1

WEST INDIES

R.C. Fredericks lbw Sarfraz Nawaz	12
C.G. Greenidge c Wasim Bari b Sarfraz Nawaz	4
A.I. Kallicharran c Wasim Bari b Sarfraz Nawaz	16
R.B. Kanhai b Naseer	24
C.H. Lloyd (capt) c Wasim Bari b Javed Miandad	53
I.V.A. Richards c Zaheer b Parvez	13
B.D. Julien c Javed Miandad b Asif Masood	18
D.L. Murray (wk) not out	61
K.D. Boyce b Naseer	7
V.A. Holder c Parvez b Sarfraz Nawaz	16
A.M.E. Roberts not out	24
Extras (lb 10, w 1, nb 8)	19
(59.4 overs)	9–267

1/6 2/31 3/36 4/84 5/99 6/145 7/151 8/166 9/203

Bowling: Asif Masood 12–1–64–1; Sarfraz Nawaz 12–1–44–4; Naseer Malik 12–2–42–2; Parvez Mir 9–1–42–1; Javed Miandad 12–0–46–1; Mushtaq Mohammad 2–0–7–0; Wasim Raja 0.4–0–3–0

Umpires: D.J. Constant, J.G. Langridge.

Toss: Pakistan. Points: West Indies 4, Pakistan 0

SATURDAY 14 JUNE 1975
THE PRUDENTIAL CUP: ROUND THREE
GROUP A: ENGLAND vs EAST AFRICA
EDGBASTON: ENGLAND WON BY 196 RUNS

Edgbaston went from the sublime to the ridiculous in a matter of three days. East Africa's total inadequacy at this level was again cruelly exposed. It was time for them to go home and lick their wounds. There were many who questioned the wisdom of including a side so far below the strength of all others. Uganda, Tanzania and Zambia have not been back, but Kenya returned 20 years later and made a far greater impact than this combine ever did.

Harilal Shah won the toss and sent England in.

Dennis Amiss and Barry Wood, in for John Jameson, responded with an opening stand of 158. Amiss gave a couple of chances and concentration may have been a bit difficult, especially as England were assured of their semi-final place. He got to 88 before someone actually held a chance.

Wood also missed his hundred, hitting across one from Quraishy. It was Wood's Lancashire team-mate, Frank Hayes, who provided the day's highlight. In 14 overs. Hayes belted his way to 52. He hit two sixes, straight towards the pavilion, and six fours. Tony Greig missed out for the third time and 290 was a smaller total than it might have been. It was always going to be far too many for the East Africans.

John Snow showed no mercy. Back in place of Geoff Arnold, Snow took 4–5 in his first six overs. Straight and fast was enough, two victims were bowled, two were lbw. Before long East Africa was 4–21. A quick finish would have been merciful, but it took 52.3 overs for England to finish the contest. The captain, Harilal Shah,

scored his first runs for the tournament and Ramesh Sethi, showing admirable application, lasted for 32 overs. Peter Lever finally bowled him, Zulfiqar and Hamish McLeod. Not all of the crowd of 5000 saw that.

England had had a nice workout in the sunshine as a lead-up to their semi-final. The question remained whether this match, or even the previous two encounters, had been tough enough work-outs to prepare them to take on the West Indies or Australia.

ENGLAND

B. Wood b Quraishy	77
D.L. Amiss c Nana b Zulfiqar	88
F.C. Hayes b Zulfiqar	52
A.W. Greig lbw Zulfiqar	9
A.P.E. Knott (wk) not out	18
C.M. Old b Quraishy	18
M.H. Denness (capt) not out	12
Extras (b 7, lb 7, w 1, nb 1)	16
(60 overs)	5–290

Did not bat: K.W.R. Fletcher, J.A. Snow, P. Lever, D.L. Underwood

1/158 2/192 3/234 4/244 5/277

Bowling: Frasat 9-0-40-0; Pringle 12-0-41-0; Nana 12-2-46-0; Sethi 5-0-29-0; Zulfiqar 12-0-63-3; Quraishy 10-0-55-2

EAST AFRICA

Frasat Ali b Snow	0
S. Walusimba lbw Snow	7
Yunus Badat b Snow	0
Jawahir Shah lbw Snow	4
Ramesh Sethi b Lever	30
Harilal, R. Shah (capt) b Greig	6
Mehmood Quraishy c Amiss b Greig	19
Zulfiqar Ali b Lever	7
H. McLeod (wk) b Lever	0
P.G. Nana not out	8
D. Pringle b Old	3
Extras (lb 6, w 1, nb 3)	10
(52.3 overs)	94

1/7 2/7 3/15 4/21 5/42 6/72 7/76 8/79 9/88 10/94

Bowling: Snow 12-6-11-4; Lever 12-3-32-3; Underwood 10-5-11-0; Wood 7-3-10-0; Greig 10-1-18-2; Old 1.3-0-2-1

Umpires: W.E. Alley, J.G. Langridge.

Toss: East Africa. Points: England 4, East Africa 0

GROUP A: NEW ZEALAND vs INDIA
OLD TRAFFORD: NEW ZEALAND WON BY 4 WICKETS

If there was any injustice about the structure and results of the Prudential World Cup, it was that in Round Three India and New Zealand were playing for a spot in the semi-finals while the Pakistani side would just be going through the motions against Sri Lanka before going their separate ways. Neither team at Old Trafford had done anything except defeat East Africa, but the groupings designed to ensure England's progress also favoured one of these two teams.

The contest attracted only 4000 patrons to Old Trafford. For a time it seemed they might see a fairly one-sided contest. Through a slightly superior showing against England, New Zealand started the match as favourites and with the

Hadlee brothers, Dayle and Richard, and Hedley Howarth putting in good spells they reduced India to a very uncomfortable 6–101 just before lunch. The Hadlee brothers had combined early on to remove the prize victim of Sunil Gavaskar.

Finally India's policy of selecting a heap of all-rounders paid some dividends. Madan Lal and the more experienced Abid Ali turned the tide with a stand of 55. Madan Lal became McKechnie's second victim, but Abid Ali stayed on, turning a good start into a major limited-overs innings in his final international. He hit some nice shots through the covers and a couple of effective slogs, one over mid wicket from the left-armer Collinge going all the way for six.

Venkataraghavan also made an important contribution with the bat, adding 60 with Abid Ali. Their stand ensured India ended with a competitive total.

As had been the case for New Zealand in the previous two games, the innings of Glenn Turner was crucial. Probably in his hands rested the fate of who would reach the semi-finals. He and John Morrison made a positive start. In 10 overs they rattled up 45 runs, then Bishen Bedi was introduced into the attack. The folly of not selecting him against England was again soon obvious. He choked off the scoring, dismissing Morrison with his second ball and conceded only 11 runs in eight overs before tea. Geoff Howarth was unluckily run-out when a Turner straight drive

was deflected from the bowler's hand onto the stumps at the non-striker's end. When Abid Ali trapped John Parker lbw, New Zealand were 3–70 and anything but certainties.

That was as close as India got, though. Turner could not be shifted. Bedi was seen off and Brian Hastings joined his captain in a 65-run partnership for the fourth wicket. Wicketkeeper, the ill-fated Ken Wadsworth, and Richard Hadlee also contributed. At no stage did New Zealand break free, but Turner completed his hundred in 163 minutes and following two boundaries from Dayle Hadlee the Kiwis reached their target with seven balls and four wickets to spare. Turner had struck thirteen boundaries in his 114 not out.

INDIA

S.M. Gavaskar c R.J. Hadlee b D.R. Hadlee	12
F.M. Engineer (wk) lbw, R.J. Hadlee	24
A.D. Gaekwad c Hastings b R.J. Hadlee	37
G.R. Viswanath lbw McKechnie	2
B.P. Patel c Wadsworth b H.J. Howarth	9
E.D. Solkar c Wadsworth b H.J. Howarth	13
S. Abid Ali c H.J. Howarth b McKechnie	70
Madan Lal c & b McKechnie	20
M. Amarnath c Morrison b D.R. Hadlee	1
S. Venkataraghavan (capt) not out	26
B.S. Bedi run out	6
Extras (b 5, w 1, nb 4)	10
(60 overs)	230

1/17 2/48 3/59 4/81 5/94 6/101 7/156 8/157 9/217 10/230

Bowling: Collinge 12–2–43–0; R.J. Hadlee 12–2–48–2; D.R. Hadlee 12–3–32–3; McKechnie 12–1–49–3; H.J. Howarth 12–0–48–2

NEW ZEALAND

G.M. Turner (capt) not out	114
J.F.M. Morrison c Engineer b Bedi	17
G.P. Howarth run out	9
J.M. Parker lbw Abid Ali	1
B.F. Hastings c Solkar b Amarnath	34
K.J. Wadsworth (wk) lbw Madan Lal	22
R.J. Hadlee b Abid Ali	15
D.R. Hadlee not out	8
Extras (b 8, lb 5)	13
(58.5 overs)	6–233

Did not bat: B.J. McKechnie, H.J. Howarth, R.O. Collinge

1/45 2/62 3/70 4/135 5/185 6/224

Bowling: Madan Lal 11.5–1–62–1; Amarnath 8–1–40–1; Bedi 12–6–28–1; Abid Ali 12–2–35–2; Venkataraghavan 12–0–39–0; Solkar 3–0–16–0

Umpires: W.L. Budd, A.E. Fagg.

Toss: India. Points: New Zealand 4, India 0

GROUP B: AUSTRALIA vs WEST INDIES
THE OVAL: WEST INDIES WON BY 7 WICKETS

The sell-out crowd that packed into the old south London ground witnessed a feast of exciting cricket, albeit virtually all of it was from one side. The West Indies in what was for them almost a home game demolished the Australians with a brilliant display of calypso cricket in its purest form. That is, incisive fast bowling followed by spectacular strokeplay. Neither side could forfeit its semi-final berth by losing this match, but the Australians must have been worried by their second-rate showing.

Riding high on the excitement of their wonderful win against Pakistan, Clive Lloyd's side played with exhilaration and supreme confidence right from the moment the West Indian captain won the toss and sent Australia in to bat. The third day of World Cup cricket, although starting cloudy and a bit cooler, again encouraged shirtsleeves and later bare torsos. The crowd was in a very buoyant mood well before the start of play. Some had paid scalpers 10 times the face value for a ticket while others had found their entrance by less accepted means, like hiding in the back of beer trucks. They absolutely exploded into life in the first over when Rick McCosker failed to keep down a lifting Julien delivery on the leg side and Roy Fredericks dived forward at leg slip to scoop up the low catch. Alan Turner found Andy Roberts an altogether more difficult proposition from the Sri Lankan trundlers and probably imagined his pads were made of paper when he got his knee in front of a very fast, straight delivery.

On what was really a fairly slow wicket Ian and Greg Chappell responded in their best fighting family tradition. Both fell within seven runs and six balls of each other to Keith Boyce who sent down a fine spell of pacy outswing. At 4–56 the West Indies were riding high and better still when a left-hand pick and lightning right-hand throw by Gordon Greenidge found Doug Walters short of his ground. Run-out seven was hardly a score to crown the day you had been awarded an MBE.

This was cricket at breakneck speed and it could not last. West Australian pair Rod Marsh and Ross Edwards restored a sense of sanity to proceedings without quite putting the game back on an even keel by adding 99 for the sixth wicket. Strangely, considering their reputations, it was Edwards who dominated the scoring, a leg-side pick-up shot off Lloyd registering the first Australian boundary just prior to lunch.

Salad was taken at 5–76, after which the West Australian rebuilding exercise continued. It lasted until the introduction of young Viv Richards. Edwards twice lofted him for four, deep towards the boundary at wide mid-on. He gave himself room for a third such blow, only to miss a faster straight ball. Roberts was recalled. He struck Thomson on the forearm and smashed out Lillee's leg-stump stump. Again the crowd exploded, Englishmen just as jubilant as the West Indians this time at seeing the Aussie pacemen receive some of their own medicine. Roberts had Ashley Mallett caught behind the next ball, leaving Rod Marsh stranded on 52 with no partners left to help him push the total beyond 192. His side had wasted 6.2 overs.

A target of 193 at just over three runs per over might have produced a sedate response from many sides. Not from the West Indians on this day, however. Once Lillee and Thomson fired in a few bouncers the challenge was always going to be met. Greenidge was trapped by a big inswinger from Max Walker with the total on 29. The left-handed Guyanese pair of Alvin Kallicharran and Roy Fredericks then took the game by the scruff of the neck with a series of flashing shots; cuts, hooks and back-foot drives sending the ball in all directions.

It was all great entertainment and it built to a tremendous climax. In an astonishing display, little 160 cm tall 'Kalli' belted Dennis Lillee for 35 runs from 10 balls. He got himself moving with a cracking drive through the covers and

AUSTRALIA

R.B. McCosker c Fredericks b Julien	0
A. Turner lbw Roberts	7
I.M. Chappell (capt) c Murray b Boyce	25
G.S. Chappell c Murray b Boyce	15
K.D. Walters run out	7
R. Edwards b Richards	58
R.W. Marsh (wk) not out	52
M.H.N. Walker lbw Holder	8
J.R. Thomson c Holder b Richards	1
D.K. Lillee b Roberts	3
A.A. Mallett c Murray b Roberts	0
Extras (lb 9, w 1, nb 6)	16
(53.4 overs)	192

1/0 2/21 3/49 4/56 5/61 6/160 7/173 8/174 9/192 10/192

Bowling: Julien 12–2–31–1; Roberts 10.4–1–39–3; Boyce 11–0–38–2; Holder 10–1–31–1; Lloyd 4–1–19–0; Richards 6–0–18–2

WEST INDIES

R.C. Fredericks c Marsh b Mallett	58
C.G. Greenidge lbw Walker	16
A.I. Kallicharran c Mallett b Lillee	78
I.V.A. Richards not out	15
R.B. Kanhai not out	18
Extras (b 4, lb 2, w 3, nb 1)	10
(46 overs)	3–195

Did not bat: C.H. Lloyd (capt), B.D. Julien, D.L. Murray (wk), K.D. Boyce, V.A. Holder, A.M.E. Roberts

1/29 2/153 3/159

Bowling: Lillee 10–0–66–1; Thomson 6–1–21–0; Walker 12–2–41–1; G.S. Chappell 4–0–13–0; Mallett 11–2–35–1; I.M. Chappell 3–1–9–0

Umpires: H.D. Bird, D.J. Constant.

Toss: West Indies. Points: West Indies 4, Australia 0

reached his 50 with a slash that sent the ball high, wide and handsome to the third-man boundary. Lillee continued to bowl short. Kallicharran kept hooking. One he picked up and hit finer, ever so sweetly over the boundary at the Pavilion End. When at last he finally mistimed a hook he had somewhat dented the Australian fast bowler's reputation. Kallicharran's 78 included a six and 13 fours. He had added 124 for the second wicket with his fellow Guyanese left-hander.

Forty runs and a few overs later Viv Richards pulled Ian Chappell away to Compton's corner for four, heralding another joyous black invasion of an English cricket ground. The West Indies had romped home by seven wickets, leaving them to return to The Oval in four days time to play New Zealand in the supposedly easier semi-final. As they filed out of the ground the West Indian supporters sang, 'We killed a kangaroo ... we killed a kangaroo ... eeeiii-adio, we killed a kangaroo'. The Australians were criticised for having a naive approach to limited-overs cricket. They had to travel to Leeds to tackle a confident, strongly supported England team.

GROUP B: PAKISTAN vs SRI LANKA
TRENT BRIDGE: PAKISTAN WON BY 192 RUNS

The Sri Lankans came back to earth with a thud in Nottingham after their fine showing against Australia. They were totally unable to contain the talented Pakistani strokeplayers and when they batted could make little of the array of wrist spinners confronting them.

In front of the smallest crowd of the tournament there was only token satisfaction for Majid Khan's side, as well. When Imran Khan returned to the team dressing-room following his exams at Oxford he found there was still an atmosphere of stunned disbelief at the loss against the West Indies. The pros and cons were being debated endlessly. They had a place in the semi-finals at their beck and call but had failed to grasp it.

When Sadiq Mohammad and Majid went out to open the batting at the invitation of Tennekoon it was quickly evident the pressure was off. Sadiq was dropped on 1, but it was the Sri Lankans' only look-in. Against friendly bowling the pair traded shot for shot, adding 159 in 32 overs. Once the openers were separated Zaheer took centre stage, caressing the ball square on both sides as he raced towards his century in 27 overs. He dominated a stand of 88 with Mushtaq. Eventually Zaheer fell just three runs short, playing

PAKISTAN

Sadiq Mohammad c Opatha b Warnapura	74
Majid Khan (capt) c Tennekoon b D.S. de Silva	84
Zaheer Abbas b Opatha	97
Mushtaq Mohammad c Heyn b Warnapura	26
Wasim Raja c Opatha b Warnapura	2
Javed Miandad not out	28
Imran Khan b Opatha	0
Parvez Mir not out	4
Extras (b 4, lb 4, w 2, nb 5)	15
(60 overs)	6–330

Did not bat: Wasim Bari (wk), Asif Masood, Naseer Malik

1/159 2/168 3/256 4/268 5/318 6/318

Bowling: Opatha 12–0–67–2; Pieris 9–0–54–0; G.R.A. de Silva 7–1–46–0; D.S. de Silva 12–1–61–1; Kaluperuma 9–1–35–0; Warnapura 8–0–42–3; Ranasinghe 3–0–10–0

SRI LANKA

E.R. Fernando (wk) c & b Javed Miandad	21
B. Warnapura b Imran Khan	2
A.P.B. Tennekoon (capt) lbw Naseer	30
M.H. Tissera c Wasim Bari b Sadiq	12
P.D. Heyn c Zaheer b Javed Miandad	1
A.N. Ranasinghe b Wasim Raja	9
H.S.M. Pieris lbw Parvez	16
A.R.M. Opatha c Zaheer b Sadiq	0
D.S. de Silva b Imran Khan	26
L.W. Kaluperuma not out	13
G.R.A. de Silva c Wasim Raja b Imran Khan	0
Extras (lb 1, w 3, nb 4)	8
(50.1 overs)	138

1/5 2/44 3/60 4/61 5/75 6/79 7/90 8/113 9/135 10/138

Bowling: Asif Masood 6–2–14–0; Imran Khan 7.1–3–15–3; Javed Miandad 7–2–22–2; Naseer Malik 6–1–19–1; Sadiq Mohammad 6–1–20–2; Wasim Raja 7–4–7–1; Mushtaq Mohammad 5–0–16–0; Parvez Mir 6–1–17–1

Umpires: A. Jepson, T.W. Spencer.

Toss: Sri Lanka. Points: Pakistan 4, Sri Lanka 0

on from Opatha late in the innings. Imran missed out on the run feast altogether. Perhaps his focus was still on his university papers.

Faced with a daunting target of 331, Sri Lanka went bravely for their shots as they had against Australia. However, this time it didn't work. They missed the injured Duleep Mendis and Sunil Wettimuny, not yet recovered from their pounding from Thomson, and slipped quickly from 1–44 to 6–79. Somachandra de Silva, who had a solid tournament, offered a little late resistance before Imran cleaned up what Javed Miandad and the other spinners had left behind. The Sri Lankan innings closed when Imran had last man, Ginigalgodage de Silva caught by Wasim Raja from the first ball of his eighth over, finishing the Prudential Cup for themselves and their unfortunate opponents.

WEDNESDAY 18 JUNE 1975
THE PRUDENTIAL CUP SEMI-FINALS

The tables at the end of the preliminary rounds of the Prudential Cup were as follows:

GROUP A	P	W	L	Pts	GROUP B	P	W	L	Pts
England	3	3	0	12	West Indies	3	3	0	12
New Zealand	3	2	1	8	Australia	3	2	1	8
India	3	1	2	4	Pakistan	3	1	2	4
East Africa	3	0	3	0	Sri Lanka	3	0	3	0

FIRST SEMI-FINAL: AUSTRALIA vs ENGLAND
HEADINGLEY: AUSTRALIA WON BY 4 WICKETS

This abrupt 65 over game of cricket will forever be known as 'Gilmour's Match'. The young Newcastle all-rounder, coming into the Australian side for the first time in the tournament, fully exploited conditions which were favourable to his bowling style. Almost single-handedly Gilmour dashed the hope of the home supporters that England would win the Prudential Cup. It was a sad day for Yorkshire and England, especially as their exit came courtesy of the dreaded warriors in baggy green caps.

Headingley, or more particularly their ground staff, had a habit of turning out some rather strange wickets for major matches in the 1970s and this one was up there with the weirdest of them. In 1972 the previously little known disease fuserium became an identity overnight when it shaved . . . I mean, destroyed, all the grass on the pitch for the deciding Test against Australia. In a happy coincidence, at the same time England recalled Derek Underwood, a bowler perfectly suited to the grassless and bounceless, turning pitch.

There was no sign of fuserium or Underwood this day. The wicket, the same one used for the Australia vs Pakistan match 10 days earlier, was emerald green. It looked badly underprepared, as if the ground staff had only found out the day before that they had to make a pitch at all and had to quickly water, roll and cut an old one. Underwood was left out and England's attack included John Snow, Geoff Arnold, Peter Lever and Chris Old—each bowler of the type to relish such conditions. As if to order, the early-morning sunshine disappeared and a cool wind sprung up, sending low grey scudding clouds over Headingley. The ground filled to capacity, this time there were few Pakistanis or West Indians, and the home side could be assured of crowd support.

A couple of things then put a glitch in the plans of the locals. Australia recognised a green top wicket as a green top, too, and omitted spinner Ashley Mallett for left-arm swing bowler Gary Gilmour. In addition Ian Chappell won the toss and asked England to bat in those typically northern English conditions.

Gilmour shared the new ball with Dennis Lillee ahead of Jeff Thomson and Max Walker. The 23-year-old had never expected such a quick promotion, but Chappell's reading of the situation was perfect. Gilmour immediately began darting the ball very late in to the right-handers. Lillee got bounce and cut, repeatedly passing the edge. Gilmour kept a fuller length and with the first ball of his second over he pinned the hapless Dennis Amiss to his stumps. The crack of a cover drive to the boundary by Barry Wood gave the crowd their first chance for a big cheer, only for them to be quietened again when another full-length Gilmour delivery cannoned off the opener's pads onto his stumps to make the score 2–11.

Tony Greig, who had a miserable tournament with the bat, tried to counterattack. Gilmour responded with one that went the other way. Greig drove, edged and Marsh, diving horizontally at full length past Ian Chappell, provided photographer Patrick Eagar with one of the game's best-known action shots.

Frank Hayes, hitting one sweet on drive, and Keith Fletcher, hanging on for grim death, took the total to 33 before Gilmour, obviously bowling his 12 over spell in one hit, utterly broke the back of the England innings. Hayes, Fletcher and Alan Knott were all trapped lbw by balls straightening down the line. The crowd groaned, but each batsman gave umpire David Constant an easy decision by falling across the crease. Knott said the static sightscreen at the grandstand end gave the batsman a poor view of a left-arm over the wicket bowler. Gilmour just gave a contented smile. The bank clerk had 6–14.

Chris Old edged Max Walker to Greg Chappell to make it 7–37. A sub-50 total looked a possibility, but Gilmour's spell was soon finished and the maligned English captain, Mike Denness, was trying to make a fight of it. He lost John Snow caught behind down the leg-side on the stroke of lunch, but managed to take the total to 73 before an exaggerated Walker inswinger bowled him. Each run was precious and Geoff Arnold's method of hanging out a vertical bat proved as effective as any of the more accepted techniques. A couple of edged fours were of frustration to the Australians until Walker found

favour from Bill Alley against Peter Lever. England all out 93. England stunned.

But just as Gilmour, Walker and Lillee revelled in the strange Headingley surface, so, too, would Snow, Old and Arnold. Alley and Constant were soon called on to adjudicate again on balls seaming late and thumping into pads. In the eighth over, with Australia's score on 17, Geoff Arnold received an affirmative answer against Turner. On 24 Snow, after no-balling and running on the pitch problems, got it right against Ian Chappell. Eight runs later he repeated the dose to Greg.

If 3–32 gave the Yorkshire faithful some cheer, the start of local boy Chris Old's spell then sent them into ecstasy. Old required no umpire's assistance as he smashed the stumps of Rick McCosker, Ross Edwards and Rod Marsh in eight balls. The three dismissals, particularly the sight of Edward's middle stump flying, induced a sort of stolid Yorkshire-style hysteria. Despite the odds, England now looked likely winners.

Doug Walters remained, phlegmatic, gum chewing, joking. Out to join him came the Newcastle bank clerk. Like Walters, Gilmour wore a long-sleeved jumper to keep out the chill wind, yet he immediately warmed to his task. He felt he had nothing to lose. His day had already been quite a good one. 'I always assumed if I went out and hit the ball nothing could go wrong,' he later commented. So when the ball was overpitched or off line he swung hard. England had taken their six wickets without the involvement of a fieldsman. When the ball started flying their slips could not catch it. Gilmour struck five boundaries. Walters hit a terrific straight drive to the Kirkstall Lane end and struck a perfect square cut off Arnold. The pressure eased. A scampered leg bye from the fourth ball of the 29th over took the seventh wicket stand to 55, and this exciting sudden-death semi-final was over. Australia, criticised from pillar to post throughout the tournament, were relieved to be through. They may not have shown too much knowledge about one-day cricket, except for one fairly important thing: under Ian Chappell they knew how to win.

England was devastated by its inability to again make runs against Australian pacemen.

Their selectors were within a couple of weeks of making wholesale changes to the make-up of the national team.

The post-mortems included plenty of criticism of the pitch. Denness did not like the uneven bounce. Jim Laker wrote, 'I don't like condemning wickets ... But ...' George Cawthray, the head groundsman, defended his creation suggesting the atmosphere was responsible for the way the seam and swing bowlers dominated. Other Englishmen bemoaned their bad luck with the toss.

ENGLAND

D.L. Amiss lbw Gilmour	2
B. Wood b Gilmour	6
K.W.R. Fletcher lbw Gilmour	8
A.W. Greig c Marsh b Gilmour	7
F.C. Hayes lbw Gilmour	4
M.H. Denness (capt) b Walker	27
A.P.E. Knott (wk) lbw Gilmour	0
C.M. Old c G.S. Chappell b Walker	0
J.A. Snow c Marsh b Lillee	2
G.G. Arnold not out	18
P. Lever lbw Walker	5
Extras (lb 5, w 7, nb 2)	14
(36.2 overs)	93

1/2 2/11 3/26 4/33 5/35 6/36 7/37 8/52 9/73 10/93

Bowling: Lillee 9–3–26–1; Gilmour 12–6–14–6; Walker 9.2–3–22–3; Thomson 6–0–17–0

AUSTRALIA

A. Turner lbw Arnold	7
R.B. McCosker b Old	15
I.M. Chappell (capt) lbw Snow	2
G.S. Chappell lbw Snow	4
K.D. Walters not out	20
R. Edwards b Old	0
R.W. Marsh (wk) b Old	5
G.J. Gilmour not out	28
Extras (b 1, lb 6, nb 6)	13
(28.4 overs)	6–94

Did not bat: M.H.N. Walker, D.K. Lillee, J.R. Thomson

1/17 2/24 3/32 4/32 5/32 6/39

Bowling: Arnold 7.4–2–15–1; Snow 12–0–30–2; Old 7–2–29–3; Lever 2–0–7–0

Umpires: W.E. Alley, D.J. Constant.

Toss: Australia

SECOND SEMI-FINAL: NEW ZEALAND vs WEST INDIES
THE OVAL: WEST INDIES WON BY 5 WICKETS

Not unnaturally, there was less attention paid to the semi-final in the south of the country than the one holding the nation riveted at Leeds. Yet a goodly 12,000 turned up at The Oval to witness the West Indies continue their inexorable progress into the final at Lord's. This game failed to go the full distance either, but it lasted more than 90 overs and had a pace to it more akin to what is usual at a cricket match. New Zealand just about did the sum of their talents justice against Clive Lloyd's powerful unit without totally convincing anyone that they deserved to be there ahead of Pakistan.

Lloyd won the toss and asked the Kiwis, who were without Richard Hadlee, to bat. This was a decision of habit rather than one based on the conditions. The south of England was bathed in sunshine and the pitch at The Oval was flat and hard. Bernard Julien struck quickly, trapping John Morrison lbw with an inswinger that straightened down the line. At the same time further up the M1 Gary Gilmour was making that type of dismissal a habit and the day his own.

Julien, too, would end with excellent figures, but nothing as spectacular as the Australian's.

Certainly there was no sign of a collapse at this stage. Andy Roberts started with a fiery spell but Glenn Turner and Geoff Howarth, who was enjoying the familiar surroundings of his county home, consolidated. They took the total to 1–92 at the lunch break off 29 overs, an excellent platform from which to build a total to really challenge the West Indies. But while they had withstood the Roberts barrage once, they failed to do so a second time. A brilliant diving slips catch by Rohan Kanhai removed Turner and the dismissal of the New Zealand captain once more precipitated disaster. Howarth just made it to his half century before becoming Roberts' second victim. Then Julien ripped through the middle order. With the exception of Brian Hastings, the Kiwi resistance crumbled. Only 66 runs were added after lunch in 23 overs while nine wickets fell to a succession of fairly soft strokes. Julien and Vanburn Holder had the figures, but Roberts had done the psychological damage.

The West Indies was 159 runs away from a place in the final. They, too, lost their first wicket with eight runs on the board, Roy Fredericks holing out at square leg off Dayle Hadlee. Gordon Greenidge was in his best form of the tournament, however, and Alvin Kallicharran was again irrepressible. The pair had to overcome an accurate spell by Richard Collinge. Once he was seen off the shots started flowing.

Greenidge was relieved to be back to something approaching his best form, while Kallicharran batted as beautifully as he had against Australia without resorting to quite the same artistic savagery even when Dayle Hadlee, against all logic, tried him out with a few short deliveries. They were promptly dealt with. Greenidge and Kallicharran added 125 for the second wicket, taking their side to within 26 runs of victory. The never-say-die spirit of New Zealand had kept them in the tournament and even though their fate was now sealed they were

not quite finished. Big Collinge came back, banging the ball hard into and, more than once, through the top of the wicket.

He got his large frame down low to hold a checked drive from Kallicharran, forced Greenidge into a hook from a ball too far up to him, and got the last lbw of the tournament when Viv Richards, like so many others that day, misjudged an inswinger from a left-arm paceman. When young Brian McKechnie had Clive Lloyd caught at square leg they had lost four wickets while advancing just 18 runs. Given another 40 to chase there might have been some drama, but Rohan Kanhai and Julien only needed to put together a stand of eight runs, which they duly did with 20 overs still to spare.

The New Zealanders, with a couple of exceptions, packed their bags and headed for home with their heads held high. The West Indies prepared for a Lord's final that they believed had been their destiny since the day the sun shone on the welcoming Duke of Edinburgh's shining silver pate.

NEW ZEALAND

G.M. Turner (capt) c Kanhai b Roberts	36
J.F.M. Morrison lbw Julien	5
G.P. Howarth c Murray b Roberts	51
J.M. Parker b Lloyd	3
B.F. Hastings not out	24
K.J. Wadsworth (wk) c Lloyd b Julien	11
B.J. McKechnie lbw Julien	1
D.R. Hadlee c Holder b Julien	0
B.L. Cairns b Holder	10
H.J. Howarth b Holder	0
R.O. Collinge b Holder	2
Extras (b 1, lb 5, w 2, nb 7)	15
(52.2 overs)	158

1/8 2/98 3/105 4/106 5/125 6/133 7/139 8/155 9/155 10/158

Bowling: Julien 12–5–27–4; Roberts 11–3–18–2; Holder 8.2–0–30–3; Boyce 9–0–31–0; Lloyd 12–1–37–1

WEST INDIES

R.C. Fredericks c Hastings b Hadlee	6
C.G. Greenidge lbw Collinge	55
A.I. Kallicharran c & b Collinge	72
I.V.A. Richards lbw Collinge	5
R.B. Kanhai not out	12
C.H. Lloyd (capt) c Hastings b McKechnie	3
B.D. Julien not out	4
Extras (lb 1, nb 1)	2
(40.1 overs)	5–159

Did not bat: D.L. Murray (wk), K.D. Boyce, V.A. Holder, A.M.E. Roberts

1/8 2/133 3/139 4/142 5/151

Bowling: Collinge 12–4–28–3; D.R. Hadlee 10–0–54–1; Cairns 6.1–2–23–0; McKechnie 8–0–37–1; H.J. Howarth 4–0–15–0

Umpires: W.L. Budd, A.E. Fagg.

Toss: West Indies

SATURDAY 21 JUNE 1975
THE PRUDENTIAL CUP FINAL
AUSTRALIA vs WEST INDIES
LORD'S: WEST INDIES WON BY 17 RUNS

The lead-up to the greatest cricketing show on earth was everything the promoters would have

wished. NW8 buzzed with excitement as ticket touts, newsmen, photographers, officials and, somewhere in there, players practising were caught up in the thrills and tension of a true cup final. There was even a little bit of controversy to add some extra spice. Derrick Robbins, a wealthy promoter of private tours to South Africa, called the Prudential Cup 'rubbish' and a 'travesty'. He claimed to have first proposed a world cup of first-class matches more along the lines of the 1912 fiasco. He was especially upset at what happened in the game at Headingley: 'If that match had gone over two innings, we would have had a true result.' Mr Robbins was speaking from Cape Town, but he was an Englishman.

All that was quickly forgotten when Saturday 21 June dawned with the bluest skies and an unending sun that demanded cricket. Satellites were not numerous or sophisticated enough to make the World Cup final the significant global television event it later became. Fans in the Caribbean had to be content with radio coverage. In Australia the Australian Broadcasting Commission made a special satellite booking allowing them to televise the majority of the match live and in colour into every household. In 1975 that was an occasion as historic as the game itself. Those who settled for the evening in front of their television or radio knew they would be in for a long night. One hundred and twenty overs of cricket looked likely to extend well into the early morning in Australia, especially when the team selections revealed both sides were packed with pacemen. There was not a short run-up, nor a spinner, in sight.

Lord's was filled to its 27,000 capacity as Gordon Greenidge and Roy Fredericks made their way out behind Ian Chappell's Australians as the clock approached 11 am. Chappell had won the toss and asked the West Indies to bat. Chasing a target seemed to be becoming the favoured option of the toss-winning captain. Clive Lloyd also tended to follow that practice, although he stated he was a little surprised by his counterpart's decision because the conditions seemed so favourable to batsmen.

The West Indies, as crowd and bookmakers favourites, were perhaps under a little more pressure than the Australians. Even by this stage of the tournament Doug Walters felt the Aussies had a fairly relaxed attitude. 'We did not have any team meetings or make any special plans for the final,' he says. 'Ian Chappell won the toss, sent the West Indies in and hoped Lillee, Thomson, Gilmour and Walker would blast them out for 120. Failing that, I suppose he wanted to know the target we would have to chase.'

Walters was on his third tour of England. For Rick McCosker on his first trip everything was new and exciting. 'It was all a fairy story to me,' McCosker says. 'I was just chuffed to be there. There was a special atmosphere brought about by this huge din that lasted all day. It was like a carnival.'

In contrast to the Australians, Clive Lloyd said everyone in his side was quite tense. Greenidge admits to being so nervous and excited his entry on to the ground is now a bit of a blur, but he and Fredericks didn't have much trouble getting the score to 12. The wicket was true and there was no perceptible movement off the seam or in the air.

Then Lillee, bowling from the Nursery End, sent down a bouncer to the left-handed Fredericks. An instinctive hooker, he struck it sweetly and fine, rocketing the ball over the fine-leg boundary. The West Indian supporters broke into a spontaneous roar. Fredericks, though, started to walk towards the pavilion. Lillee's bouncer had just angled back into him, causing Fredericks to have to lean back further and then overbalance slightly on the pivot with the shot. That, his decision to wear rubber-soled shoes, and the English habit of leaving the grass uncut and unrolled within the batting creases threw his feet from under him and onto the stumps. It was an astonishing, genuine and classic case of six and out and it occurred on the game's greatest and newest stage.

Kallicharran announced his arrival by starting off where he finished at The Oval. A glorious cover drive off Gilmour was followed by a pull to the grandstand. But Greenidge, perhaps becoming even more overcome by the occasion, had stalled. The team's momentum went with him and Kallicharran, perhaps for just a moment, was distracted. He tried an off-balance cut against Gilmour and only succeeded in edging the ball to Rod Marsh. In the 10th over the West Indies were 2–27.

Rohan Kanhai, having seen it all, looked in command of his emotions. Lloyd has stated how important his experience was in controlling the situation within the team. He got off the mark with a boundary, too, a classic cover drive on the up off Thomson, who had relieved Lillee. He also hit another fine cover shot off Walker before the big medium pacer quietened him with balls that jumped and struck the splice of his bat. The total was taken to 50 in the 18th over, but it had progressed no further when Greenidge edged a low catch behind off Thomson. The opener, still in his funny blue towelling hat, was disappointed, but he consoled himself with the fact that the sting had been taken out of the new ball for the strokeplayers to follow.

Whatever Greenidge's thoughts, the West Indian innings at 3–50 was in the balance. Ian Chappell recognised this and immediately brought back Lillee into the attack. Lloyd responded with a clip off his toes to the square-leg boundary in front of the Tavern Stand. Lillee challenged with a bouncer and Lloyd hooked him for a perfect six in the same direction. Another pull/hook was mistimed, but Ross Edwards failed to hold the low chance at mid wicket. A crucial miss. The West Indies went to lunch at 3–91 off 28 overs.

Kanhai remained scoreless for 11 overs either side of the interval. Lloyd, however, kept the runs coming single-handedly. A fine leg glance to the pavilion off Thomson brought up the 100 and the 50-run partnership in 49 minutes, Kanhai having contributed just six of those. Ten minutes later the West Indian captain lofted Walker down the ground to record his own half century in under an hour with seven fours and that one six.

Big 'Tangles' Walker's tidy first seven over spell became a distant memory as Lloyd took it upon himself to lift the run rate. There were more dropped catches, another to Edwards at deep point off Greg Chappell and one to Lillee at fine leg off the now despairing Walker. Both times Kanhai was the beneficiary. Lloyd needed no further assistance. He smacked Walker, now bowling around the wicket, off the front foot

over square leg into the waving, cheering throng in the grandstand for his second six. That brought up the 100 partnership in 85 minutes and was followed by two slashing square cuts and a lofted cover drive all to the boundary off the same bowler. Walker, thought of as someone suited to English conditions, conceded 71 runs from his allotted 12 overs, including 49 from his last five.

No bowler was immune. Gilmour was lifted to mid wicket for another four to take Lloyd to 99. A stunning square drive, just for a single to the now protected point boundary, raised the most amazing century in 100 fantastically entertaining minutes off just 82 balls with two sixes and twelve fours.

'I guess you would call my fielding position off-side sweeper now,' Rick McCosker says. 'I remember Lloyd hitting that ball straight to me. I was right on the boundary and it was struck with such power I am certain that a yard either side of me I wouldn't have been able to cut it off. I thought, "How hard did he hit that?" He had so much power.'

Television commentator, Jim Laker, normally very restrained, was in uncontained rapture at Lloyd's superb exhibition. Of course, he was still slightly more subdued than the spontaneous Caribbean festival that was erupting among West Indian fans. Even the Australian team acknowledged Lloyd's mastery. 'At the time Ross Edwards missed that catch we weren't too pleased,' Doug Walters says. 'At this distance I don't mind so much, though. Lloyd's innings still holds up as one of the best ever seen in one-day cricket. He certainly played magnificently.'

English batting legend Denis Compton compared Lloyd's innings to Australian Stan McCabe's startling 232 in the Trent Bridge Test of 1938. Tony Lewis wrote of an innings of 'surpassing talent and power'. John Arlott's tribute spoke of 'relaxed majesty' and his ability to strike the ball 'mightily and as he willed'.

Soon after the cacophony of cans and bugles died down Kanhai got them going again when he drove Walters wristly to the point boundary to complete his own invaluable fifty. Then, after 36 overs and a 149-run stand with Kanhai, Lloyd's magnum opus was over. Unfortunately its ending was a bit anti-climactic. A leg-side flick off Gilmour, a low take by Marsh, an appeal, the umpires consulted and 'Dickie' Bird raised his finger. Lloyd was unsure, but he proudly ambled away to a thunderous standing ovation befitting the performance.

Suddenly, Gilmour was on song from the Nursery End. He bowled Kanhai through the gate and repeated the dose to young Viv Richards. At 6–209 in the 46th over the West Indies were in danger of not seeing out their overs. It was Keith Boyce who regained the initiative. He took a liking to Thomson's bowling and hit up a quick-fire 34 before mistiming a full toss off the same bowler. With Bernard Julien holding firm, Boyce and then Deryck Murray struck out with freedom. The wicketkeeper pulled Lillee over square leg for another six before a leading edge made him Gilmour's fifth victim.

Vanburn Holder's cue-end swipe and an overthrow from the final ball of the innings left the Australians a massive 8–291 to chase. At 4.00 pm, Gilmour, rightly content again with his efforts, led the side from the field. He was followed by 10 furrowed brows all of which registered the enormity of the task in front of them.

The Australians required 4.86 runs per over for the duration of their innings if they were to reach their target. Rick McCosker and Alan Turner opened with a stand of 25 before Boyce ran a leg-cutter up the slope to have McCosker caught at second slip for seven.

Ian Chappell immediately settled in with typical fidgety determination and found that Turner had warmed to his task. The Australian captain could hardly hope to emulate his West Indian counterpart, but still unleashed some fine shots. A pull off Julien was followed by a cracking cover drive. Chappell lofted Boyce over mid-on for another four and Turner hooked Holder down to the Tavern boundary.

At 1–81 from 20 overs Australia had built the foundation they needed. Seeing his fast medium bowlers punished, Lloyd brought himself into the attack. Chappell played his first ball quietly to the on side and called Turner for a single. The left-hander hesitated a moment, then took off.

Viv Richards raced in and in one movement picked up the ball and with an underarm flick scored a direct hit on the stumps. It was close, but 'Dickie' Bird gave Turner out.

That signalled the start of the most bizarre period of the match. Clive Lloyd said his side noticed quite early that the Australians had some suicidal running tendencies. After Turner's demise the Chappell brothers added 26 runs in four overs up to tea, Greg Chappell hitting a terrific on drive and a pull for four. The break was taken at 2–107 from 25 overs. It was already 6 pm in St John's Wood and 3 am in the eastern states for the bleary-eyed still watching on television in Australia.

Soon after the interval Ian Chappell glanced Andy Roberts to the pavilion rails. A couple of stolen singles took the partnership to 34. When Ian Chappell pushed a Roberts delivery to point there was a momentary misfield, a change in the call, then a brilliant recovery by Richards who this time picked up, swivelled and threw down the stumps from side-on. Greg Chappell just kept running towards the pavilion.

An Ian Chappell straight drive for three off Roberts brought up the Australian captain's 50 in 100 minutes with four fours. Now, though, he was playing second fiddle to Walters who was in prime form. Pulls and cuts brought boundaries off Holder. One deflected off umpire Tom Spencer's leg. Such was its force it left him with a bleeding cut for the rest of the game.

Again Australia fought back to level terms, only to muck up between wickets. After 38 overs it was 3–162 when Lloyd began his 10th over. Ian Chappell pushed to mid wicket. There was hesitation. The fieldsman, inevitably, was Richards. Chappell went through but the throw to Lloyd found him a metre short. The cans and bugles rang out.

'A lot has been made of our running between wickets,' Doug Walters says, 'but the need to chase such a big total meant we had to chance short singles. Then run-outs are always on. Especially when someone like Viv Richards is in such good form with their throwing arm.'

'It wasn't just the number of run-outs,' Rick McCosker says. 'It was who they were and when they occurred. Richards ran-out three key players. I believe it made the difference in the end. It's funny, probably the two best out-fieldsmen on the ground were Richards and Ross Edwards. Roscoe had a bad day, Richards was brilliant. If the game had been played again the situation could just as easily have been reversed.'

From that point the Australian innings started to subside. After another beautiful cover drive Walters took one chance too many off Lloyd: 'I was happy with the way I batted. All the time, though, the match seemed to be slipping away. I tried to hit a straight one to the on side and missed.' Ross Edwards, Rod Marsh, Gary Gilmour and Max Walker hit out as effectively as they could, but succumbed to Keith Boyce and the pressure of the required run rate.

When Walker became the fourth batsman to be run-out in the innings, another direct-hit victim looking for a run to square leg that wasn't there, Australia were 9–233. The crowd was already charging onto the ground at every oppor-tunity. They had danced all over the place when Marsh was clean bowled, and Rohan Kanhai was swamped when he caught Gary Gilmour at deep square leg just in front of the grandstand. Now it seemed half the 27,000 were lined up at the boundary rope anticipating the end.

The last wicket pair of Dennis Lillee and Jeff Thomson required 59 runs from just 43 balls, supposedly an impossible task. Just as impossible as the one Murray and Roberts tackled at Edgbaston. Thomson straight drove the first ball of Roberts ninth over for four, then clipped him off his toes to square leg for another. Lillee lofted Holder over mid-on for still another boundary and the field spread to all corners. A sharp single to square leg gave Richards the opportunity for another direct-hit run-out, but he missed and the resultant overthrow brought up the Australian 250.

Every appeal by the fieldsmen led to another pitch invasion. When Thomson was caught at cover by Fredericks off a no-ball there was abso-lute mayhem. Fredericks threw at the stumps for a run-out, missed and there was no sign of anyone backing up. Nobody could find the ball. Jim Laker suggested the Australians could have run 10! When the crowd was finally persuaded to leave the arena and the ball was returned, Thomson was given three runs. Lloyd, who had not heard Tom Spencer's no-ball call, had to ask what was going on.

Even the neutral English spectators found it hard to bear the tension. With the field spread and the ground now mostly in evening shadow, the requirement was getting steeper. Eighteen were needed off nine balls when Thomson swung and missed at Holder. He just sort of wandered out of his crease looking for the ball and the chance of a run at the same time. When he saw that Murray had it in his gloves he dived back for his crease. Too late. Murray scored yet another direct hit. Thomson was the fifth run-out victim and the Prudential Cup had a winner at 8.43 pm on the longest day of the year.

No-one dwelt on that thought. Despite their obvious exhaustion, players and umpires sprinted for safety, Murray risking self-impalement with a clutch of stumps as he ran. An area in front of the pavilion was secured by rope and police enforcement. The Duke of Edinburgh stepped forward. Clive Lloyd was called up to the podium. He received both the Man of the Match award and the World Cup. The latter trophy was held aloft. The West Indian captain admits to this being his greatest moment in cricket.

'We were disappointed at having got so close and not quite making it,' McCosker says. 'But there was also the feeling that we had competed well and we were proud to be there on such a fantastic day in front of such a fantastic crowd. We were also absolutely exhausted. We had got there early in the morning and by the time we left the ground after having showers and a few drinks it was midnight.

'The two teams stayed together and had a few beers. It was a nice moment, with both sides feeling they had been part of a special event.'

WEST INDIES	
R.C. Fredericks hit wicket b Lillee	7
C.G. Greenidge c Marsh b Thomson	13
A.I. Kallicharran c Marsh b Gilmour	12
R.B. Kanhai b Gilmour	55
C.H. Lloyd (capt) c Marsh b Gilmour	102
I.V.A. Richards b Gilmour	5
K.D. Boyce c G.S. Chappell b Thomson	34
B.D. Julien not out	26
D.L. Murray (wk) c & b Gilmour	14
V.A. Holder not out	6
Extras (lb 6, nb 11)	17
(60 overs)	8-291

Did not bat: A.M.E. Roberts

1/12 2/27 3/50 4/199 5/206 6/209 7/261 8/285

Bowling: Lillee 12-1-55-1; Gilmour 12-2-48-5; Thomson 12-1-44-2; Walker 12-1-71-0; G.S. Chappell 7-0-33-0; Walters 5-0-23-0

AUSTRALIA	
R.B. McCosker c Kallicharran b Boyce	7
A. Turner run out	40
I.M. Chappell (capt) run out	62
G.S. Chappell run out	15
K.D. Walters b Lloyd	35
R.W. Marsh (wk) b Boyce	11
R. Edwards c Fredericks b Boyce	28
G.J. Gilmour c Kanhai b Boyce	14
M.H.N. Walker run out	7
J.R. Thomson run out	21
D.K. Lillee not out	16
Extras (b 2, lb 9, nb 7)	18
(58.4 overs)	274

1/25 2/81 3/115 4/162 5/170 6/195 7/221 8/231 9/233 10/274

Bowling: Julien 12-0-58-0; Roberts 11-1-45-0; Boyce 12-0-50-4; Holder 11.4-1-65-0; Lloyd 12-1-38-1

Umpires: H.D. Bird, T.W. Spencer.

Toss: Australia

POST-MORTEM

The cricketing world was unanimous in its approval of the 1975 World Cup final. Jack Fingleton, a hard-bitten Australian cricketer journalist who had played in the bodyline series, called it 'a game never to be forgotten, in line with the Brisbane tied Test against the West Indies'. John Arlott suggested, 'The entertainment was prodigious'. Nobody could disagree.

Australia had less time to wait than even Clive Lloyd to forget the World Cup. The next Wednesday they began preparation for the main objective of their tour with a match against Kent at Canterbury. They went on to win the four-Test series against England 1–0, thus retaining the Ashes. That was also a well-attended series, further boosting the coffers of the TCCB during an almost ideal summer. Once all the sums had been done the Prudential World Cup registered a surplus of £244,784. Takings from the Lord's final itself were £117,000. A tidy profit for what was considered a risky venture. A subcommittee set up by the International Cricket Conference decided the future of the World Cup. That was easy, too. Everyone would be back in four years, although there was consideration given to lifting the number of contestants to 10.

3

The Second Prudential World Cup, 1979:

Richards Lightens the Gloom

The cricket world of the Prudential World Cup in 1979 was a very different place from the one it had been in 1975. Some would say the sport had finally started to grow up. Others might suggest it had lost some of its essential charm and aspects that were unique and valuable. Each argument is correct in its own right. Certainly cricket would never be the same again after the events of 1977.

I refer, of course, to the setting up of World Series Cricket by Australian media magnate Kerry Packer. In a bid to take control of televised cricket in Australia, Packer signed the best players in the world for sums of money far in excess of anything the game's established authorities believed they could afford to give them.

The problems associated with leading cricketers' meagre financial rewards could be no better exemplified than by the events that immediately followed the 1975 World Cup. The whole tournament was an unqualified success with 160,000 spectators filing through the turnstiles to witness the 15 cricket matches. This included the full house at the Lord's final, all 27,000 of whom were right royally entertained by the 22 protagonists on the day.

Yet the fantastic efforts of the winning side over the concentrated and enervating two weeks were rewarded with a mere £350 per man, plus the splitting of the £4000 prize money and the honour and glory. The captain for one was not impressed by the non-recognition from the admittedly always cash-strapped West Indian Board. Lloyd was at least partly satisfied when the Guyanese government organised a motorcade through Georgetown and presented each team member with a commemorative gold chain.

When Packer came along with his cheque-book the West Indians signed almost en masse. So, too, did most of the Australians who had also started to wonder at their recompense in relation to the massive crowds they attracted to cricket grounds and the enormous television audiences that followed them. Packer was in no way buying into a game that was in its death throes, even though his media empire has perpetuated that myth over the years. He was mainly concerned with the lucrative television rights. When he secured those he was prepared to hand back the control of international cricket and cricketers to the original authorities. So poorly paid were the players, though, that it is now obvious that if Packer had not stepped in another entrepreneur soon would have. They were ripe for the picking.

The Cricket War, as it has been called, split the game's fraternity, ruptured many friendships and created a lot of ill will. However, it all seems small potatoes in comparison to the wheeling and dealing that goes on in the cutthroat business world of the 1990s. A modern economic rationalist would wonder how the game ever ran as it did before 1977.

The truce was called in May 1979, only a couple of weeks before the second Prudential World Cup. It came as no surprise. ICC officials had spoken with Packer early in 1979 and the big man had gone to 'have lunch' with the Australian authorities during the poorly attended Australia vs Pakistan Test at the MCG in March.

The second World Cup, like the first one, was to be fought out in England over the period of a fortnight in early to mid-June. Some suggested

World Cup Final 1979 — Viv Richards during his magnificent innings of 138 not out against England.

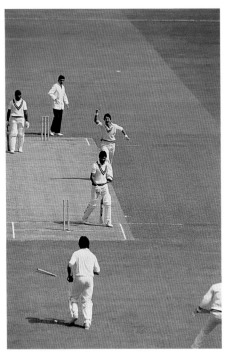

New Zealand vs Pakistan, World Cup 1983 round two — Richard Hadlee takes the wicket of Zaheer Abbas for a duck.

(Allsport/Adrian Murrell)

Roger Binny (India) takes a catch during the match at Chelmsford that ended Australia's 1983 World Cup hopes.

(Allsport/Adrian Murrell)

Sandhu of India avoids a bouncer from Malcolm Marshall during the 1983 final.

(Allsport/Adrian Murrell)

Andy Roberts (West Indies) out lbw to Kapil Dev as India head towards their amazing victory in the 1983 final.

(Allsport/Adrian Murrell)

Celebrations as Australia beats England by seven runs to claim the 1987 World Cup.   (Allsport/Adrian Murrell)

Three players central to Australia's successful 1987 World Cup campaign: Allan Border (capt); David Boon and Dean Jones scoring runs in the Calcutta final. (Allsport/Adrian Murrell) (Allsport/Chris Cole) (Allsport/Chris Cole)

the West Indies, as the holders of the trophy should have been the hosts the second time around. Even Clive Lloyd felt that the geography and climate of the Caribbean might make the effective running of the tournament difficult. The Indian authorities quickly revealed their interest in taking a turn at being hosts, but had to wait a little longer.

A similar format and time frame to that used in 1975 were agreed upon. The tournament would again constitute a schedule of 15 matches, contested between eight teams. In the Round One matches each side in two groups of four would play against the others. The top two teams in each group would then contest the semi-finals, followed by a final at Lord's three days later between the semi-final winners. Prudential Assurance, as major sponsor again, kicked in £250,000. Six of the eight teams were the current Test playing nations. South Africa, even more isolated than in 1975, was not considered.

Sri Lanka, as it did in 1975, and Canada made up the numbers. They earned their spot by being finalists in the International Cricket Conference Trophy. That tournament, played on grounds in the English Midlands, preceded the World Cup by only a couple of weeks. Its purpose was to fill those World Cup places and to encourage associate member countries to strive for recognition against the major cricketing nations. Despite their loss to Israel in a walkover, Sri Lanka's victory in the ICC final surprised no-one. They were getting very close to full Test status and in fact they followed their 1979 World Cup campaign with a nine match first-class tour of England. The promotion of Canada, on the other hand, was quite a shock.

As in 1975, innings would be of 60 overs duration, bowlers were permitted a maximum of 12 overs and any bouncer that flew above the batsman's head was to be called a no-ball. The weather, so kind four years earlier, was still not to be trusted and each game had two reserve days attached to it. In 1975 not one reserve day was used. This time it was to be quite a different story.

The ICC, at their 1978 meeting, offered no guidance to individual countries as to what their selection policy should be regarding players contracted to World Series Cricket. The game's authorities had lost out badly when taken to court by some Packer players in 1977 for restraint of trade. They had no desire to return there. Any real chance of embarrassment in the matter receded further when Packer and the Australian authorities signed their truce. It meant that every side, with the exception of the Australians, would virtually be at full strength for the tournament.

The West Indies were red-hot favourites to retain the title. Since their great victory in 1975 they had built a side with awesome fast-bowling firepower. In support of the still very formidable Andy Roberts were Michael Holding, Joel Garner and Colin Croft. All four were fast bowlers of the most intimidating type, capable of devastating pace. Batsmen had their composure challenged on a number of levels, not least being that each paceman had such a long run-up that matches might not be finished until the dulled light of late evening. To compensate for this new-found threat of four express fast bowlers in the one side, batsmen had recently started to wear helmets with some regularity in a design familiar today.

The West Indian batting, too, had matured into something to be envied. Left-handed opener Roy Fredericks had retired, but into his place had stepped the aggressive young Barbadian, Desmond Haynes. Clive Lloyd had lost none of his powers either as batsman or astute captain and motivator. Most imposing of all when assessing the West Indies prospects was that their line-up now contained clearly the best batsman in the world. Four years on, Viv Richards had emerged as the most entertaining, powerful and aggressive strokeplayer imaginable. He had stamped his presence on the previous tournament with his fielding in the final. This time he would be able to let his bat do the talking.

The West Indies side of 1979 was arguably as good as any that has played the game. In 1984, with the addition of the superb Malcolm Marshall to the starting 11, they were pretty special, too, but hardly more so than this squad for the second World Cup. The young Marshall was in the party, but could not break into the final line-up. The likes of Wayne Daniel and Sylvester Clarke did not even get that far. The captain initially was concerned as to how his three non-WSC members would blend in with the bulk of the side. He need not have worried.

The West Indies' worthy opponents in the 1975 final could boast no such equal development. Despite the settlement with Packer, the Australian authorities were obliged to stay with the players who had remained faithful to their cause between 1977 and 1979. That meant they were captained by the inexperienced 25-year-old Western Australian, Kim Hughes. Hughes had only recently secured the job when he replaced the injured Graham Yallop for the second Test of the brief series against Pakistan. He led what amounted to a 'B' side which was considered 20–1 outsiders to win the tournament. It was a team that was supposed to have loads of potential. However, most of that was never realised and many had only a couple of weeks left as Australian players. Some of the names from that World Cup squad and the follow-up tour of India make for excellent quiz questions for cricket trivia buffs. Is all-rounder Graeme Porter the most obscure cricketer to wear a baggy green cap this side of the Second World War? Maybe so, but he did top the bowling averages for the whole tournament.

Not everyone was without a future. Fast bowler Rodney Hogg who had taken a record-breaking 41 wickets in the recent Ashes series, had his moments of success in the early 1980s. He arrived in England with an anti-hero fanfare to rival Jeff Thomson's from the previous World Cup. Hogg bowled very fast and very straight and had fair hair like Thomson. But it was curly and he also had a great tendency to fall over in his follow through, which never was a concern for Thommo.

Kim Hughes batted brilliantly at times and captained Australia off and on between 1979 and 1984, without ever convincing everyone of his suitability for the role. Eventually he resigned in tears in Brisbane after a bitter defeat by the West Indies. And a lower profiled left-handed batsman named Allan Border was emerging from the second string pack on his way to a reasonably

respectable career of 156 Tests and 11,000 runs. This was the first of seven eventual trips to England for Border wearing Australian colours.

The names left out of the Australian line-up were far more impressive than those in it. Greg and Ian Chappell, Dennis Lillee, Jeff Thomson, and Rod Marsh would have to wait until the next southern summer to reclaim their rightful places at the forefront of Australian cricket.

Under Mike Brearley, England looked a much stronger contender this time around. They had demolished Australia 5–1 in the Test series in Australia, having lost just a handful of players to World Series Cricket. They had, however, been defeated 2–1 in a three match one-day series down-under. This time they were drawn in the same group as their traditional rivals and were scheduled to meet them on the opening day of the tournament at Lord's in a sell-out match. But in reality it was Pakistan, not Australia, who posed the greatest threat to English progress in Group B.

England have probably never had a better side since than the one which represented them between 9 and 23 June 1979. Geoff Boycott was properly rehabilitated and well-managed by Brearley. Ian Botham had emerged as a match-winning all-rounder. He and Bob Willis gave the English pace attack a bite it has often lacked in the two decades since. David Gower and Graham Gooch added class to the middle-order batting and some youthful zest. Members of the support cast like Derek Randall, Mike Hendrick and Chris Old were also quite worthy.

Much attention surrounded the young Ian Botham. The powerful Somerset all-rounder had completed an almost unbroken sequence of fantastic feats since his debut on the international stage against Australia at Trent Bridge in 1977. He had belted centuries, smashed stumps and taken blinding catches seemingly at will over a two-year period. Some English supporters almost believed he would win them the World Cup by himself. Such was Botham's confidence he might just about have imagined it, too.

New Zealand's semi-final berth in 1975 had accelerated their growing stature as a force to be reckoned with in international cricket. In 1979

Glenn Turner had just returned to the side after a self-imposed break, but he was no longer captain. The veteran batsman Mark Burgess assumed that role. Nor could Turner take his position as number one in the batting order for granted. The left-handed opening combination of John Wright and Bruce Edgar had recently done sterling service and they offered a far better long-term bet than the older and sometimes reluctant Turner.

The most obvious sign of progress in New Zealand cricket, however, had been the growth in status and expertise of the fast bowler Richard Hadlee. Hadlee was now a fast bowler and hard-hitting lower order batsman of the highest calibre. A stunning spell by Hadlee at Wellington in February 1978 led to England being skittled for 64. That effort had given New Zealand cricket the fillip of a historic and long-awaited first Test win against the mother country. It was a superb effort by Hadlee and there were many more to follow.

Pakistan did a full circle by reinstating Asif Iqbal as captain just prior to the tournament. In 1975 he took over the role from Intikhab Alam. This time he replaced Mushtaq Mohammad. Pakistan, like the West Indies, picked virtually all their World Series Cricket players. They would again be a formidable contender.

They also had a brilliant fast bowling all-rounder as their spearhead and inspiration. Imran Khan had elevated his rating almost in unison with Hadlee and Botham. The turning point in Imran's career had been a mighty 12-wicket bowling return in a Test in Sydney early in 1977 which, like Hadlee's spell in Wellington a year later, led his side to a first-ever win over a previously revered opponent.

Pakistan still boasted their collection of fine batsmen like Majid Khan, Zaheer Abbas and Sadiq Mohammad. Added to that was the precocious talent of Javed Miandad, already at 22 a veteran of his second World Cup. This aggressive, cheeky, irritating fellow sought to rival Viv Richards as the best batsman in the world.

India, too, had reinstated their captain from the previous tournament. Srinivas Venkataraghavan assumed the leadership role from Sunil Gavaskar, who by now was his side's number one batsman and most obvious choice as captain. He was in the midst of a prolific couple of years of Test century making, but there had been rumours of him flirting with the professional troupe of Kerry Packer. The captaincy was taken away, but he kept his place in the side. Wicket-keeper Syed Kirmani, who Packer had also attempted to woo, was dropped from the side altogether. He responded to the news by jumping in a taxi and asking the driver to take him anywhere at all. Wherever they drove, Kirmani did eventually come back.

Poor old Venkat had hardly inspired his team to any great degree four years before. Now his role was further compromised because his selection was based more on a political decision than on cricketing merit. He knew that and so did his team.

Gavaskar would be the batting key to any prospective Indian success. Gundappa Viswanath was still a fine player and Dilip Vengsarkar had established his place in the middle-order. But the Indian bowling resources looked thin, despite the emergence of a young all-rounder whose talent matched that of Botham, Hadlee and Imran. Unlike the other three emerging champions, the Kapil Dev of 1979 was new to English wickets and weather conditions and he had only a few days to acclimatise for the concentrated program of Limited-Over Internationals in a side which was unlikely to be full of help and harmony.

After the World Cup, though, he would immediately have the opportunity to further that experience in a meaningful way. With the English authorities now confident of the success of the World Cup, India, rather than Australia, was to compete in the follow-up four match Test series. Australia was not needed as a back-up guarantee, nor with its emaciated line-up was it an assured attraction.

Sri Lanka completed its four-year cycle from one World Cup preparation to the next with another unofficial mini test series against the West Indies. Anura Tennekoon retained the nucleus of the talent he had four years earlier. This time they were more worldly wise in the cricketing sense. They had established themselves as the dominant team amongst the ICC associate countries and felt ready to compete with the best the rest of the world could offer. Besides which, Jeff Thomson would not be bowling to them.

Canada's line-up boasted names with a cricketing ring to them like Chappell, Marshall, Patel and Walters. But this team, largely made up of expatriate West Indians, was expected to make about the same impact as the East Africans had in 1975. That is, none. A schoolteaching left-arm medium pacer, John Valentine, had bowled impressively throughout the ICC Trophy matches and the team had fought hard by scoring a losing 264 in the final against Sri Lanka. Despite the nature of the tournament the trip was costing the Canadian players money. Kerry Packer hadn't come near them.

The weather throughout the ICC Trophy matches had been miserable, but so it had been in the lead-up four years before. That was not necessarily a bad omen. Talk of worldwide petrol shortages might have been less encouraging and the split caused by World Series Cricket had hardly had time to heal. The feelings between the teams and players variously affected and variously cashed up was an unknown, potentially volatile quantity. Dennis Lillee, working as a journalist, had all sorts of trouble getting into Lord's when he tried to wish the Australians good luck before their opening day clash with England. He was three times denied entry by various officials and when he was finally received into the Australian dressing-room the response of several players was distinctly chilly.

When non-WSC Australia played the WSC enriched Pakistan side in March there was a lot of ill-temper between the teams. At least everyone was on their best behaviour at Buckingham Palace and in the Long Room at Lord's where the players enjoyed their wine, roast beef and Prince Philip in fine form. All the teams lined up together for a massed photograph the type of which has now become almost as big a tradition as the tournament itself, but unlike 1975 there were no loosened ties. That had nothing to do with greater acceptance of formality. It was just too overcast and chilly. But once Australia and England lined up against each other at Lord's in their traditional garb in front of a full house only one thing really mattered.

SATURDAY 9 JUNE 1979
THE PRUDENTIAL CUP: ROUND ONE
GROUP B: ENGLAND vs AUSTRALIA
LORD'S: ENGLAND WON BY 6 WICKETS

When England meet Australia at Lord's the ground will fill to capacity. It will fill for a Limited-Over International or a Test match. It will fill if the weather is hot or cold. I have seen it full when soaked in glorious sunshine and I have seen it filled when most people in the crowd were getting a thorough soaking.

This capacity gathering had to endure a continuance of the cold, drizzly and cloudy weather that seemed in a permanent holding pattern over the whole country. But despite the unbroken steel grey canopy they still created a special buzz of anticipation. It wasn't just brought about by the cheery confrontational T-shirts on the chests of the opposing supporters.

England was going into the match as red-hot favourites and that at the game's headquarters is a very rare occurrence. Whatever the strength of Kim Hughes' side, they most likely would have won if this had been a Test. Australia has lost only one such encounter there this century.

With 12 of the 14 players in the English squad recent Australian tourists, some in the dressing-room commented that it was like the start of the Ashes tour again. Mike Brearley won the toss and sent the Australians in to bat. He said he thought the wicket contained some moisture. The decision may also have been influenced after his county side, Middlesex, had been demolished for 107 by Yorkshire just three days earlier when they batted first in a Benson and Hedges Cup quarter-final.

The inexperienced Australians had their pre-tournament preparations badly interrupted by the weather. In their warm-up games they thrashed New Zealand, lost to strong county side, Kent, and had matches against Hampshire and Middlesex ruined by rain. Not surprisingly, Andrew Hilditch and Rick Darling were tentative against Mike Hendrick and Bob Willis armed with the new ball. In the still gloomy conditions they scratched around for just 14 runs in the first 10 overs before settling properly to their task and lifting the total to 56 from 21 overs.

Willis then returned to trap the increasingly aggressive Darling for 25. Border, who was to end up with a Test average of just on 100 at Lord's, fought tenaciously to keep his wicket intact and stayed with the more comfortable Hilditch until lunch was reached at 1–97 after 36 overs. Brearley's decision had seemingly back-fired and many thought the English captain was becoming desperate when he resorted to bringing Geoff Boycott and his gentle seamers into the attack.

The controversial opening batsman from Yorkshire had had a miserable Test tour of Australia and at 38 years his selection in the World Cup squad had been no certainty. Now he looked almost ridiculous charging in still wearing his England cap at an unusual angle. But lo and behold, in the first over after the interval Hilditch, still three runs short of a deserved half century, dragged a delivery onto his stumps. The crowd erupted for the first time. Boycott stood mid-pitch, his arms aloft. Border and Kim Hughes had taken the total to 111 when Hughes saw an opportunity to lift the scoring. He belted Boycott towards the mid-wicket boundary where Mike Hendrick ran in, dived forward and held an excellent low outfield catch. After a spell of six overs Brearley was finished with him but Boycott had served a very useful purpose.

Border and Graham Yallop lifted the score to 131, but it was still a hard graft and the dwindling overs became something of an issue. Run-outs had bedevilled the young Australians during the recent Ashes series. They had escaped unscathed until lunch, even though 'Kamikaze Kid' Darling had riskily taken on David Gower's arm a couple of times. Now Yallop challenged Derek Randall at cover and lost. The Australian innings continued its downward spiral when Bob Taylor, who had a bad day and earlier missed two stumpings, finally held Border from an edge off the left-arm spin of Phil Edmonds. Edmonds bowled a very tidy spell, but he hurt his back so badly he was assisted from the field at the end of the Australian innings.

A mix-up left Gary Cosier stranded in the middle of the pitch when Taylor removed the bails. All-rounder Trevor Laughlin and Rodney Hogg were also run-out victims, leaving many to wonder what it was about Australians, Prudential World Cup matches, Lord's and run-outs. Hogg's dismissal made it nine such dismissals in two starts at this venue. Since lunch eight wickets had fallen for 56 and it was left to tail enders Alan Hurst and Geoff Dymock to hold on and bat out the overs. When the 60th had been completed they had only pushed the total up to a fairly inadequate 9–159. The English bowling had been tight and done its job, but the fielding and outcricket had been brilliant, which is not something in which English teams have often had an advantage over Australia.

Australia looked to have blown their chances by setting a target of just 160 in 60 overs, but Rodney Hogg and Alan Hurst had other ideas. Boycott was trapped in front by Hogg, whose first burst of four overs was very fast. David Frith noted the irony of a cricket match where Boycott took more wickets than he scored runs. The English glitch became a tremor when Hurst, an underrated back-up to Hogg but such an appalling batsman he would fit beautifully into the current England lower order, had Derek Randall caught behind wafting outside the off stump.

England 2–5 suggested a fight to the finish. Hogg, though, was prone to fizzle out as quickly as he fired up. Graham Gooch joined Mike Brearley and their stand of 108 virtually settled the issue. Gooch had already scored 1000 runs for his county in all competitions through April and May and was soon into his stride. He struck the ball powerfully to the boundary six times on his way to a half century in two and three-quarter hours. Gooch's strike rate was excellent, but the tempo of the game was slowed by Kim Hughes' meticulous and persistent field adjustments. Australia had gone in without a spinner and Hogg in particular was slow to complete an over.

Perhaps Hughes was praying for the rain that always threatened but never came. Australian hope only flickered again when bustling all-rounder Trevor Laughlin had Brearley caught behind by Kevin Wright and won an lbw decision in his next over against Gooch. Four for 124 was a worse position than Australia had been in. However, David Gower and Ian Botham had no intention of running out themselves or anyone

else. They added the 36 runs required for victory in brisk time, Gower scoring elegantly, Botham in muscular fashion. The target was reached with nearly 13 overs to spare.

Wisden, giving the English point of view, suggested the day was an absorbing one. For the Australian supporters, there or at home watching television this time on the Ten Network because Kerry Packer said the BBC coverage was not up to the required standard, it was cold, grey and depressing and made them pine once more for the return of their WSC stars. They had witnessed this second-string team choke too often like this to hold any more faith in their ability.

Gooch was named Man of the Match by Fred Titmus.

AUSTRALIA

A.M.J. Hilditch b Boycott	47
W.M. Darling lbw Willis	25
A.R. Border c Taylor b Edmonds	34
K.J. Hughes (capt) c Hendrick b Boycott	6
G.N. Yallop run out	10
G.J. Cosier run out	6
T.J. Laughlin run out	8
K.J. Wright (wk) lbw Old	6
R.M. Hogg run out	0
A.G. Hurst not out	3
G. Dymock not out	4
Extras (b 4, lb 5, w 1)	10
(60 overs)	9–159

1/56 2/97 3/111 4/131 5/132 6/137 7/150 8/153 9/153

Bowling: Willis 11–2–20–1; Hendrick 12–2–24–0; Old 12–2–33–1; Botham 8–0–32–0; Edmonds 11–1–25–1; Boycott 6–0–15–2

ENGLAND

J.M. Brearley (capt) c Wright b Laughlin	44
G. Boycott lbw Hogg	1
D.W. Randall c Wright b Hurst	1
G.A. Gooch lbw Laughlin	53
D.I. Gower not out	22
I.T. Botham not out	18
Extras (lb 10, nb 11)	21
(47.1 overs)	4–160

Did not bat: P.H. Edmonds, R.W. Taylor (wk), C.M. Old, M. Hendrick, R.G.D. Willis

1/4 2/5 3/113 4/124

Bowling: Hogg 9–1–25–1; Hurst 10–3–33–1; Dymock 11–2–19–0; Cosier 8–1–24–0; Laughlin 9.1–0–38–2

Umpires: D.J. Constant, B.J. Meyer.

Toss: England. Points: England 4, Australia 0

GROUP B: PAKISTAN vs CANADA
HEADINGLEY: PAKISTAN WON BY 8 WICKETS

The Canadian team that confronted Pakistan at Headingley contained such a strong West Indian contingent it should have been no surprise that they relished fast bowling. Barbadian born 39-year-old Glenroy Sealy exhibited typical Caribbean enthusiasm when he put away the first ball of the match from Imran Khan for a leg-side four. After their captain and wicketkeeper Mauricette had won the toss and elected to bat, Sealy and Chris Chappell went on to add an impressive 54 runs for the first wicket. Chappell later stated that making runs against the likes of Imran and fellow paceman

Sarfraz Nawaz made the personal expense of travelling to England worthwhile.

Like Australia in the other Group B match, Canada built a really useful platform, reaching 2–103 at one point. But their progress was eventually slowed, especially by Majid Khan's slow-medium off spin. Majid conceded just one run per over, while Asif Iqbal's little inswingers made quite a mess of Canada's middle order. Opener Sealy went on to make 45, but again like Australia, the Canadian innings really went nowhere in its later stages. They were pleased to last their allotted 60 overs, but their last seven wickets added a meagre 36 runs and 139 was never likely to challenge a Pakistani team desperate to make up for the shocking disappointments of 1975.

Left-armer, John Valentine, who had done so well in the ICC Trophy matches and ended this game with very respectable figures, soon yorked Majid. Then Sadiq Mohammad and Zaheer Abbas added 57 before Chappell ran out Zaheer with a direct-hit throw to the bowler's end. That was the Canadians' last success. Sadiq remained firm, Haroon Rashid dominated the scoring and the 140 runs required for victory were achieved with eight wickets and 20 overs to spare when a single was taken from the first ball of Patel's final over.

Sadiq's sound effort, punctuated with his trademark shots square of the wicket, earned him the Man of the Match award. Always an entertainer, the youngest Mohammad brother could give the bat handle a vigorous twirl between deliveries. On the 1978 tour of England he became one of the first players to bat in a helmet in a Test match. Whether it would have afforded him much protection if struck is debateable, however. He batted with the motorbike-style headgear on back to front for quite some time.

CANADA

C.J.D. Chappell c & b Sikander	14
G.R. Sealy c & b Asif Iqbal	45
F.A. Dennis c Wasim Bari b Sarfraz Nawaz	25
M.P. Stead c Zaheer b Asif Iqbal	10
C.A. Marshall b Imran Khan	8
J.C.B. Vaughan c & b Asif Iqbal	0
B.M. Mauricette (capt-wk) c Zaheer b Sarfraz Nawaz	15
Tariq Javed st Wasim Bari b Majid	3
J.M. Patel b Sarfraz Nawaz	0
C.C. Henry not out	1
Extras (lb 10, w 5, nb 3)	18
(60 overs)	9-139

Did not bat: J.N. Valentine

1/54 2/85 3/103 4/110 5/110 6/129 7/134 8/138 9/139

Bowling: Imran Khan 11-1-27-1; Sarfraz Nawaz 10-1-26-3; Mudassar Nazar 4-1-11-0; Sikander Bakht 12-5-18-1; Majid Khan 11-4-11-1; Asif Iqbal 12-2-28-3

PAKISTAN

Majid Khan b Valentine	1
Sadiq Mohammad not out	57
Zaheer Abbas run out	36
Haroon Rashid not out	37
Extras (b 1, lb 3, w 1, nb 4)	9
(40.1 overs)	2-140

Did not bat: Javed Miandad, Asif Iqbal (capt), Mudassar Nazar, Imran Khan, Sarfraz Nawaz, Wasim Bari (wk), Sikander Bakht

Bowling: Valentine 9-3-18-1; Vaughan 5-1-21-0; Henry 5-0-26-0; Patel 11.1-0-27-0; Sealy 6-0-21-0; Stead 4-0-18-0

Umpires: H.D. Bird, A.G.T. Whitehead.

Toss: Canada. Points: Pakistan 4, Canada 0

GROUP A: INDIA vs WEST INDIES
EDGBASTON: WEST INDIES WON BY 9 WICKETS

The first century of the 1979 Prudential World Cup by Gordon Greenidge swept the West Indies to an easy victory over India in their opening encounter at Edgbaston. The pattern of the whole match was fairly predictable from the moment Clive Lloyd won the toss and sent the Indian batsmen in to cope with his awesome battery of fast bowlers.

Gavaskar had come a long way since his bizarre batting display on the corresponding day four years before. He had emerged as a superb opening batsman and was now a wonderful technician with the ability to counter any form of bowling, including West Indian speed. In the Caribbean early in 1976 he had scored centuries in two of the four Tests. Then in six Tests back in India between December and February, Gavaskar had amassed an astonishing 732 runs from the West Indians, who were admittedly without their WSC players.

The little opener started confidently putting away Andy Roberts' first delivery for four. He rated the Antiguan the best bowler he ever faced. Soon a mistimed hook off the same bowler steepled the ball and Michael Holding safely judged the catch. The multitude of flags which were waved vigorously by the thousands of Indian supporters after that first ball now went sadly limp. And they were just about at half-mast soon after when Holding removed Anshuman Gaekwad and Dilip Vengsarkar caught low at third slip with the total still only 29. It was the turn of the equally enthusiastic West Indians to lift the roof of the Hollies Stand.

Gundappa Viswanath handled the situation and the frequent short of a length deliveries well, defending competently and scoring freely with flicks, cuts and glides. But he lost Brijesh Patel to a foolish run-out and when Mohinder Amarnath was brilliantly caught behind by Deryck Murray off Colin Croft half the Indian side was gone for 77 and a total rout seemed on the cards.

Some previous Indian sides might have folded completely to the onslaught of such pace, and there was never any prospect of a full recovery. However, Viswanath eventually found a couple of worthy partners in the all-rounders, young Kapil Dev and Karsan Ghavri. They pushed the total beyond 150, then a clinking delivery from Holding breached Viswanath's defence and all resistance seemed over. It wasn't quite, because skipper Venkataraghavan and the unlikely figure of Bishen Bedi added a joyous 27 runs for the last wicket. Bedi, who liked to give himself quite a bit of room when facing fast bowling hit Holding for a boundary which got the flags going again. There were still seven overs of the Indian innings remaining when Roberts spoiled the fun by having Bedi caught

at slip, leaving the West Indies a straightforward target of 191 to win.

The simplicity of the task was exemplified by the ease with which Gordon Greenidge and Desmond Haynes added 138 for the first wicket. The Indian attack, so lacking in firepower, still sent down more no-balls than their West Indian counterparts. Greenidge, often a solemn character, was determined to make up for a modest first World Cup and this was his best opportunity. After settling himself for a few overs, he hit the ball with fearsome strength off the back foot through the off side and dominated the scoring during his stand with Haynes.

Kapil Dev, in front of the wider cricketing audience for the first time, impressed as a bowler with a lot more spunk than is normally associated with Indian pacemen. He trapped Haynes lbw three short of a half century. That, of course, only brought in Richards who cruised along to ensure Greenidge reached his deserved century. He really enjoyed the hundred, but perhaps not the buffeting he received from the dozens of well-wishers who invaded the ground supposedly to congratulate him. Greenidge was named Man of the Match and everyone thought the choice obvious, despite Holding's devastating exploits with the ball.

Bedi had lost his mesmeric powers. Ghavri, Amarnath and Venkataraghavan lacked penetration. The West Indies reached their objective with eight and a half overs to spare. India,

INDIA	
S.M. Gavaskar c Holding b Roberts	8
A.D. Gaekwad c King b Holding	11
D.B. Vengsarkar c Kallicharran b Holding	7
G.R. Viswanath b Holding	75
B.P. Patel run out	15
M. Amarnath c Murray b Croft	8
Kapil Dev b King	12
S.C. Khanna (wk) c Haynes b Holding	0
K.D. Ghavri c Murray b Garner	12
S. Venkataraghavan (capt) not out	13
B.S. Bedi c Lloyd b Roberts	13
Extras (b 6, lb 3, w 3, nb 4)	16
(53.1 overs)	190

1/10 2/24 3/29 4/56 5/77 6/112 7/119 8/155 9/163 10/190

Bowling: Roberts 9.1–0–32–2; Holding 12–2–33–4; Garner 12–1–42–1; Croft 10–1–31–1; King 10–1–36–1

WEST INDIES	
C.G. Greenidge not out	106
D.L. Haynes lbw Kapil Dev	47
I.V.A. Richards not out	28
Extras (lb 6, nb 7)	13
(51.3 overs)	1–194

Did not bat: A.I. Kallicharran, C.H. Lloyd (capt), C.L. King, D.L. Murray (wk), A.M.E. Roberts, J. Garner, M.A. Holding, C.E.H. Croft

1/138

Bowling: Kapil Dev 10–1–46–1; Ghavri 10–2–25–0; Venkataraghavan 12–3–30–0; Bedi 12–0–45–0; Amarnath 7.3–0–35–0

Umpires: D.G.L. Evans, J.G. Langridge.

Toss: West Indies. Points: West Indies 4, India 0

humiliated in 1975 looked to be in deep trouble again. The flags were down. It was the sound of Caribbean bugles, drums, whistles and hand-held bells that filled the Birmingham evening air.

Sitting in the pavilion, 21-year-old Malcolm Marshall, who had suffered recent bowling humiliations in India, wrote that he found the ease of his teams's win particularly satisfying.

GROUP A: NEW ZEALAND vs SRI LANKA
TRENT BRIDGE: NEW ZEALAND WON BY 9 WICKETS

The remarkable similarity in the scores in the two Group A matches meant that a close result was nowhere to be found on the opening day of the 1979 Prudential World Cup.

At Trent Bridge everyone nodded approvingly and noted the improvement in the Sri Lankan batting, but they did not last their 60 overs and the total of 189 proved as inadequate as that of the other three countries who had gone in first on this typically overcast and chilly early English summer's day. Wisely, in view of their battering at the hands of Jeff Thomson in 1975, the Sri Lankans willingly adopted the new-fashioned batting helmets after Mark Burgess had won the toss and invited Anura Tennekoon's side to bat.

That did cause a problem or two for the scorers, who had all sorts of difficulty identifying one busy Sri Lankan from another. It is still fairly safe to assume that Tennekoon did complete a competent half century which seemed to set his side up for a competitive total. He and Roy Dias added 50 runs for the third wicket, taking the score to a very promising 2–107. But like Australia

at Lord's and Canada at Headingley, the under-dogs flattered to deceive. Both Tennekoon and Dias fell to Warren Stott, whose sole international appearance this was. The rest of the batsmen had no real idea how to boost the run rate later in the innings and stumbled and fell from 4–149 to 8–154. Tony Opatha and D.L.S. de Silva gave the total a bit of a boost, although it hardly seemed enough.

The Sri Lankan medium pacers made little impression on Glenn Turner and John Wright as the Kiwis began their reply. The total had already reached 64 before Wright mistimed a catch to the Sri Lankan captain at mid-on off left-arm spinner Ginigalgodage de Silva. A further 126 runs were required when Geoff Howarth joined Turner and this pair were able to achieve their objective with more than 12 overs to spare. Turner never missed an opportunity to spend time at the crease when there were easy runs to be made and he was always likely to be not out at the end of this innings. Howarth's main difficulty arose from a strained hamstring that necessitated the assistance of a runner. He scored as freely as Turner

SRI LANKA	
B. Warnapura c & b McKechnie	20
S.R.de S. Wettimuny b Cairns	16
A.P.B. Tennekoon (capt) b Stott	59
R.L. Dias c & b Stott	25
L.R.D. Mendis c Turner b Troup	14
D.S. de Silva c Burgess b Stott	6
S.A. Jayasinghe (wk) run out	1
S.P. Pasqual b Hadlee	1
A.R.M. Opatha b McKechnie	18
D.L.S. de Silva c Wright b McKechnie	10
G.R.A. de Silva not out	2
Extras (lb 13, w 2, nb 2)	17
(56.5 overs)	189

1/26 2/57 3/107 4/137 5/149 6/150 7/150 8/154 9/178 10/189

Bowling: Hadlee 12–3–24–1; Troup 10–0–30–1; Cairns 12–1–45–1; McKechnie 10.5–2–25–3; Stott 12–0–48–3

NEW ZEALAND	
G.M. Turner not out	83
J.G. Wright c Tennekoon b G.R.A. de Silva	34
G.P. Howarth not out	63
Extras (lb 7, w 2, nb 1)	10
(47.4 overs)	1–190

Did not bat: J.V. Coney, M.G. Burgess (capt), W.K. Lees (wk), B.J. McKechnie, B.L. Cairns, R.J. Hadlee, L.W. Stott, G.B. Troup

1/64

Bowling: Opatha 7–1–31–0; D.L.S. de Silva 8–2–18–0; Warnapura 7–0–30–0; D.S. de Silva 9–0–42–0; G.R.A. de Silva 12–1–39–1; Pasqual 4.4–0–20–0

Umpires: W.L. Budd, K.E. Palmer.

Toss: New Zealand. Points: New Zealand 4, Sri Lanka 0

and even belted Somachandra de Silva for a clean six on his way to an unbeaten 63. His stylish pulling and driving in the face of some physical adversity earned Howarth the Man of the Match award just ahead of his more experienced batting partner.

WEDNESDAY 13 JUNE, THURSDAY 14 JUNE 1979
THE PRUDENTIAL CUP: ROUND TWO
GROUP B: ENGLAND vs CANADA
OLD TRAFFORD: ENGLAND WON BY 8 WICKETS

The ghost of Abe Bailey, still smarting from the disasters of 1912, finally took out his wrath on Round Two of the 1979 tournament. What had threatened in Round One became an unpleasant reality four days later when rain covered the country. It was worse in the west and south than the north, as only at Headingley could the match be completed in a day.

Across the Pennines, though, at Old Trafford, no play was possible on the Wednesday. Heavy rain soon caused Barry Meyer and John Langridge to abandon proceedings and when everyone, including a mere sprinkling of spectators, turned up on the Thursday there was a further delay of an hour.

For some unexplained reason, Canadian captain Mauricette elected to bat first in what *Wisden* called 'farcical conditions'. Bob Willis said none of the England team could believe Mauricette's decision and that they felt sorry for their opponents. That pity did not extend to generosity in the bowling, however. In an astonishing display of miserly economy the English seamers dismissed Canada for 45. Perhaps coming from the 1975 Sunil Gavaskar school for batting in Limited-Over Internationals, survival was the Canadians' only objective and they at least managed to do this for 40 overs. Number 3 batsman Franklin Dennis lasted for 31 of those overs before misjudging the bounce of a short ball from Bob Willis. That caused him to overbalance and fall on his wicket.

Willis' figures were superb, but Chris Old's were even better. His 4–8 from 10 overs remains one of the best analyses from any World Cup tournament. The Canadian innings lasted just 157 minutes and they became the first and remain the only World Cup side to be dismissed for less than 60. On another miserable Manchester day only Ian Botham held a catch. It did not matter much because six of the last seven batsmen were bowled, the stumps flying spectacularly in all directions from the rain-softened turf. The last six wickets fell for eight runs. Extras were equal second top score.

CANADA

G.R. Sealey c Botham b Hendrick	3
C.J.D. Chappell lbw Botham	5
F.A. Dennis hit wicket b Willis	21
Tariq Javed lbw Old	4
J.C.B. Vaughan b Old	1
C.A. Marshall b Old	2
B.M. Mauricette (capt-wk) b Willis	0
M.P. Stead b Old	0
J.M. Patel b Willis	1
R.G. Callender b Willis	0
J.N. Valentine not out	3
Extras (lb 4, nb 1)	5
(40.3 overs)	45

1/5 2/13 3/25 4/29 5/37 6/38 7/41 8/41 9/42 10/45

Bowling: Willis 10.3–3–11–4; Hendrick 8–4–5–1; Botham 9–5–12–1; Miller 2–1–1–0; Boycott 1–0–3–0; Old 10–5–8–4

ENGLAND

J.M. Brearley (capt) lbw Valentine	0
G. Boycott not out	14
D.W. Randall b Callender	5
G.A. Gooch not out	21
Extras (w 3, nb 3)	6
(13.5 overs)	2–46

Did not bat: D.I. Gower, I.T. Botham, G. Miller, R.W. Taylor (wk), C.M. Old, R.G.D. Willis, M. Hendrick

1/3 2/11

Bowling: Valentine 7–2–20–1; Callender 6–1–14–1; Stead 0.5–0–6–0

Umpires: J.G. Langridge, B.J. Meyer.

Toss: Canada. Points: England 4, Canada 0

More heavy rain delayed the start of the England innings for another three and a half hours. It was 7 pm before Geoff Boycott and Mike Brearley made their way out to the wicket in brief but welcome sunshine and not long after the hour when Brearley was on his way back. The Canadians had no hope of protecting their total, but they retained their unadulterated enthusiasm. That was quickly rewarded when John Valentine straightened one on the English captain.

Callender then bowled the out of form Derek Randall. England were 2–11 and potential embarrassment loomed.

Again it was Graham Gooch who ended the fuss, hitting out effectively in the gathering gloom. The match aggregate of 91 runs is a World Cup all-time low, as is the playing time of just three hours and thirty-five minutes. Old was named Man of the Match.

GROUP B: AUSTRALIA vs PAKISTAN
TRENT BRIDGE: PAKISTAN WON BY 89 RUNS

As it did four years earlier, the clash between these two countries loomed as a crucial contest to see who would progress through to the semi-finals. Unlike 1975, this time nearly all the best cricket came from Pakistan and on the second day they emerged comfortable and relieved winners by 89 runs.

Rain delayed the start for an hour. Then Kim Hughes won the toss and invited Asif Iqbal and his side to bat. Hughes' major spearhead, Rodney Hogg, was out of the starting eleven. The continuing cold and damp was causing all sorts of bronchial problems for the asthmatic fast bowler, although some reports suggested a muscle strain stopped him from playing. His partner in crime, Alan Hurst, now led the way. Hurst had bowled brilliantly in the ill-tempered two match Test series against Pakistan in Australia in March, but here just a couple of months later the responsibility of being his country's number one fast bowler seemed to distract him.

'I'd got it into my head that I could get a few of these guys out by bowling short,' Hurst later said to Gideon Haigh in *The Cricket War*. 'I kept at them and they kept hammering me. I was stupid and I don't use it as an excuse, but it was really made worse by the inexperience of the side. I had the adrenalin flowing and I got no guidance at all.'

Trent Bridge was certainly not the WACA. Majid Khan could not believe his luck and took a heavy toll on the wayward Hurst, who sent down a quota of five wides and four no-balls as well as the misplaced short stuff. Hughes might

have despaired, but fortunately Hogg's replacement, that obscure West Australian, Graeme Porter, and left-armer Geoff Dymock stemmed the run flow with some sensible line and length bowling. Both Majid and his opening partner Sadiq were dismissed when the total was on 99. Then Gary Cosier, bowling medium-paced swing and cut off about five paces, removed Zaheer Abbas and Haroon Rashid cheaply.

When Pakistan were 4–152 Australia would have considered they were back in the contest. At selection Australia had brought in left-handed batsman Jeff Moss for all-rounder Trevor Laughlin. That meant Graham Yallop and Allan Border had to make up a 12-over stint between them. The idea was a poor one. Both left-armers were caned. Yallop conceded 56 runs from eight overs, Border 38 runs from just four overs.

Javed Miandad and Asif Iqbal made the most of these innocuous offerings. They lifted the score to 239 with some fine strokes and sharp running in 14 overs before being parted. When the Australian outcricket was tested by Javed and Asif's energetic batting it was found wanting. Ginger-haired wicketkeeper Kevin Wright, another with injury problems, had a bad day behind the stumps.

Another 47 runs from the last five overs left the Australians needing 287 to have any hope of progressing to the semi-finals. Andrew Hilditch and Rick Darling scored 17 runs while they negotiated five overs of a Pakistan attack without the injured Sarfraz Nawaz before play was halted for the day.

Kim Hughes' team had everything to play for on a cold grey Thursday at Trent Bridge but they were never really in the hunt. Imran Khan soon had Darling caught behind and when Sikander Bakht bowled Allan Border for a duck Australia were 2–24 and right behind the eight ball. Hilditch had batted well at Lord's and it was Hughes' vice-captain who again held the innings together as best he could. He added 71 with Graham Yallop in 21 overs, giving the scoreboard respectability without causing the Pakistanis any real angst. Eventually Hilditch fell to

Mudassar's persistence and Yallop missed a straight one from Majid.

The Australian innings limped along from there until Kevin Wright, trying to score the 90 runs still required from three overs, edged Imran to Wasim Bari from the first ball of the 58th over. The result had long been a formality. At least there had only been one run-out.

Asif Iqbal's sprightly innings, his tidy bowling and astute captaincy earned him the Man of the Match award.

PAKISTAN

Sadiq Mohammad c Moss b Porter	27
Majid Khan b Dymock	61
Zaheer Abbas c & b Cosier	16
Haroon Rashid c Wright b Cosier	16
Javed Miandad c Border b Cosier	46
Asif Iqbal (capt) c sub (D.F. Whatmore) b Hurst	61
Wasim Raja c Moss b Border	18
Imran Khan not out	15
Mudassar Nazar not out	1
Extras (b 6, lb 4, w 5, nb 10)	25
(60 overs)	7–286

Did not bat: Wasim Bari (wk), Sikander Bakht

1/99 2/99 3/133 4/152 5/239 6/268 7/274

Bowling: Porter 12-3-20-1; Dymock 12-3-28-1; Cosier 12-1-54-3; Hurst 12-0-65-1; Yallop 8-0-56-0; Border 4-0-38-1

AUSTRALIA

W.M. Darling c Wasim Bari b Imran Khan	13
A.M.J. Hilditch c Sadiq b Mudassar	72
A.R. Border b Sikander	0
K.J. Hughes (capt) lbw Sikander	15
G.N. Yallop b Majid	37
J.K. Moss run out	7
G.J. Cosier c & b Majid	0
K.J. Wright (wk) c Wasim Bari b Imran Khan	23
G.D. Porter c Sadiq b Majid	3
G. Dymock lbw Sikander	10
A.G. Hurst not out	3
Extras (b 1, lb 5, w 8)	14
(57.1 overs)	197

1/22 2/24 3/46 4/117 5/136 6/137 7/172 8/175 9/193 10/197

Bowling: Asif Iqbal 12-0-36-0; Majid Khan 12-0-53-3; Mudassar Nazar 12-0-31-1; Imran Khan 10.1-2-29-2; Sikander Bakht 11-1-34-3

Umpires: H.D. Bird, K.E. Palmer.

Toss: Australia. Points: Pakistan 4, Australia 0

GROUP A: INDIA vs NEW ZEALAND
HEADINGLEY: NEW ZEALAND WON BY 8 WICKETS

India's complete inadequacy at 60 overs per side cricket was again cruelly exposed, this time by New Zealand at Headingley, in the only second round match to be completed on the originally scheduled playing day.

Venkataraghavan lost the toss once more and his team was required to bat when the wicket gave the greatest assistance to New Zealand's competent pace attack. The Indians had to graft nearly all the way. Richard Hadlee made the first breakthrough, but Brian McKechnie, only available because he had no rugby commitments with the All Blacks, and burly inswinger Lance Cairns did the most damage.

Gavaskar batted for 44 overs at a pace not much above his crawl at Lord's in 1975. He had greater cause to be circumspect than during that debacle, though. There was a damp and heavy atmosphere over Leeds and Gavaskar's wicket was obviously a key to the result. He had a let-off early, Hadlee missing a sharp caught and bowled, then settled down to play an anchor role. Gundappa Viswanath's early dismissal was a blow. After 20 overs India were 2–50. Soon they were 3–53.

It took an enterprising knock by Brijesh Patel to give the innings a bit of momentum. At 3–104 India had almost fought back to level terms only for big left-arm paceman Gary Troup, a direct replacement for Richard Collinge, to bowl both Patel and Mohinder Amarnath in quick succession.

Kapil Dev and Karsan Ghavri chipped in with runs of value, lifting the total from the pathetic to the vaguely competitive. Hadlee finally got Gavaskar caught behind and this time there was no last wicket bonus from Bedi. The omission of accomplished wicketkeeper-batsman Syed Kirmani again looked a costly move by the Indian selectors. India was again unable to bat out its 60 over allocation and could only set New Zealand 183 for victory.

The heavy cloud cover had lifted and batting conditions had eased by the time left-handed pair Bruce Edgar and John Wright established themselves at the crease in pursuit of the runs that would assure New Zealand a semi-final berth.

None of the Indian bowlers could make any impact as Wright and Edgar gradually built a solid platform for victory. It was sensible rather than exciting stuff from the young pair. They put on exactly 100 before Wright hit a return catch to Mohinder Amarnath. Burgess must have been a little concerned about the run rate because he sent in Lance Cairns to smack the ball around a bit. That came unstuck when Cairns was quickly run-out, but Glenn Turner had enough experience of limited-overs cricket to know what was required.

Turner moved positively into his work and with Edgar becoming more fluent saw New Zealand to victory with no further alarms and three overs to spare. The opener's unbeaten 84 was considered the feature of a fairly plain day and thus earned him the Man of the Match award.

INDIA	
S.M. Gavaskar c Lees b Hadlee	55
A.D. Gaekwad b Hadlee	10
D.B. Vengsarkar c Lees b McKechnie	1
G.R. Viswanath c Turner b Cairns	9
B.P. Patel b Troup	38
M. Amarnath b Troup	1
Kapil Dev c & b Cairns	25
K.D. Ghavri c Coney b McKechnie	20
S.C. Khanna (wk) c Morrison b McKechnie	7
S. Venkataraghavan (capt) c Lees b Cairns	1
B.S. Bedi not out	1
Extras (lb 8, w 5, nb 1)	14
(55.5 overs)	182

1/27 2/38 3/53 4/104 5/107 6/147 7/153 8/180 9/181 10/182

Bowling: Hadlee 10–2–20–2; Troup 10–2–36–2; Cairns 11.5–0–36–3; McKechnie 12–1–24–3; Coney 7–0–33–0; Morrison 5–0–19–0

NEW ZEALAND	
J.G. Wright c & b Amarnath	48
B.A. Edgar not out	84
B.L. Cairns run out	2
G.M. Turner not out	43
Extras (lb 3, nb 3)	6
(57 overs)	2–183

Did not bat: J.V. Coney, M.G. Burgess (capt), J.F.M. Morrison, B.J. McKechnie, W.K. Lees (wk), R.J. Hadlee, G.B. Troup

Bowling: Amarnath 12–1–39–1; Bedi 12–1–32–0; Venkataraghavan 12–0–34–0; Ghavri 10–1–34–0; Kapil Dev 11–3–38–0

Umpires: W.L. Budd, A.G.T. Whitehead.

Toss: New Zealand. Points: New Zealand 4, India 0

GROUP A: WEST INDIES vs SRI LANKA
THE OVAL: MATCH ABANDONED

On a clear day at The Oval you can see three aeroplanes in the sky following the River Thames as their flight path. One is about to touch down at Heathrow, the other is straight overhead and the third is beginning its landing approach. On a bad day you cannot see any planes. Rather, you look up at three big black clouds. One has just rained on you and drifted away, one is

currently dousing you and the cricket ground and one is getting ready to pour some more on you.

On 13, 14 and 15 June 1979 when the cricketers of West Indies and Sri Lanka gazed up into the sky they saw black clouds not aeroplanes. There were, in fact, a couple of breaks in the weather, but subsequent downpours soon dampened the thought of any prospect of play.

Each side was given two points for turning up. In their own way these were historic. Sri Lanka received their first-ever points in the World Cup and also became the first team to take any off the West Indies. There were a few smiles amongst the Sri Lankan players at that. Although unlikely, mathematically it was now possible for Clive Lloyd's side to miss a place in the semi-finals. This was the only no-result match in the World Cup until rain arrived at an opportune time for Pakistan when they were playing England in Adelaide on 1 March 1992.

SATURDAY 16 JUNE 1979
THE PRUDENTIAL CUP: ROUND THREE
GROUP B: ENGLAND vs PAKISTAN
HEADINGLEY: ENGLAND WON BY 14 RUNS

This tight, fluctuating encounter, played before a full house, proved to be the best round-robin match of the tournament. Both England and Pakistan were assured of a semi-final berth, but the winning side would probably avoid the West Indies in the semi-finals and therefore improve its chances of reaching the final.

Like many games between England and Pakistan, this one had a special edge to it. The supporters of both sides on the terraces added plenty of enthusiasm and noise and increased the tension for the players. There were so many Pakistani fans, Bob Willis suggested the entire city of Bradford must be closed. Later in the day, unfortunately, police dogs would be needed to separate the worst elements of both sides when fighting broke out. The weather had improved from mid-week, however the conditions still favoured the bowlers. Asif Iqbal sent England in to bat when he won the toss.

Irregular bounce and movement off the seam proved his reading of the wicket correct. Even without the services of the still injured Sarfraz Nawaz, Pakistan quickly broke through. In a trice the home side were 2–4, Mike Brearley and Derek Randall both edging seaming deliveries to Wasim Bari.

Geoff Boycott was fairly familiar with such conditions. He held firm for an hour and a half and put on 47 valuable runs with the more enterprising Graham Gooch. They appeared to have weathered the worst of the storm when Boycott was trapped in front by Majid Khan. That was rarely a popular decision in Yorkshire. Sadiq Mohammad then held an excellent catch at deep gully from a Gooch slash off Sikander Bakht. Ian Botham and David Gower got going, but became the second and third victims of Majid's seemingly innocuous flat off spin. Asif Iqbal had England in further trouble when he removed Phil Edmonds and held a return catch off Chris Old.

Bob Willis came to the wicket to the noise and chanting of Pakistani supporters delirious at an England scoreline of 8–118. With the ball still moving around, Willis plonked his long left leg down the wicket so far across his off stump that he often played the ball inside out. As many deliveries were missed and edged as were struck, but with Bob Taylor holding fast at the other end a few overs were consumed and the total began to rise a little.

Imran was champing at the bit trying to convince Asif to put him on and finish the innings. Meanwhile Willis was dropped by Sikander Bakht, skewed a few more runs in unlikely directions between extra cover and third man and then was bowled by Sikander for an invaluable 24. He had added 43 with Taylor, who with Mike Hendrick batted out the innings.

England had set Pakistan a target of 166 from their allotted 60 overs. Despite the ongoing assistance for seam bowlers from the wicket, Sadiq and Majid promptly took the score to 27. Derbyshire seamer, Hendrick, who had beaten the bat more than once, suddenly began putting the ball in exactly the right spot. In five phenomenal overs six wickets fell for seven runs. There was panic in the Pakistani dressing-room with players running in all directions and equipment flying through the air. Hendrick, well supported by

Botham, took four wickets in eight balls, each one a batsman of real quality. This time the English sections of the crowd were ecstatic as Pakistan at 6–34 seemed beyond recall.

But there was great batting depth in their line-up and Hendrick was finally seen off by Asif, playing with a stick of rhubarb according to Bob Willis, and Wasim Raja. They re-established a semblance of sanity to the Pakistani innings, adding 52 runs in the process. Raja went lbw to Old but Imran, suffering badly from nerves, then stayed with his captain leaving Asif to play the shots while he held firm. The Pakistani captain reached his invaluable half century, the only one of the match, in an hour and three quarters. Each run was now greeted with wild cheering, but Bob Willis' next delivery to Asif after he completed his fifty was a brutish lifter which was edged to Mike Brearley at slip.

At 8–115, Pakistan looked to Imran as their main hope. He and Wasim Bari had plenty of overs in hand. Brearley reverted to his part-time seamers rather than entrust the ball to his spinner Phil Edmonds. The tension became almost unbearable as Imran and Wasim added 30, closing the target to within 20 runs. Brearley's use of Geoff Boycott as a bowler would have been seen as a sign of desperation if Pakistan had got home. As it turned out, the England captain was hailed as a genius. On 145, still bowling in

his cap around the wicket, Boycott induced an ill-advised cut shot from Wasim Bari to an inswinger. Bob Taylor had had another poor day behind the stumps but this time he held the inside edge superbly.

Brearley set the field back on the boundary for Imran and brought it in for last man Sikander Bakht. Imran took the singles on offer. The Pakistani's crept to within 14 runs. Imran said the tension was so great and the crowd so silent at times you could hear a pin drop. The last ball of Boycott's fifth over was a widish half-volley. Sikander launched himself at it. He hit it well, but in the air towards deep mid-off. There stood Hendrick. He leapt in the air and clutched at the ball with his right hand. It stuck, giving England their precious and thrilling victory. Imran, unbeaten on 21, was distraught, as was Sikander. The Pakistanis had been unable to secure victory in another close World Cup match. Imran believed he batted with great determination, others thought he looked out of form. After the game many inconsolable Pakistani supporters questioned the approach of the great all-rounder. Whatever the rights and wrongs, at least Pakistan knew they had not forfeited a semi-final place this time.

For his sensational spell of bowling and grand finale catch, Mike Hendrick was named Man of the Match by Brian Close.

ENGLAND

J.M. Brearley (capt) c Wasim Bari b Imran Khan		0
G. Boycott lbw Majid		18
D.W. Randall c Wasim Bari b Sikander		1
G.A. Gooch c Sadiq b Sikander		33
D.I. Gower b Majid		27
I.T. Botham b Majid		22
P.H. Edmonds c Wasim Raja b Asif		2
R.W. Taylor (wk) not out		20
C.M. Old c & b Asif		2
R.G.D. Willis b Sikander		24
M. Hendrick not out		1
Extras (lb 3, w 7, nb 5)		15
(60 overs)		9–165

1/0 2/4 3/51 4/70 5/99 6/115 7/115 8/118 9/161

Bowling: Imran Khan 12-3-34-1; Sikander Bakht 12-3-32-3; Mudassar Nazar 12-4-30-0; Asif Iqbal 12-3-37-2; Majid Khan 12-2-27-3

PAKISTAN

Majid Khan c Botham b Hendrick		7
Sadiq Mohammad b Hendrick		18
Mudassar Nazar lbw Hendrick		0
Zaheer Abbas c Taylor b Botham		3
Haroon Rashid c Brearley b Hendrick		1
Javed Miandad lbw Botham		0
Asif Iqbal (capt) c Brearley b Willis		51
Wasim Raja lbw Old		21
Imran Khan not out		21
Wasim Bari (wk) c Taylor b Boycott		17
Sikander Bakht c Hendrick b Boycott		2
Extras (lb 8, w 1, nb 1)		10
(56 overs)		151

1/27 2/27 3/28 4/30 5/31 6/34 7/86 8/115 9/145 10/151

Bowling: Willis 11-2-37-1; Hendrick 12-6-15-4; Botham 12-3-38-2; Old 12-2-28-1; Edmonds 3-0-8-0; Boycott 5-0-14-2; Gooch 1-0-1-0

Umpires: W.L. Budd, D.G.L. Evans.

Toss: Pakistan. Points: England 4, Pakistan 0

GROUP B: AUSTRALIA vs CANADA
EDGBASTON: AUSTRALIA WON BY 7 WICKETS

The Australians and Canadians filled in the Saturday before their flights back home with a cricket match. Even though the weather was half decent only about 1200 people filed into Edgbaston and a number of those might have turned up to see if even Canada would be too good for Kim Hughes' forlorn team.

Hughes won the toss and sent the Canadians in. Opener Glenroy Sealy reacted by smashing four boundaries off the first over of the match from Rodney Hogg. He defended the opening two deliveries before unleashing three powerful pull shots in a row and an exquisite leg glance from the sixth ball. Hogg conceded another 10 runs from his second over before he took his long-sleeved sweater and retired to the outfield, his reputation somewhat damaged by a 39-year-old.

Sealy and Chris Chappell extended their opening stand to 44, but again what followed them was inadequate. Geoff Dymock and Graeme Porter showed far greater control than

Hogg and Alan Hurst, a schoolteacher by profession, showed he had learnt quickly from his excesses against Pakistan. He reaped the reward of bowling a much fuller length, his pace eventually proving too much for five of the Canadians. Hurst was named Man of the Match. After the breakneck start only Vaughan provided any real resistance and the Canadians, having lost their last five wickets for eight runs, were all out by lunch.

Australia's reply started with a flurry as well, 12 runs coming from the first over before John Valentine removed Rick Darling with a shooter. He also took an excellent catch at square leg to dismiss Andrew Hilditch, but by then the Australians were halfway towards their target of 106. That was achieved in just 26 overs for the further loss of Allan Border, allowing both teams to pay their respects to each other and organise their departures nice and early. The Australians were leaving with their tails between their legs.

CANADA

G.R. Sealy c Porter b Dymock	25
C.J.D. Chappell lbw Hurst	19
F.A. Dennis lbw Hurst	1
Tariq Javed c Wright b Porter	8
S. Baksh b Hurst	0
J.C.B. Vaughan b Porter	29
B.M. Mauricette (capt-wk) c Hilditch b Cosier	5
J.M. Patel b Cosier	2
R.G. Callender c Wright b Hurst	0
C.C. Henry c Hughes b Hurst	5
J.N. Valentine not out	0
Extras (b 4, lb 5, w 1, nb 1)	11
(33.2 overs)	105

1/44 2/50 3/51 4/51 5/78 6/97 7/97 8/98 9/104 10/105

Bowling: Hogg 2-0-26-0; Hurst 10-3-21-5; Dymock 8-2-17-1; Porter 6-2-13-2; Cosier 7.2-2-17-2

AUSTRALIA

A.M.J. Hilditch c Valentine b Henry	24
W.M. Darling lbw Valentine	13
A.R. Border b Henry	25
K.J. Hughes (capt) not out	27
G.N. Yallop not out	13
Extras (lb 1, nb 3)	4
(26 overs)	3-106

Did not bat: G.J. Cosier, K.J. Wright (wk), G.D. Porter, R.M. Hogg, G. Dymock, A.G. Hurst

1/23 2/53 3/72

Bowling: Valentine 3-0-28-1; Callender 3-0-12-0; Henry 10-0-27-2; Vaughan 6-0-15-0; Patel 4-0-20-0

Umpires: D.J. Constant, J.G. Langridge.

Toss: Australia. Points: Australia 4, Canada 0

GROUP A: INDIA vs SRI LANKA
OLD TRAFFORD: SRI LANKA WON BY 47 RUNS

In some ways this match provided the most significant result of the tournament. Although the game had no bearing on the World Cup itself, Sri Lanka's win, the first by an associate ICC member over a full ICC member, gave a lot of

weight to that country's push for full Test status, something they achieved within a couple of years. It also condemned India to a pointless tournament, leaving them level with lowly Canada. At that moment it was probably a fair assessment of India's achievements in Limited-Over Internationals.

Further rain delayed the start of the match, and when proceedings got under way Venkataraghavan won the toss and sent the Sri Lankans in. They were without their respected captain, Anura Tennekoon, who had strained a hamstring at practice the day before, but still had no trouble coping with the unimpressive Indian bowling.

Sidath Wettimuny and Roy Dias added an enterprising 96 runs in 25 overs for the second wicket, charming a small crowd with their wristy strokeplay. Duleep Mendis, who had been hospitalised by Jeff Thomson, and Wettimuny, whose older brother Sunil had also been pummeled, made sure their efforts were not wasted. He belted the Indian medium pacers for three big sixes on the way to the third half century of the innings. Mohinder Amarnath picked up three wickets, but that hardly stemmed the run flow as Mendis and the young left-hander, Pasqual, added 52 in seven overs.

At the end of their 60 overs Sri Lanka had made 5–238, a worthy total. However, it was not necessarily one to daunt the Indians. Sri Lanka's bowling also had few credentials and was considered far inferior to their batting.

The Indians had all of Sunday to stew over their run chase. It did not appear to concern them unduly early on, though, when Sunil Gavaskar and Anshuman Gaekwad had an opening partnership of 60. India went to lunch on 2–117, requiring a further 122 runs from the remaining 25 overs.

It was soon after the interval that things started to go amiss. Gundappa Viswanath's wicket was pivotal to the Indian effort. He foolishly ran himself out and Sri Lanka saw an opening. Somachandra de Silva, a fast leg spinner of a style not dissimilar to India's own recent champion, Bhagwat Chandrasekhar, took advantage. He dismissed Dilip Vengsarkar and then bowled Brijesh Patel and Mohinder Amarnath. The Indian middle order started to crumble under the pressure. They were unable to establish any sort of a partnership and the innings began to subside, much as it had in every World Cup match so far.

Tony Opatha had made no impact with the new ball, but stand-in captain Bandula Warnapura brought him back into the attack at just the right time. Opatha bowled with increased pace and picked up the wickets of Karsan Ghavri and wicketkeeper Surinder Khanna. Then, from the first ball of his 11th over, the opening bowler had last man Bishen Bedi caught behind. India were all out with nearly six overs still to go. Sri Lanka had claimed a merited and historic

SRI LANKA	
B. Warnapura (capt) c Gaekwad b Amarnath	18
S.R. de S. Wettimuny c Vengsarkar b Kapil Dev	67
R.L. Dias c & b Amarnath	50
L.R.D. Mendis run out	64
R.S. Madugalle c Khanna b Amarnath	4
S.P. Pasqual not out	23
D.S. de Silva not out	1
Extras (lb 8, w 2, nb 1)	11
(60 overs)	5–238

Did not bat: S.A. Jayasinghe (wk), A.R.M. Opatha, D.L.S. de Silva, F.R.M. Goonatillake

1/31 2/127 3/147 4/175 5/227

Bowling: Kapil Dev 12-2-53-1; Ghavri 12-0-53-0; Amarnath 12-3-40-3; Bedi 12-2-37-0; Venkataraghavan 12-0-44-0

INDIA	
S.M. Gavaskar c Dias b Warnapura	26
A.D. Gaekwad c sub (G.R.A. de Silva) b D.L.S. de Silva	33
D.B. Vengsarkar c D.L.S. de Silva b D.S. de Silva	36
G.R. Viswanath run out	22
B.P. Patel b D.S. de Silva	10
Kapil Dev c Warnapura b D.L.S. de Silva	16
M. Amarnath b D.S. de Silva	7
K.D. Ghavri c Warnapura b Opatha	3
S.C. Khanna (wk) c Dias b Opatha	10
S. Venkataraghavan (capt) not out	9
B.S. Bedi c Jayasinghe b Opatha	5
Extras (lb 10, w 3, nb 1)	14
(54.1 overs)	191

1/60 2/76 3/119 4/132 5/147 6/160 7/162 8/170 9/185 10/191

Bowling: Opatha 10.1-0-31-3; Goonatillake 9-1-34-0; Warnapura 12-0-47-1; D.L.S. de Silva 12-0-36-2; D.S. de Silva 11-1-29-3

Umpires: K.E. Palmer, A.G.T. Whitehead.

Toss: India. Points: Sri Lanka 4, India 0

47 run victory. The small cluster of Sri Lankan enthusiasts who came to Old Trafford this special Monday celebrated with their proud team. Duleep Mendis was named Man of the Match.

India quietly eased themselves off the arena. Behind the closed doors of their dressing-room there was a lengthy and fairly sombre post-mortem. They had lots to talk about. India's sole success in six World Cup starts in 1975 and 1979 had been their win over East Africa. Their innings totals this time had all been similar and inadequate: 190, 182 and 191 in 53.1, 55.5 and 54.1 overs respectively.

GROUP A: NEW ZEALAND vs WEST INDIES
TRENT BRIDGE: WEST INDIES WON BY 32 RUNS

It is a measure of the general estimation of the qualities of these two sides that New Zealand were considered to have done quite well to get within 32 runs of the mighty West Indians. The Kiwis were described as 'plucky', 'efficient', 'competent', 'underrated' and 'good fighters'. The trouble was Clive Lloyd's side was all that and a whole lot more, and only early on and very briefly did this game for top spot in Group A look like being close.

New Zealand were still without Geoff Howarth, whose hamstring had not healed. Mark Burgess won the toss and sent the West Indies in to bat. The belief was that the Caribbean team preferred to chase runs than bat first. That and the prospect of Richard Hadlee taking advantage of any favourable bowling conditions on the ground where he played county cricket would have been the determining factors in Burgess' decision.

Hadlee was a little erratic early, but he won an lbw decision against Desmond Haynes. Jeremy Coney's gentle little swing deliveries always looked easy pickings for quality batsmen. When he came on second change Viv Richards' eyes probably lit up. But the great man underestimated Coney's worth and with the total on 61 he holed out to the New Zealand captain.

Burgess kept deep-set, defensive fields and tried to unsettle the West Indies with constant bowling changes. Gordon Greenidge and Alvin Kallicharran built a worthwhile stand of 56, which took the West Indies to 2–117. The opener felt in good fettle, got to 65 in 33 overs and saw no reason why he should not complete his second century in as many innings. But Greenidge, too, paid insufficient heed to Coney's wiles and edged to Bruce Edgar.

Hadlee returned and bowled a fiery spell which thrilled the crowd. The West Indian total built steadily without their strokemakers ever really breaking loose. At the 55 over mark Clive Lloyd was still at the crease with his side on 7–204. An easily forgotten aspect of the great West Indian sides of this era is the fact that most of their fast bowlers were quite competent batsmen. The West Indian captain, who was later named Man of the Match, finally found a worthy partner in big Joel Garner. Lloyd took control, Garner held firm and 40 runs were added in the final five overs.

Without Howarth's attractive strokeplay 245 was always going to be too many for New Zealand against the West Indies' prize attack. They kept Lloyd's side out in the field for the full 60 overs but battled to maintain a run rate above three per over rather than the required four. Michael Holding proved particularly difficult to get away.

Coney and Glenn Turner had a promising stand, Burgess played some nice shots and Hadlee clubbed the ball around for a while to take the score above the 200 run respectability mark. When the innings concluded Brian McKechnie and Ewan Chatfield were at the crease. They were unable to make any real attempt to score the runs necessary, but were probably not overly concerned. New Zealand conceded top place in their group to their opponents, however their place in the semi-finals had already been assured and they knew they would not be facing the West Indies again at least until the final.

WEST INDIES

C.G. Greenidge c Edgar b Coney	65
D.L. Haynes lbw Hadlee	12
I.V.A. Richards c Burgess b Coney	9
A.I. Kallicharran b McKechnie	39
C.H. Lloyd (capt) not out	73
C.L. King lbw Cairns	12
D.L. Murray (wk) c Coney b Chatfield	12
A.M.E. Roberts c Lees b Cairns	1
J. Garner not out	9
Extras (b 5, lb 7)	12
(60 overs)	7–244

Did not bat: M.A. Holding, C.E.H. Croft

1/23 2/61 3/117 4/152 5/175 6/202 7/204

Bowling: Hadlee 11–2–41–1; Chatfield 11–0–45–1; Cairns 12–1–48–2; Coney 12–0–40–2; McKechnie 11–0–46–1; Morrison 3–0–12–0

NEW ZEALAND

B.A. Edgar run out	12
J.G. Wright c Lloyd b Garner	15
J.V. Coney c Garner b King	36
G.M. Turner c Lloyd b Roberts	20
J.F.M. Morrison c Murray b Garner	11
M.G. Burgess (capt) c Richards b Roberts	35
W.K. Lees (wk) b Croft	5
R.J. Hadlee b Roberts	42
B.J. McKechnie not out	13
B.L. Cairns b Holding	1
E.J. Chatfield not out	3
Extras (lb 14, w 4, nb 1)	19
(60 overs)	9–212

1/27 2/38 3/90 4/91 5/138 6/143 7/160 8/199 9/202

Bowling: Roberts 12–2–43–3; Holding 12–1–29–1; Croft 12–1–38–1; Garner 12–0–45–2; King 12–1–38–1

Umpires: H.D. Bird, B.J. Meyer.

Toss: New Zealand. Points: West Indies 4, New Zealand 0

WEDNESDAY 20 JUNE 1979
THE PRUDENTIAL CUP SEMI-FINALS

At the end of the preliminary rounds of the 1979 World Cup the Group tables finished as follows:

GROUP A	P	W	L	NR	Pts
West Indies	3	2	0	1	10
New Zealand	3	2	1	0	8
Sri Lanka	3	1	1	1	6
India	3	0	3	0	0

GROUP B	P	W	L	Pts
England	3	3	0	12
Pakistan	3	2	1	8
Australia	3	1	2	4
Canada	3	0	3	0

FIRST SEMI-FINAL: ENGLAND vs NEW ZEALAND
OLD TRAFFORD: ENGLAND WON BY 9 RUNS

The weather finally turned on its 1975 best for the two mid-week semi-finals and the cricketers of the four teams involved responded accordingly with a fine display of all the best aspects of the limited-overs game.

Old Trafford was filled to its 22,000 capacity for the clash between England and New Zealand. The English supporters crammed into the saucer-shaped arena were hoping to cheer their side one step further than they had gone four years before. They eventually got what they wanted, but the Kiwis made them apprehensive on more than one occasion before the favourites sneaked home.

Unlike Headingley 1975, there was no 'pitchus horribilis' for this encounter. Sunshine and a dry flat wicket ensured most if not all the day's allocation of 120 overs would be needed. Mark Burgess won the toss and, as was his and every other captain's habit, inserted the opposition. His spearhead, Richard Hadlee, responded with a superb opening spell. Geoff Boycott survived a sharp chance to wicketkeeper Warren Lees from the second ball he faced off Gary Troup before Hadlee had the opener well caught at third slip by the fit again Geoff Howarth in the fifth over of the day.

It was the start New Zealand wanted. England had included debutant batsman Wayne Larkins

51

at the expense of their spinner, Phil Edmonds, and it was the newcomer who joined Mike Brearley with the score on 13. Larkins middled the ball well from the moment he arrived at the crease. His placement, though, was lacking. His captain, too, was fairly circumspect and the pair occupied 16 overs while adding 25 before Larkins' tough initiation ended when he holed out at cover off Brian McKechnie.

Burgess had put in place his deep field setting by now, ensuring few if any boundaries were conceded. Brearley, who would take Burgess' deep set field theory to excess in Australia the following winter, continued to accumulate in singles. Gooch arrived and played shots. Often he had to be content with singles, as well. One six off McKechnie altered the pattern. Gooch danced down the wicket and thumped the ball straight. It soared towards and then through the sightscreen at Stretford End, leaving a neat hole that Gooch says he checked every time he played on the ground and was not mended for 10 years.

Brearley, now helmetless and hatless, went to his solid half century but he could barely extend it and in the 34th over was caught behind cutting at Jeremy Coney. Three for 96 suggested a game in the balance. That balance swung the way of the Kiwis almost immediately when David Gower took on Lance Cairns' arm going for a sharp second run and lost. Gooch and Ian Botham then lifted the tempo of the England innings, adding 47 runs in just 10 overs. Cairns then struck again, this time as a bowler. A loud appeal for lbw against Botham when he essayed a massive hook at a ball that kept low was answered in the affirmative as he and Gooch set off for a leg bye.

Derek Randall had probably held his place in the side through his brilliant fielding. His tournament scores in the preliminary rounds batting at number 3 had been 1, 5 and 1. 'Arkle' came in now at 5–145 and played his chip and run role to perfection. Gooch finally chopped a wide one from McKechnie onto his stumps and Troup had Chris Old caught behind for a duck. England were now 7–178 and a substandard total loomed as a possibility.

As he did against Pakistan, Bob Taylor came in at a crucial time to play an important small innings. The 38-year-old greying, immaculate little keeper ran well with the busy Randall and once lifted Cairns over long-on for six to the delight of the big Mancunian crowd. Randall also put one into the crowd off Cairns. The suffering bowler ran-out Taylor in the last over with a direct underarm hit, but New Zealand had conceded 25 runs in their final three overs. England finished on 8–221 and knew now they were well in the contest.

Some English scribes were not confident that the required run rate of 3.7 per over was enough of an ask and the ease with which John Wright and Bruce Edgar got the Kiwi reply under way suggested their pessimism could be well founded. They put on 47 in 16 overs and then Edgar became the first of four batsmen in the New Zealand innings to be given out lbw. Chris Old won that decision. Geoff Howarth was the next 11 runs later, his dismissal being a real blow to the Kiwis' chances. Geoff Boycott came on as second change. He went around the wicket. Howarth received a full toss. He went to sweep the ball to square leg, missed and was given out. Even the Lancastrians were pleased with yet another bonus Boycott wicket.

Coney and Wright lifted the score into three figures. But Coney became the third lbw victim and Wright, after a fine display, was sent back on a second run by Glenn Turner and fell foul of a superb throw from the revitalised Randall. He rocketed the ball in 60 yards from deep square leg. Bob Willis related how relieved he was to catch it and successfully remove the bails.

New Zealand were now struggling a little at 4–112. Another Randall inspired run-out, this time Mark Burgess making the misjudgment, left them an even worse 5–132. Bob Willis wrenched his knee in a bowling foothold so badly it kept him out of the final, but he had time to complete his 12-over spell and win a critical lbw decision against the experienced Glenn Turner.

The game was slipping away, but Hadlee, Lees and Cairns would not give in. Forty-three runs were required from the last five overs. Lees hit Hendrick long, hard and high to mid-on. Boycott manoeuvred under the ball, then held the catch. However, with his feet over the boundary rope the shot counted for six. Botham bowled Hadlee, another crucial dismissal. Cairns, an immensely powerful man, retaliated by hoisting the English all-rounder into the crowd at mid wicket. Twenty-five runs were still needed from the final 18 deliveries.

Botham and Hendrick were both limping, yet they managed to keep the ball right up on a yorker length at the business end of the innings. Cairns smacked a catch hard and low to mid wicket off Hendrick. Brearley held on without fuss. McKechnie and Lees pushed on, scraping together another 13 precious runs until the second-last over of the match when Hendrick sent down the perfect yorker to the New Zealand wicketkeeper. McKechnie and Troup needed 14 runs off the final over from Botham. If Greg Chappell had witnessed McKechnie's failure to

get more than four runs with his partner from this over he may later have refrained from his regrettable underarm instruction to his younger brother in a later limited-overs tournament. Six more well-directed deliveries and England could celebrate their advance into the Prudential Cup final.

For the second consecutive World Cup New Zealand bowed out at the semi-final stage. This time they had got to within an agonising nine runs of their objective. There was plenty of 'hard luck, old boy' attitude to their efforts amongst the press, but the Kiwis' final total of 9–212 was identical to the one they scored off the West Indies at Trent Bridge four days earlier. As it did in that game, the score indicated a batting line-up that was not quite good enough.

Graham Gooch's important innings earned him his second Man of the Match award in 11 days.

ENGLAND

J.M. Brearley (capt) c Lees b Coney		53
G. Boycott c Howarth b Hadlee		2
W. Larkins c Coney b McKechnie		7
G.A. Gooch b McKechnie		71
D.I. Gower run out		1
I.T. Botham lbw Cairns		21
D.W. Randall not out		42
C.M. Old c Lees b Troup		0
R.W. Taylor (wk) run out		12
R.G.D. Willis not out		1
Extras (lb 8, w 3)		11
(60 overs)		8–221

Did not bat: M. Hendrick

1/13 2/38 3/96 4/98 5/145 6/177 7/178 8/219

Bowling: Hadlee 12–4–32–1; Troup 12–1–38–1; Cairns 12–2–47–1; Coney 12–0–47–1; McKechnie 12–1–46–2

NEW ZEALAND

J.G. Wright run out		69
B.A. Edgar lbw Old		17
G.P. Howarth lbw Boycott		7
J.V. Coney lbw Hendrick		11
G.M. Turner lbw Willis		30
M.G. Burgess (capt) run out		10
R.J. Hadlee b Botham		15
W.K. Lees (wk) b Hendrick		23
B.L. Cairns c Brearley b Hendrick		14
B.J. McKechnie not out		4
G.B. Troup not out		3
Extras (b 5, w 4)		9
(60 overs)		9–212

1/47 2/58 3/104 4/112 5/132 6/162 7/180 8/195 9/208

Bowling: Botham 12–3–42–1; Hendrick 12–0–55–3; Old 12–1–33–1; Boycott 9–1–24–1; Gooch 3–1–8–0; Willis 12–1–41–1

Umpires: J.G. Langridge, K.E. Palmer.

Toss: New Zealand

SECOND SEMI-FINAL: PAKISTAN vs WEST INDIES
THE OVAL: WEST INDIES WON BY 43 RUNS

If the semi-final at Old Trafford provided a classic limited-overs nip and tuck contest, then the match at The Oval was the sumptuous batting feast. The West Indian side must have marvelled at the transformation of the south London ground from the wet, gloomy hole of 10 days before to the sun-drenched buzzing venue that greeted them this time.

An almost equal mix of West Indians, Pakistanis and neutrals created a fantastic, noisy cosmopolitan atmosphere which demanded great cricket. The 20,000 fans saw Asif Iqbal win the toss and predictably send the West Indies in. The Pakistani captain had Sarfraz Nawaz back at the helm with Imran Khan and he must have been hopeful his new-ball pair could provide an early breakthrough. Sarfraz had been brilliant against the West Indies in 1975. On this day, though, he was obviously underdone and could find neither line nor length. David Lemmon compared his profligacy with that of Alan Hurst against Pakistan at Trent Bridge. Imran bowled with genuine pace, but in Gordon Greenidge's estimation was too short.

Greenidge and Desmond Haynes took full advantage. They punished anything loose with the utmost vigour, Greenidge continuing his especially fine form. Mudassar Nazar was introduced into the attack and Haynes on 32 top-edged him towards Imran at fine leg. The all-rounder momentarily lost sight of the ball against the crowd background, and moving late, he missed the important catch. It was Pakistan's only real opportunity for 30 overs as Greenidge and Haynes put on 132 for the first wicket. Finally Asif brought himself on and got Greenidge to edge the ball to Wasim Bari standing up.

Viv Richards and Clive Lloyd played some blazing strokes as the bowlers conceded on average five or six runs an over. Asif caught Haynes off his own bowling and later bowled Richards. However, it was Majid Khan who did most to stem the torrent of runs. In the midst of the batting carnage going on all around him, Majid sent down his quiet little offspinners at no more than two an over.

Collis King dominated a stand of 49 with Alvin Kallicharran. King's aggressive cameo was to prove the perfect warm-up for Saturday's festivities, but in this case it was a material help towards the West Indies' total of 6–293, which was easily the best of the tournament so far.

The West Indies had started this match as clear favourites with the bookmakers and after setting Pakistan 294 to win were virtually unbackable. Michael Holding started with a very fast spell, including a few bouncers to soften the batsmen's resolve. The tactic worked when Sadiq Mohammad was caught behind with the score on just 10. But Greenidge at second slip dropped Majid and soon the West Indian pacemen were finding the wicket as slow and unresponsive as had Sarfraz and Imran.

Majid and Zaheer Abbas took full advantage. In a dazzling display the pair added 166 runs in 36 overs. On their day either could be the most enchanting strokeplayer in the world. At The Oval their sublime batting thrilled all with the exception of the West Indians. For the first time in any World Cup contest, Clive Lloyd was worried. Pakistan got themselves into a position where they required five runs an over with nine wickets in hand. On such a day this was a very gettable target. Lloyd admitted that the tea break arrived at just the right time. It allowed his side to regroup and reassess their tactics.

They agreed to concentrate on a restrictive leg-stump line of attack. Colin Croft the meanest and, regarding action, ugliest member of the Caribbean pace quartet and Viv Richards were entrusted with the job. Both responded magnificently. Richards' first over cost 12 runs, but next over Zaheer's superb 93 was ended by a brilliant diving leg-side catch by wicketkeeper Deryck Murray. Imran believes Asif then made a grave tactical error at this point by sending in the inexperienced Haroon Rashid. He could not give Majid enough of the strike and eventually it was the established batsman who mistimed a ball to Kallicharran in the covers.

Croft then picked up his third wicket from 12 balls in his spell from the Vauxhall End when he trapped Javed Miandad lbw first ball. From 1–176 Pakistan had slipped to 4–187. Asif came in and tried to resurrect the run rate. He attempted to blast Richards for six and was dropped on the boundary. He tried again and was caught by Holding. Finally, with the total on 6–220, Imran walked to the wicket. At Headingley everything had depended on him. Now it did again. Already, though, he felt defeated and soon became Richards' third victim when the off spinner held a spectacular caught and bowled chance.

Andy Roberts made the denouement a brief one and at 8.10 pm Pakistan were all out 43 runs short of the West Indies total in the 57th over of their innings. Imran and perhaps most of his team-mates felt sickened by the result. Their compatriots filed out of the ground on a beautiful evening wondering what had gone wrong. With a sensational win within their grasp they had lost 9–74. As in the corresponding fixture in 1975, Pakistan's temperament had failed them at exactly the wrong moment.

The West Indies were relieved but believed, as did most cricket followers, that justice was being done by them progressing to the final. Whether justice was done by John Edrich's

choice of the Man of the Match is another matter. Greenidge, who admittedly played a fine innings, got the nod ahead of Majid, who also bowled well, and Zaheer who made 20 extra runs. It is rare that the Man of the Match comes from the losing side but not for the adjudicator to pick someone who fulfils the same team role that he used to.

WEST INDIES

C.G. Greenidge c Wasim Bari b Asif	73
D.L. Haynes c & b Asif	65
I.V.A. Richards b Asif	42
C.H. Lloyd (capt) c Mudassar b Asif	37
C.L. King c sub (Wasim Raja) b Sarfraz Nawaz	34
A.I. Kallicharran b Imran Khan	11
A.M.E. Roberts not out	7
J. Garner not out	1
Extras (b 1, lb 17, w 1, nb 4)	23
(60 overs)	6–293

Did not bat: D.L. Murray (wk), M.A. Holding, C.E.H. Croft

1/132 2/165 3/233 4/236 5/285 6/285

Bowling: Imran Khan 9-1-43-1; Sarfraz Nawaz 12-1-71-1; Sikander Bakht 6-1-24-0; Mudassar Nazar 10-0-50-0; Majid Khan 12-2-26-0; Asif Iqbal 11-0-56-4

PAKISTAN

Majid Khan c Kallicharran b Croft	81
Sadiq Mohammad c Murray b Holding	2
Zaheer Abbas c Murray b Croft	93
Haroon Rashid run out	15
Javed Miandad lbw Croft	0
Asif Iqbal (capt) c Holding b Richards	17
Mudassar Nazar c Kallicharran b Richards	2
Imran Khan c & b Richards	6
Sarfraz Nawaz c Haynes b Roberts	12
Wasim Bari (wk) c Murray b Roberts	9
Sikander Bakht not out	1
Extras (lb 9, w 2, nb 1)	12
(56.2 overs)	250

1/10 2/176 3/187 4/187 5/208 6/220 7/221 8/228 9/246 10/250

Bowling: Roberts 9.2-2-41-2; Holding 9-1-28-1; Croft 11-0-29-3; Garner 12-1-47-0; King 7-0-41-0; Richards 8-0-52-3

Umpires: W.L. Budd, D.J. Constant.

Toss: Pakistan

SATURDAY 23 JUNE 1979
THE PRUDENTIAL CUP FINAL
ENGLAND vs WEST INDIES
LORDS: WEST INDIES WON BY 92 RUNS

Phil Edmonds returned to London from Old Trafford in the same car as his captain. The two did not always see eye to eye. Edmonds was not selected in the semi-final so it was not surprising that the atmosphere in the car was tense.

According to Edmonds, his captain was clearly intimidated by the pressure of leading his country against the might of the West Indies. It was something he never had to do in a Test match. The left-arm spinner reveals that Brearley kept repeating, 'How can we possibly beat the West Indies?'

Edmonds does not go any further than this or indicate what suggestions he might have offered

except to say that he thought Brearley had a poor match tactically. From the word go, however, he was up against it. In addition to the quality of the opposition Brearley had to try and cover shortcomings in his own side. Bob Willis, try as he might, had insufficient time to recuperate from his knee injury. He agonised over the decision right up to the morning of the big match and even tried his knee out in the nets before he succumbed to the discomfort and had to inform Chairman of Selectors, Alec Bedser of his withdrawal.

That left the English selectors in a quandary. At the time of the nomination of their 14-man squad there were many who chastised them for including an extra batsman at the expense of another pace bowler like in-form Essex left-armer, John Lever. The folly of their policy was quickly apparent because Mike Gatting was not selected in any games. Nor was there any confidence in the second spinner, Geoff Miller, so England, with the extra batsman in the final, would have to make do once again with overs from the likes of Geoff Boycott and Graham Gooch. Boycott had done a sterling job during the tournament, taking five important and inexpensive wickets. But he had not had to bowl against the West Indies and was also now troubled by a sore back.

Boycott had tried wearing a helmet for the first time in the nets prior to the big match, but his decision whether to use it had to wait as Mike Brearley won the toss. He had asked a few of his closest lieutenants what he should do and then, like everyone else in the tournament except the Canadian captain Mauricette, he asked the opposition to bat.

An air of expectancy filled the ground. The weather, although not as good as in 1975, promised to be fine throughout. There would be high cloud with some sunny breaks. It would be a day very comfortable for players and spectators alike. The West Indian players who were lucky enough to be involved for the second time were just as exhilarated and nervous as they had been four years earlier. They had no real selection or injury problems and maintained the same eleven for the entire tournament. The West Indies went into the game as clear-cut favourites. A punter could get 9–4 on England taking out the final. Once they were at the ground the English team really believed they could win. 'We knew the West Indies had a great side,' England wicketkeeper Bob Taylor recalls, 'but because it was a one-day game we thought we had a very good chance.'

The match had long been a sell-out, and 25,000 spectators crammed into Lord's. The bells and rhythms of the West Indian fans rang through the ground early and then continued non-stop. People milled outside the ground in St John's Wood Road, hoping to buy a stray ticket

from a tout, to just catch a glimpse of the players or action, or even to absorb some of the atmosphere of the great event.

'It was a fantastic atmosphere,' says Bob Taylor. 'There were plenty of West Indians in the crowd, a lot more than seem to go to matches in England today. But the majority were still right behind us and that helped. It was a big day, a cricketer's equivalent of the football World Cup. There were a few nerves before the game in the dressing-room. However, once you are on the ground and into the game you just get on with it.'

Brearley's decision to bowl had met with a mixed reaction, but there was plenty of movement off the seam early on and the ball regularly beat the edge of the bats of Gordon Greenidge and Desmond Haynes. Mike Hendrick was moving his leg-cutter up the slope. Maiden overs were enthusiastically applauded by hopeful English supporters. Greenidge had batted beautifully throughout the tournament. Today, though, he seemed slightly overawed by the occasion, as he had been in 1975. A call for a short single to mid wicket was misjudged. Randall swooped and scored a direct hit with his underarm throw. Greenidge did not even have to look at the umpire to know his fate.

Viv Richards was another who failed with the bat in the previous World Cup final. His form in this tournament had been patchy and off his second ball he had to withstand a confident lbw shout. A clip off his pads to the grandstand boundary off Chris Old was an isolated stroke of quality as the champion batsman struggled to find his touch.

Richards was able to hang on but Haynes, after working his way to 20, edged Old to Hendrick at second slip. The West Indies were an uneasy 2–36. Brearley thought it a good opportunity to use up some overs from Boycott. When he conceded just one run in his first over, it seemed the veteran, bad back and all, could once more do the job required.

The pattern of Limited-Over Internationals today is that batting becomes more restrained after the 15th over as it signals the end of fielding restrictions outside the circle. Richards saw the

15th over of this match as the time to open up. He smashed Old to mid-on with a stand-up pull and next ball played a perfect cover drive to the Mound Stand boundary.

Spinner Phil Edmonds was introduced. He concentrated on a leg-side attack and once more Richards was obliged to go on the defensive. The 50 was passed, but Alvin Kallicharran, almost a shadow of the batsman who dominated in 1975, soon misjudged the line of a ball from Hendrick and was bowled behind his legs.

The comparisons with 1975 continued. Then, Lloyd had come in at 3–50; today the total was 3–55 and another rescue job was required. He grabbed a single first ball, but at no time looked to take control as he had against the Australians. Instead he let Richards, who had been on 22 when Lloyd came in, continue to dominate. Boycott came back on from the Pavilion End. This time Richards relished his around the wicket inswing. A short ball was crashed into the Tavern concourse for six. The next was a full toss struck sweetly through square leg for four more.

The fourth wicket stand carried the total to 99 when Old lifted English spirits once more. Lloyd finally unleashed a powerful straight drive. The Yorkshireman stooped, put down his left hand and came up with an astonishing caught and bowled. It was no more than his side deserved. They had fielded in exemplary fashion all morning.

The home crowd sensed an upset and the possibility of a complete West Indian collapse. Collis King was coming in at number six and his record was hardly imposing. 'We thought we had one end open,' Bob Taylor says. 'But how wrong we were. Collis got going straight away.' Richards passed his 50 with an edge off Ian Botham wide of second slip to the pavilion rail. It had been scored out of 109 from 71 balls in 89 minutes. King started fluently enough with 19 runs off five overs, including one cracking back-foot drive through the covers and the West Indies were 4–125 at lunch off 34 overs leaving the game nicely poised.

Brearley still had to get through more overs with his fill-in bowlers. He brought them on straight after lunch. It was to prove the crucial phase of the match. Richards and King turned their attention first to Gooch. King swept him for four and Richards, also playing a sweep, hit him for his second six, this time into the Mound Stand. Next Richards stepped right away from his leg stump and cracked Edmonds through the covers for four more.

The stand was growing quickly and alarmingly for the English team and its supporters. And things would get a whole lot worse for them before they got better. King, who had struggled in a short stint with Glamorgan, had been impressive in his matching of Richards stroke for stroke. Now, though, with Richards just six short of his century, the Barbadian all-rounder, who still plays league cricket in Yorkshire, took total control.

As expensive as Gooch and Boycott had been, Brearley was looking for too much by asking Wayne Larkins to bowl. The English captain could not have done worse if he had used himself. Larkins came on and in the 47th over of the innings conceded 16 runs. King twice deposited juicy long hops into the Grandstand for six, the first one bringing King to his wonderful half century and raising the 200. From the second Randall was lucky to get the ball back from the excited dancing crowd. On television Jim Laker spoke of the futility of England not picking a recognised fifth bowler. Boycott returned and received similar treatment. King crashed him off the back foot through the covers, clipped him off his toes over square leg for six and belted a front-foot cover drive for four more towards the Mound Stand. Fifteen runs came from that over.

Edmonds was recalled and soon put an end to the mayhem, King holing out to Randall on the deep square-leg boundary. The fieldsman joined the applause for King as soon as the catch was held. Randall knew his unbelievable innings of 86 off 67 balls in 77 minutes including three sixes and 10 fours, had ruined England's chances. King had added 139 with Richards in just 21 overs, leaving the score on 5–238. He left the arena to a huge ovation. This was the greatest moment of King's career.

'It's easy after the event, I know,' says Bob Taylor. 'However, it really was asking too much of second-string bowlers to keep a tight rein on Viv Richards and Co. in a World Cup final. Goochie maybe, but never Geoff Boycott and Wayne Larkins. It turned the game. You sensed even as they came on to bowl that Richards and King were going to get into them. They played shots all around the wicket, every shot in the book.'

King had been dismissed in the 51st over of the innings. In the 52nd Richards went to the hundred that had temporarily been put on hold. An on drive from an Old full toss raised the three figures in 129 balls. Richards raised his bat and cap as the sun shone. An Antiguan flag fluttered at the front of the Tavern in proud response.

It was a magic moment. Richards knew, though, that his job was not done. For the rest of the innings only five more runs were scored by batsmen other than the Antiguan champion. Andy Roberts, Joel Garner and Michael Holding were all dismissed for ducks. Roberts was brilliantly caught by Brearley on the mid-wicket boundary. Richards took his turn to blaze. Hendrick conceded 14 runs in the 60th over. A flat-bat straight drive had nearly decapitated the umpire, Barry Meyer, as well as the bowler. Then from the final ball of the innings came his pièce de résistance. Hendricks fired in the ball full and straight. Richards was already moving straight across his stumps. He picked the ball up and swatted it straight over square leg for a most ridiculous six. 'A front foot straight drive executed at right angles,' was how *World of Cricket 1980* described it.

The West Indies had finished on 9–286, just five runs short of their wonderful effort in 1975. Eighty-six of those runs had been conceded by Boycott, Gooch and Larkins, although Clive Lloyd believed nobody would have been able to contain King on that day. Richards batted three and a half hours for his unbeaten 138 and hit three sixes and 11 fours.

England began their reply at 3.35 pm. The pairing of Boycott and Brearley had been a dismal failure in this World Cup, but the wicket was now dry and sound and the obdurate pair got themselves entrenched. Boycott looked in trouble against Holding, who was again fearsome

with the new ball. In the seventh over the England captain struck Roberts to the point boundary. Then a pull shot went square through Garner's fingers for four more, lifting the pressure for the moment.

Brearley was let off again in the 15th over when Lloyd dropped him at second slip. Boycott, who had taken 17 overs to reach double figures, hooked Croft and after 19 overs England were 0–55. Richards was becoming agitated at the missed opportunities and lack of a breakthrough. He was brought on to bowl and after his first over snatched his cap off umpire 'Dickie' Bird. Next over he threw the ball back like a bullet at Deryck Murray behind the stumps.

Both batsmen were reduced to scoring mostly in singles so that England went to tea at 0–79 from 25 overs. At that point 208 runs were needed from 35 overs. The West Indian fans had gone quiet, but Lloyd was not concerned. 'I thought they would have opened with Gooch,' he told 'Dickie' Bird at tea. 'They are scoring only at three an over and that's not bad for us.' A foundation had been established, but the need to accelerate straight after the interval was obvious. Yet inside the England dressing-room the sentiment according to Brearley was 'keep it going like it is'. He says that Botham told him not to take too many chances and that Randall assured him with, 'It's magic'. Edmonds, as was often the case, was a dissenter and voiced his disapproval of the scoring rate.

After the break, with the light gradually starting to deteriorate, the runs continued to come in singles. The hundred partnership was raised in the 32nd over. Boycott advanced on Richards and hit him to Lloyd at mid-on. He leapt and dropped his second catch. The cynical suggested he had done so on purpose. In 13 overs after tea Boycott and Brearley added a further 50 runs. It was good solid stuff, but it made the task of the following batsmen impossible. Brearley knew Richards should have been attacked, however he conceded only 35 runs from his 10 overs. Gooch wrote in his autobiography, 'In hindsight they should never have opened together'. Bob Taylor agrees: 'Boycott and Mike Brearley were too much the same in their batting styles. We should have opened with at least one strokeplayer, like Gooch himself.'

Boycott hit Roberts through the covers on the up and guided him to third man for boundaries. Both men reached their half century. But the run rate was creeping up all the time. Every single increased it further. Lloyd said he knew that each over the pair stayed together it was 'another nail in the English coffin'.

Brearley finally hooked Holding straight high to King at square leg and Boycott, too, could not control a cross-batted shot off the same bowler. Gooch, England's best batsman in the competition, came in to join Randall facing the awesome task of scoring 151 runs in 20 overs.

He gave it his best shot. Garner was struck hard and high to the mid-on boundary. Gooch unleashed pulls and further drives. In 43 balls he and Randall put on 48 runs in energetic fashion, lifting the score to 2–183 and maintaining the faint prospect of an English miracle. Then Joel Garner snuffed it out in an instant. Gooch had hit a couple of fine drives while scoring 32 in 28 balls. Then Randall swiped once too often at Colin Croft and was bowled. From the first ball of the next over Gooch played all over a Garner yorker and England were 4–183. Four balls and three runs later David Gower backed away, making room for a cut, and saw his off stump knocked back. Then from the final ball of this sensational over Garner completed Larkins' misery for the day by delivering yet another spot-on yorker.

Botham intended to go down fighting and he hooked hard and high to fine leg. There was his Somerset colleague and friend Viv Richards running hard and taking a brilliant catch. Botham's miserable four were the only runs scored by a fast bowler in the entire match. England 7–188. Now Garner went to work again. From the fourth ball of his next over he flattened Old's off stump. Like Gower he had totally misjudged the line and length of the ball. Did he see it? Perhaps not. It was now quite late in the evening and the hand of the giant Barbadian was coming down from above the sightscreen at the Nursery End. Gooch said the ball was coming out of the darkening trees. When Bob Taylor was caught behind first ball, Garner with that heavy-footed run and galumphing action had taken 5–4 in 11 balls. 'By the time I got in we were already dead and buried,' says Bob Taylor. England were 9–192 and the World Cup was in effect over.

Croft completed the last rites a few moments later when he bowled Hendrick. The Derbyshire seamer became the fifth English batsman out for no score. The last eight wickets had fallen for 11 runs. The West Indies had won the Prudential Cup for the second time, on this occasion defeating England by a clear-cut margin of 92 runs. West Indian supporters who had overflowed onto the ground with some regularity during the afternoon now charged from every direction in joyous celebration.

'We participated in the celebrations,' says Bob Taylor. 'I don't know about now, but then all the teams fraternised. The one gap in my career was that I never got to play a Test against the West Indies even though I was picked 57 times for England. This was the only big match I got to compete against that great side, so that made it special for me, too.'

Young Malcolm Marshall, watching in the dressing-room, had been tense and nervous all day, more so, he admitted, than the actual players in the game. He was exultant when he received his winner's medal with the rest of the team. Gordon Greenidge reveals the celebrations were as hectic and joyous as they had been four years before. He felt prouder this time because his own contribution in the four matches played had been far more significant.

Clive Lloyd believed the win totally unified West Indian cricket again in the post-Packer era. He wondered, though, how much the game's authorities had learned when he was originally offered a captain's winning bonus of just £50 by the Board's representative, Clyde Walcott.

England, the majority of the 25,000 crowd and everyone else watching on the BBC felt disappointed but proud. Brearley later wrote of his opponents, 'I cannot believe that in the history of the game there had been a side better equipped for one-day cricket'. The English have always revered the gallant defeat. By 1992, when they had lost two more finals, pride at just participating in the event was starting to wear thin. By then only the result really mattered. I should know. I support Geelong Football Club in the AFL.

Viv Richards was named Man of the Match. Denis Compton called it a 'joyous exhibition' and also wrote, 'The Don at his best could not have been more impudently superior'.

WEST INDIES	
C.G. Greenidge run out	9
D.L. Haynes c Hendrick b Old	20
I.V.A. Richards not out	138
A.I. Kallicharran b Hendrick	4
C.H. Lloyd (capt) c & b Old	13
C.L. King c Randall b Edmonds	86
D.L. Murray (wk) c Gower b Edmonds	5
A.M.E. Roberts c Brearley b Hendrick	0
J. Garner c Taylor b Botham	0
M.A. Holding b Botham	0
C.E.H. Croft not out	0
Extras (b 1, lb 10)	11
(60 overs)	9–286

1/22 2/36 3/55 4/99 5/238 6/252 7/258 8/260 9/272

Bowling: Botham 12-2-44-2; Hendrick 12-2-50-2; Old 12-0-55-2; Boycott 6-0-38-0; Edmonds 12-2-40-2; Gooch 4-0-27-0; Larkins 2-0-21-0

ENGLAND	
J.M. Brearley (capt) c King b Holding	64
G. Boycott c Kallicharran b Holding	57
D.W. Randall b Croft	15
G.A. Gooch b Garner	32
D.I. Gower b Garner	0
I.T. Botham c Richards b Croft	4
W. Larkins b Garner	0
P.H. Edmonds not out	5
C.M. Old b Garner	0
R.W. Taylor (wk) c Murray b Garner	0
M. Hendrick b Croft	0
Extras (lb 12, w 2, nb 3)	17
(51 overs)	194

1/129 2/135 3/183 4/183 5/186 6/186 7/188 8/192 9/192 10/194

Bowling: Roberts 9-2-33-0; Holding 8-1-16-2; Croft 10-1-42-3; Garner 11-0-38-5; Richards 10-0-35-0; King 3-0-13-0

Umpires: H.D. Bird, B.J. Meyer.

Toss: England

POST-MORTEM

Whatever the weather miseries of the second round of the 1979 Prudential World Cup, the tournament was once more considered a fantastic success overall. The ICC certainly liked it enough. They agreed that a Limited-Overs World Cup would now be a regular tournament, played every four years.

The financial returns were attractive to the officials from every country. Prudential had put in their £250,000, while gate receipts were up from £188,000 to £359,000. Attendance was down from 160,000 to 132,000, a factor blamed entirely on the inferior weather. The West Indies took away £10,000 in prizemoney, plus the £100 bonus for Clive Lloyd being winning captain. (Walcott had come back later and doubled his original offer).

Although celebrations had been whole-hearted, within a few days everyone was back on the treadmill. The next Thursday, 27 June, Ian Botham, Viv Richards and Joel Garner were team-mates again as Somerset tackled Worcestershire.

4

The Third Prudential World Cup, 1983: Tournament of the Boilovers

Just as the 1979 World Cup followed in the wake of the controversial World Series Cricket, so too did the 1983 tournament fall into the shadow of a greater issue.

South African authorities, frustrated by their ongoing isolation from the rest of the cricketing world, had been flying incognito to various countries, bringing out their chequebooks and signing players to make tours of their country. They secured the services of 'rebel' teams from England early in 1982 and Sri Lanka and the West Indies 12 months later. The players involved were banned by their home boards for varying periods. English players, including Graham Gooch and John Emburey, missed three years of Test and Limited-Overs International cricket for their willingness to receive large amounts of rand. The West Indian and Sri Lankan players originally received 25-year and lifetime bans, so seriously did their countries view players venturing into the then-forbidden territory.

This was a completely different matter from the World Series Cricket intrusion. The implications went much further than television and cricket. The potential existed for the cricket world to be split between black and white nations. Further complications arose from the fact that Zimbabwe, formerly Rhodesia, now had a democratically elected majority government and their representative teams were welcome all over the cricketing world. On the other side of the coin, certain conservative elements of the Marylebone Cricket Club were calling for a side representing them to be sent to South Africa. In a final bizarre twist, South African born players

like Allan Lamb had qualified for England and were establishing themselves in the Test side in the absence of the banned rebels.

These problems meant that England, the West Indies and Sri Lanka had reduced resources to draw upon for the 1983 Prudential Cup, although none would be decimated as the Australians of 1979 had been.

The scheduling of Limited-Over Internationals had grown dramatically since the last World Cup. Between the first two tournaments there had been 28 recognised matches. In the four years since England had met the West Indies at Lord's until the first match of the 1983 Prudential World Cup, another 122 encounters were added to the list. Many of those could be accounted for by the plethora of matches played in Australia each year under the title of the World Series Cup. Now the other Test nations had embraced the concept as well. They relished the instant popularity of the one-day games and the money they brought in. In Australia one-day cricket reached the peak of its appeal in the early 1980s and doubts about the future of Test cricket were at their most serious.

The time was right to increase the number of World Cup matches. At their 1982 meeting the ICC agreed that, in each group, all sides should play each other twice. This was to reduce the chances of a 'freak result caused by the weather'. No mention of money there. A couple of extra days were added to the fixture list and the number of days available for each match was reduced from three to two. The semi-finals and final were an exception, with three days still available for each. It was felt that the 1979 finalists should be seeded into two separate groups. This meant that England for the third time did not have to meet the West Indies in the preliminary rounds. The groups would be made up of the seven current Test-playing nations, Sri Lanka having been added to that company, and Zimbabwe, who had defeated Bermuda in the 1982 ICC Trophy final.

Games were unchanged at 60 overs per innings with a limitation of 12 overs per bowler. They were due to start at 10.45 am each day. For the first time in the World Cup competition fielding restrictions, as we have come to know and love them today, were enforced. In this tournament they took the form of two 30-yard semi-circles with the fieldsmen inside and outside set at specific numbers at various times during an innings. Umpires were told to be strict in their interpretation of wides and bouncers to prevent any attempts at negative bowling tactics. The extra matches also meant that venues away from the major Test grounds would have to be used this time. The best of the county grounds like Swansea, Taunton, Leicester, Bristol, Worcester, Southampton, Tunbridge Wells and Chelmsford were to be used to spread the World Cup gospel further around the country.

Prudential Assurance lifted their sponsorship to £500,000, double that of 1979, but at the same time announced that three times was enough and that they would have no involvement with the competition in 1987. This left the door open to other countries who were keen to stage the tournament.

Prize money was also increased. The members of the winning team would go home £20,000 richer. Most people believed, with justification, that the West Indies would collect that cash, continue their dominance of the competition and secure the World Cup for the third time. The Caribbean juggernaut had sustained its run of success in an almost unbroken fashion since their 1979 win. They clearly stood head and shoulders above every other side in the world, despite the fact their squad did not include a specialist spinner.

Clive Lloyd returned as leader for the last time, seeking to complete a hat-trick of trophies which would set a precedent unlikely ever to be matched. While the batting remained a real attraction, it was the quartet of pacemen which seemed likely to dominate all comers. A couple of the faces had changed, but the formula was the same: sustained blistering speed, which eventually wore down a batsman's resolve. Colin Croft had gone the way of the South African rebels, but into his place stepped Malcolm Marshall—if anything faster than Croft and probably more skilful.

Andy Roberts, Michael Holding and Joel Garner remained. Graham Gooch thought too much county cricket had blunted Roberts' edge in 1979 and he would soon be replaced, but Roberts had become a canny bowler who had adapted beautifully to the demands of the limited-overs game. Holding, despite a knee operation, and Garner had several years of batting demolition ahead of them yet. Wayne Daniel and Winston Davis squeezed into the squad as heirs apparent to the next two spots in the fast bowling production line. The West Indies completed their bowling quota now with the tight straight breaks of Viv Richards and Larry Gomes rather than the medium pace of Collis King. King, like Croft, was prepared to take the consequences of accepting South African rand.

One thing definitely unchanged since 1979 was that Viv Richards maintained his position as the batsman with the highest rating in the world. Now carrying the title the 'Master Blaster', the tremendous range and power of Richards' strokes were undiminished from four years before. Lloyd was now pushing 40 but his form was better in 1983 than it had been in the previous World Cup. Gordon Greenidge and Desmond Haynes remained firmly entrenched as the world's premier opening pair, while left-hander Larry Gomes had come into the line-up to provide middle-order stability.

Lloyd's right-hand man, Deryck Murray, had been replaced in 1980, much to the disgust of his fans in Trinidad. But the man who now stood in his stead, Jeffrey Dujon, was a more than worthy replacement. The Jamaican bore comparison with Murray as a wicketkeeper, but was in a higher class as a stylish middle-order batsman. He injected further quality into a side which had even more right to start the World Cup as favourites than their successful predecessors. Most thought that way. Bookmakers had them 11–8 on. The West Indies arrived in England having just completed fairly comprehensive Test and limited-over series victories in the Caribbean over India.

England had overcome the loss of its South African rebels with moderate success. Fast-bowling veteran Bob Willis was at the helm of a team which had had to plug several holes over the previous 18 months. Willis himself was in form as consistent as any from his long and distinguished career and he was closing in fast on the 300 Test wicket mark. He had led an unsuccessful campaign in Australia, although he was not likely to have his position as captain questioned in the immediate future. Test series against Australia were not yet the demoralising contests for England they became in the 1990s and Willis' side returned home with some positives. David Gower had responded to his appointment as Willis' deputy with a brilliant Ashes tour, scoring prolifically in both Tests and Limited-Overs Internationals. His batting won him the honour of the International Cricketer of the Year in Australia for 1982–83.

Allan Lamb had also proved himself a genuine run-making acquisition while Ian Botham's powers, in England at least, were as threatening as ever. The limited-over game almost seemed custom-made for a man of Botham's belligerent talents, yet his record in the shorter game remained far inferior to that in Tests. The 1983 World Cup offered him another opportunity to redress that balance. His team, despite the loss of their defectors, attracted a lot of local money which made them 7–2 second favourites to go one step further than 1979 and claim the trophy at Lord's on 25 June.

The top-order English batting was less settled despite the obduracy of Chris Tavare, but quality pace bowling support for the aging Willis seemed to be flowering. Graham Dilley's progress would be watched with interest, while young Norman Cowans had created a big impression in Australia.

Pakistan's two previous World Cup campaigns had been marred by the frustration of missed opportunities. This one was in trouble before the team even assembled in England. Imran Khan remained Pakistan's main strike bowler, his batting had developed to the point where he was now a major contributor in the middle order, and since his appointment as captain he had unified his team into a force in world cricket. However, such a mighty effort was starting to take a toll. Imran had been diagnosed as having stress fractures of the shin and, despite a two-month rest in the lead-up to the World Cup, he would not be able to bowl in the tournament. After weighing up conflicting advice he finally decided to make himself available just as a batsman.

Imran's fast inswing bowling would be missed, as the pace back-up of Tahir Naqqash and Rashid Khan was modest. Not that the Pakistani attack would be totally without merit. The last word used to describe Sarfraz Nawaz as a cricketer would be modest, and much interest surrounded Abdul Qadir. His wheeling, fizzing leg breaks had revitalised the belief that wrist-spin could be a viable commodity at the top level of the game. Qadir had attracted rave reviews during the tight series between England and Pakistan in 1982.

Also emerging as a star during that three-match contest was opening batsman Mohsin Khan, who made an attractive and match-winning 200 in the Lord's Test. Mohsin assumed the mantle of number one opener following the departure of Majid Khan. Majid's partner, Sadiq, the last of the Mohammad clan, was also gone, but Zaheer Abbas, Wasim Raja and the ever-present nuisance, Javed Miandad, remained.

Another fixture to return was New Zealand opener, Glenn Turner. There was not much international cricket left in him and he had made himself unavailable for the follow-up Test series against England, but there is no doubting he had made a significant contribution to New Zealand's admirable progress in 1975 and 1979. Geoff Howarth led the Kiwis this time and they looked as competent as their predecessors, if not more so.

Richard Hadlee's powers had not waned in any way and his seam support in Ewan Chatfield, Lance Cairns and Martin Snedden was more than respectable. Howarth himself was an accomplished middle-order batsman with a fine blend of experience and achievement in English conditions. The Crowe brothers, Jeff and Martin, were establishing their reputations on the world stage and John Wright and Bruce Edgar had become a solid fixture as an opening combination.

The cricketing world of Kim Hughes had fluctuated quite vigorously since 1979, both as captain and batsman, and worse would follow, but in 1983 he was back in England as leader of Australia again with a second, far more realistic chance of glory. This time Dennis Lillee would not have to request entry into any dressing-room. He would be trying to make his mark on the tournament on the playing field. It was to be his last tour of England and his first lengthy outing since knee surgery the previous November.

His mates from the 70s, wicketkeeper Rod Marsh and Sri Lankan scourge Jeff Thomson, were also in the Australian squad this time. Lillee, Thomson, Rod Hogg and newcomer Geoff Lawson formed a pace quartet which was supposed to challenge the West Indian fast bowling supremacy. Lawson, tall with a long toe drag and plenty of speed, was the bowler who now arrived with the big reputation. He had just secured 34 wickets in the recently completed Ashes series. The clearest assessment of Australia's improved chances was shown by their rating as 6–1 equal third favourites with Pakistan. The one doubt was the threat to team harmony. The cloud of World Series Cricket had not yet properly dissipated from over the Australian dressing-room. In addition, South African authorities were looking for new recruits. A number of Australian players were targets and the South Africans were offering them substantial amounts of money which would have been something of a distraction. Meantime the Australian Cricket Board was trying to protect its men from such temptations.

Greg Chappell had a neck injury and decided to stay with his family in Queensland, but if Hughes maintained his recent form Chappell would hardly be missed. Hughes had topped the averages and aggregates against England and had in his batting line-up vice-captain David Hookes, also successful against England, and Allan Border, quietly emerging as the grittiest batsman in world cricket. Graham Yallop, Graeme Wood and Kepler Wessels, along with Border, Hookes and Marsh, completed the largest set of left-handed batsmen ever to wear the baggy green cap in one team. Trevor Chappell ensured his famous Australian cricket family did not completely miss out on all the fun of the World Cup. He had an important spare-parts role within Hughes' side. Tom Hogan beat Bruce Yardley for the sole spinner's place. Yardley promptly retired when his fellow West Australian took the spot he craved.

India began the 1983 Prudential Cup as 66–1 outsiders and it was no wonder. Their limited-overs form guide made depressing reading. There had been a sprinkling of victories since Kapil Dev had taken over the leadership reins from Sunil Gavaskar, but nothing to suggest that the embarrassments of 1975 and 1979 could be turned into victory in the whole competition. The very idea seemed ludicrous. David Frith's preview in *Wisden Cricket Monthly* suggested: 'If their pride is not important enough to spur them to wholehearted effort this time, they might as well give way to other would-be participants in 1987.'

Like Botham, Hadlee and Imran before him, Kapil Dev had developed into a fantastic all-rounder, full of charisma and wonderful attacking cricket. By himself he should have ensured at least an improved performance from India. Sunil Gavaskar, with the departure of Geoff Boycott, now stood alone as the world's greatest batting technician. He was not pleased to lose the captaincy again, but did not let that stand in the way of his thirst for big scores.

His brother-in-law Gundappa Viswanath was no longer in the team and would be missed. However, there were consolations. Mohinder Amarnath's batting recently in the West Indies had been a revelation, Sandeep Patil's strokeplay was exciting and handsome enough to attract movie producers and Kris Srikkanth had an approach to opening the batting that was 13 years ahead of its time. His attitude was that the harder and shinier the ball, the further it was meant to be hit.

Spin and guile were out, medium pace and swing were in. Kapil Dev and a variety of support staff like Amarnath, Roger Binny, Madan Lal and Balwindersingh Sandhu would do the bulk of the Indian bowling this time.

Of the three countries so far affected, Sri Lanka could least afford to lose their South African 'rebels'. Despite their country's elevation to full Test match status, lack of depth remained an issue and the loss of talents like Tony Opatha and Bandula Warnapura would be felt. They had, however, under the guidance of former Australian spinner and coach Peter Philpott and West Indian legend Sir Garfield Sobers, already made some impact on the Limited-Over International stage with wins over Australia, India, Pakistan and England.

Their bowling lacked any real speed and would rely more on accuracy, Somachandra de Silva's wrist spin offering the most serious test of anyone's batting technique. Duleep Mendis, now captain, and Roy Dias had dabbled with the South African prospectus. This pair of short, stocky strokeplayers, were clearly Sri Lanka's best batsmen and their eventual availability was crucial to their team being able to make any impact on the competition.

In previous World Cups the eighth team— East Africa in 1975 and Canada in 1979—did little more than make up the numbers. Indications were that, although Zimbabwe might struggle to win the tournament, and they were rated at 1000–1 outsiders, they would be competitive and might, like Sri Lanka before them, give a few frights to any of the big boys who were off their guard.

Their captain, Duncan Fletcher, was a more than capable all-rounder, batting left-handed and bowling tight medium pace. He led a side several of whose members had first-class experience with Rhodesia in the South African Currie Cup. Best credentialled were wicketkeeper batsman Dave Houghton, who went on to become a stalwart of Zimbabewe's earliest forays into the international cricketing brotherhood; John Traicos, an Egyptian-born off spinner with Greek parents, who had played in South Africa's last few Tests before isolation in 1970; Kevin Curran, an all-rounder who went on to a long and successful career with English county sides Gloucestershire and Northhamptonshire; and a very talented 17-year-old schoolboy batsman on the trip for experience named Graeme Hick. The now traditional Buckingham Palace reception made a big impression on the teenage Zimbabwean. He nervously forgot his protocol, said, 'Hi' when introduced to the Queen and spent the afternoon drinking champagne and scoffing his beloved cashew nuts.

When the Australians practised against New Zealand at Arundel prior to the tournament they had to call off the game because of a hailstorm that covered the ground in ice in 15 minutes. Bats were put away for cameras. In *Wisden Cricket Monthly*, David Gower described his occupation as a cricketer as a 'joke', so little play was there in May. Once again there was the fear that the World Cup might be rained out of existence if 9 June did not bring about a change. Some were not even optimistic that there would be enough time for grounds to dry before the start of the tournament, even if the rain did stop in time.

But when the four sides involved on the first day at The Oval and Swansea turned up at the grounds they must have wondered what all the fuss was about. The weather was perfect for cricket.

THURSDAY 9 JUNE 1983
THE PRUDENTIAL CUP: ROUND ONE
GROUP A: ENGLAND vs NEW ZEALAND
THE OVAL: ENGLAND WON BY 106 RUNS

England opened their campaign at The Oval on a Thursday rather than Lord's on a Saturday. It made no real difference to Bob Willis' side, which ran out convincing winners. Unlike 1975 and 1979, however, the ground was nowhere near full for the host country's opening match. Nine and a half thousand was only a fair turn-up.

New Zealand's restrictive tactics of the previous tournament had been undermined to an extent by the rule changes to field restrictions, and when they had to bowl first they conceded runs freely. Those restrictions had been an innovation first tried in the Australian World Series Cup. Another 'gimmick' idea 'imported' from Australia was the setting up of a replay screen at The Oval for this match, but it caused some problems, only received mixed acceptance and by the end of the day was being switched off when left-handers were facing the Vauxhall End.

New Zealand had defeated England five times in limited-overs matches during the southern summer and must have approached this contest with some confidence. Bob Willis won the toss and batted, but Lance Cairns soon broke through for the Kiwis, sending Graeme Fowler back to the pavilion caught at slip from a late-moving delivery when there were just 13 runs on the board.

Richard Hadlee, less of a tearaway paceman now, was as testing and accurate as ever, but David Gower and Chris Tavare added 66 for the second wicket before Gower was caught on the mid-wicket boundary. Then the generally stolid Kent opener stayed with Allan Lamb until Ewan Chatfield dismissed him with the total on 117. That set loose Mike Gatting and Lamb, who demolished the New Zealand attack in a fourth-wicket partnership of 115 in just 16 overs. Martin Snedden came in for some severe punishment. Once Lamb pulled him high into the crowd. Young Martin Crowe was also very expensive.

In one wayward over he conceded 23 runs. Lamb struck his second six, straight to the pavilion. A brief interruption for rain failed to stem the batting momentum. On resumption Gatting hit the next two balls for four. He had been in and out of the England side for the past five years. This time he scraped in ahead of Derek Randall because of his part-time bowling. Gatting was exhilarated by the energy of the partnership. He and Lamb were taking twos from hits straight to fieldsmen on the boundary in a fashion for which Dean Jones would later become famous.

Finally Snedden, the first bowler ever to concede 100 runs in a World Cup match, gained a modicum of revenge by bowling both Gatting and Lamb, but that was not before the South African had completed his powerful century in 103 balls. It was Lamb's third in Limited-Over Internationals and, like the other two, it won him the Man of the Match award.

Hadlee won the points in his personal duel with Ian Botham, but Graham Dilley's late flurry of hitting meant that England added a phenomenal 203 from their last 25 overs. Ninety runs came from the last 10 overs, while Gould and Dilley had added 44 in 23 balls.

Any hope New Zealand had of scoring the 323 runs they needed for victory soon evaporated. Willis and Dilley sent down very fast opening spells which were too much for Glenn Turner, Bruce Edgar and John Wright. Edgar was the first to go, caught behind by Ian Gould diving in front of first slip, and when Turner was trapped in front and Wright, mistiming a pull, fell within three runs of each other New Zealand were 3–31. From that point there was really nowhere to go. Geoff Howarth succumbed to Vic Marks before tea. At the break New Zealand was 4–71 from 25 overs.

The wickets continued to fall at regular intervals in the last session and when New Zealand was 8–138 an early finish seemed likely. Ironically it was Martin Crowe, assisted by Martin Snedden, who kept the match going, without ever looking likely to alter the result. They had conceded an astonishing 156 runs in 18 overs between them. Now they added 52 runs for the ninth wicket. That gave the 20-year-old Crowe an outside chance to make his first hundred in international company. When Gatting snaffled Snedden, last man Ewan Chatfield held firm too, and the landmark got closer. Finally, however, just three runs short of his personal target, Crowe was run out backing up too far.

ENGLAND

G. Fowler c Coney b Cairns	8
C.J. Tavare c Edgar b Chatfield	45
D.I. Gower c Edgar b Coney	39
A.J. Lamb b Snedden	102
M.W. Gatting b Snedden	43
I.T. Botham c Lees b Hadlee	22
I.J. Gould (wk) not out	14
G.R. Dilley not out	31
Extras (lb 12, w 1, nb 5)	18
(60 overs)	6–322

Did not bat: V.J. Marks, P.J.W. Allott, R.G.D. Willis (capt)

1/13 2/79 3/117 4/232 5/271 6/278

Bowling: Hadlee 12–4–26–1; Cairns 12–4–57–1; Snedden 12–1–105–2; Chatfield 12–1–45–1; Coney 6–1–20–1; Crowe 6–0–51–0

NEW ZEALAND

G.M. Turner lbw Willis	14
B.A. Edgar c Gould b Willis	3
J.G. Wright c Botham b Dilley	10
G.P. Howarth (capt) c Lamb b Marks	18
J.V. Coney run out	23
M.D. Crowe run out	97
W.K. Lees (wk) b Botham	8
R.J. Hadlee c Lamb b Marks	1
B.L. Cairns lbw Botham	1
M.C. Snedden c Gould b Gatting	21
E.J. Chatfield not out	9
Extras (b 2, lb 4, w 4, nb 1)	11
(59 overs)	216

1/3 2/28 3/31 4/62 5/85 6/123 7/136 8/138 9/190 10/216

Bowling: Willis 7–2–9–2; Dilley 8–0–33–1; Botham 12–0–42–2; Allott 12–1–47–0; Marks 12–1–39–2; Gatting 8–1–35–1

Umpires: B.J. Meyer, D.O. Oslear.

Toss: England. Points: England 4, New Zealand 0

GROUP A: PAKISTAN vs SRI LANKA
ST HELENS, SWANSEA: PAKISTAN WON BY 50 RUNS

The people of Wales were provided with an absolute run feast when World Cup cricket came to Swansea. Pakistan and Sri Lanka hit 626 runs in the 120 overs of cricket, batsman after batsman enjoying the favourable conditions and the less than imposing bowling on offer. The match aggregate of 14 wickets for 626 runs is still the second highest in the World Cup, and Pakistan's 5–338 was at the time the highest innings total ever recorded in that competition.

What made it seem especially meritorious at the time was that Duleep Mendis won the toss and sent Pakistan in on a wicket that contained a lot of early moisture. But neither the wicket nor the bowling of Ashantha de Mel and big Vinothen John gave the opening batsmen Mudassar Nazar and Mohsin Khan any significant trouble. They put on 88 in 26 overs and then Mohsin and Zaheer Abbas added a further 68 in 14 overs. The stylish opener was finally removed just after lunch for 82, but Javed Miandad and Zaheer comfortably lifted the total to 229. Zaheer was also dismissed for 82. It was then that the fun began.

John had come back for his second spell and bowled Mohsin. As if to punish him for that impudence, Javed and his captain smashed John for 42 runs from his last three overs. One of those went for 23 and Imran, obviously trying to limit the amount of running on his sore shin, belted 22 of those including four fours and a six. Some of the shots were out of the textbook, others were the invention of the batsmen. Ninety-six runs were put on for the fourth wicket in nine overs of batting mayhem. de Mel finally won an lbw shout against Javed, but he too had been punished severely, his last two overs costing 30. Javed's 72 lasted 54 balls and contained three sixes.

It was great entertainment and few expected Sri Lanka to seriously challenge a target of 339.

Nor did they really, but they showed, as they had bravely against Australia eight years before, that chasing large totals did not overwhelm them. The wicket was now in excellent condition and most of the bowling was unthreatening. Even Zaheer Abbas was called on to send down a few deliveries, which he and probably the batsmen would have enjoyed.

The Sri Lankans were never up with the required run rate, nor were there any big partnerships. Twenty-one-year-old opener Brendon Kuruppu did best with a fighting innings that lasted 33 overs and included two more sixes. His stand with Arjuna Ranatunga took the score to a promising 3–142 before Zaheer ran out the youngster with a direct hit from mid wicket. Roy Dias and Duleep Mendis had both missed out, so

that once Ranatunga and Kuruppu were dismissed the challenge slipped badly. At 7–180 the margin of defeat seemed likely to be a large one. But wicketkeeper Guy de Alwis batted through the remainder of the innings. He and John were still unbeaten when the 60 overs were up. It was 8.15 pm and Sri Lanka were still 50 runs short of their requirement. Their 9–288 was the highest losing World Cup score at the time.

Six batsmen completed half centuries in this match. Mohsin Khan's name was the one eventually picked from the hat to receive the Man of the Match award. Yet on a day and in a form of the game custom-made for batsmen, who could deny that Sarfraz Nawaz's figures of 3–40 from his 12 overs was the most impressive performance?

PAKISTAN

Mudassar Nazar c de Silva b Ratnayake	36
Mohsin Khan b John	82
Zaheer Abbas c Kuruppu b de Mel	82
Javed Miandad lbw de Mel	72
Imran Khan (capt) not out	56
Ijaz Faqih run out	2
Tahir Naqqash not out	0
Extras (b 4, lb 4)	8
(60 overs)	5–338

Did not bat: Wasim Bari (wk), Rashid Khan, Shahid Mahboob, Sarfraz Nawaz

1/88 2/156 3/229 4/325 5/332

Bowling: de Mel 12-2-69-2; John 12-2-58-1; Ratnayake 12-0-65-1; Ranatunga 9-0-53-0; De Silva 10-0-52-0; Samarasekera 5-0-33-0

SRI LANKA

S.R. de S. Wettimuny c Rashid Khan b Sarfraz Nawaz	12
D.S.B.P. Kuruppu run out	72
R.L. Dias b Rashid Khan	5
L.R.D. Mendis (capt) b Tahir Naqqash	16
A. Ranatunga c & b Mudassar Nazar	31
M.A.R. Samarasekera run out	0
D.S. de Silva c Wasim Bari b Sarfraz Nawaz	35
A.L.F. de Mel c Tahir Naqqash b Shahid	11
R.G. de Alwis (wk) not out	59
R.J. Ratnayake c Mudassar Nazar b Sarfraz Nawaz	13
V.B. John not out	12
Extras (lb 8, w 10, nb 4)	22
(60 overs)	9–288

1/34 2/58 3/85 4/142 5/143 6/157 7/180 8/234 9/262

Bowling: Sarfraz Nawaz 12-1-40-3; Shahid Mahboob 11-0-48-1; Tahir Naqqash 8-0-49-1; Rashid Khan 12-1-55-1; Ijaz Faqih 12-1-52-0; Mudassar Nazar 4-0-18-1; Zaheer Abbas 1-0-4-0

Umpires: K.E. Palmer, D.R. Shepherd.

Toss: Sri Lanka. Points: Pakistan 4, Sri Lanka 0

GROUP B: AUSTRALIA vs ZIMBABWE
TRENT BRIDGE: ZIMBABWE WON BY 13 RUNS

According to Australian wicketkeeper Rod Marsh, Australia just about got what it deserved in this historic World Cup upset. Kim Hughes' side apparently had been lackadaisical in their preparation and they felt turning up at Trent Bridge would be enough for them to win. Well it wasn't.

They fell foul of a more determined

Zimbabwe side who looked as though they had more to play for. After the match Kim Hughes admitted Australia had been 'outplayed'. On the day he was right. However, certain members of the Australian side were embarrassed that they had been caught so badly unawares. The Zimbabwean amateurs had defeated the best that Australia could put in the field and most scribes had to go back to the loss against Holland in 1964 for a result of equal humiliation.

Nothing extraordinary looked likely at lunch, after Hughes had won the toss and sent Zimbabwe in to bat. Hughes started confidently with three slips to Lawson, but it was Dennis Lillee, coming on first change, who got the breakthrough. He claimed his 100th wicket in Limited-Over Internationals when in the 18th over he severed the solid opening partnership between Ali Shah, who knicked an outswinger, and Grant Paterson, who top-edged a hook. The clouds rolled in after a sunny start and even Graham Yallop and Allan Border, those bowling bunnies of 1979, took three wickets between them. Yallop had the dangerous Dave Houghton caught behind for a duck. Marsh juggled the catch and it took a conference between Hughes, Marsh and umpire David Constant before Houghton was sent on his way. He had also removed Jack Heron in the same fashion the previous ball to give Rod Marsh his 100th catch in Limited-Over Internationals. The fifth wicket fell right on the interval. Zimbabwe were 5–94 and the small crowd, remembering the authentic minnow efforts of East Africa and Canada, must have imagined a straightforward result for Australia. Ladbrokes by now had Australia at unbackable odds.

In the session after lunch, though, the mood of the game began to change. The Australians had not been fielding at their best and as the innings progressed things got worse. Much to the frustration of the fieldsmen and bowlers concerned, five chances were missed during the 60 overs. The Zimbabwean captain, Duncan Fletcher, benefited twice and was eventually able to take advantage of the let-offs. Taking the attack up to the bowlers, the left-hander hit hard and effectively. He put on 70 runs with young Kevin Curran in 15 overs and an unbroken 75, then a World Cup record, with Iain Butchart in 12 overs. The reputations of the four Australian fast bowlers counted for little as the Zimbabweans batted through to the end of the innings at 6–239.

Australia's fielding and bowling efforts had got them into some strife. A poor reflection of their out cricket was the concession of 31 extras. They must have imagined they had the resources to score at four runs per over for 60 overs against a lowly rated attack. Graeme Wood and Kepler Wessels started comfortably enough. Their opening stand realised 61 until Fletcher had Wood caught behind, umpire Merv Kitchen, in his first international, sending the West Australian on his way. Two runs later and captain removed captain. Hughes, brilliantly caught by a diving Shah on the leg side, found his day had gone from bad to worse. At tea Australia was 2–77 from 25 overs and after the interval Wessels and David Hookes lifted the score to 2–114. Once more Australia seemed well on course.

But Zimbabwe were much sharper in the field than Australia had been. They maintained the pressure on the batsmen, ensuring the run rate was always a factor and made the most of their chances. Wessels, who had got bogged down by a leg-stump attack after a solid innings was run out by a marvellous throw from Heron. Fletcher picked up two more victims in Hookes, well caught at cover, and Graham Yallop. When Yallop went to an amazing catch on the boundary by Pycroft, who juggled the ball while looking into the sun, the score was 5–138 and Australia required nearly eight an over to win. Curran and Butchart got rid of Border and Geoff Lawson cheaply. In the cool late-afternoon Nottingham sunlight, the underdogs gathered in groups were all smiles while, one after another, the Australians bowed their heads and trudged away.

Standing at the non-striker's end, Marsh was disgusted by what he saw. Australia was 7–176 and staring absolute humiliation in the face. Rodney Hogg, who despite the doubts about his resilience was now on his third visit to England in Australian colours, found the necessary competitive edge to hang in with Marsh. They had to fight for every run they could muster as the Zimbabweans threw themselves around in the field. The score mounted beyond 200, but the overs dwindled away. The run requirement got harder and harder. Fifty-three were needed from five overs, then 23 had to be hit from the last one. Marsh reached his 50 with a six, but, when the 360th ball had been delivered Australia was still 13 runs short of the Zimbabwean total.

Fletcher's team had reaped the benefit of all the determined preparation they had put in and the captain, himself, was rewarded for his efforts

with the Man of the Match award. In the Australian dressing-room the cloud still hanging overhead from the World Series Cricket split grew darker and larger.

ZIMBABWE	
A.H. Shah c Marsh b Lillee	16
G.A. Paterson c Hookes b Lillee	27
J.G. Heron c Marsh b Yallop	14
A.J. Pycroft b Border	21
D.L. Houghton (wk) c Marsh b Yallop	0
D.A.G. Fletcher (capt) not out	69
K.M. Curran c Hookes b Hogg	27
I.P. Butchart not out	34
Extras (lb 18, w 7, nb 6)	31
(60 overs)	6–239

Did not bat: P.W.E. Rawson, A.J. Traicos, V.R. Hogg

1/55 2/55 3/86 4/86 5/94 6/164

Bowling: Lawson 11–2–33–0; Hogg 12–3–43–1; Lillee 12–1–47–2; Thomson 11–1–46–0; Yallop 9–0–28–2; Border 5–0–11–1

AUSTRALIA	
G.M. Wood c Houghton b Fletcher	31
K.C. Wessels run out	76
K.J. Hughes (capt) c Shah b Fletcher	0
D.W. Hookes c Traicos b Fletcher	20
G.N. Yallop c Pycroft b Fletcher	2
A.R. Border c Pycroft b Curran	17
R.W. Marsh (wk) not out	50
G.F. Lawson b Butchart	0
R.M. Hogg not out	19
Extras (b 2, lb 7, w 2)	11
(60 overs)	7–226

Did not bat: D.K. Lillee, J.R. Thomson

1/61 2/63 3/114 4/133 5/138 6/168 7/176

Bowling: Hogg 6–2–15–0; Rawson 12–1–54–0; Butchart 10–0–39–1; Fletcher 11–1–42–4; Traicos 12–2–27–0; Curran 9–0–38–1

Umpires: D.J. Constant, M.J. Kitchen.

Toss: Australia. Points: Zimbabwe 4, Australia 0

GROUP B: INDIA vs WEST INDIES
OLD TRAFFORD: INDIA WON BY 34 RUNS

In its own way, this result was just as big a surprise as the match at Trent Bridge. It took a little longer, as a delayed start meant the game lasted into the second day, but it was no less warmly received for that.

India, the great World Cup underachievers, was thought no match for the West Indies by anyone. Even they probably approached this game in Manchester with apprehension. Their only glimmer of optimism came from an isolated victory in a Limited-Over International in Berbice just a couple of months earlier. The conditions encountered in Guyana that day could not have been more different than those that greeted both sides at Old Trafford. The heat and humidity had been replaced by Manchester grey. This was not a venue or a colour normally associated with Indian batting heroics.

There was nothing in the early stages to suggest that the status quo of 1975 and 1979 would be altered. Damp weather and conditions

held up play until shortly after the scheduled lunch interval. Then Clive Lloyd won the toss and with a smile told Kapil Dev his side could bat. Kapil demanded his top order blunt the firepower of the West Indian pacemen, but it would be no easy task as the light was poor and the wicket remained moist and conducive to sideways movement.

Sunil Gavaskar, Kris Srikkanth and Mohinder Amarnath, who had batted brilliantly against this attack in the Caribbean, all fought hard before falling to catches by the athletic wicketkeeper Jeffrey Dujon. After 22 overs India was 3–76 and a total of around 180–190, India's par in a World Cup match, seemed likely. However, the next 10 overs saw Sandeep Patil and Yashpal Sharma take the attack up to the West Indians, paying particular attention to Viv Richards and Larry Gomes. The runs came freely before Gomes struck twice, bowling Patil and having the Indian captain caught by Richards.

There was to be no turning back this time, though. Sharma was playing the innings of his life and he found a worthy partner in Roger Binny. Pulling fiercely and driving whenever the ball was up, Sharma raced past his fifty and added an invaluable 73 runs in 15 overs for the sixth wicket with Binny. After Binny shuffled in front of his stumps the recovery continued when Madan Lal joined Sharma. By the time Michael Holding ended the number 5's superb 120-ball effort India was well on the way to 262, their highest score in this competition.

'It gave us something to defend. Defend it we were going to—with body and soul,' said Kapil Dev in his autobiography *By God's Decree*. However, as the day drew to a close and rain clouds built up again on the horizon, the West Indian openers were making more than satisfactory progress. They put on 49 runs in even time. Then Haynes was run out going for a sharp single in the 14th over and seven runs and four overs later Greenidge was bowled by one from Balwindersingh Sandhu that cut back.

The West Indies ended the day on 2–67 from 22 overs, a position of no more than equality with India, yet the press the next morning looked at the West Indian batting line-up and still considered Lloyd's team would win.

Conditions on the Friday were improved, but there was no drying from a weak sun and the West Indian batsmen found it hard to time the succession of medium pacers on a wicket that did encourage flamboyant strokeplay. Roger Binny put in a superb spell. He lifted the spirits of his team immeasurably when he had Richards caught behind early on. It was a key wicket which set the pattern for most of the rest of the innings. Richards' dismissal left the West Indies 3–76. Soon they were 8–130 and the game appeared over. Binny had removed Lloyd, then Dujon, caught at mid-off, cheaply. Gomes was run out going for a third run and Marshall was stumped off a ball from the left-arm spin of Ravi Shastri that turned a long way.

Michael Holding survived a chance on the boundary and held on with Andy Roberts for a while until Shastri struck again. Roberts and Garner needed to add 106 for the 10th wicket if the West Indies were to steal the match. There were still lots of overs left and Roberts was already settled at the crease. Garner, too, established himself and soon the runs began to flow. Both batsmen used their height to get well forward and their strength to give the ball an occasional hefty thump. Garner hit Shastri for a four, then a six next ball, and Kapil removed him from the attack.

Against the odds they took the total to 200, then soon after completed their 50-run stand. Garner hit Sandeep Patil for another six.

INDIA

S.M. Gavaskar c Dujon b Marshall		19
K. Srikkanth c Dujon b Holding		14
M. Amarnath c Dujon b Garner		21
S.M. Patil b Gomes		36
Yashpal Sharma b Holding		89
Kapil Dev (capt) c Richards b Gomes		6
R.M.H. Binny lbw Marshall		27
Madan Lal not out		21
S.M.H. Kirmani (wk) run out		1
R.J. Shastri not out		5
Extras (b 4, lb 10, w 1, nb 8)		23
(60 overs)		8-262

Did not bat: B.S. Sandhu

1/21 2/46 3/76 4/125 5/141 6/214 7/243 8/246

Bowling: Holding 12-3-32-2; Roberts 12-1-51-0; Marshall 12-1-48-2; Garner 12-1-49-1; Richards 2-0-13-0; Gomes 10-0-46-2

WEST INDIES

C.G. Greenidge b Sandhu		24
D.L. Haynes run out		24
I.V.A. Richards c Kirmani b Binny		17
S.F.A.F. Bacchus b Madan Lal		14
C.H. Lloyd (capt) b Gomes		25
P.J.L. Dujon (wk) c Sandhu b Binny		7
H.A. Gomes run out		8
M.D. Marshall st Kirmani b Shastri		2
A.M.E. Roberts not out		37
M.A. Holding b Shastri		8
J. Garner st Kirmani b Shastri		37
Extras (b 4, lb 17, w 4)		25
(54.1 overs)		228

1/49 2/56 3/76 4/96 5/107 6/124 7/126 8/130 9/157 10/228

Bowling: Kapil Dev 10-0-34-0; Sandhu 12-1-36-1; Madan Lal 12-1-34-1; Binny 12-1-48-3; Shastri 5.1-0-26-3; Patil 3-0-25-0

Umpires: B. Leadbeater, A.G.T. Whitehead.

Toss: West Indies. Points: India 4, West Indies 0

Eventually thoughts turned to the West Indies' magnificent win over Pakistan in 1975 when Roberts and Deryck Murray guided their side home. Murray and Roberts had put on 64. Garner and Roberts added 71, still a World Cup record for the last wicket, and were within 35 runs of a miracle. Indian brows were furrowed. Gavaskar suggested Kapil bring back his young spinner Shastri, into the attack, forcing the two tail enders to hit against the spin.

It was a risk, there were 36 balls remaining, but from the first delivery of Shastri's sixth over Garner swung hard. Syed Kirmani, back from his taxi ride, had the bails off in a flash. The wicketkeeper jumped in instantaneous glee. Big Joel just lowered his head and walked away. He had only been out of his ground for an instant. India had completed its best win in Limited-Over Internationals. It was only their second-ever victory in this competition. The West Indies had suffered their first-ever defeat. Yashpal Sharma was named Man of the Match.

SATURDAY 11 JUNE
THE PRUDENTIAL CUP: ROUND TWO
GROUP A: ENGLAND vs SRI LANKA
TAUNTON: ENGLAND WON BY 47 RUNS

Sri Lanka stayed out west, this time in the cider country of Somerset, greeting the English team who travelled down the M4 from London. And as they did at Swansea, the Sri Lankans turned on a great spectacle, this time for a sell-out crowd. The formula was the same: weak bowling that was belted in all directions and a spirited batting reply that entertained, but inevitably fell significantly short of the required target.

The ground was packed. People had been queuing since the early hours of the morning and the gates were opened soon after eight o'clock. Bob Willis won the toss and, bucking what had been the limited-overs norm, elected to bat as he had done at The Oval. His openers, Graeme Fowler and Chris Tavare gave England another positive start on a very friendly batting surface. Neither player was able to turn that start into anything substantial and it was only when the in-form Allan Lamb joined David Gower that the fireworks really began.

The pair traded stroke for stroke while adding 96 runs. Lamb was first to his fifty but went no further as he became over-ambitious against Rumesh Ratnayake. Mike Gatting did not last long, finding himself in the middle of the pitch looking for a second run to square leg which Gower had no interest in. That brought Ian Botham to the wicket on his home county ground. The capacity crowd responded enthusi-astically to his entrance, expecting something special from their favourite all-rounder.

In a way they got it, but not as they would have wished. Botham had been in only a couple of balls and had still not scored when there was confusion between himself and Gower. A mad scramble for the stumps and a charge for the crease found the local hero short of his ground. England, 2–174 prior to Lamb's dismissal, was now 5–194.

Ian Gould's bubbly enthusiasm and busy batting had won a place in the side ahead of specialist wicketkeeprs like Bob Taylor. This day, the favourite of his brief England career, he fulfilled his obligations to perfection, supporting Gower and giving him the strike as often as possible while his fellow left-hander continued to flay the bowling. The combination worked perfectly and added 98 runs for the sixth wicket. Gower completed his thrilling century and went on to 130. He hit 12 fours and five glorious sixes, three of which sailed over long-on into the new grandstand. Two were from successive deliveries from Rumesh Ratnayake.

Gower and Gould fell within a few runs of each other, but as he had done at The Oval, Graham Dilley flogged a tiring attack to good effect. His 17-ball innings included five fours. England scored 105 runs from their last 10 overs and finished on 9–333, another massive score for

Sri Lanka to chase. No bowler came in for special treatment, they were all unable to stem the run flow and conceded 5.5 runs per over. The innings contained just three maidens, all sent down by Ashantha de Mel.

The Sri Lankans began their reply against a fired up Willis and Dilley. Soon the latter was making inroads. Brendon Kuruppu, who had batted so well against Pakistan, was caught at first slip by Gatting and Roy Dias, aiming a furious flat-footed drive, was brilliantly held two-handed at second slip by a high-leaping Botham. At 2–17 all hope for Sri Lanka was really lost, but they pressed on regardless. Duleep Mendis and Sidath Wettimuny were able to fashion a recovery and keep up with the required run rate. Mendis hooked Willis for six, giving the members in the new pavilion another close look at the ball. Paul Allott found out how difficult it was for a medium pacer to bowl on the flat Taunton wicket. Nor could Botham make any impression.

But it was another hometown boy, off spinner Vic Marks, who settled the issue once and for all. He broke the 75-run Wettimuny and Mendis stand and when he removed Ranjan Madugalle Sri Lanka were 5–117 in the 32nd over. From that point the batsmen were generally in control. Arjuna Ranatunga, Somachandra de Silva, de Mel and the consistent Guy de Alwis all made good runs, the bulk of which still came from the bowling of Allott and Botham. Marks, on the other hand, continued to pick up wickets. By the conclusion of his 12-over spell he had five and they were all upper and middle-order batsmen. de Silva was stumped by the beaming Gould. It was a rare treat. Gould's success was only the sixth stumping in World Cup matches to that point.

Dilley ended the game with the final ball of his 11th over when he bowled Vinothen John. Sri Lanka who finished 47 runs short of their target, had played in two matches within three days where 1245 runs had been scored. It was a run orgy enough to make bowlers wonder at the reason for their existence.

ENGLAND

G. Fowler b John	22
C.J. Tavare c de Alwis b Ranatunga	32
D.I. Gower b de Mel	130
A.J. Lamb b Ratnayake	53
M.W. Gatting run out	7
I.T. Botham run out	0
I.J. Gould (wk) c Ranatunga b Ratnayake	35
G.R. Dilley b de Mel	29
V.J. Marks run out	5
P.J.W. Allott not out	0
Extras (lb 11, w 9)	20
(60 overs)	9–333

Did not bat: R.G.D. Willis (capt)

1/49 2/78 3/174 4/193 5/194 6/292 7/298 8/333 9/333

Bowling: de Mel 12–3–62–2; John 12–0–55–1; Ratnayake 12–0–66–2; Ranatunga 12–0–65–1; de Silva 12–0–65–0

SRI LANKA

S. Wettimuny lbw Marks	33
D.S.B.P. Kuruppu c Gatting b Dilley	4
R.L. Dias c Botham b Dilley	2
L.R.D. Mendis (capt) c Willis b Marks	56
R.S. Madugalle c Tavare b Marks	12
A. Ranatunga c Lamb b Marks	34
D.S. de Silva st Gould b Marks	28
R.G. de Alwis (wk) not out	58
A.L.F. de Mel c Dilley b Allott	27
R.J. Ratnayake c Lamb b Dilley	15
V.B. John b Dilley	0
Extras (lb 12, w 2, nb 3)	17
(58 overs)	286

1/11 2/17 3/92 4/108 5/117 6/168 7/192 8/246 9/281 10/286

Bowling: Willis 11–3–43–0; Dilley 11–0–45–4; Allott 12–1–82–1; Botham 12–0–60–0; Marks 12–3–39–5

Umpires: M.J. Kitchen, K.E. Palmer.

Toss: England. Points: England 4, Sri Lanka 0

GROUP A: NEW ZEALAND vs PAKISTAN
EDGBASTON: NEW ZEALAND WON BY 52 RUNS

This was another two-day 'one-day' match. Persistent Birmingham drizzle delayed the start of the game until 1.45 pm and a later delay of 90 minutes meant only 56 overs could be completed on the Saturday. It was therefore on Sunday the 12th that New Zealand asserted their dominance over Pakistan with a win that threw Group A wide open.

Despite the fact that every Round One match had been won by the side batting first and that he was unavailable to take any advantage that might be gained from the wicket, Imran sent New Zealand in to bat when he won the toss. His opening attack could not make the early break-through, although it would have if Wasim Bari had not uncharacteristically put down two catches off Bruce Edgar. The left-hander and Glenn Turner provided the Kiwi innings with an excellent platform during their opening stand of 57. It was the introduction of Abdul Qadir, brought into the side at the expense of Tahir Naqqash, that created some anxiety amongst the New Zealanders for the first time.

In a superb spell the leg spinner not only stemmed the run flow but snapped up four prize wickets. The Kiwis, quite unused to this form of bowling, gave the indication that they had no idea which way the ball would turn. John Wright was caught behind, Lance Cairns promoted to belt the spinner out of the attack, was bowled having a slog; and Geoff Howarth became the seventh batsman to be stumped in a World Cup game.

New Zealand slipped to 5–120, but the rain returned for another 90 minutes. Qadir was restricted by the wet ball, besides which he could

not bowl forever. On the resumption Jeremy Coney and Martin Crowe were able to fashion a reasonable recovery. By the close New Zealand had fought their way to 8–211 from 56 overs. The Kiwis were able to make the most of their remaining four overs on the Sunday, adding a further vital 27 runs. Wicketkeeper Warren Lees scored the bulk of those, running and hitting furiously, and New Zealand had a competitive 238 on the board.

There were plenty of Pakistani supporters at Edgbaston and they cheered the arrival of Mohsin Khan and Mudassar Nazar to the crease. The noise quickly subsided, though, in Richard Hadlee's first over. By its completion Pakistan was 2–0, Mohsin and Zaheer Abbas both falling to the champion fast bowler. Mohsin was given out lbw to the third ball, Zaheer lost his off stump on the sixth. A target of 239 had quickly moved from competitive to mountainous. In the next over the peak got even higher when Lees pulled off a fantastic catch to send Mudassar on his way, still without a run on the board.

Imran, who was completely frustrated by his being unable to match himself properly against another champion all-rounder, did little to improve his side's fortunes before hooking loosely and becoming Hadlee's third victim. Six for 60 promised an early and embarrassing finish

NEW ZEALAND	
G.M. Turner c Wasim Bari b Rashid Khan	27
B.A. Edgar c Imran Khan b Abdul Qadir	44
J.G. Wright c Wasim Bari b Abdul Qadir	9
B.L. Cairns b Abdul Qadir	4
G.P. Howarth (capt) st Wasim Bari b Abdul Qadir	16
J.V. Coney c Ijaz b Shahid	33
M.D. Crowe c Mohsin Khan b Rashid Khan	34
R.J. Hadlee c Wasim Bari b Sarfraz Nawaz	13
J.G. Bracewell lbw Rashid Khan	3
W.K. Lees (wk) not out	24
E.J. Chatfield not out	6
Extras (lb 20, w 4, nb 1)	25
(60 overs)	9–238

1/57 2/68 3/80 4/109 5/120 6/166 7/197 8/202 9/223

Bowling: Sarfraz Nawaz 11-1-49-1; Shahid Mahboob 10-2-38-1; Rashid Khan 11-0-47-3; Mudassar Nazar 12-1-40-0; Abdul Qadir 12-4-21-4; Ijaz Faqih 1-0-6-0; Zaheer Abbas 3-0-12-0

PAKISTAN	
Mohsin Khan lbw Hadlee	0
Mudassar Nazar c Lee b Cairns	0
Zaheer Abbas b Hadlee	0
Javed Miandad lbw Chatfield	35
Imran Khan (capt) c Chatfield b Hadlee	9
Ijaz Faqih c Edgar b Coney	12
Shahid Mahboob c Wright b Coney	17
Wasim Bari (wk) c Edgar b Coney	34
Abdul Qadir not out	41
Sarfraz Nawaz c Crowe b Chatfield	13
Rashid Khan c & b Cairns	9
Extras (b 5, lb 6, w 3, nb 2)	16
(55.2 overs)	186

1/0 2/0 3/0 4/22 5/54 6/60 7/102 8/131 9/158 10/186

Bowling: Hadlee 9-2-20-3; Cairns 9.2-3-21-2; Chatfield 12-0-50-2; Crowe 2-0-12-0; Coney 12-3-28-3; Bracewell 11-2-39-0

Umpires: H.D. Bird, B. Leadbeater.

Toss: Pakistan. Points: New Zealand 4, Pakistan 0

for the Pakistanis and their aggrieved fans, who vented their anger inappropriately by throwing the occasional missile at New Zealand fieldsmen.

Once more Qadir saved face for his team, this time with the bat. Wasim Bari and Shahid Mahboob had pushed the total over three figures, but it was Qadir who ensured the team's overall runs per over coefficient was not damaged beyond repair. Qadir was never going to win the game and ran out of partners in the 56th over, however, but he top-scored for Pakistan, was only three runs short of the highest score in the match and batted well enough after his great bowling spell to lift his standing above all the other Man of the Match contenders.

After the game Imran was critical of just about everyone, particularly his batsmen and the umpire, Barrie Leadbeater. He had a bad day.

GROUP B: AUSTRALIA vs THE WEST INDIES
HEADINGLEY: WEST INDIES WON BY 101 RUNS

The last thing the disgruntled Australians needed was to meet the West Indies on the rebound on a wicket that was an uneven greentop. Kim Hughes might suggest such luck was the story of his life as Australian captain, because that is exactly what happened.

This was another match affected by bad weather on the Saturday. In complete contrast to the rain and general misery that delayed the start until 3.30 pm on the first day, Australia's batting capitulation occurred during a spell of brilliant sunshine on Sunday. What quickly became obvious was that the improvement in the weather had not changed the character of the wicket. It remained firmly entrenched in the brute class. The modern era has shown such tracks are almost custom-made for tall aggressive West Indian fast bowlers.

Not that the West Indies got first use of it. In fact Malcolm Marshall and Joel Garner did not get any use of it at all, missing out on the match with injuries. They were replaced by Wayne Daniel and debutant, the ultimately ill-fated Winston Davis. By the end of the game the Australians might have preferred it if Garner and Marshall had been fit.

Australian players who had inspected the pitch pre-match were reminded of the surface provided for the astonishing Test at Headingley in 1981. Then their bogeys were Ian Botham and Bob Willis. When the match got under way after Kim Hughes had won the toss, it seemed the main problem was getting the ball and the bowler's feet within the legal parameters of a cricket pitch. Wide followed no-ball followed wide as the new ball was sprayed about. Jeff Thomson, who was often guilty of such sins, could not be held responsible. He sat watching from the pavilion, replaced in the Australian eleven by Ken MacLeay.

There would be more interruptions for bad light and drizzle and so difficult were the conditions that even the occasional delivery in the right place brought a result. Rodney Hogg broke through first, having Gordon Greenidge caught at square leg, and when Geoff Lawson had Desmond Haynes caught behind and removed Viv Richards' off stump the West Indies were 3–32 and in real trouble. Clive Lloyd and Larry Gomes began the recovery, but the total was still only 78 when the West Indian captain was trapped lbw by MacLeay.

Faoud Bacchus had limited success as a West Indian player, but at Headingley this day he put together a precious innings of 47 which turned the match in the favour of his team. He and the imperturbable if lucky Gomes added 76 as the day drew to a close. Bacchus didn't quite make it to stumps, becoming another victim of part-timer Graham Yallop, but by then the West Indies on 5–160 from 42 overs were well back in the contest. On the Sunday Gomes pushed and deflected his way to 78 as the West Indies increased their score by 92 runs in the 18 overs available. Michael Holding and Daniel hit out in muscular fashion and added 41 runs in four belligerent overs before Holding was run-out from the final ball of the innings.

Australia needed 253 to win and they were none too confident. In that famous Test match two years earlier they had failed to chase 130 against an attack less lethal than the one they were about to face. The intention was to come out with all guns blazing, but all that Graeme Wood did was go down in a screaming heap. With the score on 18 a Holding delivery leapt off a length and hit Wood flush on the cheekbone. Although wearing a helmet he had no visor, according to the recollection of his captain. Wood was knocked unconscious and had to be carried from the field on a stretcher. The Australians were critical of the time it took for on-field assistance to arrive for the left-handed opener.

Wood was taken straight to Leeds Infirmary, where he was diagnosed with concussion and kept in overnight for observation. Fortunately there was no bone damage. Back at Headingley, Kim Hughes counterattacked with two sensational hooked sixes off Wayne Daniel's first two balls. Winston Davis came on and quickly had Hughes edging to Clive Lloyd at first slip. Kepler Wessels was out of sorts and soon left, but David Hookes and Graham Yallop took up where Hughes left off. The two strokeplayers traded blow for blow for eight exhilarating overs which realised 59 runs and seemed to place Australia in a position where they might reach 253.

Alas, their batting was an act of desperation rather than one of calculated aggression. Both were dismissed within two runs of each other, Yallop to a desperate hook, and the remaining executions were swift. Davis was nigh on unplayable as the ball flew at all angles. The Australian tail had no stomach for such an unequal contest and halfway through the 31st over the match had ended. Eight wickets fell for 37 runs. Davis had 1–37 at one stage from five overs. He finished with 7–51 and became the first bowler to take seven wickets in a Limited-Over International. He was named Man of the Match by Brian Close. The next day the headlines read, 'The Davis Cup'.

Both captains complained that the wicket was totally unsuitable for the game. Lloyd said, 'What are they trying to do to sides containing genuine fast bowlers by playing the match up here? Getting us to knock each other out?' After the game it was decided that the pitch used should be dug up, relaid and not used again until the following season. Graeme Wood thought the idea a sensible one.

WEST INDIES

C.G. Greenidge	c Wood b Hogg	4
D.L. Haynes	c Marsh b Lawson	13
I.V.A. Richards	b Lawson	7
H.A. Gomes	c Marsh b Lillee	78
C.H. Lloyd (capt)	lbw MacLeay	19
S.F.A.F. Bacchus	c Wessels b Yallop	47
P.J.L. Dujon (wk)	lbw Lawson	12
A.M.E. Roberts	c Marsh b Lillee	5
M.A. Holding	run out	20
W.W. Daniel	not out	16
Extras	(b 1, lb 9, w 10, nb 11)	31
(60 overs)		9–252

Did not bat: W.W. Davis

1/7 2/25 3/32 4/78 5/154 6/192 7/208 8/211 9/252

Bowling: Lawson 12-3-29-3; Hogg 12-1-49-1; MacLeay 12-1-31-1; Lillee 12-0-55-2; Yallop 5-0-26-1; Border 7-0-31-0

AUSTRALIA

G.M. Wood	retired hurt	2
K.C. Wessels	b Roberts	11
K.J. Hughes (capt)	c Lloyd b Davis	18
D.W. Hookes	c Dujon b Davis	45
G.N. Yallop	c Holding b Davis	29
A.R. Border	c Lloyd b Davis	17
K.H. MacLeay	c Haynes b Davis	1
R.W. Marsh (wk)	c Haynes b Holding	8
G.F. Lawson	c Dujon b Davis	2
R.M. Hogg	not out	0
D.K. Lillee	b Davis	0
Extras	(b 1, lb 4, w 5, nb 8)	18
(30.3 overs)		151

1/18 2/55 3/114 4/116 5/126 6/137 7/141 8/150 9/151

Bowling: Roberts 7-0-14-1; Holding 8-2-23-1; Davis 10.3-0-51-7; Daniel 3-0-35-0; Gomes 2-0-10-0

Umpires, D.J. Constant, D.G.L. Evans.

Toss: Australia. Points: West Indies 4, Australia 0

GROUP B: INDIA vs ZIMBABWE
GRACE ROAD LEICESTER: INDIA WON BY 5 WICKETS

After yet another delayed start, Zimbabwe were totally unable to reproduce the batting and bowling form that took them to their sensational victory on the Thursday. In the battle of the giant killers, India came out on top very comfortably.

Again there was drizzle and again the spectators, including the large Indian contingent inside the ground, had to wait until after lunch for some action. They made up such a large percentage of the crowd that some PA announcements were in Hindi. What cricket they did eventually see only provided mediocre entertainment.

Kapil Dev sent Zimbabwe in on a very green wicket and their batsmen struggled against the seaming and swinging ball. Madan Lal in particular achieved plenty of late movement. Zimbabwe received the benefit of a few missed chances, as they did against Australia, but could not capitalise on them or lift the run rate significantly. After Ali Shah became the first of a record-equalling five victims behind the wicket for Syed Kirmani, Grant Paterson and Jack Heron lifted the score to 1–55. Neither batsman looked in total control, so it was no surprise when wickets began to fall with some regularity.

Dave Houghton and Iain Butchart did best down the order without ever increasing the run rate to a point that seemed likely to worry India. It took 34 overs to reach 100. Houghton was caught behind trying to accelerate, Curran was run out while still in the middle of the pitch, and when John Traicos was run out from the fourth ball of the 52nd over Zimbabwe were all out for 155. India required just over 2.5 runs per over from their 360-ball allocation to go to the top of Group B.

Zimbabwe had to take early wickets if they were to make a game of it. They were without one fast bowler, Vince Hogg, who was suffering a back strain, and then Peter Rawson, who quickly got rid of Sunil Gavaskar and Kris Srikkanth, went down with a similar complaint at the start of his sixth over. Zimbabwe continued to impress with their fielding, but once Mohinder Amarnath and Sandeep Patil began to build their 69-run partnership it was never enough.

Patil scored his 50 at a run a ball. Curran conceded 15 runs in one over. The Indians began to race to their target. A couple more wickets fell, but halfway through the 38th over Yashpal Sharma hit Ali Shah to the boundary and Kapil Dev's side had completed a comfortable win. The Indian captain, leading a team that had previously been World Cup easybeats, noted that the Indian fielding had been poor and that his players were starting to get a little complacent. Madan Lal beat Patil for the Man of the Match award.

ZIMBABWE

A.H. Shah c Kirmani b Sandhu		8
G.A. Paterson lbw Madan Lal		22
J.G. Heron c Kirmani b Madan Lal		18
A.J. Pycroft c Shastri b Binny		14
D.L. Houghton (wk) c Kirmani b Madan Lal		21
D.A.G. Fletcher (capt) b Kapil Dev		13
K.M. Curran run out		8
I.P. Butchart not out		22
R.D. Brown c Kirmani b Shastri		6
P.W.E. Rawson c Kirmani b Binny		3
A.J. Traicos run out		2
Extras (lb 9, w 9)		18
(51.4 overs)		155

1/13 2/55 3/56 4/71 5/106 6/114 7/115 8/139 9/148 10/155

Bowling: Kapil Dev 9–3–18–1; Sandhu 9–1–29–1; Madan Lal 10.4–0–27–3; Binny 11–2–25–2; Shastri 12–1–38–1

INDIA

K. Srikkanth c Butchart b Rawson		20
S.M. Gavaskar c Heron b Rawson		4
M. Amarnath c sub (G.E. Peekover) b Traicos		44
S.M. Patil b Fletcher		50
R.J. Shastri c Brown b Shah		17
Yashpal Sharma not out		18
Kapil Dev (capt) not out		2
Extras (w 2)		2
(37.3 overs)		5–157

Did not bat: R.M.H. Binny, Madan Lal, S.M.H. Kirmani, B.S. Sandhu

1/13 2/32 3/101 4/128 5/148

Bowling: Rawson 5.1–1–11–2; Curran 6.5–1–33–0; Butchart 5–1–21–0; Traicos 11–1–41–1; Fletcher 6–1–32–1; Shah 3.3–0–17–1

Umpires: J. Birkenshaw, R. Palmer.

Toss: India. Points: India 4, Zimbabwe 0

MONDAY JUNE 13th
THE PRUDENTIAL CUP: ROUND THREE
GROUP A: ENGLAND vs PAKISTAN
LORD'S: ENGLAND WON BY 8 WICKETS

Lord's was filled to capacity, which is rare for a Monday, for this clash of World Cup arch rivals, England and Pakistan. The crowd, who at least got plenty of sunshine for their troubles, expected another tooth and nail struggle but a goodly number of them, that is, Pakistani supporters, were to be sadly disappointed. England was at its best and steamrollered Imran's side by eight wickets with plenty of overs to spare.

For the players it was now go, go go. The number of preliminary matches may have been doubled, but the time frame had not. One match quickly followed another so that there was little time to savour or enjoy an achievement. No wonder some cricketers find it hard to recollect what happened in games during their limited-overs career.

Imran elected to bat this day, but his side was almost immediately in trouble as Bob Willis and Graham Dilley gained every assistance from a fast wicket. It was the English captain who twice struck early. Mohsin Khan mishooked to a diving Tavare at mid-on after struggling for 45 minutes and Mansoor Akhtar edged behind. He had been brought in to allow Zaheer Abbas to slip down the order. Both players were back in the grand old pavilion by the time the score reached 33. Willis' first spell realised 2–12 from nine overs.

It could have been worse. The camera showed Mudassar had been short of his ground following a run-out attempt by Ian Botham at the bowler's end. The umpire, though, gave the benefit of the doubt to the batsman. Javed Miandad struck Paul Allott for two consecutive fours. Then wicketkeeper Ian Gould, who had caught Mansoor, snapped up Javed, beaten by Botham, and Mudassar, swinging too hard at Allott, as his second and third victims. That left Pakistan a precarious 4–67. They were 4–72 at lunch off 33 overs.

Javed was back on the ground soon after his dismissal. As if a stress-fractured shin was not enough, Imran also got hit on the toe, had to call for a runner and later was unable to field. Dilley exerted enormous pressure in his four-over spell from the Pavilion End after lunch. He failed to take a wicket, but his pace was extreme and his accuracy exemplary. After one express delivery Imran was so surprised he turned to Allan Lamb and said in amazement, 'What's going on, then?'.

Although Imran survived the Dilley onslaught and a chance to Gould, he could not get going and then suffered the indignity of being a passive witness to his own run-out. His runner, Javed, on the way for a second run was sent back too late by Zaheer. England was once more jubilant to have Pakistan 5–96 with fewer than 20 overs remaining.

Zaheer was now in good touch, but still Pakistan struggled. Off spinner Vic Marks, who had again been tidy, picked up Wasim Raja and when Abdul Qadir became the second run-out victim of the day Pakistan was 7–118. Finally Sarfraz Nawaz and Wasim Bari held on with Zaheer. The bespectacled champion attacked to good effect so that the run rate for the first time was lifted above three per over. At the 40-over mark the score had been 4–87. Twenty overs later the total had been increased by 106.

Graeme Fowler and David Gower soon had England progressing comfortably towards their target of 194. Fowler had lost his opening partner, Chris Tavare at 15, but he could sit back and watch his new partner again unveil his wide array of exquisite strokes. Gower scored 48 of the 78-run partnership he had with his fellow left-hander in 22 overs. The lack of bowling depth was a problem for Pakistan. The rarely used Mansoor had to send down a full quota of 12 overs. In fact he took the second wicket of the English innings, the last captured by Pakistan, when David Gower, his concentration finally deserting him, holed out to Sarfraz at mid wicket.

Fowler found difficulty in timing his strokes and was missed three times, but it hardly mattered. He just kept giving the in-form batsmen the strike as much as possible. After a close call for lbw against a Qadir wrong 'un, Allan Lamb took up where Gower left off. Abdul Qadir often troubled Lamb. On this day, though, the South African scored freely off him. The game was finished when Lamb put the leg spinner over long-off for six, lifting his tournament average above the 100 mark in the process. England had asserted a clear dominance over their opponents, although one, Zaheer Abbas, was recognised by adjudicator John Murray as Man of the Match.

PAKISTAN

Mohsin Khan c Tavare b Willis	3
Mudassar Nazar c Gould b Allott	26
Mansoor Akhtar c Gould b Willis	3
Javed Miandad c Gould b Botham	14
Zaheer Abbas not out	83
Imran Khan (capt) run out	7
Wasim Raja c Botham b Marks	9
Abdul Qadir run out	0
Sarfraz Nawaz c & b Botham	11
Wasim Bari (wk) not out	18
Extras (b 5, lb 8, w 3, nb 3)	19
(60 overs)	8–193

Did not bat: Rashid Khan

1/29 2/33 3/49 5/96 6/112 7/118 8/154

Bowling: Willis 12–4–24–2; Dilley 12–1–33–0; Allott 12–2–48–1; Botham 12–3–36–2; Marks 12–1–33–1

ENGLAND

G. Fowler not out	78
C.J. Tavare lbw Rashid Khan	8
D.I. Gower c Sarfraz Nawaz b Mansoor Akhtar	48
A.J. Lamb not out	48
Extras (b 1, lb 12, w 2, nb 2)	17
(50.4 overs)	2–199

Did not bat: M.W. Gatting, I.T. Botham, I.J. Gould (wk), V.J. Marks, G.R. Dilley, P.J.W. Allott, R.G.D. Willis (capt)

1/15 2/93

Bowling: Rashid Khan 7–2–19–1; Sarfraz Nawaz 11–5–22–0; Wasim Raja 3–0–14–0; Mudassar Nazar 8–0–30–0; Abdul Qadir 9.4–0–53–0; Mansoor Akhtar 12–2–44–1

Umpires: B.J. Meyer, A.G.T. Whitehead.

Toss: Pakistan. Points: England 4, Pakistan 0

GROUP A: NEW ZEALAND vs SRI LANKA
PHOENIX COUNTY GROUND, BRISTOL: NEW ZEALAND WON BY 5 WICKETS

New Zealand made three changes to the side which defeated Pakistan on the Saturday and Sunday. It did not undermine their strength. On the back of a sensational bowling spell by Richard Hadlee, New Zealand cruised home by five wickets with more than 20 overs to spare.

The Sri Lankans, still hanging about in the west country, were sent in and might have hoped, after their batting efforts against Pakistan and England, that they could set the Kiwis a big total to chase. They had lost Sidath Wettimuny by the time the score reached 16, Hadlee striking in his first spell. Brendon Kuruppu and Roy Dias set about establishing the innings base, but it was not until Duleep Mendis and Ranjan Madugalle got together that Sri Lanka really looked like getting anything close to the 280s they had hit at Swansea and Taunton.

Madugalle completed a pleasing half century. He and Mendis had seen their side through to 3–144 when Hadlee struck again soon after lunch, ending a productive 71-run partnership in 20 overs. Sri Lanka's tail had boosted their previous efforts. However, this time they were not able to quell the threat of New Zealand's champion. Hadlee dismissed the young left-hander Ranatunga before he had scored and stage-managed a late collapse which saw four wickets fall for 10 runs. In addition to Hadlee's outstanding spell, Ewan Chatfield's economy played an important part in Sri Lanka being restricted to 206.

New Zealand were concerned by the threat of rain. There were a few spots here and there so Glenn Turner and John Wright cracked 89 runs in 17 overs off the inadequate Sri Lankan pace attack. The Kiwis had a hiccup, slipping to 3–110 when Ashantha de Mel and Somachandra de Silva combined for a triple breakthrough. Neither really looked like getting rid of Geoff Howarth.

The New Zealand captain was at his stylish, stroke-filled best, scoring very freely. His side were 3–120 from 25 overs at tea and his 66-run partnership with Jeff Crowe sealed the result, although neither was at the wicket when the win was achieved. It was left to Ian Smith, brought in as wicketkeeper for Warren Lees, to hit the winning boundary off Vinothen John.

Five weeks after the match the Sri Lankan manager wrote to the English Test and County Cricket Board announcing that Ashantha de Mel and not Rumesh Ratnayake had dismissed Howarth. But both scorers were convinced that they had observed Ratnayake perform the deed. Perhaps the Sri Lankans were unsure of the identity of some New Zealand batsmen.

No-one had any real trouble identifying Hadlee as Man of the Match.

SRI LANKA

S. Wettimuny lbw Hadlee	7
D.S.B.P. Kuruppu c Hadlee b Chatfield	26
R.L. Dias b Chatfield	25
L.R.D. Mendis (capt) b Hadlee	43
R.S. Madugalle c Snedden b Coney	60
A. Ranatunga lbw Hadlee	0
D.S. de Silva b Coney	13
R.G. de Alwis (wk) c Howarth b Snedden	16
A.L.F. de Mel c & b Hadlee	1
R.J. Ratnayake b Hadlee	5
V.B. John not out	2
Extras (lb 6, w 1, nb 1)	8
(56.1 overs)	206

1/16 2/56 3/73 4/144 5/144 6/171 7/196 8/199 9/199 10/206

Bowling: Hadlee 10.1–4–25–5; Snedden 10–1–38–1; Chatfield 12–4–24–2; Cairns 7–0–35–0; Coney 12–0–44–2; M.D. Crowe 5–0–32–0

NEW ZEALAND

G.M. Turner c Mendis b de Silva	50
J.G. Wright lbw de Mel	45
G.P. Howarth (capt) c Madugalle b Ratnayake	76
M.D. Crowe c de Alwis b de Mel	0
J.J. Crowe lbw John	23
J.V. Coney not out	2
I.D.S. Smith (wk) not out	4
Extras (lb 6, w 3)	9
(39.2 overs)	5–209

Did not bat: R.J. Hadlee, B.L. Cairns, M.C. Snedden, E.J. Chatfield

1/89 2/99 3/110 4/176 5/205

Bowling: de Mel 8–2–30–2; John 8.2–0–49–1; Ratnayake 12–0–60–1; de Silva 9–0–39–1; Ranatunga 2–0–22–0

Umpires: H.D. Bird, D.R. Shepherd.

Toss: New Zealand. Points: New Zealand 4, Sri Lanka 0

GROUP B: AUSTRALIA vs INDIA
TRENT BRIDGE: AUSTRALIA WON BY 162 RUNS

The cricketing world seemed to be returning to a state of equilibrium after Australia thrashed India in Nottingham. Despite the upheavals of the first day of the tournament there was only ever one side in this contest, as India was totally outclassed. The only real surprise came from the fact that the Australian heroes were the previously unsung third Chappell brother Trevor, and Western Australian swing bowler Ken MacLeay.

Kim Hughes won the toss and elected to bat. He left out Jeff Thomson again and also, this time, the great Dennis Lillee, who was still underdone after his knee-troubled southern summer. At 34 there were those who considered this a sign the great man's career was almost at an end. Lillee and Hughes were not on the best of terms. At one net session the legendary fast

bowler sent down nothing but bouncers at his captain.

India had its worries, too. Sunil Gavaskar reported unfit and was left out of the side. He and Kapil Dev were not seeing eye to eye. And that complacency problem had not been dealt with, either.

Of more immediate concern to the Indian captain, was the fact that Chappell, in the side as a replacement opener for the concussed Graeme Wood, got Australia away to a flyer. He lost his out-of-form opening partner Kepler Wessels to a poor stroke in the third over with the score on just 11, but when joined by Hughes, Chappell went on a spree that rattled the Indians.

The sun shone, the wicket was good and Chappell and Hughes ran for everything. There was an element of risk involved, but the Indians were way off the mark in the field. Roger Binny put down a caught and bowled chance when Chappell was on 27. None of the throws could hit the stumps. The partnership prospered and 144 runs were added in 29 overs. Hughes had been badly out of form in the lead-up matches and had failed against Zimbabwe and the West Indies. He was under pressure from team manager, Phil Ridings, to elevate Graham Yallop in the order and demote himself to number 5. To his great relief at Trent Bridge he went to his fifty in 80 balls with three fours.

The relief might just have broken his concentration because he was out soon after and when David Hookes was caught at cover misjudging a Madan Lal slower ball four runs later, Australia could still have contrived another collapse. Chappell, though, was set upon a bigger milestone. He raced on to his century, his first in international cricket and the second by an Australian in World Cup matches. By the time he holed out at point off Mohinder Amarnath he had seen the 200 raised in 40 overs and hit 13 fours in 131 balls.

Kapil Dev was not suffering from complacency. He kept the pressure on for the remainder of the innings and finished with five wickets, but his team-mates were below par. Allan Border, who gave two chances, stayed until the score was

254 and Yallop batted through, ensuring a 300-plus total from the previously beleaguered Australians.

Without Gavaskar, India's task of chasing 321 was always going to be a difficult one. Kris Srikkanth hit about with his usual dash, registering five boundaries in the first six overs of the innings. Geoff Lawson and Rodney Hogg were quite expensive, but the Indians were always in trouble. Lillee had been replaced by fellow West Australian, Tom Hogan. A left-arm spinner, he fired in darts at leg stump from around the wicket that restricted the freedom of India's strokeplayers. Rain and bad light interruptions interfered with any momentum that the Indians tried to build. MacLeay took great advantage of this. He kept the ball on a full length, moved it a little and waited for the batsmen to overreach their ambition. Sandeep Patil was bowled between bat and pad and Yashpal Sharma found out how high the tall MacLeay could reach to take a caught and bowled.

The Indians were 6–66 after 22 overs, having lost 4–9 at the start of MacLeay's spell. They were all out after 37.5 overs for 158 . Kapil Dev had hit out and top-scored. Generally, though, it was a reminder of the bad old days. At least the complacency was gone. Trevor Chappell received the Man of the Match award.

AUSTRALIA

K.C. Wessels b Kapil Dev	5
T.M. Chappell c Srikkanth b Amarnath	110
K.J. Hughes (capt) b Madan Lal	52
D.W. Hookes c Kapil Dev b Madan Lal	1
G.N. Yallop not out	66
A.R. Border c Yashpal b Binny	26
R.W. Marsh (wk) c Sandhu b Kapil Dev	12
K.H. MacLeay c & b Kapil Dev	4
T.G. Hogan b Kapil Dev	11
G.F. Lawson c Srikkanth b Kapil Dev	6
R.M. Hogg not out	2
Extras (b 1, lb 14, w 8, nb 2)	25
(60 overs)	9-320

1/11 2/155 3/159 4/206 5/254 6/277 7/289 8/301 9/307

Bowling: Kapil Dev 12-2-43-5; Sandhu 12-1-52-0; Binny 12-1-52-1; Shastri 2-0-16-0; Madan Lal 12-0-69-2; Patil 6-0-36-0; Amarnath 4-0-27-1

INDIA

R.J. Shastri lbw Lawson	11
K. Srikkanth c Border b Hogan	39
M. Amarnath run out	2
D.B. Vengsarkar lbw MacLeay	5
S.M. Patil b MacLeay	0
Yashpal Sharma c & b MacLeay	3
Kapil Dev (capt) b Hogan	40
Madan Lal c Hogan b MacLeay	27
R.M.H. Binny lbw MacLeay	0
S.M.H. Kirmani (wk) b MacLeay	12
B.S. Sandhu not out	9
Extras (b 1, lb 4, w 3, nb 2)	10
(37.5 overs)	158

1/38 2/43 3/57 4/57 5/64 6/66 7/124 8/126 9/136 10/158

Bowling: Lawson 5-1-25-1; Hogg 7-2-23-0; Hogan 12-1-48-2; MacLeay 11.5-3-39-6; Border 2-0-13-0

Umpires: D.O. Oslear, R. Palmer.

Toss: Australia. Points: Australia 4, India 0

GROUP B: WEST INDIES vs ZIMBABWE
NEW ROAD, WORCESTER: WEST INDIES WON BY 8 WICKETS

Zimbabwe came out of this game with nearly as much credit as the winners. For much of the day at the world's most beautiful cricket ground, they challenged the world champions before the West Indies' depth in quality saw them through. In the end the margin was substantial, yet when Clive Lloyd's side was 2–23 chasing 218 another massive upset was being contemplated. Again Zimbabwe proved their worth as competitors in the World Cup.

Lloyd won the toss and would not even have had to tell his opposite number, Duncan Fletcher, that his side would be sent in to bat. The move paid immediate dividends. Ali Shah chopped a ball from Andy Roberts onto his stumps and when Grant Paterson edged a Michael Holding screamer to Jeff Dujon Zimbabwe was 2–7 and a complete rout was on the cards.

That possibility had been quelled by lunch, but the Zimbabweans were still struggling at 4–70 from 33 overs. Andy Pycroft had hit the first boundary of the day, a nice drive through the covers off Winston Davis. Davis and Wayne Daniel held their places, with Joel Garner's side strain and Malcolm Marshall's injury still a worry. With the score on 35 Pycroft tried to take a sharp single to Viv Richards. Not wise. Jack Heron hung on for 41 minutes before scoring, and batted 108 minutes for 12 before being stumped off Larry Gomes' third ball.

Against Australia Zimbabwe had gone to lunch in trouble and recovered. Now, as then, it was captain Fletcher who led the way. He and Dave Houghton added 92 runs for the fifth wicket, 55 of them coming from the slows of Gomes and Richards. Fletcher was dropped twice, by Davis on 25 and then Dujon on 44, but he went to a fine fifty in 48 balls. Houghton finally edged a Roberts outswinger in the 50th over. The Zimbabwean captain once more batted until the end of the innings. Zimbabwe added 34 runs from the last four overs to ensure they were in with a chance.

Vince Hogg was still suffering from his back complaint, but Peter Rawson had recovered. He quickly had Desmond Haynes caught behind and after a brief flurry of strokes trapped Viv Richards in front. By now the light was not good and play was interrupted a couple of times. Gordon Greenidge and Larry Gomes needed to be at their best. Gomes was regularly beaten outside the off stump and Greenidge was subdued. Like Chappell and Hughes at Trent Bridge, they initially built the scoreboard with a series of sharply taken singles. They had no other choice as the pressure was maintained.

After the 50 was passed in 19 overs strokes began to replace pushes and the Zimbabwean bowlers lost a little of their edge. Greenidge powered ahead of his partner. Partnership land-

ZIMBABWE

A.H. Shah b Roberts	2
G.A. Paterson c Dujon b Holding	4
J.G. Heron st Dujon b Gomes	12
A.J. Pycroft run out	13
D.L. Houghton (wk) c Dujon b Roberts	54
D.A.G. Fletcher (capt) not out	71
K.M. Curran b Roberts	7
I.P. Butchart lbw Holding	0
G.E. Peekover not out	16
Extras (b 1, lb 23, w 7, nb 7)	38
(60 overs)	7–217

Did not bat: P.W.E. Rawson, A.J. Traicos

1/7 2/7 3/35 4/65 5/157 6/181 7/183

Bowling: Roberts 12–4–36–3; Holding 12–2–33–3; Daniel 12–4–21–0; Davis 12–2–34–0; Gomes 8–0–42–1; Richards 4–1–13–0

WEST INDIES

C.G. Greenidge not out	105
D.L. Haynes c Houghton b Rawson	2
I.V.A. Richards lbw Rawson	16
H.A. Gomes not out	75
Extras (b 1, lb 8, w 9, nb 2)	20
(48.3 overs)	2–218

Did not bat: S.F.A.F. Bacchus, C.H. Lloyd (capt), P.J.L. Dujon (wk), W.W. Daniel, A.M.E. Roberts, M.A. Holding, W.W. Davis

1/3 2/23

Bowling: Rawson 12–1–39–2; Curran 10.3–1–37–0; Butchart 9–1–40–0; Fletcher 4–0–22–0; Traicos 9–0–37–0; Shah 4–0–23–0

Umpires: J. Birkenshaw, D.G.L. Evans.

Toss: West Indies. Points: West Indies 4, Zimbabwe 0

marks were passed—50, 100, 150—and Greenidge completed his second World Cup century. He had hit one six and just five fours. He and Gomes completed an unbroken 195-run partnership which was then an all-wicket record for the World Cup, beating Rick McCosker and Alan Turner's 182 runs against Sri Lanka at The Oval in 1975. The West Indies finally romped home with 11.3 overs to spare. Greenidge, perhaps starting a medal collection, was the nominated Man of the Match.

WEDNESDAY JUNE 15th
THE PRUDENTIAL CUP: ROUND FOUR
GROUP A: ENGLAND vs NEW ZEALAND
EDGBASTON: NEW ZEALAND WON BY 2 WICKETS

Following six days on the merry-go-round the eight sides were back to the starting point again. There had been a lot of cricket and there was a lot more to come. Realistically, seven sides remained in the hunt for a semi-final berth. Only Sri Lanka was without a win and, mathematically, if it won all its three games, it could make it, too.

As the teams entered the mid-week Round Four, the only unbeaten side was England. However by the end of the day it also had tasted defeat. At Edgbaston, New Zealand turned the tables, converting a 106-run defeat on the opening day of the tournament into an exciting narrow wicket victory this time. It was their first win over England in England in any international.

Graeme Fowler, more confident after his innings against Pakistan, and Chris Tavare gave England a nice, positive start of 63 from 19 overs. Bob Willis, after winning the toss, saw an opportunity for Ian Botham to regain a bit of batting confidence and score some quick runs against the slower bowling of Jeremy Coney and John Bracewell. The all-rounder made every attempt to bludgeon the ball, but after scoring 12, which included one chance as well as one four and one six, he hit a low scorcher straight back at Bracewell which the off spinner held.

The change in the order made no difference to David Gower who continued on his merry way. He and Fowler put England in a position where another 250-plus total seemed likely. From 2–117, though, the innings sort of lost its way. While the England captain blamed over-confidence, Gower suggested the innings was poorly paced. Gower was in the best position to judge as he saw eight partners come and go, their failures almost certainly denying him yet another century. It was Lance Cairns, bowling wrong-footed inswing, who put the Kiwis on top. He disposed of Allan Lamb, Mike Gatting and Ian Gould in quick succession, leaving England on 6–162.

Gower finally found support from Vic Marks and Graham Dilley. He cruised into the nineties in 96 balls, having hit four sixes and six fours on the way. Gower dominated the scoring in the latter part of the innings, compiling 52 runs out of the 72 scored. Seven for 233 with a few overs left still offered the chance of a very decent total. But that was about as far as it got. In an instant Richard Hadlee and Ewan Chatfield had polished off the last three wickets for one run to leave Gower high and dry. England were all out and had wasted 28 deliveries.

New Zealand had plenty of work in front of it to get the 235 they required for victory and Bob Willis, perhaps annoyed at making a duck, gave the Kiwis a double setback. He got rid of Glenn Turner in his first over and Bruce Edgar in his second with only three runs on the board. Both decisions prompted some debate, especially the second where there was doubt whether the ball carried.

The wicket was not entirely to be trusted, so it was hard work to bring about a recovery. Willis finished his spell, but Paul Allott bowled Jeff Crowe to make it 3–47. The younger Crowe, Martin, made 20 out of a stand of 28 with his resilient captain before he was bowled by Vic Marks. With the Kiwis 4–75, England was in control.

It was Jeremy Coney who finally became the kind of partner Geoff Howarth had been looking for. The New Zealand captain, who was recovering from a bout of dysentery, and the future New Zealand captain added a very important 71 runs in 15 overs before Howarth's fine innings of 60 came to an unfortunate end, run out when trying to take a second run to Dilley's strong throw from fine leg.

Ian Smith soon went, but Coney was still there as a potential match winner. He and Hadlee changed the direction of the game. They put on 70 at five runs per over to take New Zealand to the brink of victory. Willis wasn't finished,

though. He came back to bowl Hadlee and won an lbw decision against Cairns with four runs still needed. Allott bowled the last over of the match. Bracewell and Coney contrived three runs from four balls, including two byes from the second delivery, to level the scores. Then Bracewell cracked the Lancastrian seamer to the mid-on boundary to give Geoff Howarth's side victory in the closest match of the tournament so far. For his guiding-light innings, something he would make a bit of a speciality, Jeremy Coney won the Man of the Match award.

England's award was a post-match chastisement from their Chairman of Selectors, Peter May. He called them 'arrogant' and 'undisciplined'.

ENGLAND

G. Fowler c J.J. Crowe b Chatfield	69
C.J. Tavare c Cairns b Coney	18
I.T. Botham c & b Bracewell	12
D.I. Gower not out	92
A.J. Lamb c J.J. Crowe b Cairns	8
M.W. Gatting b Cairns	1
I.J. Gould (wk) lbw Cairns	4
V.J. Marks b Hadlee	5
G.R. Dilley b Hadlee	10
P.J.W. Allott c Smith b Hadlee	0
R.G.D. Willis (capt) not out	0
Extras (b 4, lb 10, w 1)	15
(55.2 overs)	234

1/63 2/77 3/117 4/143 5/154 6/162 7/203 8/233 9/233 10/234

Bowling: Hadlee 10-3-32-3; Cairns 11-0-44-3; Coney 12-2-27-1; Bracewell 12-0-66-1; Chatfield 10.2-0-50-2

NEW ZEALAND

G.M. Turner lbw Willis	2
B.A. Edgar c Gould b Willis	1
G.P. Howarth (capt) run out	60
J.J. Crowe b Allott	17
M.D. Crowe b Marks	20
J.V. Coney not out	66
I.D.S. Smith (wk) b Botham	4
R.J. Hadlee b Willis	31
B.L. Cairns lbw Willis	5
J.G. Bracewell not out	4
Extras (b 2, lb 22, w 1, nb 3)	28
(59.5 overs)	8–238

Did not bat: E.J. Chatfield

1/2 2/3 3/47 4/75 5/146 6/151 7/221 8/231

Bowling: Willis 12-1-42-4; Dilley 12-1-43-0; Botham 12-1-47-1; Allott 11.5-2-44-1; Marks 12-1-34-1

Umpires: J. Birkenshaw, K.E. Palmer.

Toss: England. Points: New Zealand 4, England 0

GROUP A: PAKISTAN vs SRI LANKA
HEADINGLEY: PAKISTAN WON BY 11 RUNS

Although Round Four did not quite provide the upsets of Round One, there was plenty of excitement in Group A. The day after England and New Zealand fought out their thriller in Birmingham, further up the M1 in Leeds Sri Lanka made life very uncomfortable for Imran Khan and his Pakistani team. Twice during the match the Sri Lankans appeared to be well on the road to a great victory. However, they were unable to sustain the pressure, and, much to the relief of the stressed captain of Pakistan, his side hung on by 11 runs.

It was a grey morning at Headingley when Duleep Mendis won the toss and elected to bowl. While not the dangerous minefield that the Australians and West Indians had played on, there was still plenty of assistance for the bowlers and Ashantha de Mel took full advantage. He moved the ball around and got rid of both openers. When Rumesh Ratnayake replaced de Mel he got Javed Miandad lbw and then won another decision against Ijaz Faqih. Pakistan was 5–43 and in big trouble.

Shahid Mahboob only ever played one Test, so he is not well remembered. He was selected for a number of Limited-Over Internationals in this period, though, and put in some useful performances. None was more valuable than this one. He and Imran lifted Pakistan out of their precarious position by adding 144 runs in 36 overs. It was a World Cup record for the sixth wicket until beaten by Kenyans Maurice Odumbe and Alpesh Vadher in 1999 and it could not have come at a more opportune time. Both batsmen offered sharp chances, but the Sri Lankan fieldsmen could not take advantage. By the time de Mel came back to claim his fourth wicket by dismissing Shahid, Pakistan was back in the contest.

As the 60 over mark closed in Imran dominated the scoring and completed his invaluable century. It was the first by a Pakistani in the World Cup and contained 11 fours. de Mel's five wicket haul was the first by a Sri Lankan in the World Cup. It was a far cry from the days when the entire team battled to get five wickets.

Despite the early loss of Brendon Kuruppu, Sri Lanka batted confidently in their pursuit of 236. The Imran-less attack still lacked punch. Worse than that, they had completely lost their radar. Mansoor, proving what a non-bowler he really was, sent down five wides in one over. The batting conditions had settled down and Sidath

Wettimuny, Roy Dias and Duleep Mendis showed composure in taking their side to 1–86 at tea off 25 overs and later to 2–162. They were just 74 runs away from a win with 13 overs to play. But if the Pakistani pace attack lacked bite, there could be no such criticism of their spinner. Imran had to fight to get the unfashionable leggie, Abdul Qadir, into his side for a limited-overs tournament. Qadir repaid his captain's faith by bowling Pakistan to victory over New Zealand at Edgbaston and he now turned this match around decisively.

With Wasim Bari an ever-present threat and accomplice behind the stumps, Qadir grabbed five cheap wickets, including 4–16 in his last four overs. Sri Lanka lost 7–37 in a terrible hurry. de Silva was run-out from mid wicket and de Alwis edged Qadir to slip. Sri Lanka slumped to 9–199. They now seemed certain to lose. But de Mel was not going to waste his five-wicket haul without a fight. He and Vinothen John got stuck in and put on 25 runs for the last wicket. Twelve more were needed with nine balls remaining. de Mel drove hard at Sarfraz. Imran was at long-off and he held the catch. There was a collective sigh in Urdu.

Qadir's match-winning spell got him the nod for the Man of the Match award ahead of other candidates like Imran, Shahid and the brave de Mel.

PAKISTAN

Mohsin Khan c Ranatunga b de Mel	3
Mansoor Akhtar c de Alwis b de Mel	6
Zaheer Abbas c Dias b de Mel	15
Javed Miandad lbw Ratnayake	7
Imran Khan (capt) not out	102
Ijaz Faqih lbw Ratnayake	0
Shahid Mahboob c de Silva b de Mel	77
Sarfraz Nawaz c Madugalle b de Mel	9
Abdul Qadir not out	5
Extras (b 1, lb 4, w 4, nb 2)	11
(60 overs)	7–235

Did not bat: Wasim Bari (wk), Rashid Khan

1/6 2/25 3/30 4/43 5/43 6/187 7/204

Bowling: de Mel 12-1-39-5; John 12-1-48-0; Ratnayake 12-2-42-2; Ranatunga 11-0-49-0; de Silva 12-1-42-0; Wettimuny 1-0-4-0

SRI LANKA

S. Wettimuny c Shahid b Rashid Khan	50
D.S.B.P. Kuruppu b Rashid Khan	12
R.L. Dias st Wasim Bari b Abdul Qadir	47
L.R.D. Mendis (capt) c Wasim Bari b Abdul Qadir	33
R.J. Ratnayake st Wasim Bari b Abdul Qadir	1
R.S. Madugalle c Abdul Qadir b Shahid Mahboob	26
A. Ranatunga c Zaheer Abbas b Abdul Qadir	0
D.S. de Silva run out	1
R.G. de Alwis (wk) c Javed Miandad b Abdul Qadir	4
A.L.F. de Mel c Imran Khan b Sarfraz Nawaz	17
V.B. John not out	6
Extras (lb 8, w 17, nb 2)	27
(58.3 overs)	224

1/22 2/101 3/162 4/162 5/166 6/166 7/171 8/193 9/199 10/224

Bowling: Rashid Khan 12-4-31-2; Sarfraz Nawaz 11.3-2-25-1; Shahid Mahboob 10-1-62-1; Mansoor Akhtar 1-0-8-0; Ijaz Faqih 12-0-27-0; Abdul Qadir 12-1-44-5

Umpires: D. Oslear, A.G.T. Whitehead.

Toss: Sri Lanka. Points: Pakistan 4, Sri Lanka 0

GROUP B: AUSTRALIA vs ZIMBABWE
COUNTY GROUND, SOUTHAMPTON: AUSTRALIA WON BY 32 RUNS

It was down on the south coast that the Australians recovered a little of the pride they had lost a week earlier at the hands of Zimbabwe. They won comfortably enough by 32 runs, without impressing anyone that they were likely to make much impression against the West Indies or England.

Like Pakistan and Sri Lanka, Australia and Zimbabwe played on the Thursday instead of Wednesday. There was no sign of interruption after Kim Hughes won the toss and batted. He had originally said that Graeme Wood might be unfit to play, but the West Australian walked to the centre at the start of play with Trevor Chappell, not Kepler Wessels.

Wood showed no ill-effects as he and Chappell started brightly with 46 runs in 10 overs. Wood could have been run out on 16, but it was Monday's centurion who went first. Wood continued on with his captain in a productive second-wicket partnership of 78. Hughes fell to the accurate off spin of John Traicos and Australia went to lunch on 2–145 from 37 overs. They briefly forfeited their sound position straight after the interval when Traicos ended Wood's worthy effort and David Hookes was caught on the same total at mid-off from a wild

uncultured swing at Duncan Fletcher.

Sensible batting and running by Allan Border and the consistent Graham Yallop were the feature of their 69-run stand that took the score from 150 to 219. Then Rod Marsh was able to swing his arms with some freedom and hit two sixes on the way to an invaluable 35 not out which guided Australia to a score of 7–272 and a position of some strength.

That was always going to be enough, even though Grant Paterson and Robin Brown put on 48 in 13 overs for the first wicket. Andy Pycroft and Jack Heron were both victims of poor running between the wickets. Pycroft was run out going for a quick single by a throw from Rod Marsh to the bowler's end. When Tom Hogan bowled the bogeyman from the first match, Duncan Fletcher, Zimbabwe was 5–109. They would never get 273 from there. Despite that Dave Houghton and Kevin Curran were not going to let the Australians have an early finish to the afternoon. They put on 103 in 17 overs. Houghton showed just what a good player he was. In 110 minutes he hit nine fours and a six off Chappell.

There were a few furrowed brows amongst the Australians and the 4000 strong crowd was

AUSTRALIA

G.M. Wood c Rawson b Traicos		73
T.M. Chappell c Traicos b Rawson		22
K.J. Hughes (capt) b Traicos		31
D.W. Hookes c Brown b Fletcher		10
G.N. Yallop c Houghton b Curran		20
A.R. Border b Butchart		43
R.W. Marsh (wk) not out		35
K.H. MacLeay c Rawson b Butchart		9
T.G. Hogan not out		5
Extras (lb 16, w 2, nb 6)		24
(60 overs)		7–272

Did not bat: D.K. Lillee, R.M. Hogg

1/46 2/124 3/150 4/150 5/219 6/231 7/249

Bowling: Hogg 9-2-34-0; Rawson 9-0-50-1; Fletcher 9-1-27-1; Butchart 10-0-52-2; Traicos 12-1-28-2; Curran 11-0-57-1

ZIMBABWE

R.D. Brown c Marsh b Hogan		38
G.A. Paterson lbw Hogg		17
J.G. Heron run out		3
A.J. Pycroft run out		13
D.L. Houghton (wk) c Hughes b Chappell		84
D.A.G. Fletcher (capt) b Hogan		2
K.M. Curran lbw Chappell		35
I.P. Butchart lbw Hogg		0
P.W.E. Rawson lbw Hogg		0
A.J. Traicos b Chappell		19
V.R. Hogg not out		7
Extras (b 1, lb 10, w 1, nb 10)		22
(59.5 overs)		240

1/48 2/53 3/79 4/97 5/109 6/212 7/213 8/213 9/213 10/240

Bowling: Hogg 12-0-40-3; Lillee 9-1-23-0; Hogan 12-0-33-2; MacLeay 9-0-45-0; Border 9-1-30-0; Chappell 8.5-0-47-3

Umpires: D.G.L. Evans, R. Palmer.

Toss: Australia. Points: Australia 4, Zimbabwe 0

brought to life until three lbw shouts were upheld within seven balls, ruining any lingering Zimbabwean hopes in the gathering gloom. From the last ball of an over Chappell finally got rid of the determined Kevin Curran. One run later in the next over Rodney Hogg got the umpire's nod against Ian Butchart and Peter Rawson off successive deliveries. With Houghton also gone,

caught at short mid-off, Zimbabwe slipped to 9–213. Vince Hogg and John Traicos held on until the second-last ball of the overs allotment, but they were a source of frustration, not a threat to victory.

Houghton's 84 was considered the highlight of the day. Roy Marshall gave him the Man of the Match award.

GROUP B: INDIA vs WEST INDIES
THE OVAL: WEST INDIES WON BY 66 RUNS

A sunny Kennington Oval and a fast wicket were seemingly tailor-made for a West Indian side continuing to build their momentum as the Prudential Cup moved into its business phase. They comfortably accounted for India in this, the Wednesday Group B fixture, their key batsmen hitting form and their pace attack being too much for the Indians.

India was without Gavaskar again. This time he was just left out of the side, a decision as controversial inside and outside the team as Australia's omission of Lillee had been. In Joel Garner's case injury was still the problem.

Clive Lloyd won the toss and, for the first time in the World Cup, elected to bat. This decision was greeted with immense pleasure by the large West Indian contingent out of the 12,000 who were attracted to The Oval by the prospect of revenge against India and a warming, almost Caribbean-style sun.

Those West Indian fans did not enjoy the prompt dismissal of Gordon Greenidge, caught at first slip off Kapil Dev. They were far better entertained by a century partnership between Desmond Haynes and the previously out-of-form Viv Richards. The wicket had pace, but the bounce was unreliable, so the mighty Antiguan was circumspect at first. It took quite a while for him to play with any freedom and, even as he later acknowledged, his strokes were more restrained than normal.

Haynes eventually got a ball from the innocuous looking Amarnath which lifted alarmingly and Richards was joined by Clive Lloyd, another batsman yet to make an impression in this World Cup. The powerful left-hander lifted Roger

Binny over mid wicket for six and in 14 overs added 80 runs with Richards.

Their stand took the West Indies to a very healthy 2–198 in the 45th over. Then Lloyd was left stranded in mid-pitch by a misunderstanding with his partner as Kirmani threw down the stumps. The West Indies now struggled to accelerate. Richards went to his deserved century and also deposited one delivery onto the roof of the Surrey Members' pavilion. Eventually he was caught behind in the 52nd over, his 119 containing just six fours and the one six—a low rate of boundaries for the 'Master Blaster'. The four West Indian fast bowlers found it just as hard to play big shots and only 59 runs came from the last 10 overs, Larry Gomes again holding things together as the innings concluded on 9–282.

It was a worthy total and India had a very difficult chase. The wicket was rock hard and the ball flew when Andy Roberts, Malcolm Marshall, Michael Holding and Winston Davis bent their backs. The West Indian supporters loved that. Roberts got both openers, Kris Srikkanth and Ravi Shastri caught behind by the time the scoreboard reached 21.

Amarnath, displaying the fortitude he had shown in the Caribbean a few months earlier, was joined by Dilip Vengsarkar in a brave 68-run stand in 21 overs. Then the spite in the pitch finally took its toll. Marshall unleashed a ball to Vengsarkar which reared and struck him in the chin. Marshall has indicated that Vengsarkar was never his favourite opponent, although there was no suggestion he gained any pleasure from decking him.

Vengsarkar took no further part in the match. Indeed, he did not play again in the tournament. But Amarnath went on. Battered from pillar to post, struck about the elbow, knuckles and even the face, he resisted and hooked bravely at every opportunity for three hours. His captain rated him the best player of express fast bowling in the world. It was an opinion he would not change, even after Amarnath scored one run from six innings in the home Test series against the West Indies four months later.

Sandeep Patil also fought hard and Kapil Dev continued to strive for victory. India got to 5–193, but the overs were starting to run out.

Michael Holding returned and picked up a couple of quick wickets. When Kapil Dev was dismissed India needed 71 runs from just eight overs. Haynes, Dev's catcher, showed the delight of a man who believed a match was won. He was right. India scored only four of the 71 runs they needed. Sandhu was run out from the first ball of the 54th over, leaving the West Indies winners by 66 runs. Only those at the ground were witnesses to this West Indian revenge. The television coverage was blacked out because of a strike by the Association of Broadcasting Staffs.

Everyone outside The Oval had to be told that Viv Richards was Man of the Match.

WEST INDIES

C.G. Greenidge c Vengsarkar b Kapil Dev	9
D.L. Haynes c Kapil Dev b Amarnath	38
I.V.A. Richards c Kirmani b Sandhu	119
C.H. Lloyd (capt) run out	41
S.F.A.F. Bacchus b Binny	8
P.J.L. Dujon (wk) c Shastri b Binny	9
H.A. Gomes not out	27
A.M.E. Roberts c Patil b Binny	7
M.D. Marshall run out	4
M.A. Holding c sub (K. Azad) b Madan Lal	2
W.W. Davis not out	0
Extras (lb 13, w 5)	18
(60 overs)	9–282

1/17 2/118 3/198 4/213 5/239 6/240 7/257 8/270 9/280

Bowling: Kapil Dev 12-0-46-1; Sandhu 12-2-42-1; Binny 12-0-71-3; Amarnath 12-0-58-1; Madan Lal 12-0-47-1

INDIA

K. Srikkanth c Dujon b Roberts	2
R.J. Shastri c Dujon b Roberts	6
M. Amarnath c Lloyd b Holding	80
D.B. Vengsarkar retired hurt	32
S.M. Patil c & b Gomes	21
Yashpal Sharma run out	9
Kapil Dev (capt) c Haynes b Holding	36
R.M.H. Binny lbw Holding	1
Madan Lal not out	8
S.M.H. Kirmani (wk) b Marshall	0
B.S. Sandhu run out	0
Extras (b 3, lb 13, nb 5)	21
(53.1 overs)	216

1/2 2/21 3/130 4/143 5/193 6/195 7/212 8/214 9/216

Bowling: Roberts 9-1-29-2; Holding 9.1-0-40-3; Marshall 11-3-20-1; Davis 12-2-51-0; Gomes 12-1-55-1

Umpires: B.J. Meyer, D.R. Shepherd.

Toss: West Indies. Points: West Indies 4, India 0

SATURDAY JUNE 18th
THE PRUDENTIAL CUP: ROUND FIVE
GROUP A: ENGLAND vs PAKISTAN
OLD TRAFFORD: ENGLAND WON BY 7 WICKETS

Saturday provided beautiful weather and reassurance for English fans that everything really was on course in their World Cup campaign. Most of England's cricket was disciplined and displayed only the positive aspects of arrogance. Pakistan, in contrast, looked lacklustre and rarely seemed to have the upper hand.

If it is sunny in Manchester then the whole of England is usually basking, and that brings out the fans. The gates were closed soon after the

start of play and 20,000, many of them baring their chests, a couple of streakers showing a little more, saw Pakistan struggle to build a competitive score only for their bowlers to fail to make any impression on the in-form English batsmen.

The wicket was a little on the low and slow side, but the outfield was fast and Imran Khan decided to bat after he won the toss. As at Lord's, Mudassar Nazar and Mohsin Khan were merely intent on survival as they withstood an early barrage from Bob Willis and Graham Dilley. The English captain, in prime bowling form, conceded just seven runs in his first six overs, while Dilley picked up the first two wickets, despite straining a muscle at the top of his right thigh in his third over. He had Mudassar caught behind down the leg side and then removed Zaheer Abbas, the Man of the Match at Lord's, one run later with a beauty that lifted and separated.

At 2–34 Pakistan had more securing work to do. Mohsin wanted to be the backbone and scored at barely one an over. Javed Miandad, however, was in good touch. He alone kept the score rate reasonable. After 30 overs he finally lost Mohsin, well caught by Vic Marks. Three overs later it was lunch and Pakistan was 3–101. Imran was not on song this day at all, nor was Wasim Raja. Both were caught at long-off, choosing the wrong ball from off spinner Marks to try and boost the scoring.

Javed finally found a partner of equal intent in Ijaz Faqih, only ever called Ijaz on Western television and radio. Ian Botham's bowling had looked very ordinary again. His fielding, as it had been at Taunton, would be his day's saviour. Javed and Ijaz were looking in control when in the 51st over Ijaz guided Willis behind point. Javed called for a single. Botham moved to his left, picked the ball up in his right hand and in one motion threw down the stumps with a mighty 20-metre pelt that caught Javed short of his ground.

It was an inspirational piece of work that thrilled the crowd, the England players and Botham himself, in equal measure. Botham's joy was evidenced by the fact that he thought the effort worth a punch of the air and a spit on the ground.

Pakistan was 6–169 and again battling to set a worthy target. Ijaz kept going until the end of the innings, playing some energetic cover drives with his left foot pointing at mid-on. He added valuable runs with Sarfraz Nawaz and Abdul Qadir. Pakistan put on 43 from their last six overs, enabling them to reach 8–232.

Imran's side needed early wickets, but without their captain's pace and skill they never looked like getting any. Graeme Fowler and Chris Tavare had an opening partnership of 115 in 30 overs. Their work was effective rather than exciting. The tackling of a streaker by umpire Don Oslear provided as much entertainment as any of the strokeplay by the Lancastrian and his partner from Kent. Fowler completed his third half century of the tournament. Tavare got his first before falling to the wiles of Zaheer. Qadir's leg spin had been Pakistan's main hope and he was introduced as soon as it was obvious the pacemen would have little impact. However, there was precious little in the wicket for him, either.

A 52-run partnership between Allan Lamb and Mike Gatting saw England home in the 58th over. Lancastrian Roy Tattersall made hometown hero Graeme Fowler Man of the Match.

PAKISTAN

Mohsin Khan c Marks b Allott		32
Mudassar Nazar c Gould b Dilley		18
Zaheer Abbas c Gould b Dilley		0
Javed Miandad run out		67
Imran Khan (capt) c Willis b Marks		13
Wasim Raja c Willis b Marks		15
Ijaz Faqih not out		42
Sarfraz Nawaz b Willis		17
Abdul Qadir run out		6
Wasim Bari (wk) not out		2
Extras (b 3, lb 14, w 2, nb 1)		20
(60 overs)		8–232

Did not bat: Rashid Khan

1/33 2/34 3/87 4/116 5/144 6/169 7/204 8/221

Bowling: Willis 12-2-37-1; Dilley 12-2-46-2; Allott 12-1-33-1; Botham 12-1-51-0; Marks 12-0-45-2

ENGLAND

G. Fowler c Javed Miandad b Mudassar Nazar		69
C.J. Tavare c Wasim Raja b Zaheer Abbas		58
D.I. Gower c Zaheer Abbas b Mudassar Nazar		31
A.J. Lamb not out		38
M.W. Gatting not out		14
Extras (b 1, lb 15, w 7)		23
(57.2 overs)		3–233

Did not bat: I.T. Botham, I.J. Gould (wk), V.J. Marks, G.R. Dilley, P.J.W. Allott, R.G.D. Willis (capt)

3/181

Bowling: Rashid Khan 11-1-58-0; Sarfraz Nawaz 10.2-2-22-0; Abdul Qadir 11-0-51-0; Ijaz Faqih 6-0-19-0; Mudassar Nazar 12-2-34-2; Zaheer Abbas 7-0-26-1

Umpires: H.D. Bird, D.O. Oslear.

Toss: Pakistan. Points: England 4, Pakistan 0

GROUP A: NEW ZEALAND vs SRI LANKA
COUNTY GROUND, DERBY: SRI LANKA WON BY 3 WICKETS

At Derby, on arguably the ugliest cricket ground in the world, New Zealand blew what looked an obvious chance to secure a semi-final berth when they lost to Sri Lanka. The Sri Lankans, who had been thrashed in New Zealand in both Test and Limited-Over Internationals in March, were overjoyed at this, their second-ever World Cup win.

Derbyshire is the spiritual home of the English medium pace seamer and this Saturday produced the sort of steamy, sunny weather and green wicket that used to delight the Les Jacksons and Cliff Gladwins of this world. Duleep Mendis was therefore very pleased to win the toss and send New Zealand in to bat.

Sure enough, Ashantha de Mel got the ball to start hooping and darting around straight away. John Wright, a Derbyshire player, should have been familiar with the conditions. A loose shot and a diving Guy de Alwis removed him for a duck and with Glenn Turner also caught off an out swinger in the same over New Zealand had made a horrendous start at 2–8. Rumesh Ratnayake also got into the act, providing a double breakthrough, getting rid of Geoff Howarth and Martin Crowe after they had briefly hinted at a recovery.

That left New Zealand 4–47 and Bruce Edgar and Jeremy Coney had to rebuild the innings. They were never able to bat with any real confidence against the unerring accuracy of wrist spinner Somachandra de Silva whose economy rate of less than one run per over was remarkable. They still put together 41 runs worth of recovery when de Silva gained another double breakthrough. Both Edgar and Coney were caught in his leg-trap, the latter being wonderfully held by a diving substitute, Susil Fernando.

At 6–91 hopes of that recovery were disappearing fast, especially when de Mel came back on after lunch and in quick succession got rid of the dangerous hitters Richard Hadlee and Lance Cairns, in addition to wicketkeeper Warren Lees, who had reclaimed his spot from Ian Smith. That made it 10–71 in the last two games for the Sri Lankan paceman, a sensational couple of days work.

New Zealand were 9–116 and almost out of the contest. However, de Mel's spell was finished so Sri Lanka's second-string bowlers were charged with the responsibility of getting out either Martin Snedden or Ewan Chatfield. Snedden would later open the batting in the 1987 World Cup. This time he and his poorly credentialled partner approached their task with real aggression to put on 65 precious runs for the last wicket. The left-handed Snedden dominated the scoring until charging for a second run he failed to beat a spot on throw from mid-on. The fielder, de Mel, could almost claim it as his 11th wicket since Thursday.

The hundreds of Sri Lankan supporters amongst the healthy crowd watched nervously as their team began the pursuit of the 182 runs they needed. Sidath Wettimuny was an early casualty to a swinging Cairns yorker and on 49 Crowe got through the defence of Arjuna Ranatunga. The New Zealand bowlers did not seem to be getting the same assistance as their Sri Lankan counterparts, though. Hadlee had been seen off without taking a wicket.

Brendon Kuruppu and Duleep Mendis added a crucial 80 runs for the third wicket. Kuruppu reached his 50 in 32 hard-fought overs. He hit 10 fours and with Dias had taken Sri Lanka to a position where victory seemed inevitable when Snedden held a hard-hit caught and bowled. Chatfield trapped Mendis one run later suggesting the Sri Lankan middle-order choke had started again. The collywobbles lasted until they were 7–161 and defeat loomed as a real possibility.

Fortunately Dias had held on throughout the 5–32 collapse. He continued to bat sensibly and with de Alwis made sure the win was not thrown away this time. From the second-last ball of the 53rd over Sri Lanka completed their win. de Alwis had made unbeaten fifties in the first two World Cup matches, but his 11 runs at Derby were far more valuable. Certainly those happy flag-waving Sri Lankan supporters appreciated them.

de Mel was David Allen's choice for the Man of the Match award.

NEW ZEALAND

G.M. Turner c Dias b de Mel	6
J.G. Wright c de Alwis b de Mel	0
G.P. Howarth (capt) b Ratnayake	15
M.D. Crowe lbw Ratnayake	8
B.A. Edgar c Samarasekera b de Silva	27
J.V. Coney c sub (E.R.N.S. Fernando) b de Silva	22
R.J. Hadlee c Madugalle b de Mel	15
W.K. Lees (wk) c Ranatunga b de Mel	2
B.L. Cairns c Dias b de Mel	6
M.C. Snedden run out	40
E.J. Chatfield not out	19
Extras (b 4, lb 5, w 11, nb 1)	21
(58.2 overs)	181

1/8 2/8 3/32 4/47 5/88 6/91 7/105 8/115 9/116 10/181

Bowling: de Mel 12–4–32–5; Ratnayake 11–4–18–2; Ranatunga 10–2–50–0; de Silva 12–5–11–2; Samarasekera 11.2–2–38–0; Wettimuny 2–0–11–0

SRI LANKA

S. Wettimuny b Cairns	4
D.S.B.P. Kuruppu c & b Snedden	62
A. Ranatunga b Crowe	15
R.L. Dias not out	64
L.R.D. Mendis (capt) lbw Chatfield	0
R.S. Madugalle c Lees b Snedden	6
M.A.R. Samarasekera c Lees b Hadlee	5
D.S. de Silva run out	2
R.G. de Alwis (wk) not out	11
Extras (b 1, lb 4, w 10)	15
(52.5 overs)	7–184

Did not bat: A.L.F. de Mel, R.J. Ratnayake

1/15 2/49 3/129 4/130 5/139 6/151 7/161

Bowling: Hadlee 12–3–16–1; Cairns 10–2–35–1; Snedden 10.5–1–58–2; Chatfield 12–3–23–1; Crowe 4–2–15–1; Coney 4–1–22–0

Umpires: D.J. Constant B Leadbeater.

Toss: Sri Lanka. Points: Sri Lanka 4, New Zealand 0

GROUP B: AUSTRALIA vs WEST INDIES
LORD'S: WEST INDIES WON BY 7 WICKETS

Lord's was packed to the rafters on a sunny Saturday for a big clash between Australia and the West Indies. It could have been 1975 all over again. Only seven players remained in the two teams from that magical day eight years before, three Australians and four West Indians. This day they would participate in another run-filled and entertaining game of cricket, if not one that was anywhere near as close at the finish.

Much to the Australians' relief they found the wicket at Lord's flat, and encouraging of strokes. Kim Hughes won the toss and, unlike at Headingley, had no problem with the idea of taking first use. Docile pitch or not, Malcolm Marshall as the fastest bowler in the world could conjure up something to test the opening batsmen. By the 10th over he had got them both. Trevor Chappell was caught behind with the total on 10 and when it was 37 Graeme Wood was bowled.

David Hookes and Kim Hughes responded as they did at Headingley with a counterattack full of aggressive and daring shots. Hughes, still batting at number 3, had strained a hamstring muscle stretching for overthrows in the ninth over so badly that he required a runner for the remainder of his innings. Hookes struck out at anything loose, dominating the scoring for 26 overs. Captain and vice-captain, their differences temporarily put aside, added 101 runs in that time, both completing half centuries. Jeff Dujon had just failed to grasp a difficult chance off Hookes when the South Australian was on 10. It was costly. The score was 138 before he took one risk too many and skyed a ball from Winston Davis.

The innings lost some impetus following Hookes' dismissal. Hughes lasted while 38 more runs were scored, but was bowled as he tried to take advantage of Larry Gomes' flat off spin. Allan Border made little progress and Graham Yallop was circumspect after two lucky let-offs. Desmond Haynes and Marshall failed to grasp lofted opportunities.

When only 40 runs were put on between the 40th and 50th overs Australia seemed headed for a sub-par total in conditions so totally in favour of batsmen. It was left to the veteran wicket-keeper Rod Marsh to strike the telling blows the Australians required from the final overs. Out of a 64-run stand with Yallop he belted 37 runs from 26 balls, picking Michael Holding of all people as his unlikely target. He pulled Holding into the Mound Stand for six, hooked the next easily anticipated shorter faster ball into the Tavern for another six, then straight drove the following ball to the Nursery End boundary to make it 16 runs from three balls. A 'perfect post-script' said *Wisden Cricket Monthly*. Australia had added 77 in the last 10 overs.

That Marsh's hitting and Yallop's unbeaten 52 were very much required quickly became evident as the West Indies began their reply. Geoff Lawson was out of the Australian side with a groin strain and Ken MacLeay, the hero at Trent Bridge, had been dropped. Into the side came Dennis Lillee and Jeff Thomson. This was the last time the legendary speed demons would share an international stage together.

Sadly, it was no triumph. Thomson shared the new ball with Rod Hogg. While Hogg earned respect, Thomson conceded runs freely to Haynes and Gordon Greenidge. If the West Indian speed quartet could get little help from the wicket then there was not much hope for the aging Lillee and Thomson. It was Tom Hogan who finally broke the opening stand. After 18 overs, with the score on 79, the left-arm spinner caused Haynes to drag a ball onto his stumps.

Haynes may have been disappointed, but few in the crowd were. The Barbadian's dismissal allowed them to be treated to 27 overs of sublime batsmanship from two of the best players in the world. Viv Richards announced his arrival with a straight hit that sailed over the boundary at long-on. He later deposited another Hogan

delivery to the same spot and heaped the igno-miny onto Thomson by stepping away and clouting a leg-side delivery for another six over extra cover. Greenidge, whose taste in caps this time led to the wearing of an unlabelled baggy maroon number, was just as impressive, hitting eight fours during his three-hour stay at the wicket.

After the 200 was raised and 124 runs had been added, Greenidge finally rewarded Hogg for his perseverance. Rod Marsh said, 'We didn't bowl all that badly; it was simply that they batted so beautifully.' There was no follow-up collapse to revive Australian hopes. Larry Gomes played second fiddle to Richards while another 38 runs were added, then Lloyd, knowing there were overs to spare, tried to give the Antiguan enough strike to reach his 100. When that was no longer possible the West Indian captain promptly finished the match with a trademark big lofted drive off Chappell's medium pace. Richards had to be satisfied with an unbeaten 95 from 117 balls, striking nine fours along with those three sixes. It was enough to win him the Man of the Match award.

The spectators, many of them neutral, walked away content. During the day of unbroken sunshine, they had seen nine wickets for 549 runs off 120 overs, less 13 balls. It was the type of cricket which once made Hogg suggest that, to save a lot of sweat and pain, bowlers should be replaced in one-day games with bowling machines.

AUSTRALIA	
G.M. Wood b Marshall	17
T.M. Chappell c Dujon b Marshall	5
K.J. Hughes (capt) b Gomes	69
D.W. Hookes c Greenidge b Davis	56
G.N. Yallop not out	52
A.R. Border c & b Gomes	11
R.W. Marsh (wk) c Haynes b Holding	37
T.G. Hogan not out	0
Extras (b 1, lb 18, w 6, nb 1)	26
(60 overs)	6-273

Did not bat: J.R. Thomson, D.K. Lillee, R.M. Hogg

1/10 2/37 3/138 4/176 5/202 6/266

Bowling: Roberts 12-0-51-0; Marshall 12-0-36-2; Davis 12-0-57-1; Holding 12-1-56-1; Gomes 12-0-47-2

WEST INDIES	
C.G. Greenidge c Hughes b Hogg	90
D.L. Haynes b Hogan	33
I.V.A. Richards not out	95
H.A. Gomes b Chappell	15
C.H. Lloyd (capt) not out	19
Extras (b 3, lb 18, w 1, nb 2)	24
(57.5 overs)	3-276

Did not bat: S.F.A.F. Bacchus, P.J.L. Dujon (wk), M.D. Marshall, A.M.E. Roberts, M.A. Holding, W.W. Davis

1/79 2/203 3/228

Bowling: Hogg 12-0-25-2; Thomson 11-0-64-0; Hogan 12-0-60-1; Lillee 12-0-52-0; Chappell 10.5-0-51-1

Umpires: K.E. Palmer, A.G.T. Whitehead.

Toss: Australia. Points: West Indies 4, Australia 0

GROUP B: INDIA vs ZIMBABWE
NEVILL GROUND, TUNBRIDGE WELLS: INDIA WON BY 31 RUNS

Tucked away in a lovely setting in the provincial town of Tunbridge Wells in Kent, India and Zimbabwe played out one of the more remarkable games of cricket of any World Cup. The transformation of the Indian innings from ruination to success and the legendary innings by Kapil Dev that got them there are part of the folklore of this premier limited-overs cricket competition.

It is still hard to imagine how a side that was 5–17 after 13 overs could recover to make 8–266 and then go on to win the match that would determine their chances of continuing in the competition. Kapil Dev indicated from the start of the tournament that he was a man on a mission and on this day his resolve was put to its most severe test. To his and his countrymen's great delight, he came through with flying colours. For Zimbabwe they had to suffer a disappointment of equal magnitude.

On the colourful, rhododendron-encircled ground Kapil Dev won the toss and elected to bat. Even the moisture in the wicket could not distract him from his objective to bat first and build a total that would bring India's run rate on line with Australia's. Kim Hughes' side remained India's main challenger for a semi-final berth.

Kapil admitted to a slight nagging doubt about his side's chances of getting 300 on that wicket, and from the commencement of play it looked as if such ambitions were mere fantasy. Peter Rawson's first ball of the day lifted and ripped past the outside edge of the bat of the recalled Sunil Gavaskar. From the last delivery in that first over Gavaskar played across the line and the Zimbabwean shout for lbw was answered in the affirmative.

It was the beginning of a procession. Mohinder Amarnath and Kris Srikkanth could not score a run until the third over, then in Rawson's third over Amarnath was given out caught behind. On the same score Srikkanth, still not off the mark, tried to hit Kevin Curran straight down the ground. The shot was badly mistimed and skyed over mid-off. Iain Butchart ran around and held a nicely judged catch. That made India 3–6. Three runs later Sandeep Patil touched a ball from Curran down the leg side.

Kapil said he came in at this stage in a trance-like state. More likely he was stunned to have his World Cup dreams almost in tatters. Soon he lost Yashpal Sharma, the hero of the Round One win against the West Indies, as well. Rawson had found another outside edge in his seventh over. India had reached their nadir of 5–17.

It was Roger Binny who joined his captain in stopping the rot and brought the contest back to being a fair one between bat and ball. They put on 60 in 14 overs, the wicket slowly drying and easing all the time. There were no fireworks at this stage. Both batsmen were content to build their partnership with pushes and deflections.

Then Binny went lbw to the off spinner John Traicos, and with Ravi Shastri caught playing a reckless stroke one run later India were 7–78 and again heading for ignominious defeat. The spectre of the inglorious campaigns of 1975 and 1979 must have haunted the veteran Madan Lal as he approached his skipper. He promised to stay put while Kapil scored the runs and up to lunch was as good as his word.

The 100 and Kapil's 50 were reached from the same shot in the 36th over and India lunched on 7–106. When Kapil entered the dressing-room he was intent on blasting his top-order batsmen. He found they had anticipated his wrath and had all disappeared into the dining room, leaving him with a glass of water to cool down.

The lunch break had further eased the wicket and upon the resumption Kapil changed his original plan, which had been to just try and last out the 60 overs. The small ground and the better batting conditions encouraged him to counter-attack. Almost immediately the runs began to flow. Another 34 were added in brisk time until Curran struck again, having Madan Lal caught behind. Syed Kirmani, the hairless wicketkeeper, entered with the score still precarious on 8–140.

Kapil said by now he had progressed from a

trance to a daze. So he unleashed a furious assault on all the bowlers. From the next 18 deliveries he faced, the Indian captain struck three fours and three sixes. Kapil admitted one pull for six off Curran into the hospitality tents was mistimed. The Zimbabwean gave him a verbal serve. Kapil replied with the suggestion Curran should try another short ball. He did. It sailed right out of the ground and Kapil showed Curran his bat.

The onslaught continued. So brutal was Kapil's strokeplay it became too much for his first bat. The ninth-wicket pair added an unbroken 126 runs in 16 overs. Kirmani's share was 24. There was no real sign of a mishit until he had reached 140. Soon after, the crowd was applauding. Kapil asked the umpire Barry Meyer why. Meyer explained that Kapil had hit the highest score ever in the World Cup. His 175 not out was India's first World Cup century and beat Glenn Turner's 171 against East Africa in 1975. His innings containing six sixes and 16 fours was spread over three hours. Kapil's score has since been passed, however the ninth-wicket partnership record remains unbeaten.

Zimbabwe, full of hope when India were 5–17, now needed 267 to keep their semi-final

aspirations alive. There was no reason to think they could not achieve that target, except that the Indians had gained a big psychological boost from their captain's performance. Pressure and run-outs haunted the Zimbabweans throughout their brave pursuit. Robin Brown and Grant Paterson put on 44 for the first wicket, then two wickets fell in three overs. The second was after a scramble that found Jack Heron short of his ground for the second game in a row. Brown, too, was badly run out and Duncan Fletcher was beautifully caught on the boundary by Kapil Dev.

At 6–113 Zimbabwe should have accepted defeat. Curran for one could not. As if trying to match Kapil's display, he struck the ball with increasing vigour. He and Iain Butchart put on 55 for the seventh wicket. Briefly the game flickered as Zimbabwe made it to 8–230. Finally Curran had to take one risk too many and when Kapil held Traicos off his own bowling a remarkable day was over with India 31 runs in front.

Wrapped up in two sweaters against the cool of the evening, Kapil accepted his Man of the Match Award from Mike Denness without a word. Perhaps he was still in a trance.

INDIA

S.M. Gavaskar lbw Rawson	0
K. Srikkanth c Butchart b Curran	0
M. Amarnath c Houghton b Rawson	5
S.M. Patil c Houghton b Curran	1
Yashpal Sharma c Houghton b Rawson	9
Kapil Dev (capt) not out	175
R.M.H. Binny lbw Traicos	22
R.J. Shastri c Pycroft b Fletcher	1
Madan Lal c Houghton b Curran	17
S.M.H. Kirmani (wk) not out	24
Extras (lb 9, w 3)	12
(60 overs)	8–266

Did not bat: B.S. Sandhu

1/0 2/6 3/6 4/9 5/17 6/77 7/78 8/140

Bowling: Rawson 12–4–47–3; Curran 12–1–65–3; Butchart 12–2–38–0; Fletcher 12–2–59–1; Traicos 12–0–45–1

ZIMBABWE

R.D. Brown run out	35
G.A. Paterson lbw Binny	23
J.G. Heron run out	3
A.J. Pycroft c Kirmani b Sandhu	6
D.L. Houghton (wk) lbw Madan Lal	17
D.A.G. Fletcher (capt) c Kapil Dev b Amarnath	13
K.M. Curran c Shastri b Madan Lal	73
I.P. Butchart b Binny	18
G.E. Peckover c Yashpal b Madan Lal	14
P.W.E. Rawson not out	2
A.J. Traicos c & b Kapil Dev	3
Extras (lb 17, w 7, nb 4)	28
(57 overs)	235

1/44 2/48 3/61 4/86 5/103 6/113 7/168 8/189 9/230 10/235

Bowling: Kapil Dev 11–1–32–1; Sandhu 11–2–44–1; Binny 11–2–45–2; Madan Lal 11–2–42–3; Amarnath 12–1–37–1; Shastri 1–0–7–0

Umpires: M.J. Kitchen, B.J. Meyer.

Toss: India. Points: India 4, Zimbabwe 0

MONDAY JUNE 20th
THE PRUDENTIAL CUP: ROUND SIX
GROUP A: ENGLAND vs SRI LANKA
HEADINGLEY: ENGLAND WON BY 9 WICKETS

Interest in the final preliminary round of the 1983 World Cup was centred elsewhere than Leeds. Sri Lanka could not make the semi-finals and England could not miss out.

In this match Sri Lanka batted and bowled as if their thoughts had already turned to home. Bob Willis won the toss and sent Duleep Mendis' side in. Sidath Wettimuny made the bulk of the early runs and the total reached 25 before a wicket fell. Willis and Norman Cowans, brought in for the injured Graham Dilley and given the downhill run, had offered the batsmen little freedom. When the wickets started to fall they did so with a clatter.

Ian Botham, too, was fired up. He had been irked by criticism of his World Cup performances in the press. Kapil Dev's innings might have been a bit of a spur, as well. A confident caught behind appeal against Wettimuny was turned down. Botham indicated some disappointment. Ultimately he would not be denied. Ranatunga, whose World Cup day would eventually come, was dismissed for his third duck of the tournament and Wettimuny was given out lbw. With Paul Allott also grabbing a couple of quick wickets, Sri Lanka lost 6–29 as they slipped to 6–54.

What little interest remained was quickly disappearing. The lower half of the order showed some fight. Mike Gatting had a bit of a bowl. Vic Marks got two wickets before anything got serious. Rumesh Ratnayake and Vinothen John added 33 for the last wicket, which allowed the innings to last beyond the 50-over mark.

England needed 137 to win. Ashantha de Mel again got some movement, but this time the edges were missed. Chris Tavare and Graeme Fowler were soon moving towards the target. Fowler looked in good touch. He swung one ball from Ratnayake over square leg for six and hit a number of other fine shots. David Gower also played a nice little cameo when he came to the wicket in the 16th over following the demise of Tavare to the worthy de Mel. From that point the end came quickly. Somachandra de Silva, who had conceded less than one run per over from a full spell against New Zealand, was now clouted for 29 runs from three overs. A single off Ranatunga's first ball and the game had finished prior to the tea break. England had won with 215 balls to spare.

Richard Hutton, who is prone to occasional eccentricities, gave the Man of the Match award to Willis for his 'leadership'.

SRI LANKA

S. Wettimuny lbw Botham	22
D.S.B.P. Kuruppu c Gatting b Willis	6
A. Ranatunga c Lamb b Botham	0
R.L. Dias c Gould b Cowans	7
L.R.D. Mendis (capt) b Allott	10
R.S. Madugalle c Gould b Allott	0
D.S. de Silva c Gower b Marks	15
R.G. de Alwis (wk) c Marks b Cowans	19
A.L.F. de Mel c Lamb b Marks	10
R.J. Ratnayake not out	20
V.B. John c Cowans b Allott	15
Extras (b 5, lb 2, w 3, nb 2)	12
(50.4 overs)	136

1/25 2/30 3/32 4/40 5/43 6/54 7/81 8/97 9/103 10/136

Bowling: Willis 9–4–9–1; Cowans 12–3–31–2; Botham 9–4–12–2; Allott 10.4–0–41–3; Gatting 4–2–13–0; Marks 6–2–18–2

ENGLAND

G. Fowler not out	81
C.J. Tavare c de Alwis b de Mel	19
D.I. Gower not out	27
Extras (b 1, lb 3, w 3, nb 3)	10
(24.1 overs)	1–137

Did not bat: A.J. Lamb, M.W. Gatting, I.T. Botham, I.J. Gould (wk), V.J. Marks, P.J.W. Allott, R.G.D. Willis (capt), N.G. Cowans

1/68

Bowling: de Mel 10–1–33–1; Ratnayake 5–0–23–0; John 6–0–41–0; de Silva 3–0–29–0; Ranatunga 0.1–0–1–0

Umpires: B. Leadbeater, R. Palmer.

Toss: England. Points: England 4, Sri Lanka 0

GROUP A: NEW ZEALAND vs PAKISTAN
TRENT BRIDGE: PAKISTAN WON BY 11 RUNS

This was a winner take all contest. For both sides victory, plus in Pakistan's case a slight improvement in their run rate, would ensure second place in Group A behind England. The New Zealanders must have been kicking themselves for losing to Sri Lanka and not securing their spot prior to this match. Pakistan, although weakened, still had plenty of mercurial talent capable of dominating any side. By the end of the day New Zealand would have some more self-kicking to do.

Imran Khan, hardly able to believe his side was still a viable finalist after their up-and-down form, won the toss and elected to bat in front of a 5000 strong crowd full of Pakistani supporters. The top order struggled to get the run rate up against the accuracy of Richard Hadlee and Lance Cairns. The opening partnership of 48 between Mudassar Nazar and Mohsin Khan took 20 overs. Mohsin then tried to smash dibbly dobblering Jeremy Coney out of the ground, only to get as far as Lance Cairns at deep mid-on.

Javed Miandad also struggled for timing. Mudassar left six runs after Mohsin, deflecting another Coney delivery into his stumps and Javed spoilt his lunch playing Hadlee on after surviving for 19 overs. At the break Pakistan was 3–126 from 42 overs, well below its run requirement. Whatever Imran and Zaheer consumed during the interval certainly fortified them. Upon the resumption they suddenly and very effectively went on the attack. Imran hit out, Zaheer played his graceful shots. It was brilliant batting that thrilled the crowd and came at a perfect time for Pakistan.

Zaheer completed a century in exactly two hours. Imran scored at faster than a run per minute. They took an astonishing 47 runs from Hadlee's last five overs and 147 runs were scored in 75 minutes. In 60 overs Pakistan had scored 3–261. Their run rate was 4.01 for the tournament, higher than New Zealand's. The Kiwis would have to win if they were to reach the semi-finals.

They did not get the start they wanted. Glenn Turner, in his final appearance for his country, was caught behind off Sarfraz Nawaz with the score on just 13. Thirty-one runs later John Wright hit out at Abdul Qadir and was held by Imran. At tea New Zealand were 2–76 from 25 overs. Geoff Howarth looked in good form and perhaps he held the destiny of his side in his own hands.

He added a further nine runs with Martin Crowe at the start of the last session, then Imran brought on Zaheer. 'Zed' stayed with an authentic first-ball loosener, a chest-high full toss. Howarth swiped it away straight to Javed at square leg. Jack Bannister called it 'the "sucker dismissal" of the competition'. It was a big setback for the Kiwis, who really struggled after that.

Crowe got to 43 before hitting across the line against Mudassar's medium pace. Bruce Edgar missed out and Richard Hadlee completed what by his standards was an ordinary day when he, too, fell to the underrated Mudassar. From 7–152 Coney and Warren Lees had to stop the procession. They did by adding 35. However, progress slowed and 75 runs were needed from just eight overs when John Bracewell joined Coney.

Pakistan were almost planning their semi-final strategies when Bracewell started to strike out at the medium pace of Sarfraz and Rashid Khan. Fifty-three runs were added in five overs. Bracewell and Coney had reduced the target to a gettable 22 from three overs when the off spinner hooked hard and high at Sarfraz. The last ball of the 58th over sailed into the deep at square leg. Bracewell's timing was better than his placement. He picked out Mohsin right on the boundary.

Now only one wicket remained. Coney needed to farm the strike. He completed his fifty. It was a meaningless milestone. At the start of the last over 13 runs were required for victory. Coney and Chatfield took a single from Sarfraz's first ball. Javed's throw missed the stumps. The 10th wicket pair looked for another run but hesitated. Imran quickly retrieved the ball and threw it to Wasim Bari, who gleefully removed the bails. Coney was stranded.

The Pakistani supporters did not have to be told of the significance of the result. Joyously laughing and bouncing, they ran from all directions straight at the players and umpires. David Evans was knocked flying. Merv Kitchen found

a brandished stump was a useful deterrent to the invaders.

Imran Khan, thrilled with the turn of events, gratefully received the Man of the Match award. New Zealand had missed a semi-final berth in World Cup for the first time.

PAKISTAN

Mohsin Khan c Cairns b Coney	33
Mudassar Nazar b Coney	15
Javed Miandad b Hadlee	25
Zaheer Abbas not out	103
Imran Khan (capt) not out	79
Extras (b 1, lb 2, w 2, nb 1)	6
(60 overs)	3-261

Did not bat: Ijaz Faqih, Shahid Mahboob, Sarfraz Nawaz, Abdul Qadir, Wasim Bari (wk), Rashid Khan

1/48 2/54 3/114

Bowling: Hadlee 12-1-61-1; Cairns 12-1-45-0; Chatfield 12-0-57-0; Coney 12-0-42-2; Bracewell 12-0-50-0

NEW ZEALAND

G.M. Turner c Wasim Bari b Sarfraz Nawaz	4
J.G. Wright c Imran Khan b Abdul Qadir	19
G.P. Howarth (capt) c Javed Miandad b Zaheer Abbas	39
M.D. Crowe b Mudassar Nazar	43
B.A. Edgar lbw Shahid Mahboob	6
J.V. Coney run out	51
R.J. Hadlee c Mohsin Khan b Mudassar Nazar	11
B.L. Cairns c Imran b Abdul Qadir	0
W.K. Lees (wk) c sub (Mansoor Akhtar) b Mudassar	26
J.G. Bracewell c Mohsin Khan b Sarfraz Nawaz	34
E.J. Chatfield not out	3
Extras (lb 8, w 5, nb 1)	14
(59.1 overs)	250

1/13 2/44 3/85 4/102 5/130 6/150 7/152 8/187 9/246 10/250

Bowling: Rashid Khan 6-1-24-0; Sarfraz Nawaz 9.1-1-50-2; Abdul Qadir 12-0-53-2; Ijaz Faqih 6-1-21-0; Shahid Mahboob 10-0-37-1; Mudassar Nazar 12-0-43-3; Zaheer Abbas 4-1-8-1

Umpires: D.G.L. Evans, M.J. Kitchen.

Toss: Pakistan. Points: Pakistan 4, New Zealand 0

GROUP B: AUSTRALIA vs INDIA
COUNTY GROUND, CHELMSFORD: INDIA WON BY 118 RUNS

To the Australians it was unthinkable, to the Indians a cricketing delight, literally against the odds. A full house at the well-appointed Essex County Ground in Chelmsford witnessed an inglorious batting display by Kim Hughes' side which condemned them to an unexpected early departure from the 1983 Prudential Cup.

Despite their obvious improvement from 1975 and 1979, India was not expected to win this match. Certainly the Australians were confident. They had thrashed India seven days earlier and several of their players felt they would remain a very manageable combination. Kim Hughes must have been one. He withdrew from the match to rest his injured thigh so that it would be ready for the semi-final clash. David Hookes took over the leadership reins.

Kapil Dev was pleased when he won the toss and he elected to bat on what seemed an excellent wicket. Geoff Lawson, back in the side at the expense of Dennis Lillee, began proceedings with a wide. It would be the first of 24 illegal deliveries. Kris Srikkanth was quickly into his stride and 27 runs were briskly accumulated. His partner was still out of sorts, though, and Gavaskar soon mistimed a ball to Trevor Chappell in the covers. The 50 was up in the 11th over when Srikkanth drove Thomson for four through the off side. Then the aggressive opener from Tamil Nadu pulled the same bowler hard to mid wicket where Allan Border held the catch at the second attempt.

Thomson struck again to have Mohinder Amarnath caught behind which left India 3-65.

It was a good comeback by the blond-haired slinger as, like Lawson, he had also started with a wide. However, the worst culprit in that regard was Rodney Hogg whose indiscretions during the Indian innings included 15 no-balls and three wides.

Right on the lunch break Sandeep Patil was removed. India went into the pavilion on 4–119 from 30 legitimate overs. Kapil Dev used his Tunbridge Wells approach after lunch, but it only worked until the total was 157. He then mis-hooked a fast lifter from the inaccurate Hogg and was easily caught at mid-off. Seventeen runs later anchorman and top scorer Yashpal Sharma was gone, also caught at mid-off. India was 6–174 and the innings threatened to fade away. It didn't fade and it didn't rally, either. Everyone got a few runs. No-one got a lot. There was a run-out, there was an lbw. One partnership was worth 33, another 17. Kim Hughes tried to control the field placings from the pavilion. Rod Marsh told him where he could go. The upshot was that after 56 overs, less one ball, India were all out for 247.

Australia felt unintimidated by the task in front of them. They had smashed India for 320 at Trent Bridge. Then Chappell had made a fine century. This time Balwindersingh Sandhu had the same batsman caught in the gully from a ball that lifted off a length in his first over. That displeased the youngest Chappell brother, who was another on his final international outing, to such an extent that he demolished an entire set of cups and saucers on the dressing-room table with his bat and ruptured a water cooler with another piece of crockery. He was fined and later apologised. Graeme Wood and Graham Yallop then seemed to consolidate Australia's push for the 248 required for a semi-final berth. They added 43 to take the total to 1–46 by the start of the 16th over when Roger Binny was introduced.

Kapil Dev said that the medium pacer knew how to trouble left-handers. In this case he did so to the extent that three left-handers were dismissed in three overs. Wood was caught behind in the first, Hookes was bowled by a pearler in the second and Yallop was caught and bowled off a skyed shot in the third. When Madan Lal had Rod Marsh lbw from the first ball of the next over Australia had collapsed to 5–52. Madan Lal struck once more when MacLeay hit out and Gavaskar held a sharp slips catch. The afternoon tea must have tasted bitter to the Australians and things got worse when Tom Hogan hit a catch straight to cover straight after the break.

India had recovered from 7–78 to 8–266 at Tunbridge Wells. Australia were now 7–78 as well, and Allan Border would need to play an innings as great as Kapil's if Australia were to survive. Great player as Border was, it was never on. Border never gave up, but the wicket was keeping low now and he could not do the impossible. Australia's last hope vanished when the future captain was bowled from the first ball of Madan Lal's ninth over. Thomson was also bowled from the next delivery leaving India victorious by 118 runs. The whole fiasco had taken less than 40 overs.

There was plenty of flag-waving and whistling from the terraces when the win was completed. India had made it to the semi-finals. The same India that had been the joke of the previous two tournaments had knocked out Australia.

There was no joy in the Australian camp. David Hookes' only day ever as captain of his country had not gone very well. To make matters worse, the next day Hughes disappeared back to Australia without saying goodbye to most of his team. He blamed his team for the mess that their World Cup campaign had become. Many of his team blamed him for a poor and uncommunicative captaincy. It was hardly a climate for success.

Roger Binny was probably not even aware of his opponents' problems. He just cherished his Man of the Match award and the opportunity he would have to play England in the semi-finals.

INDIA

S.M. Gavaskar c Chappell b Hogg	9
K. Srikkanth c Border b Thomson	24
M. Amarnath c Marsh b Thomson	13
Yashpal Sharma c Hogg b Hogan	40
S.M. Patil c Hogan b MacLeay	30
Kapil Dev (capt) c Hookes b Hogg	28
K. Azad c Border b Lawson	15
R.M.H. Binny run out	21
Madan Lal not out	12
S.M.H. Kirmani (wk) lbw Hogg	10
B.S. Sandhu b Thomson	8
Extras (lb 13, w 9, nb 15)	37
(55.5 overs)	247

1/27 2/54 3/65 4/118 5/157 6/174 7/207 8/215 9/232 10/247

Bowling: Lawson 10-1-40-1; Hogg 12-2-40-3; Hogan 11-1-31-1; Thomson 10.5-0-51-3; MacLeay 12-2-48-1

AUSTRALIA

T.M. Chappell c Madan Lal b Sandhu	2
G.M. Wood c Kirmani b Binny	21
G.N. Yallop c & b Binny	18
D.W. Hookes (capt) b Binny	1
A.R. Border b Madan Lal	36
R.W. Marsh lbw Madan Lal	0
K.H. MacLeay c Gavaskar b Madan Lal	5
T.G. Hogan c Srikkanth b Binny	8
G.F. Lawson b Sandhu	16
R.M. Hogg not out	8
J.R. Thomson b Madan Lal	0
Extras (lb 5, w 5, nb 4)	14
(38.2 overs)	129

1/3 2/46 3/48 4/52 5/52 6/69 7/78 8/115 9/129 10/129

Bowling: Kapil Dev 8-2-16-0; Sandhu 10-1-26-2; Madan Lal 8.2-3-20-4; Binny 8-2-29-4; Amarnath 2-0-17-0; Azad 2-0-7-0

Umpires: J. Birkenshaw, D.R. Shepherd.

Toss: India. Points: India 4, Australia 0

GROUP B: WEST INDIES vs ZIMBABWE
EDGBASTON: WEST INDIES WON BY 10 WICKETS

Little hinged on this game except that the West Indies needed a decent work-out in the lead-up to the semi-finals. They had to send down their full complement of overs so the six bowlers worked up a decent sweat. The batting was a different story. No-one below number 4 even got their pads on because the openers Desmond Haynes and Faoud Bacchus refused to give up their position at the batting crease until the match was completed.

There were three changes to the West Indies line-up from the game against Australia. Gordon Greenidge, Andy Roberts and Michael Holding were all rested for Gus Logie, Wayne Daniel and the recovered Joel Garner. It was Garner who did the early damage after Duncan Fletcher had won the toss and elected to bat on what looked a fine wicket. The total had reached 17 when in the fourth over 'Big Bird' had Grant Paterson caught by Viv Richards and next ball Jack Heron found one of the worst ways possible to avoid being run out.

There were a few wides and no-balls floating around which helped Robin Brown and Andy Pycroft lift the total to 41. Then Malcolm Marshall and Daniel ripped out three more

batsmen while one run was being added. In the 23rd over Zimbabwe was 5–42 and their final innings in the tournament looked in ruins.

Fletcher and Kevin Curran developed a hard-fought stand that temporarily halted the slide. They had put on 37 for the sixth wicket when Richards claimed the Zimbabwean captain as the first of his three victims. Curran was not one of them. The all-rounder again impressed with his determination and ability to score runs against quality bowling. He smacked Garner for six over long-off, a rare feat, put on 55 for the ninth wicket with Peter Rawson and reached a fine 62 before being bowled in the final over of the innings. Rawson's ineffective last-ball slog against Daniel neatly terminated the Zimbabwean effort right at the end of the 60th over for 171.

Haynes and Bacchus put the Zimbabwean batting into perspective. They were rarely troubled on a sound batting surface. Runs were taken freely off the pace bowlers, Haynes scoring the bulk of his off the front foot, Bacchus concentrating on back foot strokes. Only John Traicos' offspin really stemmed the flow, his full quota of 12 overs costing just 24 runs.

Either batsman could have made a century,

neither quite did. It was the Barbadian who had his nose in front when the winning run was scored from the first ball of the 46th over of the innings, but the Guyanan beat him for the Man of the Match award.

The West Indies won with nearly 15 overs to spare, the early finish allowing them to quickly turn their attention to their semi-final clash on Wednesday with Pakistan at The Oval.

ZIMBABWE

R.D. Brown c Lloyd b Marshall	14
G.A. Paterson c Richards b Garner	6
J.G. Heron c Dujon b Garner	0
A.J. Pycroft c Dujon b Marshall	4
D.L. Houghton (wk) c Lloyd b Daniel	0
D.A.G. Fletcher (capt) b Richards	23
K.M. Curran b Daniel	62
I.P. Butchart c Haynes b Richards	8
G.E. Peckover c & b Richards	3
P.W.E. Rawson b Daniel	19
A.J. Traicos not out	1
Extras (b 4, lb 13, w 7, nb 7)	31
(60 overs)	171

1/17 2/17 3/41 4/42 5/42 6/79 7/104 8/115 9/170 10/171

Bowling: Marshall 12–3–19–2; Garner 7–4–13–2; Davis 8–2–13–0; Daniel 9–2–28–3; Gomes 12–2–26–0; Richards 12–1–41–3

WEST INDIES

D.L. Haynes not out	88
S.F.A.F. Bacchus not out	80
Extras (lb 1, w 3)	4
(45.1 overs)	0–172

Did not bat: A.L. Logie, I.V.A. Richards, H.A. Gomes, C.H. Lloyd (capt), P.J.L. Dujon (wk), J. Garner, M.D. Marshall, W.W. Daniel, W.W. Davis

Bowling: Rawson 12–3–38–0; Butchart 4–0–23–0; Traicos 12–2–24–0; Curran 9–0–44–0; Fletcher 8.1–0–39–0

Umpires: H.D. Bird, D.J. Constant.

Toss: Zimbabwe. Points: West Indies 4, Zimbabwe 0

WEDNESDAY 22 JUNE 1983
THE PRUDENTIAL CUP SEMI-FINALS

At the end of the preliminary rounds of the 1983 World Cup the group tables finished as follows:

GROUP A	P	W	L	Pts	R/R
England	6	5	1	20	4.67
Pakistan	6	3	3	12	4.01
New Zealand	6	3	3	12	3.92
Sri Lanka	6	1	5	4	3.75

GROUP B	P	W	L	Pts	R/R
West Indies	6	5	1	20	4.31
India	6	4	2	16	3.87
Australia	6	2	4	8	3.81
Zimbabwe	6	1	5	4	3.49

Both tables had a nice symmetrical look to them, but New Zealanders must cry every time they study the Group A result. Missing the semi-finals by a run rate of 0.08 has got to hurt. With the preliminary rounds as a form guide, England and the West Indies would start the semi-finals as big favourites.

FIRST SEMI-FINAL: ENGLAND vs INDIA
OLD TRAFFORD: INDIA WON BY 6 WICKETS

Of all the let-downs that English cricket teams and supporters have suffered during the various World Cups, and there have been plenty, none could have been more demoralising than this six-wicket defeat at Old Trafford. Bob Willis' side had been utterly convincing in the preliminary rounds, but they were so comfortably beaten by the underdogs, India, that there was a great gnashing of English teeth.

Like most other English cricket disasters over

the years, the result provided the opportunity for a bit of a whinge. The wicket provided for the occasion was bare of grass, low and slow. Some English players felt that the ground staff had unintentionally played into India's hands with conditions similar to those when Kapil Dev's side defeated the West Indies in Round One. Not that there was a soul in the packed ground who considered it would have a significant influence on the result when Graeme Fowler and Chris Tavare smoothly took England to 0–69 after 17 overs.

Bob Willis had won the toss and all was set fair on a warm sunny day. Fowler had been in great form throughout the tournament. Tavare's had been a sound if unspectacular back-up role to the Lancastrian. On semi-final day both were at their best, striking seven boundaries between them and running smartly for singles and twos. Balwindersingh Sandhu conceded runs freely.

As at Chelmsford, it was the introduction of Roger Binny which altered the direction of the match. He immediately had Tavare caught behind from a defensive push and 15 runs later Fowler was bowled middle stump by one that kept low. England's batting became more hesitant. Kapil Dev introduced Mohinder Amarnath and Kirti Azad. Their captain had originally meant them to share a spell of 12 overs but they so completely choked off England's supply of runs either side of lunch, and picked a few wickets, that Kapil was thrilled to be able to keep them going. All through, he did so over by over, just waiting until they were hit around. That moment never came.

David Gower, so productive in the preliminary games, flashed outside the off stump at Amarnath, edged and was well taken by wicket-keeper Syed Kirmani. It was 3–107 and the home team's position was just starting to deteriorate. Allan Lamb in 1982 had feasted on the tame offerings of the Indian bowlers. He and Mike Gatting added 34 and promised more to put England back in a position where again they could push towards a formidable score. Then Lamb swept at a ball which rolled away off his pad. Gatting called his South African born partner through for a single. There was a slight hesitation and Yashpal Sharma at short fine-leg

swooped and threw down the wicket with Lamb short of his ground at the bowler's end.

It was an unnecessary dismissal that provided India with a real opening. Ian Botham stepped away to thump the ball through point only to miss a delivery that nearly bounced twice before it hit his leg-stump. Gatting left a gap between bat and pad and an Amarnath off-cutter cartwheeled his off stump. The situation for England was now becoming critical. Slow low wicket or not they were making a hash of their later overs. At the 50 over mark they were 6–169, and that added up to a sorry tale of 6–100 from their last 33 overs. Only 55 runs were scored from the 24 overs sent down by Azad and Amarnath. At one stage there was an hour's cricket without one shot piercing the five men stationed on the boundary. Ian Gould's run-out and Vic Mark's inability to keep out Kapil Dev saw a further decline to 8–177.

Only the fast bowlers were left. Fortunately one of those was Graham Dilley, whose broad-shouldered left-handed batting had already been a contributing factor to England's success in the past couple of weeks. With Paul Allott and Bob Willis in tow, Dilley gave the England innings a boost when it appeared they may fall short of the 200 mark. No English supporters minded that the bulk of these runs were scored off the edge. For the first time the Indian fielding lagged with a few errors and overthrows. Kapil Dev's final over contained four wides and when Willis had his off stump neatly removed by his opposite number from the last ball of the 60th over, England had 213 runs to protect.

Like England, India had a good start and then stumbled. Sunil Gavaskar showed his best form of competition, even outpacing the normally frenetic Kris Srikkanth. The slow wicket dulled the new-ball threat of Willis and Dilley and they moved nicely to 46 in the 14th over. As if in sympathy with each other, both were gone in consecutive overs, Paul Allott and Ian Botham doing the important damage. India was 2–50 and the game lay in the balance.

Mohinder Amarnath and Yashpal Sharma had to resurrect the chase. It was no easy task while Botham, Allott and Marks kept it tight and either side of tea the runs dried up. The tension was perceptible as both teams strove to achieve the advantage over their opponents that would carry them through to the World Cup final. There were big shouts against Sharma for a run-out and then a caught behind. India fought to 2–107 from 38 overs, but despite the half-century stand neither batsman was comfortable. Amarnath survived two close shaves in the next over when he mishit off spinner Marks into space and then substitute fieldsman, Derek Randall dived at square leg only to disclaim what at first looked a catch.

It was as if England had missed their chances. Amarnath and Sharma now began the necessary acceleration. Amarnath hit Allott straight for six and Sharma bravely swiped the first ball of a new spell from Willis over mid wicket for another six. They had built their stand to 92 in 29 overs when Amarnath became the third run-out victim of the day, trying for a second run that was not there.

India still required 72 for victory and it could have been difficult. However, Sandeep Patil's entrance changed the game's complexion one last time. On the same ground where he had caned Willis for 24 runs off one over a year before, the Indian movie star made people wonder why so many other batsmen had struggled. He drove with impressive freedom, rapidly closing in on the target and bringing dejection into the English ranks. Patil and Sharma had lifted the total by 63 runs in nine overs when the latter slashed a short ball from Willis towards third man. Allott, in front

of his home crowd, took a fantastic catch, but it was too little too late. Sharma had had a great day and his side was within nine runs of victory.

Lots of Indian fans miscounted, because when eight of those runs had been scored they charged on to the field in premature celebration. Remembering what happened to Merv Kitchen and his fellow semi-final umpire, David Evans, two days before at Trent Bridge, Don Oslear grabbed a stump to protect himself. Neither he nor the spectators came to any real harm and after a few minutes clearing time the game was able to restart.

India had six wickets and more than five overs to spare when Willis put all his fieldsmen on the boundary on the pavilion side of the ground and let Patil hit the ball to the rope towards the outer so that everyone could get off in safety. A small contingent of English hooligans tried to disrupt the Indian celebrations. Luckily any nastiness was avoided and the players could shower their delirious fans with champagne. Those few thousand were able to share the moment with their heroes, while in India millions more were thrilled at the prospect of their team playing in the final when on previous occasions they had never even gained a sniff of that possibility. They had won by a significant margin in the end. One that broached no argument.

To top off the Indian joy Mohinder 'Jimmy' Amarnath was named Man of the Match.

ENGLAND	
G. Fowler b Binny	33
C.J. Tavare c Kirmani b Binny	32
D.I. Gower c Kirmani b Amarnath	17
A.J. Lamb run out	29
M.W. Gatting b Amarnath	18
I.T. Botham b Azad	6
I.J. Gould (wk) run out	13
V.J. Marks b Kapil Dev	8
G.R. Dilley not out	20
P.J.W. Allott c Patil b Kapil Dev	8
R.G.D. Willis (capt) b Kapil Dev	0
Extras (b 1, lb 17, w 7, nb 4)	29
(60 overs)	213

1/69 2/84 3/107 4/141 5/150 6/160 7/175 8/177 9/202 10/213

Bowling: Kapil Dev 11-1-35-3; Sandhu 8-1-36-0; Binny 12-1-43-2; Madan Lal 5-0-15-0; Azad 12-1-28-1; Amarnath 12-1-27-2

INDIA	
S.M. Gavaskar c Gould b Allott	25
K. Srikkanth c Willis b Botham	19
M. Amarnath run out	46
Yashpal Sharma c Allott b Willis	61
S.M. Patil not out	51
Kapil Dev (capt) not out	1
Extras (b 5, lb 6, w 1, nb 2)	14
(54.4 overs)	4–217

Did not bat: K. Azad, R.M.H. Binny, Madan Lal, S.M.H. Kirmani (wk), B.S. Sandhu

1/46 2/50 3/142 4/205

Bowling: Willis 10.4-2-42-1; Dilley 11-0-43-0; Allott 10-3-40-1; Botham 11-4-40-1; Marks 12-1-38-0

Umpires: D.G.L. Evans, D.O. Oslear.

Toss: England

SECOND SEMI-FINAL: PAKISTAN vs WEST INDIES
WEST INDIES WON BY 8 WICKETS

A Pakistan team without the services of their captain's bowling and their fighting batting hero, Javed Miandad, stricken down by influenza, played their semi-final against the West Indies as if they had already run their race in this tournament. The great win against New Zealand really turned out to be their final because the West Indies, seemingly en route to their third world crown, were rarely troubled.

Most teams would not select The Oval as their choice of venue to face the West Indies in England. It has the fastest and bounciest wicket in the country and in 1983, with the West Indies having the fastest and bounciest bowlers in the world, run-making was going to be a difficult assignment. Many of the capacity crowd who filled the historic old ground would have hoped for a repeat of the classic run feast of 1979. It soon became obvious that was not going to be the case.

Unlike four years before, winning the toss in 1983 did not mean an automatic insertion of the opposition. But when Clive Lloyd made the correct call on a fine but humid South London morning the prospect of early moisture, pace, bounce and lateral movement proved too great a temptation and he reverted to his old habit.

Almost immediately it was evident his choice had been the right one. Joel Garner, back in the side and wanting to keep the likes of Winston Davis and Wayne Daniel at arm's length, was a very difficult proposition for Mudassar Nazar and Mohsin Khan. He repeatedly beat the outside edge and both batsmen looked at nothing more than survival against the new ball. Mohsin took a single from a leg glance in the sixth over. It was his first run.

After another six overs the total had limped to 23 when Mudassar offered a tame caught and bowled chance to Garner who gratefully accepted. Pakistan's problems were magnified when Ijaz Faqih came in at number 3. He was never going to be an adequate replacement for Javed and despite a couple of brave hook shots was soon edging Michael Holding behind to leave Pakistan struggling at 2–34.

Zaheer Abbas' most memorable innings in a long and illustrious career were against flat bowlers on flat wickets. Then he could compile the most attractive centuries and double centuries imaginable. Dodging and weaving bullets fired by express West Indians on fiery surfaces was never his strong point. With Mohsin playing a purely passive role, Zaheer came in to withstand the awesome firepower of Holding and Malcolm Marshall. Often his head was not behind the line of the ball, but he survived and in the 25th over, along with all the Pakistani supporters, relaxed a little for the first time when Larry Gomes' off spin was introduced into the attack.

The runs did begin to tick over at last and on the verge of the lunch break Mohsin and Zaheer had taken their stand to 54 in 12 overs and the total to 2–88. That suggested a satisfactory start until in the 31st over, the last before the break, all the Pakistanis were put off their food when Zaheer moved down the wicket, tried to drive Gomes to mid wicket, missed and was bowled off his pads.

After the interval Mohsin and Imran continued to make use of the pace respite. They put on 51 in 16 overs and Pakistan reached 3–139, which gave the illusion of mild strength. They were merely in the eye of the storm. Marshall returned and in his second over set Pakistan right back on their heels. From the second ball the Pakistani captain nicked an outswinger and from the fifth left-hander Wasim Raja was caught in front of his stumps.

Five overs and 20 runs later Marshall ended Shahid Mahboob's World Cup campaign when the all-rounder hit softly to mid wicket. Shahid had already been pinged on the helmet by the same bowler and seemed relieved to get off the ground. Marshall had taken 3–3 in 14 balls to really break the back of the Pakistani effort. It was fast bowling of the highest quality. Sarfraz was caught off a skier. Mohsin hung on until there were just three overs remaining. Finally, after four hours vigilance, 70 runs, one four, which resulted from a misfield, 43 singles and plenty of barracking he swung across the line at Andy Roberts and was bowled.

Pakistan's tail enders also managed to hold out against the fearsome late-innings pace onslaught. However, after 60 overs, despite the fact they were only eight wickets down, they finished with their lowest total in the competition. The whole innings contained just two boundaries.

The West Indies only needed 185 to reach their third final out of three. Pakistan required a miracle. Unfortunately there was no-one qualified to provide it. Rashid Khan put in a fine effort with the new ball and in the 11th over trapped Gordon Greenidge lbw with a delivery that kept low. By then the total had reached 34. It had been 29 when Abdul Qadir was introduced to a loud fanfare in the 10th over.

The leg spinner's early overs were impressive. He troubled both Desmond Haynes and Viv Richards. They failed to spot his wrong 'un and Richards was nearly caught at short leg. Haynes hit two fours to mid wicket before misreading another wrong 'un, driving over the top of the ball and being bowled.

That was 2–56 in 20 overs. At tea it was 2–72. In the last session the Qadir threat seemed to have evaporated. His percentage of loose deliveries increased, or at least Richards made it appear that they had. In front of a big noisy crowd on a warm day at one of his most productive venues Richards turned up the batting heat in the final session. He blasted the bowling in his most masterly fashion. Imran set two mid wickets and two mid-ons to curb his strength and stop the run flow. Richards still cracked the ball through and over the fieldsmen with immense power.

Richards reached his 50 in 30 overs and went on to an unbeaten 80 which contained 11 fours and one six. He eased back to allow Larry Gomes to reach his 50, a noble gesture which made his Man of the Match award all the more deserved. When the ball was engulfed by the charging West Indian fans following the winning boundary hit off Zaheer, Richards and Gomes had put on 132 and carried their side to an emphatic victory with 12 overs to spare.

Christopher Martin-Jenkins, who complained about The Oval crowd's joyous reaction to news of England's demise at Old Trafford, thought the result a dress rehearsal for what would happen at Lord's the next Saturday. The West Indies had looked half a class above their opposition, wrote the editor of *The Cricketer*. The one glitch was the groin injury sustained by Lloyd when in the field.

Once again the witnesses to this game were restricted to those who actually attended. The people at home were frustrated by another strike which caused a television blackout.

PAKISTAN

Mohsin Khan b Roberts		70
Mudassar Nazar c & b Garner		11
Ijaz Faqih c Dujon b Holding		5
Zaheer Abbas b Gomes		30
Imran Khan (capt) c Dujon b Marshall		17
Wasim Raja lbw Marshall		0
Shahid Mahboob c Richards b Marshall		6
Sarfraz Nawaz c Holding b Roberts		3
Abdul Qadir not out		10
Wasim Bari (wk) not out		4
Extras (b 6, lb 13, w 4, nb 5)		28
(60 overs)		8–184

Did not bat: Rashid Khan

1/23 2/34 3/88 4/139 5/139 6/159 7/164 8/171

Bowling: Roberts 12-3-25-2; Garner 12-1-31-1; Marshall 12-2-28-3; Holding 12-1-25-1; Gomes 7-0-29-1; Richards 5-0-18-0

WEST INDIES

C.G. Greenidge lbw Rashid Khan		17
D.L. Haynes b Abdul Qadir		29
I.V.A. Richards not out		80
H.A. Gomes not out		50
Extras (b 2, lb 6, w 4)		12
(48.4 overs)		2–188

Did not bat: C.H. Lloyd (capt), S.F.A.F. Bacchus, P.J.L. Dujon (wk), A.M.E. Roberts, M.D. Marshall, J. Garner, M.A. Holding

1/34 2/56

Bowling: Rashid Khan 12-2-32-1; Sarfraz Nawaz 8-0-23-0; Abdul Qadir 11-1-42-1; Shahid Mahboob 11-1-43-0; Wasim Raja 1-0-9-0; Zaheer Abbas 4.4-1-24-0; Mohsin Khan 1-0-3-0

Umpires: D.J. Constant, A.G.T. Whitehead.

Toss: West Indies

SATURDAY 25 JUNE 1983
THE PRUDENTIAL CUP FINAL
INDIA vs WEST INDIES
LORD'S: INDIA WON BY 43 RUNS

There could hardly have been a cricket fan in the world who was not pleased for the previously maligned Indians for making it to a World Cup final. Against all predictions they had defeated Australia, Zimbabwe and the West Indies in the preliminary rounds and then upset all the scribes and pundits by knocking out England in the semi-final at Old Trafford.

It was nice for them and nice for cricket, because they were a lovely bunch of fellows who had done jolly well for themselves and their country. But now it would be all over. This was the final and underdogs do not win finals against juggernauts. It was a miracle that Kapil Dev's side had made it to Lord's on Saturday 25 June 1983. Lightning would not strike twice and by the early evening or even the middle of the afternoon the West Indies would have in their keeping another Prudential World Cup.

So confident was West Indian fast bowler Malcolm Marshall of the outcome of the tournament and final that he put on order a BMW sports car he intended to pay for with his World Cup winnings. No-one told him not to. He was only echoing the sentiments of the rest of the cricket community. Marshall's actions hinted at arrogance. Did they also suggest a modicum of complacency? If they had, Kapil Dev would have identified them.

Many Indians were satisfied just to have made it to Lord's. Fans flew in from all corners of the globe so they could say they saw their team play in a World Cup final. Four came from Belgium and paid £70 each for their precious tickets. Three more had hidden all night in the Lord's toilets only to be found by police tracking dogs and ejected. Others risked life and limb on the ground's outer wall, perhaps briefly fooling police who are more used to people trying to get out of a walled establishment than into it. Not everyone made it or found a ticket tout. Lord's still only held 25,000. Those who were successful were overjoyed. The original odds on India even reaching Lord's had been very long, the Indian team hastily arranged a cocktail party to which friends and ex-players were invited. They didn't have much notice. Early in the tournament the Indian players and management couldn't assume they would still be in London at that time.

There had been early-morning rain in St John's Wood and the streets were still wet when those fans who were too excited to sleep arrived at the ground bright and early. The gates were opened at 9.15 and everyone started to file in. Well before 11 am the ground was completely full and the sun was shining in all its glory. 'Lord's, groomed like a high-born lady,' wrote *Wisden*.

Neither side changed the line-up from its semi-final wins. A question mark hung over Clive Lloyd's groin, but he strode confidently to the wicket at the appointed time with Kapil Dev, called correctly at the toss and told his opponent that India would bat first. Sunil Gavaskar and Kris Srikkanth followed out the West Indians to a rousing reception—a great, if nerve-racking, moment for both of them.

Gavaskar took strike. Andy Roberts, the most experienced of the Caribbean pace quartet, was entrusted with the new ball. He opened from the Nursery End. Gavaskar, a tiny figure, looked incongruous facing big powerful fast bowlers. They seemed sure to break him in half. Often the little Indian champion relished the split-second contest against the best and fastest in the world. He had taken double centuries off them and would do so again, but this was not his day or his tournament. Both batsmen strove to do nothing more than survive the opening salvos from Roberts and Joel Garner. The score was only two in the fifth over when the bravely helmetless and hatless Gavaskar checked an off-drive and was caught behind. It was Roberts' first wicket in three finals.

Gavaskar's dismissal was a blow both for the confidence of the Indian team and for their fans. Mohinder Amarnath, such an accomplished batsman against fast bowling, was greeted with a Garner bouncer. Srikkanth took that as a cue to begin to return fire. Soon he cut Garner over the slips for the first four of the match. Then he turned his attention to Roberts. An on-drive raced into the milling spectators in the Grandstand. A few balls later and the Antiguan was hooked for six into the Warner Stand, bringing a vigorous flag-waving response from several quarters. He climaxed his trio of brilliant shots in Roberts' next over when he crouched on one knee and drove the ball forward of point to the boundary at the speed of light.

With Amarnath settling in to his task, momentarily at least, India suggested a competitive total could be within their capabilities. The match at Lord's the week before between the West Indies and Australia had produced 549 runs and there was no reason to think this might not also be a high-scoring affair. India reached 1–59 in 19 overs and Srikkanth, who ran a second run backwards all the way, had scored 38 in 57 balls when Malcolm Marshall, who had started to cause trouble as soon as he replaced Roberts, had him walking in front of a very fast and straight delivery.

Run-making was harder work, at least until Larry Gomes' off spin brought its usual relief. His first over was a maiden, but soon Amarnath hit him through the covers for four and moving down the wicket, drove him for another. Michael Holding bowled a wild one that eluded Jeffrey Dujon and went unhindered for four wides to the Nursery end. Faoud Bacchus might have run out Yashpal Sharma with a direct hit. A vibrant crowd danced, sang and whistled. The atmosphere inside the ground was fantastic.

Amarnath and Sharma lasted until the 30th over, their 31-run stand lifting the total to a neat 90. Lunchtime loomed and India could suggest they had done a fair morning's work. However, quality fast bowlers are always capable of producing an unplayable delivery out of nowhere and Michael Holding did just that. Bowling from his short run, the Jamaican sent down a ripsnorter

that cut back and succinctly removed Amarnath's off stump. As if that was not enough to ruin the Indians' midday meal, two runs later Sharma tried to belt Gomes 'inside out' through the off side, only to hit a catch straight at Gus Logie who was substituting for Desmond Haynes. Two for 90 had slipped to 4–92.

At lunch it was 4–100 from 32 overs and consensus suggested India were doing no more than they could against superior opposition. The growing dominance of the West Indies continued after the interval. Gomes was still on and Kapil Dev eased him twice to the on-side boundary, then unwisely tried to belt him for six, reaching only as far as the safe-handed Holding in the deep. One run and one over later, Kirti Azad hit a simple catch to square leg off Roberts. At 6–111 in the 36th over, India had lost 4–21 and their innings was sagging badly.

Sandeep Patil, late hero of the semi-final and always aggressive in intent, tried to regain some Indian initiative and showed his captain how to put Gomes into the crowd for six. There was no significant partnership, however. Roger Binny soon went the same way as Azad, and after Madan Lal hit Gomes for another six, Patil thoroughly mistimed a pull shot off Garner to leave India 8–153. Eight runs later Marshall broke through Madan Lal's defence and India had lost 7–71 in 15 inglorious overs.

Syed Kirmani and Balwindersingh Sandhu had 15 overs available for their last-wicket partnership. To the surprise of some they used 10 of them. The stand featured 22 runs and a thump on the helmet for Sandhu courtesy of another Marshall fireball. Sandhu survived and 'Dickie' Bird told Marshall what he thought of bouncers to number 11 batsmen. In fact the Sikh finally outlasted Kirmani when, like Amarnath, the Indian wicketkeeper received a delivery from Holding, bowling from the Nursery end, that would have challenged any batsman on Earth. India was all out for 183 in the 55th over.

It was 3.15 pm. The West Indies were sure to win, but at least the paying customers could feel satisfied that close to six hours cricket would be provided for their money.

A slight haze covered the afternoon sun as

Haynes and Gordon Greenidge began the pursuit of 184. It cooled proceedings slightly and quelled the atmosphere a little. Kapil Dev kept his dressing-room speech short, admitting to limited confidence for the task ahead. In the other dressing-room Marshall was relaxing and taking it easy. He did not expect to have to bat and settled back to dream about his new BMW. India were now at odds of 100–1 to win the match.

Greenidge had missed out in the 1975 and 1979 finals. Another chance now presented itself and Sandhu appeared to offer the chance of a few early comfortable runs. Haynes thought so and drove him to the extra-cover boundary. Then the man in the maroon patka sent down his second over to the man in the baggy maroon cap. Greenidge lifted his bat out of the way of a ball outside the off stump. Suddenly it jagged back and hit his off stump. The opener could not believe his own error of judgment. The West Indies was 1–5 and Greenidge's three finals had realised 13, 9 and 1, a poor return for such a great batsman.

A champion took the place of the great batsman at the wicket and almost from the moment he arrived assumed his trademark role of dominance. Sandhu dropped short. Richards silently and sweetly pulled the ball to mid wicket for four. He had been made Man of the Match in 1979 for his supreme 138 not out and this time was coming out of the blocks as if he wanted to top that performance. Two drives, one to the off and one to the on, reduced the margin by eight more runs and showed the Indian captain who was in charge.

Madan Lal was introduced. Richards welcomed him by sending the ball to all points for three more fours in four balls. The 50 was raised in no time, then out of the blue Haynes, wanting a piece of the boundary action, drove loosely at Madan Lal and was caught by Binny in the covers. It was thought that might stem the run flow for a while, especially when Lloyd pulled up lame going for his first single, a simple trot to a shot to third man. Haynes came back straight away as his captain's runner. It was easy to believe the Barbadian knew he would be needed and that Lloyd had carried the injury into the match. Even if that were so, Kapil made no fuss and allowed the runner.

Besides which, Kapil Dev soon had other things to occupy him. 'Dickie' Bird says that when Haynes was caught Kapil came up to him and said, 'Do you know, we will win after all? They think it is too easy.' Most would have thought he was still being a bit optimistic, but they may have had their doubts a few moments later.

Madan Lal bowled the 14th over of the innings. Richards pulled at a short ball and sent it sailing over mid wicket towards the noisy throng in the grandstand. They roared their approval just as Kapil turned, eyes skyward, following the ball's trajectory. Quickly the inadequacy of Richards' timing was evident. Kapil ran hard for 25 metres and judged the ball's descent perfectly. His eyes never left their objective and he held a very important catch. Richard's innings of 33 had contained seven stunning boundaries. But while each shot to the rope seemed to indicate his side's superiority, Richards' dismissal gave the first glimpse of their fragility. The West Indies were 3–57 and for the first time since Srikkanth's early assault Indian noise drowned out West Indian noise.

It was a pivotal moment. Lloyd was really struggling. 'Dickie' Bird thought he should have retired hurt. Lloyd was intent on helping his side win a match that, unbelievably was no longer there for the taking. He and Larry Gomes took their time for a few overs and added nine runs, just trying to consolidate things. Gomes had been shackled by Binny. Now he took a liberty outside the off stump at Madan Lal, edged the ball and Gavaskar held the slips catch into his stomach.

The twist was quickly gaining momentum. Gomes had gone in the 18th over. From the first ball of the 19th Lloyd lunged painfully at Binny. The attempted drive was ill-conceived and lobbed straight to mid-off. The West Indies were 5–66 and a cricket match had been turned on its head. The medium pacers were swinging the ball and Lloyd's batsmen were not handling them well. Bacchus and Dujon batted in rearguard mode, surviving six overs until the tea break where the West Indies could regroup and refocus.

Marshall was no longer dreaming of BMWs. He had the pads on and had to think about batting.

Three balls into the final session of the 1983 Prudential Cup final Marshall was thinking very hard about his batting. He was the incoming batsman crossing over with the outgoing Bacchus, who without addition had slashed at a wide ball from Sandhu, only to edge a catch to the diving Kirmani. The West Indies had lost 5–16 to plummet to 6–76. Dujon hit Sandhu over square leg for the fourth and last six of this low-scoring match. It was the sole boundary in a 43-run partnership with Marshall that revived West Indian hopes. 'This is going to be tough,' Dujon had told the fast bowler when he arrived at the wicket. They took no more risks than their three runs per over requirement necessitated.

Playing straight and running hard, they seemed to have everything under control when Kapil reintroduced Amarnath for the 42nd over at the Nursery end. Dujon went to play his first delivery, then pulled his bat away, only for the ball to follow him a little. It glided off the edge of the bat and down into his stumps. Dujon was devastated, not being able to believe his misfortune. He bent over and thumped his open palm on the ground.

It was 7–119 and all the recognised batsmen were gone. Soon Marshall joined them. His 73-minute vigil ended when he moved down the wicket to Amarnath, followed the ball as it moved away down the slope and guided it to Gavaskar at slip. The bowler whom Lloyd had hoped would provide the easiest runs for his side was winning the game for India. The West Indies were 60 runs short of their objective when Garner joined Roberts. These two had put on 71 in the opening match of the tournament against India with some uninhibited free hitting.

This time there was a lot more at stake and two runs after Marshall was out Roberts, the cool calm Antiguan, so often the lower order batting hero in a tight situation, shuffled in front to Kapil and was adjudged lbw. Now it was 9–126 and India was on the verge of the greatest boilover in what had been a competition full of upset results.

It did not come straight away. Garner and Holding clung on to the hope of another Caribbean miracle for seven overs and 28 minutes. They pushed a few runs here and there edging 14 closer to the target. The requirement was 44 runs from 49 balls as Amarnath ran in to deliver the final ball of his seventh over. It was short of a length. Holding swung hard across it and was struck on the pads. Amarnath, Kirmani and 750 million watching the special telecast live in India let out an almighty appeal. 'Dickie' Bird acknowledged the irresistible plea. Up came a crooked right finger. India were the winners of the 1983 Prudential Cup.

Everyone ran in every direction except poor Holding, who stood rooted at the crease, not stunned at the decision but at his fate. It was a mistake because the invading hordes knocked him flying, resulting in a twisted ankle which kept the fast bowler out of county cricket for several days.

The contrast between Indian joy and West Indian despair could not have been more marked. Some West Indian players broke down and cried. 'We were dreadful,' Lloyd lamented. He retired on the spot and had to be talked into continuing by his team-mates and the West Indian Board of Control. Gradually the pain dulled amongst the vanquished, but it would not be forgotten. They gathered their composure and went to acknowledge and share a drink with the team that had defeated them on the day on their merits.

Kapil announced the moment of victory as the most joyous in his life. The celebrations started instantly and were to last for quite some time. There was more joy yet. Amarnath, who had charged straight down the wicket and grabbed a stump once 'Dickie' Bird had given Holding out, was presented with an even more valuable souvenir: the Man of the Match award from Mike Brearley for his important innings and carpet-sweeping seven-over spell of 3–12. Not all the rewards were silverware, either. As a bonus each player was given £1150 by the Indian Board. In India it was 1 am on the Sunday morning when the match finished. Instantly 26 June became a public holiday.

The Indian team danced and sang all night at the Westmoreland Hotel. In the streets of London there was much the same tune as thousands of Indian expatriates revelled in the proud moment. And the mood was the same all over India, with sitars, drums, whistles, rhythmic handclapping all beating out the same happy tune. In *A History of Indian Cricket*, Mihir Bose wrote of the cohesion within the team, resulting, partially at least, from the success of players from the northern part of India and their support for a captain from the same region. That may be so, but to an outsider the 1983 World Cup final will always be a game where a 66–1 underdog turned the tables on the acknowledged best team in the world in another wonderful game of limited-overs cricket.

INDIA

S.M. Gavaskar c Dujon b Roberts	2
K. Srikkanth lbw Marshall	38
M. Amarnath b Holding	26
Yashpal Sharma c sub (A.L. Logie) b Gomes	11
S.M. Patil c Gomes b Garner	27
Kapil Dev (capt) c Holding b Gomes	15
K. Azad c Garner b Roberts	0
R.M.H. Binny c Garner b Roberts	2
Madan Lal b Marshall	17
S.M.H. Kirmani (wk) b Holding	14
B.S. Sandhu not out	11
Extras (b 5, lb 5, w 9, nb 1)	20
(54.4 overs)	183

1/2 2/59 3/90 4/92 5/110 6/111 7/130 8/153 9/161 10/183

Bowling: Roberts 10–3–32–3; Garner 12–4–24–1; Marshall 11–1–24–2; Holding 9.4–2–26–2; Gomes 11–1–49–2; Richards 1–0–8–0

WEST INDIES

C.G. Greenidge b Sandhu	1
D.L. Haynes c Binny b Madan Lal	13
I.V.A. Richards c Kapil Dev b Madan Lal	33
C.H. Lloyd (capt) c Kapil Dev b Binny	8
H.A. Gomes c Gavaskar b Madan Lal	5
S.F.A.F. Bacchus c Kirmani b Sandhu	8
P.J.L. Dujon (wk) b Amarnath	25
M.D. Marshall c Gavaskar b Amarnath	18
A.M.E. Roberts lbw Kapil Dev	4
J. Garner not out	5
M.A. Holding lbw Amarnath	6
Extras (lb 4, w 10)	14
(52 overs)	140

1/5 2/50 3/57 4/66 5/66 6/76 7/119 8/124 9/126 10/140

Bowling: Kapil Dev 11–4–21–1; Sandhu 9–1–32–2; Madan Lal 12–2–31–3; Binny 10–1–23–1; Amarnath 7–0–12–3; Azad 3–0–7–0

Umpires: H.D. Bird, B.J. Meyer.

Toss: West Indies

POST-MORTEM

The fastest after-effect of the 1983 World Cup was that the editor of *Wisden Cricket Monthly*, David Frith, literally ate his own words. He said he would on behalf of everyone who maligned the Indians prior to the tournament. After a reader of his magazine challenged him to do so, Frith consumed the offending piece with good grace.

The boilover World Cup, the last to be held in England for 16 years, had been an outstanding success. The increase in the number of games had been a worthwhile innovation, as the figures revealed: 232,000 people attended the matches, up from 132,000, and gate takings amounted to over £1 million.

The growing prestige of the World Cup meant there was close scrutiny of teams and players who underperformed. Kim Hughes' Australians were perhaps the most disappointing combination over the two weeks and the flak flew when they returned home. David Hookes copped a hefty fine for airing his thoughts publicly on who he thought should be in charge of the side. Worse than that, he was left out of the Test team for the next two summers. Australian cricket had still not bottomed out. Despite the efforts of Phil Ridings in England, several stars had already been secured for the next 'rebel' tour of South Africa.

That the West Indies were hurting there was no doubt. They soon rallied, however, and under Clive Lloyd the following October they thrashed India 3–0 in a six-match Test series and hammered them 5–0 in the Limited-Over Internationals. It may have given the Caribbean champions some satisfaction to exact such a revenge. I am not sure, though, that they would not have willingly swapped any of those victories for a winner's medal at Lord's on Saturday 25 June.

The ICC had a meeting following the tournament where they called for tenders to be submitted by the end of the year to host the 1987 competition.

5

The Reliance World Cup, 1987:
The Australian Revival

Speak to any Australian, New Zealand or English players about their tours of the subcontinent in the 1950s and 1960s and they will regale you with horror stories of illness and poor hygiene. Former Australian Test batsman and current Test match referee Peter Burge said his greatest achievement on three tours of India and Pakistan was to arrive home each time with his health intact. Others revelled in the cultural exotica of the two countries and all had enough bizarre experiences to provide plenty of material for their various biographers.

By the 1980s the situation had improved, but there were still problems with transport, climate and accommodation, especially outside the major cities. In addition, a siege mentality lingered amongst many Western players as to the treatment they had received at the hand of the umpires from that part of the world.

So when the July 1984 ICC meeting voted 16–12 in favour of the fourth World Cup being staged in India and Pakistan there were doubters who feared the whole thing could be an organisational fiasco. An example of the type of difficulties that might arise occurred when Australia met India at Jamshedpur in October 1984. The match started three hours late because the baggage of both sides was still in transit on the road from Trivandrum.

The behaviour of volatile crowds was also a concern and both India and Pakistan had a history, some of it quite recent, of games being disrupted and even ruined by poorly behaved elements in big crowds.

The authorities from India and Pakistan worked hard to win the votes they needed at the ICC meeting. What clinched the deal ahead of England's bid to again stage the tournament was the guarantee that all full ICC member countries involved would receive £75,000 plus expenses from participating in the tournament. The English Test and County Cricket Board could not match that.

That was the easy part settled. The greatest issue to be resolved was whether English players who had toured, played or coached in South Africa would be allowed into India or Pakistan by the governments of the day. There was lots of toing-and-froing and political grandstanding over this. Graham Gooch was a particular target. He had a rotten tour of the West Indies in 1986, being subjected to much local criticism for his visits to the forbidden land. There was no guarantee he or John Emburey would be granted visas to enter India. If they had been refused England would not have participated in the 1987 World Cup and Australia and New Zealand might have also withdrawn in support. Then the cricket world would have been split into two along lines of race and colour, something that is still too awful to contemplate.

Eventually sanity sort of prevailed. The Indian government said it would accept players with South African connections if they publicly denounced apartheid. This allowed the tournament to go ahead with all teams participating. The problem did not go away, though. When Graham Gooch was made captain of England for the 1988–89 tour of India local politicians considered him unacceptable and the tour was called off.

The July 1984 ICC meeting, after voting in

favour of India and Pakistan hosting the 1987 World Cup, had to address the issue of the shorter daylight hours in that part of the world. The first idea was that each innings would be limited to 60 overs, as previously, and that every game would go into a second day. The folly of this was obvious and two years later was corrected. Innings were reduced from 60 to 50 overs in the hope each game would be completed in a day, so establishing in the premier competition the now standard length of an innings in all Limited-Over Internationals. Two days were still available for each game.

Play was scheduled to start at 9 am to help finish the matches before the quickly darkening evenings. Each side was required to complete its 50 overs within an allotted three and a half hours or face financial penalties. The West Indies had to pay close attention to that if they were not to return home out of pocket.

Neutral umpires were selected to officiate for the first time, also. Each preliminary round match would be controlled by one specially appointed official from an overseas panel and a leading Indian umpire for matches in Pakistan and a leading Pakistani umpire for the games in India.

What all this did was stimulate extra interest and perhaps a greater sense of anticipation than if the tournament had been held once more in England. In August 1986 the Indian and Pakistan authorities secured the big sponsor they needed. The Indian company Reliance was forthcoming with the sponsorship money that had been sought and would provide the winner's trophy. This was a lavish product of gold, silver and diamonds and would be the featured prize of the Reliance Cup final.

Further worldwide interest arose from the fact that there were no clear-cut favourites to win the trophy. In 1983 India had set a precedent for outsiders to come from nowhere, hit their straps over the concentrated two-week period, and snatch victory against the odds.

India had not emerged as a powerhouse since their triumph under Kapil Dev. There had been moments of triumph, but plenty of defeats and frustrations. A win in the World Championship

of Cricket limited-overs tournament in Australia early in 1985 echoed the Prudential Cup success. At other times, particularly at home against England in 1984–85, their performances were poor. One noticeable and seemingly permanent change following the 1983 win was that Indian crowds had ditched the slower, more sophisticated spectacle of Test cricket for the thrills and spills of the limited-overs game.

Their challenge for a prestigious win at home and participation in an impossibly crowded and exciting final in Calcutta would be led by their charismatic captain and leading all-rounder Kapil Dev. He had lost the captaincy and even his place in the side against England, only to regain it and then the leadership again soon after. He carried a lot on his shoulders as his team's leader, highest wicket taking and most penetrative bowler, and fastest-scoring batsman. He would finish the tournament as hero or villain. The passionate Indian fans would allow nothing in between.

The great Sunil Gavaskar used the Reliance Cup as his swansong. This little champion had pushed himself to the top of the Test match tree in terms of run aggregate and Test centuries. Gavaskar passed Sir Donald Bradman's 29 Test century record in 1984 and by the time of the World Cup had lifted his quota to a still unbeaten 34 tons. He had become the first batsman to clock over 10,000 Test runs and finished with an average of over 50, a true measure of a batsman's quality. There had been plenty of limited-over achievements, too, but his World Cup record was modest in comparison with everything else. The greying 38-year-old opener had one last chance to correct that situation.

India's attack in 1983 was successfully based on medium-paced bowlers who could move the ball around in English conditions. On their home turf they would return to their traditional dependence on spinners. Left-arm Sikh, Maninder Singh, and blossoming all-rounder Ravi Shastri, also left-arm orthodox, were key players in the side. Dilip Vengsarkar and Mohammad Azharuddin were attractive and successful middle-order batsmen who ensured India's rating with the bookmakers was much higher than the 66–1 it had been prior to the 1983 tournament.

What threw open the competition more than anything else was the diminishing power of the West Indies as a force in Limited-Overs Internationals. Now led by Viv Richards, the Caribbean side remained the best in the longer form of the game, but the gap between the two forms of cricket was widening. Bouncers were now outlawed by the ruling that deemed any ball above the batsman's shoulder be called a no-ball. This quelled some of the threat of the West Indian pacemen. In addition, almost a completely new set of speedsters had to be found. Michael Holding was recently retired and Joel Garner and Malcolm Marshall were unavailable due to injury. The second line of pacemen like Tony Gray, Winston Benjamin and Patrick Patterson would have to make plenty of adjustments to foreign wickets and conditions very quickly.

Clive Lloyd had been two and a half years out of the game. He would be missed and so too would Gordon Greenidge, not retired but nursing a gammy knee. Since the heady days of the early 1980s Richie Richardson had developed into a fine back-foot slayer of wayward bowlers and the little Trinidadian Gus Logie thrilled crowds, as much with his athletic catching as his stylish run-making. Much would depend on Greenidge's reliable opening partner, Desmond Haynes, and the captain, Richards, who was still considered the premier batsman in the world.

Richards' side had missed out in the two Limited-Over Tournaments held in Australia in the first months of 1987. Those losses indicated a reduction of West Indian dominance and the seeming emergence of a quality England side. To the time of writing, the 1986–87 Ashes tour of Australia was England's last period of sustained success. They had a fine time of it down under, led by Mike Gatting, winning everything on offer against an admittedly demoralised Australian team.

Like the West Indies they would have to do without a couple of important players. David Gower and Ian Botham decided a winter at home was more desirable than this four-week sojourn, although the follow-up Test tour of Pakistan was possibly more of a discouraging factor. Gower had not taken a break from the game since the start of the 1978 English season, so he was entitled to a bit of long-service leave. Botham had let slip a quip about not wanting to send his mother-in-law to Pakistan after he returned from the country in 1984. His decision not to make the trip might have been mutually appreciated. The English tabloid journalists did not really want to go and made their feelings plain and the BBC, wrongly thinking the facilities would be inadequate, at first refused to televise the matches until the final.

One player who did agree to attend was the sometimes reluctant tourist, Graham Gooch. A match-winning opener, especially in Limited-Over Internationals, Gooch had his ups and downs as an international batsman. When on song, though, he could win a limited-overs match off his own very ample bat. Gatting's hold on the captaincy in the lead up to the World Cup looked much more secure than it actually was but he was at his peak as a thumping middle-order batsman and had been a big success in India three years earlier.

English supporters might have been more apprehensive about their bowling attack. The pace of Phil DeFreitas, Gladstone Small and Neil Foster suggested honest competence, not blistering firepower. John Emburey could be relied upon for accuracy in the spin department. His ability to claim wickets was more open to question. As England's chief spinner he had taken a total of none in five Tests against Pakistan.

England was in Group B. This time it would have to face the West Indies in the preliminary rounds, as well as Pakistan and Sri Lanka.

Pakistan, like India, had the burden of extra pressure matched by home-ground advantage as Imran Khan led them into another campaign where their likely level of success was very hard to assess. The 35-year-old Pakistani captain also suggested the month-long concentration of Limited-Over Internationals would see him out of international cricket. This added to the romance of the occasion.

Imran had taken some time to recuperate from his 1983 injuries. He was bowling effectively again, if at a slightly reduced pace, but his ability to send down lethal, prodigious inswingers was unaffected. He now had at his side an heir apparent in Wasim Akram, a left-handed all-rounder of immense potential as a pace bowler and lower order hitter. With Abdul Qadir's leg spin expected to be a handful on Pakistan's pitches, it was thought Imran's attack was the best equipped in the competition.

Zaheer Abbas and Mohsin Khan were finished, which imposed an even greater run-making responsibility on Javed Miandad. There was no suggestion he did not relish that opportunity. Javed was in a rich vein of form and prior to the tournament had threatened to pull out if he did not receive a pay rise. His most recent Test innings before the World Cup was 260 against England at The Oval. Salim Malik had emerged as a typically precocious Pakistani middle-order talent, and since his return from injury Imran was a far more reliable run-maker. Jack Bannister, an English cricket commentator and bookmaker, thought Pakistan was 2–1 favourites to win the final.

Allan Border brought an Australian side whose recent form had been as low as at any time in its history. They had not won a Test series since January 1984. In the years since there had been mass retirements, tearful captaincy resignations and South African defections which decimated the quality of the side. The West Indies, England and even New Zealand had all triumphed over this once-proud cricketing nation. At times it seemed only their tough little captain was holding the team together, and he had threatened to quit a couple of times too.

Border's batting during this period was often astonishing in its resilience against overwhelming odds. Fast bowling or slow, he sold his wicket dearly and on several occasions rescued losing causes almost single-handedly. He now had Bob Simpson as team coach to try and give the side direction and to develop a strong cooperative work ethic. It remained to be seen if Simpson's tactics and approach would have any impact.

Border seemed to have the nucleus of a team blossoming with talent. Dean Jones had already made his mark, Geoff Marsh was noted for his

dedication and had been an instant success at international level in both forms of the game. Steve Waugh carried a reputation as an excellent limited-overs all-rounder and David Boon, despite a poor 1986–87 Ashes series, remained the batting pride of Tasmania.

Less certain were the bowling resources at Border's disposal. Beanpole left-arm paceman Bruce Reid had quickly established his rating as the team's main strike bowler. Craig McDermott was the fastest bowler in the party and still young enough to be a developing talent. That also meant much of his potential was as yet unfulfilled. Beyond that pair the bowling responsibilities would be shared between all-rounders Waugh and Simon O'Donnell, Border himself and his off spinners, Peter Taylor and Tim May.

On paper the Australians looked to have the easier run in Group A, having to overcome two of India, New Zealand and their 1983 nemesis, Zimbabwe, to reach the semi-finals. Of course, everyone thought Australia had a fairly easy draw in 1983 and that did not do them any good. Such was the pessimism pervading the Australian cricket community that Channel 9, despite having the Australian television rights to the 1987 World Cup, showed no inclination to provide any direct telecasts of the tournament. They touted the feeble excuse that the expected picture quality was too low.

Of all the teams missing players from the Reliance Cup, none was harder hit than New Zealand, which had to strive for victory without the services of their premier bowler Richard Hadlee. As well as Hadlee, whose decision was controversial because he told the press of his unavailability before informing New Zealand's cricket authorities, Bruce Edgar and Jeremy Coney had retired. Jeff Crowe was the captain of a team still expected to give a good account of themselves.

Crowe's younger brother Martin, about to embark upon his second World Cup tournament, was rated in the top five batsmen in the game at the time. A real stylist, Crowe had shown an ability to compile centuries against top-quality opposition of varying types. His would be the wicket most wanted by opposing attacks. John

Wright's stability at the top of the batting order could have an influence and Ken Rutherford, in Limited-Overs Internationals at least, was revealing his talent for positive batsmanship.

Without Hadlee, medium pacers Ewan Chatfield, Martin Snedden and Willie Watson would share a far greater burden. Chatfield, the cricketer who literally came back from the dead, had uncanny accuracy and was rarely collared. He was the most experienced of the trio. Danny Morrison was sharp but untried, raw in the ways of containment and unlikely to be used often in this form of cricket just yet.

Since the 1983 World Cup Sri Lanka had secured their first couple of Test victories, one each over India and Pakistan. Duleep Mendis retained the captaincy, becoming a more rounded figure as the seasons progressed. He, fellow batting aggressor Roy Dias, and rotund young left-hander Arjuna Ranatunga, would be expected to score the bulk of the quick runs needed by Sri Lanka to make up for lack of penetration in their bowling.

They would still be calling the likes of Rumesh Ratnayake, Vinothen John and Ashantha de Mel to threaten their opposition. It was an unlikely prospect on England's fairly sympathetic wickets and was even less so on the hard-baked, often grassless surfaces of India and Pakistan.

Holland had given Zimbabwe a decent run for their money in the ICC Trophy final in July 1986, but there was never any real doubt that the African nation would make their deserved return to their second World Cup. Their prodigy from 1983, Graeme Hick, had decided to follow his cricketing destiny in England, first with Worcestershire and later with England. His talent would be missed, as would that of retired captain and important all-rounder Duncan Fletcher.

Thirty-nine-year-old off spinner John Traicos had assumed the leadership mantle. His experience was an asset to the Zimbabweans and he could be expected to trouble batsmen with his accuracy on the finger-spinner friendly wickets of the subcontinent.

Traicos' vice-captain was Dave Houghton who had a key role to play as wicketkeeper—

batsman. Others back four years on for more run-making fun were openers Grant Paterson, Robin Brown and Ali Shah, Andy Pycroft, all-rounder Iain Butchart and the fiercely competitive Kevin Curran. Curran and Butchart would be required to do plenty of bowling. Peter Rawson was remembered as Zimbabwe's best new-ball exponent in 1983. He retained his place in the line-up but had a new offsider to nurture in the developing Eddo Brandes.

The venues for each of the World Cup games had been carefully selected to assuage fears about hygiene and organisation. Determined that their showpiece tournament would be a success, the Indians and Pakistanis were leaving nothing to chance. Each venue had to receive a stamp of approval from a TCCB or an ACB representative if it was to be added to the venue list. Once these locations had been accepted, the policy was to take the matches all over the subcontinent. That would involve the players travelling far greater distances than they had in the tournaments in England. To compensate for this and the need to recover from long, perhaps arduous journeys, the 27 Reliance Cup matches were extended over four weeks rather than crammed into two, as they had been in 1983. Again, everyone would play other group members twice.

The extent of the travel was yet another worry and there were still plenty of frowns as the sides began to file into India and Pakistan at the end of September. Sri Lanka, which hardly had to move from match to match in 1983, had a very strenuous itinerary this World Cup as they had to flit from one corner of Pakistan to the next. The Australians impressed all observers with their willingness to get out and practise in the heat, so acclimatising themselves to prevailing conditions. It immediately contrasted with the attitude that had gone before them.

Another more obvious contrast was the match selected to open the Reliance Cup. Instead of England leading the way at beautiful Lord's or the austerely traditional Oval, it would be Pakistan doing battle with Sri Lanka at the Niaz Stadium in Hyderabad. This ground was put on the world cricketing map when Mudassar Nazar and Javed Miandad put on 451 against India in

1982–83. The greatest threat to an interruption of play was not chilly May rain in this notably hot location, but maybe a dust storm from the Thar Desert.

THURSDAY 8 OCTOBER, FRIDAY 9 OCTOBER and SATURDAY 10 OCTOBER 1987
THE RELIANCE CUP: ROUND ONE
GROUP B: PAKISTAN vs SRI LANKA
NIAZ STADIUM, HYDERABAD: PAKISTAN WON BY 15 RUNS

Although an unlikely venue for the opening of the world's major cricket tournament, Hyderabad turned on an excellent cricket match for the start of the Reliance Cup.

Pakistan was in the grip of World Cup fever. The whole country seemed to stop to watch Imran's side fight it out with their Group B opponents. There was a passionate belief that this side would have the honour of bringing that gold and silver trophy to Pakistan after the final in Calcutta on 8 November. Sri Lanka was seen as just the first stepping stone to that national triumph, and so it eventually proved this day. But the Sri Lankans put up a great fight and their trio of up and coming batsmen nearly ruined the Pakistani plan at the first time of asking.

A 9 am start did not deter Imran and he had no hesitation in electing to bat after he won the toss. It proved the correct decision. The Sri Lankan opening bowlers betrayed some nervousness, conceding 18 extras in the first nine overs. Ijaz Ahmed and Ramiz Raja batted capably enough with a stand of 48 before Ijaz was caught behind off Rumesh Ratnayake. Nineteen runs later Rumesh caught Mansoor Akhtar off his namesake, Ravi Ratnayake, to leave Pakistan 2–67. Ramiz and Javed Miandad then took control of the innings with a stand of 113. Ramiz provided the solidity, taking 30 overs to reach his half century, while Javed attacked and improvised his way to an excellent century in 96 balls.

Javed's 103 was his fifth hundred in Limited-Over Internationals, but his first in the World Cup. He hit six fours and won the Man of the Match award. After the departure of this pair the run-making momentum was maintained to the completion of the 50 overs. The two Ratnayakes had each picked up a couple of wickets.

Neither they nor any other Sri Lankan was able to halt the steady run flow.

Pakistan had finished with 6–267, the equivalent of which off 60 overs would have been 320. It was an imposing chase for the Sri Lankans, many of whom were inexperienced, and it did not start off well. Roshan Mahanama, quickly into his stride, lost partners Brendon Kuruppu, caught behind at 29, Roy Dias, bowled by the mesmerising Abdul Qadir at 57, Arjuna Ranatunga, also bowled, this time by off spinner Tauseef Ahmed on 100, and his captain Duleep Mendis, disastrously run out just three runs later. Sri Lanka at 4–103 was quickly slipping to defeat.

Twenty-one-year-old Mahanama was joined by the equally youthful left-hander Asanka Gurusinha. They added 79 runs for the fifth wicket in impressive fashion. Mudassar Nazar was made to suffer, conceding seven runs per over throughout his spell. Imran became annoyed as the standard of fielding slipped. Mahanama had guided his side to within 86 runs of their target and hit seven fours and the first six of the tournament when he was caught from a long hop off Mansoor Akhtar's only over.

Gurusinha was bowled by the deserving Abdul Qadir, which meant that only Aravinda de Silva, another 21-year-old, stood between Pakistan and victory. He pressed on, adding valuable runs with the two Ratnayakes. The Sri Lankans closed in, but the overs available were running dangerously low. Imran returned and settled the issue when he bowled de Silva with a full toss, his 100th wicket in Limited-Over Internationals. The challenge had gone and Don Anurasiri's run-out from the second ball of the final over was merely academic. Pakistan had the start it needed.

PAKISTAN

Ramiz Raja c R.J. Ratnayake b Anurasiri	76
Ijaz Ahmed c Kuruppu b R.J. Ratnayake	16
Mansoor Akhtar c R.J. Ratnayake b J.R. Ratnayake	12
Javed Miandad b J.R. Ratnayake	103
Wasim Akram run out	14
Salim Malik not out	18
Imran Khan (capt) b R.J. Ratnayake	2
Salim Yousuf (wk) not out	1
Extras (lb 15, w 1, nb 9)	25
(50 overs)	6–267

Did not bat: Mudassar Nazar, Abdul Qadir, Tauseef Ahmed

1/48 2/67 3/180 4/226 5/259 6/266

Bowling: John 10–2–37–0; R.J. Ratnayake 10–0–64–2; J.R. Ratnayake 9–0–47–2; de Silva 10–0–44–0; Anurasiri 10–0–52–1; Gurusinha 1–0–8–0

SRI LANKA

D.S.B.P. Kuruppu (wk) c Salim Yousuf b Imran Khan	9
R.S. Mahanama c Javed Miandad b Mansoor Akhtar	89
R.L. Dias b Abdul Qadir	5
A. Ranatunga b Tauseef Ahmed	24
L.R.D. Mendis (capt) run out	1
A.P. Gurusinha b Abdul Qadir	37
P.A. de Silva b Imran Khan	42
J.R. Ratnayake c Salim Yousuf b Wasim Akram	7
R.J. Ratnayake c Mudassar Nazar b Wasim Akram	8
V.B. John not out	1
S.D. Anurasiri run out	0
Extras (b 7, lb 14, w 7, nb 1)	29
(49.2 overs)	252

1/29 2/57 3/100 4/103 5/182 6/190 7/209 8/223 9/251 10/252

Bowling: Imran Khan 10–2–42–2; Wasim Akram 9.2–1–41–2; Mudassar Nazar 9–0–63–0; Abdul Qadir 10–1–30–2; Tauseef Ahmed 10–0–48–1; Mansoor Akhtar 1–0–7–1

Umpires: V.K. Ramaswamy, S.J. Woodward.

Toss: Pakistan. Points: Pakistan 4, Sri Lanka 0

GROUP B: ENGLAND vs WEST INDIES
MUNICIPAL STADIUM, GUJRANWALA: ENGLAND WON BY 2 WICKETS

Limited-overs cricket is almost designed to provide exciting finishes. This fluctuating encounter in a small ground rarely used in international cricket was one of two absolute thrillers played on the first Friday of the tournament. England won in unlikely fashion from the third ball of the last over of the match, condemning the West Indies to their second consecutive World Cup defeat. As this loss followed their poor performances in Australia there was no doubt that for the first time in many years the West Indies were not an insurmountable force.

Not that they really should have lost this match. An English middle-order collapse left them needing 34 runs with two wickets left from the last three overs. Unbelievably, Courtney Walsh cracked and Allan Lamb hit England home.

For those making the 130-kilometre journey from Lahore it was an early start on the road to Gujranwala—5 am for some to make the impressive Municipal Stadium on time. By the start of play a healthy neutral crowd was in. Soon the heat, pollution and humidity of the holiday Friday would affect the players of both sides as they strove to gain ascendancy. The wicket, bare apart from an occasional tuft of grass, was so hard the umpires had trouble getting the stumps into it. There was no chance it would deteriorate, so Mike Gatting had no problem with sending the opposition in to bat after he won the toss.

His bowlers were the ones with problems. They were sweating so profusely they struggled to find a dry spot on their whites to shine the ball. Nevertheless, Phil DeFreitas soon got through Carlisle Best with the new ball. His partner and fellow Barbadian, Desmond Haynes, was also subdued taking 18 overs to make 19 before being run out by a diving John Emburey who made good a wayward throw from Chris Broad.

The West Indian total was 2–53 by then, Richie Richardson being quickly into his stride. He was joined by his captain Viv Richards who began the acceleration when he hit Derek Pringle's second and third deliveries to the boundary, both trademark on-drives. Pringle undid all the good work of DeFreitas, who was so affected by the heat he vomited in the middle of one spell, and Emburey, who bowled with impeccable control if still not taking a wicket. The Antiguans have played some awesome partnerships. This, though, would not be one of them. Neil Foster had bowled them both by the time the score was 122, Richards' dismissal, playing on a back-foot off-side drive, was almost as trademark as his boundary shots.

The loss of wickets slowed the run rate. It was 4–151 after 40 overs and Jeff Dujon and Gus Logie were concentrating on consolidation. Dujon had one lucky escape when a sweep off the back of his bat was caught by Downton only for the token appeal to be rejected. Then, as if a bell had gone for a final lap, the strokes were unleashed again. The bowlers and fielders began to wilt in the Gujranwala heat. Foster, despite bowling Logie, lost control for an over and Pringle was treated like a novice.

Pringle bowled the 49th over of the innings to Roger Harper. Chris Broad at mid-off failed to stop the first ball going through his legs for four. Two balls later Harper smacked him for six over the leg side and hit two more boundaries, one off a no-ball to third man and the other straight past the bowler. The over cost 22. Nine more runs for the wicket of Harper were contrived from Gladstone Small in the 50th over, to leave England a target of 244 for victory. Ninety-two had come from the final 10 overs.

The heat of the day was at its fiercest as England began their chase. Broad did not have to suffer it for long. Courtney Walsh quickly had him caught behind. Tim Robinson was also making little headway when Harper ran him out in the 17th over. It was another astonishing display of the Guyanan's fielding talents. Immediately upon his arrival Gatting added some urgency to the batting. His aggression infected Gooch and the runs began to flow freely from the pacemen, who were as badly affected by the heat as their English counterparts.

Gooch and Gatting added 58 in nine overs to put their team in a strong position. Then within four balls they undid all their good work. Not for the first time, Carl Hooper benefited from the batsmen relaxing mentally after having seen off the fast-bowling threat. Now, sending down medium pacers he had developed while playing club cricket in Melbourne, Hooper had Gatting dancing over and around a straight ball and

Gooch chasing a wide delivery. Allan Lamb looked out of sorts and Pringle hit the ball with about 10 per cent of the power that had been dealt out to him. Paul Downton was run out after Lamb turned down a call for a leg bye. The wicketkeeper gave up the cause when he might have made his ground. That mix-up left England 6–131 from 37 overs, a long way from their objective.

Emburey is credited with kick-starting the innings again. His ungainly whacking brought him 22 runs in 13 balls, including a flat pull for a straight six off Patrick Patterson. Ninety-one runs were still needed from 10 overs and an attempt at another six saw Patterson knock back Emburey's leg-stump. With Lamb pushing singles, DeFreitas took over Emburey's role and hit 23 from five overs. From the last ball of the 47th over he also emulated the off spinner's dismissal so when Foster joined Lamb the equation was 34 from three overs.

It looked an unlikely proposition, but Walsh was really suffering now and Lamb had set a personal precedent some months before in Australia when he took 18 runs from the final Bruce Reid over to win a World Series Cup match. He took 15 from the tiring Jamaican's six deliveries. Patterson conceded just six from the 49th over, allowing Walsh 13 runs to play with in the last.

Lamb scored two from the first ball, then slip drove the second, a full toss, for four to third man. The third delivery was meant to follow Lamb as he stepped away to hit the ball through the gaps in the off side. Walsh overcompensated and the ball shot past Dujon down the leg side to the boundary for four wides. Walsh's next ball was a no-ball and Lamb took the single on offer. It was down to two runs from four balls. Only one was needed. Foster moved down the wicket, played another cultured slip drive and the ball went away for the four that won the match for England.

Walsh bent over, distraught and tearful, his hands on his knees. The future captain, taker of more than 400 Test wickets and possibly most level-headed member of the side had conceded 29 runs from his last nine balls. Derek Pringle would have been sympathetic. Lamb finished on 67 from 68 balls. He too was exhausted, had to be helped from the ground and later said he

would not have lasted another over. He won the Man of the Match award.

WEST INDIES

D.L. Haynes run out	19
C.A. Best b DeFreitas	5
R.B. Richardson b Foster	53
I.V.A. Richards (capt) b Foster	27
P.J.L. Dujon (wk) run out	46
A.L. Logie b Foster	49
R.A. Harper b Small	24
C.L. Hooper not out	1
W.K.M. Benjamin not out	7
Extras (lb 9, nb 3)	12
(50 overs)	7–243

Did not bat: C.A. Walsh, B.P. Patterson

1/8 2/53 3/105 4/122 5/205 6/235 7/235

Bowling: DeFreitas 10–2–31–1; Foster 10–0–53–3; Emburey 10–2–22–0; Small 10–0–45–1; Pringle 10–0–83–0

ENGLAND

G.A. Gooch c Dujon b Hooper	47
B.C. Broad c Dujon b Walsh	3
R.T. Robinson run out	12
M.W. Gatting (capt) b Hooper	25
A.J. Lamb not out	67
D.R. Pringle c Best b Hooper	12
P.R. Downton (wk) run out	3
J.E. Emburey b Patterson	22
P.A.J. DeFreitas b Patterson	23
N.A. Foster not out	9
Extras (lb 14, w 6, nb 3)	23
(49.3 overs)	8–246

Did not bat: G.C. Small

1/14 2/40 3/98 4/99 5/123 6/131 7/162 8/209

Bowling: Patterson 10–0–49–2; Walsh 9.3–0–65–1; Harper 10–0–44–0; Benjamin 10–1–32–0; Hooper 10–0–42–3

Umpires: A.R. Crafter, R.B. Gupta.

Toss: England. Points: England 4, West Indies 0

GROUP A: INDIA vs AUSTRALIA
CHEPAUK GROUND: MADRAS (CHENNAI): AUSTRALIA WON BY 1 RUN

In contrast to their celebrating rivals across the western frontier, India had to suffer an agonising single-run defeat as their World Cup defence got under way. The sight of Maninder Singh's off stump cartwheeling out of the ground with two runs needed for victory stunned the capacity crowd into silence, but sent the Australian party into raptures. It was another magnificent match with a finish that was loaded with coincidence. Almost exactly a year earlier a game on the same ground between the same two countries had ended in Test cricket's second tie. The last batsman dismissed in that emotional cauldron was also Maninder Singh.

The heat in Madras was no less forgiving than that in Gujranwala when Kapil Dev won the toss and told Allan Border his side could take the 9 am batting start. The early-morning dew which prompted the decision of the Indian captain had no apparent slowing effect on the batting of Geoff Marsh and David Boon. They launched the Australian innings in very impressive fashion, raising 110 runs in 25 overs, until Ravi Shastri had Boon lbw with the Tasmanian one short of

his 50. Boon didn't agree with umpire Dave Archer's decision and discussed it heatedly with a few Indian players on his way out.

Dean Jones lifted the run tempo even further. He attacked the bowling from the moment of his arrival and dominated the 64-run partnership with the reliable Marsh. His 35-ball innings included several big hits, one of which was changed from a four to a six by Hanif Mohammad, the match adjudicator, during the lunch break. That became a far more significant event in retrospect than it seemed at the time. After Jones had fallen to the spin of Maninder Singh, Marsh and Allan Border lifted the total beyond 200 by the 40th over. A massive score loomed, but the Australian middle order stumbled as they tried to accelerate.

Marsh fell to Manoj Prabhakar after completing his third century in Limited-Over Internationals. All three had been against India. This one, worth a Man of the Match award, had taken three and a half hours and included one six and seven fours. His stamina in the hot airless stadium while facing 141 deliveries was phenomenal. When Simon O'Donnell was run out from the last ball of the innings Australia had set India 271 to win.

Sunil Gavaskar began as if reaching that requirement was the simplest thing in the world. His strokeplay delighted Henry Blofeld, who called Gavaskar's back-foot drive off Craig McDermott's first over 'The stroke of the year'. McDermott's third over contained three more boundaries, a drive through mid wicket, a square cut and a square drive. Off spinner Peter Taylor came on for the 10th over of the innings. Gavaskar sweetly drove his first ball over mid-off for four and in his second over the little Indian champion swatted Taylor back over his head for a big six. Fifty thousand supporters roared as one. In the same over Taylor had a modicum of revenge when Gavaskar holed out to Bruce Reid. India, through the efforts of the same man who once batted through 60 overs for 36 runs, had got away to a flying 69 in 12 overs.

Kris Srikkanth and Limited-Overs International debutant Navjot Singh Sidhu took up where Gavaskar left off, continuing to trade in fours and sixes. Sidhu, in sensational form, hit five balls over the boundary. Three of those were big drives off the suffering Taylor. He and Srikkanth added a further 52 and then Dilip Vengsarkar stayed with the debutant until the score reached 207. They added 76 in 11 overs and India were cruising, needing 64 more runs in 13 overs with eight wickets standing.

McDermott had conceded 31 in his first four overs. Now he yorked Sidhu and bowled Mohammad Azharuddin slogging across the line. Vengsarkar was caught at mid-on and Shastri offered a simple caught and bowled to the Queenslander.

Despite the Australian comeback the equation still got down to 15 runs from four overs with four wickets standing. In 1983 the outcome would have been obvious. However, this Australian side had maintained its standards in the field and would not relent.

Jones and Border ran out Roger Binny and Prabhakar respectively with direct hits. When the last over started Maninder and Kiran More needed to score six more runs for the final wicket. Twenty-two-year-old Steve Waugh, building his reputation as the 'iceman' in tight finishes, was given the responsibility of bowling the 50th over. Maninder got two to fine leg from the first ball and two more to third man from the third ball. He tried to win it from the fifth with a big drive. The clatter of timber was followed by the silence of 50,000 spectators.

Australia celebrated after the match at the Taj Coromandel Hotel in a fashion so enthusiastic

AUSTRALIA

D.C. Boon lbw Shastri	49
G.R. Marsh c Azahruddin b Prabhakar	110
D.M. Jones c Sidhu b Maninder Singh	39
A.R. Border (capt) b Binny	16
T.M. Moody c Kapil Dev b Prabhakar	8
S.R. Waugh not out	19
S.P. O'Donnell run out	7
Extras (lb 18, w 2, nb 2)	22
(50 overs)	6–270

Did not bat: G.C. Dyer (wk), P.L. Taylor, C.J. McDermott, B.A. Reid

1/110 2/174 3/228 4/237 5/251 6/270

Bowling: Kapil Dev 10–0–41–0; Prabhakar 10–0–47–2; Binny 7–0–46–1; Maninder Singh 10–0–48–1; Shastri 10–0–50–1; Azharuddin 3–0–20–0

INDIA

S.M. Gavaskar c Reid b Taylor	37
K. Srikkanth lbw Waugh	70
N.S. Sidhu b McDermott	73
D.B. Vengsarkar c Jones b McDermott	29
M. Azharuddin b McDermott	10
Kapil Dev (capt) c Boon b O'Donnell	6
R.J. Shastri c & b McDermott	12
K.S. More (wk) not out	12
R.M.H. Binny run out	0
M. Prabhakar run out	5
Maninder Singh b Waugh	4
Extras (lb 7, b 2, w 2)	11
(49.5 overs)	269

1/69 2/131 3/207 4/229 5/232 6/246 7/256 8/256 9/265 10/269

Bowling: McDermott 10–0–56–4; Reid 10–0–35–0; O'Donnell 9–1–32–1; Taylor 5–0–46–1; Waugh 9.5–0–52–2; Border 6–0–39–0

Umpires: D.M. Archer, H.D. Bird.

Toss: India. Points: Australia 4, India 0

they might have won the whole tournament in one game. Expatriate Australians turned up from everywhere in the hotel lobby to share in the success. Border's team had been strongly motivated by Zaheer Abbas' newspaper call that the Australians were no better than 'a schoolboy side'. They had also developed a bit of niggling rivalry with India in recent times and were well prepared by their coach Bobby Simpson. This was not a reverse of the upset that befell Australia in 1983, but it did give them some real momentum, not unlike India's win over the West Indies in Round One of the last Prudential Cup.

GROUP A: NEW ZEALAND vs ZIMBABWE
FATEH MAIDAN, HYDERABAD: NEW ZEALAND WON BY 3 RUNS

The Saturday fixture of the first round provided a match the equal of the two last-over thrillers played on the Friday. Hyderabad could hardly boast it was hosting the feature event of the tournament. However, there would be no complaints about the Saturday-afternoon entertainment put on by the New Zealanders and Zimbabweans.

New Zealand tried to shore up their limited resources by opening with Martin Snedden after John Traicos had won the toss and sent them in to bat. At the first time of asking it proved a real success. Taking the opportunity to exploit the open spaces while the fieldsmen were kept up close by the restrictive circle, Snedden used his ungainly left-handed technique to pinch hit some early runs. He scored the majority of a 59 opening stand with John Wright and then helped his side to an impressive 1–143 in partnership with the stylish Martin Crowe.

Peter Rawson finally ended Snedden's 95-ball escapade and his 84-run stand with Crowe. John Traicos then applied the brakes to the New Zealand scoring. He choked off Crowe's run flow and wickets began to fall. Once Snedden had gone the Kiwis only added a further 99 for the rest of the innings. Their final total of 7–242 looked no better than par for the course.

It seemed much better than that once Snedden and Ewan Chatfield began to knock over the Zimbabwean top order. The openers Robin Brown and Ali Shah were removed with only 10 on the board. Andy Pycroft stayed with Dave Houghton for a 51-run stand until suffering a recurrence of the 1983 run-out disease and six runs later Willie Watson dismissed the dangerous Kevin Curran.

The wickets continued to tumble to Watson and left-arm spinner Stephen Boock, so that in the 23rd over Zimbabwe were an inglorious 7–104. The curly haired wicketkeeper-batsman Houghton was unbeaten and had reached an accomplished fifty in 62 balls with his second driven six off John Bracewell. He was joined by Iain Butchart, who was capable, but not more so than those who had come before him. In the next 20 overs Butchart showed his team-mates how to support a batsman in prime form.

Houghton was racing towards his 100, taking runs at will from an attack that had lost its earlier edge. Another six, this time a pull from off spinner Dipak Patel, took him to 80. Soon after he swept Boock for four to bring him his worthy 100 in 107 balls out of 156. By the 40th over the target was a far more accessible 69 runs. A chance to long-off allowed Houghton to continue his heroic assault. He faced Snedden at the start of the 47th over with 36 runs still required. Four balls later and the target was 22. Houghton hit three leg-side boundaries and a straight drive for two then lofted the fifth ball over mid-on. Martin Crowe turned, ran and at full stretch held what was acknowledged as the catch of the tournament.

Eddo Brandes was immediately run out. Butchart passed his 50 and he and Traicos took the game into the final over when, like India's last-wicket pair, six runs had to be squeezed out. They had only made two of those by the fourth ball. A big swing by Butchart missed, the ball hit his pad, there was confusion and the all-rounder was run out. His side's brave revival failed by just three runs. Dave Houghton's 141 runs and one stone loss of weight in the heat had been in vain. The Man of the Match award was his sole consolation.

NEW ZEALAND

M.C. Snedden c Waller b Rawson	64
J.G. Wright c Houghton b Traicos	17
M.D. Crowe c & b Rawson	72
A.H. Jones c Brandes b Shah	0
J.J. Crowe (capt) c Brown b Curran	31
D.N. Patel b Ali Shah	0
J.G. Bracewell not out	13
I.D.S. Smith (wk) c Brown b Curran	29
S.L. Boock not out	0
Extras (b 4, lb 5, w 4, nb 3)	16
(50 overs)	7-242

Did not bat: W. Watson, E.J. Chatfield

1/59 2/143 3/145 4/166 5/169 6/205 7/240

Bowling: Curran 10-0-51-2; Rawson 10-0-62-2; Brandes 7-2-23-0; Traicos 10-2-28-1; Butchart 4-0-27-0; Ali Shah 9-0-42-2

ZIMBABWE

R.D. Brown c J.J. Crowe b Chatfield	1
A.H. Shah lbw Snedden	5
D.L. Houghton (wk) c M.D. Crowe b Snedden	141
A.J. Pycroft run out	12
K.M. Curran c Boock b Watson	4
A.C. Waller c Smith b Watson	5
G.A. Paterson c Smith b Boock	2
P.W.E. Rawson lbw Boock	1
I.P. Butchart run out	54
E.A. Brandes run out	0
A.J. Traicos (capt) not out	4
Extras (lb 8, w 1, nb 1)	10
(49.4 overs)	239

1/8 2/10 3/61 4/67 5/86 6/94 7/104 8/221 9/221 10/239

Bowling: Chatfield 10-2-26-1; Snedden 9-0-53-2; Watson 10-2-36-2; Bracewell 7-0-47-0; Patel 5-0-27-0; Boock 8.4-0-42-2

Umpires: Mahboob Shah, P.W. Vidanagamage.

Toss: Zimbabwe. Points: New Zealand 4, Zimbabwe 0

TUESDAY 13 OCTOBER and WEDNESDAY 14 OCTOBER 1987
THE RELIANCE CUP: ROUND TWO
GROUP B: ENGLAND vs PAKISTAN
CLUB GROUND, RAWALPINDI: PAKISTAN WON BY 18 RUNS

Originally scheduled for the Monday, this match was postponed after a downpour left the outfield saturated. The England management complained at the early abandonment, but should have been more unhappy with the late batting panic that cost them the match the next day when it appeared they would win.

They had no excuses. Mike Gatting won the toss and asked Pakistan to bat when the outfield was still damp and slow. He had beaten Javed Miandad rather than Imran Khan at the call of the coin. The Pakistani captain was suffering from food poisoning and although he batted, he was not fit to bowl.

At the home of the Pakistani President, General Zia, half an hour away from the Presidential Palace in Islamabad, England put on an early fielding display unfit to show any spectator, let alone a powerful military leader. While their bowlers tried to take advantage of helpful conditions two straightforward catches were missed. Gladstone Small and Derek Pringle moved the new ball around and Neil Foster quickly had

Mansoor Akhtar edging to the keeper. Rameez Raja and Salim Malik took some advantage of the fielding lapses before Chris Broad drilled a direct-hit throw from mid-off to run out Rameez at the bowler's end.

Salim, playing to win, and Javed had to work hard to add a further 61 runs. They lasted until the 31st over when Australian umpire Tony Crafter gave Javed out lbw to Phil DeFreitas. This was a rare form of dismissal for Javed in Pakistan and he quickly showed his dislike for it, indicating that he had been struck above the pad. He dwelt at the crease for some time and found that the gathered English players were advising him where he could find the pavilion. Javed raised his bat at Gatting in a repeat of his 1981 anti-Dennis Lillee pose before Bill Athey, on the field as a substitute, finally ushered him gently away in the direction Crafter had originally intended.

Pakistan was still struggling when the ailing Imran came in at 4-123 two overs after the Javed incident. He held firm, in more ways than one, while Ijaz Ahmed attacked. The youngster scored his 59 at a run a ball and hit a six and six fours. He nearly cleaned up Gatting with the bat when it slipped from his hands playing a sweep and flew out to square leg. The fifth-wicket pair added 79, lifting the total beyond 200. Both were dismissed by Gladstone Small, Imran leaving the ground and going straight back to bed.

John Emburey began the final over of the innings with figures of 0–36 from nine overs. The total was a manageable 7–224. Six balls later Pakistan was 15 runs better off. Abdul Qadir hit a four and a straight six and Pakistan, so long struggling with their run rate, had somehow finished with a competitive 239.

Graham Gooch and Broad launched the England reply with a solid opening of 52 in 14 overs. Neither of the two left-arm pacemen, Wasim Akram and Salim Jaffer, could make the breakthrough. It was left to Qadir, his confidence already high, to bowl Gooch. Broad struggled once Qadir and off spinner Tauseef were working in tandem. He and Robinson added a further 40 runs, but when the left-hander was bowled by Tauseef half England's quota of overs had been consumed and they were still 148 runs from their target.

Even though Gatting injected the batting with some greater urgency, Robinson was still slug-gish and the runs per over requirement was kept constantly around seven rather than being reduced. Finally the Nottinghamshire opener's 21-over vigil ended when he hit out at Qadir and was bowled. Lamb's entrance heralded a change in the game's tempo. He and his captain silenced the large crowd with some vigorous strokeplay and daring running between wickets. Gatting was stranded mid-pitch in the 42nd over only for Mansoor Akhtar's throw to miss the stumps at the bowler's end. Next ball Lamb had to dive back to regain his ground to avoid being run out.

Fifty-four runs were needed from eight overs when Gatting stepped right away from his stumps to hit Salim Jaffer through the off-side and was bowled. The English press groaned at their captain's misjudgment. Later Martin Johnson would blame Gatting's stroke for setting England on the road to defeat. However, there was no immediate sign that it would prove to be so costly. Lamb and Pringle reduced the equation to 34 runs from four overs with six wickets standing. A tight finish seemed in prospect. Sixteen balls later the match was over.

Lamb fell lbw trying to sweep Qadir, Emburey did sweep but was run out going for a second run, Paul Downton swept also, only to top-edge a catch to the keeper Salim Yousuf. Three wickets had fallen in four balls and

PAKISTAN

Mansoor Akhtar c Downton b Foster	6
Rameez Raja run out	15
Salim Malik c Downton b DeFreitas	65
Javed Miandad lbw DeFreitas	23
Ijaz Ahmed c Robinson b Small	59
Imran Khan (capt) b Small	22
Wasim Akram b DeFreitas	5
Salim Yousuf (wk) not out	16
Abdul Qadir not out	12
Extras (lb 10, w 3, nb 3)	16
(50 overs)	7–239

Did not bat: Tauseef Ahmed, Salim Jaffer

1/13 2/51 3/112 4/123 5/202 6/210 7/210

Bowling: DeFreitas 10–1–42–3; Foster 10–1–35–1; Small 10–1–47–2; Pringle 10–0–54–0; Emburey 10–0–51–0

ENGLAND

G.A. Gooch b Abdul Qadir	21
B.C. Broad b Tauseef Ahmed	36
R.T. Robinson b Abdul Qadir	33
M.W. Gatting (capt) b Salim Jaffer	43
A.J. Lamb lbw Qadir	30
D.R. Pringle run out	8
J.E. Emburey run out	1
P.R. Downton (wk) c Salim Yousuf b Abdul Qadir	0
P.A.J. DeFreitas not out	3
N.A. Foster run out	6
G.C. Small lbw Salim Jaffer	0
Extras (b 6, lb 26, w 8)	40
(48.4 overs)	221

1/52 2/92 3/141 4/186 5/206 6/207 7/207 8/213 9/221 10/221

Bowling: Wasim Akram 9–0–32–0; Salim Jaffer 9.4–0–42–2; Tauseef Ahmed 10–0–39–1; Abdul Qadir 10–0–31–4; Salim Malik 7–0–29–0; Mansoor Akhtar 3–0–16–0

Umpires: A.R. Crafter, R.B. Gupta.

Toss: England. Points: Pakistan 4, England 0

England had slipped from 4–206 to 7–207. The three England fast bowlers, caught up in the frenzy, hit and dived around the place which resulted in two more run-outs and an lbw from a full toss to wrap up the match. Pakistan, who had suffered all those disappointments against England in the Prudential World Cups, were thrilled that their opponents could also panic when under the pressure of closing overs. Abdul Qadir added to the local joy by being named Man of the Match. General Zia enjoyed the result. He gave the Pakistani players a cheque for 100,000 rupees as a sign of gratitude for the win.

GROUP B: SRI LANKA vs WEST INDIES
NATIONAL STADIUM, KARACHI: WEST INDIES WON BY 191 RUNS

The West Indian captain, Viv Richards, was probably very annoyed by his side's narrow loss against England. Four days later he found the perfect way to exorcise his frustration; beat an innocuous Sri Lankan attack into utter submission. In 125 scintillating balls he put Kapil Dev's remarkable 175 at Tunbridge Wells in the previous Prudential Cup into second place on the list of highest-ever World Cup scores. He added 182 with Desmond Haynes for the third wicket and 116 with Gus Logie for the fourth. Despite the reduction in this tournament of each innings to 50 overs, the West Indies made 4–360, at the time the highest-ever World Cup total.

In a match scheduled for Tuesday and played on Tuesday, Duleep Mendis gave his opposite number first use of the wicket in the National Stadium in front of the smallest crowd of the tournament. When Ravi Ratnayake bowled Carlisle Best and then had Richie Richardson caught behind first ball Mendis must have nodded his head in self-approval. Later there might have been greater regret.

Richards joined Haynes at 2–45. The West Indian captain avoided the hat-trick then took control. He and Haynes used commonsense at first to ensure the Sri Lankans were kept at bay. Once their position was established they let loose and the Sri Lankans lost all semblance of control. Richards reached his first 50 in 62 balls, 35 balls later he was celebrating his century. Still the mayhem continued, along the ground or in the air. Richards was unerring in his ability to strike the ball with immense power right off the middle, although he ensured the majority of his strokes were played with a straight bat. Ratnayake conceded 44 runs in two overs.

Ashantha de Mel, so effective in England, was treated with contempt, 97 runs flowed during his 10-over stint.

Overshadowed by his captain's innings, Haynes reached his own hundred at almost a run per ball. When Asanka Gurusinha finally bowled him, the Barbadian had hit one six and nine fours. His partnership with Richards had taken 177 balls. The stand between Richards and Logie lasted less than an hour. Logie gave his captain the strike and Richards raced from 100 to 150 in just 15 balls. Finally, going for his seventh six, the Antiguan holed out to Roshan Mahanama. His final 81 runs had come from just 33 deliveries. In addition to his six sixes Richards had struck 16 wonderful fours.

Sri Lanka needed 7.2 runs per over to win. As if to continue the theme of the day, Mahanama and Brendon Kuruppu hit 24 runs from the first eight balls of the innings. When Mahanama was caught behind from Courtney Walsh's third ball Sri Lanka's charge ceased. They slipped to 3–57 and then opted for batting practice. Richards thought to save his main bowlers for more important contests so that even Richardson bowled some overs. Off spinner Roger Harper conceded 1.5 runs per over during his stint. The futility of limited-overs matches when one side gives up was again in evidence during much of the Sri Lankan innings. Richards' display was something special, but it ruined the second half of the game. The West Indian captain was made Man of the Match.

WEST INDIES	
D.L. Haynes b Gurusinha	105
C.A. Best b Ratnayake	18
R.B. Richardson c Kuruppu b Ratnayake	0
I.V.A. Richards (capt) c Mahanama b de Mel	181
A.L. Logie not out	31
R.A. Harper not out	5
Extras (b 4, lb 8, w 4, nb 4)	20
(50 overs)	4–360

Did not bat: P.J.L. Dujon (wk), C.L. Hooper, W.K.M. Benjamin, C.A. Walsh, B.P. Patterson

1/45 2/45 3/227 4/343

Bowling: John 10–1–48–0; Ratnayake 8–0–68–2; Anurasiri 10–0–39–0; de Mel 10–0–97–1; de Silva 6–0–35–0; Ranatunga 2–0–18–0; Gurusinha 4–0–43–1

SRI LANKA	
R.S. Mahanama c Dujon b Walsh	12
D.S.B.P. Kuruppu (wk) lbw Patterson	14
A.P. Gurusinha b Hooper	36
P.A. de Silva c Dujon b Hooper	9
A. Ranatunga not out	52
L.R.D. Mendis (capt) not out	37
Extras (b 1, lb 2, w 6)	9
(50 overs)	4–169

Did not bat: R.S. Madugalle, J.R. Ratnayake, A.L.F. de Mel, V.B. John, S.D. Anurasiri

1/24 2/31 3/57 4/112

Bowling: Patterson 7–0–32–1; Walsh 7–0–23–1; Harper 10–2–15–0; Benjamin 4–0–11–0; Hooper 10–0–39–2; Richards 8–0–22–0; Richardson 4–0–22–0

Umpires: V.K. Ramaswamy, S.J. Woodward.

Toss: Sri Lanka. Points: West Indies 4, Sri Lanka 0

GROUP A: AUSTRALIA vs ZIMBABWE
CHEPAUK GROUND, MADRAS (CHENNAI): AUSTRALIA WON BY 96 RUNS

Talk prior to this match centred on the possibility of Zimbabwe repeating their shock victory from the opening round in 1983. It was not to be. Australia were a totally different outfit from the rabble of four years before and had no trouble in comfortably accounting for Zimbabwe.

Not only did Australia play on the same arena where they had beaten India on the previous Friday, but they were sent in to bat by John Traicos on exactly the same wicket. Again the early start offered the bowlers morning moisture and Kevin Curran quickly had David Boon caught behind. Ten runs later it was 2–20 when Dean Jones for once over-estimated his admittedly gazelle-like running ability. Then in the next over left-arm debutant Malcolm Jarvis dropped a dollied caught and bowled chance from Allan Border who was on 1.

Border was too fine a player to not take advantage of such a let-off. With the reliable and in-form Geoff Marsh he put on 113 in 20 overs. The left-handed Australian captain repeatedly punched the ball through the on side as the Zimbabwean bowling drifted on to his pads. He faced 88 balls and passed 4000 runs in Limited-Over Internationals before being caught in the deep off Iain Butchart. Geoff Marsh and Simon O'Donnell fell soon after, then wicketkeeper

Greg Dyer and Steve Waugh rallied the cause with a well-timed 47-run stand. Waugh finished with 45 in 40 balls before becoming the third of four run-out victims. A few runs from Peter Taylor at the end of the innings lifted Australia to 9–235 from their 50 overs.

That was almost the total Zimbabwe had set Australia at Trent Bridge in 1983. Then it proved just enough. This time, on a wicket of variable bounce, it was enough with plenty to spare. The opening partnership between Grant Paterson and Robin Brown realised 13 runs in nine overs. O'Donnell bowled Brown as soon as he came on, Paterson was run out and so, almost inevitably, was Andy Pycroft. Kevin Curran, fighting all the way, top-scored, but he became the second of O'Donnell's four victims. Debutant Tim May's off spin was more rewarding than Peter Taylor's. When the South Australian picked up a couple of wickets, including Hyderabad hero Dave Houghton, Zimbabwe were quickly sliding to defeat. They were able to hang on until the 43rd over, however their run rate was barely above three an over when it needed to be at least four and a half. Traicos used the captain's prerogative and promoted himself from 11 to 10 in the batting order. It made no difference. Craig

McDermott and Steve Waugh shared 13 overs and conceded just 20 runs between them.

Waugh's all-round effort won him the Man of the Match award.

AUSTRALIA

G.R. Marsh c Curran b Ali Shah		62
D.C. Boon c Houghton b Curran		2
D.M. Jones run out		2
A.R. Border (capt) c Ali Shah b Butchart		67
S.R. Waugh run out		45
S.P. O'Donnell run out		3
G.C. Dyer (wk) c Paterson b Butchart		27
P.L. Taylor not out		17
C.J. McDermott c Brown b Curran		1
T.B.A. May run out		1
Extras (w 8)		8
(50 overs)		9–235

Did not bat: B.A. Reid

1/10 2/20 3/133 4/143 5/155 6/202 7/228 8/230 9/235

Bowling: Curran 8-0-29-2; Jarvis 10-0-40-0; Rawson 6-0-39-0; Butchart 10-1-59-2; Traicos 10-0-36-0; Ali Shah 6-0-32-1

ZIMBABWE

R.D. Brown b O'Donnell		3
G.A. Paterson run out		16
D.L. Houghton (wk) c O'Donnell b May		11
A.J. Pycroft run out		9
K.M. Curran b O'Donnell		30
A.C. Waller c & b May		19
A.H. Shah b McDermott		2
P.W.E. Rawson b Reid		15
I.P. Butchart c Jones b O'Donnell		18
A.J. Traicos (capt) c & b O'Donnell		6
M.P. Jarvis not out		1
Extras (b 2, lb 3, w 3, nb 1)		9
(42.4 overs)		139

1/13 2/27 3/41 4/44 5/79 6/97 7/97 8/124 9/137 10/139

Bowling: McDermott 7-1-13-1; Reid 7-1-21-1; O'Donnell 9.4-1-39-4; Waugh 6-3-7-0; May 8-0-29-2; Taylor 5-0-25-0

Umpires: Khizar Hayat, D.R. Shepherd.

Toss: Zimbabwe. Points: Australia 4, Zimbabwe 0

GROUP A: INDIA vs NEW ZEALAND
KARNATAKA STATE C.A. GROUND, BANGALORE: INDIA WON BY 16 RUNS

India left Australia and their disappointing defeat at Madras behind and travelled west into the hills to meet New Zealand at Bangalore. They had another 50,000 supporters in the ground to noisily urge them on and this time the fans did not go home disappointed.

The result of this Wednesday match of Round Two was seen as crucial to the fate of both sides. India could hardly afford to go down a second time, while New Zealand were lucky to get away with a win over Zimbabwe and had to convince punters of their viability as a finals prospect.

After Jeff Crowe had won the toss and sent India in to bat, Kris Srikkanth convinced everyone of his suitability as a mental asylum patient when he ran out Sunil Gavaskar and then himself in the opening overs of the match. Again the early start meant the outfield was slow when India began their innings. With the bounce in the wicket inconsistent the top order stressed itself. Srikkanth, who was coasting up the pitch when Ken Rutherford threw down the stumps, had committed his double kamikaze by the eighth

over. Two overs and five runs later Dilip Vengsarkar checked a drive and hit the ball straight back to Willie Watson. India were teetering at 3–21.

Navjot Sidhu led the recovery. Uninhibited in his strokeplay as he had been at Madras, the young Sikh dominated a 65-run stand with Mohammad Azharuddin, no mean feat in itself. A sweet straight drive off left-arm spinner Stephen Boock was one of four sixes struck by Sidhu in 71 balls. Each one brought a big roar from the crowd, but they went as quiet as they had been during the early collapse, when Dipak Patel started to eat his way through the Indian middle order. The off-spinning Kenyan, recruited by New Zealand from Worcestershire, dismissed Azharuddin, Sidhu and Ravi Shastri to leave India a still-precarious 7–170 from 42 overs.

Kapil Dev, in his best Tunbridge Wells trance-like state, and Kiran More had eight overs to try and raise a worthy target. They got 82 in 51 balls. Kapil went to 72 in 58 balls with one six and four fours. Again there were fireworks, literally, the 50,000 being reasonably satisfied with a total of 252.

Unlike India, New Zealand got away to a good start. Rutherford had come in to open in place of John Wright, suffering from influenza. He batted well and Martin Snedden once more proved to be of value as a restrained pinch-hitter. Even when Martin Crowe was drawn out of his crease by Maninder Singh and controversially given out stumped by West Indian umpire Dave Archer, the Kiwis kept in touch. Rutherford and Andrew Jones took them to 2–146. However, the spin trio of Maninder, Laxman Shivaramak-

rishnan and Ravi Shastri, who all turned away from the right-hander, kept the runs in check.

Eventually that meant too many were required from too few overs. Batting had to become more reckless, which led to rash shots and run-outs. Of the last six batsmen who made it to the crease, only wicketkeeper Ian Smith got into double figures. New Zealand were within 16 runs of their requirement. It was an effort of respectability, not one that looked like upsetting the cheering crowd. The charismatic Kapil Dev won the Man of the Match award for his important captain's innings.

INDIA	
K. Srikkanth run out	9
S.M. Gavaskar run out	2
N.S. Sidhu c Jones b Patel	75
D.B. Vengsarkar c & b Watson	0
M. Azharuddin c Boock b Patel	21
R.J. Shastri c & b Patel	22
Kapil Dev (capt) not out	72
M. Prabhakar c & b Chatfield	3
K.S. More (wk) not out	42
Extras (lb 4, w 2)	6
(50 overs)	7–252

Did not bat: L. Shivaramakrishnan, Maninder Singh

1/11 2/16 3/21 4/86 5/114 6/165 7/170

Bowling: Chatfield 10–1–39–1; Snedden 10–1–56–0; Watson 9–0–59–1; Boock 4–0–26–0; Bracewell 7–0–32–0; Patel 10–0–36–3

NEW ZEALAND	
M.C. Snedden c Shastri b Azharuddin	33
K.R. Rutherford c Srikkanth b Shastri	75
M.D. Crowe st More b Maninder	9
A.H. Jones run out	64
J.J. Crowe (capt) c Vengsarkar b Maninder	7
D.N. Patel run out	1
J.G. Bracewell c Maninder b Shastri	8
I.D.S. Smith (wk) b Prabhakar	10
S.L. Boock not out	7
W. Watson not out	2
Extras (b 5, lb 9, w 5, nb 1)	20
(50 overs)	8–236

Did not bat: E.J. Chatfield

1/67 2/86 3/146 4/168 5/170 6/189 7/206 8/225

Bowling: Kapil Dev 10–1–54–0; Prabhakar 8–0–38–1; Azharuddin 4–0–11–1; Shivaramakrishnan 8–0–34–0; Maninder 10–0–40–2; Shastri 10–0–45–2

Umpires: D.M. Archer, H.D. Bird.

Toss: New Zealand. Points: India 4, New Zealand 0

FRIDAY 16 OCTOBER, SATURDAY 17 OCTOBER, SUNDAY 18 OCTOBER and MONDAY 19 OCTOBER
THE RELIANCE CUP: ROUND THREE
GROUP B: PAKISTAN vs THE WEST INDIES
GADDAFI STADIUM, LAHORE: PAKISTAN WON BY 1 WICKET

On the previous Tuesday Pakistan had enjoyed laying to rest the disappointments they had suffered at the hands of England in the previous World Cups. Now, three days later, Pakistan stole the show against the West Indies, whom they also could not beat in 1975, 1979 or 1983. What is more, this was another thriller and it was the West Indies who succumbed to the

pressure of a tense finish.

Abdul Qadir emerged as a late hero by hitting a six in the final over and scoring the winning two runs from the last ball of the match. Courtney Walsh, who was again the suffering bowler, was developing into some kind of unfortunate tragic figure.

The queues had formed tightly and early.

Soon Gaddafi Stadium was filled for this clash between two of the most talented and exciting cricket teams in the world. Desmond Haynes and debutant Phil Simmons kept the crowd pretty quiet during the first part of the day with an impressive opening partnership. Neither the rehabilitated Imran Khan nor Wasim Akram could shift the in-form Barbadian or the newcomer, selected to replace Carlisle Best. Simmons hit eight fours during his run-per-ball 50 and he shared in a partnership of 91 with Haynes.

Both openers fell within six runs of each other and the rest of the West Indians struggled to build on the excellent base provided for them. Richards was an exception. He never threatened a repeat of his Karachi massacre, but batted fluently to reach another half century. When the West Indies reached 4–169 a testing total looked likely. Imran, though, showed the food poisoning had not affected his fitness and he returned to have his opposite number caught and then dismissed Roger Harper next ball. Akram also had a better second spell, securing the important wickets of Carl Hooper and Jeff Dujon. Eventually the West Indies fell three balls short of batting out their overs.

Needing 217 to win, Pakistan lost Mansoor Akhtar and Salim Malik cheaply before Rameez Raja and Javed Miandad added 64 runs for the third wicket in a struggling partnership. Harper dismissed Rameez to claim his 50th wicket in Limited-Over Internationals, Walsh bowled Ijaz Ahmed and when Carl Hooper held a catch off his own bowling six runs later to get rid of Miandad Pakistan were 5–110 from 35 overs and in deep trouble.

Imran, as he had at Rawalpindi, then played a steadying role while wicketkeeper Salim Yousuf went for his shots. He amazingly survived three chances in three balls from the luckless Eldine Baptiste before reviving his side's fortunes, dominating a 73-run stand with Imran in 11 overs. Yousuf went on to 56, the highest score in the match, in 49 balls with seven telling fours. He got his side within 21 runs of victory with four wickets in hand when Hooper finally held a chance off Walsh in the 48th over. Patrick Patterson then sent down a classic 49th over which saw Akram caught and Tauseef Ahmed run out while only two runs were conceded.

That left Qadir and Salim Jaffer with the unlikely task of hitting 14 runs from the final over for the last wicket. Walsh would have thought he had little to worry about when only two singles were scored from his first two balls. The equation was reduced to 10 runs required from three balls when Qadir launched into Walsh and hit him back down the ground and over the boundary for six. The crowd was ecstatic. Walsh and Richards now feared the worst. Qadir squeezed two more runs from the fifth ball. Two more were needed from the last ball to win the match, although one would have tied the scores and given Pakistan victory on the fewer wickets lost rule.

Walsh ran in to Qadir, who had scored all but one run from the final over so far. He arrived at the bowling crease and stopped. Jaffer was already halfway up the wicket. Walsh could have ended the match there and then with a simple flick of the wrist. Instead he warned the number 11 for his transgression and went back to bowl again. This time the ball was delivered and Qadir sliced it behind point for the two runs that gave Pakistan a wonderful victory.

Walsh's hands were on his knees again. Richards lay flat on the ground. Soon they both had to charge towards the sanctuary of the dressing-room as the invading hordes took over the arena. Qadir was their objective and without some aid he could have been trampled by the army of well-wishers. Despite the leg spinner's heroics, Salim Yousuf received the Man of the Match award. Qadir had to be satisfied with a gift worth £20,000 from a very happy and wealthy businessman.

Eden Gardens, Calcutta, 1987; Allan Border is carried aloft by his team-mates.   (Patrick Eugar)

Grahame Hick's up and down career was mirrored by his form in the 1992 World Cup. Here he is bowled by
Sri Lankan Champaka Ramanayake.   (Ballarat Courier)

Desmond Haynes, the last of the West Indian 'old guard' still making runs during the 1992 tournament.

(Murray Pioneer)

The 1992 World Cup was Ian Botham's last hurrah on the international stage. He had his moments on and off the field.

(Ballarat Courier)

Zimbabwe's 1992 campaign, like their others, was one of disappointment interspersed with an occasional highlight. Here they are on their way to heavy defeat against Australia in Hobart. (Rick Smith)

Wasim Akram takes the wicket of Allan Lamb during the 1992 World Cup final. 'One of the best balls I've ever bowled' Akram would later state. (Allsport/Adrian Murrell)

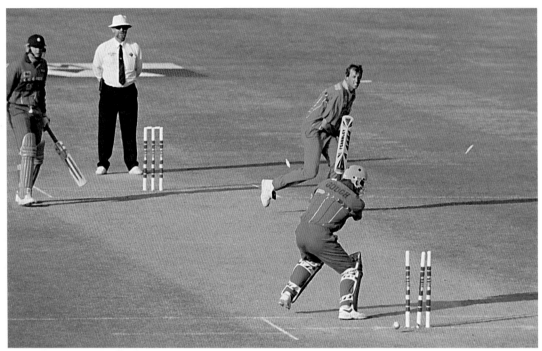

Craig Matthews bowls Darren Gough. South Africa easily won this match against the English players who struggled for form throughout the 1996 World Cup.   (Allsport/Mike Hewitt)

West Indian Shivnarine Chanderpaul in action against Australia.   (Allsport/Shaun Botterill)

WEST INDIES

D.L. Haynes b Salim Jaffer		37
P.V. Simmons c & b Tauseef Ahmed		50
R.B. Richardson c Ijaz Ahmed b Salim Jaffer		11
I.V.A. Richards (capt) c Salim Malik b Imran Khan		51
A.L. Logie c Mansoor Akhtar b Salim Jaffer		2
C.L. Hooper lbw Wasim Akram		22
P.J.L. Dujon (wk) lbw Akram		5
R.A. Harper c Mansoor Akhtar b Imran Khan		0
E.A.E. Baptiste b Imran Khan		14
C.A. Walsh lbw Imran Khan		7
B.P. Patterson not out		0
Extras (b 1, lb 14, w 2)		17
(49.3 overs)		216

1/91 2/97 3/118 4/121 5/169 6/184 7/184 8/196 9/207 10/216

Bowling: Imran Khan 8.3-2-37-4; Wasim Akram 10-0-45-2; Adbul Qadir 8-0-42-0; Tauseef 10-2-35-1; Jaffer 10-0-30-3; Salim Malik 3-0-12-0

PAKISTAN

Rameez Raja c Richards b Harper		42
Mansoor Akhtar b Patterson		10
Salim Malik c Baptiste b Walsh		4
Javed Miandad c & b Hooper		33
Ijaz Ahmed b Walsh		6
Imran Khan (capt) c Logie b Walsh		18
Salim Yousuf (wk) c Hooper b Walsh		56
Wasim Akram c Richardson b Patterson		7
Abdul Qadir not out		16
Tauseef Ahmed run out		0
Salim Jaffer not out		1
Extras (b 5, lb 12, w 7)		24
(50 overs)		9-217

1/23 2/28 3/92 4/104 5/110 6/183 7/200 8/202 9/203

Bowling: Patterson 10-1-51-2; Walsh 10-1-40-4; Baptiste 8-1-33-0; Harper 10-0-28-1; Hooper 10-0-38-1; Richards 2-0-10-0

Umpires: A.R. Crafter, S.J. Woodward.

Toss: West Indies. Points: Pakistan 4, West Indies 0

GROUP B: ENGLAND vs SRI LANKA
SHAHI BAGH STADIUM, PESHAWAR: ENGLAND WON ON FASTER SCORING RATE

The use of 21 different venues around India and Pakistan meant there was plenty of travelling to do for those involved in the 1987 Reliance Cup. Sri Lanka had to cope with more packing and travelling than anyone else, this time scooting from the southern coast of Pakistan in Karachi to Peshawar in the northwest corner of the country, near the Khyber Pass. The fatigue brought on by the constant disruption and annoyance of uncomfortable travelling may have partially accounted for Duleep Mendis' side underperforming in the tournament.

Certainly, on the Saturday of Round Three England had as much trouble with the weather as they did with the friendly bowling and tame batting of their opponents. Even as Gatting won the toss and elected to bat, thunderclouds were building up to the west of the city. Three-quarters of an hour into the contest a few big spots of rain landed on Messrs Gupta and Ramaswamy. It looked as if Graham Gooch had to convince the two umpires that it was worth staying out on the ground. Meantime he and Chris Broad were setting England up for a big score with a strong opening partnership.

Gooch was at his fluent and powerful best on a flat wicket. Broad again struggled for timing and eventually, after taking 60 balls to make 28, misjudged a slog at Ravi Ratnayake. Gatting not only changed his line-up and his habit of bowling first, he also promoted himself in the batting order to good effect. While Gooch went on to 84 in 100 balls with eight fours, Gatting clubbed and clipped his way to 58 in 63 balls.

The England captain added 76 in 12 overs with Allan Lamb to take the England innings well beyond 200 with plenty of overs to come. The ground was bathed in sunshine, but the clouds swelled and closed in. In this volatile part of the world a big clap of thunder during the lunch break had nervous patrons worrying about terrorist attacks. Outside the ground there was a political demonstration.

Indeed, the crowd in the ground was a small one, leaving plenty of room on the bare concrete terraces. They might have been entertained by the ongoing slaughter of the bowlers. Gatting was bowled by Rumesh Ratnayake to make it 3–218. Emburey came in ahead of Bill Athey and with Lamb stepped up the tempo even further. In five overs the South African and the South African 'rebel' added 66. Lamb was at his punishing best, hitting two sixes and three fours in just 58 balls. Emburey faced just 19 balls and hit a six and three fours. One hundred and one runs came from the final ten overs.

The Sri Lankans looked out of their depth and were never likely to get the 297 runs needed to win. The only real chance they had was for the match to get washed out and that remained a possibility. Another part of Peshawar was awash. If the Sri Lankan innings did not contain 25 overs the game would be declared to have 'no result' and would be started again the following day. England moved at great speed, running between overs and refusing to take drinks breaks. Sri Lanka still lost three early wickets. When Gooch completed the 25th over of the innings, everything could go back to a regular 1987 on-field pace.

Then the rains arrived and everyone beat a hasty retreat. However, there was no washout and after having their innings reduced by five overs and their target to 267 Sri Lanka resumed batting. Arjuna Ranatunga and Ranjan Madugalle put on 62 for the fourth wicket either side of the interruption. But on a wicket that stayed lower as the day wore on, neither they nor the batsmen who followed could score with the necessary energy. Emburey and fellow off spinner Eddie Hemmings conceded just 57 runs from 20 overs. Gatting even gave Bill Athey, Chris Broad and eventual Man of the Match Allan Lamb a bowl. That might have entertained the English team. Otherwise the cricket was pointless and it might have been better if the rain had returned.

ENGLAND	
G.A. Gooch c & b Anurasiri	84
B.C. Broad c de Silva b J.R. Ratnayake	28
M.W. Gatting (capt) b R.J. Ratnayake	58
A.J. Lamb c de Silva b J.R. Ratnayake	76
J.E. Emburey not out	30
C.W.J. Athey not out	2
Extras (lb 13, w 5)	18
(50 overs)	4–296

Did not bat: D.R. Pringle, P.R. Downton (wk), P.A.J. DeFreitas, E.E. Hemmings, G.C. Small

1/89 2/142 3/218 4/289

Bowling: J.R. Ratnayake 9–0–62–2; John 10–0–44–0; de Silva 7–0–33–0; R.J. Ratnayake 10–0–60–1; Anurasiri 8–0–44–1; Ranatunga 6–0–40–0

SRI LANKA	
R.S. Mahanama c Gooch b Pringle	11
D.S.B.P. Kuruppu (wk) c Hemmings b Emburey	13
A.P. Gurusinha run out	1
R.S. Madugalle b Hemmings	30
A. Ranatunga lbw DeFreitas	40
L.R.D. Mendis (capt) run out	14
P.A. de Silva c Emburey b Hemmings	6
J.R. Ratnayake c Broad b Emburey	1
R.J. Ratnayake not out	14
V.B. John not out	8
Extras (b 2, lb 9, w 6, nb 3)	20
(45 overs)	8–158

Did not bat: S.D. Anurasiri

1/31 2/32 3/37 4/99 5/105 6/113 7/119 8/137

Bowling: DeFreitas 9–2–24–1; Small 7–0–27–0; Pringle 4–0–11–1; Emburey 10–1–26–1; Hemmings 10–1–31–2; Gooch 2–0–9–0; Athey 1–0–10–0; Broad 1–0–6–0; Lamb 1–0–3–0

Umpires: R.B. Gupta, V.K. Ramaswamy.

Toss: England. Points: England 4, Sri Lanka 0

GROUP A: INDIA vs ZIMBABWE
WANKHEDE STADIUM, BOMBAY: INDIA WON BY 8 WICKETS

A clatter of wickets, a burst of runs and by 2 pm everyone could pack up and go home as India made short work of Zimbabwe in perhaps the most featureless contest of the 1987 Reliance Cup. The 22,000 who turned up at Wankhede Stadium made no complaints at being short-changed. They were gratified enough by their heroes dominance of the Africans.

John Traicos thought batting first would give his side their best chance of victory. The other four Group A matches in India had all been won by the team who had set a target. What was essential to success was that top-order wickets were not lost while there was early humidity, moisture and movement. Zimbabwe failed to achieve that prerequisite. All-rounder Manoj

Prabhakar took the new-ball, swung it appreciably and in a devastating spell claimed four wickets in 17 balls to leave Zimbabwe in tatters. Dave Houghton had quickly come down to earth, being bowled for a duck. Kevin Curran was caught behind and also failed to score.

Only Andy Pycroft stood firm. So often a disappointment, he was the sole Zimbabwean batsman to do himself justice this day. Pycroft came in at 2–12 and was last out in the 45th over after making a gallant 61 in 102 balls. He and second game left-arm seamer, Malcolm Jarvis, took the score from 9–99 to 135 before Ravi Shastri finally had Pycroft stumped. The wicket had flattened out and after Prabhakar's burst every other wicket in the match was taken by a spinner. The 10th-wicket stand of 36 was the highest of the innings. Nevertheless, Zimbabwe

had made their lowest total in World Cup competition.

It certainly made little impression on India. They wanted to lift their run rate, conscious of the fact that a strong rate might be valuable if things got tight on their group table. Sunil Gavaskar began the assignment by dealing solely in boundaries for his first 36 runs. He lasted 51 balls and put on 76 for the first wicket with Kris Srikkanth before becoming the day's third stumping victim. Traicos also removed Srikkanth and withstood the Indian onslaught well. The other bowlers were flayed and after an hour and 40 minutes India had completed their second Reliance Cup victory in the 28th over. Prabhakar, at the crease with a rampant Dilip Vengsarkar when the winning runs were scored, was named Man of the Match.

ZIMBABWE

G.A. Paterson b Prabhakar	6
K.J. Arnott lbw Prabhakar	1
D.L. Houghton (wk) b Prabhakar	0
A.J. Pycroft st More b Shastri	61
K.M. Curran c More b Prabhakar	0
A.C. Waller st More b Maninder Singh	16
I.P. Butchart c Shivaramakrishnan b Maninder Singh	10
A.H. Shah c More b Maninder Singh	0
M.A. Meman run out	19
A.J. Traicos (capt) c Gavaskar b Shivaramakrishnan	0
M.P. Jarvis not out	8
Extras (b 2, lb 6, w 6)	14
(44.2 overs)	135

1/3 2/12 3/13 4/13 5/47 6/67 7/67 8/98 9/99 10/135

Bowling: Kapil Dev 8–1–17–0; Prabhakar 8–1–19–4; Maninder Singh 10–0–21–3; Azharuddin 1–0–6–0; Shivaramakrishnan 9–0–36–1; Shastri 8.2–0–28–1

INDIA

K. Srikkanth c Paterson b Traicos	31
S.M. Gavaskar st Houghton b Traicos	43
M. Prabhakar not out	11
D.B. Vengsarkar not out	46
Extras (lb 1, w 4)	5
(27.5 overs)	2–136

Did not bat: N.S. Sidhu, M. Azharuddin, Kapil Dev (capt), R.J. Shastri, K.S. More (wk), L. Shivaramakrishnan, Maninder Singh

1/76 2/80

Bowling: Curran 6–0–32–0; Jarvis 4–0–22–0; Butchart 3–0–22–0; Traicos 8–0–27–2; Meman 6.5–0–34–0

Umpires: Mahboob Shah, D.R. Shepherd.

Toss: Zimbabwe. Points: India 4, Zimbabwe 0

GROUP A: AUSTRALIA vs NEW ZEALAND
NEHRU STADIUM, INDORE: AUSTRALIA WON BY 3 RUNS

A 30 overs per side slather-and-whack contest reached a thrilling climax from which Australia once more emerged victorious. The breakneck cricket was brought about by heavy rain, the first at Indore in October for 35 years, which flooded the ground on the Sunday and made it still unfit at the start of the Monday. Even when play began over three hours late the run-ups and outfield were very wet. New Zealand's assistant

manager Glenn Turner argued that the match should be abandoned. The day before, groundsmen had been knee-deep in water as they used picks and an assortment of other implements to clear blocked drains.

Jeff Crowe sent the Australians in to bat. Soon the in-form Geoff Marsh drove at Snedden and was caught by Crowe stationed as the sole slip. That brought together Dean Jones and

David Boon who batted with uninhibited freedom to add 117 runs in 98 balls. They reached their century stand in 11 overs and were particularly severe on off spinners John Bracewell and Dipak Patel. Boon used his feet beautifully to club Patel down the ground, while a pull sweep by Jones off Bracewell sent the ball sailing over the admittedly short mid-wicket boundary and out of the stadium. He had got off the mark by playing a reverse sweep from the same bowler.

Fieldsmen lost their footing on a few occasions, but there was never any risk of serious injury. Patel exacted a modicum of revenge when Jones, after making 52 in 49 balls, lofted a full toss to a juggling Ken Rutherford deep on the on side. Boon continued on at a run a ball to 87, when he lofted Martin Snedden straight, only for Wright to take a fine diving catch to the left of the sightscreen. The Tasmanian had added 37 with Allan Border. The captain played all sorts of strokes for 26 balls to take his side to the verge of 200 when the overs ran out. Steve Waugh, just 22 years old and already a Limited-Overs International veteran, passed the 1000-run landmark less than two years after his debut.

New Zealand's target of 200 would require 6.66 repeating runs per over. They were given a perfect start, too, by Rutherford and Wright who put on 83 in just 12 overs. Rutherford danced at Craig McDermott and cracked him over mid-on for six. He danced again at Simon O'Donnell, but failed to pick his slower ball and was bowled. O'Donnell had Wright caught behind 11 runs later, which left much of the responsibility for scoring with Martin Crowe. He responded magnificently, racing to 58 in 46 balls and shared short productive partnerships with Andrew Jones and Patel.

When the final over began Crowe was on strike and seven runs were needed with four wickets in hand. If the bowler had been the 1987 version of Courtney Walsh the Kiwi win would have been a formality. Waugh was a different proposition. He had already bowled his magical final 'iceman' over against India. He said he had

watched Kapil Dev bowling at the end of an innings for India and had learned from that champion all-rounder how to approach the pressure task.

Crowe admits he choked on the first ball, failing to decide whether to hit it straight or over the off side. The compromise was a lofted drive which swirled over cover. Geoff Marsh ran around from his off-side sweeping position and held a nicely judged running catch. 'What had I done?' Crowe lamented in his autobiography, *Out on a Limb*. He confessed that on his return to the dressing-room he put his head in his hands and sulked and that he was so distressed by his dismissal and the result that he did not bat well for the rest of the tournament.

Despite Crowe's untimely departure the game was still there to be won. Ian Smith, who had crossed with Crowe while the ball was in the air, had and would score Test centuries during a long and successful career. At Indore seven runs would have been enough to make him a hero. Waugh fired in a quick yorker. Smith played over and around the ball, which cannoned off his pads and onto his stumps. Seven runs were still needed with only four balls and two wickets left. Singles were scored from the third and fourth balls. From the fifth Willie Watson backed away and slapped the ball as hard as he could. He made contact but hit the ball straight back up the pitch to Waugh. Snedden, backing up, as he had to, had no chance of getting back. Watson needed to hit a six to win the match from the final ball. An underarm would have ensured against that. Instead, Waugh bowled straight and full and restricted Watson to a single. The Australian hero was surrounded by his teammates and submitted to bear hugs and back slaps that would have done Merv Hughes proud. Border admitted Waugh was the only one in the side who did not seem to have legs of jelly at the climax.

Since the start of play the sun had shone throughout. Now the Australians, almost certain of a semi-final berth, were basking in it. David Boon received the Man of the Match award.

AUSTRALIA

D.C. Boon c Wright b Snedden	87
G.R. Marsh c J. Crowe b Snedden	5
D.M. Jones c Rutherford b Patel	52
A.R. Border (capt) c M. Crowe b Chatfield	34
S.R. Waugh not out	13
T.M. Moody not out	0
Extras (b 1, lb 5, w 2)	8
(30 overs)	4-199

Did not bat: S.P. O'Donnell, G.C. Dyer (wk), C.J. McDermott, T.B.A. May, B.A. Reid.

1/17 2/134 3/171 4/196

Bowling: Snedden 6-0-35-2; Chatfield 6-0-28-1; Watson 6-0-34-0; Patel 6-0-45-1; Bracewell 6-0-51-0

NEW ZEALAND

K.R. Rutherford b O'Donnell	37
J.G. Wright c Dyer b O'Donnell	47
M.D. Crowe c Marsh b Waugh	58
A.H. Jones c Marsh b McDermott	15
J.J. Crowe (capt) c & b Reid	3
D.N. Patel run out	13
J.G. Bracewell c & b Reid	6
I.D.S. Smith (wk) b Waugh	1
M.C. Snedden run out	1
E.J. Chatfield not out	0
W. Watson not out	2
Extras (b 4, lb 5, w 4)	13
(30 overs)	9-196

1/83 2/94 3/133 4/140 5/165 6/183 7/193 8/193 9/195

Bowling: McDermott 6-0-30-1; Reid 6-0-38-2; May 6-0-39-0; O'Donnell 6-0-44-2; Waugh 6-0-36-2

Umpires: D.M. Archer, Khizar Hayat.

Toss: New Zealand. Points: Australia 4, New Zealand 0

TUESDAY OCTOBER 20th, WEDNESDAY OCTOBER 21st, THURSDAY OCTOBER 22nd, FRIDAY OCTOBER 23rd
RELIANCE CUP: ROUND FOUR
GROUP B: PAKISTAN vs ENGLAND
NATIONAL STADIUM, KARACHI: PAKISTAN WON BY 7 WICKETS

Pakistan celebrated a sound win over England and ensured their place in the semi-finals in front of an enthusiastic if at times badly behaved gathering at the National Stadium in Karachi.

It was a victory based around the performances of two quality bowlers, a partnership between two quality batsmen and two ill-advised sweep shots by Englishmen. The day before the game the sweeping was being done by soldiers with metal detectors which reminded everyone that the security and efficiency of the tournament could not be taken for granted. The conscientiousness of the local organisers was commendable and may have spilled over to Imran Khan who generously offered England the chance to bat first on a flat wicket on a very warm morning.

If Salim Yousuf had held an edge from Tim Robinson Imran would have made the breakthrough he sought in the first over. Instead he had to wait until Graham Gooch, after a couple of typically powerful strokes, top-edged a shovel hook to Wasim Akram, one of two fieldsmen placed for the shot, when the score was 26. Robinson struggled on without ever looking in form until in Abdul Qadir's second over his cut missed a straight top-spinner.

England were an unimpressive 2-52 when Mike Gatting joined Bill Athey. In the next 24 overs it seemed as if the third-wicket pair had put their side into a match-winning position. After Yousuf had missed a stumping and Javed Miandad dropped him in slips the English captain put on 135 with his stylish Yorkshire partner. Athey was in particularly fine form. Noted journalist Scyld Berry rated his 86 the equal of any English innings in the tournament. He got off the mark first ball with a boundary glided through slips off Wasim Akram. Later he drove Tauseef Ahmed for six over long-on and pulled Salim Malik for another six.

Gatting, who had further unpleasant words with Javed during his 65-ball innings, hit Qadir for six over long-on and England reached 2-187 with 13 overs to go. Finally Athey incurred the wrath of the entire English press contingent when he hit two boundaries and then played a reverse sweep at Tauseef and was bowled. That one rash moment spoiled 102 balls of exquisite batting that included four fours as well as the two sixes. In the next over Gatting swept in orthodox fashion at Qadir and top-edged a simple catch to Yousuf. Now Imran and Qadir really went to work.

John Emburey was bemused by the spinner and hit on the full in front of his stumps, Paul Downton nicked a well-pitched outswinger from the Pakistan captain and Allan Lamb had his leg stump removed by one that swung in late as he attempted a cut. Two for 187 had become 7–206. The capacity crowd was very pleased. Imran stood tall and wiped his brow.

Neil Foster and Phil DeFreitas put together a few handy runs to halt a complete collapse, but England could hardly have been satisfied with a return of 7–57 from those final 13 overs. The wicket showed no sign of dying, as had occurred in other games, and the weather remained on the side of the batsmen.

England had to get an early breakthrough if they were to protect 244. Foster had Rameez Raja lofting a shot to square leg when he was six, only for Gatting to drop the straightforward chance. This allowed Rameez and Mansoor Akhtar to put on 61 for the first wicket, which gave Pakistan exactly the start they wanted.

Salim Malik and Rameez were then able to take full control against an out of sorts English attack. Rameez had two more let-offs, a close stumping call off Emburey and another dropped chance on 62 to Athey at mid-on off Eddie Hemmings. He took full advantage of the opportunities he had been given by going on to complete his first Limited-Overs International 100 and added 167 in 29 overs with the polished Malik.

The Pakistani pair ran England ragged. Rameez's innings of 113 included 62 singles as well as five fours. Malik hit 43 singles and seven stylish boundaries in an innings which lasted 92 balls. The greatest threat to Pakistan's progress towards victory came from some of their own irresponsible spectators who, perhaps tiring of seeing one single after another, started throwing substantial missiles on to the playing field. Play was held up for 10 minutes while the boundary edge was cleared. Gatting handed one rock to umpire Ramaswamy, who held it up as if it were a second new ball. The English bowlers might have shown more penetration if such a change had been made. DeFreitas had been ill after his first spell, although it was Gladstone Small whose accuracy had been most off-colour.

Rameez and Malik clinically reduced the target. With 20 overs to go Pakistan required 128. Ten overs later 65 were required and the rate was almost identical. Neither batsman made it right through to the end. It did not matter. Ijaz

ENGLAND

G.A. Gooch c Akram b Imran Khan	16
R.T. Robinson b Abdul Qadir	16
C.W.J. Athey b Tauseef	86
M.W. Gatting (capt) c Salim Yousuf b Abdul Qadir	60
A.J. Lamb b Imran Khan	9
J.E. Emburey lbw Abdul Qadir	3
P.R. Downton (wk) c Salim Yousuf b Imran Khan	6
P.A.J. DeFreitas c Salim Yousuf b Imran Khan	13
N.A. Foster not out	20
G.C. Small run out	0
E.E. Hemmings not out	4
Extras (lb 7, w 4)	11
(50 overs)	9–244

1/26 2/52 3/187 4/187 5/192 6/203 7/206 8/230 9/230

Bowling: Imran Khan 9-0-37-4; Wasim Akram 8-0-44-0; Tauseef Ahmed 10-0-46-1; Abdul Qadir 10-0-31-3; Salim Jaffer 8-0-44-0; Salim Malik 5-0-35-0

PAKISTAN

Rameez Raja c Gooch b DeFreitas	113
Mansoor Akhtar run out	29
Salim Malik c Athey b Emburey	88
Javed Miandad not out	6
Ijaz Ahmed not out	4
Extras (lb 6, w 1)	7
(49 overs)	3–247

Did not bat: Imran Khan (capt), Salim Yousuf (wk), Wasim Akram, Abdul Qadir, Tauseef Ahmed, Salim Jaffer

1/61 2/228 3/243

Bowling: DeFreitas 8-2-41-1; Foster 10-0-51-0; Hemmings 10-1-40-0; Emburey 10-0-34-1; Small 9-0-63-0; Gooch 2-0-10-0

Umpires: A.R. Crafter, V.K. Ramaswamy.

Toss: Pakistan. Points: Pakistan 4, England 0

Ahmed hit the winning run from the last ball of the 49th over to give Pakistan their fourth victory in as many starts. For once a bowler was recognised ahead of batsmen, Imran receiving the Man of the Match award. More cash flowed the way of the Pakistanis.

GROUP B: SRI LANKA vs WEST INDIES
GREEN PARK, KANPUR: WEST INDIES WON BY 25 RUNS

Unlike the earlier Viv Richards exhibition match in Karachi, this clash at Kanpur was reasonably close at certain stages. Eventually the West Indies won, which meant their clash with England at Jaipur would in effect be a knockout quarter-final. Sri Lanka's long south-eastern journey seemed to agree with a few of their players who put up their best performance since Round One. Possibly it was because they were a little bit closer to home.

Richards elected to bat after he won the toss. His side found that the wicket was very slow and that the Sri Lankan finger spinners Don Anurasiri, Aravinda de Silva and Sridharan Jeganathan were difficult to score from. Between them they picked up four good wickets and conceded just 122 runs from their combined 30 overs. It was little de Silva, later to emerge as one of the best batsmen in the world, who claimed the prize scalp of Richards.

Desmond Haynes and Phil Simmons got the West Indies away to a steady start of 62. Haynes became the first victim of the spin trio and Richie Richardson could make little progress against the slow low turn. However, without ever breaking loose, Simmons hit strongly when the opportunity presented itself. He batted 37 overs, faced 122 balls and hit 11 fours before being fourth out at 155. Into Simmons' shoes stepped fellow Trinidadian Gus Logie. He batted throughout the remainder of the innings using a wide range of shots, some with names, others without. The 22 put on in the final overs by Logie and Courtney Walsh were invaluable as the West Indies reached 8–236 from their 50 overs.

Sri Lanka's reply took a long time to get going. Almost immediately Patrick Patterson bowled Roshan Mahanama for a duck. There were no further shocks and Brendon Kuruppu batted steadily if a little slowly. It was not until the short robust left-hander, Arjuna Ranatunga, asserted himself that Sri Lanka looked at all likely to get anywhere near 237. He hit Courtney Walsh for two consecutive sixes, but his assault

WEST INDIES

D.L. Haynes b Anurasiri	24
P.V. Simmons c Madugalle b J.R. Ratnayake	89
R.B. Richardson c Mahanama b Jeganathan	4
I.V.A. Richards (capt) c R.J. Ratnayake b de Silva	14
A.L. Logie not out	65
C.L. Hooper st Kuruppu b de Silva	6
P.J.L. Dujon (wk) c Kuruppu b J.R. Ratnayake	6
R.A. Harper b J.R. Ratnayake	3
W.K.M. Benjamin b R.J. Ratnayake	0
C.A. Walsh not out	9
Extras (b 2, lb 7, w 7)	16
(50 overs)	8–236

Did not bat: B.P. Patterson

1/62 2/80 3/115 4/155 5/168 6/199 7/213 8/214

Bowling: J.R. Ratnayake 10-1-41-3; John 5-0-25-0; R.J. Ratnayake 5-0-39-1; Jeganathan 10-1-33-1; Anurasiri 10-1-46-1; de Silva 10-0-43-2

SRI LANKA

R.S. Mahanama b Patterson	0
D.S.B.P. Kuruppu (wk) c & b Hooper	33
J.R. Ratnayake lbw Benjamin	15
R.S. Madugalle c Haynes b Harper	18
A. Ranatunga not out	86
L.R.D. Mendis (capt) b Walsh	19
P.A. de Silva b Patterson	8
R.J. Ratnayake c Walsh b Patterson	5
S. Jeganathan run out	3
V.B. John not out	1
Extras (b 2, lb 11, nb 10)	23
(50 overs)	8–211

Did not bat: S.D. Anurasiri

1/2 2/28 3/66 4/86 5/156 6/184 7/200 8/209

Bowling: Patterson 10-0-31-3; Walsh 9-2-43-1; Benjamin 10-0-43-1; Harper 10-1-29-1; Hooper 8-0-35-1; Richards 3-0-17-0

Umpires: Amanullah Khan, Mahboob Shah.

Toss: Sri Lanka. Points: West Indies 4, Sri Lanka 0

was almost single-handed. Apart from Simmons and Logie, no West Indians passed 24 and Ranatunga's brave fight was the only Sri Lankan innings over 33. The man who would later captain his country to their greatest triumph in international cricket reduced the target to 72 runs in eight overs, then 37 from 24 deliveries.

Then at such a crucial time, he was deprived of the strike and the run flow was stemmed. From the next 18 balls only nine runs were scored. Sri Lanka required 28 from the 50th and last over of the innings. Ranatunga was still in and Walsh had an over left to bowl. Richards had no wish to submit himself, his team or Walsh to extra torment and called on Winston Benjamin to do the job. The over cost two.

Ranatunga's 92-ball innings had been a mighty effort. However, Simmons was named Man of the Match.

GROUP A: INDIA vs AUSTRALIA
FEROZ SHAH KOTLA, NEW DELHI: INDIA WON BY 56 RUNS

Australia came back to earth with a thud as they were totally outbatted by the Indians in front of an excited packed house at the Feroz Shah Kotla ground on the Thursday match of Round Four.

The Australian brains trust got a few things wrong for this particular match. Allan Border won the toss and, even though his side had been successful in each of their three matches batting first, elected to bowl. Then, in the belief that Indian batsmen play spin better then pace and because the boundaries were short, Tim May was omitted for the 20-year-old South Australian seamer, Andrew Zesers.

Neither tactic worked and Border later admitted that perhaps he and his fellow selectors were wrong. Right from ball one the Indians went for their shots and showed themselves to be in prime form. When Kris Srikkanth was caught behind off Craig McDermott's second ball in the 10th over the total was already 50. He had played the shot of the morning. A square drive off Bruce Reid, reminiscent of the one that he crashed to the point boundary in the 1983 final off Andy Roberts. Sunil Gavaskar continued to sign off from international cricket with a series of beautiful shots. This innings amounted to 61 before he chopped a Simon O'Donnell delivery onto his stumps, bent down, handed over a bail and left contentedly to tumultuous applause from an appreciative throng of more than 40,000.

Navjot Sidhu also took advantage of the fast outfield and short boundaries. His third consecutive half century included a trademark straight six off young Zesers, who despite the onslaught, was as economical as any of the Australian bowlers. Sidhu was third out at 167, and Kapil Dev did not last long before becoming McDermott's third victim. The third and fourth half centuries of the innings were scored by Dilip Vengsarkar and Mohammad Azharuddin. Their 65-run stand for the fifth wicket in 10 overs was a treat. Vengsarkar's 63 lasted 59 balls. Azharuddin's 54 not out, which included a memorable on-drive off Reid in the final over and one six, another straight drive, this time off Steve Waugh, took just 47 balls.

Azharuddin was still going strong when the 50 overs were up and it was to be wondered what sort of a total India would have finished with if the matches were still of 60 overs duration. Australia had an awesome task in front of them if they were to score the 290 required to keep their unbeaten record intact. For a time Geoff Marsh and David Boon gave the impression that such an assignment was quite reasonable. They had no more trouble with medium pace than had the Indians and added 88 in 18 overs. Boon was his usual pugnacious self, using hooks, pulls and cuts to good effect.

The spinners were much harder to handle. Maninder Singh was introduced by Kapil Dev in the 16th over, Ravi Shastri in the 17th. Maninder immediately looked threatening. In his second over the Sikh lured Marsh out to drive with a beautifully flighted delivery that spun a long way past the outside edge of his bat and presented Kiran More with a straightforward stumping. Sixteen runs later Boon, who had hit seven fours in 55 balls, backed away to cut Shastri. The ball went through to More and there was a confident appeal for a catch. Umpire Khalid Aziz gave Boon out.

The Tasmanian showed his astonishment at the decision and when he slowly walked away he was booed by sections of the crowd and had something to say back to a few spectators. Australia never really made a serious challenge to India's total from that point. The two spinners slowed the run rate, conceding just 69 from their 20 overs. Maninder had Border caught at long-on and Australia in the 32nd over were slipping at 3–135. Kapil rested his main spinner for a couple of overs, brought him back on and Maninder instantly had Dean Jones caught at cover. Once more he had beaten a quality batsman with flight. Australia were 4–164 in the 36th over.

After a worthwhile 53-ball innings, Steve Waugh became Kapil's first victim of the tournament. He had watched Azharuddin, brought into the attack after paceman Chetan Sharma broke down, remove O'Donnell's leg stump with a yorker. Azharuddin went on to claim the Man of the Match Award and the best bowling figures with 3–19. His catch off his own bowling had stopped a very hot straight drive from McDermott from drilling him between the eyes. When Azharuddin removed Reid, Australia were all out with an over to go for 233, the game long since out of their reach. The Feroz Shah Kotla ground can be a featureless stadium of high wire fences and bland concrete terraces. On this day, with 40,000 celebrating an important win, it was a sea of noise, colour and happiness. India, like their western neighbours, now seemed certain of their semi-final place.

INDIA

K. Srikkanth c Dyer b McDermott	26
S.M. Gavaskar b O'Donnell	61
N.S. Sidhu c Moody b McDermott	51
D.B. Vengsarkar c O'Donnell b Reid	63
Kapil Dev (capt) c Dyer b McDermott	3
M. Azharuddin not out	54
R.J. Shastri c & b Waugh	8
K.S. More (wk) not out	5
Extras (b 1, lb 6, w 11)	18
(50 overs)	6–289

Did not bat: M. Prabhakar, Chetan Sharma, Maninder Singh

1/50 2/125 3/167 4/178 5/243 6/274

Bowling: O'Donnell 9-0-45-1; Reid 10-0-65-1; Waugh 10-0-59-1; McDermott 10-0-61-3; Moody 2-0-15-0; Zesers 9-1-37-0

AUSTRALIA

G.R. Marsh st More b Maninder	33
D.C. Boon c More b Shastri	62
D.M. Jones c Kapil Dev b Maninder	36
A.R. Border (capt) c Prabhakar b Maninder	12
S.R. Waugh c Sidhu b Kapil Dev	42
T.M. Moody run out	2
S.P. O'Donnell b Azharuddin	5
G.C. Dyer (wk) c Kapil Dev b Prabhakar	15
C.J. McDermott c & b Azharuddin	4
A.K. Zesers not out	2
B.A. Reid c Sidhu b Azharuddin	1
Extras (lb 11, w 8)	19
(49 overs)	233

1/88 2/104 3/135 4/164 5/167 6/182 7/214 8/227 9/231 10/233

Bowling: Kapil Dev 8-1-41-1; Prabhakar 10-0-56-1; Maninder 10-0-34-3; Shastri 10-0-35-1; Sharma 7.1-0-37-0; Azharuddin 3.5-0-19-3

Umpires: Khalid Aziz, D.R. Shepherd.

Toss: Australia. Points: India 4, Australia 0

GROUP A: NEW ZEALAND vs ZIMBABWE
EDEN GARDENS, CALCUTTA: NEW ZEALAND WON BY 4 WICKETS

Zimbabwe once more challenged New Zealand without being able to clinch their first victory of the Reliance Cup. The cricket was competitive if unspectacular. A contest in many parts of the world between these two sides would be hard to sell. Not in Calcutta, where 50,000 cricket-mad inhabitants of the massive crowded city would front up to Eden Gardens to watch a match between Greenland and Liechtenstein.

Jeff Crowe sent Zimbabwe in to bat and his side had an immediate breakthrough, Grant Paterson being run out for a duck. There were no further early dramas as the other opener, Ali Shah, settled in to play a solid innings. He let his partner, Kevin Arnott, do the bulk of the scoring. The pair had added 81 and Arnott had completed his half century when Shah changed his call mid-run and left his partner stranded. Still Shah soldiered on, lasting until the 35th over, by which time the score was only 121. The New Zealanders may have been disappointed by his dismissal because it opened the way for Dave Houghton and Andy Pycroft to up the tempo of the innings. Houghton once more demonstrated his relish for Kiwi bowling by racing to 50 in 58 balls. This time he went no further, but his confidence rubbed off on Pycroft, who took over the major strokeplaying role towards the closure of the innings.

Zimbabwe's 227 was hardly an imposing total to pursue, especially when Kevin Curran and Malcolm Jarvis failed to make an early

breakthrough. Then Eddo Brandes and Ali Shah gave the match a shake as New Zealand slipped from 0–37 to 3–56. The Crowe brothers, Martin and captain, Jeff, responded with a partnership of 69. Martin was seen as the key and he cruised to 58 off as many deliveries. His dismissal, caught in the deep by Iain Butchart when sweeping Ali Shah, the best of the Zimbabwean bowlers, left New Zealand 4–125. The game looked wide open again and it might have been if Jeff Crowe had not played his best innings of the competition.

Crowe was able to let his side cling to a faint hope of making the semi-finals. He batted two hours for his 88, hit eight fours in 105 balls and was still at the crease with Ian Smith when the winning runs were scored off Jarvis in the 48th over. The New Zealand captain was an obvious choice for the Man of the Match award.

ZIMBABWE	
G.A. Paterson run out	0
A.H. Shah c M. Crowe b Watson	41
K.J. Arnott run out	51
D.L. Houghton (wk) c M. Crowe b Boock	50
A.J. Pycroft not out	52
K.M. Curran b Boock	12
A.C. Waller not out	8
Extras (lb 7, w 6)	13
(50 overs)	5–227

Did not bat: I.P. Butchart, E.A. Brandes, A.J. Traicos (capt), M.P. Jarvis

1/1 2/82 3/121 4/180 5/216

Bowling: Snedden 10–2–32–0; Chatfield 10–2–47–0; Patel 10–0–52–0; Watson 10–1–45–1; Boock 10–1–44–2

NEW ZEALAND	
K.R. Rutherford b Brandes	22
J.G. Wright b Shah	12
M.D. Crowe c Butchart b Shah	58
D.N. Patel c Arnott b Brandes	1
J.J. Crowe (capt) not out	88
A.H. Jones c Jarvis b Traicos	15
M.C. Snedden b Jarvis	4
I.D.S. Smith (wk) not out	17
Extras (b 1, lb 5, w 4, nb 1)	11
(47.4 overs)	6–228

Did not bat: S.L. Boock, W. Watson, E.J. Chatfield

1/37 2/53 3/56 4/125 5/158 6/182

Bowling: Curran 2–0–12–0; Jarvis 7.4–0–39–1; Brandes 10–1–44–2; Shah 10–0–34–2; Butchart 8–0–50–0; Traicos 10–0–43–1

Umpires: Khizar Hayat, P.W. Vidanagamage.

Toss: New Zealand. Points: New Zealand 4, Zimbabwe 0

SUNDAY OCTOBER 25th, MONDAY OCTOBER 26th and TUESDAY OCTOBER 27th
RELIANCE CUP: ROUND FIVE
GROUP B: PAKISTAN vs SRI LANKA
THE IQBAL STADIUM, FAISALABAD: PAKISTAN WON BY 113 RUNS

Sri Lanka went back over the western border to Pakistan just so their bowlers could suffer another merciless caning at the hands of opposition batsmen. Only briefly were they in the hunt at the Iqbal Stadium and the superior depth in talent of

the Pakistanis became more and more obvious as the day wore on. This win by the home side ensured they would top Group B and could play their semi-final at Lahore.

Salim Malik followed up his fine innings

against England with an even 100 at Faisalabad. He saw his team through a mini-collapse when they lost three wickets between 64 and 77 and went on to complete his century in 85 balls with 10 fours.

Imran Khan elected to bat in the hope that his strokeplayers would score quickly enough to put Sri Lanka out of the contest. Once more Duleep Mendis got very little bite out of his new-ball bowlers as Mansoor Akhtar and Rameez Raja moved through the opening overs in relative comfort. It was the spinners, Don Anurasiri and Sridharan Jeganathan, who caused the brief flutter by removing an opener each. Javed Miandad's run-out then lifted Sri Lankan hopes further.

Almost as quickly Malik and Wasim Akram dampened them down again. Promoted up the order, Akram boosted the run rate and twice hit the ball for six with mighty left-handed swipes. Malik added 60 with Akram, a further 60 with Ijaz

Ahmed, whose 30 runs took just 18 balls, and 67 with Imran. Pakistan put on 154 in their final 15 overs and their total of 297 was their highest in the tournament to date.

Imran was unable to complete his fourth over because of an injured ankle, but he had already put Sri Lanka on the back foot by having Brendon Kuruppu caught behind. Nor did his absence from the bowling crease inspire the Sri Lankan batsmen to deeds of great daring. The innings just stuttered along. No-one was able to score with enough freedom to get anywhere near Pakistan's total. Tauseef Ahmed bowled with great economy. Arjuna Ranatunga completed his second consec-utive half century and added 80 runs with his captain for the fifth wicket, but both fell to the wrist spin of Abdul Qadir, whose fascinating bowling was just about the best feature of some tame after-noon cricket. Salim Malik received the Man of the Match award.

PAKISTAN			SRI LANKA	
Rameez Raja c & b Anurasiri	32		R.S. Mahanama run out	8
Mansoor Akhtar b Jeganathan	33		D.S.B.P. Kuruppu (wk) c Salim Yousuf b Imran Khan	0
Salim Malik b Ratnayake	100		J.R. Ratnayake run out	22
Javed Miandad run out	1		R.S. Madugalle c Salim Yousuf b Manzoor Elahi	15
Wasim Akram c Ranatunga b de Silva	39		A. Ranatunga c & b Abdul Qadir	50
Ijaz Ahmed c & b John	30		L.R.D. Mendis (capt) b Abdul Qadir	58
Imran Khan (capt) run out	39		P.A. de Silva not out	13
Manzoor Elahi not out	4		A.L.F. de Mel b Abdul Qadir	0
Salim Yousuf (wk) not out	11		S. Jeganathan c Salim Yousuf b Javed Miandad	1
Extras (lb 6, w 2)	8		V.B. John not out	1
(50 overs)	7-297		Extras (b 4, lb 4, w 6, nb 2)	16
			(50 overs)	8-184

Did not bat: Abdul Qadir, Tauseef Ahmed

1/64 2/72 3/77 4/137 5/197 6/264 7/285

Bowling: Ratnayake 10-0-58-1; John 8-0-53-1; de Mel 10-0-53-0; Jeganathan 9-1-45-1; Anurasiri 7-0-45-1; de Silva 6-0-37-1

Did not bat: S.D. Anurasiri

1/4 2/11 3/41 4/70 5/150 6/173 7/173 8/179

Bowling: Imran Khan 3.2-1-13-1; Wasim Akram 7-0-34-0; Manzoor Elahi 9.4-0-32-1; Tauseef Ahmed 10-0-23-0; Abdul Qadir 10-0-40-3; Salim Malik 7-1-29-0; Javed Miandad 3-0-5-1

Umpires: R.B. Gupta, S.J. Woodward.

Toss: Pakistan. Points: Pakistan 4, Sri Lanka 0

GROUP B: ENGLAND vs WEST INDIES
SAWAI MAN SINGH STADIUM, JAIPUR: ENGLAND WON BY 34 RUNS

There was great English joy in Jaipur as a second win over the West Indies virtually ensured Mike Gatting's team a place in the semi-finals. Even though both sides had one more match, this game amounted to what was effectively a quarter-final

and England's pleasure was matched by West Indian disappointment, especially as a large proportion of the margin of defeat could be attrib-uted to a surfeit of wides.

Some of those were illegal bouncers from fast

bowlers, while Carl Hooper totally lost control of his slow medium swingers during his short and unsuccessful spell. Viv Richards had sent England in to bat on a wicket that was greener than most and contained a lot of early-morning moisture. Gatting would also have bowled if he had won.

Rather than take advantage of the wicket, Patrick Patterson and Winston Benjamin sprayed the ball around. Courtney Walsh, on the other hand, conceded fewer runs in his 10-over spell than he had off those horrendous 10 deliveries at Gujranwala and Lahore. He cut the ball off the wicket prodigiously without having any luck.

Patterson achieved the first breakthrough when he got through Robinson's defence after half an hour and snapped his off stump in half. Robinson had been missed by Jeff Dujon when he was six and the West Indian wicketkeeper also dropped a catch off Bill Athey. In stifling Rajastan heat Gooch settled to build an important innings. He dominated an opening stand of 35 with Robinson, one of 55 with Athey for the second wicket and another of 64 runs with Mike Gatting for the third. England were 2–151 at the start of the 31st over, having scored 71 runs from their previous 10 overs, and potentially on target for a score of around 300. Richards having lost some faith in his bowlers, used the captain's prerogative and claimed the ball himself.

It paid immediate dividends. The sweep shot again proved a dangerous choice for the English captain, Gatting missing a straight ball. Gooch and Allan Lamb were then becalmed so that by the 40th over only another 35 runs had been added. At least another collapse had been avoided. Patterson came back to dismiss both Gooch, eight short of his century after seven fours in 137 balls, and Lamb. By now, though, the runs were flowing again. John Emburey and Phil DeFreitas unleashed an assault on some more loose deliveries. The big off spinner hit four fours in 16 balls and 83 runs were made in the final 10 overs, including 51 in the last five.

Only DeFreitas kept the pressure on the West Indian top order as they began their pursuit of the 270 runs they required for victory. Neil Foster and Gladstone Small were expensive early and the runs were being conceded at five per over. DeFreitas removed Desmond Haynes and Emburey bowled

Phil Simmons with an arm ball in the 13th over with the total already on 65. In partnership with his fellow Antiguan Richie Richardson, the West Indian captain Richards thrilled the crowd for the next 17 overs while 82 runs were added. They brought up the 100 in the 21st over, which was quicker than England had. The wicket had dried into a batsman's paradise. Off spinner Eddie Hemmings and a more controlled Foster suddenly found their line and length to dry up all but nine runs for five overs. Then Richards and Richardson broke loose again. Richards had already hit Emburey for one six when he swept Hemmings hard and high for six more. Off the next ball he repeated the dose, this time a top edge just clearing the fieldsman on the boundary.

The captain had just reached his fifty and the West Indies was 2–147, needing 123 to win off 20 overs with eight wickets in hand. The heat remained intense, several bowlers were unwell and there were thoughts that England might start to wilt. Instead, Richards stepped back to cut Hemmings, missed a ball that was tossed up slower and higher and was bowled. Gus Logie joined Richardson and there were no immediate signs of tremors in the West Indian camp. They reduced the target to 88 when Logie played the tournament's favourite shot off Emburey, only to top edge the ball to Hemmings.

At the start of the 41st over the West Indies still appeared to be in control. Another 65 runs and they would condemn England to an early exit from the competition. Six wickets were still in hand, one of them being Richardson's. Six runs later and both Carl Hooper and Jeff Dujon had been caught behind by Paul Downton, the one to dismiss Hooper off DeFreitas being a fine diving effort.

The pressure was now starting to build. Roger Harper guided the ball to backward point. Richardson called him for a sharp run to Hemmings, the oldest and chubbiest player on the field. In the middle of a sweltering afternoon and with everything to play for, Hemmings moved quickly, picked up the ball one-handed and threw down the stumps at the bowler's end with the agile Harper still stretching for the crease. The West Indian challenge was fading. Richardson went on to top score in the match, beating Gooch's total by one run in 130 balls with one six and eight fours. Then he fell to another fine catch behind by Downton. From the first ball of the 49th over, with his side still needing another 35 runs Winston Benjamin was caught by Foster off DeFreitas. The West Indies had lost 6–30 in eight overs to hand over the

match. Beneath one of the 'Pink' City's ancient castles which overlook the ground, Graham Gooch received his Man of the Match award. It was a worthy reward for a fine innings. The English also celebrated the contribution of the unfashionable Eddie Hemmings with enthusiasm.

ENGLAND

G.A. Gooch c Harper b Patterson	92
R.T. Robinson b Patterson	13
C.W.J. Athey c Patterson b Harper	21
M.W. Gatting (capt) lbw Richards	25
A.J. Lamb c Richardson b Patterson	40
J.E. Emburey not out	24
P.A.J. DeFreitas not out	16
Extras (b 5, lb 10, w 22, nb 1)	38
(50 overs)	5–269

Did not bat: P.R. Downton (wk), N.A. Foster, E.E. Hemmings, G.C. Small

1/35 2/90 3/154 4/209 5/250

Bowling: Patterson 9–0–56–3; Walsh 10–0–24–0; Benjamin 10–0–63–0; Harper 10–1–52–1; Hooper 3–0–27–0; Richards 8–0–32–1

WEST INDIES

D.L. Haynes c Athey b DeFreitas	9
P.V. Simmons b Emburey	25
R.B. Richardson c Downton b Small	93
I.V.A. Richards (capt) b Hemmings	51
A.L. Logie c Hemmings b Emburey	22
C.L. Hooper c Downton b DeFreitas	8
P.J.L. Dujon (wk) c Downton b Foster	1
R.A. Harper run out	3
W.K.M. Benjamin c Foster b DeFreitas	8
C.A. Walsh b Hemmings	2
B.P. Patterson not out	4
Extras (lb 7, w 1, nb 1)	9
(48.1 overs)	235

1/18 2/65 3/147 4/182 5/208 6/211 7/219 8/221 9/224 10/235

Bowling: DeFreitas 9.1–2–28–3; Foster 10–0–52–1; Emburey 9–0–41–2; Small 10–0–61–1; Hemmings 10–0–46–2

Umpires: Mahboob Shah, P.W. Vidanagamage.

Toss: West Indies. Points: England 4, West Indies 0

GROUP A: INDIA vs ZIMBABWE
GUJARAT STADIUM, AHMEDABAD: INDIA WON BY 7 WICKETS

While England and the West Indies fought out their fluctuating 'quarter-final' at Jaipur, India and Zimbabwe were engaged in a lacklustre affair to the south. There was little attractive batting from either side, even though India were supposed to be striving to lift their run rate above that of Australia.

The wicket that Kapil Dev asked John Traicos' side to bat on was slow and low. It made stroke-making difficult, especially against the intelligent left-arm spin of Ravi Shastri and Maninder Singh. Not that they were required to break the opening partnership, Ali Shah took his turn to be the victim of a Zimbabwean top-order run-out in the second over of the match. Kevin Arnott joined the recalled Robin Brown and he stuck around for 43 overs while compiling a sound if unadventurous 60.

While there were no prospects of a major collapse, there was no major acceleration, either. Dave Houghton, capable of the aggression required, got out just at the wrong time and Kevin

Curran, also potentially a fast scorer, was out of form and out of the side. Chris Waller helped Arnott add 67 for the fifth wicket, which ensured the spectators would have their fill of cricket for the day.

Chasing 192, the only 50-over sub-200 first innings total of the Reliance Cup, Kapil Dev ordered his team try and win in 38 overs so as to lift their run rate above Australia. Strangely Sunil Gavaskar, who had been batting in such positive fashion, reverted to Lord's 1975 type and occupied the crease for 114 balls for his 50. Kapil twice sent out messages to the veteran opener to increase his scoring, but to no avail. The old feud between India's two greatest players briefly simmered again. The crowd was also a bit annoyed and behaved in such an unruly fashion that play had to be held up. 'Dickie' Bird, umpiring his 100th Limited-Over International would have been upset. 'Stones on ground. Not my fault, that!'

Gavaskar had lost his opening partner, Kris Srikkanth, early. He might have felt encumbered by the turgid pitch and the need to establish a platform for victory. In such circumstances John Traicos was almost inevitably miserly in his run concessions. Navjot Sidhu completed his fourth consecutive half century, batting altogether more fluently than his partner. Peter Rawson, another recalled to the Zimbabwean side, dismissed Sidhu and, in the 35th over, Gavaskar. By then India were 3–132 and well on the way to victory. Kapil still

had a point to prove. Coming in at number 5 he put his bat where his mouth was and in 25 balls smashed the game towards its obvious destiny. Three sixes helped dissipate the anger of the Indian captain, even if they were not quite enough to lift his team's run rate above that of the Australians. With eight overs still to be bowled Kapil could claim his Man of the Match award and announce to the press his disappointment with Gavaskar's tardiness.

ZIMBABWE	
R.D. Brown c More b Sharma	13
A.H. Shah run out	0
K.J. Arnott b Kapil Dev	60
A.J. Pycroft c More b Sharma	2
D.L. Houghton (wk) c Kapil Dev b Shastri	22
A.C. Waller c Shastri b Maninder	39
I.P. Butchart b Kapil Dev	13
P.W.E. Rawson not out	16
E.A. Brandes not out	3
Extras (b 1, lb 12, w 9, nb 1)	23
(50 overs)	7–191

Did not bat: A.J. Traicos (capt), M.P. Jarvis

1/4 2/36 3/40 4/83 5/150 6/155 7/184

Bowling: Kapil Dev 10–2–44–2; Prabhakar 7–2–12–0; Sharma 10–0–41–2; Maninder 10–1–32–1; Shastri 10–0–35–1; Azharuddin 3–0–14–0

INDIA	
K. Srikkanth lbw Jarvis	6
S.M. Gavaskar c Butchart b Rawson	50
N.S. Sidhu c Brandes b Rawson	55
D.B. Vengsarkar not out	33
Kapil Dev (capt) not out	41
Extras (lb 6, w 3)	9
(42 overs)	3–194

Did not bat: M. Azharuddin, R.J. Shastri, K.S. More (wk), M. Prabhakar, Chetan Sharma, Maninder Singh

1/11 2/105 3/132

Bowling: Brandes 6–0–28–0; Jarvis 8–1–21–1; Shah 8–0–40–0; Traicos 10–0–39–0; Rawson 8–0–46–2; Butchart 2–0–14–0

Umpires: D.M. Archer, H.D. Bird.

Toss: India. Points: India 4, Zimbabwe 0

GROUP A: AUSTRALIA vs NEW ZEALAND
PANJAB C.A. STADIUM, CHANDIGARH: AUSTRALIA WON BY 17 RUNS

Allan Border's Australians secured their place in the Reliance Cup semi-finals with this 17-run win over the disappointing New Zealanders at Chandigarh. Through their hard work and determination they had gone further than the better credentialled 1983 team, which was all credit to their captain and to their coach, Bobby Simpson.

There was also great Aussie satisfaction in the humidity of the northern Indian city with the success of Geoff Marsh. His work ethic and support of Border in his new role as vice-captain were beyond reproach. Without Marsh's individual contribution of 126 not out it is quite possible that Australia would have been defeated and their finals spot placed in some jeopardy.

There was not much thought of that while Dean Jones and Marsh were building a powerful second-wicket partnership of 126 in 26 overs. Allan

Border had restored the batting first option after winning the toss and would have been gratified at the response of his vice-captain and the brash Victorian. Marsh and David Boon had opened against Martin Snedden and Ewan Chatfield in their usual competent fashion until the 10th over when the West Australian hit the ball to point, Boon went looking for a run, was sent back and found well short when Jeff Crowe threw to the bowler Chatfield.

Jones soon made light of the Australian disappointment with his usual busy aggression. The run rate remained an issue, though, and despite the form of Marsh and Jones, Australia struggled to keep it ahead of India. Jones reached 50, then in the 36th over struck Willie Watson for a huge six over mid wicket. That might have been the signal for him to cut loose but from the next ball, his 80th of the innings, Jones attempted a drive and was caught behind. Allan Border too, wanted to boost that run rate and seven runs later he unleashed a big booming drive at Snedden that only deflected the ball onto his off stump. Mike Veletta, on his international debut, dropped his first ball beside the pitch, got into a terrible muddle with his partner and was run out as Martin Crowe ran in and broke the bowler's stumps.

The Australian middle order had fallen away badly. Six wickets went down for 50 as the total reached an unimposing 7–201 after 45 overs. Tim May added a few useful runs, lifting his side to 8–232 at the start of the final over of the innings. It was to be bowled by Chatfield, considered to be amongst the most frugal bowlers in the world. That opinion was confirmed by his figures at that stage of 9–2–33–2. Marsh had completed his second century of the tournament and was looking for every opportunity to attack. In one of life's surprises, Chatfield offered him every chance. A delivery drifted onto Marsh's pads. The batsman lifted it high over the leg-side boundary for six. The next ball was in the same place and achieved the same result. Chatfield conceded 19 runs in his desperate final over. Marsh finished 126 not out and became the third player after Glenn Turner and Sunil Gavaskar to carry his bat through a World Cup innings. He hit three sixes and 12 fours.

New Zealand had a chase that was their last chance to resurrect their campaign. They needed to get 252 and started well. Martin Snedden opened again instead of Rutherford. The left-handed coupling, one an orthodox batsman and the other a promoted tail ender, realised 72 runs in 17 overs. Snedden was not afraid to use the old-fashioned slog. He belted Craig McDermott for four through mid-on, using a horizontal bat to a ball pitched short of a length outside the off-stump. Snedden finally deflected Steve Waugh onto his stumps, which was a setback, although not as big as the one that occurred 10 runs later. Martin Crowe was still regarded as the Kiwis' leading batsman and most obvious match winner. At Indore he had failed his team at a crucial moment with an error of judg-

ment. In front of 25,000 at Chandigarh he was again dismissed at a critical moment, this time, however, without any blame to himself.

John Wright hit a straight drive off Waugh as sweet as a nut. The all-rounder put down his hand. The ball flicked through his fingers and cannoned into the stumps at the bowler's end. Crowe saw the danger an instant too late and, backing up, was about five centimetres out of his ground when the bails came off. Wright and Ken Rutherford maintained the healthy challenge. They added a further 45 runs and Wright completed his 50.

Shot-making and risk-taking had to be maintained if the target was to be reached in time. Eventually that took its toll on the batsmen. On 127 Wright hit a full toss straight back at Andrew Zesers off a leading edge. Even while Rutherford and Jeff Crowe put on 46 the pressure was still evident. Rutherford hooked McDermott, only to pick out Jones running in at fine leg. Border brought himself on to bowl left-arm spin. In seven tidy overs he caught and bowled his opposite number, Jeff Crowe, and had Dipak Patel stumped. Now the Kiwis were 6–186 and their challenge was starting to falter.

From the last 10 overs 72 runs had been required. John Bracewell, Ian Smith and Stephen Boock would not give up and took the total within 30 of their target. Now risks had to be taken with running, as well. Bracewell and Boock were run out. Last wicket pair Willie Watson and Ewan Chatfield put on another precious 13. They were within 18 of victory but only nine balls remained when Waugh sent down the fourth delivery of the 49th over. It was full. Watson dug it out and the ball rolled towards mid-on. The last wicket pair had to run on everything. Both batsmen took off, Border swooped and, with one stump to aim at, threw down the wicket underarm from close range. New Zealand's last seven wickets had gone down for 61 in 11 overs.

Australia's middle-order collapse had forfeited their top position in Group A, but they felt little disappointment. An assured semi-final berth was achievement enough on this day.

AUSTRALIA

G.R. Marsh not out	126
D.C. Boon run out	14
D.M. Jones c Smith b Watson	56
A.R. Border (capt) b Snedden	1
M.R.J. Veletta run out	0
S.R. Waugh b Watson	1
G.C. Dyer (wk) b Chatfield	8
C.J. McDermott lbw Chatfield	5
T.B.A. May run out	15
A.K. Zesers not out	8
Extras (lb 10, w 7)	17
(50 overs)	8–251

Did not bat: B.A. Reid

1/25 2/151 3/158 4/158 5/175 6/193 7/201 8/228

Bowling: Snedden 10-0-48-1; Chatfield 10-2-52-2; Boock 10-1-45-0; Bracewell 4-0-24-0; Patel 8-0-26-0; Watson 8-0-46-2

NEW ZEALAND

M.C. Snedden b Waugh	32
J.G. Wright c & b Zesers	61
M.D. Crowe run out	4
K.R. Rutherford c Jones b McDermott	44
J.J. Crowe (capt) c & b Border	27
D.N. Patel st Dyer b Border	3
J.G. Bracewell run out	12
I.D.S. Smith (wk) c Boon b Waugh	12
S.L. Boock run out	12
W. Watson run out	8
E.J. Chatfield not out	5
Extras (b 1, lb 7, w 4, nb 2)	14
(48.4 overs)	234

1/72 2/82 3/127 4/173 5/179 6/186 7/206 8/208 9/221 10/234

Bowling: McDermott 10-1-43-1; Reid 6-0-30-0; Waugh 9.4-0-37-2; Zesers 6-0-37-1; May 10-0-52-0; Border 7-0-27-2

Umpires: Khizar Hayat, D.R. Shepherd.

Toss: Australia. Points: Australia 4, New Zealand 0

FRIDAY OCTOBER 30th and SATURDAY OCTOBER 31st
RELIANCE CUP: ROUND SIX
GROUP B: ENGLAND vs SRI LANKA
NEHRU STADIUM, PUNE: ENGLAND WON BY 8 WICKETS

England suffered few moments of uncertainty as they marched through to their rightful place in the semi-finals. They comfortably accounted for Sri Lanka, who packed their bags for home without a point for all their travelling and efforts. At Pune they mostly looked a tired and uninspired team, something for which the England team were extremely grateful.

They were less grateful at having to field first after having lost the toss on a rough outfield in front of a restless crowd that half-filled the Nehru Stadium. Duleep Mendis' correct call was virtually his last success as his country's captain. The Sri Lankan openers, batting first for the only time in the tournament, were restrained early by the accuracy of Phil DeFreitas and Gladstone Small. They might have been in a parlous position if the England fieldsmen had been in any sort of catching form. After Roshan Mahanama hit DeFreitas' first ball of the day through the leg side for four, Graham Gooch dislocated a finger while dropping a slips catch from the fifth ball of the opening over.

In the 14th over, with the crowd booing and the total on a subdued 2–31, wicketkeeper Paul Downton dropped the struggling Roy Dias. Dias had just been recalled to the side and offered Downton the most straightforward of chances. The afternoon's entertainment may have been sadly curtailed if the catch had been held, for Dias went on to provide the Sri Lankan innings with its only real degree of substance. Just when everyone was starting to lose interest he swept Jaipur hero, Eddie Hemmings, for six. Later, a drive off John Emburey cleared the boundary at long-off and then Dias picked up a ball from Small so perfectly that it sailed over mid wicket for his third six. Some critics rated that shot the best of the competition.

Dias added 88 in 22 overs with the tall, accomplished Asanka Gurusinha. When Sri Lanka reached 2–113 there was a possibility of them setting England a testing target. The partnership was broken when the 'Guru' hit the ball to mid-on and ran a single. Unfortunately Dias did not move and when Gatting's throw to Downton left Gurusinha run out by the length of the pitch the Sri Lankans went in to their shell again.

They were 4–144 at the start of the 40th over, struggling to get their run rate up to four per over. The Sri Lankans managed to achieve that at least by adding 74 from the final 60 deliveries. Dias completed his 105-ball innings, containing six fours as well as the three sixes, and Ranjan Madugalle, Aravinda de Silva and Sridharan Jeganathan chipped in. England's contribution amounted to four dropped catches.

The wicket had provided some turn, but there was nothing to suggest England would not make the 219 they required to win.

Gooch's early-morning finger injury had been repaired well enough by the team physiotherapist, Laurie Brown, for him to open with Tim Robinson. He immediately hit Ravi Ratnayake's first ball through mid-off for four and then settled in to play

a typically powerful innings. Robinson, too, was in prime form and the pair rattled up a partnership of 123 in 23 overs. They struck 14 boundaries between them. Gooch's sharp chance to mid wicket was the only blemish before he hit a return catch off the leading edge to the accurate Jeganathan from his 79th ball. Jeganathan also bowled Robinson on the sweep for his equally impressive 55. That double breakthrough was the end of Sri Lankan success for the Reliance Cup.

Bill Athey and Gatting quickly took up where the opening pair had left off. They attacked with confidence and raced towards their objective. Aravinda de Silva was crunched, Ashantha de Mel was pulverised and when the partnership had put on 87 by the second ball of the 42nd over England had completed their victory. Graham Gooch, with a knack for being recognised, beat all other contenders for the Man of the Match award.

SRI LANKA

R.S. Mahanama c Emburey b DeFreitas		14
J.R. Ratnayake lbw Small		7
A.P. Gurusinha (wk) run out		34
R.L. Dias st Downton b Hemmings		80
L.R.D. Mendis (capt) b DeFreitas		7
R.S. Madugalle c sub (P.W. Jarvis) b Hemmings		22
P.A. de Silva not out		23
A.L.F. de Mel c Lamb b Hemmings		0
S. Jeganathan not out		20
Extras (lb 3, w 3, nb 5)		11
(50 overs)		7–218

Did not bat: V.B. John, S.D. Anurasiri

1/23 2/25 3/113 4/125 5/170 6/177 8/180

Bowling: DeFreitas 10–2–46–2; Small 10–1–33–1; Foster 10–0–37–0; Emburey 10–1–42–0; Hemmings 10–0–57–3

ENGLAND

G.A. Gooch c & b Jeganathan		61
R.T. Robinson b Jeganathan		55
C.W.J. Athey not out		40
M.W. Gatting (capt) not out		46
Extras (b 1, lb 13, w 3)		17
(41.2 overs)		2–219

Did not bat: A.J. Lamb, J.E. Emburey, P.R. Downton (wk), P.A.J. DeFreitas, N.A. Foster, E.E. Hemmings, G.C. Small

Bowling: Ratnayake 8–1–37–0; John 6–2–19–0; de Mel 4.2–0–34–0; Jeganathan 10–0–45–2; Anurasiri 10–0–45–0; de Silva 3–0–25–0

Umpires: D.M. Archer, Khizar Hayat.

Toss: Sri Lanka. Points: England 4, Sri Lanka 0

GROUP B: PAKISTAN vs WEST INDIES
NATIONAL STADIUM, KARACHI: WEST INDIES WON BY 28 RUNS

The West Indies did everything they could to reassert pressure on semi-finals contender England in their best performance of the Reliance Cup. However, their 28-run win over Pakistan was too little too late and this excellent victory would finish as merely a consolation for a team that let their destiny fall into the hands of others.

The West Indian loss in the 1983 final had been seen as an temporary aberration. The format of the side under Viv Richards in the 1987 Reliance Cup

revealed that, in the limited-overs format of the game, the Caribbean decline was real enough. This was the first time they had failed to reach the final, let alone the semi-finals.

Richards won the toss and elected to bat. Phil Simmons was dismissed early, but Richie Richardson was soon demonstrating he had retained his form from Jaipur. His stand of 65 with Desmond Haynes provided the innings with the type of base which Viv Richards is able to brutally exploit. He and his fellow Antiguan tore into the Pakistani attack to the tune of 137 runs in 23 overs. They were assisted by some lackadaisical fielding which resulted in dropped catches and bonus runs for the West Indies. Perhaps the Pakistani fieldsmen were distracted by the clashes between police and students in the crowd and the tear gas that drifted over the ground.

Richardson struck Imran down the ground for a rare six off the Pakistani captain. He hit one other ball into the crowd and eight fours as he stroked his way to 110 in 136 balls. Richards brought up his 1000th World Cup run during his 74-ball innings which ended when he was bowled by left-arm paceman, Wasim Akram. He and Abdul Qadir would prove the best of the Pakistani bowlers. Imran also came back strongly to pick up three wickets, while also concerning himself with his team's slow over rate. Heavy fines loomed at one stage, a problem exacerbated by wayward bowling and plenty of wides. The West Indies could only add a further 37 runs after Richards and Richardson were separated, although this was enough to temporarily lift their run rate above England who were listening hard to the goings on at the National Stadium during their own match in Pune.

Pakistan's tardiness with their over rate carried into the early batting of their openers. Mudassar Nazar and Rameez Raja had put on just 26 after 10 overs. From there they were able to accelerate and they had got their rate up to four per over by the time Mudassar was bowled by off spinner Roger Harper with the total on 78. Rameez and Salim Malik put on another 50 and Pakistan reached 1–128. It was an excellent platform, but this was the sort of day Imran had come to dread. His later batsmen were not on task and could not maintain the challenge. A few sharp shocks by Patrick Patterson and Winston Benjamin saw Pakistan decline from 5–202 to 9–208.

Both camps would have been dissatisfied with the eventual result. Pakistan could not have been happy with such a performance as a lead-up to a semi-final clash and the West Indies must have wondered what could have been if they had consistently played as well as they did this day. Still, it was a nice way to finish. Especially as for Viv Richards this was his farewell World Cup match. Richie Richardson was a clear-cut choice for the Man of the Match award.

WEST INDIES	
D.L. Haynes c Imran Khan b Mudassar Nazar	25
P.V. Simmons b Wasim Akram	6
R.B. Richardson c Abdul Qadir b Imran Khan	110
I.V.A. Richards (capt) b Wasim Akram	67
A.L. Logie c Mudassar Nazar b Imran Khan	12
R.A. Harper b Wasim Akram	2
C.L. Hooper not out	5
W.K.M. Benjamin c Mudassar Nazar b Imran Khan	0
P.J.L. Dujon (wk) not out	1
Extras (b 3, lb 10, w 16, nb 1)	30
(50 overs)	7–258

Did not bat: C.A. Walsh, B.P. Patterson

1/19 2/84 3/221 4/242 5/248 6/255 7/255

Bowling: Imran Khan 9-0-57-3; Wasim Akram 10-0-45-3; Qadir 10-1-29-0; Mudassar Nazar 10-0-47-1; Salim Jaffer 6-0-37-0; Salim Malik 5-0-30-0

PAKISTAN	
Mudassar Nazar b Harper	40
Rameez Raja c Hooper b Patterson	70
Salim Malik c Richards b Walsh	23
Javed Miandad b Benjamin	38
Ijaz Ahmed b Benjamin	6
Imran Khan (capt) c Harper b Walsh	8
Salim Yousuf (wk) b Patterson	7
Wasim Akram lbw Patterson	0
Abdul Qadir not out	8
Shoaib Mohammad b Benjamin	0
Salim Jaffer not out	8
Extras (b 4, lb 6, w 10, nb 2)	22
(50 overs)	9–230

1/78 2/128 3/147 4/167 5/186 6/202 7/202 8/208 9/208

Bowling: Patterson 10-1-34-3; Walsh 10-1-34-2; Harper 10-0-38-1; Benjamin 10-0-69-3; Richards 10-0-45-0

Umpires: R.B. Gupta, V.K. Ramaswamy.

Toss: West Indies. Points: West Indies 4, Pakistan 0

GROUP A: AUSTRALIA vs ZIMBABWE
BARABATI STADIUM, CUTTACK: AUSTRALIA WON BY 70 RUNS

The third Friday match in Round Six of the Reliance Cup saw Australia comfortably account for Zimbabwe. It was a solid pre-semi-final workout, however the Australians still had to wait for the result of the India vs New Zealand game on the Saturday to find out whether they would finish in top or second place in Group A.

Allan Border called incorrectly, but found that his side were still going to bat first. John Traicos wanted them to take first use of the green and lively track prepared at the Barabati Stadium. Geoff Marsh and David Boon were unfazed by the juice in the wicket, nor did Peter Rawson or Malcolm Jarvis cause them much concern with the new ball. Maintaining their excellent tournament record, they added 90 in 23 overs before Marsh was run out.

With such a good start, Dean Jones was an ideal man to come in at number 3. He and Boon had to work for their runs as Traicos extracted some turn from the moist surface. They still added 58 in 10 overs until Iain Butchart and wicketkeeper Dave Houghton ended Boon's resistance, which had included a six and nine fours. Craig McDermott's pinch-hitting promotion failed and Border soon rewarded Traicos' persistence so that Australia had slid from 1–148 to 4–170. Jones was still in, ticking the score over rather than taking control. Mike Veletta was to the forefront with a busy innings during which he put on 78 with Jones. His 43 was of real benefit to his side and to his own cause.

They batted just quickly enough to lift Australia's rate one hundredth of a run per over ahead of India's. Jones completed his fifty, his

third of the competition, hitting just one six and one four on the way. Australia put 266 on the board, which considering the conditions was no mean feat.

Zimbabwe were quickly in trouble. Chris Waller was cracked on the bridge of the nose by a ball from Bruce Reid that lifted from a length and forced him to temporarily retire hurt. Ali Shah and Kevin Curran, back in the side again, were then put on the defensive by the Australian pacemen who were threatening on the grassy wicket.

It took nearly 30 overs for Zimbabwe to reach a reasonable platform of 1–89 and then they threw the position away. Off spinner Tim May had Curran caught in the 27th over and then trapped Dave Houghton lbw in the 29th. Zimbabwe were 4–97, chasing runs at nine per over against the fastest improving team in the competition. Soon it was obvious this was another example of a limited-overs match that would benefit from some sort of forfeiture rule being available to bail everyone out from having to play over after over of pointless cricket. Boon was given a bowl. It was for entertainment rather than tactical reasons and cost 17 runs. Waller returned to the batting crease showing no serious ill effects from the blow to his nose and he finished equal top score for his side.

After Australia had won by 70 runs David Boon was announced as Man of the Match. Back

AUSTRALIA	
D.C. Boon c Houghton b Butchart	93
G.R. Marsh run out	37
D.M. Jones not out	58
C.J. McDermott c Rawson b Traicos	9
A.R. Border (capt) st Houghton b Traicos	4
M.R.J. Veletta run out	43
S.R. Waugh not out	10
Extras (b 3, lb 3, w 6)	12
(50 overs)	5–266

Did not bat: S.P. O'Donnell, G.C. Dyer (wk), T.B.A. May, B.A. Reid

1/90 2/148 3/159 4/170 5/248

Bowling: Rawson 9-0-41-0; Jarvis 6-0-33-0; Shah 7-0-31-0; Brandes 10-1-58-0; Traicos 10-0-45-2; Butchart 8-0-52-1

ZIMBABWE	
A.H. Shah b Waugh	32
A.C. Waller c Waugh b McDermott	38
K.M. Curran c Waugh b May	29
A.J. Pycroft c Dyer b McDermott	38
D.L. Houghton (wk) lbw May	1
I.P. Butchart st Dyer b Border	3
P.W.E. Rawson not out	24
E.A. Brandes not out	18
Extras (lb 5, w 6, nb 2)	13
(50 overs)	6–196

Did not bat: K.J. Arnott, A.J. Traicos (capt), M.P. Jarvis

1/55 2/89 3/92 4/97 5/139 6/156

Bowling: McDermott 10-0-43-2; Reid 9-2-30-0; Waugh 4-0-9-1; O'Donnell 7-1-21-0; May 10-1-30-2; Border 8-0-36-1; Jones 1-0-5-0; Boon 1-0-17-0

Umpires: Mahboob Shah, P.W. Vidanagamage.

Toss: Zimbabwe. Points: Australia 4, Zimbabwe 0

in Australia there was another announcement. Cricket fans up to this final match had had to be satisfied with nothing more than a 60-second report on the sports section of the news. At last Channel 9 agreed to show an hour of delayed highlights of both semi-finals.

GROUP A: INDIA vs NEW ZEALAND
VIDARBHA C.A. GROUND, NAGPUR: INDIA WON BY 9 WICKETS

In front of a big crowd three Indian batsmen turned on fireworks for 32.1 overs so that their side charged to the top position of their group and could look forward to a home semi-final in the Wankhede Stadium in Bombay (Mumbai). Chasing a respectable if modest 221, Kris Srikkanth, Mohammad Azharuddin and a supposedly ailing Sunil Gavaskar struck boundary after boundary to completely demoralise the Kiwi attack. India had needed to reach their target in 42.2 overs. That was more than enough time.

There was little prospect of anything remarkable while New Zealand steadily built their total after Jeff Crowe won the toss and chose to bat first. John Wright, again a consistent performer, and another left-hander in for his first game in the tournament, Phil Horne, gave New Zealand a steady opening. That stayed the nature of the innings up until the 42nd over. The Kiwis reached 4–181. Each batsman had got a start without properly capitalising. Ravi Shastri had just dismissed top scorer, the stylish Dipak Patel, when paceman Chetan Sharma began his sixth over. The first three balls contained little of real note, but Ken Rutherford was bowled from the fourth. 6–182 suggested a few problems arising and they worsened when Sharma bowled wicketkeeper Ian Smith first ball.

Ewan Chatfield joined Martin Snedden. The innings was quickly disintegrating and Chatfield faced a hat-trick ball from a rampant Sharma with the frenzied crowd behind him. A charging run, a whipping action and a set of shattered stumps, followed immediately by an explosion of special Indian joy, meant that Sharma had completed the first World Cup hat-trick.

That ended the 42nd over. After the euphoria had subsided Snedden and Willie Watson rallied and added 39 from the last eight overs to give their side's total a modicum of substance.

Once India got under way it was shown up to really only be a modicum. Eighteen runs came off the first two overs. Then from Chatfield's third over Gavaskar, supposedly ill with a temperature over 35°C, lifted the innings into warp speed. The same man who five days earlier had earned his captain's wrath by batting too slowly, put his foot down the wicket and with a scything sweep of the bat clouted the ball over the mid-wicket boundary for six. Next ball an effortless straight drive registered another six that scattered a few patrons in a VIP box. Gavaskar followed that with another drive, this time a one-bounce four over mid-off. Finally, he clipped a full toss to the square-leg boundary to make it 20 runs from four balls.

From that point the tempo rarely eased. The 50 was raised after eight overs. While Gavaskar continued to charm as he raced towards his first century in 106 Limited-Over Internationals, Srikkanth became even more dominant. The arms of umpires Bird and Shepherd must have tired, such was the regularity that they had to signal fours and sixes. Willie Watson, who ironically came out of the massacre best, claimed, 'It was just like bowling in the TV highlights'. Six overs after the 50 had been reached the crowd was cheering the Indian 100. Finally Srikkanth's 58-ball extravaganza ended when Watson had him caught by Rutherford in the 17th over. He had hit three sixes and nine fours and the total was 136.

Azharuddin maintained the tempo, as he had to. Gavsakar, by now feeling the effects of his illness, slowed a little in the nineties. Then from his 85th ball the most prolific century-maker in Test cricket pushed the New Zealand debutant, young paceman Danny Morrison, through mid wicket for two to complete his 100. It was the second-fastest century ever scored in the World Cup. Azharuddin hit the first ball of Chatfield's fifth over, the 33rd of the innings, over mid wicket for four to terminate India's astonishing batting heroics. They had comfortably achieved both their objectives. Gavaskar had hit three

sixes and 10 fours in his 103 not out. He still had to share the Man of the Match award with the hat-trick man, Sharma.

NEW ZEALAND

J.G. Wright run out	35
P.A. Horne b Prabhakar	18
M.D. Crowe c Pandit b Azharuddin	21
K.R. Rutherford b Sharma	26
J.J. Crowe (capt) b Maninder	24
D.N. Patel c Kapil Dev b Shastri	40
M.C. Snedden run out	23
I.D.S. Smith (wk) b Sharma	0
E.J. Chatfield b Sharma	0
W. Watson not out	12
Extras (lb 14, w 7, nb 1)	22
(50 overs)	9–221

Did not bat: D.K. Morrison

1/46 2/84 3/90 4/122 5/181 6/182 7/182 8/182 9/221

Bowling: Kapil Dev 6–0–24–0; Prabhakar 7–0–23–1; Sharma 10–2–51–3; Azharuddin 7–0–26–1; Maninder Singh 10–0–51–1; Shastri 10–1–32–1

INDIA

K. Srikkanth c Rutherford b Watson	75
S.M. Gavaskar not out	103
M. Azharuddin not out	41
Extras (lb 1, w 2, nb 2)	5
(32.1 overs)	1–224

Did not bat: N.S. Sidhu, D.B. Vengsarkar Kapil Dev, R.J. Shastri, C.S. Pandit, M. Prabhakar, C. Sharma, Maninder Singh

1/136

Bowling: Morrison 10–0–69–0; Chatfield 4.1–1–39–0; Snedden 4–0–29–0; Watson 10–0–50–0; Patel 4–0–29–0

Umpires: H.D. Bird, D.R. Shepherd.

Toss: New Zealand. Points: India 4, New Zealand 0

WEDNESDAY NOVEMBER 4th AND THURSDAY NOVEMBER 5th
THE RELIANCE CUP SEMI-FINALS

At the conclusion of the preliminary rounds of the 1987 World Cup the group tables finished as follows:

GROUP A	P	W	L	Pts	R/R	GROUP B	P	W	L	Pts	R/R
INDIA	6	5	1	20	5.39	PAKISTAN	6	5	1	20	5.01
AUSTRALIA	6	5	1	20	5.19	ENGLAND	6	4	2	16	5.12
NEW ZEALAND	6	2	4	8	4.88	WEST INDIES	6	3	3	12	5.16
ZIMBABWE	6	0	6	0	3.76	SRI LANKA	6	0	6	0	4.04

FIRST SEMI-FINAL: AUSTRALIA vs PAKISTAN
GADDAFI STADIUM, LAHORE: AUSTRALIA WON BY 18 RUNS

The case for Pakistan winning this semi-final seemed irresistible. Excellent lead-up form, a side laden with talent, home-ground and home-crowd advantage and an opponent with little success behind them prior to this competition. Many felt Australia had done well to reach the semi-finals and that, subconsciously, they would be satisfied with that.

This semi-final was a very special event for the Pakistani team and the people of their

country. The intensity and the passion were tangible. Nothing mattered in the streets of the cities and the villages other than the Reliance Cup would be theirs after the final at Eden Gardens. The cricket fans of Pakistan, and that was virtually the entire population, saw the win as the destiny of their side. Imran reiterated his belief that his main ambitions centred around Test cricket. But he knew how much this tournament meant to the people of his country and he wanted to go out of the game with this one final honour. The only doubts arose from the thought that previous Pakistani teams had fallen at the semi-final hurdle and that the enormous local enthusiasm might add extra pressure to a team with an occasionally questionable collective temperament.

The concrete terraces were covered early by 40,000-plus fans when Allan Border won the toss and elected to bat. Australia made no change to the team that won at Cuttack while Pakistan brought in Mansoor Akhtar for Mudassar Nazar, who had a neck injury, and off spinner Tauseef Ahmed for Shoaib Mohammad. Imran believed the need to change the side and the loss of the toss were bad omens.

Geoff Marsh and David Boon gave Imran even further worries by getting Australia away to yet another excellent start. Salim Jaffer was very expensive and fellow left-armer, Wasim Akram, who had been in doubt because of a foot injury, also struggled. Marsh showed the occasion affected him when he was nearly out to the second ball of the day. He edged Imran to second slip only for Mansoor to take the ball on the half-volley. A flowing cover drive by the same batsman for four off a wide Akram half-volley indicated the malady was temporary.

The Australian openers had put together a partnership of 73 in 18 overs when Marsh pushed Tauseef to square leg. He took off for a single but Boon sent him back. Salim Malik threw down the stumps with Marsh still well short. That brought the day's first big cheer and made Malik a very popular fellow.

Dean Jones had to survive a close lbw shout when Abdul Qadir's leg spin was introduced. Boon then put the Pakistani in his place by crashing him through the covers for four with a perfect front-foot drive. The run-out had not improved the fortunes of Imran's team. A top-spinning Qadir wrong 'un flipped up off Jones' pad and whacked wicketkeeper Salim Yousuf in the mouth. He had to leave the ground for treatment. Javed Miandad took over his role with a smile and a bit to say. When there was a close call for a run-out he smashed all three stumps out of the ground, sending them flying metres. It

was spectacular, but Jones had made his ground.

Pakistan had even more troubles. Boon danced down the wicket and drove the ball straight back at Tauseef. The caught and bowled chance burst through the off spinner's fingers, cracking his left thumb on the way. More time was consumed while Tauseef was repaired. There was still plenty of noise coming from the stands. The ladies cheered and squealed at Imran even when he was not directly involved with the play. 'Imran we'll miss you' and 'King Khan' they waved on homemade signs, but the 'Tiger' of Pakistan was only interested in the cricket.

Jones and Boon brought up the Australian 100 from 135 balls. Jones twice square cut the wayward Jaffer for four and Boon raised his half century with a two to fine leg off Malik. Malik's unlikely little cutters provided the breakthrough in the 31st over to end the second-wicket partnership of 82 between the stocky Tasmanian and his Victorian partner. Boon went walking to a ball that drifted down leg side. Javed was just quick enough to punch out the middle stump, ending Boon's 91-ball resistance.

Next over Jones stepped away to cut Tauseef, missed and was bowled. Three for 155 looked a bit better than 1–155 for the locals. Border and Mike Veletta repaired the damage with a fourth wicket stand of 60, albeit at a slower rate; only 56 runs came between the 30th and 40th overs. Veletta was the busier of the two, although Border's square cut off Imran for four was a feature shot. In the 42nd over the Australian captain drove Akram into the covers. He took off for a single, but he had hit the ball too well and straight at Mansoor. When the stumps were thrown down Border kept on running towards the pavilion.

Steve Waugh and Veletta added another 21, until the West Australian gave himself room to drive Imran in the 47th over and lost his leg stump. He could have been proud of his 50 ball knock. Instead Veletta walked away holding his head and grimacing. He might have known what was to follow. In the same over Simon O'Donnell was struck on the pad and the ball fell at his feet. Waugh ran for a single, O'Donnell did not move. Imran rolled the ball back to Malik who removed a bail, then put it back on the stumps. Waugh kept walking but the umpires ruled that the batsmen had crossed and that O'Donnell was out.

Waugh neatly edged a four past the outstretched glove of Miandad, then in the same over Dyer was bowled off stump by a full-length delivery. In the 49th over Imran completed the set by taking out Craig McDermott's middle stump to leave Australia 8–249. It was a mighty fightback by the Pakistani captain.

He still had to find a bowler to finish the innings and had miscalculated so that the expensive, nervous Salim Jaffer would be required to finish the job. Final-over Steve 'Master' Waugh awaited the left-armer with relish. His first delivery landed on off stump on a length. Waugh made a mighty swing and lofted the ball over long-on for six. Jaffer's next ball was wide of off stump. Waugh dragged it through mid-on with a cross-bat thump that gave the boundary fielders no chance. Two full tosses brought two more twos, then from the final delivery Waugh clipped a leg-stump half volley square. The fieldsman ran around, lost his white hat and let the ball through his hands for four. Eighteen runs had come from the 50th over and Imran's disgust as he led his team off the field was obvious to all.

Pakistan's passage to the Reliance Cup final was no longer a certainty. They required 268 to win at 5.36 per over. Their strong batting line-up was capable enough, although the Australians now scented a chance at a boilover akin to the 1983 Lord's final. The bubbling soon intensified when disaster struck from the third ball of the innings. Mansoor clipped McDermott off the back foot to cover. Rameez took off. Mansoor, who had gone a few steps, sent him back. Border returned the ball to the bowler, who turned around and broke the stumps with Rameez struggling to get back. It was a costly mistake as Rameez's recent scores had been 42, 113, 32 and 70.

Malik had also been in form and in Reid's first over he followed an edged four with an authentic cover drive. He did the bulk of the scoring while the total reached 37 in the ninth over. Mansoor, totally out of sorts, then tried to

hit to square leg a full-pitched McDermott delivery which struck his off stump. The silence that dismissal caused was, if anything, greater when Malik chipped Waugh's first ball straight to mid-off off the bat's leading edge. Pakistan after 10.1 overs were 3–38. Imran was coming in to a crisis.

It was not the farewell Imran was hoping for and it could have got much worse the very next ball. An lbw shout was turned down. Replays showed the decision could easily have gone the way of the bowler. Miandad was also lucky when a catch off Reid flew between the keeper and Boon, standing at about third slip. Pakistan's requirement had increased to 6.5 runs per over.

The captain knew the time was nigh. He glanced Waugh for four and lofted him with just enough force to clear mid wicket for another boundary. An on-driven four by Imran off O'Donnell brought up the 100 in the 27th over. Imran completed his fifty in 73 balls with four fours. He reached 58 and had put on 112 with Miandad when Border came on to bowl the 36th over. Imran swung hard, the ball went between the batsman and the stumps. Border and Dyer appealed for a stumping and a catch. 'Dickie' Bird gave Imran out caught behind. Pakistan doubted the merit of the decision, although there was some evidence of a bottom edge.

A lot of responsibility now rested with Miandad, who brought up his half century in 79 balls. It was Akram, however, who tried to accelerate the scoring. He slapped McDermott straight down the ground for six and swept Border away into the cheering masses for a second six. McDermott responded with a leg-stump yorker to leave Pakistan 5–177 in the 39th over. The assignment was getting tougher and tougher. Seventy-six runs were needed from nine overs when 19-year-old Ijaz Ahmed clipped a Reid leg-stump half-volley in the air straight to Jones at deep square leg.

Miandad remained as the last hope. Two runs to square leg off Waugh took the total to 200 in the 43rd over and his invention, the upward nudge shot, brought two more runs straight after. Only 56 were still required from 37 balls when he slogged at Reid and lost his off stump. He had visibly tired during his innings, fatigued by having had to keep wicket and by the looming disappointment for his team. Yousuf and Qadir fought on, getting closer if not quite within striking distance. Yousuf and then Jaffer slogged at McDermott and were caught behind.

Tauseef faced up to the last ball of the 49th over, tentative and in pain from his throbbing thumb. He hung his bat out to a McDermott delivery and feathered an edge to Dyer. While the Australians ran and embraced each other, everyone else in the stadium was despondent. At McDermott's Man of the Match presentation the smiles from the dignitaries, including General Zia, were impressive but strained. This was a defeat that was not in the Pakistani script. Imran had retired in defeat. Well, retired for a while.

AUSTRALIA	
G.R. Marsh run out	31
D.C. Boon st Javed Miandad b Salim Malik	65
D.M. Jones b Tauseef Ahmed	38
A.R. Border (capt) run out	18
M.R.J. Veletta b Imran Khan	48
S.R. Waugh not out	32
S.P. O'Donnell run out	0
G.C. Dyer (wk) b Imran Khan	0
C.J. McDermott b Imran Khan	1
T.B.A. May not out	0
Extras (b 1, lb 19, w 13, nb 1)	34
(50 overs)	8–267

Did not bat: B.A. Reid

1/73 2/155 3/155 4/215 5/236 6/236 7/241 8/249

Bowling: Imran Khan 10-1-36-3; Salim Jaffer 6-0-57-0; Wasim Akram 10-0-54-0; Abdul Qadir 10-0-39-0; Tauseef Ahmed 10-1-39-1; Salim Malik 4-0-22-1

PAKISTAN	
Mansoor Akhtar b McDermott	9
Rameez Raja run out	1
Salim Malik c McDermott b Waugh	25
Javed Miandad b Reid	70
Imran Khan (capt) c Dyer b Border	58
Wasim Akram b McDermott	20
Ijaz Ahmed c Jones b Reid	8
Salim Yousuf (wk) c Dyer b McDermott	21
Abdul Qadir not out	20
Salim Jaffer c Dyer b McDermott	0
Tauseef Ahmed c Dyer b McDermott	1
Extras (lb 6, w 10)	16
(49 overs)	249

1/2 2/37 3/38 4/150 5/177 6/192 7/212 8/236 9/247 10/249

Bowling: McDermott 10-0-44-5; Reid 10-2-41-2; Waugh 9-1-51-1; O'Donnell 10-1-45-0; May 6-0-36-0; Border 4-0-26-1

Umpires: H.D. Bird, D.R. Shepherd.

Toss: Australia

SECOND SEMI-FINAL: INDIA vs ENGLAND
WANKHEDE STADIUM, BOMBAY: ENGLAND WON BY 35 RUNS

Australia had shattered the promoters' dream of an all subcontinental final. That did not upset India. They fancied their chances against Australia at Eden Gardens, especially after the mauling they gave their bowlers at New Delhi. All they had to do was overcome England in the Bombay semi-final on Thursday to fulfil their dream of winning a second consecutive World Cup, this time in front of their own adoring public.

England, happy to have a few days extra preparation because they were able to stay in India rather than travel to Lahore, looked at the Wankhede Stadium wicket and were suspicious and critical. It was about 40 metres long, devoid of grass, red brown in colour and promised a complete absence of bounce. It appeared custom-made for the Indian left-arm spinners. Gooch saw it and spent an hour in the nets practising his sweep shot against local bowlers.

Bombay's big day dawned, cloudy, airless, humid and stiflingly hot. The ground's 45,000 capacity was stretched to the limit. It made for an intimidating spectacle, as Wankhede's covered stands almost lean over the smallish playing arena. The noisy, seething spectators according to Eddie Hemmings were 'breathing down your neck'. The effect was increased by the wire fences. They were designed to keep the spectators out, but gave the players the feeling they were performing in a cage.

Against Zimbabwe, Manoj Prabhakar had swung the ball disconcertingly in the hot and heavy atmosphere. What to do if the toss was won? The English hierarchy were split on whether to bat or bowl. In the end it did not matter. Gatting called incorrectly. To this day he does not know what his decision would have been had he won. Kapil Dev sent England in.

India were without Dilip Vengsarkar, incapacitated with the type of stomach upset which more commonly affects visitors to the country. Wicketkeeper Kiran More returned while Chandrakant Pandit retained his place as a batsman. England's side was unchanged from their previous match.

Kapil's hoped-for swing was not there and, apart from a throat-clearing shout for lbw, Graham Gooch and Tim Robinson were not troubled by the new ball. Early progress was slow and after 10 overs only 20 runs were on the board. Robinson twice got Prabhakar away to the boundary, a clip to square leg and a drive over cover. When Maninder Singh came on the fun really began.

His first ball turned a metre away from Gooch, scooting through about five centimetres above the ground. Next ball Gooch bent low and swept hard. The ball shot away to fine leg for four. Gooch's assessment was right. From then he went on sweeping, paddling and pulling against the left-arm spin. Robinson's departure in the 13th over, stumped going for a drive, made no difference. With the ball spinning away prodigiously, Kapil was slow to plug up the leg-side gaps and the runs were coming freely out there.

Bill Athey battled to come to terms with the conditions. He could only contribute four runs to a 39-run second-wicket stand with Gooch in nine overs before inside edging Chetan Sharma to More. Then Gooch found a like-minded partner in his captain and they swept the Indians to distraction. Shot after shot went onto the vacant leg side, fine, behind and in front of square leg. Gooch had reached his fifty in the 19th over off 64 balls. He brought up the 100 with yet another bent-knee sweep, taking his own score to 60.

Azharuddin came on and Gatting varied the strokeplay with a square cut for four. Gooch had reached 82 when he finally mishit a sweep, only for Kris Srikkanth to miss the skyed chance as he ran in the same direction as the ball. A few overs later the Essex man pushed Kapil to deep mid-on and ran the single that brought up his

impressive 100 out of 3–157 in the 38th over. Next, he back cut the same bowler for four while at the other end Gatting brought out the reverse sweep and hit Ravi Shastri for four more to third man.

Gatting went to his fifty when he put Maninder fine for another boundary. It had taken 59 balls and included four fours. An edged drive through slip for four more from a full toss took the stand to 117 in 19 overs. Next ball, however, Gatting went so far across to the off that his sweep only brought the ball back onto the leg stump. England were 3–196 in the 41st over. Gooch finally went a couple of overs later, held under his chin by a relieved Srikkanth on the square-leg boundary. He had hit 11 fours in 136 balls. Kapil's late wickets could not stop Allan Lamb guiding England to 6–254 by the time of their compulsory closure. On this wicket, like Australia in Lahore, England knew they were in with a big chance.

The biggest roar of the day came in response to Gavaskar's stylish leg glance to the fine-leg boundary to open his scoring in Philip DeFreitas' first over. A few minutes later joy turned to horror as the little opener's off stump was sent cartwheeling. DeFreitas had nipped the ball back between bat and pad. Most Indians believed Gavaskar would bat for them one more time. As events turned out this was his final departure from the international arena and, unlike Imran, he was never called back.

It was an inspirational start by DeFreitas and it made Srikkanth and Navjot Sidhu more circumspect. Srikkanth played and missed three consecutive deliveries and was dropped by wicketkeeper Paul Downton off Gladstone Small when he was 10. He and Sidhu eventually added 51 without hitting a boundary. A missed slog at Neil Foster removed Srikkanth and 15 runs later it was 3–73 when Sidhu was caught in the covers by Athey off the same bowler.

India, like Pakistan the day before, could feel their Reliance Cup dreams slipping away. Pandit and Azharuddin responded by attacking Hemmings as soon as the off spinner was introduced. Sweeping was again the fashion, although Azharuddin's boundary that brought up the 100 in the 25th over was nearly caught at square leg by a brave Small. The tactic worked. Hemmings conceded 27 runs from three overs and was removed from the attack.

Pandit failed to take advantage of that when a slower full toss from Foster hit him on the foot right in front of the stumps. That brought the Indian captain in at 4–121. He french cut Foster just past his leg stump, one of several similar shots that day on the stay-down pitch. A flick to fine leg off DeFreitas got a better result.

After a few overs from Gooch, Gatting brought back Hemmings. Kapil swung him away for yet another leg-side four and India were starting to close in. Kapil and Azharuddin had put on 47 in 5.2 overs when Hemmings insisted Gatting put a fieldsman on the mid-wicket boundary. He had been urging him to do so for some time and was not pleased that it took so long to get a response. Eventually Gatting himself went out there. The very next ball Kapil hit hard and high in that direction. The English captain said his entire cricket career flashed in front of him as he waited for the ball to descend. Nevertheless, the crucial catch was safely held. Kapil had faced just 22 balls for his 30.

Azharuddin pushed John Emburey to point to bring up his 50 in 60 balls. His job was far from finished and he was still there with Shastri to raise the 200. The sweeping swipe was still popular and such a hit right off the middle by

Shastri left India a very gettable 51 runs to win from nine overs with five wickets standing.

Now, though, the game changed decisively. Azharuddin was given out lbw by umpire Steve Woodward when he swept at a straight and full Hemmings top-spinner. Azharuddin hit seven fours in 74 balls. His dismissal seemed to induce an Indian panic. One run later More chipped a catch back to Emburey, who nonchalantly caught the ball one-handed high to his right. Prabhakar stepped away to cut Small and was caught behind off the bottom edge. Sharma slogged his first ball from Hemmings into the deep where Lamb took an excellent outfield catch low down.

It was all left up to Shastri. From the non-striker's end he had witnessed the suicidal batting that had reduced his side to 9–219. India still needed 36 and only non-batsman Maninder was left with him. There were 33 deliveries remaining, but Shastri pulled out the harikari sword as well. Another hoik off Hemmings skyed the ball to square leg where Downton judged the catch perfectly. The old traditional rivals, England and Australia were through. The subcontinental rivals were out.

India had lost their last five wickets for 15 in 33 balls. Hemmings share was 4–21 in 34 balls. Thank goodness his captain had finally agreed with his field placement. Gooch won the Man of the Match award and allowed himself the luxury

ENGLAND	
G.A. Gooch c Srikkanth b Maninder	115
R.T. Robinson st More b Maninder	13
C.W.J. Athey c More b Sharma	4
M.W. Gatting (capt) b Maninder	56
A.J. Lamb not out	32
J.E. Emburey lbw Kapil Dev	6
P.A.J. DeFreitas b Kapil Dev	7
P.R. Downton (wk) not out	1
Extras (b 1, lb 18, w 1)	20
(50 overs)	6–254

Did not bat: N.A. Foster, E.E. Hemmings, G.C. Small

1/40 2/79 3/196 4/203 5/219 6/231

Bowling: Kapil Dev 10-1-38-2; Prabhakar 9-1-40-0; Maninder 10-0-54-3; Sharma 9-0-41-1; Shastri 10-0-49-0; Azharuddin 2-0-13-0

INDIA	
K. Srikkanth b Foster	31
S.M. Gavaskar b DeFreitas	4
N.S. Sidhu c Athey b Foster	22
M. Azharuddin lbw Hemmings	64
C.S. Pandit lbw Foster	24
Kapil Dev (capt) c Gatting b Hemmings	30
R.J. Shastri c Downton b Hemmings	21
K.S. More (wk) c & b Emburey	0
M. Prabhakar c Downton b Small	4
Chetan Sharma c Lamb b Hemmings	0
Maninder Singh not out	0
Extras (b 1, lb 9, w 6, nb 3)	19
(45.3 overs)	219

1/7 2/58 3/73 4/121 5/168 6/204 7/205 8/218 9/219 10/219

Bowling: DeFreitas 7-0-37-1; Small 6-0-22-1; Emburey 10-1-35-1; Foster 10-0-47-3; Hemmings 9.3-1-52-4; Gooch 3-0-16-0

Umpires: A.R. Crafter, S.J. Woodward.

Toss: India

of a smile. When Kapil had been racing along with Azharuddin, fireworks were being let off continuously in the stands. Once things went wrong, however, Wankhede was as quiet as Gaddafi had been the day before. The fans could be blamed for the loss, too, to the extent that all through the Indian innings they were madly calling for sixes. They were drunk on the type of batting their team had exhibited at Nagpur. Kapil got the official blame. He was relieved of the captaincy for the second time.

SUNDAY 8 NOVEMBER 1987
THE RELIANCE CUP FINAL
AUSTRALIA vs ENGLAND
EDEN GARDENS, CALCUTTA: AUSTRALIA WON BY 7 RUNS

The absence of their own team did nothing to deter the cricket fans of Calcutta. The World Cup final was an event, whoever the combatants, and the Indians selected Australia as the team to support. The English press believed it was because they had knocked out India while Australia had eliminated India's rivals, Pakistan. They do not realise that every other country will support whoever is playing against England. Always have, always will.

So 70,000, 80,000, 90,000 or however many fill that massive stadium were there in force for a match that, whatever the result, would see a new country celebrating the holding of cricket's most prestigious limited-overs trophy. The scalpers had to cut their ticket prices. India's semi-final defeat had cost them thousands of rupees.

There was plenty of radio coverage worldwide. Australians, suddenly very interested in cricket again, had to be satisfied with that and some more delayed television highlights of the conclusion of the match. The only live coverage was on Sky television in hotels. Despite images to the contrary, not all Australians live in public bars. Once more the words and pictures came via the BBC. Tony Lewis, Jack Bannister and Ray Illingworth competed with buzzing voices coming from crossed telephone lines. Did this mean there were Indians not actually watching the final?

The wicket provided for the big game was still slow, but far better than the one for the Bombay semi-final. Its preparation had been overseen by Les Burdett, curator at the Adelaide Oval, who was invited over by the Bengal Cricket Association.

All players involved were impressed, excited and even overwhelmed by the atmosphere, the occasion and the vibrancy of the stadium. This was not Lord's, but everyone celebrated the difference and the most cynical doubters had to admit Eden Gardens was in its own way a venue worthy of the World Cup final. Australian coach Bob Simpson has rated this ground the equal of any in the world. Mike Veletta is another who was very impressed. 'We had an early rise because of the 9 am start,' he says. 'It was an exciting day and the whole team was thrilled just to be involved. There were thousands of people milling around as we drove in the bus to the ground. We had worked so hard to get to the final and this was a celebration of the success we had in the tournament.

'It was the only time I played at Eden Gardens so I only ever saw it full. It is a fantastic arena with a good surface and the Indian authorities had done a great job in getting everything organised.'

The day dawned fine and hot, but far more comfortable than steamy Bombay (Mumbai). Border won an important toss. Both he and his counterpart had wanted to bat first. The team line-ups were unchanged from their semi-final wins. England started the match as the bookmaker's favourite.

The value of Gatting's incorrect call was emphasised when David Boon and Geoff Marsh got Australia away to a flyer. Gladstone Small and Phil DeFreitas seemed affected by the occasion and were unable to control the new ball. Boon, in particular, took advantage. Small's first over contained two no-balls and cost 11 runs. DeFreitas dropped short. One ball had Boon in trouble, the next was pulled for four. Another shot off his toes brought four more. After nine overs the total was already 48 and Boon was outscoring his partner three to one. Between them the two West Indian born new-ball bowlers conceded 67 runs and Gatting decided not to risk them using their full quota of overs.

Neil Foster came on first change at the Pavilion End and immediately made Boon and Marsh work harder for their runs. The next nine overs realised just 27. Then Foster moved a leg-cutter through Marsh's defence and Australia was 1–75. Foster's first eight overs cost him just 16 so that after 25 overs the score was just 1–95. The off spinners John Emburey and Eddie Hemmings had been introduced. Jones pulled the latter for six and lofted a Graham Gooch medium pacer down the ground for four.

Drinks were taken at the end of the 34th over with Australia 1–150. There were wickets in hand, but the projected target was now closer to 230 than the 270 it might have been after 10 overs. The break in play fortified England's attack. Jones clipped Hemmings to Bill Athey at mid wicket straight after the break. Border's concern with the run rate was clear when Craig McDermott was promoted with the sole purpose of clouting some quick runs. He slogged Gooch for consecutive fours, but a few balls later missed a straight yorker from the same bowler. Two runs later Boon top-edged a sweep off Hemmings and wicketkeeper Paul Downton held the catch running back. Australia were 4–168 in the 39th over. The innings now lay in the balance. Boon had hit seven fours in 125 balls for his fifth half century of the competition.

Border was joined by Veletta and the pair quickly reasserted Australia's control. Busy and bustling, they put on 73 in 10 overs. Veletta, who made his unbeaten 45 in just 31 balls, glanced, swept and ran like a terrier. His placement was a feature of perhaps the most important innings of his life. 'I had to play my shots straight away,' Veletta says. 'AB and I got the partnership going

with singles and then we hit out and took the odd chance towards the end of the innings. The spinners bowled a straight line so it was better to sweep them rather than back away and hit the ball to the off, which I only did a couple of times. I think the combination of a left- and right-hand batsman mucked up their line a bit.'

Gooch's eighth over cost 12 and the 200 was raised in the 44th over. A total of 79 was taken from the last 10 overs, including 11 from the luckless DeFreitas in the 50th. 'Two hundred and fifty-three was 20 more than we thought we would get in the middle of the innings,' Veletta says. 'More than that, though, a flurry of runs at the end gives the team a lift and puts them in a positive frame of mind when they go out to field. We knew we were in with a chance with 253 on the board, but also knew that we had a lot of hard work in front of us.'

It did not take much work to get rid of Tim Robinson. His first ball was the third of the innings. McDermott bowled a fullish length, the ball cut back and Robinson, immobile at the crease, was trapped right in front. There was talk the Australian and English teams had asked for Tony Crafter and 'Dickie' Bird to officiate in the final. Quite rightly, the tournament officials insisted on neutrals and Ram Babu Gupta and Mahboob Shah got the job, which they handled competently. Robinson's lbw was one of the day's easier decisions.

Border had a half chance to run out Athey in the fourth over. The Yorkshireman responded with a nice glance for four in the next over. McDermott was bowling quickly enough to extract some lift from the slow wicket, but he could do nothing about a trademark Gooch on-drive to a half-volley pitched on middle stump. The opener pulled Reid for another boundary, then the left-armer slid the ball past his outside edge. Veletta added to the value of his batting by saving runs with some energetic work at square leg.

Simon O'Donnell, hiding the fact that he was very ill, dived desperately at fine leg to save two runs, then in the 18th over brought a ball back into Gooch that won a second lbw decision. It was 2–66, so Athey and Gooch had consolidated well without scoring at the rate needed to win the match.

Gatting's task was to lift that rate. He got off the mark with an off-side glide for four off Waugh, then selected young off spinner Tim May as the object of his batting brutality. He reverse swept and drove the South Australian for a seven-run return, then lofted him down the ground. Waugh on the boundary judged the catch perfectly. Unfortunately the force of the hit caused him to take two steps back. Waugh looked at his feet and threw the ball back in disgust. He had stepped over the rope and the shot would count as six. After four expensive overs May was removed from the attack.

England reached their hundred in the 25th over. Gatting and Athey had added 69 in 14 overs when Border brought himself on to bowl. England was 2–135. Without any assessment of the left-arm spinner Gatting reverse swept Border's first ball. It flew from the top edge onto his shoulder and dollied in the air to wicket-keeper Greg Dyer. In an instant every English scribe and follower had a scapegoat for the eventual loss. Chairman of Selectors, Peter May, a known opponent of the reverse sweep, closed his eyes. An over or so later the shot may have been a worthwhile risk. The judgmental error was to try it off Border's first ball. Veletta said, 'I was surprised. They were batting well and it was unnecessary.'

Athey, stylish and unhurried reached his 50 in 92 balls. When he and Allan Lamb paused for the day's last break for drinks England wanted 102 from 15 overs. Upon the resumption Lamb escaped when Dyer missed a stumping off Border. England had to keep pressing desperately for runs. Going for a third run, Athey failed by a whisker to beat Waugh's throw. He had become one of over 60 run-out dismissals throughout the tournament. Athey, who had assumed the role of the innings' cornerstone hit just two fours in 103 balls. His dismissal left England on 4–170 in the 39th over.

Downton came in ahead of Emburey. He looked uncertain as to whether he should support Lamb or hit out to reduce the deficit. He hit a four, was dropped in the deep by a diving

McDermott and then holed out to O'Donnell at long-off. Five for 188 in the 42nd over. All of Emburey's expertise in the unorthodox was required. He played his special step-away square slash at McDermott. The ball flew over point. Veletta was well placed but the low sun was not. A brave attempt at the catch failed. 'The sun was in my eyes,' Veletta says, 'but AB still was not impressed when the catch went down.'

The ask was getting tougher all the time. It was down to 38 required from 24 balls. Lamb pulled hard at Waugh, missed and ran a leg bye, another single to Emburey and Lamb tried the pull again. The ball hurried through and he was bowled. England felt it was over. Two more singles at the start of the 48th over did nothing to boost their hopes. Then Emburey swatted hard to mid wicket and ran. Boon did not have to move and his throw to McDermott was spot-on. England 7–220 needed 34 from 15 balls and were out of it. The Indians thought so. They were cheering and dancing to a result that pleased them.

DeFreitas just ignored all this and smashed McDermott's next ball over extra cover for four. No-one took a great deal of notice. Next ball he wound up and cracked the ball over the sight-screen for six. Now people were watching. From the sixth ball the seamer stepped right away and lifted the ball over mid wicket for four more. 'I think Craig was bowling to get wickets and put the ball on the wrong length,' Veletta says. 'DeFreitas gave us a bit of a fright. It got pretty nerve-racking out there.'

Waugh, however, was not so easy to hit. DeFreitas used the same tactics and did not connect properly once. There was laughter when an outrageous slower ball barely bounced over his stumps. Then an inside edge was caught on the half-volley by Dyer. When DeFreitas did connect he merely lobbed a catch to Reid deep on the off side.

It was left to the two fast bowlers, Small and Foster, to get 17 from the final over. They pushed hard and collected a brave but forlorn nine. Australia had won the Reliance Cup by seven runs.

'I fielded the last ball and foolishly threw it

back in,' Veletta says. 'In the end the only souvenir I got from the match was a bail from Greg Dyer. I also got all the players to sign my bat. Otherwise there are just the memories. I'm not a great watcher of cricket, so I've never even sat through a video of the game.'

Within minutes the smiling short on top, long at the back, 'mullet' haired Australians were being feted and photographed in the darkness. For the long-suffering Border, carried in triumph on the shoulders of his team-mates, it was his sweetest moment in the game. The crowd stayed to cheer the Australians as they displayed their trophy on a lap of honour. They were then treated to a fantastic fireworks display which signalled the close of the 1987 World Cup. It was a spectacular conclusion to a wonderful tourna-

ment. Some original doubters were now sorry the carnival was over. David Frith in *Wisden Cricket Monthly* wrote, 'Australia is back! And the cricket world is better for it.'

'We had plenty of plans to celebrate and there was a function put on for us back at the hotel,' Veletta says. 'I remember Simon O'Donnell doing a bit of singing, but it was a big day and by midnight I had conked out. I think the majority of the team were the same. We were able to celebrate a bit more over the next couple of days.'

In the Oberoi Grand Hotel most people had forgotten that David Boon won the Man of the Match award. This was a victory for every member of the Australian team.

AUSTRALIA

D.C. Boon c Downton b Hemmings	75
G.R. Marsh b Foster	24
D.M. Jones c Athey b Hemmings	33
C.J. McDermott b Gooch	14
A.R. Border (capt) run out	31
M.R.J. Veletta not out	45
S.R. Waugh not out	5
Extras (b 1, lb 13, w 5, nb 7)	26
(50 overs)	5-253

Did not bat: S.P. O'Donnell, G.C. Dyer (wk), T.B.A. May, B.A. Reid

1/75 2/151 3/166 4/168 5/241

Bowling: DeFreitas 6-1-34-0; Small 6-0-33-0; Foster 10-0-38-1; Hemmings 10-1-48-2; Emburey 10-0-44-0; Gooch 8-1-42-1

ENGLAND

G.A. Gooch lbw O'Donnell	35
R.T. Robinson lbw McDermott	0
C.W.J. Athey run out	58
M.W. Gatting (capt) c Dyer b Border	41
A.J. Lamb b Waugh	45
P.R. Downton (wk) c O'Donnell b Border	9
J.E. Emburey run out	10
P.A.J. DeFreitas c Reid b Waugh	17
N.A. Foster not out	7
G.C. Small not out	3
Extras (b 1, lb 14, w 2, nb 4)	21
(50 overs)	8-246

Did not bat: E.E. Hemmings

1/1 2/66 3/135 4/170 5/188 6/218 7/220 8/235

Bowling: McDermott 10-1-51-1; Reid 10-0-43-0; Waugh 9-0-37-2; O'Donnell 10-1-35-1; May 4-0-27-0; Border 7-0-38-2

Umpires: R.B. Gupta, Mahboob Shah.

Toss: Australia

POST-MORTEM

Australian World Cup joy was tempered by the announcement that 24-year-old all-rounder Simon O'Donnell was diagnosed with cancer soon after his return home. The life-threatening lymphatic tumour in his rib cage had to receive exhausting chemotherapy treatment. Happily, a couple of months later O'Donnell was given the all clear, to the relief of the entire cricket

community. O'Donnell successfully resumed his career at the start of the 1988–89 season, although his perspective on life had been slightly altered.

At least that saga had a positive ending. The same could not be said of Mike Gatting's clash with umpire Shakoor Rana during the acrimonious Pakistan vs England Test series which immediately followed the World Cup. The petty feud between the two countries sullied the game and the finger-pointing incident went a long way towards ending Gatting's tenure as captain. It also distracted attention away from the great job India and Pakistan did as co-hosts of the 1987 Reliance Cup. The tournament was a success in virtually every aspect and did great credit to the organisers.

6

Benson and Hedges World Cup, 1992:
Imran's Cornered Tigers

Nineteen ninety-two was the year coloured uniforms, replay screens, night cricket under lights and tobacco advertising came to the World Cup. It was also the year that the South African issue dominated the headlines in the lead-up to the tournament. Fortunately, this time it was for all the right reasons.

To contest the World Cup in Australasia seemed a logical progression after the success of the first migration to India and Pakistan in 1987 and as a follow-up to the exciting win by Allan Border's team in the Reliance Cup final in Calcutta. Yet there was reluctance from the Australian authorities to commit themselves. Not even a World Cup was going to interfere with their schedule of a Test series and the precious, television-friendly World Series Cup. Some even questioned the likelihood of the financial success of a World Cup in Australia and New Zealand.

It was New Zealand Cricket Council chairman Bob Vance who showed most enthusiasm for the idea, finally convincing his Australian counterparts at an ICC meeting in London in 1987 of the merit of the proposal.

Another ICC meeting in July 1989 ratified the joint submission that the 1992 World Cup would be played with the two countries as co-hosts. A schedule of matches was drawn up which included the same eight teams that participated in the competition in 1983 and 1987, except that this time the tournament would be played as a full round robin, each side meeting all the others once and four teams progressing to the semi-finals. This caused an increase in the number of games from 27 to 31.

All seemed set until the political situation in South Africa began to change. When Nelson Mandela was released from gaol he gave his blessing for South Africa to return to the international cricketing fold. The ICC re-admitted them at their meeting in July 1991, although chairman, Colin Cowdrey suggested they would not be able to be included in the 1992 World Cup.

Mandela's advice was sought on the matter. He wrote to Cowdrey suggesting South Africa's inclusion would assist reconciliation and be a reward for the ground-breaking racial integration by South African cricket authorities. British Prime Minister John Major and his Australian counterpart, Bob Hawke, were also involved in negotiations. Most people liked the idea and in October it was agreed that a ninth side be included in the tournament. That necessitated a re-draw which increased the number of matches still further to 39. The publicity the move brought to the competition was invaluable.

Once all that was sorted out the rules for the 1992 Benson and Hedges World Cup could be studied more closely. Each innings was once again limited to 50 overs. Fielding restrictions were increased in the first 15 overs with only two men allowed outside the circles during that time. The players' uniforms would be coloured and would bear their names on the back. A selection of games at suitable venues were to be partially played under lights at night. Two white balls were used each innings because of a problem with the greying and fading of just one. Most controversially, the tight scheduling allowed only one day to be set aside for each fixture and if rain interfered with a side batting second their lost overs were only to be compensated by the lowest scoring overs of their opponents. It looked a dangerous and potentially unfair rule even at its inception.

And the possibility of problems with rain was increased by scheduling the tournament right at the end of the southern summer in late February and March, after all the other Australian Test and limited-over commitments had been cleared.

Despite the amount of cricket they had already played that summer, the form of the Australian side in 1991–92 under Allan Border had been excellent and at the start of the Benson and Hedges World Cup they were red-hot favourites to take the trophy for the second time running. They had the measure of India and the West Indies in the World Series Cup and had thrashed India 4–0 in a five-match Test series.

David Boon was in the midst of a fantastic run of form with the bat. The consistency of the powerful Tasmanian in the short and longer versions of the game was to be marvelled at. Against India he peeled off four Test centuries and one more in a Limited-Over International. His opening partner, Geoff Marsh, had a leaner time and had lost his Test place, but the popular deputy had been recalled for the World Cup. Mark Taylor, Dean Jones, possibly the greatest limited-overs batsman in the world and on the verge of becoming a specialist in that form of the game, Border and the Waugh twins, Mark and Steve, suggested a line-up capable of many match-winning totals in conditions that would suit them.

Like Boon, paceman Craig McDermott had just completed a fine domestic summer with oodles of wickets. With support from Merv Hughes, Mike Whitney, a fit-again Bruce Reid, off spinner Peter Taylor and the all-rounders it was easy to see why this unit, well drilled by Bob Simpson, began the tournament so likely, in the eyes of many to be the team to beat. Sharp running between wickets and error-free fielding were keynotes to recent successes and likely to feature again.

Australia's opponent in the 1987 final, England, under manager Mickey Stewart and captain, Graham Gooch, had embraced much of the Simpson ethos of discipline and hard work. After a strong showing against the West Indies and New Zealand in recent months they were very confident of a strong showing in the 1992 World Cup.

Since his leadership appointment in 1990, Gooch had responded with a welter of runs and was an important component at the top of the order. Although 38, his willingness to train and keep fit was standing him in good stead. Gooch's philosophy meant that no place could be found for David Gower. However, Ian Botham, who arrived late in New Zealand because he had a part to play in a children's pantomime, was included.

Botham was just one of a squad bursting with all-rounders and middle-order batsmen. There was no specialist opener selected to accompany Gooch and the word was that Botham would be used to launch the innings in an attacking style that was perhaps four years ahead of its time. Graeme Hick's reputation as a batsman with the ability to massacre mediocre bowling preceded him, while Alec Stewart, the son of the team's manager, had adopted the important dual role of wicketkeeper-batsman and had been a revelation at the end of the English season and in New Zealand. For the likes of Gooch, Allan Lamb and Ian Botham, this was a last chance at the ultimate limited-overs prize.

The winning of the World Cup was Imran Khan's final ambition in cricket, too. The all-rounder wanted to do it for himself, his team, his country and the cancer hospital he wanted to have built in Pakistan. His squad was filled with talent, not least his own which, if diminishing slightly, was still formidable. There had been plenty of comings and goings in the lead-up to the World Cup as Pakistan tried to get the balance of their 14-man squad just right. A big loss was the back injury to Wasim Akram's new-ball partner Waqar Younis. The stress fractures were diagnosed at the start of the competition and were only partially compensated for by the late availability of Javed Miandad, who had just recovered from a back injury.

Since the disappointing loss in the semi-final in Lahore in 1987, which at the time was thought to be Imran's farewell match, Salim Malik had become a quality performer in the Pakistani middle order and Ramiz Raja, an aggressive opener, also had an impressive record in Limited-Over Internationals. Imran, starting the tournament with a shoulder injury, could still deliver a lethal inswinger, while his heir apparent, Wasim Akram, swung the ball late at fast left-arm. His hitting in a tight situation was a real bonus to Pakistan.

India must have felt that they had been in Australia forever by the time the World Cup began. They had been playing cricket in that country since the previous November and by February had only a few wins in the World Series Cup to show for their efforts. Much attention centred on the wunderkind batting of Sachin Tendulkar. At 18, the youngster from Bombay had already shown the skill and temperament to flourish at the highest level and Indian fans in particular waited for him to make an impact on the premier limited-overs tournament.

At the other end of his career was all-rounder Kapil Dev. Like Botham and Imran, this would be the last showcase of his great talents. He had just become the second bowler in history to pass the 400 Test wicket mark. Kapil's fast-medium swingers were the cutting edge of the Indian attack. To neutral spectators, though, it was his middle-order hitting that was the greatest attraction. Disappointed at losing the 1987 semi-final in Bombay after the triumph of 1983, the pressure was on the respected Indian captain, Mohammad Azharuddin, to get plenty of runs himself and to lead his team successfully. Indian fans would accept nothing less.

While holding on to their status as the best Test side in the world, the past six years had seen a decline in the West Indies as a force in the limited-overs version of the game. They, like India, were familiar with conditions in Australia, although the selectors made some changes to the squad that competed in the World Series Cup to the one for the World Cup.

Viv Richards had hoped to use the tournament as his swansong, but the selectors opted to leave him out, hoping that the new captain, Richie Richardson, could establish his authority over the team. The World Cup squad was boosted with the inclusion of experienced players like Roger Harper, Phil Simmons and Winston Benjamin. Malcolm Marshall's wise head was another asset to Richardson, although the champion fast bowler had lost a lot of his sting with the new ball.

Eagerly anticipated was the batting of the rival to Tendulkar's status as world prodigy, Brian Lara. The stylish Trinidadian left-hander had a pedigree as impressive as Tendulkar's and was at about the same stage of his career. Desmond Haynes and Richardson would be expected to be the best performed West Indian batsmen, while Curtly Ambrose remained a fearsome opponent when armed with a new ball. Interestingly, the value of Courtney Walsh in this form of cricket had diminished in the eyes of the West Indian selectors at this stage. Early in 1992 it was unsure if his time would come again.

Although rated only a 14–1 chance to win the World Cup, New Zealand were thrilled with their role as joint hosts, had prepared thoroughly and might be a handful on their own wickets. The Kiwi's had been outclassed by England only weeks before, but Martin Crowe and his brains trust still had a few tricks up their sleeves and hoped to make an impact on the competition.

If New Zealand were to have any success, Crowe himself, a batsman among the world's elite, would have to score plenty of runs. There was some talent behind him, too, in the shape of John Wright, Ken Rutherford and Mark Greatbatch, but the best feature of the attack looked to be its steadiness, which was hardly inspiring. The medium pace of Willie Watson was supported by the fast-medium pace of Chris Cairns and Danny Morrison, the slow-medium pace of Gavin Larsen and Rod Latham and the flat darting off spin of Dipak Patel.

The possible promotion of Zimbabwe to full ICC membership and hence eventual Test status was welcomed by the Sri Lankans, as they would no longer be viewed as the underlings of the international fold. An isolated win against other countries still gave cause for special celebration in Colombo, but they gave no indication that they would have any impact on the Benson and

Hedges World Cup. As with New Zealand, their bowling looked to lack the necessary punch to restrict quality opposition to a losing total.

Aravinda de Silva was captain for the World Cup and clearly his side's classiest batsman in a well-credentialled line-up which included chunky left-hander Arjuna Ranatunga. Hashan Tillerkeratne, Sanath Jayasuriya and Asanka Gurusinha were also accomplished left-handers with their best days ahead of them, while Roshan Mahanama's style and technique at the top of the order complemented the aggression of the left-handers well.

The Sri Lankan bowling resources were thin. Rumesh Ratnayake, Pramodya Wickremasinghe and Champaka Ramanayake had fair credentials at best as pace bowlers. They may have been able to defend substantial totals, but not modest ones. Sri Lanka would find by the end of the tournament that their geographical knowledge of Australasia was excellent. As in 1987, they had plenty of international criss-crossing to do.

Zimbabwe had made the best possible start when they entered the competition in 1983 by defeating Australia. They had been worthy winners again of the ICC Trophy. To the start of the 1992 campaign, though, that initial victory was still their only World Cup success. Dave Houghton would hope to remedy that. His individual effort against New Zealand in 1987 had brought Zimbabwe closest to their second win. Now Houghton was captain, taking on that role at the expense of his wicketkeeping duties which he had handed over to the promising left-handed opening batsman, Andy Flower. Teenager Alistair Campbell was another Zimbabwean batsman of great promise having the opportunity to see how he measured up against the best in the world.

Eddo Brandes offered the greatest likelihood of breaking through with the new ball. The most reliable member of the Zimbabwean attack, however, was still John Traicos. Only a few months short of his 45th birthday, the metronomic accuracy of his off spin was a byword. Traicos remained as lean and fit as when he played three Tests for South Africa back in 1970.

Like many others, Traicos was probably astounded when South Africa achieved sudden re-acceptance into the outside cricketing world. And he and his peers were excited by the prospect of pitting their skill against the former exiles. The side was led by Kepler Wessels, who like Traicos had now represented two countries. Wessels had already played over 50 Limited-Over Internationals for Australia between 1982 and 1985. Seven years later the selection of his team had caused an uproar in South Africa. Three favourite sons who had done themselves great credit through the years of isolation, Clive Rice, Jimmy Cook and Peter Kirsten, were all omitted from the South African side. Following much protest a spot was found for Kirsten. Cook was selected for a couple of later Tests, but Rice, a great all-rounder who captained the side in South Africa's first sanctioned match on their return in India, was finished as an international cricketer when he had hardly started.

Many of Wessels' players were new names and faces to fans outside South Africa. One whose arrival in Australasia was eagerly anticipated was fast bowler Allan Donald. 'White Lightning' had a reputation as one of the quickest bowlers in the world. An exciting spectacle as a thoroughbred in the Michael Holding and Dennis Lillee mould, Donald's bowling would be a talking point amongst the batsmen in each of the other eight sides before this tournament was over.

The teams in their pretty blues, greens, yellows and reds lined up on the deck of the HMAS *Canberra* on Sydney Harbour for the now almost traditional pre-tournament group photo. Another shot at Circular Quay with the Opera House as a backdrop featured the captains, with Border and Gooch nursing the glass orb that was the object of their desire.

The weather for Sydney was a little gloomy, which summed up the attitude of some of the participants and those covering the tournament at this early stage. A complaints department would have been very busy after the black-tie dinner that launched the competition. Too expensive, poorly arranged and uninspiring was the view of the critics after the event. Ian Chappell wrote the guests would have been better off to spend their money on a harbour cruise. Wasim Akram called the photo session a shambles and the price of the dinner 'immoral'. Ray Martin hosted without the support of the type of quality offsider he had when introducing Australian television coverage of the 1999 World Cup.

The only memorable moment came when joint chairman of the organising committee, Malcolm Gray, said that the room contained the most extraordinary collection of cricketing talent, 'with the possible exception of when Sir Donald Bradman dines alone'. Three days later a selection of that talent, sans Bradman, was on display. The Benson and Hedges World Cup was under way.

SATURDAY 22 FEBRUARY 1992
NEW ZEALAND vs AUSTRALIA
EDEN PARK, AUCKLAND: NEW ZEALAND WON BY 37 RUNS

Australia had only to play one of their matches in New Zealand, and after the tournament favourites were well beaten by the better-prepared Kiwis in this one they would be glad not to have to come back.

After some pre-match hype that included the distribution of thousands of party hooters to the big parochial crowd and a parade with sets of giant stumps, dancing girls and Sir Richard Hadlee being driven around holding that precious glass trophy, Martin Crowe won the toss and elected to bat. Craig McDermott opened with a wide, sent another one down second ball then bowled John Wright behind his legs with the first legal delivery of the tournament.

When Ian Healy brilliantly caught Rod Latham low to his right the home side was 3–53 after 15 overs and there was no indication that the Australians would be set a difficult target. Some signs were not good for Allan Border's side, though. Tom Moody had already dropped a simple waist-high chance at first slip and the bowlers, supposedly slightly underdone in the shorter version of the game, were unwisely dropping the ball short.

This meant Martin Crowe could put his powerful pull shot and the short boundaries at backward square leg to good use. It almost brought him unstuck when a diving Dean Jones nearly brought off the catch of the season at deep square leg. Otherwise time and again, even with two fieldsmen protecting the boundary, short balls were pummelled to the fence. A Ken Rutherford version of the shot off Steve Waugh raised the 100 in the 28th over as the acceleration began.

Off spinner Peter Taylor bowled a poor spell. Crowe belted yet another short delivery between two leg-side boundary sweepers to bring him to his fifty in the 31st over. The milestones continued. The 100 partnership arrived in the 38th over with still another pulled four by Crowe off Bruce Reid. For variety, the next ball was driven through mid-off, also for four.

The deepening frown on Border's brow grew darker when the Australian captain failed to hold a swirling chance running back at square leg given by his opposite number. A direct-hit underarm throw by Mark Waugh which ran out Rutherford ended the excellent 118-run stand. However, it failed to bring any relief for Border and the Australians. Productive little partnerships between Crowe and Chris Harris, then Crowe and Ian Smith, lifted the total above 200. Healy's second wonderful catch brought in Chris Cairns and the young all-rounder mixed the verbals with the Australians, clubbed a couple of boundaries and ran like the wind to complete the single which gave Crowe his 100 in the 50th over. The Kiwi supporters invaded Eden Park in celebration, happy at the milestone and the final team total of 6–248 which included 77 from the final 10 overs.

Crowe had been no certainty to start in the World Cup because of problems with his right knee. It was another reason why seven of his 11 fours had come from back-foot pulls. The quality and aggression of the New Zealand captain's batting, in harness with Rutherford, had taken the favourites by surprise. Now, in the field, he confused their tactics further by opening the bowling with off spinner Dipak Patel.

The idea brought no immediate reward as David Boon and Geoff Marsh put on 62 for the first wicket. The pair, with Marsh in particular struggling, used up 18 overs which boosted the required run rate to a run per ball. Once Marsh was caught at cover driving Larsen, Jones attempted to lift the tempo only to be run out going for a two to square leg on Cairns' powerful arm. The decision by Khizar Hayat, which replays showed was a tight one, had a big impact on the Australian momentum.

Boon pulled Patel for four to raise the hundred in the 28th over. The Kiwis had reached the landmark at the same time. A few balls later, unaccountably, Border swung across the line at the off spinner and was caught at deep square leg by Cairns. Moody struggled and soon totally mistimed a defensive push straight back to Latham. When Mark Waugh was given out lbw hitting across a full-pitched ball from Gavin Larsen Australia were 5–125 in the 34th over and in deep trouble.

Crowe kept rotating his dibbly dobbler medium pacers in one- and two-over spells which upset the rhythm of the Australian batting. When Steve Waugh joined Boon Australia needed nearly eight per over. The sixth wicket pair also had to repair the damage caused by the collapse on a wicket playing slower and lower than in the morning. They did so to good effect, putting on 74 at a run per ball. In the 45th over Waugh stepped away and clobbered Latham straight for the only six of the match. More of the same was needed, as the ask was now up to 10 per over.

Larsen's next over decided the result. Boon, who like Crowe was starting to hobble in the later stages on his bad knee, brought up his hundred. Then Waugh tried to advance on the bowler, was checked by a shorter delivery and pushed the ball in the air back along the pitch. Larsen dived and exultantly came up with the catch. Two balls later a brilliant direct-hit throw at the bowler's end by Chris Harris ran out Boon by a metre and finished Australia's challenge. Healy and McDermott were also run-out sacrifices, Taylor was caught at mid wicket and when Reid lifted Harris to Andrew Jones on the long-on boundary, a worthy hit by the spindly non-batsman, Australia had lost five wickets in 17 balls and New Zealand had completed a sensational 37-run victory. The 25,000 strong crowd charged onto the ground again in celebration. Victory over Australia was sweet, especially so for the recently criticised, now Man of the Match New Zealand captain. He described it as one of the best days of his life.

NEW ZEALAND

J.G. Wright b McDermott	0
R.T. Latham c Healy b Moody	26
A.H. Jones lbw Reid	4
M.D. Crowe (capt) not out	100
K.R. Rutherford run out	57
C.Z. Harris run out	14
I.D.S. Smith (wk) c Healy b McDermott	14
C.L. Cairns not out	16
Extras (lb 6, w 7, nb 4)	17
(50 overs)	6–248

Did not bat: D.N. Patel, G.R. Larsen, W. Watson

1/2 2/13 3/53 4/171 5/191 6/215

Bowling: McDermott 10-1-43-2; Reid 10-0-39-1; Moody 9-1-37-1; S.R. Waugh 10-0-60-0; Taylor 7-0-36-0; M.E. Waugh 4-0-27-0

AUSTRALIA

D.C. Boon run out	100
G.R. Marsh c Latham b Larsen	19
D.M. Jones run out	21
A.R. Border (capt) c Cairns b Patel	3
T.M. Moody c & b Latham	7
M.E. Waugh lbw Larsen	2
S.R. Waugh c & b Larsen	38
I.A. Healy (wk) not out	7
C.J. McDermott run out	1
P.L. Taylor c Rutherford b Watson	1
B.A. Reid c Jones b Harris	3
Extras (lb 6, w 2, nb 1)	9
(48.1 overs)	10–211

1/62 2/92 3/104 4/120 5/125 6/199 7/200 8/205 9/206

Bowling: Cairns 4-0-30-0; Patel 10-1-36-1; Watson 9-1-39-1; Larsen 10-1-30-3; Latham 8-0-35-1; Harris 7.1-0-35-1

Umpires: Khizar Hayat, D.R Shepherd.

Toss: New Zealand. Points: New Zealand 2, Australia 0

SATURDAY 22 FEBRUARY 1992
ENGLAND vs INDIA
WACA, PERTH: ENGLAND WON BY 9 RUNS

Same date, same tournament, but almost half a world and certainly half a day away, England won a thriller against India in Perth. The Australian section of the competition was lit up both figuratively and literally as India became the first team in the World Cup to bat at night under lights. The late finish in Perth meant that most people on the east coast of Australia and virtually everyone in New Zealand had to wait until the next morning to find out the result of this tight encounter.

Graham Gooch took Ian Botham out to open with him after he won the toss and batted on a typically hard and bouncy Perth wicket. The pantomime king's booming drive over mid-off in the seventh over was an isolated blow in an inconsequential innings. Troubled, as many are by the steep bounce, he batted sluggishly for nine overs before edging a back foot drive off Kapil Dev through to Kiran More.

Robin Smith, a record-breaker with South Perth four years before, was altogether more comfortable and soon making up for the slow start. In his navy blue Test helmet rather than the sky blue of the World Cup, Smith spanked a couple of thrilling cover drives, then in the 24th over pulled left-arm spinner Ravi Shastri many a mile for a six over mid wicket that brought up the hundred. His own half century was completed four overs later.

Gooch, much more circumspect, had only once reached the boundary when he passed 50. Hampered by a knock to his leg from his own bat and using Botham as a runner, he tried to drive Shastri inside out and spooned an easy catch to cover. His replacement, Graeme Hick, hit one stunning lofted off drive then perished to a feeble push outside the off stump to Subroto Banerjee.

Pragmatic rather than fashionable, Neil Fairbrother added 60 with the in-form Smith, who pulled Banerjee for his second six. Mike Gatting estimated the blow at 100 metres. With the total on 197 Fairbrother skyed an attempted leg-side

pick shot off Javagal Srinath to Kris Srikkanth at mid-on. When a vicious Smith cut was beautifully held by Mohammad Azharuddin in the gully one run later England were 5–198 in the 44th over. Their all-rounders failed to significantly add to that and the English tally for the last seven overs was 6–39 out of an eventual 9–236.

Gooch was unsure of the overall merit of his side's total. Any lack of confidence would have been compounded by Srikkanth's attacking approach which brought him seven thumping boundaries. In the 16th over he twice pulled Phil DeFreitas for four then, unable to calm his adrenalin rush, skyed the next ball to mid-off. When Azharuddin was caught behind by a beauty from Dermott Reeve next over, 0–63 had become 2–63 and India had forfeited their advantage.

Ravi Shastri and Sachin Tendulkar doubled the score by the 30th over, the teenager looking ominously good. Then Botham put England back on top again. A perfectly pitched away cutter had Tendulkar caught behind playing forward. In the midst of a very tight spell Botham also had Tendulkar's old school chum, Vinod Kambli, chipping to a juggling Hick at mid-on. Shastri completed a solid fifty before skying a slog off DeFreitas straight up in the air. The bowler, perhaps distracted by moving batsmen, dropped the chance but retained enough composure to run out Shastri with an underarm direct hit.

The equation was reduced to 51 from seven overs. Kapil Dev smacked some powerful blows before holing out to DeFreitas at long-on. In the rush for runs Praveen Amre and More were run out and Manoj Prabhakar was bowled stepping away to drive Reeve. The last pair of Banerjee and Srinath had to conjure up another 36 in three overs. To the astonishment of the healthy English contingent in the crowd, the Indian pacemen started to strike the ball well. Banerjee lifted an off drive to the boundary and smashed Derek Pringle's last ball for six over long-on.

India needed 11 from the last over, but from the second ball messed up their running which allowed Botham to charge in from short cover and break the stumps. England sighed with relief. Botham was named Man of the Match ahead of Smith. Azharuddin saw Tendulkar's dismissal as the turning point in the game and also lamented the 13 wides sent down by his bowlers.

ENGLAND	
G.A. Gooch (capt) c Tendulkar b Shastri	51
I.T. Botham c Moore b Kapil Dev	9
R.A. Smith c Azharuddin b Prabhakar	91
G.A. Hick c Moore b Banerjee	5
N.H. Fairbrother c Srikkanth b Srinath	24
A.J. Stewart (wk) b Prabhakar	13
C.C. Lewis c Banerjee b Kapil Dev	10
D.R. Pringle c Srikkanth b Srinath	1
D.A. Reeve not out	8
P.A.J. DeFreitas run out	1
P.C.R. Tufnell not out	3
Extras (b 1, lb 6, w 13)	20
(50 overs)	9–236

1/21 2/121 3/137 4/197 5/198 6/214 7/222 8/223 9/224

Bowling: Kapil Dev 10-0-38-2; Prabhakar 10-3-34-2; Srinath 9-1-47-2; Banerjee 7-0-45-1; Tendulkar 10-0-37-0; Shastri 4-0-28-1

INDIA	
R.J. Shastri run out	57
K. Srikkanth c Botham b DeFreitas	39
M. Azharuddin (capt) c Stewart b Reeve	0
S.R. Tendulkar c Stewart b Botham	35
V.G. Kambli c Hick b Botham	3
P.K. Amre run out	22
Kapil Dev c DeFreitas b Reeve	17
S.T. Banerjee not out	25
K.S. More (wk) run out	1
M. Prabhakar b Reeve	0
J. Srinath run out	11
Extras (lb 9, w 7, nb 1)	17
(49.2 overs)	10–227

1/63 2/63 3/126 4/140 5/149 6/187 7/194 8/200 9/201

Bowling: Pringle 10-0-53-0; Lewis 9.2-0-36-0; DeFreitas 10-0-39-1; Reeve 6-0-38-3; Botham 10-0-27-2; Tufnell 4-0-25-0

Umpires: D.P. Buultjens, P.J. McConnell.

Toss: England. Points: England 2, India 0

SUNDAY 23 FEBRUARY 1992
SRI LANKA vs ZIMBABWE
PUKEKURA PARK, NEW PLYMOUTH: SRI LANKA WON BY 3 WICKETS

The first Sunday helping of the Benson and Hedges World Cup was not considered worthy of television coverage, so details of the extraordinary match at Pukekura Park in New Plymouth are left to those who actually attended the attractive North Island venue. If the 3000 or so spectators had put their heads together to contrive some sort of a tale to tell their friends about what they had seen they could not have bettered this run bonanza. The joint lack of bowling penetration cancelled out any advantage to either side so the tiny ground hosted a 625-run thriller.

Zimbabwe batted first after Aravinda de Silva had won the toss and sent them in. Their start was unremarkable as they were 3–82 when Asanka Gurusinha had Dave Houghton caught behind. Kevin Arnott's run-per-ball 52 of a partnership of 85 with young opener Andy Flower was the first indication of the day's batting dominance.

Then when powerful Andy Waller joined Flower all hell broke loose during a record-breaking unbroken stand of 145 in 13 overs. Waller raced to his 50 in 32 balls, then also a record. The Sri Lankan attack was without Rumesh Ratnayake who had a dislocated shoulder and they found it impossible to stem the run flow. Waller crunched nine fours and three sixes, one of which landed in a nearby duck pond. Flower completed his maiden century in Limited-Over Internationals.

Only the arrival of the 50-over limit stopped the entertainment, and then just temporarily. When the chase for 313 began, Sri Lankan openers Roshan Mahanama and Athula Samarasekera were quickly into their stride. Samarasekera raced to his fifty at a rate just one ball slower than Waller and 128 runs were on the board before John Traicos brought some bowling sanity to the game. The 44-year-old picked up a wicket, conceded just three runs per over and stalled Sri Lanka who slipped to 4–167, a scoreline identical to the one Zimbabwe had been.

But Traicos could only bowl 10 overs, so that even though 100 was required from the last 11 overs the return of the medium pacers again invited all-out attack. Sanath Jayasuriya in a cameo taster for 1996 smashed two sixes and two fours in 23 balls. It was the ex-captain Arjuna Ranatunga, playing his 100th Limited-Over

International, who became the match winner. He smashed his way to fifty, bringing up the milestone with a six and, after being caught off a noball, went on to make 88 in 61 balls, including the winning boundary, a pull off Malcolm Jarvis with three wickets and four balls to spare. Andy Flower, like his team-mates unable to believe they had lost after making 4–312, was named Man of the Match.

ZIMBABWE

A. Flower (wk) not out	115
W.R. James c Tillekaratne b Wickremasinghe	17
A.J. Pycroft c Ramanayake b Gurusinha	5
D.L. Houghton (capt) c Tillekaratne b Gurusinha	10
K.J. Arnott c Tillekaratne b Wickremasinghe	52
A.C. Waller not out	30
Extras (b 2, lb 6, w 13, nb 9)	30
(50 overs)	4–312

Did not bat: I.P. Butchart, K.G. Duers, E.A. Brandes, M.P. Jarvis, A.J. Traicos

1/30 2/57 3/82 4/167

Bowling: Ramanayake 10-0-59-0; Wijegunawardene 7-0-59-0; Wickremasinghe 10-1-50-2; Gurusinha 10-0-72-2; Kalpage 10-0-51-0; Jayasuriya 3-0-18-0

SRI LANKA

R.S. Mahanama c Arnott b Brandes	59
M.A.R. Samarasekera c Duers b Traicos	75
P.A. de Silva (capt) c Houghton b Brandes	14
A.P. Gurusinha run out	5
A. Ranatunga not out	88
S.T. Jayasuriya c Flower b Houghton	32
H.P. Tillekaratne (wk) b Jarvis	18
R.S. Kalpage c Duers b Brandes	11
C.P.H. Ramanayake not out	1
Extras (lb 5, w 5)	10
(49.2 overs)	7–313

Did not bat: K.I.W. Wijegunawardene, G.G.P. Wickremasinghe

1/128 2/144 3/155 4/167 5/212 6/273 7/309

Bowling: Jarvis 9.2-0-61-1; Brandes 10-0-70-3; Duers 10-0-72-0; Butchart 8-0-53-0; Traicos 10-1-33-1; Houghton 2-0-19-1

Umpires: P.D. Reporter, S.J. Woodward.

Toss: Sri Lanka. Points: Sri Lanka 2, Zimbabwe 0

SUNDAY 23 FEBRUARY 1992
PAKISTAN vs WEST INDIES
MCG, MELBOURNE: WEST INDIES WON BY 10 WICKETS

To top off run-making Sunday, the West Indies and Pakistan played out a match at the MCG where just two wickets fell for 441 runs from 96.5 overs. This game was entertaining enough for the 14,000 in attendance and the television viewers, but without the thrills and spills of New Plymouth as the West Indies always looked to have plenty in hand when they batted.

Such a crowd makes little impact on the 90,000 or so seats available at the MCG, so it was a fairly cold and cheerless venue that greeted Ramiz Raja and Aamir Sohail as they began the Pakistani innings after Richie Richardson had sent them in to bat. The pair certainly took some time to warm to their task. Sohail was only on 12 after 13 overs. He finally got Malcolm

Marshall away for a couple of fours before skying Winston Benjamin to Gus Logie in the covers.

The arrival of young Inzamam-ul-Haq failed to lift the tempo. The West Indies used both their off spinners, Carl Hooper and Roger Harper, effectively. Ramiz survived a stumping chance when he was 16 and moved from 23 to 57 in singles. Harper got rid of Inzamam in the 30th over when the total was still short of 100. At that rate Pakistan would barely top 160 after 50 overs. Javed Miandad, captaining the side in place of the injured Imran Khan even though Salim Malik had been nominated as vice-captain in the selected squad, realised the need for greater urgency. He got Ramiz out of first gear, barking orders at him and forcing him to run for short singles.

West Indian wicketkeeper David Williams missed catching both batsmen as Miandad started improvising and Ramiz finally began to hit the ball in the middle. The opener reached his 100 in 157 balls. Miandad, walking everywhere around the crease, glanced Marshall to the unguarded fine-leg boundary. He reached his fifty in 56 balls, was caught off an Ambrose delivery that was called a no-ball because it bounced above his shoulder and was still at the crease with Ramiz when the 50 overs were completed. The unbroken stand was worth 123 and the West Indies, in stark contrast to previous sides from the Caribbean, had actually completed their overs 30 minutes ahead of time.

They also reached their target ahead of schedule on the back of a brilliant innings by Brian Lara, who made 88 in 101 balls before a Wasim Akram yorker crushed his toe. The Pakistani attack without Imran Khan and Waqar Younis lacked firepower once Akram had completed his first spell. They certainly could not afford to drop Desmond Haynes on 35 and 49 as the experienced Barbadian went on to bat until the game had reached its conclusion.

Lara's was the feature innings of the day and won him the Man of the Match award. He struck 11 boundaries, all with the flourishing backlift, exquisite timing and full follow-through that are so appealing to the eye. X-rays showed no bone damage after Lara was assisted from the field with the total on 175, just seven short of the then first-wicket World Cup record set in 1975.

Two no-balled bouncers by Aqib Javed finished the match and annoyed Miandad, as did the increasing number of fielding mistakes. His opposite number was pleased that pushing Lara up the order had been effective and that his off spinners had bowled with such control.

PAKISTAN

Ramiz Raja not out	102
Aamir Sohail c Logie b Benjamin	23
Inzamam-ul-Haq c Hooper b Harper	27
Javed Miandad (capt) not out	57
Extras (b 1, lb 3, w 5, nb 2)	11
(50 overs)	2–220

Did not bat: Salim Malik, Ijaz Ahmed, Wasim Akram, Moin Khan (wk), Iqbal Sikander, Wasim Haider, Aqib Javed

1/45 2/97

Bowling: Marshall 10–1–53–0; Ambrose 10–0–40–0; Benjamin 10–0–49–1; Hooper 10–0–41–0; Harper 10–0–33–1

WEST INDIES

D.L. Haynes not out	93
B.C. Lara retired hurt	88
R.B. Richardson (capt) not out	20
Extras (b 2, lb 8, w 7, nb 3)	20
(46.5 overs)	0–221

Did not bat: C.L. Hooper, K.L.T. Arthurton, A.L. Logie, R.A. Harper, M.D. Marshall, W.K.M. Benjamin, D. Williams (wk), C.E.L. Ambrose

Lara retired hurt at 0–175

Bowling: Wasim Akram 10–0–37–0; Aqib Javed 8.5–0–42–0; Wasim Haider 8–0–42–0; Ijaz Ahmed 6–1–29–0; Iqbal Sikander 8–1–26–0; Aamir Sohail 6–0–35–0

Umpires: S.G. Randell, I.D. Robinson.

Toss: West Indies. Points: West Indies 2, Pakistan 0

TUESDAY 25 FEBRUARY 1992
NEW ZEALAND vs SRI LANKA
TRUST BANK PARK, HAMILTON: NEW ZEALAND WON BY 6 WICKETS

The most featureless match of the competition so far saw New Zealand cruise to their second win by six wickets on a humid day in Hamilton. Martin Crowe's failure suggested the Kiwis were a force as a team, not just a one-man show. Sri Lanka's batsmen, on the other hand, at no stage batted with the freedom they had on Sunday and were unable to set a challenging target.

With some humidity around, Crowe used his pacemen rather than Dipak Patel's off spin to take the new ball after he won the toss and asked Sri Lanka to bat. Roshan Mahanama's determination and technique were the platform of a sound base to the Sri Lankan innings. His stand of 70 with Aravinda de Silva took Sri Lanka to 2–120. The run-out of the Sri Lankan captain was untimely, although Mahanama and Arjuna Ranatunga put on another 52 so that at the 42-over mark a competitive score was a strong possibility. Then, against the tight bowling of Patel and Willie Watson and bedevilled by more run-outs, the innings stalled. The last eight overs produced just 34 runs for the loss of six wickets.

Even though left-handed opener John Wright had hurt his shoulder while fielding, he dominated the opening stand of 77 with Rod Latham. The two Sri Lankan spinners, Ruwan Kalpage and left-armer Don Anurasiri, reined in the scoring. Kalpage got rid of both openers and when a restrained Crowe was caught in the deep off a Pramodya Wickremasinghe long-hop the Kiwis had slipped to 3–105.

That was as close as the Sri Lankans came to winning. Ken Rutherford was dropped by Ranatunga at slip before he had scored and then put together a match-winning innings. Andrew Jones' solidity allowed Rutherford to stroke the ball with confidence and fluency. To rub salt into the Sri Lankan wound, he put Ranatunga over long-on for six. When Jones was out after a stand of 81 with Rutherford victory was clearly in sight and duly achieved with 10 balls to spare.

Rutherford was named Man of the Match. Aravinda de Silva lamented his injury list. Athula Samarasekera had damaged a hamstring and Rumesh Ratnayake's shoulder injury put him out of the tournament. A request that Graeme Labrooy might be included in the Sri Lankan squad in place of Ratnayake was granted.

SRI LANKA

R.S. Mahanama c & b Harris	80
M.A.R. Samarasekera c Wright b Watson	9
A.P. Gurusinha c Smith b Harris	9
P.A. de Silva (capt) run out	31
A. Ranatunga c Rutherford b Harris	20
S.T. Jayasuriya run out	5
H.P. Tillekaratne (wk) c Crowe b Watson	8
R.S. Kalpage c Larsen b Watson	11
C.P.H. Ramanayake run out	2
S.D. Anurasiri not out	3
G.G.P. Wickremasinghe not out	3
Extras (b 1, lb 15, w 4, nb 5)	25
(50 overs)	9–206

1/18 2/50 3/120 4/172 5/172 6/181 7/195 8/199 9/202

Bowling: Morrison 8–0–36–0; Watson 10–0–37–3; Larsen 10–1–29–0; Harris 10–0–43–3; Latham 3–0–13–0; Patel 9–0–32–0

NEW ZEALAND

J.G. Wright c & b Kalpage	57
R.T. Latham b Kalpage	20
A .H. Jones c Jayasuriya b Gurusinha	49
M.D. Crowe (capt) c Ramanayake b Wickremasinghe	5
K.R. Rutherford not out	65
C.Z. Harris not out	5
Extras (lb 3, w 3, nb 3)	9
(48.2 overs)	4–210

Did not bat: D.N. Patel, I.D.S. Smith (wk), G.R. Larsen, D.K. Morrison, W. Watson

1/77 2/91 3/105 4/186

Bowling: Ramanayake 9.2–0–46–0; Wickremasinghe 8–1–40–1; Anurasiri 10–1–27–0; Kalpage 10–0–33–2; Gurusinha 4–0–19–0; Ranatunga 4–0–22–0; Jayasuriya 2–0–14–0; de Silva 1–0–6–0

Umpires, P.D. Reporter, D.R. Shepherd.

Toss: New Zealand. Points: New Zealand 2, Sri Lanka 0

WEDNESDAY 26 FEBRUARY 1992
AUSTRALIA vs SOUTH AFRICA
SCG, SYDNEY: SOUTH AFRICA WON BY 9 WICKETS

South Africa's debut in the World Cup could not have gone better. In front of an initially enthusiastic and later subdued capacity SCG crowd of 40,000, Kepler Wessels' side annihilated an out of form and out of touch Australian side by nine wickets. If Martin Crowe had a good day at Auckland at the Australian's expense on

Saturday, Wessels' Wednesday was perfection.

From the moment the South Africans received an enormous reception when they took the field after Allan Border had won the toss and batted to the winning nudge by the captain to third man at 9.38 pm, this game was like a tribute to 22 lost years. The only act towards South

Africa lacking in generosity was Brian Aldridge's not-out decision when Geoff Marsh followed Allan Donald's first ball as it lifted outside the off stump. He clearly edged it through to wicketkeeper Dave Richardson, but the umpire was unmoved.

As if wracked by guilt, Marsh scratched around for 72 balls for 25. David Boon's conscience forced him to run himself out after looking in great form for 10 overs and Allan Border so much wanted South Africa to feel at home he let himself be bowled off his pad first ball by a beautiful inswinger to the left-hander by Adrian Kuiper.

The Australian acts of self-destruction continued unabated for almost the duration of their 49-over innings. Border's dismissal left his side on 3–76 in the 21st over. Donald's new-ball partner Meyrick Pringle had been punished by Boon before Richard Snell choked off the flow of runs. Dean Jones was caught behind from the full face of the bat off Brian McMillan. He still waited for Steve Bucknor to give him out. Tom Moody was clearly lbw to Donald when the speedster was recalled to bowl to his Warwickshire team-mate.

That left Australia 5–108 in the 33rd over. Steve Waugh and Ian Healy hinted at recovery when they put on 35 in six overs, at one stage taking 12 off an over from the expensive Pringle. Healy, though, was incapacitated by a bad hamstring strain, the result of an ambitious call for a short single by Waugh. Eventually the Australian wicketkeeper skyed a lofted drive off Donald, Waugh was caught at short cover off the verbally aggressive Brian McMillan and Peter Taylor had his leg stump neatly removed by another Donald thunderbolt.

Craig McDermott underestimated the athleticism of the cover-point fieldsman, a newcomer named Jonty Rhodes, which left Mike Whitney and Bruce Reid to bolster Australia's final total. Whitney would later write of the excitement of playing in the World Cup. One highlight must have been his off-side glide that scooted for four down to third man off the previously economical Snell.

Whitney's captain, at his most solemn during the between innings break, needed the left-arm paceman to bowl with penetration rather than scrape together a few runs. Unfortunately neither Whitney nor his team-mates could make any impression on the South African top order. There was little excitement as Wessels and Andrew Hudson went about their business at just above the three runs per over they needed to win. The television commentators resorted to informing their viewers of the beauty of the Sydney sunset and the perfect weather. A run-out chance missed by Jones and a couple of stylish cover drives by Hudson briefly roused the crowd.

An on-driven four by Wessels off Whitney raised the fifty in the 16th over, then off the last ball of the same over Boon, wicketkeeping in place of the injured Healy, put down an edged drive low to his left. Finally, in off-spinner Taylor's first over, Hudson aimed a big drive and was bowled. The crowd roared, hoping the wicket was the first of many. It was, in fact, the last of the night. Peter Kirsten was as sound as Wessels and was rarely troubled. Border brought himself on to bowl. The SCG had on occasions been kind to his left-arm spinners. This was not one of them. In the 29th over Wessels raised the South African hundred. Six overs later a square drive to the boundary off McDermott brought him to an emotional fifty.

The match was heading to an obvious conclusion, yet after 45 overs Australia had actually been one run ahead of the South Africans at the same stage. A couple of cracking off-side shots by Wessels took his side to the brink of victory. Many of the Australian fans were leaving, but not the handful of green-shirted South African fans, however. They stayed even after the game was over and the lights were out, sharing a precious moment with their victorious team.

Wessels, named Man of the Match, was also a national hero. The changes necessary to dismantle apartheid still had to pass a referendum. It was believed the big win over Australia could have a significant influence on the result of that vote. African National Congress official Steve Tshwete embraced Wessels in the dressing-room. President F.W. de Klerk congratulated Wessels over the phone back at the hotel. There were 250 faxes of congratulation at the

hotel for Wessels and the team. It was a big night for South Africa.

AUSTRALIA	
G.R. Marsh c Richardson b Kuiper	25
D.C. Boon run out	27
D.M. Jones c Richardson b McMillan	24
A.R. Border (capt) b Kuiper	0
T.M. Moody lbw Donald	10
S.R. Waugh c Cronje b McMillan	27
I.A. Healy (wk) c McMillan b Donald	16
P.L. Taylor b Donald	4
C.J. McDermott run out	6
M.R. Whitney not out	9
B.A. Reid not out	5
Extras (b 2, w 11, nb 4)	17
(49 overs)	9–170

1/42 2/76 3/76 4/97 5/108 6/143 7/146 8/156 9/161

Bowling: Donald 10–0–34–3; Pringle 10–0–52–0; Snell 9–1–15–0; McMillan 10–0–35–2; Kuiper 5–0–15–2; Cronje 5–1–17–0

SOUTH AFRICA	
K.C. Wessels (capt) not out	81
A.C. Hudson b Taylor	28
P.N. Kirsten not out	49
Extras (lb 5, w 6, nb 2)	13
(46.5 overs)	1–171

Did not bat: W.J. Cronje, A.P. Kuiper, J.N. Rhodes, B.M. McMillan, R.P. Snell, D.J. Richardson (wk), M.W. Pringle, A.A.A. Donald

1/74

Bowling: McDermott 10–1–23–0; Reid 8.5–0–45–0; Whitney 6–0–26–0; Waugh 4–1–16–0; Taylor 10–1–32–1; Border 4–0–13–0; Moody 4–0–15–0

Umpires: B.L. Aldridge, S.A. Bucknor.

Toss: Australia. Points: South Africa 2, Australia 0

THURSDAY 27 FEBRUARY 1992
PAKISTAN vs ZIMBABWE
BELLERIVE OVAL, HOBART: PAKISTAN WON BY 53 RUNS

Imran Khan called this a perfect day's cricket because he did not have to bat or bowl and his side still won easily. With so much perfection around and the weather fine, it was a surprise only 1101 people bothered to journey out to Bellerive Oval. They would have seen some enterprising batting from Man of the Match and century-maker Aamir Sohail, and from Javed Miandad. Much of the cricket, however, fell well short of Imran's tongue-in-cheek interpretation. In truth the Pakistani captain was still badly troubled by his injured shoulder.

Initially Pakistan struggled on a bouncy wicket after Dave Houghton had sent them in. Pakistan was 2–63 when Miandad joined Sohail. As he had done in Melbourne, Miandad brought a positive urgency to the batting. The score was still only 96 at the 30-over mark and only a low percentage of the runs were made in boundaries, yet he and Sohail were able to put on 145 at virtually a run per ball. Even John Traicos was unable to stem the flow this time. For much of

the partnership the pair scored at eight runs per over. Sohail was able to go on to complete his maiden century in Limited-Over Internationals. He had offered three clear-cut chances to the Zimbabwean fieldsmen after reaching fifty, but also struck 12 fours.

Zimbabwe never looked like getting near their target of 255. Even without Waqar Younis or Imran, the Pakistani attack was too accomplished. Dave Houghton admitted after the game that his batsmen could only concentrate on survival, particularly against the pace and skill of Wasim Akram who claimed his 150th wicket in Limited-Over Internationals. The top order didn't even manage to survive. Zimbabwe struggled to 3–33 and after 30 overs was out of the contest at 3–69. Andy Waller and Iain Butchart gave the total a boost by adding 79 in nine overs. All that achieved against an attack which used three spinners was respectability. Pakistan and much of the small crowd by that stage had lost interest.

PAKISTAN

Ramiz Raja c Flower b Jarvis	9
Aamir Sohail c Pycroft b Butchart	114
Inzamam-ul-Haq c Brandes b Butchart	14
Javed Miandad lbw Butchart	89
Salim Malik not out	14
Wasim Akram not out	1
Extras (lb 9, nb 4)	13
(50 overs)	4-254

Did not bat: Imran Khan (capt), Moin Khan (wk),
Iqbal Sikander, Mushtaq Ahmed, Aqib Javed

1/29 2/63 3/208 4/253

Bowling: Brandes 10-1-49-0; Jarvis 10-1-52-1; Shah
10-1-24-0; Butchart 10-0-57-3; Traicos 10-0-63-0

ZIMBABWE

K.J. Arnott c Wasim Akram b Iqbal Sikander	7
A. Flower (wk) c Inzamam-ul-Haq b Wasim Akram	6
A.J. Pycroft b Wasim Akram	0
D.L. Houghton (capt) c Ramiz Raja b Aamir Sohail	44
A.H. Shah b Aamir Sohail	33
A.C. Waller b Wasim Akram	44
I.P. Butchart c Javed Miandad b Aqib Javed	33
E.A. Brandes not out	2
A.J. Traicos not out	8
Extras (b 3, lb 15, w 6)	24
(50 overs)	7-201

Did not bat: W.R. James, M.P. Jarvis

1/14 2/14 3/33 4/103 5/108 6/187 7/190

Bowling: Wasim Akram 10-2-21-3; Aqib Javed 10-1-49-1;
Sikander 10-1-35-1; Mushtaq Ahmed 10-1-34-0;
Aamir Sohail 6-1-26-2; Salim Malik 4-0-18-0

Umpires: D.P. Buultjens, S.G. Randell.

Toss: Zimbabwe. Points: Pakistan 2, Zimbabwe 0

THURSDAY 27 FEBRUARY 1992

ENGLAND vs WEST INDIES
MCG, MELBOURNE: ENGLAND WON BY 6 WICKETS

England were launched to first-week tournament favouritism when an inept batting display by the West Indies allowed Graham Gooch's side to cruise to an easy victory. Brian Lara was hit in the box by the first ball he faced from Chris Lewis and that seemed to knock the stuffing out of not just Lara, but the entire West Indian batting line-up.

The weather in Melbourne was as clear as in Hobart, but the amount of moisture below the surface of the wicket was indicated by the dark marks left by the bowlers' footmarks and the batsmen's scratchings at the crease. Graham Gooch had read the conditions correctly when he inserted the West Indies after winning the toss.

Lewis, bowling the second over of the match with a sparsely populated Great Southern Stand as his backdrop, had Lara caught behind the ball after he struck him. In the next over Derek Pringle, straight on to a perfect line, had Desmond Haynes edging an outswinger low to Ian Botham at slip. Botham claimed the catch, the batsmen and the umpires were unsure, so Haynes stayed. Botham's immediate reaction was one of disgust. Replays were inconclusive.

With the exception of Lewis' third over which cost 11 runs, the West Indies were circumspect and their apprehension increased two overs later when Richie Richardson was too slow getting his bat out of the way of a Lewis outswinger and edged a clear catch to Botham. Carl Hooper coped neither with the pressure nor the conditions and skyed a pull off Botham to Dermot Reeve, moving in from cover.

Haynes played a couple of nice pulls, survived a chance behind to Alec Stewart, then pulled Phil DeFreitas shoulder high to Neil Fairbrother at backward square leg. That left the West Indies 4–55 in the 20th over. Despite a couple of brave blows by Keith Arthurton, who hit Phil Tufnell for a straight six and pulled DeFreitas for another six to raise his fifty, and Gus Logie, whose leg-side scoop off Botham also went into the stand, the West Indies never recovered from their poor start.

There remained an air of self-destruction about their running between wickets. Logie went wandering after an lbw shout and Malcolm Marshall responded to an Arthurton call only to find his partner had gone back. When DeFreitas held Curtly Ambrose at third man off a mis-directed slog, Lewis had his third cheap wicket and the West Indies had been dismissed for their second-lowest World Cup score.

Ambrose sorely troubled both Gooch and Botham in his opening spell. However, Malcolm Marshall was far less imposing and Gooch twice belted him through the covers for four in his fourth over. Botham was meant to be the batsman to take the initiative, but he had only made eight of an opening partnership of 50 when he pushed forward at Winston Benjamin and was caught behind. Benjamin also got Robin Smith to badly mistime a pull to Logie at square leg 21 runs later. Gooch, though, was in command and he reached his fifty in the 25th over. Hooper bowled his off spin tidily enough. Roger Harper on the other hand was punished severely by Graeme Hick for sending down a succession of long-hops.

By the time Gooch went waltzing down the pitch to Hooper and missed, an English win was only 32 runs away. Hick hastened the end by racing to his 50 at a run per ball, the milestone being reached with a lofted drive for six over extra cover. Harper got a little revenge when he dived and claimed a caught and bowled off the Zimbabwean's soft push back up the wicket. As with the Botham slips 'catch' earlier in the day, there was some doubt as to the legitimacy of the dismissal. This time, however, the batsman walked away. It made no difference. In the next over Fairbrother's educated edge flew past slip to the third-man boundary leaving the English fans, easily identifiable by their Union Jack flags and face paint, ready to claim that they would win the World Cup. Lewis won the Man of the Match award.

WEST INDIES

D.L. Haynes c Fairbrother b DeFreitas		38
B.C. Lara c Stewart b Lewis		0
R.B. Richardson (capt) c Botham b Lewis		5
C.L. Hooper c Reeve b Botham		5
K.L.T. Arthurton c Fairbrother b DeFreitas		54
A.L. Logie run out		20
R.A. Harper c Hick b Reeve		3
M.D. Marshall run out		3
D. Williams (wk) c Pringle b DeFreitas		6
C.E.L. Ambrose c DeFreitas b Lewis		4
W.K.M. Benjamin not out		11
Extras (lb 4, w 3, nb 1)		8
(49.2 overs)		10/157

1/0 2/22 3/36 4/55 5/91 6/102 7/114 8/131 9/145

Bowling: Pringle 7-3-16-0; Lewis 8.2-1-30-3; DeFreitas 9-2-34-3; Botham 10-0-30-1; Reeve 10-1-23-1; Tufnell 5-0-20-0

ENGLAND

G.A. Gooch (capt) st Williams b Hooper		65
I.T. Botham c Williams b Benjamin		8
R.A. Smith c Logie b Benjamin		8
G Hick c & b Harper		54
N.H. Fairbrother not out		13
A.J. Stewart (wk) not out		0
Extras (lb 7, w 4, nb 1)		12
(39.5 overs)		4/160

Did not bat: D.A. Reeve, C.C. Lewis, D.R. Pringle, P.A.J. DeFreitas, P.C.R. Tufnell

1/50 2/71 3/126 4/156

Bowling: Ambrose 8-1-26-0; Marshall 8-0-37-0; Benjamin 9.5-2-22-2; Hooper 10-1-38-1; Harper 4-0-30-1

Umpires: K.E. Liebenberg, S.J. Woodward.

Toss: England. Points: England 2, West Indies 0

FRIDAY 28 FEBRUARY 1992

INDIA vs SRI LANKA
HARRUP PARK, MACKAY: NO RESULT

Mackay in Queensland is a long way to go for two deliveries. The first rain in a month initially delayed the match and then, after 3000 gathered in anticipation of a 20 overs per side slogarama, it returned in all its tropical fury to quickly stymie even that prospect. The outcome must have been heartbreaking for local officials. Kris Srikkanth has made the only World Cup run ever scored in Mackay.

INDIA	
K. Srikkanth not out	1
Kapil Dev not out	0
Extras	0
(0.2 overs)	0–1

Did not bat: M. Azharuddin (capt), S.R. Tendulkar,
V.G. Kambli, P.K. Amre, A.D. Jadeja, K.S. More (wk),
M. Prabhakar, J. Srinath, S.L.V. Raju

Bowling: Ramanayake 0.2–0–1–0

SRI LANKA

R.S. Mahanama, U.C. Hathurusingha, A.P. Gurusinha,
P.A. de Silva (capt), A. Ranatunga, S.T. Jayasuriya,
H.P. Tillekaratne (wk), R.S. Kalpage, C.P.H. Ramanayake,
K.I.W. Wijegunawardene, G.G.P. Wickremasinghe

Umpires: I.D. Robinson, D.R. Shepherd.

Toss: Sri Lanka. Points: Sri Lanka 1, India 1

SATURDAY 29 FEBRUARY 1992
NEW ZEALAND vs SOUTH AFRICA
EDEN PARK, AUCKLAND: NEW ZEALAND WON BY 7 WICKETS

The uncharitable might have suggested that putting New Zealand in grey uniforms for the World Cup was appropriate because that has often been the colour of their cricket. If that had ever been the case it was certainly not so during the Benson and Hedges World Cup. Another big crowd at Eden Park was treated to innovative, aggressive, entertaining and successful cricket and nearly all of it came from the home side.

Kepler Wessels later wrote of a hangover following the wonder of the win against Australia. His top-order batsmen were indeed as sluggish as someone after a big night and were totally unable to adapt to the same dry, slow Eden Park wicket that had scuppered Australia the week before. Neither the captain, Wessels, who had won the toss, Andrew Hudson, nor young Hansie Cronje could come to terms with the accuracy and pacelessness of Willie Watson, who opened without a slip, and off spinner Dipak Patel, once more recalled to take the new ball.

When Cronje was caught behind off Chris Harris' first ball South Africa were 3–29 and into the 16th over. What they might have finished with without the contribution of Peter Kirsten is too frightening to contemplate. The 36-year-old late addition to the squad and wicketkeeper Dave Richardson shored up the middle overs of the innings with a solid partnership of 79. Trouble loomed again when Richardson's dismissal was followed by the bizarre demise of Adrian Kuiper.

He hooked at a Cairns bouncer and gloved the ball through to Ian Smith. Thinking he was out caught, Kuiper started walking away only for Kirsten to yell at him to regain his crease because umpire Piloo Reporter had called 'no-ball' for an above-the-shoulder delivery. As he tried to regain his ground the bails were removed and Kuiper was given run-out. It was much the same circumstance as when Dean Jones was controversially run out in a Test in Guyana a year earlier. On both occasions lack of clear-cut knowledge of the rules by players and umpires had affected a dismissal.

Kirsten went on to hit 10 fours before becoming Watson's second victim and it took a late rally by Richard Snell and Brian McMillan, including 15 off the final over, to set the Kiwis what looked a moderately competitive target.

Looks were deceiving, however, as 191 turned out to be a simple assignment. On the back of a stunning opening partnership of 114 in just 18 overs between Mark Greatbatch and Rod Latham, the Kiwis strolled home with more than 15 overs to spare. Greatbatch was only in the side as a replacement for the injured John Wright. Blanking out previous poor form against England, the big left-hander took a couple of sighters, then started smashing the ball in all directions. His clean uncomplicated hitting reaped Greatbatch nine fours and three big sixes, the last of which landed on the roof of the North Stand. Latham was hardly circumspect, either. He hit seven fours, too, and scored at a rate just below a run per ball.

When Greatbatch finally got too carried away and Latham had fallen to Snell, Crowe sent in Smith who promptly hit his first three balls for four and even had the temerity to dance out to Allan Donald and crack him down the ground for another boundary. The wicketkeeper then got out of the way so that his captain could come in and hit the winning runs to top off another great,

dare we say, almost perfect day. It was special for Greatbatch, who had grasped his opportunity with both hands. At his Man of the Match conference he admitted his whole innings was a bit of a blur.

SOUTH AFRICA

K.C. Wessels (capt) c Smith b Watson	3
A.C. Hudson b Patel	1
P.N. Kirsten c Cairns b Watson	90
W.J. Cronje c Smith b Harris	7
D.J. Richardson (wk) c Larsen b Cairns	28
A.P. Kuiper run out	2
J.N. Rhodes c Crowe b Cairns	6
B.M. McMillan not out	33
R.P. Snell not out	11
Extras (lb 8, nb 1)	9
(50 overs)	7–190

Did not bat: T. Bosch, A.A.A. Donald

1/8 2/10 3/29 4/108 5/110 6/121 7/162

Bowling: Watson 10-2-30-2; Patel 10-1-28-1; Larsen 10-1-29-0; Harris 10-2-33-1; Latham 2-0-19-0; Cairns 8-0-43-2

NEW ZEALAND

M.J. Greatbatch b Kirsten	68
R.T. Latham c Wessels b Snell	60
A.H. Jones not out	34
I.D.S. Smith (wk) c Kirsten b Donald	19
M.D. Crowe (capt) not out	3
Extras (b 1, w 5, nb 1)	7
(34.3 overs)	3–191

Did not bat: K.R. Rutherford, C.Z. Harris, D.N. Patel, C.L. Cairns, G.R. Larsen, W. Watson

1/114 2/155 3/179

Bowling: Donald 10-0-38-1; McMillan 5-1-23-0; Snell 7-0-56-1; Bosch 2.3-0-19-0; Cronje 2-0-14-0; Kuiper 1-0-18-0; Kirsten 7-1-22-1

Umpires: Khizar Hyatt, P.D. Reporter.

Toss: South Africa. Points: New Zealand 2, South Africa 0

SATURDAY 29 FEBRUARY 1992
WEST INDIES vs ZIMBABWE
WOOLLOONGABBA, BRISBANE: WEST INDIES WON BY 75 RUNS

Here was another match of injuries, bumps and bruises for the West Indies. This time, though, they gave as good as they got and ended up comfortable winners over Zimbabwe.

Phil Simmons, in the side because of a back injury to Desmond Haynes, opened with Brian Lara after the West Indies had been sent in to bat by Dave Houghton. The weather was fine but the spectacle of the maroon verses the red team only attracted 2000 local devotees. The stay-at-homes missed another gem of an innings by Lara. The young Trinidadian featured some more sweet cover drives as he raced to 72 at a run per ball. Simmons supported him in an opening stand of 78, then Richie Richardson and Carl Hooper added 117 to take the score to 2–220 in the 43rd over. Both batsmen were caught in the deep, one straight after the other, trying to add to their sixes tally. Keith Arthurton showed how that was best done with two blows over the boundary in the closing overs. Otherwise the West Indian tail did little to boost the final total.

The West Indian pacemen were soon clunking, smacking and crunching the Zimbabwe batsmen into submission. Andy Pycroft was hit on the cheekbone, then caught behind next ball, and Kevin Arnott had his finger bloodied and broken and had to retire hurt. With another batsman, Wayne James, already nursing a fractured finger Zimbabwe asked permission for an addition to their squad.

There were other problems. Richie Richardson deliberately took a catch at cover to remove Alistair Campbell one handed because of his injured digit and Houghton batted after receiving a pain-killing injection for a broken toe. It was he and Ali Shah, also his side's best bowler in this game, who restored respectability after Zimbabwe had been in effect 5–63. They both made half centuries and ensured the innings ran its full 50-over course. Richardson admitted that at the end his side started 'relaxing a bit'. Lara won his second Man of the Match award.

WEST INDIES

P.V. Simmons b Brandes	21
B.C. Lara c Houghton b Shah	72
R.B. Richardson (capt) c Brandes b Jarvis	56
C.L. Hooper c Pycroft b Traicos	63
K.L.T. Arthurton b Duers	26
A.L. Logie run out	5
M.D. Marshall c Houghton b Brandes	2
D. Williams (wk) not out	8
W.K.M. Benjamin b Brandes	1
Extras (b 1, lb 6, w 2, nb 1)	10
(50 overs)	8–264

Did not bat: A.C. Cummins, B.P. Patterson

1/78 2/103 3/220 4/221 5/239 6/254 7/255 8/264

Bowling: Brandes 10–1–45–3; Jarvis 10–1–71–1; Duers 10–0–52–1; Shah 10–2–39–1; Traicos 10–0–50–1

ZIMBABWE

K.J. Arnott retired hurt	16
A. Flower (wk) b Patterson	6
A.J. Pycroft c Williams b Benjamin	10
D.L. Houghton (capt) c Patterson b Hooper	55
A.C. Waller c Simmons b Benjamin	0
A.D. Campbell c Richardson b Hooper	1
A.H. Shah not out	60
E.A. Brandes c & b Benjamin	6
A.J. Traicos run out	8
M.P. Jarvis not out	5
Extras (lb 9, w 5, nb 8)	22
(50 overs)	7–189

Did not bat: K.G. Duers

1/24 2/43 3/48 4/64 5/132 6/161 7/181 (K.J. Arnott retired hurt at 2–43)

Bowling: Patterson 10–0–25–1; Marshall 6–0–23–0; Benjamin 10–2–27–3; Cummins 10–0–33–0; Hooper 10–0–47–2; Arthurton 4–0–25–0

Umpires: K.E. Liebenberg, S.J. Woodward.

Toss: Zimbabwe. Points: West Indies 2, Zimbabwe 0

SUNDAY 1 MARCH 1992

AUSTRALIA vs INDIA
WOOLLOONGABBA, BRISBANE: AUSTRALIA WON BY 1 RUN

This thrilling game arrived just in the nick of time for the locals, whose campaign was on the verge of floundering. To win a thriller like this in front of a large Sunday-afternoon television audience was crucial to the future ratings of the tournament in Australia.

It was the second time in as many World Cups that Australia had beaten India by one run. This time they were lucky on two counts. Rain took three overs off the Indian innings, but the new rain rule meant that their target was only reduced by two runs. Then when Javagal Srinath clubbed the final ball into the outfield the man in the hot seat was almost inevitably Steve Waugh, a cricketer noted for his ability to handle such a situation. He came through again, if only just.

The Gabba was far from full when Allan Border won the toss and elected to bat. His two openers, Mark Taylor and Geoff Marsh, made little impact and it was left to David Boon and Dean Jones to give the innings direction. Jones provided the feature Australian batting of the

day. His second scoring shot was a six off Srinath over long-on. However, exactly half of his 90 runs came in singles, 22 of them consecutively as Boon, Waugh and Tom Moody were made to move. Not only were Jones' batting partners kept busy. Bruce Reid and Mark Waugh had to maintain supplies of batting gloves and water throughout his 109-ball stay.

The Indian bowlers improved their figures as wickets tumbled through the final few overs and a target of 238 from 50 overs was seen as about an even money bet. They had lost Kris Srikkanth and were 1–45 in the 17th over when the rain interruption occurred. Although the mathematics of that pause was unfair on India, the damp ball at least hampered the Australians and allowed Mohammad Azharuddin to put together one of his gems. Kapil Dev was promoted to increase the run rate, but it was Sanjay Manjrekar, in partnership was Azharuddin, who put India within reach of a win.

The requirement had got to 77 off eight overs when the two Indians really began their assault.

After 10 fours in 103 balls Azharuddin fell foul of the throwing accuracy of his opposite number at short mid wicket. Manjrekar hit Merv Hughes for a four and a six and scored at better than a run per ball before being run out with 20 still needed.

Border, who later admitted to a 'monumental cock-up', found it hard to calculate the allocation each bowler was allowed with the Indian innings reduced to 47 overs and had to use Tom Moody for the final six deliveries. The tall West Australian had 12 runs to play with. After two balls he had just four left. Wicketkeeper Kiran More put two full tosses to the boundary at square leg. Then, probably trying to win the match with another four, he was bowled backing away and hitting across the line.

Manoj Prabhakar scored a single from the fourth ball and was run-out from the fifth which left Srinath having to hit a four to win the match from the last ball. Moody bowled, Srinath swung

hard and connected, sending the ball soaring into the leg-side outfield. The cries from the crowd followed the ball as it neared the boundary and Steve Waugh ran around. At full tilt Waugh reached for the catch only for the ball to hit his wrist. Like an Aussie Rules footballer, he crumbed his own dropped mark, picking the ball up as it rolled parallel to the boundary. A quick throw reached wicketkeeper Boon first bounce as Venkatapathy Raju scrambled for the third run. Television commentator, Bill Lawry screamed 'Run lad, run'. The substitute gloveman held his nerve enough to break the stumps with Raju short of his ground.

It was an agonising loss for India, who might easily have come out of their two games in Queensland with four points, but had to be satisfied with just the one from the washout in Mackay. Jones was named Man of the Match, getting the award ahead of Azharuddin by the few centimetres that Raju was run out.

AUSTRALIA

M.A. Taylor c More b Kapil Dev	13
G.R. Marsh b Kapil Dev	8
D.C. Boon (wk) c Shastri b Raju	43
D.M. Jones c & b Prabhakar	90
S.R. Waugh b Srinath	29
T.M. Moody b Prabhakar	25
A.R. Border (capt) c Jadeja b Kapil Dev	10
C.J. McDermott c Jadeja b Prabhakar	2
P.L. Taylor run out	1
M.G. Hughes not out	0
Extras (lb 7, w 5, nb 4)	16
(50 overs)	9–237

Did not bat: M.R. Whitney

1/18 2/31 3/102 4/156 5/198 6/230 7/235 8/236 9/237

Bowling: Kapil Dev 10–2–41–3; Prabhakar 10–0–41–3; Srinath 8–0–48–1; Tendulkar 5–0–29–0; Raju 10–0–37–1; Jadeja 7–0–34–0

INDIA

R.J. Shastri c Waugh b Moody	25
K. Srikkanth b McDermott	0
M. Azharuddin (capt) run out	93
S.R. Tendulkar c Waugh b Moody	11
Kapil Dev lbw Waugh	21
S.V. Manjrekar run out	47
A.D. Jadeja b Hughes	1
K.S. More (wk) b Moody	14
J. Srinath not out	8
M. Prabhakar run out	1
S.L.V. Raju run out	0
Extras (lb 8, w 5)	13
(47 overs)	10–234

1/6 2/53 3/86 4/128 5/194 6/199 7/216 8/231 9/232

Bowling: McDermott 9–1–35–1; Whitney 10–2–36–0; Hughes 9–1–49–1; Moody 9–0–56–3; Waugh 10–0–50–1

Umpires: B.L. Aldridge, I.D. Robinson.

Toss: Australia. Points: Australia 2, India 0

SUNDAY 1 MARCH 1992
ENGLAND vs PAKISTAN
ADELAIDE OVAL, ADELAIDE: NO RESULT

While rain was hampering India's progress in Brisbane, it saved the skin of their neighbours and rivals, Pakistan. An unseasonable drenching of the driest of Australia's capital cities washed

out their match with England after they had been bowled out for 74. It had not rained in Adelaide for five weeks yet only two overs were possible after lunch, much to the frustration of England.

On such things are World Cups won and lost.

Imran Khan's bad shoulder kept him out again, so it was Javed Miandad who called incorrectly at the toss, Gooch telling him Pakistan would bat. None of them could make much of the conditions as the ball seamed and jagged around. Derek Pringle finished with astonishing figures. The Pakistani's innings lasted 40 overs, but they were dismissed for their lowest World Cup total. It was a procession, the best stand being 15 for the ninth wicket.

The wicket had sweated under covers and soon Ramiz Raja drove to point off Phil DeFreitas and Inzamam-ul-Haq was caught behind first ball to leave Pakistan 2–5. Salim Malik hit three of the innings' five fours and

Mushtaq and Wasim Haider used up what turned out to be valuable time when the scoreboard read 8–47. Mushtaq played and missed at an entire over of outswingers from Dermot Reeve.

England was still able to bat prior to the lunch interval and Gooch was out again before he could get to a sandwich, given out caught behind off Akram. The left-arm paceman was unhappy with the condition of the wicket, although with so much rain around, how that might have been changed is hard to imagine. In the good old days of the World Cup everyone would have come back on Monday to finish. In 1992, though, one-day cricket literally meant one day of cricket and Pakistan and England both received one point for the 'no result'.

PAKISTAN

Ramiz Raja c Reeve b DeFreitas	1
Aamir Sohail c & b Pringle	9
Inzamam-ul-Haq c Stewart b DeFreitas	0
Javed Miandad (capt) b Pringle	3
Salim Malik c Reeve b Botham	17
Ijaz Ahmed c Stewart b Small	0
Wasim Akram b Botham	1
Moin Khan (wk) c Hick b Small	2
Wasim Haider c Stewart b Reeve	13
Mushtaq Ahmed c Reeve b Pringle	17
Aqib Javed not out	1
Extras (lb 1, w 8, nb 1)	10
(40.2 overs)	10–74

1/5 2/5 3/14 4/20 5/32 6/35 7/42 8/47 9/62

Bowling: Pringle 8.2–5–8–3; DeFreitas 7–1–22–2; Small 10–1–29–2; Botham 10–4–12–2; Reeve 5–3–2–1

ENGLAND

G.A. Gooch (capt) c Moin Khan b Wasim Akram	3
I.T. Botham not out	6
R.A. Smith not out	5
Extras (b 1, lb 3, w 5, nb 1)	10
(8 overs)	1–24

Did not bat: G.A. Hick, N.H. Fairbrother, A.J. Stewart (wk), D.A. Reeve, C.C. Lewis, D.R. Pringle, P.A.J. DeFreitas, G.C. Small

1/14

Bowling: Wasim Akram 3–0–7–1; Aqib Javed 3–1–7–0; Wasim Haider 1–0–1–0; Ijaz Ahmed 1–0–5–0

Umpires: S.A. Bucknor, P.J. McConnell.

Toss: England. Points: England 1, Pakistan 1

MONDAY 2 MARCH 1992
SOUTH AFRICA vs SRI LANKA
BASIN RESERVE, WELLINGTON: SRI LANKA WON BY 3 WICKETS

The faxes received by Kepler Wessels after this surprising defeat were a little less complimentary than those sent following the win over Australia. The condemnation was not just of the performance of his team, but also of Wessels' own batting. The hero of Sydney struggled through 94 balls at the Basin Reserve without once reaching the boundary. He said he found the wicket even slower and lower than the one used in Auckland.

He had been on three at the 10-over mark after South Africa had been sent in to bat by

Aravinda de Silva. Champaka Ramanayake's first seven overs cost just seven runs. Wessels' decision to use Adrian Kuiper as an opener instead of Andrew Hudson also failed, the all-rounder missing more deliveries than he struck before being bowled by left-arm spinner Don Anurasiri. Although the second wicket did not fall until the total was 113, Wessels and, to a lesser extent, Peter Kirsten had been so tardy that 35 overs had been completed by the time both fell within a run of each other.

The acceleration from that point was at a cost of all remaining wickets. Jonty Rhodes established himself and was batting in an enterprising fashion when Sanath Jayasuriya leapt high to hold the first of two great catches at short cover. When Allan Donald was run out from the last ball of the innings South Africa had lost 9–81 and were all out for 195.

Maybe 'White Lightning' was annoyed by his dismissal because he bowled like fury at the start of the Sri Lankan reply. They had made the long 14-hour journey from Mackay with only 12 fit players and when Donald, who sent down six wides in his two overs, yorked de Silva Sri Lanka were 3–35. That meant an uphill fight for the pre-match underdogs, one started by the solid Roshan Mahanama and Hashan Tillekaratne who put on 52. Omar Henry's removal of the Sri Lankan wicketkeeper was followed by a stand of 67 by Mahanama and Arjuna Ranatunga. The

opener finally fell in the 43rd over with 42 runs still needed.

The result was clearly going down to the wire and the cheap dismissal of Jayasuriya meant Ranatunga would have to score the bulk of the runs. He was equal to the task. South Africa's bowlers had given Sri Lanka 17 extra runs and deliveries which left Donald, one of the worst offenders, with just five runs to spare for the 50th over. A four over mid wicket by Ranatunga and a slashing square drive by Ramanayake carried Sri Lanka to victory from the second-last ball. It was the first time the Sri Lankans had won two games in a World Cup tournament, so the on-field dancing of Ranatunga and Ramanayake, as well as the singing from the group of flag-wavers in the outer, was justified. Ranatunga was named Man of the Match for an innings which lasted 73 balls and included six fours. Wessels was left to read his poisoned mail.

SOUTH AFRICA

K.C. Wessels (capt) c & b Ranatunga	40
A.P. Kuiper b Anurasiri	18
P.N. Kirsten c Hathurusingha b Kalpage	47
J.N. Rhodes c Jayasuriya b Wickremasinghe	28
M.W. Rushmere c Jayasuriya b Ranatunga	4
W.J. Cronje st Tillekaratne b Anurasiri	3
B.M. McMillan not out	18
R.P. Snell b Anurasiri	9
D.J. Richardson (wk) run out	0
O. Henry c Kalpage b Ramanayake	11
A.A.A. Donald run out	3
Extras (lb 9, w 4, nb 1)	14
(50 overs)	10–195

1/27 2/113 3/114 4/128 5/149 6/153 7/165 8/165 9/186

Bowling: Ramanayake 9-2-19-1; Wickremasinghe 7-0-32-1; Kalpage 10-0-38-1; Anurasiri 10-1-41-3; Ranatunga 6-0-26-2; Gurusinha 8-0-30-0

SRI LANKA

R.S. Mahanama c Richardson b McMillan	68
U.C. Hathurusingha c Wessels b Donald	5
A.P. Gurusinha lbw Donald	0
P.A. de Silva (capt) b Donald	7
H.P. Tillekaratne (wk) c Rushmere b Henry	17
A. Ranatunga not out	64
S.T. Jayasuriya st Richardson b Kirsten	3
R.S. Kalpage run out	5
C.P.H. Ramanayake not out	4
Extras (b 1, lb 7, w 13, nb 4)	25
(49.5 overs)	7–198

Did not bat: S.D. Anurasiri, G.G.P. Wickremasinghe

1/11 2/12 3/35 4/87 5/154 6/168 7/189

Bowling: McMillan 10-2-34-1; Donald 9.5-0-42-3; Henry 10-0-31-1; Snell 10-1-33-0; Kuiper 5-0-25-0; Kirsten 5-0-25-1

Umpires: Khizar Hayat, S.J. Woodward.

Toss: Sri Lanka. Points: Sri Lanka 2, South Africa 0

TUESDAY 3 MARCH 1992
NEW ZEALAND vs ZIMBABWE
McLEAN PARK, NAPIER: NEW ZEALAND WON BY 48 RUNS

The stupidity of the rule for rain-reduced games was exemplified by this greasy encounter on the east coast of New Zealand's North Island. One reduction followed another until finally

Zimbabwe's ask was 154 from 18 overs, which their captain Dave Houghton thought was 'bizarre' and turned out to be quite unrealistic.

There were problems right from the start and

a 75-minute delay meant that the contest began as one of 43 overs per side. When the game got under way Houghton won the toss and sent New Zealand in. After 11 overs the players were interrupted again with New Zealand 2–52. When Martin Crowe and Andrew Jones resumed the innings they had an allowance of only another 76 deliveries. Of those they received just 57 before yet another shower brought the Kiwi time allocation to an end. It turned out those 9.3 overs were enough to set up a winning total.

Aided by bowlers who struggled to control a wet ball and fieldsmen who slipped all over the place on a wet outfield, Crowe and Jones created batting mayhem by adding 110 in 57 balls. Crowe, in particular, was uninhibited in his assault on the Zimbabwean attack. Much of his hitting was through and over the leg side. When Houghton packed that half of the field Crowe stepped away and began cracking the ball over the covers. He hit Ali Shah for six over square leg and then over cover into the Centenary Stand, racing to his fifty in 31 balls which put Andy Waller's 32-ball effort earlier in the competition into second place.

The difficulties the Zimbabweans were under were highlighted when Iain Butchart slipped over twice as he ran in to bowl. He was punished as severely as anyone by Jones and Crowe, but at least had the consolation of ending the 14-over, 129 stand when Jones was beautifully caught by Waller in front of the sightscreen from another big hit.

Zimbabwe made a brave attempt to make 154 from 108 balls. Wickets kept tumbling in the overcast conditions, though, and the loss of the best hitter, Waller, to a Danny Morrison yorker was critical. Chris Cairns was belted and Dipak Patel was not used because of the wet ball. The dibbly dobblering Chris Harris and Gavin Larsen could not be collared and between them took 6–31 from eight overs. Then, when light rain returned in the 13th over, a 'no result' threatened again. Alistair Campbell skyed a ball towards Crowe and the New Zealand captain later admitted he considered deliberately dropping it. He thought the umpires might have taken the players off the ground at the break in play as the rain was getting heavier.

Much to the relief of the Kiwis, the officials consulted then allowed the game to continue. The rain eased a little and the 18 overs were completed. Crowe was named Man of the Match and even allowed himself the luxury of thoughts of a semi-final berth.

NEW ZEALAND	
M.J. Greatbatch b Duers	15
R.T. Latham b Brandes	2
A.H. Jones c Waller b Butchart	57
M.D. Crowe (capt) not out	74
C.L. Cairns not out	1
Extras (b 7, lb 6)	13
(20.5 overs)	3–162

Did not bat: K.R. Rutherford, C.Z. Harris, D.N. Patel, I.D.S. Smith (wk), G.R. Larsen, D.K. Morrison

1/9 2/25 3/154

Bowling: Brandes 5–1–28–1; Duers 6–0–17–1; Shah 4–0–34–0; Butchart 4–0–53–1; Burmester 1.5–0–17–0

ZIMBABWE	
A. Flower (wk) b Larsen	30
A.C. Waller b Morrison	11
D.L. Houghton (capt) b Larsen	10
I.P. Butchart c Cairns b Larsen	3
E.A. Brandes b Harris	6
A.J. Pycroft not out	13
A.D. Campbell c Crowe b Harris	8
A.H. Shah b Harris	7
M.G. Burmester not out	4
Extras (lb 9, w 3, nb 1)	13
(18 overs)	7–105

Did not bat: A.J. Traicos, K.G. Duers

1/22 2/41 3/63 4/63 5/75 6/86 7/97

Bowling: Morrison 4–0–14–1; Cairns 2–0–27–0; Larsen 4–0–16–3; Harris 4–0–15–3; Latham 3–0–18–0; Crowe 1–0–6–0

Umpires: D.P. Buultjens, K.E. Liebenberg.

Toss: Zimbabwe. Points: New Zealand 2, Zimbabwe 0

WEDNESDAY 4 MARCH 1992
INDIA vs PAKISTAN
SCG, SYDNEY: INDIA WON BY 43 RUNS

India's luck turned for the better in the first-ever World Cup match between cricket's two closest and most intense neighbours. The collapse of the Pakistani middle order under lights in front of an estimated television audience of 250 million left India victorious by a comfortable margin. After the game Imran Khan spoke optimistically about Pakistan's chances of reaching the semi-finals, even though they had only one win from four starts.

Ten thousand expatriate and visiting Indians and Pakistanis were in the SCG when Mohammad Azharuddin won the toss and batted. The Indians had left out their vice-captain Ravi Shastri for slow batting and it was his replacement, Ajay Jadeja, in only his second Limited-Over International, who got the Indian innings away to a positive start. Apart from the cheap removal of an out-of-touch Kris Srikkanth, who had all sorts of trouble with the accurate Aqib Javed, there was consistency at the top of the Indian order, although no-one managed to go on to a really big score.

Sachin Tendulkar put on 46 with his old school chum, Vinod Kambli. Then young leg-spinner Mushtaq Ahmed had the left-hander caught, and bowled Sanjay Manjrekar first ball to leave India 5–148. There was cause for concern for the Indians that they may not have set a worthy target in such a prestigious match. That, however, reckoned without the maturity and skill of 18-year-old Tendulkar and the smiting ability of Kapil Dev. Mushtaq had three valuable and quite cheap wickets. Kapil hit hard and to good effect to give his figures a bit of a battering while 60 runs were added in eight overs. Once Kapil put the spinner over extra cover for six on his way to 35 in 26 balls.

Tendulkar batted through to the end of the innings, called after 49 overs because of Pakistani tardiness. There were only three boundaries in an effort which still exuded class throughout its 62-ball duration.

Protecting 216 Azharuddin kept his fieldsmen in a ring around the Pakistanis to increase the pressure. It worked at the start as the absence of the injured Ramiz Raja was felt by Pakistan. A wicket each to Kapil and Manoj Prabhakar left them 2–17 and Aamir Sohail and Javed Miandad with a rebuilding assignment. It was tense stuff as they put together a partnership of 88. Javed Miandad and Indian wicketkeeper Kiran More had a tete-a-tete over the merits or otherwise of some appeals. Miandad, never one to back away from such matters, demonstrated his feelings with a high-leaping imitation of More. Both players were reported, but let off because the umpires, Peter McConnell and David Shepherd, could not understand what the protagonists had actually said to each other.

The Pakistani innings stalled in the face of a fine spell by Prabhakar. Salim Malik responded with two boundaries, then was caught behind off a perfectly pitched leg-cutter. Prabhakar gave the batsman a fiery send-off. Imran, who had tested his shoulder with a tidy eight-over spell of medium-paced inswing, entered with his side 3–127, needing 90 in 15 overs.

It was a respectable ask yet the Pakistani middle order crumbled. Imran fell foul of a running muddle, then Wasim Akram failed to pick Venkatapathy Raju's arm ball and was stumped. Javed shouldered even more pressure as his side's last hope. His had been the innings of a determined rather than in-form batsman. When, after 113 balls he stepped away to hit Javagal Srinath through the off side and edged the ball into his stumps the elation of the Indians was obvious.

The Pakistani challenge faded. Tendulkar was named Man of the Match and Pakistan would have to wait for another opportunity to restore national pride.

INDIA

A.D. Jadeja c Zahid Fazal b Wasim Haider	46
K. Srikkanth c Moin Khan b Aqib Javed	5
M. Azharuddin (capt) c Moin Khan b Mushtaq Ahmed	32
V.G. Kambli c Inzamam b Mushtaq Ahmed	24
S.R. Tendulkar not out	54
S.V. Manjrekar b Mushtaq Ahmed	0
Kapil Dev c Imran Khan b Aqib Javed	35
K.S. More (wk) run out	4
M. Prabhakar not out	2
Extras (lb 3, w 9, nb 2)	14
(49 overs)	7–216

Did not bat: J. Srinath, S.L.V. Raju

1/25 2/86 3/101 4/147 5/148 6/208 7/213

Bowling: Wasim Akram 10–0–45–0; Aqib Javed 8–2–28–2; Imran Khan 8–0–25–0; Wasim Haider 10–1–36–1; Mushtaq Ahmed 10–0–59–3; Aamir Sohail 3–0–20–0

PAKISTAN

Aamir Sohail c Srikkanth b Tendulkar	62
Inzamam-ul-Haq lbw Kapil Dev	2
Zahid Fazal c More b Prabhakar	2
Javed Miandad b Srinath	40
Salim Malik c More b Prabhakar	12
Imran Khan (capt) run out	0
Wasim Akram st More b Raju	4
Wasim Haider b Srinath	13
Moin Khan (wk) c Manjrekar b Kapil Dev	12
Mushtaq Ahmed run out	3
Aqib Javed not out	1
Extras (lb 6, w 15, nb 1)	22
(48.1 overs)	10–173

1/8 2/17 3/105 4/127 5/130 6/141 7/141 8/161 9/166

Bowling: Kapil Dev 10–0–30–2; Prabhakar 10–1–22–2; Srinath 8.1–0–37–2; Tendulkar 10–0–37–1; Raju 10–1–41–1

Umpires: P.J. McConnell, D.R. Shepherd.

Toss: India. Points: India 2, Pakistan 0

THURSDAY 5 MARCH 1992
SOUTH AFRICA vs WEST INDIES
LANCASTER PARK, CHRISTCHURCH: SOUTH AFRICA WON BY 64 RUNS

As it did against England, the West Indies batting let them down badly against South Africa, allowing Kepler Wessels to relax when the faxes came in after this game. A World Cup first like Wednesday's clash, this was also the first official contest anywhere between the two teams. It was the 100th World Cup match.

In grey weather there were few batting comforts on a bouncy pitch which encouraged fast bowling. Wessels lost the toss and was first out with the total on eight. Andrew Hudson and the consistent Peter Kirsten brought up the 50 by the 17th over before the opener was brilliantly caught by Brian Lara in the gully. Kirsten used a runner for the second half of his innings, having pulled a calf muscle on 28. He was the only one of six batsmen who reached 20 to go on to a substantial score. His 92-ball innings included just two fours before wicketkeeper David Williams took a nice catch to give Malcolm Marshall his second wicket.

There were few boundaries and only one six, a leg-side clout by Adrian Kuiper off Winston Benjamin which raised the South African 100, in a neat total of 200 from the 50 overs. Kuiper had become second top score before playing over a slower yorker from Curtly Ambrose, who along with Marshall was the most effective of the West Indian bowlers.

The team whose fast bowlers had inflicted such heartache, fingerache, thighache, ribache and occasionally headache on other teams over the years now got a bit of their own medicine as the South African speedsters ripped through the West Indian top order. It was Meyrick Pringle, not number-one speedster Allan Donald, who did the damage. After a couple of sweet square cuts Brian Lara holed out to Jonty Rhodes at point. Then Richie Richardson was trapped lbw and Carl Hooper and Keith Arthurton were caught by Wessels at slip while the score was stationary on 19. Pringle took four wickets in 11 balls without cost. Desmond Haynes survived the Pringle massacre, but had an already damaged finger so badly battered he retired hurt and intended to get hospital treatment.

Instead, when Richard Snell dismissed Malcolm Marshall and David Williams one after the other, he returned to the crease at 6–70. Gus Logie was going down fighting and punished Adrian Kuiper for a succession of boundaries. One of those raised his fifty and brief hopes of an unlikely West Indian win. But Kuiper got revenge when he removed Logie and Haynes caught behind driving in the same over. Eight for 117 soon became 136 all out, which meant the West Indies had made their lowest-ever total in the World Cup. Pringle had not even been selected in South Africa's original World Cup squad of 20. Now he was Man of the Match in a game that revitalised South Africa's whole campaign.

SOUTH AFRICA	
K.C. Wessels (capt) c Haynes b Marshall	1
A.C. Hudson c Lara b Cummins	22
P.N. Kirsten c Williams b Marshall	56
M.W. Rushmere st Williams b Hooper	10
A.P. Kuiper b Ambrose	23
J.N. Rhodes c Williams b Cummins	22
B.M. McMillan c Lara b Benjamin	20
D.J. Richardson (wk) not out	20
R.P. Snell c Haynes b Ambrose	3
M.W. Pringle not out	5
Extras (lb 8, w 3, nb 7)	18
(50 overs)	8–200

Did not bat: A.A.A. Donald

1/8 2/51 3/73 4/119 5/127 6/159 7/181 8/187

Bowling: Ambrose 10–1–34–2; Marshall 10–1–26–2; Benjamin 10–0–47–1; Cummins 10–0–40–2; Hooper 10–0–45–1

WEST INDIES	
D.L. Haynes c Richardson b Kuiper	30
B.C. Lara c Rhodes b Pringle	9
R.B. Richardson (capt) lbw Pringle	1
C.L. Hooper c Wessels b Pringle	0
K.L.T. Arthurton c Wessels b Pringle	0
A.L. Logie c Pringle b Kuiper	61
M.D. Marshall c Rhodes b Snell	6
D. Williams (wk) c Richardson b Snell	0
C.E.L. Ambrose run out	12
A.C. Cummins c McMillan b Donald	6
W.K.M. Benjamin not out	1
Extras (lb 9, w 1)	10
(38.4 overs)	10–136

1/10 2/19 3/19 4/19 5/70 6/70 7/116 8/117 9/132 10/136
Haynes retired hurt 4–50 resumed 6–70

Bowling: Donald 6.4–2–13–1; Pringle 8–4–11–4; McMillan 8–2–36–0; Snell 7–2–16–2; Kuiper 9–0–51–2

Umpires: B.L. Aldridge, S.G. Randell.

Toss: West Indies. Points: South Africa 2, West Indies 0

THURSDAY 5 MARCH 1992
AUSTRALIA vs ENGLAND
SCG, SYDNEY: ENGLAND WON BY 8 WICKETS

Australia found co-hosting a World Cup did not agree with them and for the second time they were thrashed at the SCG. The chances of the home side west of the Tasman Sea reaching the semi-finals was not looking good. What irked Australians most was that Ian Botham, a forgotten Ashes nemesis, proved a match-winner and had no trouble taking the game award.

The recipe for the Australian disaster was also horribly similar to the one of the previous week: a sound start, a disastrous middle-order collapse, and a total around 170 which the bowlers could make nothing of.

Allan Border won the toss and batted in front of another capacity SCG crowd, whose spread of support was more even than it had been the previous Thursday. Mark Taylor failed again and

David Boon, backing up too far, fell foul of a sharp piece of work by Neil Fairbrother at mid wicket in the 10th over. Tom Moody had been promoted to open at the expense of the lacklustre Geoff Marsh and he responded with an important half century. He and Dean Jones took Australia to a 2–106 in 28 overs when the Victorian was brilliantly caught at point by the athletic Chris Lewis off a well-timed cut shot.

Even after Moody had gloved a ball from left-arm spinner Phil Tufnell back on to his stumps while sweeping there was no sense of imminent disaster. Border and Steve Waugh carried Australia to 4–145 in the 38th over when the ghosts of 1981 rose up from the grave. Initially it seemed Australia had been let off when Waugh was dropped at short cover, but from the fifth ball Botham duplicated Adrian Kuiper's inswinger to Border and achieved the same result.

That was only the pantomime king's warm-up. In his next over, the 40th of the innings, Ian Healy clipped a catch to mid wicket. Two balls later Peter Taylor fell in the same way and for the same score as his top-of-the-order namesake. After a sighter Craig McDermott offered a soft catch to Phil DeFreitas at mid-on. Botham had 4–0 in seven balls. It was pitiful stuff by Australia and it must have caused a lot of Australian television viewers to switch channels. Steve Waugh's run-out in the 43rd over ended any hope of a reasonable total and when Dermot Reeve captured the prized scalp of Bruce Reid Australia had lost 6–26 in 11 overs.

Botham, not satisfied with 4–31, made the Union Jacks in the Doug Walters Stand and on the refurbished Hill wave even harder when he

and Graham Gooch put on a century opening partnership. They withstood a fast opening spell by a highly motivated McDermott, then took control. Wasim Akram had complained that batting conditions under lights could be difficult. Neither England nor South Africa had much difficulty seeing the white ball at night. Botham's promotion to opener had achieved little to this point and his previous highest score in any World Cup was 22, but he had a night out in Sydney and hit six fours in his fifty before being well caught down the leg side in the 23rd over.

Gooch went on to complete his fifty as well, and was not dismissed until victory was assured. The target was reached nine comfortable overs to spare. After the humiliations of the Ashes tour in 1990–91 and talk by the Prime Minister, Paul Keating, of Australia becoming a republic, it was a sweet moment for the proud English captain.

AUSTRALIA

T.M. Moody b Tufnell	51
M.A. Taylor lbw Pringle	0
D.C. Boon run out	18
D.M. Jones c Lewis b DeFreitas	22
S.R. Waugh run out	27
A.R. Border (capt) b Botham	16
I.A. Healy (wk) c Fairbrother b Botham	9
P.L. Taylor lbw Botham	0
C.J. McDermott c DeFreitas b Botham	0
M.R. Whitney not out	8
B.A. Reid b Reeve	1
Extras (b 2, lb 8, w 5, nb 4)	19
(49 overs)	10–171

1/5 2/35 3/106 4/114 5/145 6/155 7/155 8/155 9/163 10/171

Bowling: Pringle 9–1–24–1; Lewis 10–2–28–0; DeFreitas 10–3–23–1; Botham 10–1–31–4; Tufnell 9–0–52–1; Reeve 1–0–3–1

ENGLAND

G.A. Gooch (capt) b Waugh	58
I.T. Botham c Healy b Whitney	53
R.A. Smith not out	30
G.A. Hick not out	7
Extras (lb 13, w 8, nb 4)	25
(40.5 overs)	2–173

Did not bat: N.H. Fairbrother, A.J. Stewart (wk), D.A. Reeve, C.C. Lewis, D.R. Pringle, P.A.J. DeFreitas, P.C.R. Tufnell

Bowling: McDermott 10–1–29–0; Reid 7.5–0–49–0; Whitney 10–2–28–1; Waugh 6–0–29–1; P.L. Taylor 3–0–7–0; Moody 4–0–18–0

Umpires: S.A. Bucknor, Khizar Hayat.

Toss: Australia. Points: England 2, Australia 0

SATURDAY 7 MARCH 1992
INDIA vs ZIMBABWE
TRUST BANK PARK, HAMILTON: INDIA WON BY 55 RUNS

The 'if it's Saturday we must be in Hamilton' game turned out to be yet another frustrating exercise for the well-travelled Zimbabweans. The timing of the rain interruptions gave them virtually no chance of winning and poured further

scorn on the rule for rain-affected games. It was threatening to undermine the validity of the whole tournament.

India was back to a swings and roundabouts situation, having won points and lost points because of the rule. At least they could relish another great display by Sachin Tendulkar, whose better than a run per ball 81 dominated India's 32-over allocation. He was named Man of the Match and mastered all the Zimbabwean bowlers except John Traicos. The off spinner was 26 years older than the young Indian master and played in South Africa's last Test three years before Tendulkar's birth. Traicos handled the wet ball as well as anyone on the day. Tendulkar added an important 99 with Sanjay Manjrekar in 15 overs and hit eight fours and a six before becoming one of Mark Burmester's three victims.

With plenty of rain around, the players forsook their lunch break between innings and got straight on with the game. The Indians ran, slipped and fell all over the place as they tried to fit in 15 overs to avoid the 'no result' curse. They got in 19.1 before the umpires took them off, never to return. Ali Shah, Andy Flower and Andy Waller had batted in competent fashion to that point and there was nothing to suggest Zimbabwe would not have made another 100 runs if the extra 13 overs had been delivered. The man with the calculator told them they should have made 160 in 19 overs. Zimbabwe said nothing officially, but they were not very happy.

INDIA

K. Srikkanth b Burmester	32
Kapil Dev lbw Brandes	10
M. Azharuddin (capt) c Flower b Burmester	12
S.R. Tendulkar c Campbell b Burmester	81
S.V. Manjrekar c Duers b Traicos	34
V.G. Kambli b Traicos	1
A.D. Jadeja c Shah b Traicos	6
K.S. More (wk) not out	15
J. Srinath not out	6
Extras (lb 3, w 3)	6
(32 overs)	7–203

Did not bat: M. Prabhakar, S.L.V. Raju

1/23 2/43 3/69 4/168 5/170 6/182 7/184

Bowling: Brandes 7–0–43–1; Duers 7–0–48–0; Burmester 6–0–36–3; Shah 6–1–38–0; Traicos 6–0–35–3

ZIMBABWE

A.H. Shah b Tendulkar	31
A. Flower (wk) not out	43
A.C. Waller not out	13
Extras (b 1, lb 11, w 5)	17
(19.1 overs)	1–104

Did not bat: D.L. Houghton (capt), A.J. Pycroft, I.P. Butchart, A.D. Campbell, E.A. Brandes, M.G. Burmester, A.J. Traicos, K.G. Duers

1/79

Bowling: Kapil Dev 4–0–6–0; Prabhakar 3–0–14–0; Srinath 4–0–20–0; Tendulkar 6–0–35–1; Raju 2.1–0–17–0

Umpires: D.P. Buultjens, S.G. Randell.

Toss: India. Points: India 2, Zimbabwe 0

SATURDAY 7 MARCH 1992
AUSTRALIA vs SRI LANKA
ADELAIDE OVAL, ADELAIDE: AUSTRALIA WON BY 7 WICKETS

It was symbolic of a far better day for Australia that, even though Geoff Marsh dropped an early catch in the gully, the previously out-of-form opener made 60 on his return to the Australian side batting, after a cautious start, with his old fluency in an opening partnership of 120 with fellow Western Australian Tom Moody. As Australia were only chasing 189 the stand settled the result and capped the co-host's best performance of the tournament. It also revived their semi-final hopes.

Allan Border won the toss, sent Sri Lanka in and, perhaps in an attempt to be innovative,

opened the bowling with Steve Waugh. The medium pacer, more used to bowling at the end of the innings, made no impact but soon the Sri Lankans began to run themselves out. Roshan Mahanama was first, being slow to respond to a call from his opening partner, Athula Samarasekera.

de Silva's 62 provided the platform for a potentially competitive total. He scored 20 consecutive singles and hit only two boundaries. The Sri Lankan captain's most memorable shot was a dancing reverse sweep off Border. However, Michael Whitney, Craig McDermott, Peter Taylor and Border were so frugal the whole innings contained just eight fours and the run rate never looked likely to reach the four per over mark. When Sri Lanka attempted to lift the tempo the captain was caught on the mid-wicket boundary. The lower order became involved in three more run-outs, including one from the final ball of the innings. The scoreline slipped from 3–123 to 9–189 at the completion of the 50 overs.

Moody and Marsh only scraped together 16 runs from the first nine overs. Certain sections

of the Adelaide crowd made their feelings known about this. Marsh responded with a cover drive for four off Champaka Ramanayake and a sweep for six off left-arm spinner Don Anurasiri.

The 100 arrived in the 26th over and after the openers had been dismissed Mark Waugh and Dean Jones hit sixes on the massively long Adelaide Oval which impressed everyone. Australia won by seven wickets at the end of the 44th over and Tom Moody was named Man of the Match.

SRI LANKA

R.S. Mahanama run out	7
M.A.R. Samarasekera c Healy b Taylor	34
A.P. Gurusinha lbw Whitney	5
P.A. de Silva (capt) c Moody b McDermott	62
A. Ranatunga c Jones b Taylor	23
S.T. Jayasuriya lbw Border	15
H.P. Tillekaratne (wk) run out	5
R.S. Kalpage run out	14
C.P.H. Ramanayake run out	5
S.D. Anurasiri not out	4
Extras (b 3, lb 6, w 5, nb 1)	15
(50 overs)	9–189

Did not bat: G.G.P. Wickremasinghe

1/8 2/28 3/72 4/123 5/151 6/163 7/166 8/182 9/189

Bowling: McDermott 10–0–28–1; S.R. Waugh 7–0–34–0; Whitney 10–3–26–1; Moody 3–0–18–0; Taylor 10–0–34–2; Border 10–0–40–1

AUSTRALIA

T.M. Moody c Mahanama b Wickremasinghe	57
G.R. Marsh c Anurasiri b Kalpage	60
M.E. Waugh c Mahanama b Wickremasinghe	26
D.C. Boon not out	27
D.M. Jones not out	12
Extras (lb 2, w 3, nb 3)	8
(44 overs)	3–190

Did not bat: A.R. Border (capt), S.R. Waugh, I.A. Healy (wk), P.L. Taylor, C.J. McDermott, M.R. Whitney

3/165

Bowling: Wickremasinghe 10–3–29–2; Ramanayake 9–1–44–0; Anurasiri 10–0–43–0; Gurusinha 6–0–20–0; Ranatunga 1–0–11–0; Kalpage 8–0–41–1

Umpires: P.D. Reporter, I.D. Robinson.

Toss: Australia. Points: Australia 2, Sri Lanka 0

SUNDAY 8 MARCH 1992
NEW ZEALAND vs WEST INDIES
EDEN PARK, AUCKLAND: NEW ZEALAND WON BY 5 WICKETS

The campaign of the once mighty West Indies was falling in a heap. They were outplayed by a rampant New Zealand who completed only their second win in a Limited-Over International against the side once so obviously their superior.

There were plenty of frustrations for the West Indians: batting that just refused to gel as a unit, slogging by Mark Greatbatch that might have been stopped if short deliveries were allowed, an incorrect umpiring adjudication on a run-out and some missed opportunities in the field. In the good old days, though, none of them would have made a difference. The West Indies would still have won.

The new wicket for this match looked green to Martin Crowe so he bowled after winning the toss on an overcast morning in front of a growing crowd. He opened again with the off spin of Dipak Patel and set two short mid wickets rather than slips catchers, which sedated Desmond Haynes and Brian Lara. The West Indian openers got stuck into Gavin Larsen and Willie Watson when they came on and eventually put on 65 for the first wicket. When Lara, who went on to complete a half century in his usual stylish manner, took 14 from Larsen's first over Crowe brought his second dibbly dobbler, Chris Harris, into the attack and switched Larsen to the other end. The move brought almost immediate reward when Harris caught and bowled Haynes and the run rate was slowed again.

Patel's economy was exceptional and when Carl Hooper tried to put him out of Eden Park Greatbatch waited 10 seconds under a skyed hit before completing the catch. Keith Arthurton made a worthwhile contribution, but it was the bright innings by little wicketkeeper David Williams, which included five fours and took advantage of loose bowling by Willie Watson, that pushed the West Indies score above 200.

For three overs neither Greatbatch nor Rod Latham could lay willow on leather. Then the big left-hander began smacking the ball around in what had become his accustomed style. There was great gnashing of Ambrose's significant teeth when Greatbatch hit him for six over third man. He also danced down the wicket and smote Malcolm Marshall over extra cover and onto the roof of the West Stand for a six that Martin Crowe called 'The stroke of the World Cup'.

Greatbatch hit seven fours and three sixes during his 77-ball innings. He swung and missed plenty of times, as well. After one unsuccessful foray Ambrose put forth a few opinions as to Greatbatch's true worth. That fired the big crowd up and Winston Benjamin became a target for bottle throwers at third man. The game was stopped and the match referee Peter McDermott called for more police to be stationed in the offending area.

Upon the resumption Rod Latham was caught behind. Later, within three runs of each other Benjamin got rid of Andrew Jones, also caught behind, and Greatbatch caught at third man. The Kiwis were 3–100, the fall of wickets uncannily similar to the way they had fallen during the West Indian innings and their win far from a certainty. Or it was until Crowe put together another masterpiece. The loss of Ken Rutherford and Chris Harris on the way did not stem the flow of strokes. He mastered the off spin of Carl Hooper, then with drives and pulls put Marshall out of the attack. Patel was given not-out when a metre short of his ground, then two balls later the West Indies missed another blatant run-out chance.

It was their last opportunity to steal the match. Crowe pressed on and when he straight drove Winston Benjamin for four from the third ball of the 49th over he had struck 12 boundaries in 77 balls. The Kiwi captain had won the Man of the Match award for the third time, had a tournament batting average of 263, and his team were unbeaten on top of the Benson and Hedges World Cup qualifying table with five wins. How many perfect days should one man have?

WEST INDIES

D.L. Haynes c & b Harris		22
B.C. Lara c Rutherford b Larsen		52
R.B. Richardson (capt) c Smith b Watson		29
C.L. Hooper c Greatbatch b Patel		2
K.L.T. Arthurton b Morrison		40
A.L. Logie b Harris		3
M.D. Marshall b Larsen		·5
D. Williams (wk) not out		32
W.K.M. Benjamin not out		2
Extras (lb 8, w 7, nb 1)		16
(50 overs)		7–203

Did not bat: C.E.L. Ambrose, A.C. Cummins

1/65 2/95 3/100 4/136 5/142 6/156 7/201

Bowling: Morrison 9-1-33-1; Patel 10-2-19-1; Watson 10-2-56-1; Larsen 10-0-41-2; Harris 10-2-32-2; Latham 1-0-14-0

NEW ZEALAND

M.J. Greatbatch c Haynes b Benjamin		63
R.T. Latham c Williams b Cummins		14
A.H. Jones c Williams b Benjamin		10
M.D. Crowe (capt) not out		81
K.R. Rutherford c Williams b Ambrose		8
C.Z. Harris c Williams b Cummins		7
D.N. Patel not out		10
Extras (lb 7, w 5, nb 1)		13
(48.3 overs)		5–206

Did not bat: I.D.S. Smith (wk), G.R. Larsen, D.K. Morrison, W. Watson

1/67 2/97 3/100 4/135 5/174

Bowling: Ambrose 10-1-41-1; Marshall 9-1-35-0; Cummins 10-0-53-2; Benjamin 9.3-3-34-2; Hooper 10-0-36-0

Umpires: K.E. Liebenberg, P.J. McConnell.

Toss: New Zealand. Points: New Zealand 2, West Indies 0

SUNDAY 8 MARCH 1992
PAKISTAN vs SOUTH AFRICA
WOOLLOONGABBA, BRISBANE: SOUTH AFRICA WON BY 20 RUNS

This was the sixth match to be adversely affected by rain in the two weeks since the opening of the tournament. Pakistan were the side to suffer for choosing to bat second when they lost 14 overs from their innings while the target was reduced by just 18 runs. A Brisbane downpour stopped play at the 22-over mark when they were 2–74 chasing South Africa's 211. At the time they required 4.84 per over to win. Upon the resumption it had leapt to 8.28, and when a flurry of shots by Imran Khan and Inzamam-ul-Haq was ended by the fielding brilliance of Jonty Rhodes Pakistan's hopes of victory quickly evaporated.

Pakistan lost some sympathy because Imran Khan chose to field first even though most local forecasts and the sky itself suggested there would be rain at some stage of the match. They were hampered by injury and illness, Ramiz Raja and Javed Miandad being unavailable. South Africa's batting, which they knew was not their strength, was again only functional. Andrew Hudson got the innings away to a flyer when he hit two off-side fours in Wasim Akram's first over. He and Mark Rushmere took the total to 1–98 in the 26th over. Then the journey from the 30th to the 40th over was a wasted one and, despite some lacklustre work in the field by the Pakistanis, South Africa slipped to 5–127.

Hansie Cronje and Brian McMillan put on 71 in 78 balls to give the South African attack something to bowl at. Cronje hit five fours as 68 were put on for the final 10 overs. There was more Pakistani fielding panic. Inzamam dropped an important catch at deep mid wicket and Moin Khan hit Aqib Javed in the head when returning the ball to the bowler before he was ready. Aqib received treatment for the blow.

Aamir Sohail and Zahid Fazal, assisted by Allan Donald's waywardness, had a half-century opening stand before both fell at the same score. When Inzamam and Imran resumed they were able to take advantage of the damp ball and struck 61 runs in nine overs, lifting their partnership to 85. Then Inzamam, not yet renowned as the worst runner in world cricket, went looking for a leg bye, turned and saw Jonty Rhodes, in a fair impression of a low-flying Superman, demolish all stumps in his path. It was a spectacular dismissal which turned the game decisively.

SOUTH AFRICA

A.C. Hudson c Ijaz Ahmed b Imran Khan		54
K.C. Wessels (capt) c Moin Khan b Aqib Javed		7
M.W. Rushmere c Aamir Sohail b Mushtaq Ahmed		35
A.P. Kuiper c Moin Khan b Imran Khan		5
J.N. Rhodes lbw Iqbal Sikander		5
W.J. Cronje not out		47
B.M. McMillan b Wasim Akram		33
D.J. Richardson (wk) b Wasim Akram		5
R.P. Snell not out		1
Extras (lb 8, w 9, nb 2)		19
(50 overs)		7–211

Did not bat: M.W. Pringle, A.A.A. Donald

1/31 2/98 3/110 4/111 5/127 6/198 7/207

Bowling: Wasim Akram 10-0-42-2; Aqib Javed 7-1-36-1; Imran Khan 10-0-34-2; Sikander 8-0-30-1; Ijaz Ahmed 7-0-26-0; Mushtaq Ahmed 8-1-35-1

PAKISTAN

Aamir Sohail b Snell		23
Zahid Fazal c Richardson b McMillan		11
Inzamam-ul-Haq run out		48
Imran Khan (capt) c Richardson b McMillan		34
Salim Malik c Donald b Kuiper		12
Wasim Akram c Snell b Kuiper		9
Ijaz Ahmed c Rhodes b Kuiper		6
Moin Khan (wk) not out		5
Mushtaq Ahmed run out		4
Iqbal Sikander not out		1
Extras (lb 2, w 17, nb 1)		20
(36 overs)		8–173

Did not bat: Aqib Javed

1/50 2/50 3/135 4/136 5/156 6/157 7/163 8/170

Bowling: Donald 7-1-31-0; Pringle 7-0-31-0; Snell 8-2-26-1; McMillan 7-0-34-2; Kuiper 6-0-40-3; Cronje 1-0-9-0

Umpires: B.L. Aldridge, S.A. Bucknor.

Toss: Pakistan. Points: South Africa 2, Pakistan 0

Imran was caught behind in the same McMillan over and with 58 still needed from just five overs the hitting had to be desperate. That made the risk factor too high for a new batsman and the wickets continued to tumble, three of them to Adrian Kuiper to catches in the deep. When the 36th over had been completed Pakistan were still 20 runs short of the target. Hudson was named Man of the Match. Wessels admitted the overs reduction had helped his side.

MONDAY 9 MARCH 1992
ENGLAND vs SRI LANKA
EASTERN OVAL, BALLARAT: ENGLAND WON BY 106 RUNS

On a beautiful public holiday Monday in front of a standing-room only crowd, England made short work of Sri Lanka. It was a big weekend in Ballarat, a town not always noted for warm sunny weather, with the opening of the annual Begonia Festival coinciding with the staging of the World Cup cricket match. Melbourne's Sri Lankan community had made the journey to the old gold-mining city in force and added colour and spectacle to the day. Unfortunately the greatest contribution of their team to the entertainment was to provide bowlers fit for collaring. England built a total quite outside the scope of the Sri Lankan batsmen, their only glitch a hamstring injury to Graham Gooch.

That occurred during the fourth over of the Sri Lankan innings. Gooch, who won the toss, had missed out with the bat, too, being first out after 40 minutes to Graeme Labrooy's fourth ball in the competition. His partner, Ian Botham, had a let-off on five before clubbing five fours and two sixes in 63 balls. Graeme Hick also spent some quality time in the centre.

It was the middle order, though, that provided the real excitement. Neil Fairbrother, dropped by wicketkeeper Hashan Tillekaratne on three, top-scored and was a key factor in building the momentum of the final overs. He and Alec Stewart began striking the ball to all parts of the smallish Eastern Oval ground, the bowling green behind the old grandstand being an attraction to the big hitter. Stewart hit one six and Fairbrother two, but it was left to Chris Lewis right at the end of the innings to actually middle the ball with enough power to get it out of the ground. The all-rounder only faced six balls for his 20 not out, his audacious strokeplay boosting the

ENGLAND

G.A. Gooch (capt) b Labrooy	8
I.T. Botham b Anurasiri	47
R.A. Smith run out	19
G.A. Hick b Ramanayake	41
N.H. Fairbrother c Ramanayake b Gurusinha	63
A.J. Stewart (wk) c Jayasuriya b Gurusinha	59
C.C. Lewis not out	20
D.R. Pringle not out	0
Extras (b 1, lb 9, w 9, nb 4)	23
(50 overs)	6–280

Did not bat: D.A. Reeve, P.A.J. DeFreitas, R.K. Illingworth

1/44 2/80 3/105 4/164 5/244 6/268

Bowling: Wickremasinghe 9-0-54-0; Ramanayake 10-1-42-1; Labrooy 10-1-68-1; Anurasiri 10-1-27-1; Gurusinha 10-0-67-2; Jayasuriya 1-0-12-0

SRI LANKA

R.S. Mahanama c Botham b Lewis	9
M.A.R. Samarasekera c Illingworth b Lewis	23
A.P. Gurusinha c & b Lewis	7
P.A. de Silva (capt) c Fairbrother b Lewis	7
A. Ranatunga c Stewart b Botham	36
H.P. Tillekaratne (wk) run out	4
S.T. Jayasuriya c DeFreitas b Illingworth	19
G.F. Labrooy c Smith b Illingworth	19
C.P.H. Ramanayake c & b Reeve	12
S.D. Anurasiri lbw Reeve	11
G.G.P. Wickremasinghe not out	6
Extras (lb 7, w 8, nb 6)	21
(44 overs)	10–174

1/33 2/46 3/56 4/60 5/91 6/119 7/123 8/156 9/158

Bowling: Pringle 7-1-27-0; Lewis 8-0-30-4; DeFreitas 5-1-31-0; Botham 10-0-33-1; Illingworth 10-0-32-2; Reeve 4-0-14-2

Umpires: Khizar Hayat, P.D. Reporter.

Toss: England. Points: England 2, Sri Lanka 0

return from the last 10 overs to 106, including 73 from the last five.

For a few overs it seemed Athula Samarasekera might actually be able to lead a challenge to England's 280. He struck four boundaries within the first few overs during an opening partnership of 33. Lewis' form and confidence soon shattered that thought. He picked up four wickets in 18 balls as Sri Lanka slipped to 4–60. Neil

Fairbrother's great catch at square leg to dismiss Aravinda de Silva was the most crucial of the four. The 5000 Sri Lankans, although disappointed at the collapse, would not let their spirits be dampened. They continued to provide a great atmosphere throughout the sun-drenched afternoon long after the game ceased to be a serious contest. Chris Lewis was named Man of the Match.

TUESDAY 10 MARCH 1992
INDIA vs WEST INDIES
BASIN RESERVE, WELLINGTON: WEST INDIES WON BY 5 WICKETS

And again the stupid rain rule was needed. This time at least the side batting second was able to win, but this was a very important game in the context of the tournament and it had not been possible to let it reach a conclusion without interference. The players from all sides just shook their heads.

Mohammad Azharuddin had elected to bat on a cold, windy showery day that indicated, in Wellington at least, time for summer sports was growing short. He got the start he would have wanted, albeit that Ajay Jadeja and Kris Srikkanth were a little on the slow side during their opening partnership. Sachin Tendulkar failed for once, Curtly Ambrose being recalled to the bowling crease and producing a peach of a legcutter to have him caught behind. That meant it was the captain's turn to play the major innings and he did so in style. For 85 balls he charmed spectators and sustained his side until the 43rd over when India at 3–166 looked likely to set the West Indies a target of reasonable significance.

Then a flat-batted off-drive off Anderson Cummins was caught near the boundary by Ambrose. From that point the Indian batting went nowhere. Cummins just put the ball in the right spot and the batsmen offered a succession of catches. Seven wickets went down for 31 and the innings did not even run its full course. It was a costly collapse of the type which can cause a team to miss a semi-final place.

The West Indies were confident they could get the runs. They were more uncertain about what the deteriorating weather would do to them. The clouds threatened as they began their reply so Brian Lara set out to get as many early runs as possible. Manoj Prabhakar was his target and the medium pacer was smashed for 32 in his first three overs. Desmond Haynes was lost at 57, then at 81 after 11 overs the umpires took the players off for rain.

Richie Richardson reckoned it was no more than a mist. Fours overs and three runs were deducted for the 20-minute delay. Upon resumption it looked as if the concentration of the batsmen had been broken. Worried about the possible return of the rain, Lara, Phil Simmons, Richardson and Gus Logie thrashed and got out, leaving the West Indies 5–112. Fortunately for cricket and justice it did not return and Keith Arthurton and Carl Hooper were able to put together a match-winning partnership of 83. They steadied, saw that the sky was clearing, then took control. Both batsmen hit three fours and Arthurton completed his fifty before the win was completed in perfect sunshine. Cummins was an interesting choice as Man of the Match. Malcolm Marshall, who had just announced he would be retiring from international cricket at the end of the World Cup, was left out of the side because of an ankle injury. His international career had already finished.

INDIA

A.D. Jadeja c Benjamin b Simmons	27
K. Srikkanth c Logie b Hooper	40
M. Azharuddin (capt) c Ambrose b Cummins	61
S.R. Tendulkar c Williams b Ambrose	4
S.V. Manjrekar run out	27
Kapil Dev c Haynes b Cummins	3
P.K. Amre c Hooper b Ambrose	4
K.S. More (wk) c Hooper b Cummins	5
M. Prabhakar c Richardson b Cummins	8
J. Srinath not out	5
S.L.V. Raju run out	1
Extras (lb 6, w 5, nb 1)	12
(49.4 overs)	10–197

1/56 2/102 3/115 4/166 5/171 6/173 7/180 8/186 9/193 10/197

Bowling: Ambrose 10-1-24-2; Benjamin 9.4-0-35-0; Cummins 10-0-33-4; Simmons 9-0-48-1; Hooper 10-0-46-1; Arthurton 1-0-5-0

WEST INDIES

D.L. Haynes c Manjrekar b Kapil Dev	16
B.C. Lara c Manjrekar b Srinath	41
P.V. Simmons c Tendulkar b Prabhakar	22
R. Richardson (capt) c Srikkanth b Srinath	3
K.L.T. Arthurton not out	58
A.L. Logie c More b Raju	7
C.L. Hooper not out	34
Extras (lb 8, w 2, nb 4)	14
(40.3 overs)	5–195

Did not bat: D. Williams (wk), C.E.L. Ambrose, A.C. Cummins, W.K.M. Benjamin

1/57 2/81 3/88 4/98 5/112

Bowling: Kapil Dev 8-0-45-1; Prabhakar 9-0-55-1; Raju 10-2-32-1; Srinath 9-2-23-2; Tendulkar 3-0-20-0; Srikkanth 1-0-7-0; Jadeja 0.3-0-5-0

Umpires: S.G. Randell, S.J. Woodward.

Toss: India. Points: West Indies 2, India 0

TUESDAY 10 MARCH 1992
SOUTH AFRICA vs ZIMBABWE
MANUKA OVAL, CANBERRA: SOUTH AFRICA WON BY 7 WICKETS

Another historic encounter involving South Africa was played in the Australian capital city at the lovely Manuka Oval. Tuesday was difficult for many, so only 3000 turned up to what turned out to be a pedestrian and one-sided encounter anyway. At least the weather was good, so the better side on the day could win unencumbered. South Africa were that better side, keeping the Zimbabwean batting under wraps, then pacing themselves solidly, unspectacularly but inevitably to a seven-wicket victory.

Kepler Wessels won the toss and sent his slightly nervous neighbours in to bat. Wayne James did not last long and Andy Flower soon had to retire with a damaged finger after misjudging a cut shot at Allan Donald. He resumed his innings later, but Dave Houghton kept wicket. Worse than those setbacks was the loss of three wickets to Peter Kirsten's straight breaks in his first two overs while the total moved from 2–72 to 5–80. Houghton and Andy Waller both holed out unnecessarily to Hansie Cronje at deep mid wicket. Eddo Brandes got a measure of revenge when he clouted Kirsten for

six and there were plenty of free offerings as Meyrick Pringle and Brian McMillan sprayed plenty of wides and no-balls. There were no partnerships, though, that were able to take advantage of batsmen getting a start. Extras comfortably top scored. When Donald bowled Kevin Duers halfway through the 48th over South Africa needed just 164 to win.

A partnership of 112 between Kepler Wessels and Peter Kirsten, still nursing a recovering calf strain but in superb form, ensured that win would be a straightforward one. Wessels hit six fours in 137 balls despite a sore thumb. He had lost his opening partner Andrew Hudson at 27, bowled leg stump by a full-pitched Malcolm Jarvis delivery, and was dropped at fine leg by Kevin Duers off Mark Burmester soon after. That was Zimbabwe's final sniff until victory was just 25 runs away. Kirsten remained unbeaten when the winning run was scored with five overs and seven wickets left. Kirsten's not-out gave the 36-year-old Man of the Match a tournament batting average of 101. His side were now third on the table.

ZIMBABWE

W.R. James lbw Pringle	5
A. Flower c Richardson b Cronje	19
A.J. Pycroft c Wessels b McMillan	19
D.L. Houghton (capt-wk) c Cronje b Kirsten	15
A.C. Waller c Cronje b Kirsten	15
A.H. Shah c Wessels b Kirsten	3
E.A. Brandes c Richardson b McMillan	20
M.G. Burmester c Kuiper b Cronje	1
A.J. Traicos not out	16
M.P. Jarvis c & b McMillan	17
K.G. Duers b Donald	5
Extras (lb 11, w 13, nb 4)	28
(48.3 overs)	10–163

1/7 2/51 3/72 4/80 5/80 6/115 7/117 8/123 9/151 10/163
A. Flower retired hurt 1–26, resumed 5–80

Bowling: Donald 9.3–1–25–1; Pringle 9–0–25–1; Snell 10–3–24–0; McMillan 10–1–30–3; Cronje 5–0–17–2; Kirsten 5–0–31–3

SOUTH AFRICA

K.C. Wessels (capt) b Shah	70
A.C. Hudson b Jarvis	13
P.N. Kirsten not out	62
A.P. Kuiper c Burmester b Brandes	7
J.N. Rhodes not out	3
Extras (lb 4, w 2, nb 3)	9
(45.1 overs)	3–164

Did not bat: W.J. Cronje, B.M. McMillan, M.W. Pringle, R.P. Snell, D.J. Richardson (wk), A.A.A. Donald

1/27 2/139 3/151

Bowling: Brandes 9.1–0–39–1; Jarvis 9–2–23–1; Burmester 5–0–20–0; Shah 8–2–33–1; Duers 8–1–19–0; Traicos 6–0–26–0

Umpires: S.A. Bucknor, D.R. Shepherd.

Toss: South Africa. Points: South Africa 2, Zimbabwe 0

WEDNESDAY 11 MARCH 1992
AUSTRALIA vs PAKISTAN
WACA, PERTH: PAKISTAN WON BY 48 RUNS

This was the match of Imran Khan's 'cornered tigers', a pivotal contest in the whole competition which determined the long-term fate of these two underachieving sides. The people of Perth knew its worth and turned out in good numbers even though the mid-week day/night fixture would keep them up late.

The Pakistani captain admitted to the pressure for both teams in what amounted to a first final. The cutthroat nature of the contest strained temperaments to the full and the WACA witnessed, not for the first time, some heated exchanges between Australians and Pakistanis. In the final analysis, though, Australia's batting let them down and another total in the low 170s was that of a loser.

Imran won the toss and batted and Aamir Sohail was promptly caught behind off a Bruce Reid no-ball before he had scored. The lanky left-arm paceman often beat the edge in his opening spell without getting a wicket. The total was 78 after 20 overs before a wicket fell when an overaggressive Ramiz Raja was caught at short mid wicket off Mike Whitney. Sohail, scoring a high percentage of his eight boundaries with the pull shot, put on another 77 with Javed Miandad, who had just returned to the side after recovering from a stomach infection, so that with several overs to go Pakistan were 3–193.

From there Steve Waugh, at his canniest, caused the batting to fall away and the last six wickets could only contribute an extra 27 runs. Despite hitting Mike Whitney into the stands, Imran batted slowly, Wasim Akram was caught first ball off a slower ball and Ijaz Ahmed was run out second ball off a dropped catch. The Pakistanis had made 9–220, which was only as good or bad as their bowlers made it.

Aqib Javed made it look very good when he had Tom Moody caught at first slip and David Boon taken at third slip during an excellent opening spell. Geoff Marsh survived, but little else, and was subjected to more barracking, even from his home crowd. A French cut was his only stroke to the boundary in 91 balls. Dean Jones, however, was altogether more positive in a stand of 85 in 22 overs. The Australians found their efforts supplemented by numerous calls for wides and no-balls, as indeed had the Pakistanis in their batting innings. So frequent were the wide calls earlier in the day that at one point Border asked for clarification.

What he might have been better off requesting was for some batting advice because he was at the top of another horrendous collapse. His failure, caught at square leg, left Border a World Cup aggregate on 30 from five innings. The Australian captain came and went after Jones had been caught at long-off from leg spinner Mushtaq Ahmed and Marsh was caught behind from an Imran inswinger. Akram said the Pakistanis had their hearts in their mouths as the ball sailed towards Aqib from Jones' big hit. It was a relief to them all when an unreliable catcher held the best one-day batsman in the Australian side.

Mark Waugh showed some class, but he had precious little support as Australia lost 8–56. The latter part of the innings was not just marred by batting incompetence, but also an altercation between Mike Whitney and wicketkeeper Moin Khan, who had to be separated by Bruce Reid and umpire Piloo Reporter. It was as pointless as it was childish as Wasim Akram finished the match by bowling the Australian tail ender almost immediately after.

Both players were docked a portion of their match fees, as was Man of the Match Aamir Sohail who had disagreed with a caught-behind decision in favour of David Boon in the seventh over. Australia, who had struggled with the ball moving around in the air under lights, were not deserving of a semi-final spot according to their disappointed captain at the post-match press conference.

PAKISTAN	
Aamir Sohail c Healy b Moody	76
Ramiz Raja c Border b Whitney	34
Salim Malik b Moody	0
Javed Miandad c Healy b S.R. Waugh	46
Imran Khan (capt) c Moody b S.R. Waugh	13
Inzamam-ul-Haq run out	16
Ijaz Ahmed run out	0
Wasim Akram c M.E. Waugh b S.R. Waugh	0
Moin Khan (wk) c Healy b McDermott	5
Mushtaq Ahmed not out	3
Extras (lb 9, w 16, nb 2)	27
(50 overs)	9–220

Did not bat: Aqib Javed

1/78 2/80 3/157 4/193 5/194 6/205 7/205 8/214 9/220

Bowling: McDermott 10–0–33–1; Reid 9–0–37–0; S.R. Waugh 10–0–36–3; Whitney 10–1–50–1; Moody 10–0–42–2; M.E. Waugh 1–0–13–0

AUSTRALIA	
T.M. Moody c Salim Malik b Aqib Javed	4
G.R. Marsh c Moin Khan b Imran Khan	39
D.C. Boon c Mushtaq Ahmed b Aqib Javed	5
D.M. Jones c Aqib Javed b Mushtaq Ahmed	47
M.E. Waugh c Ijaz Ahmed b Mushtaq Ahmed	30
A.R. Border (capt) c Ijaz Ahmed b Mushtaq Ahmed	1
S.R. Waugh c Moin Khan b Imran Khan	5
I.A. Healy (wk) c Ijaz Ahmed b Aqib Javed	8
C.J. McDermott lbw Wasim Akram	0
M.R. Whitney b Wasim Akram	5
B.A. Reid not out	0
Extras (lb 7, w 14, nb 7)	28
(45.2 overs)	10–172

1/13 2/31 3/116 4/122 5/123 6/130 7/156 8/162 9/167 10/172

Bowling: Wasim Akram 7.2–0–28–2; Aqib Javed 8–1–21–3; Imran Khan 10–1–32–2; Ijaz Ahmed 10–0–43–0; Mushtaq Ahmed 10–0–41–3

Umpires: K.E. Liebenberg, P.D. Reporter.

Toss: Pakistan. Points: Pakistan 2, Australia 0

THURSDAY 12 MARCH 1992
NEW ZEALAND vs INDIA
CARISBROOK, DUNEDIN: NEW ZEALAND WON BY 4 WICKETS

It was no wonder India did not win at cricket's closest venue to the South Pole. Bitter winds swept the ground all day, making fingers numb, the ball hard and elusive in the air. Twice fieldsmen failed to touch chances from swirling, skyed shots. India, gloved and padded, batted well enough but could not restrain their in-form opponents who by the start of the 48th over of their innings had completed a record-equalling six consecutive World Cup wins. Crowe admitted that his original idea was to give other players in the squad a run in games like this. Now, in the lead-up to the semi-finals, New Zealand stuck to their strongest side to give them their best opportunity to maintain the winning habit.

Understandably fearing rain, Mohammad Azharuddin batted after he won the toss. Kris Srikkanth tried to undermine the Dipak Patel tactic and was caught on the long-on boundary from the third ball of the match. His opening partner, Ajay Jadeja, soon snapped a hamstring muscle that surely was not warmed up enough. That brought together Azharuddin and Sachin Tendulkar. The two stylists do not always come off as a pair, but when they do it is a sight to behold.

Their stand of 127 in 30 overs warmed the hearts of the 9000 hardy souls in attendance. Azharuddin reached fifty by hitting Patel for six, then trying to repeat the shot was caught by Mark Greatbatch diving forward at deep mid wicket. Tendulkar went on to 84 in 105 balls with six off-side fours before becoming another of Chris Harris' growing bag of World Cup victims. Kapil

Dev hit five fours in 17 balls, which lifted India to a very competitive score in the context of this competition.

Mark Greatbatch sensibly used the wind assistance to hit four sixes and five fours in another belligerent onslaught during the fielding restrictions of the first 15 overs. He twice clouted Kapil Dev over square leg, got to his 50 in 47 balls and with the reliable Andrew Jones had the total up to 118 before holing out to square leg in the 25th over. Martin Crowe looked supremely confident when Kiran More freakishly ran him out with a backward flick from gully. The halving of the New Zealand captain's World Cup batting average had no real detrimental affect as Jones held the chase together until victory had been achieved. Greatbatch chased Crowe's Man of the Match tally with his second award. India, possibly thinking of their warm homeland more this day than on any other during their marathon Antipodean tour, were now able to make plans for their return as a semi-final berth was out of reach.

INDIA	
A.D. Jadeja retired hurt	13
K. Srikkanth c Latham b Patel	0
M. Azharuddin (capt) c Greatbatch b Patel	55
S.R. Tendulkar c Smith b Harris	84
S.V. Manjrekar c & b Harris	18
Kapil Dev c Larsen b Harris	33
S.T. Banerjee c Greatbatch b Watson	11
K.S. More (wk) not out	2
J. Srinath not out	4
Extras (b 1, lb 4, w 4, nb 1)	10
(50 overs)	6–230

Did not bat: M. Prabhakar, S.L.V. Raju

1/4 2/149 3/166 4/201 5/222 6/223
Jadeja retired hurt at 1/22

Bowling: Cairns 8-1-40-0; Patel 10-0-29-2; Watson 10-1-34-1; Larsen 9-0-43-0; Harris 9-0-55-3; Latham 4-0-24-0

NEW ZEALAND	
M.J. Greatbatch c Banerjee b Raju	73
R.T. Latham b Prabhakar	8
A.H. Jones not out	67
M.D. Crowe (capt) run out	26
I.D.S. Smith (wk) c sub (P.K. Amre) b Prabhakar	9
K.R. Rutherford lbw Raju	21
C.Z. Harris b Prabhakar	4
C.L. Cairns not out	4
Extras (b 4, lb 3, w 4, nb 8)	19
(47.1 overs)	6–231

Did not bat: D.N. Patel, G.R. Larsen, W. Watson

1/36 2/118 3/162 4/172 5/206 6/225

Bowling: Kapil Dev 10-0-55-0; Prabhakar 10-0-46-3; Banerjee 6-1-40-0; Srinath 9-0-35-0; Raju 10-0-38-2; Tendulkar 1-0-2-0; Srikkanth 1.1-0-8-0

Umpires: P.J. McConnell, I.D. Robinson.

Toss: India. Points: New Zealand 2, India 0

THURSDAY 12 MARCH 1992
ENGLAND vs SOUTH AFRICA
MCG, MELBOURNE: ENGLAND WON BY 3 WICKETS

England won an exciting victory, overcoming a worthy opponent in South Africa, the unfair rain

regulation and a high injury attrition rate. Behind the scenes Ian Botham was beginning to grumble about the strict training routines Graham Gooch and Mickey Stewart were still forcing upon the team. The two fitness fanatics could point to a string of wins, 'Beefy' Botham to a growing casualty list.

None of those debates on cricket philosophy were evident during an entertaining afternoon and evening at the MCG. The handy Thursday crowd witnessed a great opening partnership by Kepler Wessels and Andrew Hudson after Alec Stewart, captaining England in place of the injured Gooch, won the toss and chose to bowl. It took until Hudson's drive off Derek Pringle in the fifth over for the ball to reach the new, reduced, roped-off boundary at the MCG. However, as the stand grew, bowlers were soon falling rather than wickets. Chris Lewis could not bowl at all because of a side strain, Phil DeFreitas limped off the ground at the end of each of his spells and Dermot Reeve fell in a foothole and hurt himself in his delivery stride and could not complete his stint.

Meantime when Hudson cut the expensive Gladstone Small for four in the 15th over the opening partnership was worth 50. The milestones kept totting up at a steady rate. Hudson, by far the most fluent of the pair, reached his fifty with a clip off his toes off Botham in the 26th over. Wessels took until the 32nd over, on-driving Reeve for a four that took the stand to 122. Hudson was run-out by Fairbrother but the umpire, still at this time not allowed to use a television replay, had to call not-out because the substantial torso of Botham blocked his view. Finally Graeme Hick, the seventh bowler used, induced a tame caught and bowled from Hudson to break the partnership in the 36th over at 151.

Peter Kirsten got off the mark by lifting Richard Illingworth over the rope at long-off for six. Yet the boundaries really dried up from that point. Adrian Kuiper's back-away square drive off Pringle in the 49th over was the first four in 10 overs. South Africa had to be satisfied with 236 when for a time a total in excess of 250 had beckoned.

On the still expansive MCG it remained a worthy target, but the new English captain set about balancing the odds with a positive start. He cut and drove Meyrick Pringle for fours in the eighth over which got the embryonic 'Barmy Army' singing, then raised the 50 in the 11th over with a slashing cut off Richard Snell. It was Man of the Match worthy stuff, but it came to an abrupt halt when an unscheduled shower arrived at 0–62 after 12 overs.

The 43-minute interruption reduced the target by 11 runs and the number of overs by nine. When Brian McMillan smashed Botham's middle stump and had Robin Smith caught behind cutting, and Richard Snell found the outside edge of Graeme Hick's bat on the drive England were 3–64 in the 15th over and thoughts of a win suddenly seemed fanciful.

It was as if the collapse had never happened, the way Stewart kept playing. A late cut off Snell gave him his fifty in 61 balls, and with Neil Fairbrother as an ally 68 runs were added in the next 13 overs. Jonty Rhodes' brilliance at cover point brought about a fatal hesitation in Stewart's running in the 28th over. Fairbrother assumed the roll of major run scorer, cutting, pulling and clipping the ball at varying angles to keep England within touch of the asking rate.

That rate stayed tight at about seven per over until Chris Lewis blazed 33 in 22 balls with four fours. He added 50 in six overs with Fairbrother, which took England to within 10 runs of victory. Rhodes was again the fieldsman when Lewis was run out with two overs remaining. Fairbrother reduced the odds even further with a slash drive over point and even Pringle's tame push to mid wicket off a Snell full toss in the final over could not deny England. Stewart had captained his country to victory over South Africa in the first clash between the two nations since 1965. To top off his night he was named Man of the Match. England joined New Zealand as confirmed semi-finalists.

SOUTH AFRICA

K.C. Wessels (capt) c Smith b Hick	85
A.C. Hudson c & b Hick	79
P.N. Kirsten c Smith b DeFreitas	11
J.N. Rhodes run out	18
A.P. Kuiper not out	15
W.J. Cronje not out	13
Extras (b 4, lb 4, w 4, nb 3)	15
(50 overs)	4–236

Did not bat: B.M. McMillan, D.J. Richardson (wk), R.P. Snell, M.W. Pringle, A.A.A. Donald

1/151 2/170 3/201 4/205

Bowling: Pringle 9–2–34–0; DeFreitas 10–1–41–1; Botham 8–0–37–0; Small 2–0–14–0; Illingworth 10–0–43–0; Reeve 2.4–0–15–0; Hick 8.2–0–44–2

ENGLAND

A.J. Stewart (capt-wk) run out	77
I.T. Botham b McMillan	22
R.A. Smith c Richardson b McMillan	0
G.A. Hick c Richardson b Snell	1
N.H. Fairbrother not out	75
D.A. Reeve c McMillan b Snell	10
C.C. Lewis run out	33
D.R. Pringle c Kuiper b Snell	1
P.A.J. DeFreitas not out	1
Extras (lb 3, w 1, nb 2)	6
(40.5 overs)	7–226

Did not bat: R.K. Illingworth, G.C. Small

1/63 2/63 3/64 4/132 5/166 6/216 7/225

Bowling: Donald 9–1–43–0; Pringle 8–0–44–0; Snell 7.5–0–42–3; McMillan 8–1–39–2; Kuiper 4–0–32–0; Cronje 3–0–14–0; Kirsten 1–0–9–0

Umpires: B.L. Aldridge, D.P. Buultjens.

Toss: England. Points: England 2, South Africa 0

FRIDAY 13 MARCH 1992

WEST INDIES vs SRI LANKA
BERRI OVAL, BERRI: WEST INDIES WON BY 91 RUNS

Sri Lanka's extensive travelling took them to the far-flung regions of South Australia, north-east of Adelaide by the Murray River where, in contrast to Thursday in Dunedin, they met the West Indies in sweltering 38-degree temperatures. Their previous on-road experiences gave the Sri Lankans no advantage and they were outplayed by Richie Richardson's side, who still harboured ambitions to reach the semi-finals.

Aravinda de Silva won the toss and, for some reason, condemned his side to a 50-over stint in the heat. After Brian Lara was an early casualty Phil Simmons dominated a visibly wilting Sri Lankan attack. He had substantial partnerships with Desmond Haynes and Keith Arthurton and went on to complete his highest international score. The Sri Lankans could have got rid of him on six and twice on 47, only to miss each opportunity. The Trinidadian punished those misdemeanours with nine fours and two sixes before becoming one of Chandika Hathurusingha's four victims in the 40th over with the total 197. The medium pacer, perhaps only used because of the heat, precipitated a collapse where the West Indies lost 5–31. A final burst of 40 runs from Curtly Ambrose and Winston Benjamin reasserted West Indian dominance and left Sri Lanka with an unlikely target of 269 for victory.

As they did against England, Roshan Mahanama and Athula Samarasekera gave the early impression that the chase was on with an opening partnership of 56. It was an illusion. Carl Hooper's off spin assumed Patel-like status as the runs dried up and the wickets began to fall. Ambrose, too, was exceptionally difficult to score from. Samarasekera hit five fours and a six, a greater return of boundary strokes than the rest of the batsmen put together. The demise was fairly gradual and in the end the West Indians did not have enough strength left to take the last wicket. When the 50th over was completed the Sri Lankans were still 92 runs short of what they required. At one point they had been third on the qualifying table. Now they, like India and Zimbabwe, could plan their homeward journey. Phil Simmons was named Man of the Match.

WEST INDIES

D.L. Haynes c Tillekaratne b Ranatunga	38
B.C. Lara c & b Ramanayake	1
P.V. Simmons c Wickremasinghe b Hathurusingha	110
R.B. Richardson (capt) run out	8
K.L.T. Arthurton c Tillekaratne b Hathurusingha	40
A.L. Logie b Anurasiri	0
C.L. Hooper c Gurusinha b Hathurusingha	12
D. Williams (wk) c Tillekaratne b Hathurusingha	2
C.E.L. Ambrose not out	15
W.K.M. Benjamin not out	24
Extras (lb 9, w 3, nb 6)	18
(50 overs)	8–268

Did not bat: A.C. Cummins

1/6 2/72 3/103 4/197 5/199 6/219 7/223 8/228

Bowling: Wickremasinghe 7–0–30–0; Ramanayake 7–1–17–1; Anurasiri 10–0–46–1; Gurusinha 1–0–10–0; Ranatunga 7–0–35–1; Kalpage 10–0–64–0; Hathurusingha 8–0–57–4

SRI LANKA

R.S. Mahanama c Athurton b Cummins	11
M.A.R. Samarasekera lbw Hooper	40
U.C. Hathurusingha run out	16
P.A. de Silva (capt) c & b Hooper	11
A. Ranatunga c Benjamin b Arthurton	24
A.P. Gurusinha c Richardson b Ambrose	10
H.P. Tillekaratne (wk) b Ambrose	3
R.S. Kalpage not out	13
C.P.H. Ramanayake b Arthurton	1
S.D. Anurasiri b Benjamin	3
G.G.P. Wickremasinghe not out	21
Extras (lb 8, w 14, nb 2)	24
(50 overs)	9–177

1/56 2/80 3/86 4/99 5/130 6/135 7/137 8/139 9/149

Bowling: Ambrose 10–2–24–2; Benjamin 10–0–34–1; Cummins 9–0–49–1; Hooper 10–1–19–2; Arthurton 10–0–40–2; Simmons 1–0–3–0

Umpires: D.R. Shepherd, S.J. Woodward.

Toss: Sri Lanka. Points: West Indies 2, Sri Lanka 0

SATURDAY 14 MARCH 1992
AUSTRALIA vs ZIMBABWE
BELLERIVE OVAL, HOBART: AUSTRALIA WON BY 128 RUNS

Australia showed they were still capable of crushing the underlings of international cricket with this emphatic win in Tasmania. It was probably too little too late, but enjoyed by the locals nevertheless. The omission of Geoff Marsh terminated the Australian career of Allan Border's favoured lieutenant. He was not to be missed this day, though.

Dave Houghton sent the Australians in after he won the toss. There were some showers around, but the interruption came early and the reduction to a 46-over contest had little impact on the pattern or worth of the game.

Local hero David Boon and Dean Jones carried Australia to a commendable 1–102 after Tom Moody was left stranded in the second over. Boon just failed to make his fifty, Jones reached his with his 22nd consecutive single. After he played-on to Mark Burmester and Border was stumped dashing at John Traicos, Australia were 5–144 and a total in the 170s was not out of the question. Then wicketkeeper Andy Flower dropped Steve Waugh before he had scored. It was a costly miss. He and his twin brother Mark took sudden and complete control of the game by putting on 113 in 11 exhilarating overs.

Steve deflected fine to the off and on and belted a caught and bowled chance back at Eddo Brandes. Mark scored faster, looked better and used a wider variety of strokes. They ran between wickets with the daring and instinct of twin brothers. Steve reached his fifty in 39 balls, Mark with a six over mid wicket in 32 balls. Brandes got a little of his own back on Steve with a well-pitched yorker and Ian Healy was lbw to Kevin Duers second ball, but the damage had been done. The final 10 overs lifted the total by 106.

Ali Shah and Flower, making no real attempt to chase 265, survived until the total reached 47. From the moment Shah was beaten by Bruce Reid's throw the innings became a bit of a procession. The progress of 50 runs from 47 to 97 cost seven wickets, shared around between Steve Waugh, Mike Whitney, Craig McDermott and Tom Moody. Andy Waller and Brandes struck a few isolated retaliatory blows which prolonged the afternoon's entertainment until there were just five overs left in the game. How does a number 11 batsman in a limited-overs international approach a target of 130 runs in five overs? Steve Waugh beat Mark for the Man of the Match award. Australia retained the slimmest hope of making the semi-finals.

AUSTRALIA	
T.M. Moody run out	6
D.C. Boon b Shah	48
D.M. Jones b Burmester	54
A.R. Border (capt) st Flower b Traicos	22
M.E. Waugh not out	66
S.R. Waugh b Brandes	55
I.A. Healy (wk) lbw Duers	0
P.L. Taylor not out	1
Extras (b 2, lb 8, w 2, nb 1)	13
(46 overs)	6–265

Did not bat: C.J. McDermott, M.R. Whitney, B.A. Reid

1/8 2/102 3/134 4/144 5/257 6/258

Bowling: Brandes 9-0-59-1; Duers 9-1-48-1; Burmester 9-0-65-1; Shah 9-0-53-1; Traicos 10-0-30-1

ZIMBABWE	
A.H. Shah run out	24
A. Flower (wk) c Border b S.R. Waugh	20
A.D. Campbell c M.E. Waugh b Whitney	4
A.J. Pycroft c M.E. Waugh b S.R. Waugh	0
D.L. Houghton (capt) b McDermott	2
A.C. Waller c Taylor b Moody	18
K.J. Arnott b Whitney	8
E.A. Brandes c McDermott b Taylor	23
M.G. Burmester c Border b Reid	12
A.J. Traicos c Border b Taylor	3
K.G. Duers not out	2
Extras (lb 11, w 8, nb 2)	21
(41.4 overs)	10–137

1/47 2/51 3/51 4/57 5/69 6/88 7/97 8/117 9/132 10/137

Bowling: McDermott 8-0-26-1; Reid 9-1-18-1; S.R. Waugh 7-0-28-2; Whitney 10-3-15-2; Moody 4-0-25-1; Taylor 3.4-0-14-2

Umpires: B.L. Aldridge, S.A. Bucknor.

Toss: Zimbabwe. Points: Australia 2, Zimbabwe 0

SUNDAY 15 MARCH 1992
NEW ZEALAND vs ENGLAND
BASIN RESERVE, WELLINGTON: NEW ZEALAND WON BY 7 WICKETS

In the eyes of some, particularly English and New Zealand supporters, this was a final preview. If so, the Kiwis would have claimed title favouritism after a comfortable win in the first match of a World Cup triple-header Sunday.

The result had little impact on anything other than keeping the winning habit, as both these teams had already qualified for the semi-finals. England had more injury worries, with Neil Fairbrother, prior to the game, and Derek Pringle, during it, joining the long list of the incapacitated. Ian Botham reckoned the team was exhausted.

Certainly their batting adrenalin seemed to wane as their innings progressed after Martin Crowe had sent them in. The Basin Reserve was packed and bathed in sunshine as Ian Botham, who pre-match had promised as much, attempted to do a Mark Greatbatch job on the slowest opening attack in international cricket in the twentieth century. He and Alec Stewart, again

English captain, got Chris Harris away a few times. Dipak Patel, however, was once more in total control on a patchy turning wicket. He had a stumping chance missed off Stewart and then bowled Botham, hitting across the line, in the seventh over.

His five-over spell of immaculate off spin yielded just seven runs. It was not until Willie Watson started dropping short that the runs flowed. Stewart and Graeme Hick, who twice pulled Watson for four in the 12th over and later hoisted Chris Cairns for six, added 70 in 14 overs. Then Patel returned and Stewart swept to square leg where Harris held a smart catch. Hick brought up his 50 off 62 balls and took the total to 2–135 with Robin Smith. Slowly, though, Crowe's bowlers and fieldsmen strangled the English run flow. Hick cut at Harris, far more effective in his second spell, and was caught behind by Greatbatch who was substituting for the migrained Ian Smith.

Gavin Larsen, like Patel, could not be hit. Andrew Jones had fumed when Crowe announced his decision to bowl. Now, he bowled flat off breaks almost as effectively as Patel. Allan Lamb, back in the side after a long injury lay-off, made little headway. Smith was discouraged by the low slow wicket and after he had holed out at long-on Chris Lewis pushed his first ball softly back to the bowler Watson. That left England on 5–162 in the 42nd over and try as the remaining batsmen might they could not get the bowling properly away. Attempts at big hits resulted in more outfield catches. Astonishingly, only 68 runs were scored from the final 18 overs of the innings.

Chasing 201 New Zealand were once more given an excellent start by Greatbatch who showed Botham a thing or two about belting early fours and sixes. He had lost recalled opening partner John Wright, bowled behind legs in a carbon copy of the first legal ball of the tournament, from Phil DeFreitas' first ball. The big left-hander had scoop-swiped Pringle over square leg for six when he picked out DeFreitas on the boundary in the 13th over. Botham was triumphant. He shouldn't have been. No more wickets fell for another 108 runs, by which time the result was a formality.

Crowe survived a caught-behind appeal off Hick, then cut the same bowler for four to raise the 100 in the 23rd over. That was no faster than England, but without the spin of Phil Tufnell, a star in the Tests in New Zealand, the attack was rendered increasingly ineffective on this Basin Reserve surface. Jones got to his fifty in 78 balls, then brought up the 150 in the 32nd over when he cut left-arm spinner Richard Illingworth for another four. Finally Hick threw down the bowler's stumps from point to penalise Jones' hesitation. He had hit 13 fours, seven more than the unbeaten Crowe would finish with when the winning runs were scored. The New Zealand captain had led his side to a record-breaking sequence of seven World Cup wins. Conceding the Man of the Match award to Jones would not have upset him too much.

ENGLAND

A.J. Stewart (capt-wk) c Harris b Patel	41
I.T. Botham b Patel	8
G.A. Hick c Greatbatch b Harris	56
R.A. Smith c Patel b Jones	38
A.J. Lamb c Cairns b Watson	12
C.C. Lewis c & b Watson	0
D.A. Reeve not out	21
D.R. Pringle c sub (R.T. Latham) b Jones	10
P.A.J. DeFreitas c Cairns b Harris	0
R.K. Illingworth not out	2
Extras (b 1, lb 7, w 4)	12
(50 overs)	8–200

Did not bat: G.C. Small

1/25 2/95 3/135 4/162 5/162 6/169 7/189 8/195

Bowling: Patel 10-1-26-2; Harris 8-0-39-2; Watson 10-0-40-2; Cairns 3-0-21-0; Larsen 10-3-24-0; Jones 9-0-42-2

NEW ZEALAND

M.J. Greatbatch c DeFreitas b Botham	35
J.G. Wright b DeFreitas	1
A.H. Jones run out	78
M.D. Crowe (capt) not out	73
K.R. Rutherford not out	3
Extras (b 1, lb 8, w 1, nb 1)	11
(40.5 overs)	3–201

Did not bat: C.Z. Harris, I.D.S. Smith (wk), C.L. Cairns, D.N. Patel, G.R. Larsen, W. Watson

1/5 2/64 3/172

Bowling: Pringle 6.2-1-34-0; DeFreitas 8.3-1-45-1; Botham 4-0-19-1; Illingworth 9-1-46-0; Hick 6-0-26-0; Reeve 3-0-9-0; Small 4-0-13-0

Umpires: S.G. Randell, I.D. Robinson.

Toss: New Zealand. Points: New Zealand 2, England 0

SUNDAY 15 MARCH 1992
INDIA vs SOUTH AFRICA
ADELAIDE OVAL, ADELAIDE: SOUTH AFRICA WON BY 6 WICKETS

A rain-shortened match saw South Africa clinch the third semi-final berth, leaving Australia, West Indies and Pakistan to battle for the last promotional place. The 59.1 overs of cricket played realised 361 runs at better than one per ball and contained at least four exciting innings. The win was a great achievement by the former isolates and might have tipped the balance in favour of reform at the following Tuesday's referendum.

Rain held up play until 1.15 pm, then Wessels won the toss and sent India in. If he expected a collapse similar to the one which Pakistan suffered against England in their rain-affected match in Adelaide, he was mistaken. This wicket was a belter and after Kris Srikkanth was brilliantly caught one-handed and high to his left by Peter Kirsten, batsmen held sway. Indian skipper, Mohammad Azharuddin, after his team's many unsuccessful months away from home, had nothing more to play for than pride, yet he batted beautifully for 79 at better than a run per ball. He put on 78 with Sanjay Manjrekar and 71 in eight overs with Kapil Dev.

The great all-rounder bid farewell to the World Cup stage with a 29-ball extravaganza of clean hitting including one great six off Allan Donald over fine leg. Donald picked up a couple of wickets, while Brian McMillan, carrying an injured ankle, and Adrian Kuiper withstood the batting heroics best. A few batsmen fell in the frantic closing moments of the innings, which eventually realised a neat 180 from 30 overs, including 80 from the final 10. South Africa needed exactly a run per ball plus one to reach the semi-finals.

Wessels dropped himself down the order and promoted the in-form Kirsten to open with Andrew Hudson. There were no early fireworks and at the 10-over mark the total was only 44. Then came the charge. The boundaries flowed and the required run rate decreased. Hudson survived a close run-out call on 34 and a stumping chance before he completed his third fifty in four innings with four boundaries.

Kirsten was even more impressive and hit seven fours in 84 balls. The score had reached 128 in 24 overs when his partner stepped away to drive Javagal Srinath and was bowled. Seventy-five had been needed from the final 10 overs. Kirsten was bowled charging Kapil Dev, Kuiper was run out and Jonty Rhodes lasted just three balls, although he did hit Manoj Prabhakar for an invaluable six in that brief stay.

Wessels came in to oversee the final victory push with 14 required from the last two overs. It was eight off seven balls when the South African captain drove Kapil Dev through the off side for four, reducing the final over requirement to one more boundary. A clip over mid wicket by Hansie Cronje, the youngest member of the side, secured the win from Prabhakar's first ball and led to joyous South African celebration from which they had a week to recover until their semi-final. Kirsten, once more emphasising the folly of his original omission, was Man of the Match.

INDIA

K. Srikkanth c Kirsten b Donald	0
S.V. Manjrekar b Kuiper	28
M. Azharuddin (capt) c Kuiper b Pringle	79
S.R. Tendulkar c Wessels b Kuiper	14
Kapil Dev b Donald	42
V.G. Kambli run out	1
P.K. Amre not out	1
J. Srinath not out	0
Extras (lb 7, w 6, nb 2)	15
(30 overs)	6–180

Did not bat: M. Prabhakar, K.S. More (wk), S.L.V. Raju

1/1 2/79 3/103 4/174 5/177 6/179

Bowling: Donald 6–0–34–2; Pringle 6–0–37–1; Snell 6–1–46–0; McMillan 6–0–28–0; Kuiper 6–0–28–2

SOUTH AFRICA

A.C. Hudson b Srinath	53
P.N. Kirsten b Kapil Dev	84
A.P. Kuiper run out	7
J.N. Rhodes c Raju b Prabhakar	7
K.C. Wessels (capt) not out	9
W.J. Cronje not out	8
Extras (lb 10, nb 3)	13
(29.1 overs)	4–181

Did not bat: B.M. McMillan, D.J. Richardson (wk), R.P. Snell, A.A.A. Donald, M.W. Pringle

1/128 2/149 3/157 4/163

Bowling: Kapil Dev 6–0–36–1; Prabhakar 5.1–1–33–1; Tendulkar 6–0–20–0; Srinath 6–0–39–1; Raju 6–0–43–0

Umpires: D.P. Buultjens, Khizar Hayat.

Toss: South Africa. Points: South Africa 2, India 0

SUNDAY 15 MARCH 1992
PAKISTAN vs SRI LANKA
WACA, PERTH: PAKISTAN WON BY 4 WICKETS

Despite the turnaround in their fortunes against Australia, Pakistan still had no margin for error if they were to take the last semi-final spot and could not afford a lapse against Sri Lanka. In the end they won, but without displaying the skill they had under lights against Australia. The Sri Lankans for their part, already moving in a westward direction, were probably thinking of home.

Pakistan, staying put, had a few days to prepare for the match in Perth, while Sri Lanka had winged their way straight across the Nullarbor Plain from Berri. Their bowlers could at least put their feet up for a while as Aravinda de Silva won the toss and batted. The game was only a modest local attraction and in the end turned out to have few outstanding performances.

The Pakistani pace attack misplaced its radar again and offered the Sri Lankans plenty of wides and no-balls between the occasional unplayable delivery. Wasim Akram got a swinging yorker through Roshan Mahanama, then Mushtaq Ahmed's leg spin accounted for Chandika Hathurusingha and Athula Samarasekera after the opener had put on 51 in 10 overs with his captain. The Pakistani fielding had also slipped. de Silva, who top-scored and hit 23 singles out of 43, was given one life, but some sensible batting by left-handers

Asanka Gurusinha and wicketkeeper batsman Hashan Tillekaratne lifted the total to the respectability of 213.

Pakistan had early worries when Champaka Ramanayake had the in-form Aamir Sohail caught in the gully in the second over and Imran Khan, promoting himself to the troubled number 3 spot, took 37 balls over his first two runs. The innings was not progressing quickly enough when Imran holed out to deep mid-off to his opposite number. At 3–84 and behind the run rate, an upset was on the cards. It took a century partnership and the best batting of the match from Salim Malik and Javed Miandad to ensure that did not happen. They put on 101 in 21 overs improvising, running for anything and playing the occasional boundary stroke.

Both reached their half centuries without going any further and it took until the first ball of the last over of the game, when Ijaz Ahmed straight drove Pramodya Wickremasinghe for four, for the win to be completed. Ijaz had been involved in the run-out of Inzamam-ul-Haq. It would not be the last time in their lives that the pair would have running troubles. Javed Miandad, who had top-scored and stayed until victory was only 28 runs away, was named Man of the Match.

SRI LANKA

R.S. Mahanama b Wasim Akram		12
M.A.R. Samarasekera st Moin Khan b Mushtaq Ahmed		38
U.C. Hathurusingha b Mushtaq Ahmed		5
P.A. de Silva (capt) c Aamir Sohail b Ijaz Ahmed		43
A.P. Gurusinha c Malik b Imran Khan		37
A. Ranatunga c sub (Zahid Fazal) b Aamir Sohail		7
H.P. Tillekaratne (wk) not out		25
R.S. Kalpage not out		13
Extras (lb 15, w 11, nb 6)		32
(50 overs)		6–212

Did not bat: C.P.H. Ramanayake, G.G.P. Wickremasinghe, K.I.W. Wijegunawardene

1/29 2/48 3/99 4/132 5/158 6/187

Bowling: Wasim Akram 10-0-37-1; Aqib Javed 10-0-39-0; Imran Khan 8-1-36-1; Mushtaq Ahmed 10-0-43-2; Ijaz Ahmed 8-0-28-1; Aamir Sohail 4-0-14-1

PAKISTAN

Aamir Sohail c Mahanama b Ramanayake		1
Ramiz Raja c Gurusinha b Wickremasinghe		32
Imran Khan (capt) c de Silva b Hathurusingha		22
Javed Miandad c Wickremasinghe b Gurusinha		57
Salim Malik c Kalpage b Ramanayake		51
Inzamam-ul-Haq run out		11
Ijaz Ahmed not out		8
Wasim Akram not out		5
Extras (lb 12, w 9, nb 8)		29
(49.1 overs)		6–216

Did not bat: Moin Khan (wk), Mushtaq Ahmed, Aqib Javed

1/7 2/68 3/84 4/185 5/201 6/205

Bowling: Wijegunawardene 10-1-34-0; Ramanayake 10-1-37-2; Wickremasinghe 9.1-0-41-1; Gurusinha 9-0-38-1; Hathurusingha 9-0-40-1; Kalpage 2-0-14-0

Umpires: K.E. Liebenberg, P.J. McConnell.

Toss: Sri Lanka. Points: Pakistan 2, Sri Lanka 0

WEDNESDAY 18 MARCH 1992
NEW ZEALAND vs PAKISTAN
LANCASTER PARK, CHRISTCHURCH: PAKISTAN WON BY 7 WICKETS

Pakistani Manager Intikhab Alam had indicated after the win over Sri Lanka in Perth that his team was very confident of ending New Zealand's winning streak. Despite having to readjust from the bouncy wickets of the WACA, Intikhab suggested Pakistani players were more than comfortable in the conditions they would encounter in Christchurch.

His prediction proved accurate as the Kiwis were easily beaten. The win put Pakistan in fourth spot on the qualifying table and eliminated Australia from semi-final calculations. Adding to the cross-Tasman frustration, the loss actually benefited New Zealand, as, had Australia snuck into the final four, the Kiwis would have had to play their semi-final against them in Sydney. The loss allowed them to enjoy the benefits of a home semi-final in Auckland. Martin Crowe admitted that throwing the match had been considered. The Kiwis eventually picked their best side, but it made no difference to Imran Khan's 'cornered tigers'.

Imran won the toss and bowled on a fine but breezy morning which necessitated the wearing of long-sleeved jumpers and some vigorous hand rubbing during the early overs. Aqib Javed's temper quickly warmed up when Mark Greatbatch thumped the last three balls of his first over for two fours and a big six, his 12th of the tournament, over mid wicket. The anticipation of another of the opener's joyous exhibitions made the crowd buzz.

Unfortunately for the Kiwi fans, the Pakistani pacemen had other ideas. Greatbatch became inhibited as Aqib struck back to have Rod Latham, in the side again for John Wright, caught at slip in his next over. Then, from the other end, Akram's inswinging yorker hit Andrew Jones' boot in front of middle stump. But the biggest blow came in the ninth over when Crowe clipped another of the left-armer's inswingers, this time from around the wicket, to Aamir Sohail's chest at backward square leg.

New Zealand were 3–39 and the middle-order batted as if in shock at their captain falling so cheaply. Greatbatch hit a few shots, including a cracking square cut off Akram and Rutherford hung around while 46 runs were put on. Rutherford was struggling, however, and should have been caught by wicketkeeper Moin Khan off Imran. Then in the 20th over he was sent back too late for a pushed single to cover. That precipitated a collapse which saw the Kiwis lose five wickets in eight overs. Chief architect of the collapse was Mushtaq Ahmed. The legspinner was unhittable and had Greatbatch caught sweeping and Chris Harris stumped off an off-side wide.

The innings eventually almost ran its course through the doggedness of Gavin Larsen and renowned rabbit, Danny Morrison. Neither had batted in the tournament to this point yet they managed to scrape together 44 runs in 17 overs. Morrison, lucky to survive a stumping appeal, was finally caught at slip off Akram, who picked up his fourth wicket when he yorked the retreating Larsen. A few wides and the throw to run-out Rutherford made it a busy day for the left-arm paceman. With extras equal top score on 42, the scoreboard had a strange top-to-tail look about it.

Morrison must have been excited about his batting because he bounced Aamir Sohail first ball of the Pakistani innings. The left-hander hooked the delivery down Dipak Patel's throat at fine leg, thinking he was immune because the ball was clearly above his shoulder. To Sohail's surprise and distress Steve Randell at square leg said nothing. Sohail, not the calmest of cricketers, had to bite his tongue and leave the crease. Morrison then fired out Inzamam-ul-Haq so that Pakistan were 2–9 in pursuit of 166.

The game might have become really interesting if Patel had held a sharp caught and bowled chance off Javed Miandad not long after. The let-off allowed him to dig in while Ramiz Raja unleashed a fine array of shots. Patel and Watson were tight, but Harris, still the leading wicket-taker in the competition, and Larsen ineffective. Not even 15 bowling changes by Crowe could make a difference this time. Miandad only hit one boundary in 85 balls, but he stayed while 115 runs were added with Ramiz. The opener continued on to his second Benson and Hedges World Cup hundred, then slogged the winning

boundary off Rutherford in the 45th over. He hit 16 fours in 155 balls yet was beaten for the Man of the Match award. Not by Akram, but the bouncing, whirling leg spinner Mushtaq. Straight after the game everyone sought out a television to see if Australia would defeat the West Indies and allow Pakistan to progress to the semi-finals.

NEW ZEALAND

M.J. Greatbatch c Salim Malik b Mushtaq Ahmed		42
R.T. Latham c Inzamam-ul-Haq b Aqib Javed		6
A.H. Jones lbw Wasim Akram		2
M.D. Crowe (capt) c Aamir Sohail b Wasim Akram		3
K.R. Rutherford run out		8
C.Z. Harris st Moin Khan b Mushtaq Ahmed		1
D.N. Patel c Mushtaq Ahmed b Aamir Sohail		7
I.D.S. Smith (wk) b Imran Khan		1
G.R. Larsen b Wasim Akram		37
D.K. Morrison c Inzamam-ul-Haq b Wasim Akram		12
W. Watson not out		5
Extras (b 3, lb 23, w 12, nb 4)		42
(48.2 overs)		166

1/23 2/26 3/39 4/85 5/88 6/93 7/96 8/106 9/150 10/166

Bowling: Wasim Akram 9.2–0–32–4; Aqib Javed 10–1–34–1; Mushtaq Ahmed 10–0–18–2; Imran Khan 8–0–22–1; Aamir Sohail 10–1–29–1; Ijaz Ahmed 1–0–5–0

PAKISTAN

Aamir Sohail c Patel b Morrison		0
Ramiz Raja not out		119
Inzamam-ul-Haq b Morrison		5
Javed Miandad lbw Morrison		30
Salim Malik not out		9
Extras (lb 1, w 1, nb 2)		4
(44.4 overs)		3–167

Did not bat: Imran Khan (capt), Ijaz Ahmed, Wasim Akram, Moin Khan (wk), Mushtaq Ahmed, Aqib Javed

1/0 2/9 3/124

Bowling: Morrison 10–0–42–3; Patel 10–2–25–0; Watson 10–3–26–0; Harris 4–0–18–0; Larsen 3–0–16–0; Jones 3–0–10–0; Latham 2–0–13–0; Rutherford 1.4–0–11–0; Greatbatch 1–0–5–0

Umpires: S.A. Bucknor, S.G. Randell.

Toss: Pakistan. Points: Pakistan 2, New Zealand 0

WEDNESDAY 18 MARCH 1992
ENGLAND vs ZIMBABWE
LAVINGTON SPORTS GROUND, ALBURY: ZIMBABWE WON BY 9 RUNS

While Pakistan, New Zealand and, later in the day, Australia and the West Indies were involved in their cutthroat dramatics, in Albury England and Zimbabwe wrote their own little piece of cricketing history. Unfortunately for England it was the story of another momentous and unexpected defeat, the type of which has become all too familiar in the last decade.

According to Ian Botham the main cause of Zimbabwe's first win in the 1992 World Cup, which was only their second win in three tournaments and their maiden victory over England, was the exhaustion and injuries carried into the match by the overworked English team. Those injuries and the exhaustion meant that England's batsmen could not successfully chase a total of 134.

The conditions favoured bowlers all day and the Zimbabwean batsmen were always struggling after Graham Gooch won the toss and sent them

in. England's slower bowlers, left-arm spinners Richard Illingworth and Phil Tufnell and Botham's medium pace, did most damage, picking up eight of the 10 wickets to fall. Zimbabwean captain Dave Houghton top-scored, but it took an important eighth-wicket partnership of 31 between Iain Butchart and Eddo Brandes, who came together at 7–96, to ensure a total in excess of 120.

Six thousand were in attendance at Lavington, which is on the Sydney side of Albury, the border city on the Murray River between Victoria and New South Wales. Their numbers were made up of face-painted English supporters, local enthusiasts and schoolchildren. There was little to excite the fans while Zimbabwe batted, but when Eddo Brandes trapped Gooch lbw on the first ball of the England innings they sat up and took notice.

The chicken-farming former schoolmate of Graeme Hick then hit Robin Smith's off-stump, had Allan Lamb mistiming a pull to mid-on and yorked his old school chum first ball. With Botham feathering a catch through to wicket-keeper Andy Flower off Ali Shah's medium-paced swing England were a messy 5–43 in the 15th over.

Alec Stewart and Neil Fairbrother halted the collapse by putting on 52 for the sixth wicket. It was grim stuff and lasted 24 overs. Fairbrother, suffering a stomach ailment, did not have the strength to reach the boundary once in 77 balls. Shah and John Traicos, at 44 finally bowling out of World Cup cricket, conceded just 33 in 20

miserly overs. When Shah had Stewart caught the tumble of wickets began again. The pressure on the tail-end batsmen was increased by the lack of overs left available. Fifteen were needed from the last two overs. That had been reduced to 11 when Andy Pycroft's direct hit ran out Illingworth. Then from the first ball of the final over Gladstone Small chipped Malcolm Jarvis to Pycroft at mid wicket. Schoolboys ran everywhere. Dave Houghton, who had played in the win over Australia in 1983 spoke with great emotion at the post-match press conference and Eddo Brandes struck a blow for the chicken farmers of the world when he was named Man of the Match.

ZIMBABWE

W.R. James c & b Illingworth	13
A. Flower (wk) b DeFreitas	7
A.J. Pycroft c Gooch b Botham	3
K.J. Arnott lbw Botham	11
D.L. Houghton (capt) c Fairbrother b Small	29
A.C. Waller b Tufnell	8
A.H. Shah c Lamb b Tufnell	3
I.P. Butchart c Fairbrother b Botham	24
E.A. Brandes st Stewart b Illingworth	14
A.J. Traicos not out	0
M.P. Jarvis lbw Illingworth	6
Extras (lb 8, w 8)	16
(46.1 overs)	134

1/12 2/19 3/30 4/52 5/65 6/77 7/96 8/127 9/127 10/134

Bowling: DeFreitas 8–1–14–1; Small 9–1–20–1; Botham 10–2–23–3; Illingworth 9.1–0–33–3; Tufnell 10–2–36–2

ENGLAND

G.A. Gooch (capt) lbw Brandes	0
I.T. Botham c Flower b Shah	18
A.J. Lamb c James b Brandes	17
R.A. Smith b Brandes	2
G.A. Hick b Brandes	0
N.H. Fairbrother c Flower b Butchart	20
A.J. Stewart (wk) c Waller b Shah	29
P.A.J. DeFreitas c Flower b Butchart	4
R.K. Illingworth run out	11
G.C. Small c Pycroft b Jarvis	5
P.C.R. Tufnell not out	0
Extras (b 4, lb 3, w 11, nb 1)	19
(49.1 overs)	125

1/0 2/32 3/42 4/42 5/43 6/95 7/101 8/108 9/124 10/125

Bowling: Brandes 10–4–21–4; Jarvis 9.1–0–32–1; Shah 10–3–17–2; Traicos 10–4–16–0; Butchart 10–2–32–2

Umpires: B.L. Aldridge, Khizar Hayat.

Toss: England. Points: Zimbabwe 2, England 0

WEDNESDAY 18 MARCH 1992
AUSTRALIA vs WEST INDIES
MCG, MELBOURNE: AUSTRALIA WON BY 57 RUNS

The time difference and the playing of this match as a day/night fixture meant that the Australians were put out of their misery quite quickly during the afternoon upon hearing the result from Christchurch. If anything, the disappointment seemed to galvanise them and they proved too accomplished for the West Indies in front of what built up to the biggest crowd of the tournament so far.

Australia got away to an excellent start. Allan

Border batted when he won the toss, a decision opening pair Tom Moody and David Boon relished. They combined for 27 overs in a part-nership of 107. It was Boon who led the way, moving on to the front foot with confidence to drive the fast bowlers on both sides of the wicket. After surviving a shout for a catch behind pulling at Anderson Cummins, he brought up his fifty in the 24th over.

Moody lofted Phil Simmons down the ground

for his third boundary, then in the same over was nicely caught by a diving Winston Benjamin at deep square leg. The Australian batting spluttered along once the openers had been separated. Boon took until the 46th over to complete his century, then immediately skyed an attempted slog to end his tournament with the same score he started it. He left the MCG with 4001 runs in Limited-Over Internationals to his credit. He was easily Australia's best-performed batsman, in stark contrast to his captain who finished with an average of eight. Both Boon and Border were bidding farewell to World Cup cricket. Cummins bowled Steve Waugh with a full toss and it was left to Ian Healy and Peter Taylor, who could boast that he slogged Curtly Ambrose to mid wicket for four, to get the total up to a non-committal 6–216 after 50 overs.

In good conditions under lights there was nothing really imposing about the task in front of the West Indies, and for seven overs Desmond Haynes and Brian Lara batted with authority. Then Haynes clipped a Craig McDermott full toss off the middle of his bat to Dean Jones at backward square leg. Next ball, Phil Simmons, only half forward, was given out lbw to leave the West Indies struggling at 2–27.

Richie Richardson, with the unenviable task of leading a Caribbean side gradually on the decline, battled with Lara for another 12 overs,

before being given out caught behind driving at Mike Whitney. The West Indian captain indicated the ball had struck his pad rather than his bat, but Piloo Reporter was never going to change his mind. Whitney continued to make inroads into the middle order. Keith Arthurton hit a couple of powerful drives then holed out tamely to mid-off. A brilliant full-length dive to his right by Healy removed the driving Gus Logie and Carl Hooper guided the ball to Mark Waugh, who had been put in place at slip.

One decent partnership would have kept the West Indies well in the contest because Lara was largely untroubled in his efforts to keep one end secure. He brought up his fifty and the team 100 in the 28th over with a swept four off Taylor, but could not find a worthy partner. Eventually, in the panic that was making the West Indies self-destruct he ran for a sharp single and Winston Benjamin didn't. When Benjamin swung across the line at Steve Waugh and was given out lbw both sides had become World Cup spectators. Australia had beaten the West Indies for the first time in a World Cup match and for all their early poor form had missed the cut by one point. Pakistan, by virtue of the point gained in the 'no result' in Adelaide against England, were through. David Boon was named Man of the Match.

AUSTRALIA

T.M. Moody c Benjamin b Simmons		42
D.C. Boon c Williams b Cummins		100
D.M. Jones c Williams b Cummins		6
A.R. Border (capt) lbw Simmons		8
M.E. Waugh st Williams b Hooper		21
S.R. Waugh b Cummins		6
I.A. Healy (wk) not out		11
P.L. Taylor not out		10
Extras (lb 3, w 3, nb 6)		12
(50 overs)		6–216

Did not bat: C.J. McDermott, M.R. Whitney, B.A. Reid

1/107 2/128 3/141 4/185 5/189 6/200

Bowling: Ambrose 10-0-46-0; Benjamin 10-1-49-0; Cummins 10-1-38-3; Hooper 10-0-40-1; Simmons 10-1-40-2

WEST INDIES

D.L. Haynes c Jones b McDermott		14
B.C. Lara run out		70
P.V. Simmons lbw McDermott		0
R.B. Richardson (capt) c Healy b Whitney		10
K.L.T. Arthurton c McDermott b Whitney		15
A.L. Logie c Healy b Whitney		5
C.L. Hooper c M.E. Waugh b Whitney		4
D. Williams (wk) c Border b Reid		4
W.K.M. Benjamin lbw, S.R. Waugh		15
C.E.L. Ambrose run out		2
A.C. Cummins not out		5
Extras (b 3, lb 5, w 3, nb 4)		15
(42.4 overs)		159

1/27 2/27 3/59 4/83 5/99 6/117 7/128 8/137 9/150 10/159

Bowling: McDermott 6-1-29-2; Reid 10-1-26-1; Whitney 10-1-34-4; S.R. Waugh 6.4-0-24-1; Taylor 4-0-24-0; Moody 6-1-14-0

Umpires: P.D. Reporter, D.R. Shepherd.

Toss: Australia. Points: Australia 2, West Indies 0

SATURDAY 21 MARCH & SUNDAY 22 MARCH 1992
BENSON & HEDGES WORLD CUP SEMI-FINALS

The qualifying table at the end of the preliminary rounds of the Benson and Hedges World Cup was as follows:

	P	W	L	NR	Pts	NR/R		P	W	L	NR	Pts	NR/R
New Zealand	8	7	1	0	14	+0.59	Australia	8	4	4	0	8	+0.20
England	8	5	2	1	11	+0.47	West Indies	8	4	4	0	8	+0.07
South Africa	8	5	3	0	10	+0.14	India	8	2	5	1	5	+0.14
Pakistan	8	4	3	1	9	+0.16	Sri Lanka	8	2	5	1	5	−0.68
							Zimbabwe	8	1	7	0	2	−1.14

21 MARCH, FIRST SEMI-FINAL: NEW ZEALAND vs PAKISTAN
EDEN PARK, AUCKLAND: PAKISTAN WON BY 4 WICKETS

On his great *John Lennon/Plastic Ono Band* album John Lennon sang, 'The dream is over, what can I say?' Lennon was referring to the demise of the Beatles, but Martin Crowe, a tear in his eye, could easily have expressed the same sentiment to the majority of the Eden Park crowd as he led his team on a lap of honour after this semi-final.

The Kiwis had been part of an exciting game on a wonderful occasion. In the end, though, their bowling shortcomings were exposed by the team they feared most on their own wickets. Pakistan had the answers even chasing a target of 263 and they, not New Zealand, would be at the MCG in four days time in an attempt to secure cricket's limited-overs Holy Grail.

A windy Saturday with scudding dark clouds building and threatening throughout the afternoon began with Crowe receiving his cash and car prizes as World Cup Champion Player. Heavy rain was forecast and that affected Crowe's decision when he won the toss. He wanted to bat second, but understandably feared the overs-reduction rule. So New Zealand went in first. Dozens of Kiwi flags fluttered proudly amongst the thousands cramming into the Eden Park terraces as John Wright and Mark Great-batch walked out to bat after the teams had lined up for the singing of the national anthems.

The opening pair found a hard and flat pitch that seemed to suit bashing opener Greatbatch. Wasim Akram posed their greatest threat and he twice beat Greatbatch before the left-hander slashed him over third man for six to get off the mark. He then on drove Aqib Javed into the South Stand for his 14th six of the World Cup. It was also his last. In the 10th over he motioned away, suggesting another big swing, only to be bowled leg stump on the outside, by an outrageous Aqib slower ball. Three overs later when Wright inadvisably tried to hit Mushtaq Ahmed down the ground into the wind and was caught at deep mid-on, 0–35 had become 2–39.

Crowe was immediately into his stride, which indicated there would be no repeat of Wednesday's collapse. Andrew Jones stuck around while 48 were added. During that time he never had much idea what Mushtaq was doing and was eventually trapped in front of his stumps hitting across a top-spinner. Even Steve Bucknor, holding his hat to his chest because of the strong winds, had no hesitation.

There was no New Zealand comfort in 3–87 in the 24th over and the tension increased further when Ken Rutherford took 25 deliveries to get off the mark. He was plumb lbw to an Akram no-ball. Crowe told him to go for his shots and Rutherford started lofting the spinners down the ground. Iqbal Sikander was deposited over the boundary at long-off. Crowe swept Mushtaq for a big six over square leg and the pair put on 107 in 113 balls. Akram returned and Rutherford top-edged a pull that was safely held by Moin Khan. Worse for New Zealand was that Crowe tore a hamstring as he ran through for the skyed shot. He lay on the ground and had his thigh strapped, then hit Akram for six over fine leg. Crowe continued until the 47th over when he could only watch his runner Greatbatch fall a metre short of the crease following a mix-up with Ian Smith.

Crowe's 91 in 83 balls with seven fours and three sixes rightly received a standing ovation and with Smith, Dipak Patel and Gavin Larsen continuing the good work the total increased by 91 in the final 10 overs. Two hundred and sixty-two was New Zealand's highest score for the tournament and the whole nation was brimming with confidence despite the fact that Wright, rather than Crowe, would have to lead the team in the field.

There was no indication that Pakistan would have the batting impetus to overtake such a mountain in the early stages of their innings. Aamir Sohail swept Patel to Jones in the ninth over and although no further wickets fell for some time the progress of Imran and Ramiz Raja was sedate. Imran back in his protective number 3 role hit two big sixes, one off Patel and a big on-drive off Larsen, but took 93 balls to make his 44. When he top-edged a sweep to fine leg off the medium pacer, Harris, in the 34th over Pakistan's required run rate had crept above eight per over. Salim Malik's mistimed one-handed drive to substitute fieldsman Rod Latham at cover point in the next over left 123 runs to be made from the final 15 overs.

The rain which, if it had fallen, would have destroyed any Pakistani hopes failed to support the weather forecasters and kept blowing away. Crowe, resting in the pavilion wanted the spinners recalled. However, the bowling changes and field placings were out of his hands. Uncapped youngster, 22-year-old Inzamam-ul-Haq, took charge. In the period after a drinks break where Wright ran to the pavilion and asked Crowe for a bowling plan, Inzamam took the game by the scruff of the neck. He had nearly made himself unavailable for the match because of an illness the previous night. There were no signs of that as he belted Chris Harris, Danny Morrison and even Patel to all parts. A high-elevation lofted drive off Harris must have risked attracting the rain. The hit lobbed out of reach over the boundary at long-off. Inzamam reached 50 in 31 balls and put on 87 in 10 overs with Javed Miandad when Harris's dive from short cover resulted in his run-out.

Harris' brilliant fielding temporarily lifted New Zealand's sinking spirits. There had been stooped shoulders and signs of panic in the field during Inzamam's onslaught. Another 35 was needed from the last five overs. Willie Watson bowled Akram, then Moin Khan settled the issue. He pulled a tiring Watson away for four, on bent knee drove Harris over mid-off for six, then from the final ball of the 49th over pulled him for the boundary that put Pakistan into their first World Cup final.

As the emotion of disappointment overwhelmed the Kiwis, so did the Pakistanis rejoice. Miandad had guided the younger players through with another of his beautifully engineered innings. When Moin struck the winning

NEW ZEALAND

M.J. Greatbatch b Aqib Javed		17
J.G. Wright c Ramiz Raja b Mushtaq Ahmed		13
A.H. Jones lbw Mushtaq Ahmed		21
M.D. Crowe (capt) run out		91
K.R. Rutherford c Moin Khan b Wasim Akram		50
C.Z. Harris st Moin Khan b Iqbal Sikander		13
I.D.S. Smith (wk) not out		18
D.N. Patel lbw Wasim Akram		8
G.R. Larsen not out		8
Extras (b 4, lb 7, w 8, nb 4)		23
(50 overs)		7–262

Did not bat: D.K. Morrison, W. Watson

1/35 2/39 3/87 4/194 5/214 6/221 7/244

Bowling: Wasim Akram 10–0–40–2; Aqib Javed 10–2–45–1; Mushtaq Ahmed 10–0–40–2; Imran Khan 10–0–59–0; Iqbal Sikander 9–0–56–1; Aamir Sohail 1–0–11–0

PAKISTAN

Aamir Sohail c Jones b Patel		14
Ramiz Raja c Morrison b Watson		44
Imran Khan (capt) c Larsen b Harris		44
Javed Miandad not out		57
Salim Malik c sub (R. Latham) b Larsen		1
Inzamam-ul-Haq run out		60
Wasim Akram b Watson		9
Moin Khan (wk) not out		20
Extras (b 4, lb 10, w 1)		15
(49 overs)		6–264

Did not bat: Iqbal Sikander, Mushtaq Ahmed, Aqib Javed

1/30 2/84 3/134 4/140 5/227 6/238

Bowling: Patel 10–0–50–1; Morrison 9–0–55–0; Watson 10–2–39–2; Larsen 10–1–34–1; Harris 10–0–72–1

Umpires: S.A. Bucknor, D.R. Shepherd.

Toss: New Zealand.

boundary the veteran kissed the turf. The New Zealand flags were put away and replaced by a few proud green and white ones. Imran and the Pakistani cricket team had their own dream. Inzamam-ul-Haq who batted for just 37 balls, was named Man of the Match.

22 MARCH, WORLD CUP SECOND SEMI-FINAL: ENGLAND VS SOUTH AFRICA
SCG, SYDNEY: ENGLAND WON BY 19 RUNS

No-one questioned England's right to progress through to the final of the 1992 World Cup. What annoyed the entire global cricketing community was that 12 minutes of rain turned an exciting semi-final climax into an absurdity and condemned the wet-weather rule to eternal damnation. With South Africa requiring 21 runs off 13 balls it began to rain. The batsmen, knowing what the rain rule would do to them, wanted to stay on. England suggested to umpires Brian Aldridge and Steve Randell that it was too wet to continue and eventually England accepted an offer to leave the SCG, much to the disappointment of the 30,000 strong crowd. The rain soon stopped and everyone returned, but by the time the covers were removed the umpires decreed that only one-ball remained to be bowled. Brian McMillan faced that delivery. He is a big man. However, even he couldn't hit the ball far enough to score 21 from one shot.

Wessels had checked with a local weather forecaster whether there would be any rain at the SCG that Sunday. The expert predicted a brief interruption of about 10 minutes late in the evening. The South African captain wanted to bat second and thought a late 10-minute shower was not a worthwhile deterrent to that decision. Little did he know.

Allan Donald and Meyrick Pringle, perhaps nervous because of the occasion, were so wayward the total had reached 20 by the third over with the majority of the runs extras. Then a big shout for a catch behind against Graham Gooch was upheld by umpire Steve Randell. Replays showed the South Africans were lucky to get the decision in their favour. Five overs later Ian Botham played on to Pringle.

Graeme Hick, his reputation in international cricket greater than his achievement, came in at 2–39 and the first ball received more benefit of the doubt on an lbw decision than his captain did on the caught behind. The South Africans could not believe Hick survived and were incredulous when next ball he was caught at slip off a no-ball. They were key let-offs as from that point the English batsmen took charge.

Alec Stewart had been promoted to number 3 after Robin Smith had joined the injured list with a pinched nerve in his back. He batted sensibly and steadied the innings while the relieved Hick quickly grew in confidence. They put on 71 in 14 overs and when Stewart was caught behind, Neil Fairbrother and the Zimbabwean added a further 73, also in 14 overs. The South African bowlers were being mastered and, using a cynical old West Indian trick, slowed their over rate.

The overs were reduced to a trickle, but the runs continued to flow. Hick's ultimately impressive 90-ball innings with nine fours was finally ended by a leaping Jonty Rhodes catch at point. Fairbrother was bowled by Pringle, the most effective of the South African bowlers, at the same time. It was obvious England was not going to receive their full allocation in three and a half hours so their middle order attacked with even greater vigour.

Allan Lamb, in his only innings against the country of his birth, hit one wonderful flat-batted off drive, Chris Lewis scored at better than a run per ball and Dermot Reeve smashed 25 in 14 balls including 17 in one over from his Warwickshire team-mate, Donald. Reeve's onslaught against just about the fastest bowler in the world included three consecutive lofted on drives to the foot of the old Hill, where sky-blue shirted English fans went berserk. South Africa were fined 20 per cent of their match fee for completing just 45 overs.

South Africa was scheduled to receive the same number in return and needed to score at 5.62 per over to overhaul England's formidable 6–252. Most of the Australians in the crowd were behind them and Wessels, back opening, got his side away to a brisk start. But a powerful pull was followed by a mistimed cut to Lewis at deep gully. Peter Kirsten struggled with an injured groin and had his off stump cleanly removed by a perfect Phil DeFreitas leg-cutter.

South Africa fought hard while losing wickets at crucial times. Andrew Hudson's elegant 46 was ended in the 19th over when he tried to cut Richard Illingworth's well-disguised arm ball. Adrian Kuiper hit two big straight drives off Illingworth, then three consecutive boundaries off Gladstone Small before missing a wild slog to a ball on middle stump from the left-arm spinner.

It was now 4–131, the requirement above six per over. Even though batting was not their strongest point, the South Africans kept coming. When Hansie Cronje was caught at deep square leg by Hick the requirement was 74 off nine overs. Rhodes may have held his spot in the team with his fielding ability, now he showed his batting prowess to a television-land audience of millions. Going hell for leather he broke his bat, had it replaced and smote Botham one bounce for four to square leg next ball. Rhodes slashed Small hard and high to the point boundary and the 200 mark had just been passed when he repeated the off-side shot only to find Lewis 10 metres inside the fence.

Streakers of various denominations momentarily diffused the tension of an equation of 40 runs from, supposedly, four overs. McMillan and Dave Richardson maintained the challenge. They hit and ran furiously, getting 18 from the next 11 balls, which had the English bowlers and fieldsmen just starting to wilt. Or was it their shirts clinging and hair becoming bedraggled? At night, rain is felt before it is seen.

A fiasco developed. The umpires were under more pressure to be fair to everyone than for a hairline run-out decision. There were howls of derision as the players left the field. To all but the English supporters, Gooch's men were villains avoiding a finish where they might have come off second best. The SCG scoreboard started flashing the altered requirement; 22 runs off 7 balls. There were more boos. The finish time had been brought forward to 10 pm because South Africa had only bowled 45 overs. The scoreboard changed the requirement again. Lewis had to bowl just one more delivery.

The tribute visits by the two teams back onto the ground were given quite different receptions. The crowd lauded the departing South Africans, while many unfairly jeered England. The hosts would need to support someone in the final and, like India at Calcutta in 1987, it would be the team that opposed the old imperial masters. There was no such ill will in the pavilion. Wessels admitted he would also have left the field given the same situation. The English captain, his delight at reaching the final tempered slightly by the recent anti-climax, said his heart went out to his opponents. They both should have demanded to know who wrote that rule. Graeme Hick was named Man of the Match.

ENGLAND

G.A. Gooch (capt)	c Richardson b Donald	2
I.T. Botham	b Pringle	21
A.J. Stewart (wk)	c Richardson b McMillan	33
G.A. Hick	c Rhodes b Snell	83
N.H. Fairbrother	b Pringle	28
A.J. Lamb	c Richardson b Donald	19
C.C. Lewis	not out	18
D.A. Reeve	not out	25
Extras	(b 1, lb 7, w 9, nb 6)	23
(45 overs)		6–252

Did not bat: P.A.J. DeFreitas, R.K. Illingworth, G.C. Small

1/20 2/39 3/110 4/183 5/187 6/221

Bowling: Donald 10-0-69-2; Pringle 9-2-36-2; Snell 8-0-52-1; McMillan 9-0-47-1; Kuiper 5-0-26-0; Cronje 4-0-14-0

SOUTH AFRICA

K.C. Wessels (capt)	c Lewis b Botham	17
A.C. Hudson	lbw Illingworth	46
P.N. Kirsten	b DeFreitas	11
A.P. Kuiper	b Illingworth	36
W.J. Cronje	c Hick b Small	24
J.N. Rhodes	c Lewis b Small	43
B.M. McMillan	not out	21
D.J. Richardson (wk)	not out	13
Extras	(lb 17, w 4)	21
(43 overs)		6–232

Did not bat: R.P. Snell, M.W. Pringle, A.A.A. Donald

1/26 2/61 3/90 4/131 5/176 6/206

Bowling: Botham 10-0-52-1; Lewis 5-0-38-0; DeFreitas 8-1-28-1; Illingworth 10-1-46-2; Small 10-1-51-2

Umpires: B.L. Aldridge, S.G. Randell.

Toss: South Africa.

WEDNESDAY 25 MARCH 1992
BENSON AND HEDGES WORLD CUP FINAL
ENGLAND vs PAKISTAN
MCG, MELBOURNE: PAKISTAN WON BY 22 RUNS

Imran Khan had played for Pakistan in the very first World Cup in 1975. He and his deputy Javed Miandad were the only two men to complete the marathon five-tournament journey over nearly 17 years. Apart from one or two moments of satisfaction, they had ultimately suffered disappointment in each of those competitions, getting no further than a place in the semi-finals.

Now under lights on what Imran later called, 'the best ground in front of the best crowd', they were winners, part of an erratic and inconsistent team that when both talent and temperament were in harmony could take on and master any opposition in the world. Here, in the Benson and Hedges World Cup, they had overcome a terrible start and, by winning their last four matches over 10 days, became the toast of the cricketing community and national heroes.

In the 1992 final Pakistan defeated England by 22 runs. Whatever the hitches, glitches and upsets of the Australasian version of the event, the final was a wonderful occasion which did total justice to a sporting occasion now followed by a billion television viewers. What is more, the weather was impeccable and the crowd enormous, both adding to the spectacle during a quality limited-overs cricket match.

The English view was slightly more sombre. This was their third loss in World Cup finals and the second in as many tournaments. As in 1987, they were favourites and still went down. After the defeats of 1979 and 1987 they were disappointed without being despondent. The group that was obliged to watch Imran Khan being presented with the glass trophy for winning the 1992 World Cup wore a tired and haggard look. Their long journey had just fallen short of the dreamed of success. Mature players like captain, Graham Gooch, Ian Botham and Allan Lamb had missed their last chance and the defeat hit harder for that reason.

During the match, relations between the teams were fine. It had not always been that way between Pakistan and England. That, too, might have increased the level of disappointment for the losers. Botham and Gooch did not go into the match in the friendliest frame of mind. They had walked out in disgust on Queen Elizabeth impersonator Gerry Connolly at the pre-final dinner. Australian Prime Minister Paul Keating had his say, the republic issue was raised again, none of which had anything to do with winning a cricket match except to give the neutrals in the 87,000 strong crowd greater incentive to support Pakistan.

There were speeches, songs and marches prior to the main event. Imran won the toss and batted. Gooch said he would have bowled anyway and it was England, not Pakistan, who got the start they wanted. Ramiz Raja, who opened with Aamir Sohail, had a let-off when he clipped a high-bouncing delivery outside the off stump from Chris Lewis to Graeme Hick at point. Ramiz began to walk away, but Steve Bucknor rightly called 'no-ball' for an above the shoulder delivery. The opener scrambled back into his crease while the ball was thrown at the stumps by Phil DeFreitas. Bucknor knew his stuff and called dead-ball.

Derek Pringle had missed the semi-final with a rib injury. Back in the side, he bowled an immaculate new-ball spell and soon had the left-hander, Sohail, caught behind by Alec Stewart low to his left as he pushed forward. Salim Malik was to be protected if 10 overs had not been bowled, so Imran came in at number 3 again and must have been horrified when Ramiz walked across his crease and was trapped lbw. His side was 2–24 in the ninth over with both their tournament century-makers back in the pavilion.

The two World Cup veterans, Imran and Miandad, put their heads down and tried to consume overs like it was the last day of a Test which had to be saved. The tempo dawdled along. This was colour with no movement. Pringle had two close lbw appeals rejected and three runs were added in 11 overs. When Imran on nine attempted to put DeFreitas over the on-side in the 21st over he skyed the ball towards deep mid wicket. Gooch ran back and under the ball and was still going full tilt when it descended and hit his hands. For a moment as he fell he had the ball, then it was down.

Halfway through the over allocation Pakistan were a mere 2–70 and it took 107 balls for Imran and Miandad's partnership to produce 50 runs. Many wondered at the merit of the plan, then three overs later the Pakistani captain danced down the wicket to left-arm spinner Richard Illingworth and hit him for a straight six into the Members' Stand. It was the signal for a change of intent. The scoreboard began to tick over. By the 31st over the 100 had been raised. Miandad's back got so sore he called for a runner and later he did not field. Imran cut and drove, Miandad glanced and nudged. Both batsmen reached fifty, the stand was worth 100 and still the tempo built, as it did in Auckland.

Miandad stepped away and drove a Chris Lewis full toss through the covers for four, then a few balls later over-improvised and reverse swept Illingworth softly to Botham at backward point. He had put on 139 with his captain in 31 overs and even got out of the way at just the right moment so the powerful tyro, Inzamam-ul-Haq, had enough time to make his mark. He flicked Botham to square leg and dabbed him past Alec Stewart's outstretched hand for two fours in the 42nd over.

Imran's important contribution was ended when he stepped away and clubbed Botham through the lengthening shadows to Illingworth on the long-on boundary. Again the timing was good. It left Wasim Akram with just enough leverage for some final-overs biffo. Inzamam traded flailing blows with the left-arm paceman while another 52 runs were put on in the last six overs. Akram hit four boundaries, never being averse to cross-bat heaves towards cow corner. Pringle withstood the final assault well and even picked up another wicket when Inzamam missed

a slog. Akram was run out going for a bye from the final ball of the innings without a hint of dissatisfaction. After 136 had been scored from the final 16 overs, he was happy to bowl at 249.

History was against England. No side batting second had won any of the other finals. Luck, too, seemed as if it might be favouring Pakistan. Akram, already bowling around the wicket, bounced the ball past the outside edge of Botham's bat. There was a huge appeal and, responding to the ball's deviation, Brian Aldridge gave the all-rounder out caught behind. His displeasure was matched by the crowd's joy. Botham had repeatedly referred to the Australians as 'convicts', then shown public indignation when a comedian impersonated the Queen. He should not have been surprised at the send off he received after making a duck. When Botham's head went back and he pulled a few faces Sohail indicated the direction he had to take to find the dressing-room. The east coast of Australia missed the drama, Channel 9, as ever, feeling obliged to interrupt the cricket coverage with news and current affairs programs.

Alec Stewart was struggling, as well, and edged an outswinger from Akram. This time umpire Aldridge ruled in favour of the batsman. It was of little benefit to either Stewart or his team as he soon edged another outswinger, this time off Aqib Javed, and walked away before the umpire could make a decision.

England was 2–21 and Gooch was charged with putting together a captain's innings of equal merit to Imran's. He might have succeeded, too, if he only had to face a succession of finger spinners and medium pacers. Instead, Pakistan's first change bowler was a talented leg spinner. He was introduced in the 11th over and was soon confusing both Gooch and Graeme Hick. They survived past the evening drinks break then Hick was palpably lbw to a Mushtaq wrong 'un which no-one had any right to say they would have picked. Nor was the 21-year-old who was often left out of his Pakistan domestic side, United Bank, finished there. Ten runs later in the 21st over he struck a bigger blow when Gooch top-edged a sweep and Aqib ran in and dived forward to hold an excellent catch at deep square leg. The bowler celebrated with a David Campese style 'goose' run.

If England had folded completely from a position of 4–69 it would not have come as a total surprise. That they did not could be put down to the fighting qualities of Allan Lamb and that underrated Limited-Overs International batsman, Neil Fairbrother. The Lancastrian left-hander scored at nearly a run per ball with his deflections and daring dashes between wickets. Lamb, straining his unreliable limbs, also responded well to the demands of the situation. They took 64 balls to put on 50, punished Imran severely and were scoring at the required seven per over against Ijaz Ahmed and Aamir Sohail when Akram was recalled.

In a flash he all but sealed the result. Still around the wicket, he angled the ball in to Lamb then cut it away to hit the off-stump, ending the 72-run partnership. 'It's one of the best balls I've ever bowled,' Akram would say later. Next ball a perfectly pitched inswinger to Chris Lewis slipped between bat and pad to the top of the stumps. Akram had been instructed by his captain at the start of the competition to bowl for wickets rather than containment. Never wholesomely accurate, he finished with the tournament's highest wide count and the most wickets.

Only boundaries would revive England's fortunes from 6–141 and, despite Fairbrother's brave efforts, they would not come. He and Dermot Reeve put on another 39 without really suggesting a miracle was about to happen. Then in the 43rd over, after 70 balls of total dedication, Fairbrother top-edged a pull off Aqib that lobbed easily to Moin. The requirement was now up to around 10 per over.

DeFreitas slogged hard before taking on Salim Malik's arm from deep mid wicket and losing. Illingworth briefly hit with power, too, and even managed a couple of fours before Imran, whose figures were none too impressive, bowled the final over of the 1992 World Cup.

He didn't get to complete it. From the second ball Illingworth top-edged an attempted smite. Ramiz ran around at mid-off and held the comfortable offering, then continued in a large circle with his arms aloft. At 10.18 pm Eastern Summer Time on 25 March 1992 Pakistan joined the West Indies, India and Australia as winners of the World Cup.

Ramiz's catch was followed by a session of proud men in green shirts kissing the ground. They arose with broad smiles to hug each other and anyone else who came within arm's reach. Within an instant the media had invaded the sanctity of the Pakistani gathering. Imran's immediate reaction on television was, 'You know I always felt we were going to win it even when we were struggling I always knew we were going to win it'. Wasim Akram, who was named as Man of the Match offered, 'This is the best moment of my life!' Their captain accepted the glass trophy and they ran around the boundary brandishing it casually, totally confident of its safety.

The giant MCG bowl still providing a fantastic spectacle under lights, even with the match over, exploded into life as the sky was filled with fireworks to close the tournament. It brought down the curtain on a disappointing finish for England who, heads held high, walked a thankyou lap, their honour intact. Gooch suggested it was not the end of the world, but Alec Stewart's arm around him during the presentation indicated that the disappointment, quite understandably, went deep. He admitted later, 'To be fair, Pakistan deserved to win. They played better than us today.'

There was a rousing rendition of 'Allah Hoo' in the MCG dressing-room, dancing in the streets of Lahore and in the Pakistani communities in Bradford. Imran was thrilled because of the publicity and fundraising benefit to the cancer hospital he wanted to have built in Lahore. Soon cricket would not interfere with his devotion to that cause.

PAKISTAN	
Aamir Sohail c Stewart b Pringle	4
Ramiz Raja lbw Pringle	8
Imran Khan (capt) c Illingworth b Botham	72
Javed Miandad c Botham b Illingworth	58
Inzamam-ul-Haq b Pringle	42
Wasim Akram run out	33
Salim Malik not out	0
Extras (lb 19, w 6, nb 7)	32
(50 overs)	6–249

Did not bat: Ijaz Ahmed, Moin Khan (wk), Mushtaq Ahmed, Aqib Javed

1/20 2/24 3/163 4/197 5/249 6/249.

Bowling: Pringle 10–2–22–3; Lewis 10–2–52–0; Botham 7–0–42–1; DeFreitas 10–1–42–0; Illingworth 10–0–50–1; Reeve 3–0–22–0

ENGLAND	
G.A. Gooch (capt) c Aqib Javed b Mushtaq Ahmed	29
I.T. Botham c Moin Khan b Wasim Akram	0
A.J. Stewart (wk) c Moin Khan b Aqib Javed	7
G.A. Hick lbw Mushtaq Ahmed	17
N.H Fairbrother c Moin Khan b Aqib Javed	62
A.J. Lamb b Wasim Akram	31
C.C. Lewis b Wasim Akram	0
D.A. Reeve c Ramiz Raja b Mushtaq Ahmed	15
D.R. Pringle not out	18
P.A.J. DeFreitas run out	10
R.K. Illingworth c Ramiz Raja b Imran Khan	14
Extras (lb 5, w 13, nb 6)	24
(49.2 overs)	10–227

1/6 2/21 3/59 4/69 5/141 6/141 7/180 8/183 9/208 10/227

Bowling: Wasim Akram 10–0–49–3; Aqib Javed 10–2–27–2; Mushtaq Ahmed 10–1–41–3; Ijaz Ahmed 3–0–13–0; Imran Khan 6.2–0–43–1; Aamir Sohail 10–0–49–0

Umpires: B.L. Aldridge, S.A. Bucknor.

Toss: Pakistan

POST-MORTEM

Financially, the 1992 World Cup continued the stories of success, not least through the merchandising of coloured replica team shirts. Unlike the previous tournaments, though, the organisers received only mixed reviews. The amount of travel involved and some of the accommodation provided were criticised by players and their countries' officials. When the weather behaved, the cricketers offered some great entertainment and there was genuine public pleasure that a team exuding mercurial talent was able to time its run and overcome those whose tactics were more rigid and less dynamic.

Pakistan, true to form, rumbled about Imran's attitude to his players after the World Cup win. Officially he retired due to ongoing problems with his shoulder, unofficially the players did not want him to lead them on the 1992 tour of England. Under Javed Miandad, they won the Test series but lost the one-dayers. Waqar Younis

and Wasim Akram swung the old ball late and to a full length, often scattering stumps in all directions. It made great viewing as feet rather than heads were under threat.

The Test win was sullied by accusations of ball tampering which England wanted to believe was the real reason they were beaten in the Tests and maybe even the World Cup.

The Australians were dissatisfied with their World Cup result and had a good look at where things might have gone wrong. Sri Lanka was less forgiving of those at the helm and Aravinda de Silva found he had swapped places with Arjuna Ranatunga again when he got back home.

South Africa and the West Indies went off to play a Test against each other and soon Zimbabwe joined the brotherhood of Test nations. Test cricket resumed its former eminence, but behind closed doors powerful and influential men were planning their campaigns for fours years hence.

7

The Wills World Cup, 1996:
Sri Lanka's Joy

The arguments about whether the World Cup was a viable concept were gone. They had been replaced by debate and disagreement over who should host the tournament scheduled for the southern summer of 1995–96. At the February 1993 ICC meeting there was so much ill-feeling some people felt no agreement could be reached and the gathering degenerated into what TCCB executive and former England wicketkeeper Alan Smith called 'A shambles'. Others thought the ICC might even be split, which would have left any future World Cups on shaky ground.

India and Pakistan, with the addition of Sri Lanka, wanted to run the show again. They were supported by a lot of the associate members of the ICC and Zimbabwe. The majority of the Test-playing nations favoured England's offer as proposed by the TCCB. Eventually to break the deadlock and with the guarantee that they would host the 1998 tournament, it being recommended that the World Cup be held every three years, the English contingent withdrew their bid. The ICC secretary, Lieutenant Colonel John Stephenson, an Englishman, called the gesture 'most magnanimous' and 'Gentlemanly'. South Africa was in line to hold the eighth competition in 2001.

The major economies of the world may have managed to hold inflation largely in check in the Western world in the first half of the 1990s. However, there was no such achievement on the World Cup stage. The number of participants continued to increase, this time from nine to twelve. The extra three sides were to come from the first three places in the February 1994 ICC Trophy tournament in Kenya. Eventually the United Arab Emirates, boosted by the inclusion of expatriate Indians, Sri Lankans and Pakistanis with first-class experience, hosts Kenya and third placed Holland won the treasured spots. Soon after the ICC met again and agreed on the February and March dates for the World Cup in 1996, at the same time thinking better of their once every three years plan. On reflection, the four-yearly status quo had greater appeal.

There was some slight deflation in the number of matches. Yet another new structure reduced the fixtures from 39 to 37. Groups were back in fashion, so into the As went India, Australia, West Indies, Sri Lanka, Zimbabwe and Kenya. The Bs contained Pakistan, England, New Zealand, South Africa, Holland and United Arab Emirates. The preliminary stage matches eliminated two sides from each group, the surviving eight teams progressing through to a quarter-final round, followed by semi-finals and the final. A second day was set aside for any matches that could not be finished because of rain. Umpires were allowed to call for video replay adjudication from a third umpire for stumping and run-out decisions. Otherwise the rules for the 1996 World Cup were much the same as those that had become standardised for Limited-Over Internationals across the cricket-playing globe.

The greater change was in the power of sponsorship and television rights. For the second time a tobacco company was able to offer enough financial incentive to get its name attached to a cricket World Cup. Wills was able to put its name on the tournament for a contract rumoured to cost them around $A20 million. That also bought them playing-field and stump logos. The

1996 version of coloured uniforms were also to bear the tobacco company's name. Coca-Cola was named as the official World Cup soft drink. Matches at major venues were to be played under lights, including the final at Lahore. Jagmohan Dalmiya was the game's new major powerbroker and a convenor of PILCOM, the World Cup organising committee. With everyone trying to get the best deal off everyone else there were difficulties with who was televising to whom. Not surprisingly, by the time the event began the holding out between rival companies had finished.

The South African issue had been buried by February 1996. Even members of the final 'rebel' tour there, Mike Gatting's English team of 1989–90, had their bans lifted and were available if their selectors wanted them and had been since 1992–93. There was to be no political plain sailing, though. Two issues clouded the 1996 World Cup, one being serious enough for it to cause two matches to be forfeited.

In 1995 high-profile Australian players Mark Waugh, Tim May and Shane Warne made accusations that Pakistani batsman Salim Malik had tried to bribe them during the 1994 Australian tour of Pakistan. The accusations created the greatest controversy the game has ever known and at the time of writing the matter has still not been resolved. Much initial reaction on the subcontinent was disbelieving and strained relations between Australia and the co-hosts of the 1996 World Cup. When Sri Lankan off spinner Muttiah Muralitharan was no-balled for throwing by umpire Darrell Hair in a Test in Melbourne there were cries of a conspiracy by certain sections of the press in India and Pakistan as well as Sri Lanka.

The deterioration in relations continued when, a couple of weeks before the lavish World Cup opening ceremony at Eden Gardens in Calcutta, a terrorist bomb exploded in central Colombo killing 80 people. The Australian Cricket Board requested that their match against Sri Lanka be relocated to a venue in India. When this was rejected by PILCOM, the Australian authorities announced that, despite assurances of increased security, they would not be sending a team to play in Sri Lanka. The West Indian authorities, also fearing for the safety of their players, joined Australia in boycotting their scheduled match in Sri Lanka.

Although conceding two points, Australia was installed as 5–2 favourites to win the 1996 Wills World Cup. The punters were obviously not discouraged by their disappointing showing in 1992. Since Pakistan's historic win in Melbourne in 1992 Australia had gradually asserted its dominance over all other nations in Test cricket. Mark Taylor had replaced Allan Border at the helm and added freshness and enterprise to the competitiveness that Border's regime had established.

Indeed, of the side that played in the 1987 final in Calcutta only Steve Waugh and Craig McDermott remained and the big fast bowler from Queensland was destined to send down just three more overs for his country. Trump cards in the Australian attack were now paceman Glenn McGrath, a spindly mean-hearted bowler with a killer instinct and a biting tongue and high profile, and blond leg-spinner Shane Warne. Warne, who had single-handedly reignited the public image of leg spin, was cautious about the reception he would receive on the subcontinent. Controversial at times himself, Warne was nothing less than a champion, easily the best Australian leg spinner since Bill O'Reilly and sure to be a force in the World Cup.

The Waugh brothers were at the peak of their batting powers, Mark taking up the role as an aggressive opener in partnership with his more pedestrian captain. While struggling at Test level, Michael Bevan had mastered many facets of middle-order batting in the limited-overs game. The left-hander had averaged 194 in the recently completed World Series Cup tournament in Australia, hitting the ball with precision into gaps and running with amazing speed between wickets. Tasmanian Ricky Ponting was the young batting tyro of the line-up, recently established in the team and looking to fulfil his immense potential.

The holders of the World Cup, Pakistan, had gone through various ructions and upheavals through the four years since their great victory.

They retained the talent necessary to take back to back titles, but had to withstand many pressures including the added expectation of playing at home. Captains had come, gone and returned. Allegations of pot smoking in the West Indies followed the bribery accusations. Key fast-bowling all-rounder Wasim Akram was at the helm for the 1996 World Cup, there having been five changes at the top of the Pakistani team in a year. Akram had come full circle since a player's revolt in South Africa.

He remained a wonderful bowler, fast and adaptable with plenty of variations, including a killer inswinging yorker. When both he and Waqar Younis were fit, on good terms with each other and firing on both cylinders, the new-ball pair displayed speed and skills the equal of any of the legendary fast-bowling duos in history. While Shane Warne received most plaudits for rejuvenating the art of wrist spin at the game's highest level, Mushtaq Ahmed, another with snapping fingers and supple wrists, had actually preceded him on the world stage. Almost as accurate as the Australian star, he possessed even greater variation, if anything concentrating too much on wrong 'uns.

The emergence of Saeed Anwar as an opening partner to Aamir Sohail gave Pakistan power at the start of their innings. Both left-handers approached their job with aggressive intent. While Anwar was perhaps the more stylish of the two, Sohail lost nothing in comparison of scoring capability or entertainment value. Ijaz Ahmed, Salim Malik, Inzama-ul-Haq and the recalled veteran of six World Cups, Javed Miandad, completed Pakistan's highly credentialled middle order.

Co-hosts India faced similar pressures of expectation to Pakistan. One of the motivating factors behind the success of Imran Khan's 1992 side had been the desire to match the euphoria in Pakistan that India had felt in 1983. Now fans in both countries expected nothing less than a repeat of that type of joy and placed them with Australia as official tournament favourites. Mohammad Azharuddin had been subject to waves of criticism each time India's form fell below those high levels of expectation. Yet his calm self-assuredness in times of success and failure made him a very capable captain even without considering his superb batting.

Since 1992 Sachin Tendulkar had gone from strength to strength. Even Sir Donald Bradman had compared the technique of the young Indian to himself. Tendulkar also showed the same killer instinct towards bowlers, seeking total domination while exhibiting every shot available. Like Mark Waugh, Tendulkar had been promoted to open the batting in Limited-Over Internationals. There was plenty of talent to support Tendulkar and Azharuddin. Sanjay Manjrekar, Navjot Sidhu, Ajay Jadeja and Vinod Kambli were all accomplished run-makers. They needed to be. India's bowling was of limited quality. This, despite the obvious quality of Anil Kumble, another to carry the wrist-spinning banner, and the brave determination of the medium-pace brigade, which included Javagal Srinath, the very competitive Manoj Prabhakar and Venkatesh Prasad.

Unlike 1992, England arrived to begin their World Cup campaign on a downer having lost a Test series in South Africa and the follow up one-day tournament. That summed up their fortunes for the majority of the time since their appearance in the final against Pakistan. Under the guidance of Keith Fletcher, then with Ray Illingworth in charge, England's overseas record was poor.

Mike Atherton, after three years as captain, had become a hardened 27-year-old. His own courage, dedication and concentration had earned plaudits without getting the results he or his country would have hoped. His side were bedevilled by inconsistency. No-one could doubt the occasional brilliance of the likes of Alec Stewart, Graeme Hick, Robin Smith and Graham Thorpe, yet as a collective unit they were prone to unaccountable lapses. Graham Gooch and Ian Botham were long gone and no-one of the same calibre had stepped forward take their place.

The bowling, the enthusiastic Darren Gough apart, had also made limited progress in recent times. It relied again on medium-paced seamers like Phil DeFreitas, back for his third World Cup, Angus Fraser, Dominic Cork and Peter Martin, none of whom threatened serious damage on batsmen-friendly subcontinental wickets. Nor was the spin of Neil Smith, Mike Watkinson or Richard Illingworth likely to create significant fear. Yet England's World Cup record was remarkably consistent, never having failed to reach at least the semi-final stage. The competitive spirit of this side, again bursting with all-rounders, could not be discounted.

South Africa had shown since 1992 that their achievements were based on genuine talent, not the romance of the return to international cricket. Kepler Wessels' bad knees had led to retirement. The reins were handed over to young Hansie Cronje, a designated leader if ever there was one. The success of the Proteas had been based on solid rather than spectacular batting, accurate pace bowling and brilliant fielding. Allan Donald remained one of the world's premier fast bowlers and his effectiveness had been increased through the emergence of a quality partner in Shaun Pollock. The red-headed son of the chairman of selectors and former Test paceman, Peter Pollock, had made an immediate impression during his debut series against England. At 22 he was fast and aggressive with a batting talent more in line with uncle Graeme than his father.

Another newcomer in the South African line-up was freakish left-arm spinner Paul Adams. The teenager with the 'frog in a blender action' had shown unorthodoxy was no obstacle to success. His meteoric rise attracted plenty of publicity, not least because as a Cape Coloured he set a landmark for the new direction of South African cricket.

Jonty Rhodes' athleticism and Brian McMillan's enormous safe hands set the standards for the amazingly high quality of the South African fielding. Although lacking renowned champions the Proteas' batting line-up had great depth and off-spinning all-rounder Pat Symcox at number 10 would eventually become a Test century-maker. Importantly, South Africa were coming into the tournament in prime limited-overs form.

West Indian decline had not been arrested since 1992. In addition to having limited impact on the shorter version of the game they had recently lost their crown as the world's premier Test nation to Australia. That increased the pressure on captain Richie Richardson, who had already had 12 months out of the game through emotional fatigue. While Richardson recuperated Courtney Walsh had successfully assumed the leadership role. The push from Walsh's home island, Jamaica, was that their man was the rightful captain. The Leeward Islands and more importantly the West Indian Board remained faithful to Richardson.

That created some inter-island rivalry inside the dressing-room of the type that had haunted West Indian cricket prior to its halcyon days. It also had the potential to undermine the still obvious talent within the side. Richardson had not completely recaptured his pre-hiatus run-making capacity, although his decline was nowhere near as severe as some people suggested.

Brian Lara's profile had skyrocketed when he broke the long-standing highest Test and highest first-class scores within weeks of each other in 1994. However, questions had arisen since then over his ability to handle media pressure. That included temporarily walking out during the 1995 tour of England and making himself unavailable for the World Series Cup tournament in Australia. Yet his sublime batting talent could carry all before it and was central to the West Indies' chances of success. Shivnarine Chanderpaul had emerged as a determined and consistent left-hander, and Jimmy Adams had been prolific on the tour of India 12 months before. Carl Hooper withdrew from the side at the last minute through illness and would be missed.

The cutting edge of Richardson's attack was his trio of big, mean fast bowlers. Curtly Ambrose, Courtney Walsh and Ian Bishop needed to stay fit and in form if the West Indies were to make an impact on the 1996 World Cup. Each, in the past, had shown the ability through strength and accuracy to overcome the slowness of wickets on the subcontinent. Both Walsh and Ambrose were the wrong side of 30 and the world waited for a diminishing of their powers and achievements. It was as well that no-one held their breath.

There was a sense that New Zealand had missed their chance by not getting through to the final in 1992. Now Martin Crowe's dicky knee had brought his career to an end. His departure just prior to the start of the World Cup left a big gap which could not be filled despite the batting promise of Nathan Astle and Stephen Fleming.

Also into the line-up was new captain Lee Germon, promoted to the national leadership after impressing in the role for Canterbury in New Zealand. Germon, who came in a package deal with new coach, Glenn Turner, displaced Adam Parore from behind the stumps, although the talented 24-year-old retained his place as a batsman. Like Dipak Patel before him, Roger Twose achieved instant Kiwi status by leaving England, marrying his girlfriend from New Zealand and settling there. The doughty left-hander walked straight into the side, his experience invaluable as, in addition to Crowe retiring, Mark Greatbatch had been omitted and Ken Rutherford, deposed as captain, had gone to play in South Africa.

Seam and medium pace was back in favour. The bulk of the New Zealand bowling responsibility would fall on Danny Morrison, Chris Cairns and Dion Nash, whose introduction to the big time had created a favourable impression. It was difficult to believe New Zealand had the talent to do any serious damage in the World Cup. However, they had a habit of reaching the semi-final stages and showed in 1992 they were very capable of causing an upset or two.

It was a pity for Sri Lanka that their first chance to showcase their home on the World Cup stage was marred by controversy. The boycotts by Australia and the West Indies reduced the number of matches in Colombo and Kandy from four to two. If nothing else it gave Arjuna Ranatunga's side a four-point launching pad for the quarter-finals.

The portents from the Sri Lankans' tour of Australia were not good. Heavy defeats were intermingled with controversy and ill-feeling. At home, though, they had always been a different proposition and they had their best-ever chance to really progress. Any impact would be based on taking full advantage of their aggressive

batting line-up. Ranatunga's inventiveness in the middle order was in the Javed Miandad class and extended beyond ploys whereby he would call for a runner. Relieved of the burden of captaincy, Aravinda de Silva sought opportunities to measure himself against the best batsmen in the world, while left-handers like Hashan Tillekaratne, Asanka Gurusinha and Sanath Jayasuriya were all approaching 30, often a batsman's peak age.

It was unfortunate that Sri Lanka's key bowler, Muttiah Muralitharan, now had to carry the stigma of being called for throwing. How that affected his form during the World Cup remained to be seen. The young off spinner had handled the matter with a great deal of dignity and was sure to receive sympathetic treatment from fans on the subcontinent, in India and Pakistan as well as Sri Lanka. The pressure on the umpires when Muralitharan bowled would be as great as on the bowler. Muralitharan's support was variable. Chaminda Vaas and Pramodya Wickremasinghe could be penetrative with the new ball. At other times they merely removed the shine for the spinners like Muralitharan and fellow 'offie', Kumara Dharmasena.

No-one had done any favours for Zimbabwe. They were not going to benefit from forfeits, had no home-ground advantage and were in Group A which had only one of the tournament underlings, fellow Africans Kenya, instead of two as in Group B. Now a Test nation, the Zimbabweans were prepared to risk playing in Sri Lanka in the search for precious points in an attempt to advance their languishing international status.

Andy Flower, like his predecessor a wicket-keeper-batsman, was the captain of Zimbabwe. Eleven years Flower's senior, Dave Houghton was the original choice as vice-captain, but his hopes of finishing his career on a high note were shattered by a foot injury sustained during a century innings against New Zealand. That placed a greater responsibility on the shoulders of both Flowers, Andy and Grant, who formed a very effective brotherly opening partnership. Alistair Campbell was a more accomplished batsman with four years experience behind him while Andy Waller, Dave Houghton's replacement, another former captain and a veteran of two previous World Cup campaigns, was amongst the hardest hitters in the game as he showed in the 1992 World Cup match at New Plymouth.

Eddo Brandes had left his chickens behind for another crack at cricketing glory. He would share the new ball with Heath Streak, a bowler of genuine pace well up to international class. Leg-spinning was now popular in Zimbabwe too, Paul Strang being the nation's number one practitioner. Underdogs still, they at least could boast the tournament's richest colours on their uniform, a bright crimson number that encouraged the opposition to wear their sponsor's sunglasses at all times.

Holland, for their part, if they achieved nothing else, looked nice in the only appearance to date of their bright orange World Cup uniform. Their outfit, like that of all other teams, had taken 10 days from order to availability. Their line-up contained plenty of experience. Barbados-born, Nolan Clarke, a scorer of 159 for his island against the MCC back in 1974, was now 47 and a legend in Dutch cricket. Captain for 10 years, Steve Lubbers, and Flavian Aponso were also in their forties. That must have made the others with first-class experience, paceman Paul-Jan Bakker (38), all-rounder Roland Lefebvre (33) and Australian Peter Cantrell (33) feel like striplings. Lefebvre was still contracted to county side, Glamorgan.

The oldest players in the Kenyan side, Dipak Chudasama, Asif Karim and Tariq Iqbal, were just 32. They also had in their squad the youngest player in the tournament, 17-year-old all-rounder Thomas Odoyo. The team's joy at participating in the prestigious World Cup was tempered by a dispute with the Kenyan authorities over the players' meagre daily allowance. That was resolved in time to avoid a fiasco. Seen as a potential future Test-playing nation, Kenya's viability during the World Cup was very important.

Maurice Odumbe, like Hansie Cronje a young national captain, was a classy all-rounder, but much attention would centre on Steve Tikolo. Many were keen to see how this talented

batsman, who had played first-class cricket in South Africa, acquitted himself against the world's best. With Kenya in Group A he would be up against Test-class opposition in every World Cup match.

The United Arab Emirates captain, Sultan Zarawani, and vice-captain Saeed-al-Saffer were the only native members of their side. Immediately following their 1994 ICC Trophy victory the grumbles began and soon the rules for player qualification were altered so that a repeat could not occur. But for the Wills 1996 World Cup this conglomerate of former Pakistani and Indian players would have to be accepted.

Outside the UAE and Pakistan, none of the players were very well known. Their batting strength had got them through the ICC Trophy tournament and would be their best chance of picking up a win in the World Cup. Someone had to win the game between UAE and Holland. Mazhar Hussain, a crouching low-gripping batsman, had been on a Pakistani B tour of Zimbabwe and Saleem Raza, an opener with experience against touring sides in Pakistan, were two of the batsmen Sultan Zarawani hoped would give UAE competitive totals. In their uniforms that would not have looked out of place on the 1st Alabama Musket Brigade in 1862, UAE should have set out to enjoy their few weeks in the limelight, for unlike Kenya and Holland, they definitely would not be back.

Tight security marked the lead-up to the opening ceremony at Eden Gardens in Calcutta. The terrorist attack in Colombo and the follow-up boycotts by the Australians and the West Indians of the matches in Sri Lanka made everyone a little apprehensive. Steve Waugh pointed out that the armed guards were of greater value in keeping fanatical cricket followers at bay than in protecting them from bombers or assassins.

There were only cricket fans amongst the 120,000 crammed into Eden Gardens for the opening ceremony to the 1996 Wills World Cup. Eye-witnesses said the reaction of the crowd when the Indian team was presented to them was something to behold. The spontaneous roar overwhelmed even the most battle-hardened players in the centre. It was the climax to a night that had its share of anti-climaxes. The major let-down came when the wind knocked over a mesh screen essential to the proper working of a $2 million laser light show. The announcer, who had also confused his introduction of UAE and South Africa, told disappointed patrons to talk among themselves. There were rumblings of discontent, but the riot was saved up for a couple of weeks. At least the fireworks went off with a bang.

The occasion, as it would three years later at Lord's, fell a long way short of the extravaganzas witnessed at Olympic and even Commonwealth Games. Some local government officials were so disgusted with the result they wanted Jagmohan Dalmiya arrested for wasting public money. It did, however, prime everyone for the start of the real thing in three days time. The prize at the end would be a four-kilogram 118-year-old sterling silver trophy originally made by the crown jewellers in London. After the final it was to be kept not by the victorious country but by the tournament sponsors, Wills. The World Cup wins by India in 1983, Australia in 1987 and Pakistan in 1992 meant that thereafter the tournament would always be a tantalising prospect. Favouritism would only go so far towards indicating a likely victor. Richard Hutton wrote in his editorial of the March 1996 edition of *The Cricketer International*: 'Such are the twists of form and fate that anyone can win the World Cup—except Holland, Kenya, the UAE, and probably Zimbabwe, Sri Lanka, New Zealand.' Well, Richard, your assessment of five out of those six sides was spot on.

WEDNESDAY 14 FEBRUARY 1996
GROUP B ENGLAND vs NEW ZEALAND
SARDAR PATEL STADIUM, AHMEDABAD: NEW ZEALAND WON BY 11 RUNS

New Zealand began their 1996 campaign as convincingly as they did the one in 1992. The Lee Germon-led Kiwis continued England's miserable recent run with a sound win. The New Zealand batsmen showed greater enterprise and their fieldsmen caught their catches. On four crucial occasions England did not.

In what *The Times* correspondent, Alan Lee, called 'an ugly, unkempt stadium', Mike Atherton gave New Zealand first use of the Sardar Patel Stadium pitch, even though by reputation it did not wear well. He was hoping to take advantage of the moisture still in the wicket at the 9 am start. Germon said he too would have bowled first. Soon that was the least of Atherton's concerns. In the third over of the day the sole slip fieldsman, Graham Thorpe, according to television commentator Tony Greig, 'standing too far back', dropped Nathan Astle off Peter Martin. Thorpe also put down Astle's opening partner Craig Spearman. That was not too costly because Dominic Cork held a caught and bowled chance off Spearman to complete the first dismissal of the 1996 World Cup.

The miss off Astle, though, was very expensive. He put on 96 for the second wicket in 19 overs with Stephen Fleming and went on to hit eight fours and two sixes off 132 balls while completing his third century in Limited-Over Internationals. There were more misses. Atherton and Cork were also culprits and England, in general, looked lacklustre. Their ground fielding also conceded unnecessary runs, enough to be significant by the end of the day. Perhaps worn down by a surfeit of cricket in South Africa, there were a number of injury problems from the outset of the tournament. Both Fleming and Roger Twose were caught by a more sure-handed Thorpe at deep square leg off top-edged sweeps. Then Chris Cairns scored at better than a run per ball striking four fours and a six. He took New Zealand to the verge of 200 with 10 overs remaining. From the moment he was caught at point off the accurate left-arm spinner Richard Illingworth, the batting was pedestrian. Instead of something in the vicinity of 270 the Kiwis had to be satisfied with 239, only 43 having come from those last 10 overs.

A well-pitched inswinging yorker from Dion Nash to Atherton in his first over got England away to a bad start. The England captain then walked to square leg rather than the pavilion. Graeme Hick had joined the growing list of the injured with a strained hamstring, sustained while fielding, and Atherton stayed on the ground as his runner. The trio of Alec Stewart, Hick and Atherton worked effectively in a partnership worth 99 runs. Hick dominated the stand, hitting nine fours in 101 balls.

At 1–100 England were reasonably placed. Once Hick watched his own demise, run out after a hesitation between Atherton and Neil Fairbrother at 144, they were always struggling. Like his 1992 predecessor, Martin Crowe, Germon was prepared to mix his bowlers around. England wanted 96 from their last 15 overs and had a spark of hope when Dominic Cork thrashed around for a couple of fours and a six. Nash extinguished that in the 47th over when he had the Derbyshire all-rounder caught behind and Danny Morrison had little trouble protecting the 16 runs available in the last over.

Atherton said after the game that he believed the poor catching had cost his side the match. Astle took the Man of the Match award in what was really a fairly tame opening to the sixth World Cup.

NEW ZEALAND	
C.M. Spearman c & b Cork	5
N.J. Astle c Hick b Martin	101
S.P. Fleming c Thorpe b Hick	28
R.G. Twose c Thorpe b Hick	17
C.L. Cairns c Cork b Illingworth	36
C.Z. Harris run out	10
S.A. Thomson not out	17
L.K. Germon (capt-wk) not out	13
Extras (b 4, lb 2, w 4, nb 2)	12
(50 overs)	6–239

Did not bat: D.J. Nash, G.R. Larsen, D.K. Morrison

1/12 2/108 3/141 4/196 5/204 6/212

Bowling: Cork 10–1–36–1; Martin 6–0–37–1; Gough 10–0–63–0; Illingworth 10–1–31–1; Hick 9–0–45–2; White 5–0–21–0

ENGLAND	
M.A. Atherton (capt) b Nash	1
A.J. Stewart c & b Harris	34
G.A. Hick run out	85
G.P. Thorpe b Larsen	9
N.H. Fairbrother b Morrison	36
R.C. Russell (wk) c Morrison b Larsen	2
C. White c Cairns b Thomson	13
D.G. Cork c Germon b Nash	19
D. Gough not out	15
P.J. Martin c Cairns b Nash	3
R.K. Illingworth not out	3
Extras (b 1, lb 4, w 1, nb 2)	8
(50 overs)	9–228

1/1 2/100 3/123 4/144 5/151 6/180 7/185 8/210 9/222

Bowling: Morrison 8–0–38–1; Nash 7–1–26–3; Cairns 4–0–24–0; Larsen 10–1–33–2; Thomson 10–0–51–1; Harris 9–0–45–1; Astle 2–0–6–0

Umpires: B.C. Cooray, S.G. Randell.

Toss: England. Points: New Zealand 2, England 0

THURSDAY 15 and FRIDAY 16 FEBRUARY 1996
GROUP B: SOUTH AFRICA vs UAE
CRICKET STADIUM, RAWALPINDI: SOUTH AFRICA WON BY 169 RUNS

The Emirates team would have been under no illusions as to the monumental task in front of them in trying to compete with the best cricket teams in the world after this thrashing handed out by South Africa.

Sultan Zarawani had the honour of winning the choice of innings, but nothing went right for him after that. He, like the rest of his bowlers, was flayed by the South African batsmen who compiled their highest score in a Limited-Over International. Later, the UAE captain was confident or foolhardy enough to face Allan Donald without a helmet and was hit on the head first ball. He lasted another few balls before Brian McMillan dismissed him for a duck.

Rain had washed out the scheduled first day. This time the 'no result' was avoided because a second day had been set aside. As the covers had been on the pitch for four days in the previous week Sultan Zarawani's decision to bowl was thought a sensible one. There may have been some assistance for the bowlers if those using the conditions had been of a reasonable standard.

They did not worry Gary Kirsten much. The left-handed opener batted through the innings, broke the highest individual World Cup score and at the completion of 50 overs was an agonising one run behind Viv Richards' all-time Limited-Over International record score of 189. He needed four from the last ball of the innings but, probably starting to feel a little fatigued, had to be satisfied with two. Kirsten knew at the crease he had broken Richards' 1987 World Cup record, but was unaware of the Limited-Over International record. It was the first century for South Africa in a World Cup match. Kirsten gave one chance on 118.

He and Andrew Hudson had set the domination in motion with an opening stand of 60. Kirsten and Hansie Cronje then put on 116 for the second wicket. The South African captain although hitting only one four and one six batted for just 62 balls while scoring 57. Cronje's

dismissal by his opposite number was the last Emirates success as Kirsten went to town over the last 20 overs. Daryll Cullinan, normally a very aggressive batsman, sat back while Kirsten continued on his merry way. At the completion of 50 overs the opener had struck 13 fours and four sixes from 159 balls. His partnership with Cullinan realised 145 runs for the third wicket.

Azhar Saeed and Ganesh Mylvaganam began the UAE reply as if they meant to get all of the 322 runs they needed. However, once they had been removed, brilliantly caught by wicketkeeper Steve Palframan and Brian McMillan, the rest of the batsmen got into a spot of bother. By the end of the 28th over UAE were 8–72. Donald and McMillan in particular were too much for them. Then, as if to avoid their opponents further embarrassment, South Africa eased back and Arshad Laiq and Shaukat Dukanwala were able to put on 80 in an unbroken ninth-wicket stand. That must have been more enjoyable for them than bowling. Their combined figures were 0–116 from 16 overs. Kirsten was an easy choice as Man of the Match.

SOUTH AFRICA

A.C. Hudson b Samarasekera	27
G. Kirsten not out	188
W.J. Cronje (capt) st Imtiaz Abbasi b Sultan Zarawani	57
D.J. Cullinan not out	41
Extras (b 1, lb 1, w 3, nb 3)	8
(50 overs)	2–321

Did not bat: J.H. Kallis, J.N. Rhodes, B.M. McMillan, S.M. Pollock, S.J. Palframan (wk), C.R. Matthews, A.A.A. Donald

1/60 2/176

Bowling: Samarasekera 9-2-39-1; Shehzad Altaf 3-0-22-0; Laeeq 6-0-52-0; Dukanwala 10-0-64-0; Azhar Saeed 7-0-41-0; Sultan Zarawani 10-0-69-1; Mazhar Hussain 5-0-32-0

UNITED ARAB EMIRATES

Azhar Saeed c McMillan b Pollock	11
G. Mylvaganam c Palframan b Donald	23
Mazhar Hussain b Donald	14
V. Mehra run out	2
Mohammad Aslam b McMillan	9
Arshad Laeeq not out	43
J.A. Samarasekera c Hudson b Donald	4
Sultan Zarawani (capt) c Cronje b McMillan	0
Imtiaz Abbasi (wk) c Palframan b McMillan	1
S.F. Dukanwala not out	40
Extras (w 3, nb 2)	5
(50 overs)	8–152

Did not bat: Altaf Shehzad Altaf

1/24 2/42 3/46 4/60 5/62 6/68 7/70 8/72

Bowling: Pollock 9-2-28-1; Matthews 10-0-39-0; Donald 10-0-21-3; Cronje 4-0-17-0; McMillan 8-1-11-3; Kallis 6-0-27-0; Kirsten 3-0-9-0

Umpires: S.A. Bucknor, V.K. Ramaswamy.

Toss: UAE. Points: South Africa 2, UAE 0

FRIDAY 16 FEBRUARY 1996
GROUP A WEST INDIES vs ZIMBABWE
FATEH MAIDAN STADIUM, HYDERABAD: WEST INDIES WON BY 6 WICKETS

The 1996 World Cup was struggling to provide exciting contests in its early stages and this one-sided affair in front of 27,000 enthusiasts in Hyderabad only raised the pulse rate in fits and starts. Fortunately a sparkling cameo by Brian Lara in his first match for the West Indies since his self-imposed exile gave the crowd something to cheer.

That it was no more than a 43-minute exhibition can be attributed to Zimbabwe not setting a significant challenge to the talented left-hander or his team. Andy Flower had taken first use of a sound surface, forcing the West Indies to bat under lights, but the Zimbabweans were unimpressive throughout. They scored at barely three per over for the full 50 overs, losing wickets regularly along the way, three of them to unnecessary run-outs.

Curtly Ambrose's opening over cost nine runs, including three of the four wides that were sent down during the innings. He was quickly back on target and soon had Andy Flower caught behind, the first of three wickets in a Man of the Match winning performance. Once his brother had gone, Grant Flower batted with some fluency, hitting six fours in 70 minutes while taking the total to 1–53 with Guy Whittall.

After the second Flower had been removed by Otis Gibson, Whittall's errors of judgment got Zimbabwe into trouble. He called Alistair Campbell through for a short single to mid wicket and Lara's direct-hit throw found Campbell short of his ground. Next, Whittall went for a second run to a Gibson misfield at third man, tripped on the bowler Ian Bishop's heel, dropped his bat and was beaten by the throw back to Courtney Browne. Three wickets had fallen for five runs between the 19th and 22nd overs leaving Zimbabwe to haul themselves back from 4–58.

They did so ever so slowly. Dave Houghton had confessed after a 1992 game that sometimes against high-class bowling Zimbabwean batsmen thought of little else but survival. They were doing so again. Ian Bishop was hardly touched, Roger Harper's off spin was almost as economical and when Ambrose tried a poorly executed slower ball Eddo Brandes picked out Shivnarine Chanderpaul at deep square leg. A couple of hard chances were put down and Zimbabwe were not bowled out, but the West Indies' requirement was an unthreatening 152.

Richie Richardson opened with Sherwin Campbell and the pair moved freely to 78 before

---

ZIMBABWE

A. Flower (capt-wk) c Browne b Ambrose	3
G.W. Flower c & b Gibson	31
G.J. Whittall run out	14
A.D.R. Campbell run out	0
A.C. Waller st Browne b Harper	21
C.N. Evans c Browne b Ambrose	21
S.G. Davies run out	9
H.H. Streak lbw Walsh	7
P.A. Strang not out	22
E.A. Brandes c Chanderpaul b Ambrose	7
A.C.I. Lock not out	1
Extras (lb 10, w 4, nb 1)	15
(50 overs)	9–151

1/11 2/53 3/56 4/58 5/91 6/103 7/115 8/125 9/142

Bowling: Ambrose 10-2-28-3; Walsh 10-3-27-1; Gibson 9-1-27-1; Bishop 10-3-18-0; Harper 10-1-30-1; Arthurton 1-0-11-0

WEST INDIES

S.L. Campbell b Strang	47
R.B. Richardson (capt) c Campbell b Strang	32
B.C. Lara not out	43
S. Chanderpaul b Strang	8
K.L.T. Arthurton c Campbell b Strang	1
R.A. Harper not out	5
Extras (b 5, lb 3, w 10, nb 1)	19
(29.3 overs)	4–155

Did not bat: O.D. Gibson, C.O. Browne (wk), I.R. Bishop, C.E.L. Ambrose, C.A. Walsh

1/78 2/115 3/123 4/136

Bowling: Streak 7-0-34-0; Lock 6-0-23-0; Brandes 7-0-42-0; Whittall 2-0-8-0; Strang 7.3-1-40-4

Umpires: R.S. Dunne, S. Venkataraghavan.

Toss: Zimbabwe. Points: West Indies 2, Zimbabwe 0

Anil Kumble takes the wicket of Ata-ur-Rehman in this quarter-final clash in Bangalore.   (Allsport/Shaun Botterill)

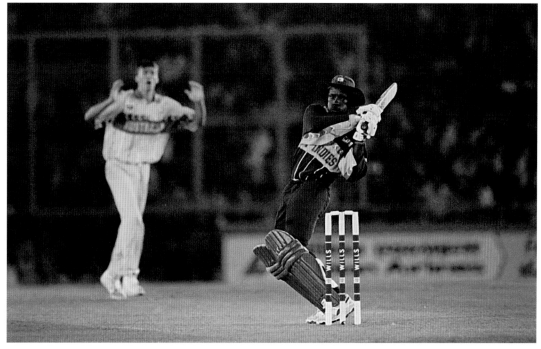

The 1996 second semi-final was Richie Richardson's last appearance for the West Indies—he played a brave, unbeaten innings.   (Allsport/Shaun Botterill)

Sadly, the 1996 India vs Sri Lanka semi-final ended prematurely when riot police were called to Eden Gardens to restore order. (Allsport/Mike Hewitt)

The 1996 World Cup final — Shane Warne drops Sri Lankan captain Arjuna Ranatunga. (Allsport/Shaun Botterill)

Arjuna Ranatunga raises his arms as his country wins the 1996 World Cup.

Australian Captain Mark Taylor during his fluent 74 in the 1996 Lahore final.   (Allsport/Mike Hewitt)

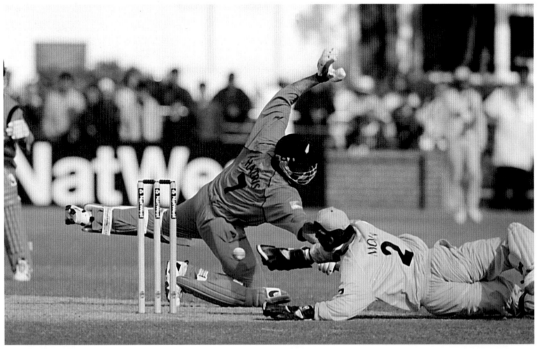

Moin Khan (Pakistan) tries to run out Chris Harris (New Zealand) during this first-round match of the
1999 World Cup.   (Allsport/Ben Radford)

Paul Strang had Richardson caught by Alistair Campbell. That brought in Lara, who was immediately into his stride. Campbell stayed with him until, just short of his 50, he failed to pick a Paul Strang wrong 'un. The leg spinner then picked up Chanderpaul and Arthurton with another wrong 'un. Strang had four wickets including three in seven balls. Even Lara was troubled enough to give a chance to slip. However, 4–136 chasing 151 is hardly cause for panic and Lara already had the measure of the medium pacers.

He pulled Heath Streak mightily for six, and drove Brandes in that exquisite and inimitable style twice through covers for four.

The crowd chanted for more and Lara turned his attention to Strang. He drove him down the ground for four, then two balls later lofted him over mid-off for six to finish the match in the most decisive fashion possible. The prodigal had returned and rushed his side to victory with 20 overs to spare.

SATURDAY 17 FEBRUARY 1996
GROUP B HOLLAND vs NEW ZEALAND
IPCL SPORTS COMPLEX GROUND, BARODA: NEW ZEALAND WON BY 119 RUNS

The lure of World Cup cricket was apparent as 20,000 turned up to witness still another one-sided contest between a fully-fledged Test nation and ICC up and comers. New Zealand and Holland probably both got out of the game what they had hoped for: one a comfortable victory and two points, the other a respectable batting performance that lasted 50 overs.

Holland made a great start after Lee Germon had won the toss and batted when Tim de Leede ran out Nathan Astle from cover point in the second over of the day. Wednesday's century-maker had been disposed of for a duck and hopes of Dutch dominance flickered. They were brief. Craig Spearman and Stephen Fleming soon took control. Neither Roland Lefebvre nor Paul Jan Bakker were able to stem the run flow that realised 118 runs in 19 overs. Spearman impressed with his eight boundaries in 59 balls, developing enough confidence in the later stages to employ the reverse sweep profitably. He was the next batsman dismissed, holing out to Bas Zuiderent at long-off from a Steve Lubbers off-spinner. On 155 the Dutch captain snared Fleming in identical fashion to give the 18-year-old Zuiderent his second catch. Ten runs later Roger Twose became over-ambitious. Marcel Schewe completed the stumping and Lubbers had a third victim.

Chris Cairns and Adam Parore paused, consolidated, then when the time was right kick-started the innings again. They hit sixes as a matter of course, five between them as 88 runs were added for the fifth wicket. Cairns got to his fifty in 38 balls. Parore took a little longer, ensuring with his captain that 300 would be attained.

A number of the Dutch players were suffering from stomach disorders and they seemed to lack the energy for such an imposing chase, let alone the skill. Peter Cantrell and Roland Lefebvre joint top-scored and handled the Kiwi attack capably enough. Cantrell, who took two excellent gully catches as a sub in the Brisbane Ashes Test of 1990–91, held the top of the innings together and hit five fours. Lefebvre was more aggressive before he heaved at Robert Kennedy and found himself lying on the pitch with his stumps rearranged.

Chris Harris was back to his dibbly dobbling best form of 1992 and at 5–102 the Dutch innings might have been swept away. Klaas van Noortwijk, at first supporting Lefebvre, went a long way towards ensuring it was not. The Man of the Match adjudicator considered Spearman's innings had been the best of the four half-century contenders for the day's award.

NEW ZEALAND

C.M. Spearman c Zuiderent b Lubbers		68
N.J. Astle run out		0
S.P. Fleming c Zuiderent b Lubbers		66
R.G. Twose st Schewe b Lubbers		25
C.L. Cairns b Cantrell		52
A.C. Parore c Clarke b Aponso		55
C.Z. Harris c Schewe b Bakker		8
L.K. Germon (capt-wk) not out		14
D.N. Patel c Schewe b Bakker		11
D.K. Morrison not out		0
Extras (lb 7, w 1)		8
(50 overs)		8–307

Did not bat: R.J. Kennedy

1/1 2/119 3/155 4/165 5/253 6/279 7/292 8/306

Bowling: Lefebvre 10–0–47–0; Bakker 10–0–51–2; de Leede 7–0–58–0; Aponso 10–0–61–1; Lubbers 9–0–48–3; Cantrell 4–0–35–1

HOLLAND

N.E. Clarke b Kennedy		14
P.E. Cantrell c Astle b Harris		45
G.J.A.F. Aponso c Astle b Harris		11
S.W. Lubbers (capt) run out		5
R.P. Lefebvre b Kennedy		45
T.B.M. de Leede lbw Harris		1
K.J.J. van Noortwijk not out		36
M. Schewe (wk) st Germon b Fleming		12
B. Zuiderent not out		1
Extras (b 3, lb 5, w 8, nb 2)		18
(50 overs)		7–188

Did not bat: E. Gouka, P.J. Bakker

1/18 2/52 3/66 4/100 5/102 6/147 7/181

Bowling: Morrison 4–1–11–0; Kennedy 10–2–36–2; Cairns 7–1–24–0; Harris 10–1–24–3; Patel 10–0–43–0; Astle 5–0–20–0; Fleming 2–0–8–1; Twose 2–0–14–0

Umpires: Khizar Hayat, I.D. Robinson.

Toss: New Zealand. Points: New Zealand 2, Holland 0

SATURDAY 17 FEBRUARY 1996
GROUP A SRI LANKA vs AUSTRALIA
R. PREMADASA STADIUM, COLOMBO: SRI LANKA WON ON FORFEIT

The Australians spent the Saturday of their first scheduled match of the World Cup at leisure in Bombay. They had held firm to their boycott after the bomb blast of 31 January in Colombo which killed 80 people. The Sri Lankan Board threatened to sue the Australian and West Indian Boards for compensation. The Sri Lankan side had net practice at the ground. It was enough to take points off Australia in the World Cup for the first time.

Umpires: Mahboob Shah, C.J. Mitchley. Points: Sri Lanka 2, Australia 0

SUNDAY 18 FEBRUARY 1996
GROUP A INDIA vs KENYA
BARABATI STADIUM, CUTTACK: INDIA WON BY 7 WICKETS

This was a day when almost everyone went home happy. The capacity crowd got the entertainment and result they wanted, the former through a great Sachin Tendulkar century, the latter through a seven wicket win. The Kenyans, although comfortably beaten, were not disgraced and at one point in their innings had worked their way to 2–161.

Mohammad Azharuddin, in his 200th Limited-Over International, won the toss and sent Kenyan in. As with other captains so far in this competition who elected to bowl, Azharuddin did not get the early breakthroughs he might have hoped for. Dipak Chudasama was soon into his stride, striking five boundaries in the first hour of play as Javagal Srinath and Manoj Prabhakar failed to make inroads.

Steve Tikolo, coming in at number 3, was also largely untroubled and dominated the scoring in a 96-run partnership with his captain, Maurice Odumbe, for the third wicket. Tikolo hit four fours and an off-driven six off left-arm spinner Venkatapathy Raju during his 83-ball innings. When Raju finally deceived him, Tikolo left the Barabati Stadium to a standing ovation from 30,000 fans. It was Raju and fellow spinner

Anil Kumble who stemmed the run flow once Tikolo was gone.

India needed exactly 200 to win and openers Tendulkar and Ajay Jadeja got 163 of them. At times Jadeja must have felt like just another one of the 30,000 spectators as his 22-year-old partner raced to fifty in 48 balls. The 100 was up by the 20th over and the stand had lasted 33 overs when a tiring Jadeja, four fours and a six in 85 balls, was caught on the boundary off Aasif Karim. There was a slight stutter as Navjot Sidhu

and Vinod Kambli failed and Tendulkar was temporarily stalled on 99. Then, once he had reached the milestone, away he went again. He had thrilled all concerned with 15 fours and a six in 134 balls when Nayan Mongia struck the winning boundary off Odumbe with eight overs to spare. Tendulkar in his 102nd Limited-Over International had completed his first World Cup century and was not a difficult choice as Man of the Match.

KENYA	
D.N. Chudasama c Mongia b Prasad	29
K.O. Otieno (wk) c Mongia b Raju	27
S.O. Tikolo c Kumble b Raju	65
M.O. Odumbe (capt) st Mongia b Kumble	26
H.S. Modi c Jadeja b Kumble	2
T.M. Odoyo c Prabhakar b Kumble	8
E.O. Odumbe not out	15
A.Y. Karim not out	6
Extras (b 2, lb 11, w 7, nb 1)	21
(50 overs)	6–199

Did not bat: D. Tikolo, M.A. Suji, R.W. Ali

1/41 2/65 3/161 4/161 5/165 6/184

Bowling: Prabhakar 5-1-19-0; Srinath 10-0-38-0; Prasad 10-0-41-1; Kumble 10-2-28-3; Raju 10-2-34-2; Tendulkar 5-0-26-0

INDIA	
A.D. Jadeja c Ali b Karim	53
S.R. Tendulkar not out	127
N.S. Sidhu c Suji b S.O. Tikolo	1
V.G. Kambli c D. Tikolo b M.O. Odumbe	2
N.R. Mongia (wk) not out	8
Extras (b 3, w 7, nb 2)	12
(41.5 overs)	3–203

Did not bat: M. Azharuddin (capt), M. Prabhakar, J. Srinath, A. Kumble, B.K.B.K.V. Prasad, S.L.V. Raju

3/182

Bowling: E.O. Odumbe 3-0-18-0; Suji 5-0-20-0; Karim 10-1-27-1; Odoyo 3-0-22-0; Ali 5-0-25-0; S.O. Tikolo 3-0-26-1; M.O. Odumbe 9.5-1-41-1; D. Tikolo 3-0-21-0

Umpires: K.T. Francis, D.R. Shepherd.

Toss: India. Points: India 2, Kenya 0

SUNDAY 18 FEBRUARY 1996
GROUP B ENGLAND vs UAE
SHAHI BAGH STADIUM, PESHAWAR: ENGLAND WON BY 8 WICKETS

It was a sad reflection on another Wills World Cup mismatch that the day's most spectacular event was the unfortunate Man of the Match, Neil Smith, being sick on the side of the pitch. It was something his father, Mike Smith, a former England captain on a tour of India, was not renowned for doing. This one-sided affair was a throw back to the matches between the major and minor sides of 1975 and failed to attract much attention from the citizens of Peshawar who, living so close to the Khyber Pass and the North-West Frontier, often have a fair bit going on in their lives anyway. The strict fast of Ramadan might have discouraged a few from going to the cricket, as well. As a mark of respect to their hosts, both teams left

the field to have their drinks break.

Phil DeFreitas, back in the side on his 30th birthday, snared the first two wickets in an impressive opening spell after Sultan Zarawani had won the toss and batted on a dry cracked pitch. Craig White broke down with an inter-costal muscle strain and Mazhar Hussain struck some boundaries so that UAE reached 2–48, but the runs dried up once the spinners could bowl to a spread field. At one stage six runs were scored off 11 overs. Vijay Mehra batted 44 minutes for one, being the first of three victims for off-spinning Smith in eight balls.

After 25 overs UAE were 5–49 and only hard work by Johanne Samarasekera and Shaukat Dukanwala got the total past 100 and made the innings last until the 49th over. Sultan Zarawani, still refusing to wear a helmet, avoided further threats to his skull, but was hardly more successful with the bat than against South Africa.

Before succumbing to the effects of a dodgy reheated pizza, Smith gave the England reply a brisk start with four boundaries in 31 balls. Even the absence of Robin Smith and Graeme Hick through injury was not going to disturb England's march to victory against the UAE

attack. While Neil Smith recovered his composure and health, Graham Thorpe scored the bulk of the remaining runs needed for the two points. He hit five fours, the win coming with a comfortable 15 overs to spare. Mike Atherton said, 'These games have a strange pressure of their own'. Maybe so, but only the players felt it. Perhaps he was referring to the pressure build up inside poor Neil Smith.

UNITED ARAB EMIRATES

Azhar Saeed lbw DeFreitas	9
G. Mylvaganam c Fairbrother b DeFreitas	0
Mazhar Hussain b Smith	33
V. Mehra c Russell b Smith	1
Mohammad Aslam b Gough	23
Arshad Laeeq b Smith	0
Saleem Raza b Cork	10
J.A. Samarasekera run out	29
Sultan Zarawani (capt) b Cork	2
S.F. Dukanwala lbw Illingworth	15
Imtiaz Abbasi not out	1
Extras (b 4, lb 4, w 4, nb 1)	13
(48.3 overs)	136

1/2 2/32 3/48 4/49 5/49 6/80 7/88 8/100 9/135 10/136

Bowling: Cork 10-1-33-2; DeFreitas 9.3-3-16-2; Gough 8-3-23-1; White 1.3-1-2-0; Smith 9.3-2-29-3; Illingworth 10-2-25-1

ENGLAND

A.J. Stewart c Mylvaganam b Laeeq	23
N.M.K. Smith retired ill	27
G.P. Thorpe not out	44
M.A. Atherton (capt) b Azhar	20
N.H. Fairbrother not out	12
Extras (b 4, lb 2, w 2, nb 6)	14
(35 overs)	2-140

Did not bat: R.C. Russell (wk), C. White, D.G. Cork, P.A.J. DeFreitas, D. Gough, R.K. Illingworth

1/52 2/109 Smith retired at 1-57

Bowling: Samarasekera 7-1-35-0; Laeeq 7-0-25-1; Raza 5-1-20-0; Azhar 10-1-26-1; Zarawani 6-0-28-0

Umpires: B.C. Cooray, V.K. Ramaswamy.

Toss: UAE. Points: England 2, UAE 0

TUESDAY 20 FEBRUARY 1996
GROUP B NEW ZEALAND vs SOUTH AFRICA
IQBAL STADIUM, FAISALABAD: SOUTH AFRICA WON BY 5 WICKETS

This poorly attended, one-sided contest at least gave an indication of who might be the team to beat from Group B. South Africa's cool and efficient demolition of New Zealand indicated their accurate and powerful bowling and brilliant outcricket were superior to anything their five preliminary round competitors might offer. From the moment Nathan Astle was run out at the bowler's end in the third over of the day the South Africans were on top and there they stayed throughout.

Even though Ramadan was officially over, the players still took their drinks off the ground. In the press box they complained that the Coca-Cola was warm. Lee Germon won the toss, batted, then found one of his openers, Craig

Spearmen, and possibly the TV replay umpire, burned his partner. Astle's early sacrifice was his second in as many matches. 'A couple of freak incidents, I hope,' he said later. After striking three boundaries Spearman was caught behind off Chris Matthews. His dismissal left New Zealand 2–17. A superb slips catch by Brian McMillan removed Roger Twose and made it 3–36. If that was the feature catch, Gary Kirsten's pinpoint throw from deep square leg and Jonty Rhodes' athleticism at cover were the ground-fielding highlights. They resulted in the direct hit run-outs of Chris Harris and Adam Parore and left New Zealand on a rather dispiriting 7–116.

Shane Thompson and Germon ensured the

avoidance of total embarrassment. Germon batted through to the completion of the 50 overs, but could do no more than push towards respectability. Allan Donald allowed no freedom at the end of the Kiwi innings while off spinner Pat Symcox had been very economical.

Any hopes New Zealand harboured of protecting 177 must have evaporated when they had dropped both South African openers by the third over of their reply. The total was 41 in the 10th over when Danny Morrison bowled Steve Palframan. The wicketkeeper had opened in place of Andrew Hudson. He did his job well in that when Hansie Cronje came in it seemed as if the sting had gone out of the bowling. The South African captain unleashed a brutal assault on the Kiwi attack, especially the medium pacers who

had been so effective four years before. Gavin Larsen went for 18 in an over as Cronje hit 11 fours and three sixes in 64 balls. One of those sixes off Thompson's off spin raised Cronje's fifty in just 36 balls.

By the time Cronje holed out off Nathan Astle his side were within 32 runs of victory and had more than 20 overs left to get them. There were no other fireworks and a couple more wickets fell, but the result was never in doubt. The Proteas won by five wickets halfway through the 38th over. Cronje, who took the time to say a few phrases to the crowd in Urdu was named Man of the Match. The South African coach, Bob Woolmer, felt his side put on an awesome display, 'The best since I've been in charge'.

NEW ZEALAND

C.M. Spearman c Palframan b Matthews	14
N.J. Astle run out	1
S.P. Fleming b McMillan	33
R.G. Twose c McMillan b Pollock	13
C.L. Cairns b Donald	9
A.C. Parore run out	27
C.Z. Harris run out	8
S.A. Thomson c Cronje b Donald	28
L.K. Germon (capt-wk) not out	31
G.R. Larsen c Cullinan b Donald	1
D.K. Morrison not out	5
Extras (lb 5, nb 2)	7
(50 overs)	9–177

1/7 2/17 3/36 4/54 5/85 6/103 7/116 8/158 9/165

Bowling: Pollock 10-1-44-1; Matthews 10-2-30-1; Donald 10-0-34-3; Cronje 3-0-13-0; Symcox 10-1-25-0; McMillan 7-1-26-1

SOUTH AFRICA

G. Kirsten lbw Harris	35
S.J. Palframan (wk) b Morrison	16
W.J. Cronje (capt) c Fleming b Astle	78
D.J. Cullinan c Thomson b Astle	27
J.H. Kallis not out	11
J.N. Rhodes c & b Larsen	9
B.M. McMillan not out	2
Extras	0
(37.3 overs)	5–178

Did not bat: S.M. Pollock, C.R. Matthews, P.L. Symcox, A.A.A. Donald

1/41 2/87 3/146 4/159 5/170

Bowling: Morrison 8-0-44-1; Cairns 6-0-24-0; Larsen 8-1-41-1; Harris 4-0-25-1; Thomson 8.3-0-34-0; Astle 3-1-10-2

Umpires: S.G. Randell, S. Venkataraghavan.

Toss: New Zealand. Points: South Africa 2 New Zealand 0

WEDNESDAY 21 FEBRUARY 1996
GROUP A SRI LANKA vs ZIMBABWE
SINHALESE SPORTS CLUB, COLOMBO: SRI LANKA WON BY 6 WICKETS

At last World Cup cricket came to Sri Lanka and their fans embraced it with a fervour. No wonder. Two of their batsmen turned on an exhilarating exhibition of power strokeplay which broke national records and to some extent brought the competition to life.

This was not quite the run feast of New Plymouth 1992, but by putting on 172 in 27

overs Aravinda de Silva and Asanka Gurusinha kept everyone in attendance royally entertained to a similar degree. Zimbabwe being prepared to travel to Colombo, were popular visitors. They were given tight and vigilant security and played the game in a fine spirit. They left without two points, though, and that would have disappointed them.

Zimbabwe batted first when Andy Flower won the toss and on a good wicket it took a long time for them to get going. Their start was marred by both openers, the Flower bothers, being run out. Andy was the first to go, victim of a direct-hit throw by Chaminda Vaas. Steve Dunne, from New Zealand, who gave the decision had not been certain to travel to Sri Lanka, either. Andy Flower might have been happier if he had not come. Dunne gave the Zimbabwean captain out without checking with the replay which suggested Flower had actually made his ground. Guy Whittall rather than the umpire was to blame for Grant Flower's run-out.

A couple of other decisions indicated Dunne might not have been entirely at ease with his situation on this day. Alistair Campbell was, however, and it was the big left-hander who gave the Zimbabwean innings some impetus. That came after Muttiah Muralitharan had been joyously welcomed to the bowling crease by his home fans. The unorthodox off spinner, recently called for throwing in Australia, then had Guy Whittall caught at long-on to make the Zimbabwean total 3–92.

Campbell added 68 with Andy Waller and went on to finish with an accomplished 75, which contained seven fours, in 102 balls. Supplemented by some effective late-over work by Craig Evans, Zimbabwe were able to set Sri Lanka a respectable target of 229.

It looked more than respectable when Heath Streak removed both openers by the fifth over. The Zimbabwean paceman's first ball of the innings had gone for four wides, and indeed his opening over cost 11 runs. In the middle of it, though, Romesh Kaluwitharana, suffering from cramp but declining a runner, slogged a catch to mid-on. Sanath Jayasuriya also went cheaply before de Silva and Gurusinha began their display.

They treated all bowlers with the same disrespect. Leg-spinner Paul Strang made no impact this time, going for more than eight per over. Gurusinha was brutal at times. He struck six powerful sixes, five of them straight hits between long-off and long-on. He brought up the 100 with his variation on a six hitting theme, a big pull over mid wicket off Streak. Gurusinha's sixth six equalled the World Cup record held by Viv Richards and Kapil Dev.

de Silva's innings was more cultured and contained only two blows over the boundary, although the first, a trademark pull off Charlie Lock, was perhaps the shot of the game and the stroke that ignited the Sri Lankans. Although still recovering from a side strain suffered in Australia, de Silva struck 10 fours in addition to his two sixes, compiling the highest score ever by a Sri Lankan in a World Cup match.

Both batsmen missed their hundreds. Gurusinha was run out because he was so

ZIMBABWE

A. Flower (capt-wk) run out	8
G.W. Flower run out	15
G.J. Whittall c Jayasuriya b Muralitharan	35
A.D.R. Campbell c Muralitharan b Vaas	75
A.C. Waller b Jayasuriya	19
C.N. Evans not out	39
H.H. Streak c de Silva b Vaas	15
P.A. Strang not out	0
Extras (b 1, lb 16, w 4, nb 1)	22
(50 overs)	6–228

Did not bat: S.G. Peall, E.A. Brandes, A.C.I. Lock

1/19 2/51 3/92 4/160 5/194 6/227

Bowling: Vaas 10-0-30-2; Wickremasinghe 8-0-36-0; Ranatunga 2-0-14-0; Muralitharan 10-0-37-1; Dharmasena 10-0-50-0; Jayasuriya 10-0-44-1

SRI LANKA

S.T. Jayasuriya b Streak	6
R.S. Kaluwitharana (wk) c Peall b Streak	0
A.P. Gurusinha run out	87
P.A. de Silva lbw Streak	91
A. Ranatunga (capt) not out	13
H.P. Tillekeratne not out	7
Extras (lb 5, w 17, nb 3)	25
(37 overs)	4–229

Did not bat: R.S. Mahanama, H.D.P.K. Dharmasena, W.P.U.J.W.U.J.C. Vaas, G.G.P. Wickremasinghe, M. Muralitharan

1/5 2/23 3/195 4/209

Bowling: Sreak 10-0-60-3; Lock 4-0-17-0; Peall 3-0-23-0; Brandes 8-0-35-0; Strang 5-0-43-0; Whittall 2-0-20-0; G.W. Flower 5-1-26-0

Umpires: R.S. Dunne, Mahboob Shah.

Toss: Zimbabwe. Points: Sri Lanka 2, Zimbabwe 0

exhausted he couldn't make the crease in time. De Silva was given out lbw 14 runs later to the disappointment of the crowd, although it did not deny him his Man of the Match award. That gave Streak his third wicket, a good return spoilt by the number of wides he sent down. The Zimbabweans won more plaudits when they stayed on the field through drizzle towards the end of the game. The Sri Lankans celebrated their victory with 13 overs to spare.

WEDNESDAY 21 FEBRUARY 1996
GROUP A INDIA vs WEST INDIES
CAPTAIN ROOP SINGH STADIUM, GWALIOR: INDIA WON BY 5 WICKETS

Under lights that highlighted the smoke from fireworks and torches, India secured an important victory which kept them apace with Sri Lanka. The game was noisily supported in large numbers, the natural attraction of a contest between the co-hosts and their high-profile opponents being boosted to even greater levels by publicity for the 'Lara vs Tendulkar' batting shoot out.

Brian Lara, greeted on the ground by many cheers and the odd racist taunt, was an early casualty and India eventually had a comfortable win. So that turned into a fizzer, yet there were few complaints. The win and a Man of the Match innings by Sachin Tendulkar compensated nicely.

Richie Richardson won the toss, batted, said he was looking for 300 and faced the new-ball himself with Sherwin Campbell. He soon lost his Barbadian partner to Javagal Srinath, whose movement and bounce troubled the batsmen in an opening spell of 2–14 from seven overs. The big blow to the West Indies was the loss of Lara in the sixth over, given out caught behind down the leg side by Pakistani umpire Khizar Hayat, a decision over which there was some doubt. Richardson and Shivnarine Chanderpaul responded with a solid stand that took the score to 2–91, then the captain's dismissal heralded the loss of three wickets in 12 balls.

Roger Harper hit a six and put on 42 with wicketkeeper Courtney Browne before there was another three wicket in 12 balls collapse, Anil Kumble's leg spin doing its share of the damage.

The West Indian fast bowlers battled through until the final ball of the innings. A total of 173 was well short of Richardson's projected target.

The loss of 8–82 meant the batting frailties of 1992 still existed in the West Indian line-up and 173 on a good wicket would have been quite inadequate against virtually any other attack. It would prove so again this time, but did not appear the case when Curtly Ambrose beat Ajay Jadeja for pace in the first over and did likewise to Navjot Sidhu in the third.

The West Indies could have further undermined the Indians from 2–15. Tendulkar on 12 was dropped at square leg, then on 22 in the 10th over he skyed a leg-side shot which dollied in the air only for wicketkeeper Browne to fumble it. That allowed the young star to put on 79 in 16 overs with Mohammad Azharuddin and another 31 with Vinod Kambli after his captain was caught in the deep. Tendulkar got to 70 in 91 balls with eight fours when he was run out following a mix-up with his old schoolmate, Kambli.

Harper caught Prabhakar off his own bowling to briefly revive West Indian hopes. Kambli and Nayan Mongia soon quashed those, taking runs with some ease off Otis Gibson, and in his later overs, Ambrose. Between them the Indian sixth wicket pair struck seven fours and a six as the winning runs were obtained before the completion of the 40th over. The announcement of Tendulkar's Man of the Match award was yet another cause for local joy.

WEST INDIES	
S.L. Campbell b Srinath	5
R.B. Richardson (capt) c Kambli b Prabhakar	47
B.C. Lara c Mongia b Srinath	2
S. Chanderpaul c Azharuddin b Kapoor	38
R.I.C. Holder b Kumble	0
R.A. Harper b Kumble	23
C.O. Browne (wk) b Prabhakar	18
O.D. Gibson b Kumble	6
I.R. Bishop run out	9
C.E.L. Ambrose c Kumble b Prabhakar	8
C.A. Walsh not out	9
Extras (lb 2, w 5, nb 1)	8
(50 overs)	173

1/16 2/24 3/91 4/99 5/99 6/141 7/141 8/149 9/162 10/173

Bowling: Prabhakar 10–0–39–3; Srinath 10–0–22–2; Kumble 10–0–35–3; Prasad 10–0–34–0; Kapoor 10–2–41–1

INDIA	
A.D. Jadeja b Ambrose	1
S.R. Tendulkar run out	70
N.S. Sidhu b Ambrose	1
M. Azharuddin (capt) c Walsh b Harper	32
V.G. Kambli not out	33
M. Prabhakar c & b Harper	1
N.R. Mongia (wk) not out	24
Extras (lb 3, w 1, nb 8)	12
(39.4 overs)	5–174

Did not bat: A.R. Kapoor, A. Kumble, J. Srinath, B.K.B.K.V. Prasad

1/2 2/15 3/94 4/125 5/127

Bowling: Ambrose 8–1–41–2; Walsh 9–3–18–0; Bishop 5–0–28–0; Gibson 8.4–0–50–0; Harper 9–1–34–2

Umpires: Khizar Hayat, I.D. Robinson.

Toss: West Indies. Points: India 2, West Indies 0

THURSDAY 22 FEBRUARY 1996
GROUP B ENGLAND vs HOLLAND
SHAHI BAGH STADIUM, PESHAWAR: ENGLAND WON BY 49 RUNS

A 500–run day was watched by a healthier Peshawar gathering than the one attending the previous Sunday when UAE were accounted for. Their reward was some energetic batting from both sides, England's being superior enough to ensure a comfortable victory.

The first all-European World Cup cricket match saw England bat first and run up what turned out to be a match-winning total after Mike Atherton had won the toss. The captain, batting down the order, missed out again, bowled dab cutting at Steve Lubbers and Alec Stewart provided Paul Jan Bakker with an early wicket. Neil Smith was back to reasonably robust health and it was his 31 in 33 balls which took advantage of the early fielding restrictions. Once he had been caught by Nolan Clarke, Graeme Hick and Graham Thorpe tore the Dutch attack apart.

Hick gave two hard chances with flat-batted drives. Otherwise he was his usual assertive self against second-string bowling. He was still not quite as impressive as Thorpe, who belted seven fours and a six in 82 balls on the way to 89. Thorpe scored the majority of the runs in a 25-over partnership with Hick worth 143 for the third wicket. A hundred beckoned for the Surrey left-hander until Roland Lefebvre, bravely struggling against injury, had an lbw shout upheld.

It was Hick, picking up the tempo with Neil Fairbrother towards the end of the innings, who did reach three figures. He had rested his strained hamstring against UAE and showed no ill effects here as he raised his second 100 in Limited-Over Internationals with a big six off Bakker. It was his second six in 133 balls and came in the 50th over of the innings.

Dominic Cork, despite being too sharp for the 47-year-old opener Clarke, conceded plenty of runs, including wides and no-balls, and it was left to the altogether more accurate DeFreitas to reduce Holland to 4–81. Tim de Leede had stroked his way impressively to a run per ball 41, but it was Klaas van Noortwijk and 18-year-old Bas Zuiderent who showed that the gap in class between the two sides was not so marked. They put on 114 for the fifth wicket in 27 overs. England's left-arm spinner Richard Illingworth, had pulled out of the side with a stomach upset and the young Dutchmen relished the diet of medium pace and off spin. They both completed half centuries, their country's first in Limited-Over Internationals. Van Noortwijk once deposited Peter Martin deep into the cheering crowd.

Top-order batsman Flavian Alponso was another down with stomach trouble and the required run rate was always demanding. When

Martin had van Noortwijk caught in the deep and Zuiderent taken by Thorpe the sting went out of the game. Hick was named Man of the Match.

ENGLAND

A.J. Stewart b Bakker	5
N.M.K. Smith c Clarke b Jansen	31
G.A. Hick not out	104
G.P. Thorpe lbw Lefebvre	89
M.A. Atherton (capt) b Lubbers	10
N.H. Fairbrother not out	24
Extras (lb 12, w 4)	16
(50 overs)	4–279

Did not bat: R.C. Russell (wk), D.G. Cork, D. Gough, P.A.J. DeFreitas, P.J. Martin

1/11 2/42 3/185 4/212

Bowling: Lefebvre 10-1-40-1; Bakker 8-0-46-1; Jansen 7-0-40-1; Aponso 8-0-55-0; Lubbers 10-0-51-1; de Leede 2-0-9-0; Cantrell 5-0-26-0

HOLLAND

N.E. Clarke lbw Cork	0
P.E. Cantrell lbw DeFreitas	28
T.B.M. de Leede lbw DeFreitas	41
S.W. Lubbers (capt) c Russell b DeFreitas	9
K.J.J. van Noortwijk c Gough b Martin	64
B. Zuiderent c Thorpe b Martin	54
R.P. Lefebvre not out	11
M. Schewe (wk) not out	11
Extras (lb 4, w 6, nb 2)	12
(50 overs)	6–230

Did not bat: G.J.A.F. Aponso, F. Jansen, P.J. Bakker

1/1 2/46 3/70 4/81 5/195 6/208

Bowling: Cork 8-0-52-1; DeFreitas 10-3-31-3; Smith 8-0-27-0; Gough 3-0-23-0; Martin 10-1-42-2; Hick -0-23-0; Thorpe 6-0-28-0

Umpires: S.A. Bucknor, K.T. Francis.

Toss: England. Points: England 2, Holland 0

FRIDAY 23 FEBRUARY 1996
GROUP A AUSTRALIA vs KENYA
INDIRA PRIYADARSHINI MUNICIPAL CRICKET GROUND, VISAKHAPATNAM:
AUSTRALIA WON BY 97 RUNS

Finally, a week after the start of the Wills World Cup, Australia got themselves onto a cricket field. It was hardly a major fixture at the Indian east coast venue which is more than a mouthful for anyone not conversant with the local dialect, but still moved attention away from boycotts, security and various perceived threats.

Mark Taylor's side would have been grateful to be able to get rid of a few cobwebs without massive pressure being exerted upon them by Kenya. While the Kenyans at no stage looked like pulling off the surprise their fellow Africans, Zimbabwe, achieved in 1983, they kept apace with their highly rated opponents at various stages of the match and went down fighting.

Maurice Odumbe decided to bowl after he won the toss and Martin Suji and Rajab Ali responded by removing Mark Taylor and Ricky Ponting by the eighth over, leaving Australia 2–26. Mark and Steve Waugh were also beaten more than once early in their innings. Once they

had become accustomed to the bowling, the lack of pace in the wicket and the heat, they established what became a record-breaking and match-winning partnership.

The twins took a heavy toll of the second-string bowlers, who conceded 159 between them from 20 overs. Mark Waugh was dropped off consecutive deliveries in the 27th over. Ali at long-off spilled a lofted drive and next ball wicketkeeper Kennedy Otieno got a glove to an edge. As Mark Waugh was already on 75 the misses probably did not alter the result. They did, however, allow 'Junior' Waugh to complete his first World Cup 100 and to go on to his equal highest score in a Limited-Over International.

He scored his 130 at just above a run per ball, often gasping for breath in the heat and humidity, and hit 14 fours and a six in the process. The partnership with Steve put on 207 for the third wicket in 32 overs, the first double century stand in the World Cup. Steve's 82 lasted 88 balls and contained five fours and one six. He drove a catch back to Suji the over after Mark had been dismissed, leaving the task of lifting the total above 300 to Stuart Law, Michael Bevan and Ian Healy.

Craig McDermott had Deepak Chudasama caught behind with a nice outswinger at the start of the Kenyan reply, only to strain a doubtful calf muscle and walk off the ground for Australia for the last time after the fifth over. Paul Reiffel then claimed the prize wicket of Steve Tikolo to leave Kenya in trouble at 2–30. They were still not overwhelmed by their opposition as Maurice Odumbe showed when he cover drove his first ball for four. That heralded the start of a 102-run stand between the Kenyan captain and his wicketkeeper, Otieno. Steve Waugh's medium pacers were treated with some disrespect. So effective was the strokeplay of the Kenyan pair that at the halfway point of the innings their score was comparable with Australia's at the same stage.

Odumbe got to his fifty in 53 balls with seven fours, then fell to Michael Bevan's, at that stage, little-known left-arm wrist spin. That was a blow to Kenya, but not as serious as the leg cramping that caused the temporary retirement of Otieno at 3–166. The wicketkeeper-batsman was suffering after 85 overs straight in the heat and had to leave the field 18 short of his 100. Although he later resumed, the Kenyans never again regained their batting momentum. Otieno added only three before being yorked by Glenn McGrath and Shane Warne kept the runs well in check. Otieno had hit eight fours and a six. Mark Waugh's innings, though, was the one the Man of the Match adjudicator rated the highest.

AUSTRALIA	
M.A. Taylor (capt) c Modi b Suji	6
M.E. Waugh c Suji b Ali	130
R.T. Ponting c Otieno b Ali	6
S.R. Waugh c & b Suji	82
S.G. Law run out	35
M.G. Bevan b Ali	12
I.A. Healy (wk) c E.O. Odumbe b Karim	17
P.R. Reiffel not out	3
S.K. Warne not out	0
Extras (b 1, w 10, nb 2)	13
(50 overs)	7–304

Did not bat: C.J. McDermott, G.D. McGrath

1/10 2/26 3/233 4/237 5/261 6/301 7/301

Bowling: Suji 10-1-55-2; Ali 10-0-45-3; Odoyo 8-0-58-0; E.O. Odumbe 4-0-21-0; Karim 10-1-54-1; M.O. Odumbe 4-0-35-0; D. Tikolo 3-0-21-0; S.O. Tikolo 1-0-14-0

KENYA	
K.O. Otieno (wk) b McGrath	85
D.N. Chudasama c Healy b McDermott	5
S.O. Tikolo c Ponting b Reiffel	6
M.O. Odumbe (capt) c Reiffel b Bevan	50
H.S. Modi b Bevan	10
E.O. Odumbe c Bevan b Reiffel	14
D. Tikolo not out	11
T.M. Odoyo st Healy b Warne	10
M.A. Suji not out	1
Extras (lb 7, w 6, nb 2)	15
(50 overs)	7–207

Did not bat: A.Y. Karim, R.W. Ali

1/12 2/30 3/132 4/167 5/188 6/195 7/206 Otieno ret hurt (82*) resumed 5–188

Bowling: McDermott 3-0-12-1; Reiffel 7-1-18-2; McGrath 10-0-44-1; S.R. Waugh 7-0-43-0; Warne 10-0-25-1; M.E. Waugh 5-0-23-0; Bevan 8-0-35-2

Umpires: C.J. Mitchley, D.R. Shepherd.

Toss: Kenya. Points: Australia 2, Kenya 0

SATURDAY 24 FEBRUARY 1996
GROUP B PAKISTAN vs UAE
JINAH STADIUM, GUJRANWALA: PAKISTAN WON BY 9 WICKETS

Pakistan had taken even longer than Australia to get on to a cricket ground in the World Cup. Their delay was because of the fast of Ramadan rather than fear of bombs. Like the Australians, Pakistan's opening fixture almost amounted to a warm-up and they had no trouble at all disposing of an inept UAE side.

Heavy overnight rain in the northern Pakistani city left the roads to the Jinah Stadium difficult and muddy and the outfield so saturated the match could not start until 12.15 pm. It had to be reduced to 33 overs per side. Pakistan included Javed Miandad. The 38-year-old veteran was making his sixth appearance in a World Cup tournament, being the sole survivor from 1975. His selection was very popular at the other end of the country in Karachi.

Eventually, Miandad would not bat as Pakistan's surge to victory came very quickly at minimal cost. They had only needed 110 to win and got them in 18 overs. Sultan Zarawani had bravely suggested his side's uninhibited batting style might be suited by the overs reduction and when Saleem Raza charged out of the blocks all guns blazing after UAE were sent in, it seemed he might be right. With the ball swinging around in the damp atmosphere, the opener cracked two fours and swung Wasim Akram away for a six over square leg in 20 balls before skying a catch to give Miandad his only real action for the game.

The only other UAE batsman to top 20 was Shaukat Dukanwala, who also hit a worthy six off Waqar Younis. In between, no-one could work out the leg-spin of Man of the Match Mushtaq Ahmed, whose three wickets came in 10 balls. The first of those was his 100th in Limited-Over Internationals. The 33rd and final over of the innings bowled by Waqar Younis was a wicket maiden.

The crowd half-filled the ground and were happy at the ease of their side's progress, making plenty of wisecracks as they jumped and waved banners. They were briefly quietened when Johanne Samarasekera got through Aamir Sohail's defence in the first over. Unfortunately Samarasekera also sent down a 12-ball over as he sprayed the new ball around. Wides were plentiful and soon Saeed Anwar and Ijaz Ahmed were moving into their work. The runs began to flow with ease. They added 105 in 106 balls, Ijaz reaching his fifty just before the win was completed with 15 overs, not much less than half the allotment, to spare.

UNITED ARAB EMIRATES

G. Mylvaganam b Mushtaq Ahmed	13
Saleem Raza c Javed Miandad b Aqib Javed	22
Azhar Saeed run out	1
Mazhar Hussain c Waqar Younis b Mushtaq Ahmed	7
Mohammad Aslam b Mushtaq Ahmed	5
Mohammad Ishaq b Wasim Akram	12
Arshad Laeeq c Ijaz Ahmed b Aqib Javed	9
J.A. Samarasekera b Waqar Younis	10
S.F. Dukanwala not out	21
Sultan, M. Zarawani (capt) b Wasim Akram	1
Imtiaz Abbasi (wk) not out	0
Extras (lb 1, w 5, nb 2)	8
(33 overs)	9–109

1/27 2/40 3/47 4/53 5/54 6/70 7/80 8/108 9/109

Bowling: Wasim Akram 7–1–25–2; Waqar Younis 7–0–33–1; Aqib Javed 6–0–18–2; Mushtaq Ahmed 7–0–16–3; Aamir Sohail 6–0–16–0

PAKISTAN

Aamir Sohail b Samarasekera	5
Saeed Anwar not out	40
Ijaz Ahmed not out	50
Extras (lb 1, w 12, nb 4)	17
(18 overs)	1–112

Did not bat: Inzamam-ul-Haq, Salim Malik, Javed Miandad, Wasim Akram (capt), Rashid Latif (wk), Mushtaq Ahmed, Waqar Younis, Aqib Javed

1/7

Bowling: Samarasekera 3–0–17–1; Arshad Laeeq 4–0–17–0; Dukanwala 3–1–14–0; Saleem Raza 3–0–17–0; Sultan Zarawani 3–0–23–0; Azhar Saeed 2–0–16–0

Umpires: B.C. Cooray, S. Venkataraghavan.

Toss: Pakistan. Points: Pakistan 2, UAE 0

SUNDAY 25 FEBRUARY 1996
GROUP B ENGLAND vs SOUTH AFRICA
RAWALPINDI CRICKET STADIUM, RAWALPINDI: SOUTH AFRICA WON BY 78 RUNS

Even without an incapacitated Allan Donald, the mean and lean South African bowling attack, supported by their intimidating fieldsmen, were far too good for England's batsmen who lacked confidence between bouts of carelessness. The decisive margin of defeat of 78 runs still flattered England. At one stage they had been 7–97 chasing 230.

No South African played a major innings, the highest score in their 230 was opener Gary Kirsten's 38, yet they hardly relaxed the psychological grip they had recently built over England. It was an edge that had netted the Proteas six wins from seven starts in Limited-Over Internationals against Mike Atherton's maligned side.

There was cloud and drizzle about when Hansie Cronje won the toss and decided to bat. Dampness had hampered England's match preparation and they had complained. That raised once more the sensitivities and disputes that raged between Pakistan and England during the 1980s and in 1992. Poor facilities had nothing to do with Robin Smith's bruised calf which prevented him from playing yet again. Smith was struck on his unprotected leg when he decided to practise with only his front pad on.

Dominic Cork missed a skyed catch off Steve Palframan which allowed the South African openers to launch the innings with a 12-over partnership of 56. They then slipped to 3–88. Gary Kirsten was run out by Alec Stewart from mid-on and Hansie Cronje was caught behind from a Darren Gough outswinger. Daryll Cullinan and 20-year-old Jacques Kallis had retrieved the situation when rain held up play for 20 minutes at 3–133. Neither batsman got going

again upon the resumption and it was left to Jonty Rhodes, as energetic at times with the bat as he is in the field, to ensure South Africa got above 200. There were no easy wickets for England to the end. Fanie de Villiers, in the side for the ailing Donald, batted last and also got to double figures before falling to Gough from the last ball of the 50th over. Gough like Cork had taken two wickets, but the big Lancastrian, Peter Martin, was the best performed of the English bowlers. Perhaps the cloud and drizzle made him feel like he was at home in Manchester.

Mike Atherton promoted himself back to the opening position and was promptly caught behind from the fourth ball of the innings. It was a setback from which England never really recovered. Neil Smith fell next, then the previously in-form Graeme Hick clipped a catch to Brian McMillan at mid wicket. The recalled de Villiers had snared both of them and England were 3–33. Graham Thorpe was relishing the scrap and momentarily his Surrey team-mate, Alec Stewart, dug in as well. Normal service was resumed on 52, however, when Stewart failed to ground his bat while strolling through for a single and Pat Symcox threw down the stumps from mid-on.

The off-spinner soon had Neil Fairbrother caught behind sweeping and it was 5–62. 'Jack'

SOUTH AFRICA	
G. Kirsten run out	38
S.J. Palframan (wk) c Russell b Martin	28
W.J. Cronje (capt) c Russell b Gough	15
D.J. Cullinan b DeFreitas	34
J.H. Kallis c Russell b Cork	26
J.N. Rhodes b Martin	37
B.M. McMillan b Smith	11
S.M. Pollock c Fairbrother b Cork	12
P.L. Symcox c Thorpe b Martin	1
C.R. Matthews not out	9
P.S. de Villiers c Smith b Gough	12
Extras (lb 1, w 5, nb 1)	7
(50 overs)	10–230

1/56 2/85 3/88 4/137 5/163 6/195 7/199 8/202 9/213 10/230

Bowling: Cork 10-0-36-2; DeFreitas 10-0-55-1; Gough 10-0-48-2; Martin 10-0-33-3; Smith 8-0-40-1; Thorpe 2-0-17-0

ENGLAND	
M.A. Atherton (capt) c Palframan b Pollock	0
N.M.K. Smith b de Villiers	11
G.A. Hick c McMillan b de Villiers	14
G.P. Thorpe c Palframan b Symcox	46
A.J. Stewart run out	7
N.H. Fairbrother c Palframan b Symcox	3
R.C. Russell (wk) c Rhodes b Pollock	12
D.G. Cork b Matthews	17
P.A.J. DeFreitas run out	22
D. Gough b Matthews	11
P.J. Martin not out	1
Extras (lb 7, w 1)	8
(44.3 overs)	10–152

1/0 2/22 3/33 4/52 5/62 6/97 7/97 8/139 9/141 10/152

Bowling: Pollock 8-1-16-2; de Villiers 7-1-27-2; Matthews 9.3-0-30-2; McMillan 6-0-17-0; Symcox 10-0-38-2; Cronje 4-0-17-0

Umpires: S.G. Randell, I.D. Robinson.

Toss: South Africa. Points: South Africa 2, England 0

Russell's determination to stay with Thorpe was already merely token resistance as the result was well in hand. Both eventually fell at 97, Thorpe at least finished with the highest individual score of the match. DeFreitas' aggression brought him a few boundaries and allowed England to reach a total the equivalent of the one UAE made against South Africa 10 days before. He too was run out when he failed to ground his bat. England was dismissed in the 45th over.

At the post-match conference a spiky Atherton called one Pakistani journalist 'a buffoon'. He would have been better looking at his own team or, with no form at all, himself. He apologised the next day. Jonty Rhodes was named Man of the Match.

SUNDAY 25 FEBRUARY 1996
GROUP A SRI LANKA vs WEST INDIES
R. PREMEDASA STADIUM, COLOMBO: SRI LANKA WON ON FORFEIT

The West Indies, like Australia, held to their promise to keep away from Sri Lanka, thus handing the hosts two points and a guaranteed place in the quarter-finals. They were concerned, though, that they would lack match practice as they had to wait eight days between games. The West Indies' worries centred on Brian Lara who was taking his turn to suffer stomach troubles.

Umpires: Mahboob Shah, V.K. Ramaswamy.
Points: Sri Lanka 2, West Indies 0

MONDAY 26 FEBRUARY 1996
GROUP B PAKISTAN vs HOLLAND
GADDAFI STADIUM, LAHORE: PAKISTAN WON BY 8 WICKETS

Sixteen thousand people turned up at the Gaddafi Stadium and Javed Miandad was not needed again! Perhaps it was the fault of the suspect spaghetti that laid low half the Dutch team with diarrhoea just before the match. Their batting was very much lacking in energy. Steve Lubbers actually missed the game, but with a bad knee, not gastric difficulty. Whatever, this was a very one-sided affair that required the employment of just four Pakistani batsmen for about 30 overs to achieve the desired result for the home side.

The first mismatch after acting Dutch captain Roland Lefebvre had won the toss and batted was 47-year-old Nolan Clarke facing Wasim Akram and a fired-up Waqar Younis with a swinging new ball. When Younis removed Peter Cantrell and Tim de Leede with consecutive deliveries Holland was a desperate-looking 3–29. A partnership of 73 between Klaas van Noortwijk and Flavian Aponso averted a rout. Both batsmen hit a six off Mushtaq Ahmed while generally batting at a tempo unsuited to limited-overs cricket. Aponso, a former Sri Lankan 'rebel' tourist of South Africa who worked in the Sri Lankan embassy in The Hague, went on to his half century. Younis finally bowled him and Lefebvre to make his haul four out of the seven wickets that fell.

Pakistan's ask was less than three per over and not even the enthusiastic Lefebvre claiming the early wicket of Aamir Sohail could make the task seem more than it was. After 14 overs Pakistan were 1–34, and below the required rate. At the completion of the 15th over the score was 1–48 and Saeed Anwar and Ijaz Ahmed had assumed control. Their urgency grew as rain clouds gathered during the afternoon. The acceleration continued even when Ijaz was caught off Cantrell. Anwar raced on to 83 off 92 balls. In addition to nine fours he hit three sixes which scattered the modest crowd as they landed. Inzamam-ul-Haq celebrated his first innings of the tournament by opening his account with a six, too. The third of Anwar's sixes, a massive strike over long-on off Erik Gouka, completed the victory. The players had not long left the field when it began to rain heavily. That dampened the presentation of the Man of the Match award to Waqar Younis.

Attendances in Pakistan remained lower than anticipated. The team might have been keeping pace with India, but their fans were behind in their commitment. With Ramadan over the blame now centred on the poor arrangements for ticket sales.

HOLLAND

N.E. Clarke c Rashid Latif b Aqib Javed	4
P.E. Cantrell c Ijaz Ahmed b Waqar Younis	17
T.B.M. de Leede c Rashid Latif b Waqar Younis	0
K.J.J. van Noortwijk c Mushtaq Ahmed b Aqib Javed	33
G.J.A.F. Aponso b Waqar Younis	58
R.P. Lefebvre (capt) b Waqar Younis	10
B. Zuiderent run out	6
E. Gouka not out	0
Extras (lb 7, w 4, nb 6)	17
(50 overs)	7–145

Did not bat: F. Jansen, M. Schewe (wk), P.J. Bakker

1/16 2/28 3/29 4/102 5/130 6/143 7/145

Bowling: Wasim Akram 10–1–30–0; Waqar Younis 10–1–26–4; Aqib Javed 9–2–25–2; Mushtaq Ahmed 10–2–27–0; Aamir Sohail 9–0–21–0; Salim Malik 2–0–9–0

PAKISTAN

Aamir Sohail c Jansen b Lefebvre	9
Saeed Anwar not out	83
Ijaz Ahmed c Lefebvre b Cantrell	39
Inzamam-ul-Haq not out	18
Extras (lb 1, w 1)	2
(30.4 overs)	2–151

Did not bat: Salim Malik, Javed Miandad, Wasim Akram (capt), Rashid Latif (wk), Mushtaq Ahmed, Waqar Younis, Aqib Javed

1/10 2/104

Bowling: Lefebvre 7–1–20–1; Bakker 7–1–13–0; Jansen 2–0–22–0; de Leede 4–0–20–0; Aponso 5–0–38–0; Cantrell 4–0–18–1; Gouka 1.4–0–19–0

Umpires: S.A. Bucknor, K.T. Francis.

Toss: Holland. Points: Pakistan 2, Holland 0

MONDAY 26 and TUESDAY 27 FEBRUARY 1996
GROUP A KENYA vs ZIMBABWE
MOIN-UL-HAQ STADIUM, PATNA: ZIMBABWE WON BY 5 WICKETS

When World Cup cricket came to Patna in the north-east corner of India the locals responded with such enthusiasm that they were rewarded with two matches for the price of one.

The 30,000 who turned up on the Monday only saw 95 balls bowled but they received, at no extra charge, a close encounter with a helicopter. The flying machine with the giant fan had been brought in to help the drying when rain soaked the ground after an hour's cricket. It had been a good hour for Kenya, and for Edward Odumbe in particular.

Andy Flower had won the toss for Zimbabwe and in cloudy conditions elected to bat. He sent in Andy Waller to open with his brother, Grant Flower, probably to reduce his own onerous duties as captain, wicketkeeper and batsman. The move did not succeed as Rajab Ali quickly made the first breakthrough. Edward Odumbe then had Guy Whittall caught by brother and captain, Maurice, and trapped Alistair Campbell lbw first

ZIMBABWE

G.W. Flower not out	25
A.C. Waller c E.O. Odumbe b Ali	3
G.J. Whittall c M.O. Odumbe b E.O. Odumbe	12
A.D.R. Campbell lbw, E.O. Odumbe	0
A. Flower (capt-wk) not out	0
Extras (lb 1, w 4)	5
(15.5 overs)	3–45

Did not bat: C.N. Evans, H.H. Streak, P.A. Strang, B.C. Strang, S.G. Peall, A.C.I. Lock

1/8 2/44 3/45

Bowling: Suji 5–1–11–0; Ali 5–0–14–1; Odoyo 3–0–10–0; E.O. Odumbe 2.5–0–8–2

KENYA

D.N. Chudasama, I.T. Iqbal (wk), K.O. Otieno, S.O. Tikolo, M.O. Odumbe (capt) H.S. Modi, E.O. Odumbe, T.M. Odoyo, A.Y. Karim, M.A. Suji, R.W. Ali

MATCH ABANDONED

ball. It was only the 16th over and Andy Flower had to come in anyway. As it turned out that was as far as the cricket got on the Monday.

Once the rain stopped every effort was made to restart the game. The idea of the helicopter was a good one. Alas, the execution was lacking. Instead of drying the ground, the wind from the rotor blades blew the covers away and deposited the water from them onto the pitch. Play was abandoned for the day and the game was declared void. According to *Wisden*, an ICC ruling directed abandoned matches like this to receive recognition as a Limited-Over International.

So to the next day; same venue, same players and umpires, seemingly same crowd, very different result. Consensus was that Kenya could have been on the verge of an upset in the Monday edition of this game. That was never an absolute certainty and on Tuesday Zimbabwe, courtesy of some brilliant Paul Strang leg spin, were well in control for most of the game.

Andy Flower had a change of heart when he won the toss again and this time he sent Kenya in. They lost Tariq Iqbal early, but Dipak Chudasama and Kennedy Otieno lifted the total to 1–60. Then four wickets went down in a

matter of moments as Kenya slipped to 5–67. Paul Strang's brother Bryan, a left-arm medium pacer, took two of those four wickets in quick succession, including Steve Tikolo.

Maurice and Edward Odumbe looked to have restored batting sanity when they added 42. It was an illusion. Paul Strang ripped the middle and lower order apart. He took three wickets in four balls, then closed the innings in the final over with two more victims in consecutive deliveries. Kenya had lost 9–74 after their solid start.

Andy Waller and Grant Flower made as if they were going to get the entire 135 runs Zimbabwe needed by themselves. They rattled up 59 in 13 overs, quickly hitting yesterday's threat, Edward Odumbe, out of the attack. Maurice was on the spot, though, and so were Asif Karim and Rajab Ali. Once Maurice Odumbe had dismissed Waller the Zimbabweans crawled to their victory, losing wickets here and there, mostly to Ali, along the way. The win was eventually achieved in lacklustre fashion in the 43rd over by five wickets. Paul Strang, having taken the best figures ever by a Zimbabwean in a Limited-Over International, was named Man of the Match.

KENYA

D.N. Chudasama run out	34
I.T. Iqbal (wk) b Lock	1
K.O. Otieno b Peall	19
S.O. Tikolo st, A. Flower b B. Strang	0
M.O. Odumbe (capt) c B. Strang b P. Strang	30
H.S. Modi b B. Strang	3
E.O. Odumbe c Campbell b P. Strang	20
T.M. Odoyo c G. Flower b P. Strang	0
A.Y. Karim lbw Strang	0
M.A. Suji c G. Flower b P. Strang	15
R.W. Ali not out	0
Extras (lb 3, w 8, nb 1)	12
(49.4 overs)	10–134

1/7 2/60 3/61 4/63 5/67 6/109 7/109 8/109 9/109 10/134

Bowling: Streak 7-2-23-0; Lock 8-2-19-1; Whittall 5-0-21-0; Peall 10-1-23-1; B.C. Strang 10-0-24-2; P.A. Strang 9.4-1-21-5

ZIMBABWE

A.C. Waller c Tikolo b M.O. Odumbe	30
G.W. Flower b Ali	45
A.D.R. Campbell c Tikolo b M.O. Odumbe	6
G.J. Whittall c E.O. Odumbe b Ali	6
A. Flower (capt-wk) lbw Ali	5
C.N. Evans not out	8
H.H. Streak not out	15
Extas: (b 3, lb 4, w 12, nb 3)	22
(42.2 overs)	5–137

Did not bat: P.A. Strang, S.G. Peall, B.C. Strang, A.C.I. Lock

1/59 2/79 3/104 4/108 5/113

Bowling: Suji 9.2-0-37-0; Ali 8-1-22-3; E.O. Odumbe 2-0-14-0; Odoyo 2-0-7-0; Karim 10-1-21-0; M.O. Odumbe 10-2-24-2; Tikolo 1-0-5-0

Umpires: Khizar Hayat, C.J. Mitchley.

Toss: Zimbabwe. Points: Zimbabwe 2, Kenya 0

TUESDAY 27 FEBRUARY 1996
GROUP B NEW ZEALAND vs UAE
IQBAL STADIUM, FAISALABAD: NEW ZEALAND WON BY 109 RUNS

Grey was the colour of both teams and also the colour of the overall interest surrounding this flat contest. New Zealand emerged from the fog to complete an easy win over UAE in what Lee Germon admitted was 'a good practice for our next match against Pakistan'. The two points they gained for their efforts at the Iqbal Stadium were enough to guarantee a place in the quarter-finals.

Visibility was not good at the scheduled start in Faisalabad. By the time the fog had lifted an hour had been lost and three overs had been deducted from each innings. Sultan Zarawani won the toss and sent New Zealand in. First-day tournament century-maker Nathan Astle was bowled by Johannes Samarasekera 10 minutes into proceedings. Stephen Fleming did not last long either, hitting a catch back to Shaukat Dukanwala after making his entire score in boundaries.

The Kiwi dominance of UAE began with the stand of 120 in 123 balls for the third wicket between Craig Spearman and Roger Twose. The opener was at his powerful best, striking 10 fours in 112 balls, while Twose, the ex-Warwickshire stalwart who may have felt some empathy with all the UAE imports, continued on towards his maiden century for New Zealand after his partner had perished to the reverse sweep.

He fell just eight runs short of the milestone after eight fours in 112 balls and it was left to Shane Thompson to give the total a final fillip. Danny Morrison came in at the fall of the eighth wicket with just two balls remaining in the innings. He faced the left-arm spin of Azhar Saeed who with three wickets was the most successful of the UAE bowlers. With no time for sighters, Morrison smacked his first ball for four then ended the innings with a six over long-on. His strike rate for the match was therefore 500!

Those extra 10 runs left UAE 277 to win in 47 overs. Some handy work from the top order, including a typical early burst of strokeplay from Saleem Raza, hinted at respectability even though a win was never a real prospect. The limited skill of the UAE middle order was once again apparent when the score slipped from 2–65 to 7–92. At that point an early finish seemed likely, but Samarasekera dominated stands with Arshad Laiq and Sultan Zarawani and the innings was able to run its meaningless course. Samarasekera, who had emigrated from Sri Lanka because of terrorist attacks near his home, at least had the pleasure of hitting seven fours in 59 balls from a Test standard attack. Twose was named Man of the Match.

NEW ZEALAND	
C.M. Spearman b Saleem Raza	78
N.J. Astle b Samarasekera	2
S.P. Fleming c & b Dukanwala	16
R.G. Twose c Mazhar Hussain b Azhar Saeed	92
C.L. Cairns c Abbasi b Sultan Zarawani	6
A.C. Parore c Azhar b Sultan Zarawani	15
S.A. Thomson not out	31
L.K. Germon (capt-wk) b Azhar Saeed	3
D.J. Nash lbw Azhar Saeed	8
D.K. Morrison not out	10
Extras (b 2, lb 12, nb 1)	15
(47 overs)	8–276

Did not bat: R.J. Kennedy

1/11 2/42 3/162 4/173 5/210 6/228 7/239 8/266

Bowling: Samarasekera 6-0-30-1; Arshad Laeeq 2-0-16-0; Dukanwala 10-0-46-1; Mazhar Hussain 3-0-28-0; Azhar Saeed 7-0-45-3; Saleem Raza 9-0-48-1; Sultan Zarawani 10-0-49-2

UNITED ARAB EMIRATES	
Azhar Saeed c Fleming b Nash	5
Saleem Raza c Kennedy b Morrison	21
Mazhar Hussain c Cairns b Thomson	29
V. Mehra c Cairns b Thomson	12
Mohammad Ishaq c Cairns b Kennedy	8
Mohammad Aslam c Twose b Thomson	1
S.F. Dukanwala c & b Cairns	8
Arshad Laeeq run out	14
J.A. Samarasekera not out	47
Sultan Zarawani (capt) c Thompson b Nash	13
Imtiaz Abbasi (wk) not out	2
Extras (lb 2, w 3, nb 2)	7
(47 overs)	9–167

1/23 2/29 3/65 4/72 5/82 6/87 7/92 8/124 9/162

Bowling: Morrison 7-0-37-1; Nash 9-1-34-2; Cairns 10-2-31-1; Kennedy 6-0-20-1; Thomson 10-2-20-3; Astle 5-0-23-0

Umpires: B.C. Cooray, S. Venkataraghavan.

Toss: UAE. Points: New Zealand 2, UAE 0

TUESDAY 27 FEBRUARY 1996
GROUP A INDIA vs AUSTRALIA
WANKHEDE STADIUM, MUMBAI (BOMBAY): AUSTRALIA WON BY 16 RUNS

Under lights in Mumbai, nearly two weeks into the tournament, the Wills World Cup finally produced a top-draw limited-overs cricket match. As in 1987 and 1992, Australia and India were involved in a great contest and if this one did not finish with the last-over dramas of the matches in Madras and Brisbane it was still rated more highly than nearly everything else in the 1996 tournament to that point.

That Australia won would have disappointed the majority of the 40,000 noisy and enthusiastic fans who crammed into the Wankhede Stadium for the ground's debut under lights. They could not, however, have questioned that the players gave them their money's worth. There were some great performances, moments of individual brilliance and a gathering tension as the climax built. For their part the players relished the knowledge of the spectators and the fantastic electric atmosphere they contributed.

With his team hungry for cricket, Mark Taylor won the toss and elected to bat. Then, unexpectedly, he took the role of chief aggressor instead of Mark Waugh in an attractive century-opening partnership. The Australian captain survived shouts for lbw and testing bowling from Javagal Srinath to loft the ball over the in field during the first 15 overs. Once he put Srinath away for six and by the time the fieldsmen were allowed outside the rings in numbers Australia were 0–74.

Venkatapathy Raju and Anil Kumble were able to stem the run flow with their accurate spin and in the 22nd over the slight looking left-armer, Raju, had Taylor caught at long-on. That signalled the start of Mark Waugh's dominance. He raised his 50 by sweeping Raju for six, then lost Ricky Ponting at 140, the Tasmanian being brilliantly caught low and one-handed by Sanjay Manjrekar off Raju at backward point. Seventeen runs later, Mark was indirectly responsible for the dismissal of his twin brother when Raju deflected a straight drive back onto the stumps with Steve, backing up, out of his ground.

So assured was Mark Waugh that he only needed someone to run with him. Stuart Law did that effectively as the total was taken from 157 to 232. Waugh reached his record-breaking second consecutive World Cup hundred in the 43rd over off 120 deliveries. He received a standing ovation which he celebrated by flat-batting Srinath over mid wicket for six to raise the Australian 200. Waugh was run-out from square leg attempting to turn a single into two after hitting eight fours and three sixes in 135 balls. It signalled an astonishing Australian collapse where they lost 7–26 through the last five overs. Venkatesh Prasad picked up a couple of those wickets in a hectic final over where four batsmen were dismissed for the addition of just two runs. That thrilled the crowd and, of course, the television sponsors who had heaps of their advertisements crammed in during that 50th over while batsmen walked in and out.

The procession of wickets temporarily continued when India began their pursuit of Australia's 258. With Craig McDermott and Paul Reiffel out of the side with injury, Damien Fleming got to share the new ball with Glenn McGrath and he made the most of his opportunity. While McGrath sent down three maidens in four overs, Fleming trapped Ajay Jadeja lbw, then bowled Vinod Kambli as the left-hander played loosely across the line.

Disaster loomed and Sachin Tendulkar's response was as brave as it was effective. McGrath paid dearly for missing a tough caught and bowled chance from the young local hero as Tendulkar took 27 runs from two of his overs. The Wankhede Stadium was alight in more ways than one and the spectacle of Tendulkar smashing the best Australia could offer on his home ground under lights was something special to behold. He lost his captain with the total on 70 when Mohammad Azharuddin played on a pull shot to a Fleming slower ball.

Still the crowd cheered, 'Sachin! Sachin! Sachin!'. He had completed his fifty from 41 balls, going from 12 to 56 in just 25 exhilarating balls. He found a solid partner in Manjrekar and paced himself in a slightly more measured fashion to build a stand of 73. Shane Warne tested both batsmen with his variation and accuracy after conceding 10 runs in his first over which included a straight-hit for six by Tendulkar from his first ball. However, it was Mark Waugh, bowling a spell of his off breaks, who gained the vital breakthrough. He saw Tendulkar move out of his crease and pushed the ball wide. It slid through to Ian Healy who completed the stumping in a flash. The adrenalin waned in Wankhede. Tendulkar's 84-ball innings included 14 fours and a six.

Australia was now confident of victory and more so four runs later when Manoj Prabhakar was run out. They still had work to do, though, as Manjrekar and wicketkeeper Nayan Mongia

added 54 in nine overs. They were scoring at a run per ball as required when Taylor recalled Warne to the attack. In the 41st over the leg spinner deceived Mongia with a flighted delivery and the wicketkeeper edged a drive to the Australian captain who had brought himself back in to slip. When Steve Waugh fiddled out Manjrekar in the next over the ask was 54 from eight overs with only three wickets in hand.

Kumble fought hard and Srinath made to slog India home. The task was quite beyond them and Fleming returned to pick up both tail enders. He bowled Kumble through his scythe from the last ball of the 48th to complete the win and claim his fifth wicket. He amongst several had put in a fine day/night's work. Mark Waugh's 126 was considered the best of that group by the Man of the Match adjudicator.

AUSTRALIA

M.E. Waugh run out		126
M.A. Taylor (capt) c Srinath b Raju		59
R.T. Ponting c Manjrekar b Raju		12
S.R. Waugh run out		7
S.G. Law c & b Kumble		21
M.G. Bevan run out		6
S. Lee run out		9
I.A. Healy (wk) c Kumble b Prasad		6
S.K. Warne c Azharuddin b Prasad		0
D.W. Fleming run out		0
G.D. McGrath not out		0
Extras (lb 8, w 2, nb 2)		12
(50 overs)		10–258

1/103 2/140 3/157 4/232 5/237 6/244 7/258 8/258 9/258 10/258

Bowling: Prabhakar 10-0-54-0; Srinath 10-1-51-0; Prasad 10-0-50-2; Kumble 10-1-47-1; Raju 10-0-48-2

INDIA

A.D. Jadeja lbw Fleming		1
S.R. Tendulkar st Healy b M.E. Waugh		90
V.G. Kambli b Fleming		0
M. Azharuddin (capt) b Fleming		10
S.V. Manjrekar c Healy b S.R. Waugh		62
M. Prabhakar run out		3
N.R. Mongia (wk) c Taylor b Warne		27
A. Kumble b Fleming		17
J. Srinath c Lee b Fleming		7
B.K.B.K.V. Prasad c Bevan b S.R. Waugh		0
S.L.V. Raju not out		3
Extras (b 5, lb 8, w 8, nb 1)		22
(50 overs)		10–242

1/7 2/7 3/70 4/143 5/147 6/201 7/205 8/224 9/231 10/242

Bowling: McGrath 8-3-48-0; Fleming 9-0-36-5; Warne 10-1-28-1; Lee 3-0-23-0; M.E. Waugh 10-0-44-1; Bevan 5-0-28-0; S.R. Waugh 3-0-22-2

Umpires: R.S. Dunne, D.R. Shepherd.

Toss: Australia. Points: Australia 2, India 0

THURSDAY 29 FEBRUARY 1996

GROUP A KENYA vs WEST INDIES
NEHRU STADIUM, POONA: KENYA WON 73 RUNS

'I have no words right now,' said Richie Richardson. As the captain of the West Indian team that had just been humiliated by none other than Kenya, that was no surprise. He, along with the entire Caribbean cricket community, must

have been stunned. February the 29th comes along every four years, but a result like this is almost once in a lifetime.

Even more surprising was the nature of the victory. Kenya, batting first, only set the West

Indies 166, yet eventually they were able to protect that total with some comfort. So lacking in passion was the West Indian batting performance that Colin Croft called for the captain and management team to be sacked mid-tournament. The Kenyans didn't care.

The match began with Dipak Chudasama hitting Curtly Ambrose for boundaries after Richardson had decided to bowl. The former dual World Cup champions looked unhappy with their lot even when early wickets fell. Courtney Walsh had claimed three victims by the 10th over and even some brave strokes by Steve Tikolo, who once pulled Walsh for six, could not halt the Kenyan slide to 6–81 on a greenish pitch.

A united West Indian side would have comfortably finished the job. This, apparently, was no such team. The tally of wide and no-balls built up, Cameron Cuffy being a serious culprit. Ian Bishop kicked the ground after a hit-wicket decision went in Tikolo's favour. Ambrose was at his sullen worst, grumbling and staring at anyone within eye range. Off spinner Roger Harper, in contrast to his fast-bowling team-mates, was on the spot and it was when he had Tikolo caught behind sweeping and Martin Suji taken at slip that the Kenyans were at their lowest point in the 23rd over. But even Harper blotted his copybook by dropping two catches.

A determined partnership of 44 between Hitesh Modi and 17-year-old Tom Odoyo seemed to provide Kenya with nothing more than respectability at the time. Modi spent nearly two hours over his runs before offering one of the four catches taken by Jimmy Adams. The Jamaican had replaced Courtney Browne and with a stumping to add to his collection on the day, he equalled Syed Kirmani's 1983 World Cup record of five dismissals for a wicketkeeper. The last of those was taken off Ambrose in the final over of the Kenyan innings. Extras finished top score, 27 of the bonus runs coming in wides and no-balls.

Michael Henderson of *The Times* called the West Indian batting response worse than an unspeakable mess. The rot set in early when Richardson was bowled by a Rajab Ali inswinger in the fourth over. Brian Lara, a hero to his oppo-

nents as much as the 5000 or so spectators in the ground, was quickly off the mark with a cover-driven four, but in the next over Suji bowled Sherwin Campbell behind his legs. With the West Indies 2–22 the Kenyans were beginning to enjoy themselves. A couple of overs later Lara, who had been batting recklessly, edged a ball to wicketkeeper Tariq Iqbal. There was a momentary fumble from the rotund gloveman, then excited glee as the magnitude of the dismissal of the number one West Indian batsman hit home.

Keith Arthurton joined the procession, running himself out when looking for a single to get off the mark. It was now 4–35 in the 10th over and thoughts were turning to an upset. Briefly, Adams and young Shivnarine Chanderpaul restored batting sanity. A pull for four by Chanderpaul off Odoyo brought up the 50 in the 17th over. Then Maurice Odumbe induced a mishit from Chanderpaul to Tikolo at backward point and normal service had been resumed. The asking rate of three runs per over at the start of the innings had crept up to over five. The Kenyan captain was getting plenty of assistance from the pitch for his off spinners. Adams batted for nearly an hour without hitting a boundary and was then caught in close off bat and pad.

Harper hit a couple of defiant blows before Iqbal held an excellent leg-side catch that gave his captain his third wicket on the way to identical figures, a maiden apart, to those the departing batsman had achieved. The crowd which included a contingent of Kenyan students was now chanting for the giant killers. They did not have to continue long enough to make themselves hoarse. From the second ball of the 36th over Cameron Cuffy lunged forward at Ali and was bowled. Kenya had defeated the West Indies by 73 runs and the cricket world was agog over perhaps the greatest upset in its history. The Kenyan players ran over to their supporters for a round of embracing. That was followed by a lap of honour.

Maurice Odumbe was named Man of the Match. 'It's like winning the World Cup. It's a dream come true,' said the justifiably thrilled Kenyan captain.

KENYA

D.N. Chudasama c Lara b Walsh	8
I.T. Iqbal (wk) c Cuffy b Walsh	16
K.O. Otieno c Adams b Walsh	2
S.O. Tikolo c Adams b Harper	29
M.O. Odumbe (capt) hit wicket b Bishop	6
H.S. Modi c Adams b Ambrose	28
M.A. Suji c Lara b Harper	0
T.M. Odoyo st Adams b Harper	24
E.O. Odumbe b Cuffy	1
A.Y. Karim c Adams b Ambrose	11
R.W. Ali not out	6
Extras (lb 8, w 14, nb 13)	35
(49.3 overs)	10-166

1/15 2/19 3/45 4/72 5/77 6/81 7/125 8/126 9/155 10/166

Bowling: Ambrose 8.3-3-21-2; Walsh 9-0-46-3; Bishop 10-2-30-1; Cuffy 8-0-31-1; Harper 10-4-15-3; Arthurton 4-0-15-0

WEST INDIES

S.L. Campbell b Suji	4
R.B. Richardson (capt) b Ali	5
B.C. Lara c Iqbal b Ali	8
S. Chanderpaul c Tikolo b M.O. Odumbe	19
K.L.T. Arthurton run out	0
J.C. Adams (wk) c Modi b M.O. Odumbe	9
R.A. Harper c Iqbal b M.O. Odumbe	17
I.R. Bishop not out	6
C.E.L. Ambrose run out	3
C.A. Walsh c Chudasama b Karim	4
C.E. Cuffy b Ali	1
Extras (b 5, lb 6, w 4, nb 2)	17
(35.2 overs)	10-93

1/18 2/22 3/33 4/35 5/55 6/65 7/78 8/81 9/89 10/93

Bowling: Suji 7-2-16-1; Ali 7.2-2-17-3; Karim 8-1-19-1; M.O. Odumbe 10-3-15-3; Odoyo 3-0-15-0

Umpires: Khizar Hayat, V.K. Ramaswamy.

Toss: West Indies. Points: Kenya 2, West Indies 0

THURSDAY 29 FEBRUARY 1996
GROUP B PAKISTAN vs SOUTH AFRICA
NATIONAL STADIUM, KARACHI: SOUTH AFRICA WON BY 5 WICKETS

South Africa gave another warning that they would take some beating in the 1996 World Cup with a thoroughly convincing performance against Pakistan in Karachi. If not the sensation that occurred in Poona, this was still an important cricket match; one that probably meant Pakistan would have to play their quarter-final in India, something they had hoped to avoid.

Their opponents confirmed their place at the top of Group B with yet another efficient display of batting, bowling and fielding. They had the restored Allan Donald back in the team, but it was Shaun Pollock and Chris Matthews who opened the attack after Wasim Akram had won the toss and batted. Pollock had Aamir Sohail dropped by Brian McMillan in the first over and it was a costly miss. It gave the left-hander the opportunity to regain form and he did so with a vengeance.

Sohail and Saeed Anwar put on 52 in 12 overs before Hansie Cronje brought himself on to bowl his medium pacers ahead of Donald. Within four balls he had Anwar caught at short cover and Ijaz Ahmed lbw. Sohail and Inzamam-ul-Haq overcame that aberration with a stand of

60 before the big man fell foul of his most common form of dismissal in World Cup matches. Cronje's throw was right on target. Sohail and Salim Malik then put on 77 as the Pakistani total grew to significant proportions.

After 'frog in a blender' spinner Paul Adams, making his tournament debut, had Malik caught behind Sohail completed his worthy hundred. He was not dismissed until he sliced Pollock high to point in the second-last over of the innings. Sohail had hit eight fours in 139 balls. The Pakistani captain boosted the latter part of the innings which finished on a worthy, but not imposing 6–242.

It certainly did not intimidate the South African top order who went after the bowling with real vigour in the first 15 overs. Neither Andrew Hudson nor Gary Kirsten were solely intent on holding the South African cause together. Hudson, just back in the side, really went for his shots, hitting six fours while scoring at a run per minute. He was bowled by Waqar Younis who quickly followed up with the wicket of McMillan who had been promoted in the order.

The two wickets made little difference to the tempo of the South African batting. When spin replaced pace Kirsten and Daryll Cullinan brought back memories of 1987 with one sweep shot after another. Mushtaq Ahmed's leg spin was mastered. However 19-year-old off spinner Saqlain Mushtaq held firm. He bowled the left-hander Kirsten and took a caught and bowled off Jacques Kallis. The match lay in the balance at 4–125 as Cronje came to the crease to join Cullinan.

They applied themselves well and stuck to the team strategy with confidence, knowing that even behind them there was batting quality. The run rate held firm as 78 was added for the fifth wicket. When Younis came back to conclude Cullinan's 76-ball, six-boundary contribution the momentum was all with the Proteas. Pakistan

were feeling the pinch. They lost their wicket-keeper Rashid Latif, to a groin strain. The wide and no-ball count became significant. Pollock and his well-set captain forcefully carried their side to an impressive victory with nearly six overs to spare.

Wasim Akram admitted to misreading the pitch and that his team had been outplayed. The experts suggested Pakistan had erred by selecting an extra batsman and only two pace bowlers. The masses in the outer at the National Stadium probably thought Javed Miandad—either omitted, retired or suffering from a bad back—would have made the difference. There was less pressure on Hansie Cronje. He could have spent some of his press conference showing off his Man of the Match award.

PAKISTAN

Aamir Sohail c Cronje b Pollock		111
Saeed Anwar c McMillan b Cronje		25
Ijaz Ahmed lbw Cronje		0
Inzamam-ul-Haq run out		23
Salim Malik c Palframan b Adams		40
Wasim Akram (capt) not out		32
Rashid Latif (wk) lbw Matthews		0
Ramiz Raja not out		2
Extras (b 1, lb 2, w 4, nb 2)		9
(50 overs)		6–242

Did not bat: Mushtaq Ahmed, Waqar Younis, Saqlain Mushtaq

1/52 2/52 3/112 4/189 5/233 6/235

Bowling: Pollock 9-0-49-1; Matthews 10-0-47-1; Cronje 5-0-20-2; Donald 8-0-50-0; Adams 10-0-42-1; McMillan 8-0-31-0

SOUTH AFRICA

A.C. Hudson b Waqar Younis		33
G. Kirsten b Saqlain Mushtaq		44
B.M. McMillan lbw Waqar Younis		1
D.J. Cullinan b Waqar Younis		65
J.H. Kallis c & b Saqlain Mushtaq		9
W.J. Cronje (capt) not out		45
S.M. Pollock not out		20
Extras (b 8, lb 4, w 6, nb 8)		26
(44.2 overs)		5–243

Did not bat: S.J. Palframan (wk), C.R. Matthews, A.A.A. Donald, P.R. Adams

1/51 2/53 3/111 4/125 5/203

Bowling: Wasim Akram 9.2-0-49-0; Waqar Younis 8-0-50-3; Mushtaq Ahmed 10-0-54-0; Aamir Sohail 6-0-35-0; Saqlain Mushtaq 10-1-38-2; Salim Malik 1-0-5-0

Umpires: S.A. Bucknor, K.T. Francis.

Toss: Pakistan. Points: South Africa 2, Pakistan 0

FRIDAY 1 MARCH 1996
GROUP A AUSTRALIA vs ZIMBABWE
VIDARBHA C.A. GROUND, NAGPUR: AUSTRALIA WON BY 8 WICKETS

Although a fully-fledged Test playing opponent, Zimbabwe gave Australia less trouble than Kenya had earlier in the tournament. Watched by one of the smallest crowds of the World Cup, the Zimbabwean batsmen could only set Australia a very mediocre target. The continuation of Mark Waugh's superb form meant the game was over with plenty of overs unused.

Andy Flower was having far more success

with the coin than the bat. He took first use of what looked a wicket full of runs, but came in with his side in trouble at 3–55 and left soon after with them in worse strife at 4–68. Only the experienced Andy Waller batted with any sign of permanency, opening and lasting until the 36th over. Glenn McGrath was miserly with the new-ball while Steve Waugh got rid of Guy Whittall and Alistair Campbell.

Craig Evans and Waller took the score to 4–106, which raised the possibility of a Zimbabwean recovery. It did not eventuate. Shane Warne and Damien Fleming easily cut through the lower order. Once Waller was run out from third man after hesitating over whether to go for a second leg bye, all worthwhile resistance ceased. Waller had hit 10 fours in 102 balls. When Warne bowled Charles Lock with what Steven Lynch in *Wisden Cricket Monthly* called a near replica of the Mike Gatting 'ball from hell', Zimbabwe had lost 6–48 to be all out in the 46th over.

Heath Streak began his new-ball spell against Mark Taylor and Mark Waugh with three maidens. However, Andy Flower would have

called for wickets not economy and Lock at the other end could not even keep a hold on the run flow. Neither could Whittall, Bryan Strang or Stephen Peall make any impact as the Australian pair ran up a opening stand of 92. Paul Strang did cause the batsmen some concern and it was the leg spinner who eventually had Taylor caught by his brother Bryan and 58 runs later snared Ricky Ponting caught and bowled. It gave the leg-spinning fraternity half the wickets to fall in the game, Shane Warne's haul of four winning him the Man of the Match award. Mark Waugh, who batted through until the winning run had been scored, facing 109 deliveries and hitting 10 fours, had been Warne's main title challenger.

ZIMBABWE	
A.C. Waller run out	67
G.W. Flower b McGrath	4
G.J. Whittall c & b S.R. Waugh	6
A.D.R. Campbell c M. Waugh b S.R. Waugh	5
A. Flower (capt-wk) st Healy b Warne	7
C.N. Evans c Healy b Warne	18
H.H. Streak c S.R. Waugh b Fleming	13
P.A. Strang not out	16
B.C. Strang b Fleming	0
S.G. Peall c & b Warne	0
A.C.I. Lock b Warne	5
Extras (lb 8, w 3, nb 2)	13
(45.3 overs)	154

1/21 2/41 3/55 4/68 5/106 6/126 7/140 8/140 9/145 10/154

Bowling: McGrath 8–2–12–1; Fleming 9–1–30–2; Lee 4–2–8–0; S.R. Waugh 7–2–22–2; Warne 9.3–1–34–4; M.E. Waugh 5–0–30–0; Law 3–0–10–0.

AUSTRALIA	
M.A. Taylor (capt) c B.C. Strang b P.A. Strang	34
M.E. Waugh not out	76
R.T. Ponting c & b P.A. Strang	33
S.R. Waugh not out	5
Extras (b 6, lb 2, w 1, nb 1)	10
(36 overs)	2–158

Did not bat: S.G. Law, M.G. Bevan, S. Lee, I.A. Healy (wk), S.K. Warne, D.W. Fleming, G.D. McGrath

1/92 2/150

Bowling: Streak 10–3–29–0; Lock 4–0–25–0; B.C. Strang 3–0–20–0; Whittall 2–0–11–0; P.A. Strang 10–2–33–2; Peall 4–0–20–0; G.W. Flower 3–0–12–0

Umpires: R.S. Dunne, D.R. Shepherd.

Toss: Zimbabwe. Points: Australia 2, Zimbabwe 0

FRIDAY 1 MARCH 1996
GROUP B HOLLAND vs UAE
GADDAFI STADIUM, LAHORE: UAE WON BY 7 WICKETS

In contrast to the way these two sides had competed against the majors of the competition, UAE cruised to an easy win over Holland, which was a repeat of what happened in the 1994 ICC Trophy semi-final. Form had suggested Holland would easily account for the disappointing Emirates team, but it was as if the UAE had been lying low while waiting for an opportunity like this. Their bowlers restrained the Dutch batsmen from any serious run-making freedom and then, inspired

by the carefree Saleem Raza, they galloped home with six overs and seven wickets in hand.

Steve Lubbers, back in the side, batted after winning the toss only for Nolan Clarke to fail again. It seemed the two years between the ICC Trophy and the World Cup had taken their toll on the 47-year-old former Barbadian and his inability to get the innings away to a bright start was disappointing. Flavian Aponso hit six boundaries as he and Peter Cantrell put on 74 for the second wicket. They had to struggle early as the new ball moved around. Shehzad Altaf, in the side for his first World Cup game, recovered from a first-ball wide and an opening-over tumble to be the personification of accuracy in his 10-over spell. The former Queensland Sheffield Shield player, Cantrell, batted on after Aponso became the first of off spinner Shaukat Dukanwala's five victims. He was able to hold the innings together but batted without any urgency for over two and a half hours.

Cantrell's slow progress meant that although Holland reached 2–148 they were already past the 40th over. The need for acceleration brought about a regular loss of wickets. Sultan Zarawani had his opposite number, Lubbers, caught by the only other UAE national in the side, Saeed-al-Saffer, while Dukanwala picked up four wickets from his last 11 balls.

After 15 overs UAE were already 0–94 in

reply to Holland's 9–216. Raza was making short work of Paul Jan Bakker and soon blasted Tim de Leede out of the attack. Batting in the city where he was born, the 31-year-old opener belted a World Cup record-equalling six sixes in addition to his seven fours in 68 fun-filled balls. When he was caught on the boundary off Lubbers and the ever-limping Roland Lefebvre removed Mazhar Hussain UAE had lost 2–3 to be 3–138.

If there was any concern, Vijay Mehra and the bearded Mohammad Ishaq did not show it. They batted with commonsense and aggression in a 99-ball match-winning partnership of 82. The boundaries flowed freely again and Ishaq, like Raza from Lahore, rejoiced at his homecoming by hitting the first two balls of Aponso's eighth over for four. That raised his fifty and took UAE to their well-deserved win. Dukanwala and Raza shared the Man of the Match award.

HOLLAND

N.E. Clarke c Mehra b Shahzad Altaf	0
P.E. Cantrell c Imtiaz Abbasi b Azhar Saeed	47
G.J.A.F. Aponso c & b Dukanwala	45
T.B.M. de Leede c & b Azhar Saeed	36
K.J.J. van Noortwijk c Sultan Zarawani b Dukanwala	26
S.W. Lubbers (capt) c Al-Saffar b Sultan Zarawani	8
R.P. Lefebvre c Mohammad Ishaq b Dukanwala	12
B. Zuiderent st Imtiaz Abbasi b Dukanwala	3
M. Schewe (wk) b Dukanwala	6
R.F. van Oosterom not out	2
P.J. Bakker not out	0
Extras (b 5, lb 15, w 11)	31
(50 overs)	9–216

1/3 2/77 3/148 4/153 5/168 6/200 7/200 8/209 9/210

Bowling: Altaf Shahzad 10–3–15–1; Samarasekera 9–1–35–0; Saeed-al-Saffar 3–0–25–0; Dukanwala 10–0–29–5; Sultan Zarawani 8–0–40–1; Saleem Raza 5–0–23–0; Azhar Saeed 5–0–29–2

UNITED ARAB EMIRATES

Azhar Saeed run out	32
Saleem Raza c Zuiderent b Lubbers	84
Mazhar Hussain c Clarke b Lefebvre	16
V. Mehra not out	29
Mohammad Ishaq not out	51
Extras (lb 7, w 1)	8
(44.2 overs)	3–220

Did not bat: J.A. Samarasekera, S.F. Dukanwala, Sultan Zarawani (capt), Saeed-al-Saffar, Imtiaz Abbasi (wk), Shehad Altaf

3/138

Bowling: Lefebvre 8–0–24–1; Bakker 8–0–41–0; de Leede 4–0–33–0; Aponso 7.2–0–47–0; Lubbers 9–0–38–1; Cantrell 8–0–30–0

Umpires: Mahboob Shah, S.G. Randell.

Toss: UAE. Points: UAE 2, Holland 0

SATURDAY 2 MARCH 1996
GROUP A INDIA vs SRI LANKA
FEROZE SHAH KOTLA GROUND, DELHI: SRI LANKA WON BY 6 WICKETS

In the context of the 1996 Wills World Cup this was a landmark match. It was a game filled with thrilling strokeplay which harvested 543 runs for only seven wickets. Not surprisingly, nearly all the heroes were batsmen. Eventually Sri Lanka

produced a couple more of those heroes which allowed them to complete a breathtaking victory against the odds in front of 25,000 dismayed Indians.

The players got better reviews than the

stadium, whose renovations for the tournament were hardly inspiring and actually reduced the ground's capacity. That left as many disappointed fans outside as there were squeezed into it. Clive Lloyd and Wes Hall were not allowed in, ticket accreditation being a shambles.

The lucky ones who got a seat soon had plenty to distract them from any discomfort or concern for those outside. Arjuna Ranatunga, sniffing the grey morning mist, offered India first use of the wicket so that Sachin Tendulkar was on show from the start. Less frenetic than during his 90 against Australia, he was just as accomplished and entertaining, building his momentum as his innings progressed. There was no batting joy for the totally out-of-touch Manoj Prabhakar, who scratched around for 10 overs before mistiming a drive to mid-off. Sanjay Manjrekar's consistency complemented Tendulkar nicely for another 14 overs while 66 runs were added. He provided an important part of the platform for Tendulkar and Mohammad Azharuddin before top-edging a sweep to wicketkeeper Romesh Kaluwitharana, who had to dive in front of the batsman to complete the catch.

The next 26 overs provided another of those special Tendulkar/Azharuddin occasions. There was a 15-minute rain interruption, after which the Sri Lankan spinners, Muttiah Muralitharan and Sanath Jayasuriya, kept the batsmen under relative control so that at the 40-over mark India was 2–172. The crowd was impatient for an acceleration and called for sixes. They got more than their fair share over the final 10 overs as the two strokeplayers indulged themselves in a run feast. The Sri Lankan fielding became slipshod. Ranatunga was obliged to bring back his medium pacers. Chaminda Vaas was punished. Ravindra Pushpakumara was slaughtered. Tendulkar reached 99 with a straight driven four off Pushpakumura in the 45th over, then pushed a single to reach his 100.

Pushpakumara also bowled the 49th over, from which 23 runs were taken. Tendulkar climaxed his innings with two fours and two sixes from the over which dented the confidence of the man labelled the Sri Lankan Waqar Younis. When he was run out by the bowler

Vaas, in the final over, Tendulkar had scored 137 at exactly a run per ball while hitting five sixes and eight fours. His partnership with his captain had put on 175, an all-wicket record for India in the World Cup. Azharuddin remained unbeaten on 72, having seen 99 runs scored from the last 10 overs. His side had set Sri Lanka the big task of making 272 to win.

The response of their openers Jayasuriya and Kaluwitharana was devastating. After three overs they had already wiped 42 off the target. Jayasuriya assaulted Prabhakar with four fours and a six off his second over. The captain of Delhi, on his home ground, had figures of 0–33 from two overs. His own crowd booed him and the proud all-rounder was banished to the outfield a broken man, soon to announce his retirement from the game. It was felt such batting could not continue, which seemed to be confirmed when Kumble held a sharp low catch at cover from a Kaluwitharana drive off Venkatesh Prasad in the first over after he replaced Prabhakar.

Jayasuriya, though, just kept going reaching his fifty in 36 balls and with Asanka Gurusinha providing busy support the total had reached 1–117 by the completion of the 15th over. Then between 129 and 141 three wickets fell as for the only time in the match a bowler got the upper hand. Anil Kumble picked up Jayasuriya caught in the deep after nine fours and two sixes and a fretting Aravinda de Silva was stumped when the leg spinner saw him coming. Gurusinha, who had played one lovely hook for six off Salil Ankola, was run out by Prasad, going for a second run. Only 23 overs had been bowled and Sri Lanka had lost four wickets. The Indians felt the time was right for a Mexican wave.

Their joy was premature. Kumble and, surprisingly, Tendulkar were the only bowlers to really cause the Sri Lankans any problems. So aggressive had been the start of the innings that Ranatunga and Hashan Tillekeratne had time to consolidate before stepping up to top gear. They put on the whole 131 Sri Lanka needed to win, only 32 of which came in boundaries. Ranatunga did not run too many sharp singles, either. Ankola missed a sliding catch at long-off. The dropping of Venkatapathy Raju left India a spinner short. Prabhakar came back for two more overs of off spin. That didn't work. The Mexican wave stopped. The ground went quiet. With eight balls to go empty drink containers began raining onto the outfield. Sri Lanka had won by six wickets and Jayasuriya was Man of the Match. His successful onslaught against the new ball would impact on the rest of the tournament.

INDIA		
M. Prabhakar c Gurusinha b Pushpakumara		7
S.R. Tendulkar run out		137
S.V. Manjrekar c Kaluwitharana b Dharmasena		32
M. Azharuddin (capt) not out		72
V.G. Kambli not out		1
Extras (b 4, lb 7, w 11)		22
(50 overs)		3–271

Did not bat: A.D. Jadeja, N.R. Mongia (wk), A. Kumble, J. Srinath, S.A. Ankola, B.K.B.K.V. Prasad

1/27 2/93 3/268

Bowling: Vaas 9–3–37–0; Pushpakumara 8–0–53–1; Muralitharan 10–1–42–0; Dharmasena 9–0–53–1; Jayasuriya 10–0–52–0; Ranatunga 4–0–23–0

SRI LANKA		
S.T. Jayasuriya c Prabhakar b Kumble		79
R.S. Kaluwitharana (wk) c Kumble b Prasad		26
A.P. Gurusinha run out		25
P.A. de Silva st Mongia b Kumble		8
A. Ranatunga (capt) not out		46
H.P. Tillekeratne not out		70
Extras (b 4, lb 9, w 3, nb 2)		18
(48.4 overs)		4–272

Did not bat: R.S. Mahanama, H.D.P.K. Dharmasena, W.P.U.J.W.U.J.C. Vaas, M. Muralitharan, K.R. Pushpakumara

1/53 2/129 3/137 4/141

Bowling: Prabhakar 4–0–47–0; Srinath 9.4–0–51–0; Prasad 10–1–53–1; Ankola 5–0–28–0; Kumble 10–1–39–2; Tendulkar 10–0–41–0

Umpires: C.J. Mitchley, I.D. Robinson.

Toss: Sri Lanka. Points: Sri Lanka 2, India 0

SUNDAY 3 MARCH 1996
GROUP B PAKISTAN vs ENGLAND
NATIONAL STADIUM, KARACHI: PAKISTAN WON BY 7 WICKETS

Pakistan comfortably accounted for an English side palpably not in the same league as the major contenders for the World Cup. Mike Atherton's team could not make anything from the return to form of their captain and his opening partnership of 147 with Robin Smith, who finally was given a clean bill of health.

A National Stadium filled with 30,000 had to wait 28 overs for any joy after Atherton, contrary to what Wasim Akram would have done, had won the toss and batted. Smith pulled Waqar Younis for a mighty six in the fourth over, seemingly trying to make up the lost time for the matches he had missed. Atherton took to leg spinner Mushtaq Ahmed and hit him out of the attack. At the halfway point of the innings England looked on target to reach their total in excess of 300. By then the strain was starting to tell on Smith's damaged calf and Dominic Cork was running for him. Finally, after hitting that one six and eight fours in 92 balls, Smith holed out to mid-on off part-time leg spinner Salim Malik. The stand had been the highest for England for any wicket against Pakistan in a Limited-Over International.

Five minutes later Smith was joined back in the pavilion by Graeme Hick who, unaccountably, was lured out of his ground second ball by Aamir Sohail. The second-string left-arm spinner followed up by removing Atherton's off stump as he tried to cut. England had lost 3–9 in three overs on an excellent batting surface and their advantage had been squandered.

Graham Thorpe and Neil Fairbrother again briefly rallied the cause, but Mushtaq returned and took 3–14 from his last five overs after 39 had been scored from his first five. When a fizzing Mushtaq wrong 'un bowled Dermot Reeve England were 7–217 and on the verge of complete collapse. That did not quite occur through the efforts of Thorpe, who worked his way through the tumble of wickets to an unbeaten 52, and Darren Gough who swiped a few handy runs.

Pakistan required a neat five per over to win and on a still sound wicket did so in relative comfort. Sohail and Saeed Anwar garnered the first 81 needed in 16 overs, the two left-handers keeping pace with each other, punctuating their batting with flowing boundary strokes. Sohail chipped a catch to Thorpe at mid wicket, but there was no follow-up panic as had been evident in the English batting once the openers were separated.

Atherton made 12 bowling changes. None made any difference. Fairbrother tore a hamstring and limped out of the tournament. Neil Smith was already out injured. Cork, although expensive, bowled with enough spark to have Anwar caught behind and later repeated the dose to Ijaz Ahmed. They had, however, scored 71 and 70 respectively and by the time Ijaz was out Pakistan were within 36 runs of victory with plenty of overs in hand.

Ijaz got out in time for Javed to bat for 30 minutes, which thrilled his parochial home-town fans. Inzamam-ul-Haq was thumping the ball to good effect so that Miandad's cameo just involved the odd push and nudge. Inzamam in his 100th Limited-Over International completed the win when he clouted Reeve for his sixth four to complete a run per ball half century.

Miandad bidding farewell to the National Stadium at last after several failed attempts at retirement was mobbed as he walked off the ground. He was given a special cash award of 600,000 rupees for his participation in six World Cups over 21 years. Sohail received the Man of the Match award for his all-round contribution over seven hours. Atherton's post-match comments amazingly indicated that England were gaining confidence from their succession of defeats against the other Test-playing nations. They had still made it through to the quarter-finals. Pakistan forfeited the chance of a home quarter-final by winning this game. The suggestions they might not have gone all out for victory were unfounded.

ENGLAND

R.A. Smith c Waqar Younis b Salim Malik	75
M.A. Atherton (capt) b Aamir Sohail	66
G.A. Hick st Rashid Latif b Aamir Sohail	1
G.P. Thorpe not out	52
N.H. Fairbrother c Wasim Akram b Mushtaq Ahmed	13
R.C. Russell (wk) c & b Mushtaq Ahmed	4
D.A. Reeve b Mushtaq Ahmed	3
D.G. Cork lbw Waqar Younis	0
D. Gough b Wasim Akram	14
P.J. Martin run out	2
R.K. Illingworth not out	1
Extras (lb 11, w 4, nb 3)	18
(50 overs)	9–249

1/147 2/151 3/156 4/194 5/204 6/212 7/217 8/241 9/247

Bowling: Wasim Akram 7-1-31-1; Waqar Younis 10-1-45-1; Aqib Javed 7-0-34-0; Mushtaq Ahmed 10-0-53-3; Aamir Sohail 10-0-48-2; Salim Malik 6-1-27-1

PAKISTAN

Aamir Sohail c Thorpe b Illingworth	42
Saeed Anwar c Russell b Cork	71
Ijaz Ahmed c Russell b Cork	70
Inzamam-ul-Haq not out	53
Javed Miandad not out	11
Extras (lb 1, w 2)	3
(47.4 overs)	3–250

Did not bat: Salim Malik, Wasim Akram (capt), Rashid Latif (wk), Mushtaq Ahmed, Waqar Younis, Aqib Javed

1/81 2/139 3/214

Bowling: Cork 10-0-59-2; Martin 9-0-45-0; Gough 10-0-45-0; Illingworth 10-0-46-1; Reeve 6.4-0-37-0; Hick 2-0-17-0

Umpires: B.C. Cooray, S. Venkataraghavan.

Toss: England. Points: Pakistan 2, England 0

MONDAY 4 MARCH 1996
GROUP A AUSTRALIA vs WEST INDIES
SAWAI MANSINGH STADIUM, JAIPUR: WEST INDIES WON BY 4 WICKETS

This West Indian turnaround was one of the game's imponderables. How does a once-proud side lose to Kenya and then four days later master the tournament favourites? While totally bewildering it almost summed up West Indian cricket in the mid-1990s. Volatile and inconsistent, yet still capable of beating anyone when their cluster of champions click together.

Richie Richardson, whose treatment by certain members of his team often seemed totally unjustified, guided the West Indies to victory, was named as Man of the Match and then announced he would be retiring from international cricket at the conclusion of the tournament. Unlike some others, his honour remained intact.

The Sawai Mansingh Stadium in the 'Pink City' in northern India still retained the aroma of the previous day's anti-mosquito spraying when Mark Taylor won the toss and batted. Curtly Ambrose and Courtney Walsh gave the first indication that this was a different West Indian team from Thursday's disorganised bunch. On a two-paced wicket they gave neither Taylor nor Mark Waugh any freedom against the new ball, sending down six maidens in tandem while conceding just eight runs in the first nine overs.

Mark Waugh, previously in such scintillating form, could not reach the boundary until the 17th over. By then he had already lost his captain and opening partner caught behind off the persevering Walsh. That four was Mark Waugh's one boundary stroke in his entire 102-minute innings which used up a lot of overs while providing a necessary solid foundation.

It was Ricky Ponting and Steve Waugh who made best use of that foundation with a third-wicket partnership of 110 from 114 balls. Although boundaries were fairly scarce, Ponting's six off Ian Bishop was one of the shots of the tournament. The young Tasmanian danced out to the paceman and lofted him over the boundary at extra cover. The urgency of the latter overs cost the Australians wickets, including three run outs, to bring their misjudgments for the competition to nine so far. Stuart Law might have been another when he backed up too far, however the bowler, Walsh, did nothing more than offer one of his icy stares. Ponting was one of the casualties, but not before he had completed his second century in Limited-Over Internationals. Surviving a close run out on 96 he eventually hit five fours as well as his six in 112 balls. Restricted for so long, the Australians were able to lift the total by 135 from the final 20 overs, including 71 from the last 10.

The task confronting the West Indies appeared difficult when they had lost both their openers by the time the score was 26. They had been unable to chase 166 against Kenya and here they were in trouble against Australia, needing 230 to have any hope of gaining a place in the quarter-finals. Sherwin Campbell was caught behind off Damien Fleming in the second over and Courtney Browne, back in the side with the added portfolio of opening batsman as well as wicketkeeper, sacrificed himself when Brian Lara called for a single that was not there.

That brought together Richardson and Lara. The two best West Indian batsmen had not always seen eye to eye. That was temporarily put behind them at least in Jaipur during an important partnership of 87. Lara was the more aggressive of the two cracking seven fours in 74 balls. Shane Warne's leg spin tested both batsmen, runs coming much more freely from the fast medium bowlers. Eventually Warne went wicketless. It was Mark Waugh, purveying his off-spin while wearing a wide-brimmed floppy hat and sunglasses, who got the breakthrough when he had Lara caught deep on the leg side by Glenn McGrath.

He also had Richardson 'caught' by Ponting on the boundary at deep mid wicket. The Tasmanian showed excellent judgment, but fell into a soft-drink advertising hoarding after holding the ball, so the shot counted for six. Waugh had genuine success when he bowled Shivnarine Chanderpaul and continued Keith

Arthurton's miserable tournament with a successful lbw shout. At 6–196 the West Indies were under pressure which without their captain may have developed into something more significant. That security allowed Jimmy Adams to hit three precious boundaries so that the winning runs were scored with seven balls to spare.

'We had a long serious meeting on Sunday and were determined to play well,' Richardson said after the match. It was a time for West Indian meetings apparently, because their Board of Control were convening to thrash out a post-mortem following the embarrassment against Kenya.

AUSTRALIA

M.E. Waugh st Browne b Harper		30
M.A. Taylor (capt) c Browne b Walsh		9
R.T. Ponting run out		102
S.R. Waugh b Walsh		57
M.G. Bevan run out		2
S.G. Law not out		12
I.A. Healy run out		3
P.R. Reiffel not out		4
Extras (lb 3, w 6, nb 1)		10
(50 overs)		6–229

Did not bat: S.K. Warne, D.W. Fleming, G.D. McGrath

1/22 2/84 3/194 4/200 5/216 6/224

Bowling: Ambrose 10-4-25-0; Walsh 9-2-35-2; Bishop 9-0-52-0; Harper 10-0-46-1; Arthurton 9-0-53-0; Adams 3-0-15-0

WEST INDIES

S.L. Campbell c Healy b Fleming		1
C.O. Browne (wk) run out		10
B.C. Lara c McGrath b M.E. Waugh		60
R.B. Richardson (capt) not out		93
S. Chanderpaul b M.E. Waugh		10
R.A. Harper lbw Reiffel		22
K.L.T. Arthurton lbw Waugh		0
J.C. Adams not out		17
Extras (lb 12, w 5, nb 2)		19
(48.5 overs)		6–232

Did not bat: I.R. Bishop, C.E.L. Ambrose, C.A. Walsh

1/1 2/26 3/113 4/146 5/194 6/196

Bowling: Reiffel 10-3-45-1; Fleming 7.5-1-44-1; McGrath 9-0-46-0; Warne 10-1-30-0; M.E. Waugh 10-1-38-3; Bevan 2-0-17-0

Umpires: Mahboob Shah, D.R. Shepherd.

Toss: Australia. Points: West Indies 2, Australia 0

TUESDAY 5 MARCH 1996

GROUP B HOLLAND vs SOUTH AFRICA
RAWALPINDI CRICKET STADIUM, RAWALPINDI: SOUTH AFRICA WON BY 160 RUNS

South Africa ended the preliminary rounds of the Wills World Cup as they began it, with a ruthless demolition of one of the promoted ICC teams. It meant that they and Sri Lanka were the only two teams to get through to the quarter-final stage unbeaten. Holland, for their part, went home with no wins, but no regrets, either.

Like the UAE bowlers three weeks before, the Dutch attack was thoroughly mauled by the South African batsmen. The absence of Roland Lefebvre forced Steve Lubbers to share the new ball with Paul Jan Bakker. Neither the off-spinning Dutch captain in his final game for his country nor any of the other bowlers could make an impression on Andrew Hudson and Gary Kirsten. The pair compiled the highest opening stand in the World Cup, passing Australian pair Rick McCosker and Alan Turner's 182 scored

against Sri Lanka at The Oval in 1975.

It was Hudson who made the most of the friendly bowling this time, going on to his second century in Limited-Over Internationals. After losing his left-handed partner at 186 he blazed his way to 161 in 132 balls with 13 fours and four sixes. Erik Gouka had conceded three consecutive sixes when he had the opener caught on the boundary going for yet another. Hudson's departure made little difference as the Proteas topped their then record Limited-Over International score against UAE by seven. It was thought by some critics that Hansie Cronje had erred by not giving some of his middle-order batsmen a chance to spend more time in the middle. So successful had South Africa been that the likes of Brian McMillan would enter the quarter-finals badly underdone.

Cronje gave eight of his bowlers a turn during the Dutch innings. There were few significant moments in an effort that managed to get just over halfway to the target of 329. Nolan Clarke, like his captain in a farewell performance, briefly turned back the clock with a couple of great shots during his hour at the crease. He and Peter

Cantrell put on 56 for the first wicket, Clarke raising the half-century stand with one of his two sixes. Once the 47-year-old had mistimed a drive to mid-off much of the interest went out of the game, even though the teenager Bas Zuiderent again demonstrated his promise. Andrew Hudson was a clear-cut Man of the Match.

SOUTH AFRICA

G. Kirsten c Zuiderent b Aponso		83
A.C. Hudson c Zuiderent b Gouka		161
W.J. Cronje (capt) c Lubbers b Cantrell		41
D.J. Cullinan not out		19
J.H. Kallis not out		17
Extras (lb 5, w 2)		7
(50 overs)		3-328

Did not bat: B.M. McMillan, S.J. Palframan (wk), S.M. Pollock, C.R. Matthews, P.L. Symcox, A.A.A. Donald

3/301

Bowling: Bakker 10–1–64–0; Lubbers 8–0–50–0; de Leede 10–0–59–0; Aponso 10–0–57–1; Cantrell 10–0–61–1; Gouka 2–0–32–1

HOLLAND

N.E. Clarke c Pollock b Donald	32
P.E. Cantrell c & b Matthews	23
T.B.M. de Leede b Donald	12
K.J.J. van Noortwijk c Palframan b Symcox	9
G.J.A.F. Aponso c Kirsten b Symcox	6
B Zuiderent run out	27
M. Schewe (wk) b Matthews	20
E. Gouka c Kallis b Pollock	19
R.F. van Oosterom not out	5
S.W. Lubbers (capt) not out	2
Extras (lb 7, w 5, nb 1)	13
(50 overs)	8-168

Did not bat: P.J. Bakker

1/56 2/70 3/81 4/86 5/97 6/126 7/158 8/163

Bowling: Pollock 8–0–35–1; Matthews 10–0–38–2; Donald 6–0–21–2; Cronje 3–1–3–0; Symcox 10–1–22–2; McMillan 4–2–5–0; Kallis 7–1–30–0; Cullinan 2–0–7–0

Umpires: Khizar Hayat, S.G. Randell.

Toss: South Africa. Points: South Africa 2, Holland 0

WEDNESDAY 6 MARCH 1996
GROUP A SRI LANKA vs KENYA
ASGIRIYA STADIUM, KANDY: SRI LANKA WON BY 144 RUNS

A veritable orgy of run-making delighted everyone in attendance as the Wills World Cup bade farewell to Sri Lanka. It was the home side who dominated the merry-making, rattling up the world record Limited-Over International total of 5–398. Between them the Sri Lankans and Kenyans belted, smashed, lofted, drilled and clobbered a total of 21 sixes and 63 fours through 100 overs where bowlers were for the most part mere fodder. The match aggregate of 652 runs also created a new World Cup record.

Sri Lanka made their runs against the same attack that had dismissed the West Indies for 93 in their previous game. They too were subject to rumours that they would allow themselves to be beaten to encourage a more favourable quarter-final situation. An opening stand of 83 in 6.3

overs by Romesh Kaluwitharana and Sanath Jayasuriya quickly dispelled that idea. In a trice they were within 10 runs of what the West Indies had made in an entire innings. It was ridiculous stuff that could not continue, except that it did.

Asanka Gurusinha and Aravinda de Silva added 183 at a run per ball in less than two hours. After the all-wicket Sri Lankan Limited-Over International record had been terminated by the 'Guru's' dismissal, de Silva went on to complete a wonderful hundred, getting to his country's highest score in a Limited-Over International, 145, before holing out off Martin Suji. He had contributed 14 fours and five sixes to the day's festivities. de Silva had been involved in a second-century stand, 106 with his captain, Arjuna Ranatunga, who had earlier lost the toss.

Ranatunga had rattled up 75 in 40 balls by the time 50 overs had been completed. He hit 13 fours and one six, having reached 50 in 26 balls, yet another World Cup record. The same bowlers who had so troubled the likes of Richie Richardson and Brian Lara had gone this day for eight, nine and even ten runs per over. Kennedy Otieno, back behind the stumps in place of Tariq Iqbal, had twice missed de Silva.

The only team who might conceivably have chased eight runs per over for 50 overs would have been Sri Lanka themselves. Kenya had no hope, but the wicket was good, the ground was small, the outfield fast so there were plenty more runs to be had. Otieno and Dipak Chudasama got

Kenya away to a good start before Muttiah Muralitharan and Chaminda Vaas inspired a collapse of 3–4. Kenya's pride would not be dimmed, however, and Steve Tikolo and Hitesh Modi earned respect with a fourth-wicket partnership of 137. Tikolo signed off from the tournament the way he opened it, with a fine innings. He was yorked by Kumara Dharmasena just four runs short of a deserved hundred, having hit eight fours and four sixes. It would have been Kenya's first century at the game's top level. The team's 7–254 was the third-highest score by a non-Test-playing nation in the World Cup. Amongst the welter of run-making and records de Silva was named as Man of the Match.

SRI LANKA

S.T. Jayasuriya c D. Tikolo b E.O. Odumbe	44
R.S. Kaluwitharana (wk) b E.O. Odumbe	33
A.P. Gurusinha c Onyango b Karim	84
P.A. de Silva c Modi b Suji	145
A. Ranatunga (capt) not out	75
H.P. Tillekeratne run out	0
R.S. Mahanama not out	0
Extras (b 1, lb 5, w 11)	17
(50 overs)	5–398

Did not bat: H.D.P.K. Dharmasena, W.P.U.J.W.U.J.C. Vaas, M. Muralitharan, K.R. Pushpakumara

1/83 2/88 3/271 4/377 5/383

Bowling: Ali 6-0-67-0; Suji 9-0-85-2; Onyango 4-0-31-0; E.O. Odumbe 5-0-34-2; Karim 10-0-50-1; D. Tikolo 2-0-13-0; M.O. Odumbe 9-0-74-0; S.O. Tikolo 5-0-38-0

KENYA

D.N. Chudasama b Muralitharan	27
K.O. Otieno (wk) b Vaas	14
S.O. Tikolo b Dharmasena	96
M.O. Odumbe (capt) st Kaluwitharana b Muralitharan	0
H.S. Modi run out	41
D. Tikolo not out	25
E.O. Odumbe c Muralitharan b Ranatunga	4
L. Onyango c sub (M. Atapattu) b Ranatunga	23
M.A. Suji not out	2
Extras (b 1, lb 9, w 7, nb 5)	22
(50 overs)	7–254

Did not bat: A.Y. Karim, R.W. Ali

1/47 2/51 3/51 4/188 5/196 6/215 7/246

Bowling: Vaas 10-0-44-1; Pushpakumara 7-0-46-0; Muralitharan 10-1-40-2; Dharmasena 10-0-44-1; Jayasuriya 7-0-34-0; Ranatunga 5-0-31-2; Tillekeratne 1-0-4-0

Umpires: R.S. Dunne, V.K. Ramaswamy.

Toss: Kenya. Points: Sri Lanka 2, Kenya 0

WEDNESDAY 6 MARCH 1996
GROUP A INDIA vs ZIMBABWE
GREEN PARK, KANPUR: INDIA WON BY 40 RUNS

The preliminary round games all finished in a rush on the same Wednesday. This one in Kanpur allowed India to finish third in Group A and set up the mouth-watering prospect of a quarter-final clash with Pakistan in Bangalore. Zimbabwe missed out on the big win required to progress to the next round. That meant another World Cup had ended without serious Zimbabwean impact.

The toss turned out to be a token exercise as

the captains of both sides wanted India to bat first. Andy Flower won at the call to complete a five–nil record in his favour. He even had luck at the fall of the coin in the unfinished game against Kenya. On four occasions, including this one, that luck did not extend to the result.

It all started promisingly for Zimbabwe, too. A clinking break back from Heath Streak shattered the stumps of Tendulkar, the man with 422 tournament runs to his credit, with the total on just five. Then by the 13th over Sanjay Manjrekar and Mohammad Azharuddin had both driven catches to Alistair Campbell at short mid wicket. Campbell took both chances well, one high and the other low. India were 3–32 and an upset loomed. Campbell had set a fielding standard that, surprisingly, the Zimbabweans were unable to maintain.

With his more illustrious former schoolmate Tendulkar gone, Vinod Kambli, who sometimes made it look as if batting was a fashion statement, took a key role with Navjot Sidhu. The left-hander put on 142 in 29 overs with Sidhu, surviving two outfield chances and a sharp caught and bowled to left-armer Bryan Strang before going on to his second hundred in Limited-Over Internationals. At 174 Streak held on to a chance offered by Sidhu off leg spinner Paul Strang, the Sikh had struck five fours in 116 balls.

While Kambli pushed on to his century, Ajay Jadeja unleashed an array of thrilling shots that brought him three fours and two sixes in 27 balls. With plenty of wickets in hand he wrought havoc on Charles Lock's final over, hitting two fours and a six from the first three deliveries. Kambli

had finally been dismissed after hitting 11 fours in 110 balls.

Zimbabwe needed to get 248 if they were to progress and Grant Flower and Andy Waller showed the proper intent by rattling up 50 in the first 10 overs. Those runs were scored off the Indian pacemen but the spin of Anil Kumble and Venkatapathy Raju proved a much more difficult proposition on a wicket getting lower and slower by the minute. Azharuddin supported his spinners with close catchers. Grant Flower was taken at silly point in Raju's first over and Waller held at silly mid-on by Tendulkar in Kumble's second over.

From then on the Zimbabweans' task became much harder. They got to 2–92 at the halfway point of their innings then lost a wicket in each of the next three overs. Guy Whittall batted an hour for 10 then was run out one ball after surviving another close run out call. Streak kept the game alive with some judicious hits without ever suggesting he was going to create a miracle. The damage had been done and partly by Jadeja, whose two wickets boosted his stocks enough to win him the Man of the Match award.

INDIA	
S.R. Tendulkar b Streak	3
N.S. Sidhu c Streak b P.A. Strang	80
S.V. Manjrekar c Campbell b Lock	2
M. Azharuddin (capt) c Campbell b B. Strang	2
V.G. Kambli c F.W. Flower b Lock	106
A.D. Jadeja not out	44
N.R. Mongia (wk) not out	6
Extras (lb 1, w 3)	4
(50 overs)	5–247

Did not bat: A. Kumble, J. Srinath, B.K.B.K.V. Prasad, S.L.V. Raju

1/5 2/25 3/32 4/174 5/219

Bowling: Streak 10–3–29–1; Lock 10–1–57–2; B. Strang 5–1–22–1; P. Strang 10–0–55–1; Peall 6–0–35–0; Whittall 3–0–19–0; G. Flower 3–0–16–0; Campbell 3–0–13–0

ZIMBABWE	
A.C. Waller c Tendulkar b Kumble	22
G.W. Flower c Azharuddin b Raju	30
G.J. Whittall run out	10
A.D.R. Campbell c & b Jadeja	28
A. Flower (capt-wk) b Raju	26
C.N. Evans c Srinath b Jadeja	6
H.H. Streak lbw Raju	30
P.A. Strang b Srinath	14
B.C. Strang lbw Srinath	3
S.G. Peall c Raju b Kumble	9
A.C.I. Lock not out	2
Extras (b 4, lb 11, w 11, nb 1)	27
(49.4 overs)	207

1/59 2/59 3/96 4/99 5/106 6/168 7/173 8/193 9/195 10/207

Bowling: Srinath 10–1–36–2; Prasad 7–0–40–0; Kumble 9.4–1–32–2; Raju 10–2–30–3; Tendulkar 6–0–23–0; Jadeja 7–0–31–2

Umpires: S.A. Bucknor, C.J. Mitchley.

Toss: Zimbabwe. Points: India 2, Zimbabwe 0

WEDNESDAY 6 MARCH 1996
GROUP B PAKISTAN vs NEW ZEALAND
GADDAFI STADIUM, LAHORE: PAKISTAN WON BY 46 RUNS

The 30th game of the Wills World Cup, the last of the preliminary round, made a greater impact on the tournament for the injuries that players suffered during it than for the result. New Zealand fast bowler Danny Morrison, tore a groin muscle and, even more significantly, Wasim Akram, already under a cloud with an injured thumb, strained a muscle in his side. Neither would play in the quarter-finals.

Workmen on the still unfinished light towers overlooking the ground got an elevated view of a fairly energetic match. The towers were originally scheduled to be working for this fixture. Now the fans of Lahore would have to wait until the final to see their cricket at night. Lahore is not the only venue to have had problems with the installation of light towers.

Morrison's appearance was merely a cameo. He limped off the field after just two expensive overs, not returning even to bat late in the game. Lee Germon had sent Pakistan in. Aamir Sohail seemed to take that as an invitation to demolish the new-ball attack. He hit 10 fours, carving the ball through and over the off side, and raced to his fifty in an hour. He was then caught in the most amazing fashion by Shane Thomson at square leg. Sohail pulled a Robert Kennedy delivery off the middle of his bat. Thomson leapt and at full stretch claimed the ball in his left hand as he fell back.

Inspiring as that was it had no real effect on the rest of the Pakistani batting. Only Javed Miandad, having another innings on the farewell Javed tour, missed out on making a worthwhile contribution when he was run out after struggling for 27 minutes. Chris Harris' brilliant work at cover brought about the mistake which prompted the crowd's big tribute for the departing batsman. Saeed Anwar, Inzamam-ul-Haq and Salim Malik

and Wasim Akram, who put on 81 in the last nine overs, more than compensated for the veteran's slow rate. Malik got to his fifty in just 42 balls, hitting six fours in that time. Akram grimaced after a pull shot, but kept batting even though it would have made little difference to the destiny of this game.

Half an hour into the New Zealand innings Rashid Latif's two catches had removed the openers. The Pakistani wicketkeeper went on to equal Syed Kirmani and Jimmy Adams' World Cup record of five dismissals in an innings, but the chances did not come quite as quickly or regularly as those first two. Lee Germon promoted himself to number 3 in the order and soon settled in, although his was a supporting role as he failed to reach the boundary in 110 minutes of batting. Stephen Fleming got there seven times during a partnership of 60 with his captain that offered the Kiwis a glimmer of hope.

There were handy contributions from the entire middle order. However, only Chris Cairns scored at a rate that would have enabled New Zealand to reach the 282 they required. He struck a six over long-on and another over cover from the spin bowling of Mushtaq Ahmed and Sohail. The left-armer was, like Malik and Ijaz Ahmed, filling in his injured captain's quota of overs. Sohail exacted some revenge when he had the Kiwi all-rounder caught behind. With Malik, who bowled a wide mixture of leg spin and medium pace, picking up Fleming and Adam Parore, and Mushtaq back to his best New Zealand did not have enough runs on the board or sufficient fit batsmen left to make the 87 they required from the final 10 overs. When Aqib Javed returned to bowl Kennedy the Kiwi's were still 47 runs short. Malik was named Man of the Match.

PAKISTAN

Aamir Sohail c Thomson b Kennedy	50
Saeed Anwar run out	62
Ijaz Ahmed c Spearman b Cairns	26
Inzamam-ul-Haq run out	39
Javed Miandad run out	5
Salim Malik not out	55
Wasim Akram (capt) not out	28
Extras (lb 5, w 5, nb 6)	16
(50 overs)	5–281

Did not bat: Rashid Latif (wk), Mushtaq Ahmed, Waqar Younis, Aqib Javed

1/70 2/139 3/155 4/173 5/200

Bowling: Morrison 2–0–17–0; Nash 10–1–49–0; Cairns 10–1–53–1; Kennedy 5–0–32–1; Astle 9–0–50–0; Thomson 6–0–35–0; Twose 8–0–40–0

NEW ZEALAND

C.M. Spearman c Rashid Latif b Aqib Javed	14
N.J. Astle c Rashid Latif b Aqib Javed	6
L.K. Germon (capt-wk) c sub (Ata-ur-Rehman) b Mushtaq Ahmed	41
S.P. Fleming st Rashid Latif b Salim Malik	42
R.G. Twose c Salim Malik b Mushtaq Ahmed	24
A.C. Parore c Mushtaq Ahmed b Salim Malik	36
C.L. Cairns c Rashid Latif b Aamir Sohail	32
S.A. Thomson c Rashid Latif b Waqar Younis	13
D.J. Nash not out	5
R.J. Kennedy b Aqib Javed	2
D.K. Morrison absent hurt	-
Extras (b 4, lb 9, w 6, nb 1)	20
(47.3 overs)	9–235

1/23 2/23 3/83 4/132 5/138 6/182 7/221 8/228 9/235

Bowling: Waqar Younis 9–2–32–2; Aqib Javed 7.3–0–45–2; Mushtaq Ahmed 10–0–32–2; Salim Malik 7–0–41–2; Ijaz Ahmed 4–0–21–0; Aamir Sohail 10–0–51–1

Umpires: K.T. Francis, I.D. Robinson.

Toss: New Zealand. Points: Pakistan 2, New Zealand 0

THE QUARTER-FINALS

The draw for the quarter-finals was determined by the relative positions of the sides in their Group tables. The top of Group A would play the fourth placed side from Group B and vice versa throughout. From here on the Wills World Cup became a straight knockout tournament. Every side had as much chance as the other whatever their number of wins in the preliminary round.

GROUP A	P	W	L	Pts	NR/R
Sri Lanka	5	5	0	10	1.60
Australia	5	3	2	6	0.90
India	5	3	2	6	0.45
West Indies	5	2	3	4	−0.13
Zimbabwe	5	1	4	2	−0.93
Kenya	5	1	4	2	−1.00

GROUP B	P	W	L	Pts	NR/R
South Africa	5	5	0	10	2.04
Pakistan	5	4	1	8	0.96
New Zealand	5	3	2	6	0.55
England	5	2	3	4	0.08
United Arab Emirates	5	1	4	2	−1.83
Holland	5	0	5	0	−1.92

SATURDAY 9 MARCH 1996

FIRST QUARTER-FINAL: SRI LANKA vs ENGLAND
IQBAL STADIUM, FAISALABAD: SRI LANKA WON BY 5 WICKETS

England had hoped that when they reached the business end of the tournament they might pull out something special. They didn't because they couldn't. No other game marked the decline of English cricket since the 1992 tournament and the improvement in Sri Lankan cricket as clearly as this one. The Sri Lankans were simply too good. Their exuberant batting, led by the astonishing Sanath Jayasuriya, totally obliterated the early England bowling and condemned them to an exit prior to the semi-finals for the first time in the history of the World Cup.

'We'll bat and try to make 300,' Mike Atherton told his team after he won the toss at the Iqbal Stadium. It was the first time England had played at the ground since Mike Gatting and Shakoor Rana had disagreed over something back in early 1988. The result this day would be less controversial, but in its own way even more disappointing for the English visitors. There was only a modest gathering in the ground when Robin Smith and Atherton began their confrontation with Chaminda Vaas and Pramodya Wickremasinghe.

Unlike the previous match, it was Atherton rather than Smith who batted with the most early aggression, the 300 a little prematurely in his sights. After half an hour he was caught behind off the left-armer Vaas. That left the African-born pair of Smith and Graeme Hick together and they just did not gel. The clear-eyed third umpire, V.K. Ramaswamy, adjudged Smith as run out from a Jayasuriya direct hit which made England 3–66, Hick having clipped off spinner Muttiah Muralitharan to Arjuna Ranatunga on the on-side eight runs earlier.

England were a miserable 4–95 at the halfway point, the sluggish progress of their innings having necessitated the promotion of the pinch hitting Phil DeFreitas. The move worked as the seamer hit out in effective if unorthodox fashion. He rattled up 67 in 63 balls with five fours and two sixes, one each off Jayasuriya and Muralitharan, before perishing as did Graham Thorpe and 'Jack' Russell to the English scourge on the subcontinent, the sweep.

Despite the efforts of DeFreitas, virtual disaster threatened again when the Sri Lankan spinners reduced England to 7–173. It was left to Dermot Reeve's improvisation and Darren Gough's muscle to put on 62 in 57 balls to give the scoreline a respectable look about it.

Plenty of World Cup matches have been won with 235 on the board. However, not any where a berserk Jayasuriya was chasing. The assault began immediately, faltered momentarily, then careered away again in decisive fashion. Jayasuriya's opening partner Romesh Kaluwitharana's innings lasted three balls. He smashed

Richard Illingworth for two fours, then was bowled behind his legs.

It made no difference to Jayasuriya. The move to open the bowling with the left-arm spin of Illingworth showed imagination and looked like it might have worked until Jayasuriya hit him for four fours off consecutive deliveries. DeFreitas was also a special target, his second over costing 22, including a six that hit a satellite dish and another that elevated the ball near the television commentators. In 30 balls Jayasuriya had reached his fifty. Gurusinha had been dropped by Gough low down before he had scored. He went on to again play a perfect secondary roll to the aggressor, sharing the plaudits for a century stand that took just 65 balls.

The crowd of two and a half thousand had witnessed about the best hour of uninhibited batting they were ever likely to see when Jayasuriya, the ball after being bowled by a no-ball, was stumped by Russell off the medium pacer, Reeve. He had made his 82 in 44 balls, being in and out by the 13th over, even before the fielding restrictions had been lifted. Jayasuriya hit 16 of those 44 balls for either a four or a six. He had offered one chance, a scorcher to square leg off Peter Martin when he was on 43.

What followed had to be a little anti-climactic. Nevertheless Aravinda de Silva and Ranatunga scored freely enough while Gurusinha held firm to make sure Jayasuriya's efforts were not wasted. When Gough had an lbw shout upheld against the Sri Lankan captain and then ended Gurusinha's resistance with a display of his soccer touch Sri Lanka were 5–198. There was no pressure on Hashan Tillekeratne or Roshan Mahanama, though, as they still had 20 overs to get the further 38 their side required. They took their time and got there with almost 10 overs to spare. Sri Lanka were through to the World Cup semi-finals for the first time. Having also picked up a couple of wickets with his left-arm sliders, Jayasuriya's Man of the Match award was never in doubt. English manager Ray Illingworth could not be so certain of his position. Sky TV conducted a post-match phone poll where 94 per cent of viewers called for him to step down. His two years at the top had not been happy ones.

ENGLAND

R.A. Smith run out	25
M.A. Atherton (capt) c Kaluwitharana b Vaas	22
G.A. Hick c Ranatunga b Muralitharan	8
G.P. Thorpe b Dharmasena	14
P.A.J. DeFreitas lbw Jayasuriya	67
A.J. Stewart b Muralitharan	17
R.C. Russell (wk) b Dharmasena	9
D.A. Reeve b Jayasuriya	35
D. Gough not out	26
P.J. Martin not out	0
Extras (lb 8, w 4)	12
(50 overs)	8-235

Did not bat: R.K. Illingworth

1/31 2/58 3/66 4/94 5/145 6/171 7/173 8/235

Bowling: Wickremasinghe 7-0-43-0; Vaas 8-1-29-1; Muralitharan 10-1-37-2; Dharmasena 10-0-30-2; Jayasuriya 9-0-46-2; de Silva 6-0-42-0

SRI LANKA

S.T. Jayasuriya st Russell b Reeve	82
R.S. Kaluwitharana (wk) b Illingworth	8
A.P. Gurusinha run out	45
P.A. de Silva c Smith b Hick	31
A. Ranatunga (capt) lbw Gough	25
H.P. Tillekeratne not out	19
R.S. Mahanama not out	22
Extras (lb 1, w 2, nb 1)	4
(40.4 overs)	5-236

Did not bat: H.D.P.K. Dharmasena, W.P.U.J.W.U.J.C. Vaas, M. Muralitharan, G.G.P. Wickremasinghe

1/12 2/113 3/165 4/194 5/198

Bowling: Martin 9-0-41-0; Illingworth 10-1-72-1; Gough 10-1-36-1; DeFreitas 3.4-0-38-0; Reeve 4-1-14-1; Hick 4-0-34-1

Umpires: Mahboob Shah, I.D. Robinson.

Toss: England

SATURDAY 9 MARCH 1996
SECOND QUARTER-FINAL: INDIA vs PAKISTAN
M. CHINNASWAMY STADIUM, BANGALORE: INDIA WON BY 39 RUNS

The organisers might have wanted this clash of the local titans to be the final, or at least the semi-final, in Calcutta. Such a game would have been a very hot affair, possibly even too hot if the passion behind this quarter-final was any indicator. For many of the 55,000 in the ground it seemed more was at stake in Bangalore than progress towards winning a cricket World Cup.

There is hardly a major cricket ground in India that could be further away from Pakistan than the Chinnaswamy Stadium and any piece of quality play by the Pakistanis all day and night was greeted by absolute silence. The Pakistani noises came from across the border in the west and they were not very pleasant after India held on for a 39-run victory. In a sort of warm-up for the negative hysteria that greeted his team's defeat in the 1999 final, effigies of Wasim Akram were burned and people turned their guns on their televisions and themselves. Tiresome accusations of bribery also surfaced.

Akram did not even play in Bangalore, not having enough time to recover from the side strain he had suffered against New Zealand. Aamir Sohail was given charge of the team for this nationally important event ahead of five other ex-captains and he got off to a bad start by losing the toss. Mohammad Azharuddin's decision to bat meant Pakistan had to bat under the lights of Chinnaswamy. At least they were supplemented by various fireworks, fires and flares during the evening.

That lay ahead. The pressure of the situation was so intense even Sachin Tendulkar was subdued, Waqar Younis sending down a testing early spell. He passed the outside edge of Navjot Sidhu's bat three times in the first over. Younis' burst only lasted four overs as he was surprisingly relieved by his captain and Tendulkar and Sidhu weathered the storm. They made steady rather than spectacular progress, taking 22 overs to put on 90, Sidhu continuing to be the more aggressive of the two. He reached his fifty in 72 balls just before Tendulkar played on to Akram's replacement, Ata-ur-Rehman.

Sanjay Manjrekar also left the scoring dominance to Sidhu. India cruised along at between four and five per over, looking to keep wickets in hand. The Sikh called for a runner as a muscle strain deteriorated during his innings and, seven runs short of a milestone century, he was deceived, swung across the line and was bowled by a Mushtaq Ahmed flipper. Never a certain selection in the Indian team, Sidhu's impressive innings had lasted 120 balls and included 11 fours. Like Manjrekar, Mohammad Azharuddin and Vinod Kambli got starts without really taking a toll on the Pakistani attack. When the Indian captain was brilliantly caught by a diving Rashid Latif in the 42nd over India were 4–200 and well short of a strong total.

Sidhu would be named Man of the Match, but it was Ajay Jadeja's short innings that changed the game. In 27 balls he cracked four fours and two sixes, ruining the figures of Younis of all people, who had been so impressive in his first spell. Javagal Srinath and Anil Kumble contributed to the final spree so that 51 runs were added from the final three overs, including 40 from Younis' last two. Jadeja had put him over long-off with a mighty drive. The bowler had Jadeja caught in the deep soon after to claim his 200th wicket in Limited-Over Internationals. However, there was little cause for celebration. Instead of chasing 250 the Pakistanis, who had been bombarded with missiles whenever they were in the outfield, now had to make 288 to win. The match referee, Raman Subba Row, also penalised them one over for their slow over rate.

Those lost six balls looked unlikely to make any difference as Saeed Anwar and Sohail implemented a Jayasuriya-style assault on Srinath and Venkatesh Prasad. Maintaining the momentum of the end of the Indian innings, they had 84 on the board by the end of the 10th over. Even the early introduction of Kumble could not halt the run flow and the nature of the loss against Sri Lanka became the uppermost thought of Indian fans.

After 32 balls of mayhem, the exhilaration of pounding bowlers became too much for Anwar and he skyed a slog off Srinath to Kumble, a local double act dismissal that thrilled the crowd. Anwar had hit five fours and two sixes and his captain for the day continued in the same vein, whacking Venkatapathy Raju for six with an extraordinary flat-batted drive over point that brought him to 50 and raised the Pakistani 100. Then Sohail let the emotion of the moment affect his concentration. Prasad was recalled, Sohail drove him for four and offered him some advice. Next ball was full and straight. The opener aimed somewhere deep on the on side and was bowled.

It had been a fatal error because it fired up Prasad who followed up by having Ijaz Ahmed caught in the deep and Inzamam-ul-Haq caught behind off the glove. From the comfort of 1–113 Pakistan had slipped to 4–132 and the rousing start had been wasted. The fight from there was well taken up by Salim Malik and Javed Miandad. They travelled at a more cautious rate, though, as the collapse had made wickets an

INDIA		
N.S. Sidhu b Mushtaq Ahmed		93
S.R. Tendulkar b Ata-ur-Rehman		31
S.V. Manjrekar c Javed Miandad b Aamir Sohail		20
M. Azharuddin (capt) c Rashid Latif b Waqar Younis		27
V.G. Kambli b Mushtaq Ahmed		24
A.D. Jadeja c Aamir Sohail b Waqar Younis		45
N.R. Mongia (wk) run out		3
A. Kumble c Javed Miandad b Aqib Javed		10
J. Srinath not out		12
B.K.B.K.V. Prasad not out		0
Extras (lb 3, w 15, nb 4)		22
(50 overs)		8–287

Did not bat: S.L.V. Raju

1/90 2/138 3/168 4/200 5/226 6/236 7/260 8/279

Bowling: Waqar Younis 10-1-67-2; Aqib Javed 10-0-67-1; Ata-ur-Rehman 10-0-40-1; Mushtaq Ahmed 10-0-56-2; Aamir Sohail 5-0-29-1; Salim Malik 5-0-25-0

PAKISTAN		
Aamir Sohail (capt) b Prasad		55
Saeed Anwar c Kumble b Srinath		48
Ijaz Ahmed c Srinath b Prasad		12
Inzamam-ul-Haq c Mongia b Prasad		12
Salim Malik lbw Kumble		38
Javed Miandad run out		38
Rashid Latif (wk) st Mongia b Raju		26
Mushtaq Ahmed c & b Kumble		0
Waqar Younis not out		4
Ata-ur-Rehman lbw Kumble		0
Aqib Javed not out		6
Extras (b 1, lb 3, w 5)		9
(49 overs)		9–248

1/84 2/113 3/122 4/132 5/184 6/231 7/232 8/239 9/239

Bowling: Srinath 9-0-61-1; Prasad 10-0-45-3; Kumble 10-0-48-3; Raju 10-0-46-1; Tendulkar 5-0-25-0; Jadeja 5-0-19-0

Umpires: S.A. Bucknor, D.R. Shepherd.

Toss: India

issue. The required run rate, once down to just above five per over, went back to nearly eight. Rashid Latif came in and hit two sixes off Kumble, then four wickets fell in a few minutes for just eight runs to settle the issue. In the 43rd over Latif was stumped, Mushtaq pushed a catch back to Kumble first ball, and Miandad, scoring at an insufficient rate, fell foul of a Jadeja throw

and the red light of the third umpire. His poignant exit from the international stage for definitely the last time momentarily distracted from the fact that India had the game in their keeping. The celebrations went outside the ground into the streets of Bangalore as car horns and whistles were overworked. There had been no second prize this day.

MONDAY 11 MARCH 1996
THIRD QUARTER-FINAL: SOUTH AFRICA vs WEST INDIES
NATIONAL STADIUM, KARACHI: WEST INDIES WON BY 19 RUNS

South Africa found how much of a waste five wins on the trot can be if the fall comes at the first hurdle of the knockout stage. Their masters were the tournament enigmas, the West Indies, who were inspired by a brilliant century from the enigma king, Brian Lara. South African coach Bob Woolmer and the captain, Hansie Cronje, both felt Lara was the difference between the two sides.

The first surprise came prior to Richie Richardson winning the toss and batting. South Africa decided to omit their fast-bowling spearhead Allan Donald and played a second spinner, Paul Adams, instead. Public interest in Karachi for this game was as limited as Saturday's clash in Faisalabad, and the country was still to some extent in cricket mourning for the loss in Bangalore.

Courtney Browne and Shivnarine Chanderpaul became the third opening pair used by the West Indies in as many matches. The young, slender left-hander Chanderpaul absorbed new ball thrust while Browne attacked. The ploy worked for a few overs while the wicketkeeper hit three fours before Craig Matthews broke through. Lara's nervousness was obvious at the start of his innings. He played and missed repeatedly during his first three overs at the wicket. Then one shot came off the middle, a square drive off Hansie Cronje, and he was away.

Lara relished the Proteas' greater emphasis on slow bowling and put off spinner Pat Symcox away for five fours in an over on his way to completing his fifty in just 45 balls. Paul Adams'

unorthodox wrist spin was also expensive. Now the pressure was on the South Africans in the field and for a while they struggled, misfields and a missed catch by Jonty Rhodes being part of an out-of-character performance.

Lara completed his splendid hundred in 83 balls and with Chanderpaul put on 138 in 25 overs. Chanderpaul perished while sweeping Brian McMillan. Symcox, changing the angle by bowling over the wicket to the left-hander and aiming at leg stump, picked up Lara when he top-edged a sweep. Lara had hit 16 fours in 97 balls and set up a big total that did not quite eventuate. The later batsmen showed far less composure against the spinners, although Keith Arthurton was able to double his tournament aggregate. A couple of hefty blows by Ian Bishop off Adams lifted the final total to a still very competitive 8–264.

It was certainly enough to inspire Curtly Ambrose and Courtney Walsh to another demanding opening salvo. It restricted South Africa to 19 runs off 10 overs and then brought about the wicket of Gary Kirsten, who broke his stumps as he set off for a single. The worst possible scenario was quickly engulfing South Africa and Andrew Hudson and Daryll Cullinan responded with a display of necessary belligerence. They put on 97 in 19 overs, Cullinan clubbing three big sixes in his innings including an inside-out drive over extra cover off Jimmy Adams to take him to his fifty. Hudson also reached the half-century landmark, having been recalled to the crease at one stage by Lara after being bowled by a no-ball from Ian Bishop. Although Adams, bowling left-arm spin at the leg stump, had both caught on the boundary attempting straight sixes, Cronje kept his side in the hunt with two shots off Walsh that did clear the boundary.

South Africa got as far as 3–186, then Cronje picked out Arthurton at mid wicket to give the part-time spinner, part-time wicketkeeper Adams his third wicket. It was not until the 41st over, though, that the match swung decisively in favour of the West Indies. Roger Harper had Rhodes pulling to Adams on the mid-wicket boundary, then next ball Brian McMillan missed a straight ball he had tried to turn to square leg. Before the end of the over Steve Palframan hit a low drive back to the bowler, which the world's most

dexterous fieldsman took low and one-handed.

From a desperate position of 7–198 Symcox struck out to good but brief effect, collaring Harper twice before failing to clear the boundary with his next attempt off Arthurton. It was South Africa's last gasp. By the time Walsh bowled Adams in the last over the task had been well beyond them. Lara was named Man of the Match. Andy Roberts attributed the win to the contrasting way the West Indians played compared to their opponents, 'instinctive' cricket winning out ahead of 'computerised science' in his opinion. As he would lose his position after the tournament, the former great fast bowler was fast running out of opportunities to back up his philosophy.

WEST INDIES	
S. Chanderpaul c Cullinan b McMillan	56
C.O. Browne (wk) c Cullinan b Matthews	26
B.C. Lara c Pollock b Symcox	111
R.B. Richardson (capt) c Kirsten b Symcox	10
R.A. Harper lbw McMillan	9
R.I.C. Holder run out	5
K.L.T. Arthurton c Hudson b Adams	1
J.C. Adams not out	13
I.R. Bishop b Adams	17
C.E.L. Ambrose not out	0
Extras (b 2, lb 11, w 2, nb 1)	16
(50 overs)	8–264

Did not bat: C.A. Walsh

1/42 2/180 3/210 4/214 5/227 6/230 7/230 8/254

Bowling: Pollock 9-0-46-0; Matthews 10-0-42-1; Cronje 3-0-17-0; McMillan 10-1-37-2; Symcox 10-0-64-2; Adams 8-0-45-2

SOUTH AFRICA	
A.C. Hudson c Walsh b Adams	54
G. Kirsten hit wicket b Ambrose	3
D.J. Cullinan c Bishop b Adams	69
W.J. Cronje (capt) c Arthurton b Adams	40
J.N. Rhodes c Adams b Harper	13
B.M. McMillan lbw Harper	6
S.M. Pollock c Adams b Harper	6
S.J. Palframan (wk) c & b Harper	1
P.L. Symcox c Harper b Arthurton	24
C.R. Matthews not out	8
P.R. Adams b Walsh	10
Extras (b 1, lb 4, w 2, nb 4)	11
(49.3 overs)	10–245

1/21 2/118 3/140 4/186 5/196 6/196 7/198 8/227 9/228 10/245

Bowling: Ambrose 10-0-29-1; Walsh 8.3-0-51-1; Bishop 5-0-31-0; Harper 10-0-47-4; Adams 10-0-52-3; Arthurton 6-0-29-1

Umpires: K.T. Francis, S.G. Randell.

Toss: West Indies

MONDAY 11 MARCH 1996
FOURTH QUARTER-FINAL: AUSTRALIA vs NEW ZEALAND
CHEPAUK STADIUM, MADRAS (CHENNAI): AUSTRALIA WON BY 6 WICKETS

On a Madras curry of an afternoon and evening, Australia outsweated New Zealand to progress through to the semi-finals of the Wills World Cup. To get there they had to produce their highest-ever score when batting second, the achievement of the target completing a match

loaded with runs and exciting strokes that thrilled the enthusiastic if relaxed capacity crowd.

New Zealand compiled their best total in a Limited-Over International against Australia without being able to go on and win. Chasing 286 Australia reached their objective with two overs and six wickets to spare. There was no surprise in the fact that the Waugh twins made a major contribution to the victory, Mark completing a World Cup record-breaking third century.

New Zealand were without Danny Morrison and knew they would need a lot of runs if they were to have a chance. They benefited from Lee Germon winning the toss and batting on a grass-less strip of concrete, which also condemned Australia to field in the heat and humidity of the afternoon.

The match opened with breakneck cricket. Craig Spearman smashed three fours in Paul Reif-fel's first over, then watched his partner Nathan Astle dance out to Damien Fleming and edge through to Ian Healy. As if liking what he saw, Spearman slashed at a wide delivery in Reiffel's next over so that New Zealand were 2–16 after 16 balls. Stephen Fleming holed out to Steve Waugh off Glenn McGrath without making an impact. That left the Kiwis on an unconvincing 3–44 as Chris Harris joined his captain, who had bravely left himself at number 3.

Neither Harris nor Germon had done anything in this tournament to suggest they would trouble the powerful Australian unit. The Aussies revised their thinking 27 overs later when the pair had put on 168. It was great batting and came out of the blue to the delight of the crowd whose sympathies lay mostly with the underdogs. No Australian bowler was spared. Shane Warne conceded 13 in an over, his most expensive in the competition. Harris twice clubbed McGrath for sixes, one over mid wicket, the other over square cover. The paceman found no assistance from the atmosphere despite the humidity and tended to drop the ball short.

Harris, with 26 runs from his previous three innings in the tournament, might not have been selected if Gavin Larsen had been fit. Steve Waugh admitted the Australians underestimated his capabilities, but they were learning quickly as the ball sailed into the outfield and the crowd. Once off Mark Waugh the ball landed in the second tier of the stands. Then Germon fell 11 short of his century after hitting 10 fours in 96 balls.

The Kiwi momentum stalled slightly from that point and they only added a further 57 runs from the last 10 overs. Harris, cramping through loss of fluids, completed his hundred in 96 balls. He went on to 130 with 13 fours and four sixes and had given two chances before being caught in the 49th over, a one-handed effort by Reiffel on the boundary from a pull off Shane Warne. Chris Cairns' dismissal had been crucial to limi-ting the Kiwi total to something below 300. It was a bonus for Australia that Michael Bevan's left-arm wrist spin had been as economical as Warne's.

While there was no doubt as to the quality of Chris Harris' innings, and he also bowled quite tidily, his effort was insufficient to win the Man of the Match award. That accolade instead went to Mark Waugh, most likely because he ended on the winning side. Between innings the Austra-lians remained confident in their own ability. They knew, however, that they had an enormous task in front of them.

Germon resorted to the 1992 tactic of opening the bowling with Dipak Patel's off spin and in the sixth over he had Mark Taylor caught behind down the leg side. Mark Waugh and Ricky Ponting consolidated the innings. When the Tasmanian was out in the 20th over the score was 2–84. The innings may have been consoli-dated, but the run rate was in desperate need of a boost.

Taylor sent in Warne to the surprise of most as a pinch hitter. He swung into his work imme-diately, only to be dropped in the deep by Patel. Nor did his innings last more than a quarter of an hour longer. However, he made the 14 deliv-eries he faced count. Harris was clouted over cover for six and Shane Thomson was also punished, so that with Mark Waugh now scoring freely, 43 were added in four and a half overs.

Even when Nathan Astle removed the trou-blesome pinch hitter it was clear control of the game had been transferred. Steve joined Mark in a quality stand of 86 that lifted the Australian confidence and run rate further. In lighting the Australians felt was not totally adequate Mark Waugh began to see the fading white ball as if it were a melon. Boundaries now punctuated the ones and twos which came at will. Mark Waugh hit a straight six off Patel that took him to 99, then completed his century in 101 balls. His second fifty had come in just 34 balls. Steve rated his twin brother's innings one of the best of his career and when it was over he had broken the record for the highest aggregate by a batsman in a World Cup tournament.

The ask when Stuart Law joined Steve Waugh was 76 in 70 balls with six wickets standing. The batting plan was to try to score the majority of the runs in singles, edging ever closer to victory. Waugh stuck pretty well to that idea.

Law, on the other hand, once he felt he had the measure of the bowlers, forgot it and opened up. The requirement was being quickly reduced when the Queenslander pulled Thomson for six. Waugh reached his fifty in 60 balls then sealed the exciting win with a leg-glanced boundary off Chris Cairns. The victory songs in the Australian dressing-room were sung with extra gusto that evening.

The four semi-finalists were all teams from Group A. Those eliminated, the four Group B sides, had been the semi-finalists of 1992.

NEW ZEALAND

C.M. Spearman c Healy b Reiffel	13
N.J. Astle c Healy b Fleming	1
L.K. Germon (capt-wk) c Fleming b McGrath	89
S.P. Fleming c S.R. Waugh b McGrath	8
C.Z. Harris c Reiffel b Warne	130
R.G. Twose b Bevan	4
C.L. Cairns c Reiffel b M.E. Waugh	4
A.C. Parore lbw Warne	11
S.A. Thomson run out	11
D.N. Patel not out	3
Extras (lb 6, w 3, nb 3)	12
(50 overs)	9–286

Did not bat: D.J. Nash

1/15 2/16 3/44 4/212 5/227 6/240 7/259 8/282 9/286

Bowling: Reiffel 4-0-38-1; Fleming 5-1-20-1; McGrath 9-2-50-2; M.E. Waugh 8-0-43-1; Warne 10-0-52-2; Bevan 10-0-52-1; S.R. Waugh 4-0-25-0

AUSTRALIA

M.A. Taylor (capt) c Germon b Patel	10
M.E. Waugh c Parore b Nash	110
R.T. Ponting c sub (R.J. Kennedy) b Thomson	31
S.K. Warne lbw Astle	24
S.R. Waugh not out	59
S.G. Law not out	42
Extras (b 1, lb 6, w 3, nb 3)	13
(47.5 overs)	4–289

Did not bat: M.G. Bevan, I.A. Healy (wk), P.R. Reiffel, D.W. Fleming, G.D. McGrath

1/19 2/84 3/127 4/213

Bowling: Nash 9-1-44-1; Patel 8-0-45-1; Cairns 6.5-0-51-0; Harris 10-1-41-0; Thomson 8-0-57-1; Astle 3-0-21-1; Twose 3-0-23-0

Umpires: C.J. Mitchley, S. Venkataraghavan.

Toss: New Zealand

THE SEMI-FINALS
WEDNESDAY 13 MARCH 1996
FIRST SEMI-FINAL: INDIA vs SRI LANKA
EDEN GARDENS, CALCUTTA: SRI LANKA WON BY DEFAULT

This may well have been World Cup cricket's darkest and saddest day. A riot by sections of the crowd as India was sliding to an inevitable defeat brought an end to the game and forced Clive Lloyd, who handled a desperately sensitive situation with firmness and commonsense, to award the game to Sri Lanka.

Arjuna Ranatunga's team would have won anyway had the match gone its course. Perhaps the greatest pity of the disturbances was that they distracted from Sri Lanka's greatest-ever crick-

eting achievement in reaching their first World Cup final.

The spectacle of 110,000 people crammed into one of cricket's greatest venues was at first an irresistible one and something special was anticipated. Those in attendance thought so too, with the added attraction being their belief India would march into the final. Later, it all went very wrong very quickly when the hosts collapsed from 1–98 to 8–120. That was too much for some to cope with. Their lack of control ruined what could have been the great advertisement for cricket in Calcutta. They embarrassed officials and brought players to tears.

Riotous celebration was the only thing on Bengali minds when two wickets fell in Javagal Srinath's opening over after Mohammad Azharuddin had won the toss and, surprisingly to some critics, elected to bowl. His reasoning was that Sri Lanka preferred to chase and he was prepared to accept the predicted risk that the wicket would turn more as the match progressed. By the fourth ball of the match Romesh Kaluwitharana, a right-hander, and Sanath Jayasuriya, a left-hander, had slashed hard and high towards third man only to be caught near the boundary.

Like a counter-punching boxer Aravinda de Silva was soon returning blows, taking a boundary nudged past slip off Anil Kumble's first over. The leg spinner shared the new ball with Srinath. In temperatures around the 35°C mark, de Silva continued to turn up the heat on the Indian bowlers. Even the loss of Asanka Gurusinha to a mistimed pull in the seventh over failed to break de Silva's stride. He took 22 off two overs by Venkatesh Prasad, striking boundaries to all parts of the ground, clean beautifully timed strokes of neat movements.

A cover drive for his 11th four in the 11th over took de Silva to his half century in 32 balls out of 3–63. Three more boundaries flowed from his bat before he edged a Kumble wrong 'un onto his middle stump in the 15th over. A score of 4–85 was still nothing to get excited about and it was the stand of 83 between Roshan Mahanama and Arjuna Ranatunga which put Sri Lanka right in the match. Without resorting to de Silva-style fireworks they compiled their runs at a consistent five per over pace, getting plenty of singles with pushes to square leg and wide of cover. That took its toll on Mahanama, who began to cramp up and was allowed to use a runner. Not only Mahanama was dehydrating. The crowd had already gone through all the drinks available for sale in the outer and had to swelter until the sting went out of the heat in the evening.

It was India's best bowler on the day/night,

Sachin Tendulkar, who broke the stand on 168, trapping Ranatunga lbw with a leg break. Fourteen runs later, in the 38th over, Mahanama, who had hardly batted in the whole tournament, collapsed again with cramp and had to be carried from the ground. He had an invaluable 58 to his name. A few late-over clouts by Chaminda Vaas and some steady scoring by Hashan Tillekeratne lifted the total to 8–251, which everyone viewed as just okay.

Totals of 270 and 280 had been inadequate in recent matches, so there was nothing to suggest India would not get very close even when Navjot Sidhu clipped Vaas to Jayasuriya in the gully in the third over. The star in the bright spotlight, Tendulkar embarked on an innings of a quality not far short of de Silva's and of equal value. With Sanjay Manjrekar as a secure partner he reached his fifty out of 1–71 in the 17th over, 110,000 people cheering spontaneously as one. By the 23rd over it was 1–98, the time for acceleration fast approaching. Jayasuriya replaced Muttiah Muralitharan and bowled his left-arm sliding spin into the bowlers' rough outside the leg stump of the right-hander. Tendulkar was struck on the pad and went looking for a leg bye. But Kaluwitharana had already gathered the ball and the third umpire showed Tendulkar's backward lunge had come too late.

At the moment the red light flashed the Indian wheels came straight off. One run and seven balls later Azharuddin pushed the ball via bat and pad back to off spinner Kumara Dharmasena. An eerie silence overtook the crowd. Manjrekar was next, bowled off his thigh, sweeping at Jayasuriya. The personal sting of the Sri Lankan opener's batting failure was being soothed by these key wickets. Srinath was promoted to pinch-hit India out of their daze. He struck one boundary, then failed to beat Muralitharan's throw to the bowler's end to make the score 5–110 in the 29th over. Collapses can be halted with commonsense, but none was in evidence in the brewing madhouse.

Ajay Jadeja, still not off the mark, swept at Jayasuriya and was bowled leg stump. Wicketkeeper Nayan Mongia went a sweeping too, lifting a de Silva off-spinner to none other than Jayasuriya at mid wicket. He leapt for joy, having been involved in six of the seven dismissals. Then facing his first ball which was the first delivery of the 35th over Aashish Kapoor carbon-copied Mongia's dismissal. India had lost 7–22 to be 8–120. Vinod Kambli went down on his haunches in an attitude of submission. Now the missiles, most of them plastic water bottles, began to rain down. The players and umpires left the field. A large percentage of the crowd had already gone home in disgust.

Many of those who remained were making their presence felt.

Kambli pleaded with Lloyd for the match to restart. There were no public announcements as to the intentions of the authorities. When they tried to resume the game after 20 minutes more missiles flew out. India was shamed out of the tournament. The crowd's attitude to their captain after the match was equally disgraceful and it took two years and a big Test century against Australia to heal the rift that developed. Aravinda de Silva was named Man of the Match.

SRI LANKA

S.T. Jayasuriya c Prasad b Srinath	1
R.S. Kaluwitharana (wk) c Manjrekar b Srinath	0
A.P. Gurusinha c Kumble b Srinath	1
P.A. de Silva b Kumble	66
R.S. Mahanama retired hurt	58
A. Ranatunga (capt) lbw Tendulkar	35
H.P. Tillekeratne c Tendulkar b Prasad	32
H.D.P.K. Dharmasena b Tendulkar	9
W.P.U.J.W.U.J.C. Vaas run out	23
G.G.P. Wickremasinghe not out	4
M. Muralitharan not out	5
Extras (lb 1, b 10, w 4, nb 2)	17
(50 overs)	8–251

1/1 2/1 3/35 4/85 5/168 6/206 7/236 8/244
Mahanama retired hurt at 5–182

Bowling: Srinath 7-1-34-3; Kumble 10-0-51-1; Prasad 8-0-50-1; Kapoor 10-0-40-0; Jadeja 5-0-31-0; Tendulkar 10-1-34-2

INDIA

S.R. Tendulkar st Kaluwitharana b Jayasuriya	65
N.S. Sidhu c Jayasuriya b Vaas	3
S.V. Manjrekar b Jayasuriya	25
M. Azharuddin (capt) c & b Dharmasena	0
V.G. Kambli not out	10
J. Srinath run out	6
A.D. Jadeja b Jayasuriya	0
N.R. Mongia (wk) c Jayasuriya b de Silva	1
A.R. Kapoor c de Silva b Muralitharan	0
A. Kumble not out	0
Extras (lb 5, w 5)	10
(34.1 overs)	8–120

Did not bat: B.K.V. Prasad

1/8 2/98 3/99 4/101 5/110 6/115 7/120 8/120

Bowling: Wickremasinghe 5-0-24-0; Vaas 6-1-23-1; Muralitharan 7.1-0-29-1; Dharmasena 7-0-24-1; Jayasuriya 7-1-12-3; de Silva 2-0-3-1

Umpires: R.S. Dunne, C.J. Mitchley.

Toss: India

THURSDAY 14 MARCH 1996
SECOND SEMI-FINAL: AUSTRALIA vs WEST INDIES
MOHALI STADIUM, CHANDIGARH: AUSTRALIA WON BY 5 RUNS

Thankfully the Chandigarh semi-final was memorable for the right reasons. The lunacy of Eden Gardens was replaced by an astonishing cricket match which was heading in one direction for much of its duration, only to be twisted violently back the other way in its closing moments.

The result was a fantastic thrill to the Australians and their supporters, but equally a bitter disappointment to the West Indies. After forfeiting a seemingly invincible position with a dreadful batting collapse it was little consolation

that they had progressed further than their previous two World Cup predecessors. The Australians had retained their rating as favourites to lift the silver trophy on Sunday 17 March and were now only one step away from repaying the confidence of those that had put money on them. Their date with Sri Lanka in Lahore would be their third appearance in a World Cup final.

Outside the subcontinent, many believed the winner of the tournament would come from this semi-final and soon after Mark Taylor won the toss and batted the West Indies almost had a stranglehold on the contest. By the 10 over mark, the eagles circling above the ground might as well have been vultures picking at the carcass of an Australian cricket team reeling at 4–15.

Curtly Ambrose immediately began the demolition of the Australian top order, taking full advantage of the two-paced wicket with his accuracy, pace and movement. He struck with the second ball of the match. A pinpoint off-cutter thumped into the stationary pads of Mark Waugh right in front of the stumps. It was a simple decision for umpire Venkataraghavan and a real boost for the West Indies to remove the most prolific batsman of the tournament so quickly.

Ian Bishop shared the new ball and in his second over Mark Taylor played it into his stumps, leaving his side 2–7. Ambrose followed up by pinning Ricky Ponting as he had Mark Waugh. Then Steve Waugh drove an undriveable Bishop delivery back onto his stumps in the 10th over. The front line had been punctured and the way to the reserves was open.

Michael Bevan had not properly established his reputation outside Australia as a top-notch limited-overs batsman by the time of the Wills World Cup. After his fighting 69 at Chandigarh the world had a better idea of his qualities. He was not alone in forcing Australia back into the contest. Stuart Law's contribution in the face of adversity was equally noteworthy. The Australian 'young guns' put on 138 in 32 overs, running feverishly for singles and twos and occasionally playing a big shot. At 4–43 Law was caught off a no-ball, an important let-off. As his confidence grew, Bevan struck off spinner Roger Harper for the only six of the match.

After 106 balls which included five fours, Law dabbed to point and Bevan charged. Law did not see him coming and was far too late to set off for what would have been a close call anyway. Once Ambrose's throw was on target Law began walking towards the pavilion.

Four overs later Bevan's step-away drive went straight to Richie Richardson at cover. He had faced 109 balls and hit four fours and a six. That made the score 6–171, so it was left to the ingenuity of Ian Healy to get the Australian total beyond the 200 mark by the end of the 50th over.

Even 207 was 25 short of what Taylor thought would be adequate on an admittedly big ground and it looked quite a modest challenge once the West Indian top order saw off the opening Australian thrust. Shane Warne, brought on as early as the seventh over, held a sharp caught and bowled when Courtney Browne punched his first ball, a long hop, back down the wicket. Then Lara, still full of form and confidence, stroked his way to 45 at a run per ball. Such was his power at times he had no trouble beating fieldsmen set in defensive positions on the boundary. With the rock-solid Shivnarine Chanderpaul Lara carried the score from 1–25 to 1–60 after 15 overs, then 1–93 in 22 before Steve Waugh, bowling around the wicket, produced a peach of a delivery. The ball pitched on off-stump, held its line and clipped the outside of the stumps. Not even Lara's immaculate defensive bat could keep it out.

Australia thought that might have signalled a West Indian capitulation. They were on the right track, but premature. Richie Richardson and Chanderpaul assumed control as another 72 were added in 20 overs. Richardson was intent on playing in a World Cup final as his farewell to international cricket and no-one was going to stand in his way, not even the square-leg umpire. The West Indian captain timed a sweep off Warne which banged into the head of umpire Cooray. The Australians should have been grateful. The head of the Sri Lankan official saved a couple of runs.

By the 42nd over most spectators at the ground and those dozing on their couches in front of the late-night television back in Australia accepted the result as a formality. Taylor had tried eight different bowlers. Another 43 runs from eight overs and Richardson would have his dream farewell. With eight wickets in hand it had to be a certainty. It mattered little when Chanderpaul, starting to cramp up, got a bit carried away and trying to belt Glenn McGrath down the ground only got as far as Damien Fleming at mid-on. Nor did the prompt removal of the all-rounders Roger Harper and Otis Gibson, the former trapped lbw on the crease by McGrath, the latter caught behind off Warne, really indicate a possible West Indian loss.

The expressions on the faces of the crowd and the players really began to change once Jimmy Adams had been given out lbw hitting across Warne. That made the West Indies 6–183, the ask now 25 from 21 balls with four wickets standing. It was still fairly straightforward but four runs later Keith Arthurton, with two runs from his previous four innings in the tournament and scoreless from six balls in this one, lifted his head and swung wildly at Fleming. His 48th over death-or-glory shot merely edged the ball through to Ian Healy and Richardson was left to get the runs with the three fast bowlers.

Seven runs later Ian Bishop played back awkwardly to a Warne flipper and Richardson had two fast bowlers left. Warne had taken 3–6 in three Man of the Match award-winning overs. However, it was up to his fellow Victorian, Fleming, to deliver the 50th over from which the West Indies required 10 runs with two wickets standing. It would last just three balls, yet such was the tension the over seemed to last an eternity. With the ground in total uproar Richardson swung the first ball away to mid wicket for four. Six required from five balls. Richardson bottom-edged a cut off Fleming's second ball along the ground to Healy and called Ambrose for the run. Healy threw down the stumps with the long

Antiguan stretching for the crease. The third umpire, Khizar Hayat, was called into action and everyone, especially the players, waited with baited breath before, to the delight of the Australians, Ambrose was shown the red light.

Australia and the West Indies have had so many wonderful contests it is a pity their off-field relations in the late 1990s have been strained. There is no better spectacle in cricket than these two proud cricketing nations going hammer and tongs at each other on a cricket field. With the demise of England as a cricketing force, Australia and the West Indies are perhaps now the game's oldest traditional rivals. The 1999 Test series in the Caribbean, for example, could not be bettered.

This semi-final at Chandigarh was another in that long line of Australia/West Indian classics and it came down to the final four deliveries to determine who would go through to Sunday's final in Lahore. There never will be a prouder West Indian cricketer than Courtney Walsh and his determination as he peered down the floodlit wicket at Fleming and belted the bottom of his bat into the blockhole was obvious. Six more runs in four balls would do it. His captain at the other end was well set. Fleming ran in and bowled. Walsh propped half forward and drove, the ball was through him in an instant and his

AUSTRALIA

M.E. Waugh lbw Ambrose	0
M.A. Taylor (capt) b Bishop	1
R.T. Ponting lbw Ambrose	0
S.R. Waugh b Bishop	3
S.G. Law run out	72
M.G. Bevan c Richardson b Harper	69
I.A. Healy (wk) run out	31
P.R. Reiffel run out	7
S.K. Warne not out	6
Extras (lb 11, w 5, nb 2)	18
(50 overs)	8–207

Did not bat: D.W. Fleming, G.D. McGrath

1/0 2/7 3/8 4/15 5/153 6/171 7/186 8/207

Bowling: Ambrose 10-1-26-2; Bishop 10-1-35-2; Walsh 10-1-33-0; Gibson 2-0-13-0; Harper 9-0-47-1; Adams 9-0-42-0

WEST INDIES

S. Chanderpaul c Fleming b McGrath	80
C.O. Browne (wk) c & b Warne	10
B.C. Lara b Waugh	45
R.B. Richardson (capt) not out	49
R.A. Harper lbw McGrath	2
O.D. Gibson c Healy b Warne	1
J.C. Adams lbw Warne	2
K.L.T. Arthurton c Healy b Fleming	0
I.R. Bishop lbw Warne	3
C.E.L. Ambrose run out	2
C.A. Walsh b Fleming	0
Extras (lb 4, w 2, nb 2)	8
(49.3 overs)	10–202

1/25 2/93 3/165 4/173 5/178 6/183 7/187 8/194 9/202 10/202

Bowling: McGrath 10-2-30-2; Fleming 8.3-0-48-2; Warne 9-0-36-4; M.E. Waugh 4-0-16-0; S.R. Waugh 7-0-30-1; Reiffel 5-0-13-0; Bevan 4-0-12-0; Law 2-0-13-0

Umpires: B.C. Cooray, S. Venkataraghavan.

Toss: Australia

stumps were shattered. Australia had won by five runs and the West Indies, so close to erasing the earlier ignominy of their defeat by Kenya, had lost an inglorious 8–37. Richie Richardson, unbeaten and within a whisker of glory, walked away. He had played his last innings for the West Indies.

Steve Waugh said the final overs were a blur, so hard was the adrenalin pumping through the Australians. Their elation and relief at so amazing a victory was all-enveloping. They laughed and danced together in a huddle, taking in the memorable moment with the entire Australian squad. 'I thought the West Indies were home and dry,' Taylor said after the game.

SUNDAY 17 MARCH 1996
WILLS WORLD CUP FINAL
AUSTRALIA vs SRI LANKA
GADDAFI STADIUM, LAHORE: SRI LANKA WON BY 7 WICKETS

There was a certain amount of trepidation about this World Cup final between Australia and Sri Lanka. Disputes and on-field controversy had marred their recent encounters and the ill-feeling surrounding Australia's boycott of their match in Colombo lingered. Arjuna Ranatunga had refused to shake Mark Taylor's hand after a World Series Cup final at the end of the Australian summer. What sort of behaviour might be on display on cricket's night of nights was cause for concern as there were members of both sides not keen to take a backward step.

In the end commonsense prevailed and the behaviour of the players was as restrained as could be hoped for. By far the greatest shock came with the ease by which Sri Lanka overcame the tournament favourites. Australian authorities had done a lot to assist Sri Lanka in gaining full Test-playing status in the early 1980s. That was nothing compared to what their defeat in this game did for cricket on the 'teardrop of India'.

The underdogs took control at the midway point of the Australian innings and did not really release their hold on the game from there. Theirs was a well-planned campaign that never faltered. It was a great credit to the coach Dav Whatmore as well as the captain, Ranatunga.

'Dav told us, "let's do the little things right and we'll see what the result is at the end of the day",' says Asanka Gurusinha. 'That was our main focus and to be honest I wasn't that conscious of the atmosphere and the pre-match build-up.'

An unimpressive Saturday night official World Cup dinner out of the way, the players of Australia and Sri Lanka woke to a Sunday of overcast skies and streets with puddles everywhere. There had been heavy overnight rain and there was no guarantee the final would start on schedule. The Australian players heard that rumour and were surprised when they were told the team buses would soon be on their way.

The covers were removed and the players completed their warm-up routines. Outside the ground the police clashed with spectators desperate to get in. As the Gaddafi Stadium filled it became clear crowd support would be with Sri Lanka and there was no shortage of their flags being waved when it was announced that Ranatunga had won the toss. It was academic how the coin fell, however, as Mark Taylor wanted to bat first on the flat rock-hard wicket and Ranatunga hoped to bowl. Both teams announced unchanged sides from their semi-final wins. Englishman David Shepherd and West Indian Steve Bucknor earned the right to officiate in cricket's showcase event. They had put on an impeccable display in the pressure-packed quarter-final between India and Pakistan and were generally regarded as the best two umpires in the world. Mistakenly, the South African national anthem was originally played beside 'Advance Australian Fair' and the Sri Lankan anthem had to be squeezed in just before the 2.30 pm start.

As if stamping his authority on the occasion,

Taylor took on the Sri Lankan opening attack of Chaminda Vaas and Pramodya Wickremasinghe. From the word go the Australian captain was finding the middle of the bat and flashing the white ball to the boundary. Mark Waugh preferred to begin sedately, looking to build towards a century as he had successfully done on three previous occasions in the tournament. From the first ball of the eighth over, though, his plan came unstuck as he clipped Vaas to an elated Sanath Jayasuriya at square leg.

Mark Waugh's demise had no effect on the confidence of Taylor and his new partner, Ricky Ponting. This was the Australian side that had so recently thrashed Sri Lanka in both the Tests and Limited-Over Internationals in Australia. Bob Simpson said pre-match the team had tried to insure against complacency. Now runs were coming freely again, especially from the captain who hit repeatedly to the leg side and once lifted Vaas over square leg for six.

By the 15-over mark the total was 1–82. Taylor raced past his fifty in 52 balls and even the introduction of Muttiah Muralitharan made no difference. At the halfway stage of the innings Australia was 1–134 and the talk was of a total around 300 that might be too much even for the in-form Sri Lankan batsmen. Ranatunga had more than one finger spinner available to try to turn the tide and introduced Aravinda de Silva as the sixth bowler.

Taylor had made 74 in 83 balls with eight fours and a six and added 101 in 19 overs with Ponting when he swept at de Silva. He made solid contact with the top half of the blade so that the ball flew towards the square-leg boundary. In place was that man Jayasuriya again and he had no trouble holding on to his second catch of the match. The dismissal of the Australian captain was the turning point of the final.

Suddenly Ponting and Steve Waugh were going nowhere against the off spinners who kept a tight line and gained some turn. Four overs and 15 runs after Taylor's dismissal, Ponting backed away to cut a sharply turning de Silva off break and was bowled middle stump. Shane Warne strode to the wicket full of big hitting intent, only to stumble forward to his sixth ball and be neatly stumped down the leg side by Romesh Kaluwitharana off Muralitharan.

Stuart Law and Steve Waugh joined in a worried assessment of the situation at a drinks-break score of 4–166 from 34 overs. Whatever they planned did no good as Waugh tried to chip Kumara Dharmasena over the in field in the next over only to loft the ball to de Silva near the long-on boundary. Australia had lost 4–33 in eight overs and disarray threatened. Michael Bevan and Law avoided that, but nine runs in the next five overs hardly eased the pressure. After 40 overs Australia was 5–178 and there had not been a boundary in the 13 overs since Taylor's dismissal. 'Everyone had their little mission during the game,' says Gurusinha. 'We didn't worry about Australia or the final, just on doing our job. Guys like Aravinda de Silva and Sanath Jayasuriya are really good spinners on their day. They can be inconsistent, but in this final they were really concentrating well.'

The push had to come and Law pulled Dharmasena cleanly and square for six. However, it was only a half charge. Law was caught at point and Ian Healy played all over a full-pitched delivery to give de Silva a third wicket. Bevan cracked a few balls away in a partnership with Paul Reiffel which included 18 from the last two overs. Ranatunga, who had bowled his various combinations of spinners right through, walked off content with his position. Sri Lanka required 242 to win the World Cup. 'We thought they might get 270 or 280 at one stage,' Gurusinha says, 'but because of the way we had been batting we were still confident and would have been so even if we had wanted 300.'

For a few minutes during the break between innings it became problematical whether the Sri Lankans would have an opportunity to pursue any runs. The Gaddafi Stadium lights went out. There had been suggestions the amount of power used by the new floodlights, the first at a Pakistani cricket ground, could place too much strain on the supply. Fortunately the lights soon came back on and the game could resume.

As the Australians took the field they noticed something different for their games in India under lights. An evening dew had come straight down and the outfield was very damp. Australia had done their pre-match practice during the day. Sri Lanka had trained under lights. They were aware of what would happen, the Australians were not.

The ball would soon become sodden and ineffective on the wet outfield, so the Australians had to take plenty of early wickets. They got two quickly. In the second over, bowled by Damien Fleming, Jayasuriya went for a two to third man on Glenn McGrath's arm and misjudged the task by the barest margin. Sri Lanka was 1–12, then 2–23 four overs later when Kaluwitharana mistimed a pull off Fleming and Michael Bevan ran around behind the square-leg umpire to hold the catch. It was the last chance accepted by an Australian fieldsman, but by no means the last chance offered.

The spectators were enjoying their night at the World Cup final and got through plenty of Mexican waves. De Silva was nearly run out and McGrath sent down a pressure-packed spell. Fleming's waywardness released some of that pressure at the other end so Taylor introduced Warne for the 11th over. This crucial over included three shots through the off side by de Silva and a delivery that hit the inside edge and whisked past Healy.

When the fieldsmen moved back at the end of 15 overs Sri Lanka was 2–71. Gurusinha lofted Mark Waugh down the ground and Fleming, sliding across the damp outfield, missed the chance. The 100 was brought up in the 21st over as Gurusinha clubbed Warne down the ground for four. The chubby faced left-hander, who would soon settle in Australia, then belted Warne for an amazing pull for six over long-off! 'It was a slow track and when I got into position to play the pull shot the ball was still coming,' Gurusinha says. 'I didn't want to hit across it because I might have mistimed it. So I hit the ball with a straight bat instead and away it went. Shane Warne was not a problem for us that night. We play him fairly well anyway and he knows it. We respect him as a fine bowler, but if the ball is loose we have always had the confidence to punish it, which is what we did in the final.'

Both batsmen reached the half-century land-mark as the prospect of a Sri Lankan victory became very real. It was the Australians who were struggling with the pressure. Gurusinha pulled Bevan and Law at deep square leg did not have to move to take the catch. It might have been better if he had, for the ball hit his hands and went straight down. The crowd enjoyed that.

After a partnership of 125 with de Silva, Gurusinha charged Reiffel and was bowled. 'We had spent a few overs just getting singles so I told Aravinda to stay there and I would have a hit, but I swung across the ball instead of straight so I missed it,' Gurusinha says. Australia hoped the reckless-looking dismissal might bring about another Chandigarh-type collapse. However lightning did not strike twice. Ranatunga came in with 95 needed from 19 overs and was immediately as assured as his partner who was progressing towards a landmark century. At first the pair batted with little urgency while ensuring the required run rate was within reach. Then Mark Waugh conceded 10 runs from an over, which left 50 to be scored from the last 10. Ranatunga drove the ball straight for four through Warne's fingers, then smashed a misdirected attempted flipper away for six and poked his tongue out at the bowler. The Sri Lankan captain was rather enjoying himself. Taylor had tried all sorts of permutations and variations, but this time nothing would work for him.

A neat glance for four off Fleming took the little Sri Lankan maestro to his century from 119 balls, only the third to be scored in a World Cup final. He joined Viv Richards and Clive Lloyd in that exclusive club and no-one could doubt the worth of his membership. 'It was one of the best innings I have ever seen,' Gurusinha says. 'The first ball he faced he just gently pushed at the ball and it scooted away through mid-off for three. I knew then everything was all right. His feet were moving. His head was still. He gave me such confidence, too. We had already shared in a couple of century partnerships during the tournament so we were confident in each other's game.'

de Silva's hundred had come as a personal bonus for he had already done enough along with Gurusinha and Ranatunga, to ensure victory.

That wonderful formality was completed when Ranatunga nudged McGrath through the vacant slips region along the ground to the third-man boundary for four from the second ball of the 42nd over. It was the shot he will best remember for his entire life.

Ranatunga and de Silva were almost instantly surrounded by their elated team-mates. The military band in attendance played a victory march. There were well-wishers everywhere as the beaming Ranatunga received the World Cup trophy from Pakistani Prime Minister, Benazir Bhutto, and de Silva accepted his enormous cheque for being named Man of the Match. During the presentations the evening mist had floated in and turned to rain. The well-wishers pressed their heroes so hard everyone went for a tumble, including Ranatunga and his precious trophy. For the lone survivor of Sri Lanka's inaugural Test, nothing could dampen the exultation of the moment.

Both captains, one in victory, the other in defeat, were gracious at the post-match conferences. Neither would be drawn into talk of previous controversies, even though Warne and the Waugh twins later refused to sign Sri Lankan

souvenir bats sent into the Australian dressing-room. In Sri Lanka most people took a holiday on the Monday to celebrate their very special achievement. Their team, who had never even got close to a semi-final berth before, were the world champions of limited-overs cricket.

'It was a great feeling,' Gurusinha says, 'although it took some time to sink in. We hadn't expected to be that successful at the start, but we had played fantastic cricket to win and in the final had beaten a great side in Australia. I don't think Australia were complacent. They had struggled to get in the final whereas we had played the best cricket in the tournament. Our top six batsmen were all in great form and the Australians knew that would be a problem for them.

'We flew back to Colombo the morning after the game. Normally the drive from the airport to the city is 40 minutes, but it took us two hours. There were millions of people out on the streets still celebrating. I think they had been up all night. We were being driven to the Presidential Palace and had full security and the Presidential fleet of cars, but there was no way we could get through all the people. They were all very happy.'

AUSTRALIA

M.A. Taylor (capt) c Jayasuriya b de Silva		74
M.E. Waugh c Jayasuriya b Vaas		12
R.T. Ponting b de Silva		45
S.R. Waugh c de Silva b Dharmasena		13
S.K. Warne st Kaluwitharana b Muralitharan		2
S.G. Law c de Silva b Jayasuriya		22
M.G. Bevan not out		36
I.A. Healy (wk) b de Silva		2
P.R. Reiffel not out		13
Extras (lb 10, w 11, nb 1)		22
(50 overs)		7–241

Did not bat: D.W. Fleming, G.D. McGrath

1/36 2/137 3/152 4/156 5/170 6/202 7/205

Bowling: Wickremasinghe 7-0-38-0; Vaas 6-1-30-1; Muralitharan 10-0-31-1; Dharmasena 10-0-47-1; Jayasuriya 8-0-43-1; de Silva 9-0-42-3

SRI LANKA

S.T. Jayasuriya run out		9
R.S. Kaluwitharana (wk) c Bevan b Fleming		6
A.P. Gurusinha b Reiffel		65
P.A. de Silva not out		107
A. Ranatunga (capt) not out		47
Extras (b 1, lb 4, w 5, nb 1)		11
(46.2 overs)		3–245

Did not bat: H.P. Tillekeratne, R.S. Mahanama, H.D.P.K. Dharmasena, W.P.U.J.W.U.J.C. Vaas, M. Muralitharan, G.G.P. Wickremasinghe

1/12 2/23 3/148

Bowling: McGrath 8.2-1-28-0; Fleming 6-0-43-1; Warne 10-0-58-0; Reiffel 10-0-49-1; M.E. Waugh 6-0-35-0; S.R. Waugh 3-0-15-0; Bevan 3-0-12-0

Umpires: S.A. Bucknor, D.R. Shepherd.

Toss: Sri Lanka

POST-MORTEM

Alan Lee's summation of the 1996 tournament in *Wisden Cricketers' Almanac* was that, despite

a handsome profit, the organisation and spirit of the Wills World Cup was not a patch on 1987.

Some of that was out of the hands of the cricket authorities; other aspects like travelling arrangements and practice facilities were within their sphere of influence. There had indeed been problems and flat moments. However, some of the cricket was sensational and no-one could question the worth of the winners, Sri Lanka.

Surprisingly Dav Whatmore soon resigned as coach of Sri Lanka, the politics of the cricket in the country of his birth taking their toll on the former Australian batsman. He returned to the position at the end of the 1999 World Cup.

Even though Australia had barely dented their reputation as one of the world's leading cricket teams by losing the final, a dramatic policy change was made soon after the tournament. Bob Simpson was replaced as Australian coach and Mark Taylor and Ian Healy's days in the limited-overs side were numbered. By the time the leading cricket nations of the world convened in England in 1999, Taylor had retired and Healy was a Test cricketer. I nearly wrote, 'only'.

8

World Cup 1999:

No Surprises Left

Twelve sides remained enough for the seventh World Cup as the competition returned to England after a 16-year break. The date and location had been agreed upon even prior to the 1996 Wills World Cup. A May and June date brought the competition into a four-yearly alignment with the first World Cup in 1975.

Restrictions on tobacco sponsorship, maybe the profile of cricket in England, or the confidence of tournament organisers, left the 1999 World Cup without a company tag. Instead the England Cricket Board received a spread of joy from a variety of sponsors. In particular from Natwest, Vodafone, Pepsi and Emirates Airlines. They were welcomed as the tournaments 'Global Partners'. It was still seen as necessary to tamper with the format and to increase the number of games played to a new record. The criticism that the 1996 format only eliminated the weaker countries in the preliminary group matches was overcome with only three sides progressing from their various groups through to the next round in 1999. That next round was the Super Sixes, a little tournament of nine matches enclosed within the bigger contest. It, too, looked to have imperfections. Sides were able to carry through some points from their round-robin games to the Super Six section, but it depended upon whom they had beaten and who else got through.

Whether that format would work more satisfactorily than the one that preceded it, only time would tell, but it was easy to pine for the schedules used in 1983 and 1987, and then the nine-sided competition of 1992. Each of those tournaments offered the fairest chance of the best side over the competition being triumphant on the day, or night, of the final.

Such a big impression had been created by the New Zealand and Sri Lankan innovations of 1992 and 1996 that the world waited with baited breath for the new revolutionary and trend-setting tactics of 1999. Editorials and feature articles in newspapers, periodicals and on the Internet were devoted to the prospect that some current cricket brain was at play trying to connive an unorthodox tactic that would put all opposition sides in a spin. It was easily forgotten that Imran Khan's 1992 Pakistanis had won by having brilliant skills and peaking at the right time.

The newcomers to the program were Scotland and Bangladesh. They and Kenya won their places ahead of the United Arab Emirates and Holland by virtue of their ICC Trophy triumphs in Kuala Lumpur in 1997. The inclusion of these nations, while worthy in the cause of cricketing globalisation, was hardly seen as likely to have a big impact on the popularity of the 1999 World Cup. The spreading of the cricketing gospel was considered so essential that instead of all the games being played in England there were two in Edinburgh and one each in Dublin, Cardiff and Amsterdam. Of far greater immediate import than this were the attempts by the marketing arm of the England Cricket Board to sell the World Cup product to a sceptical English populace.

This was to be the 'Carnival of Cricket' World Cup, which meant lots of music and colour. Leading cricketers modelling their country's colourful uniforms were joined in photo shoots by various celebrities, notably blonde

English bombshell Caprice. There was an official World Cup logo. Australian journalist Martin Blake called the yellow-and-green Australian uniform 'hideous' when he saw it in a warm-up game at Worcester. South Africa wore upside down Y-fronts. Uniforms had sponsors' logos, their countries emblems and were now numbered as well as named. Equally as blond as Caprice, rock guitarist Dave Stewart provided the 'hit' song, 'All Over the World', which was supposed to capture the hearts of the nation and lure them to the cricket grounds around the country from Friday 14 May until the final at Lord's on Sunday 20 June. Two videos accompanied the song. A Royal Albert Hall concert was mooted then cancelled due to a lack of big-name attractions. Woman were targeted as a prospective audience. It was a far cry from the formal receptions of 1975 and looked a lot of effort for little result as early ticket sales were slow. By the start of March the only sell-out matches were the final and the England vs South Africa game at The Oval. There was no soccer World Cup to compete with, but the FA Cup and the football Premiership were still to be resolved when England met Sri Lanka at Lord's on 14 May.

The ongoing mediocrity of the performances of the English team was another factor restraining early public interest. Crowd troubles in India and the West Indies in the months before the World Cup had given the game some bad publicity. However possibly the most significant negative influence were the lingering accusations that bookmakers from the Indian subcontinent had infiltrated player ranks.

The issue of bribes and match-fixing had not been fully resolved. The revelation that Shane Warne and Mark Waugh had taken money from bookmakers years before and that the Australian authorities, after finding out and punishing the pair, then covered the information up, brought the game in that country into disrepute. The ICC had met and discussed the issue in New Zealand, showing resolve but little prompt action. Meanwhile in Pakistan accusations and counter-accusations continued to fly in all directions, inside and outside courtrooms. None of this enhanced the good name of cricket.

The choice of the first part of the English summer for the program of matches was a risk both with ticket sales and the games themselves. The weather at that time of year is unreliable. In 1975 the gods had been kind and the Prudential Cup was unaffected. They were less co-operative in 1979 and some matches went into a second day. England, though, made the final. That might have been a consideration for the authorities setting up the 1999 competition.

It did not, however, make the host team tournament favourites. That honour fell to Hansie Cronje's South Africans who began the competition at 3–1, ahead of Australia at 7–2. Scotland was rated a 500–1 chance and Bangladesh 1000–1. This was considered to be a very open World Cup, but not that open.

The Proteas, who were placed along with England, India, Sri Lanka, Zimbabwe and Kenya in the tougher looking Group A, brought form and confidence to the World Cup. Over the southern summer they had thrashed the West Indies at home in both the Test and the limited-overs series. Then, in February and March they had made short work of New Zealand in New Zealand.

A featured strength of the South African side was the bevy of genuine all-rounders in the line-up, as opposed to the bits and pieces cricketers touted as all-rounders by other countries. Jacques Kallis and Shaun Pollock at 23 and 25 years of age respectively were emerging as a combined powerhouse in world cricket. Either could hold his place in the South African one-day side for his batting or bowling. More than that, they were exciting and aggressive players capable of energetic and athletic fielding of the type which can win one-day games.

That they were rated below Jonty Rhodes only served to prove that South Africa's busy and positive middle-order batsman was rated as highly as any cover fieldsman who has ever played the game. The South African batting could have been labelled a tad colourless at times. However, recent form had indicated that the problem would be resolved, especially if the powerful Daryll Cullinan could be kept away from Shane Warne. And then there was Allan Donald.

The champion paceman was reaching the late middle age of his fast bowling career. He had become a middle of the innings rather than a new-ball bowler in Limited-Over Internationals. But such were Donald's pace and skill that whoever avoided his thundering, silken charges would have been very relieved. One bad day had cost South Africa dearly in 1996. Some believed they might stumble at the wrong time again. The other 11 sides hoped that would be the day the Proteas played them.

Grim-faced Steve Waugh provided a stark contrast to the receptive, friendly but all-seeing countenance of the captain of the 1996 runners-up, Australia. Waugh had taken over from Mark Taylor as official captain of Australia's limited-overs side in 1997–98. They were in Group B, and one of themselves, Pakistan, New Zealand or the West Indies would miss promotion to the Super Sixes, presuming Scotland and Bangladesh were out of their league. Waugh's elevation seemed to correspond with a deterioration in his own form and fitness in the branch of the game where he had first established a worldwide reputation. A torn hamstring in the World Series Cup had severely curtailed his appearances during the early months of 1999. It also gave Shane Warne the opportunity to impress as a bright captain with his finger on the pulse.

Nevertheless, Waugh regained his place at the helm of the Australian one-day side. In the Caribbean he had to withstand some appalling treatment by overexcited and incensed crowds. His reputation as one of the game's most resilient characters and greatest students was undiminished by those events. Some, like Martin Crowe, felt his captaincy was a weak link; others suggested he was Australia's greatest asset.

That overlooked the brilliance of Glenn McGrath, the equal of any bowler in the world; the accuracy of Shane Warne whose powers in one-day cricket were not as diminished as at Test level; the audacious opening batting of Adam Gilchrist which, when complemented by the grace and strokeplay of Mark Waugh, launched Australian innings at breakneck speed. Nor could the enigmatic Michael Bevan be forgotten. The batsman with the highest average in the world in limited-overs cricket was able to brilliantly control the closing overs of an innings and rarely failed to score off any ball received. It beggared belief that his techniques were found so wanting in the longer version of the game.

The holders of the trophy, Sri Lanka, arrived in England as even greater outsiders than when they snared the World Cup just over three years earlier. Fatigue, injury and the onset of cricketing old age were offered as reasons for Sri Lanka's inconsistency over the southern summer. They had rarely been a match for England or Australia in the World Series Cup and with an attack based around controversial off spinner Muttiah Muralitharan, were thought unlikely to be suited to English wickets in May and June.

When the prospect of the MCC outlawing sledging became a topical issue, Arjuna Ranatunga, whose clashes with Alec Stewart in a one-day match in Adelaide in January had been most unpleasant, had plenty to say on the matter. With Javed Miandad retired the rotund Sri Lankan captain assumed the position as the game's leading on-field stirrer. He would have been quite prepared to further annoy all cricket followers outside his own country if it meant holding up the game's leading limited-overs trophy again in 1999.

He still had plenty of batting talent on call. Sanath Jayasuriya's left-handed belligerence would be suited to the smallest English grounds. Little Aravinda de Silva on his day was the equal of any batsman in the world, and in Australia and during the Pepsi Cup 21-year-old Mahela Jaya-wardene had revealed a precocious talent that suggested a budding champion. Happily, too, a return to England reduced the amount of travelling this weary team would have to complete. In 1987 and 1992 they spent more time in airports than on cricket grounds.

England had banked on experience and bowlers who might be able to take advantage of seaming wickets in their World Cup 1999 squad selection. There was as much discussion on who was left out as on who was included. As with Steve Waugh in Australia there were those in England of the opinion that better captains were available for limited-overs matches than Alec

Stewart. Unlike Australia, that is the norm in English thinking. That Mark Ramprakash's improved consistency at Test level had not yet translated into limited-overs selection was a surprise. The extent of Graham Thorpe's recovery from back injury in cool May conditions might be an influential factor when determining England's fate. Whatever England's overall level of success, the prospect of Graeme Hick batting against Kenya was exciting. The lime tree at Canterbury had been declared unwell. An on-song Hick could have demolished it even before its time was up.

Darren Gough's fitness and degree of accuracy were seen as crucial to England's bowling penetration. In the helpful dampness of May and early June, though, the old warhorse Angus Fraser threatened a few surprises as a last international hurrah.

Hot and cold and often controversial, Pakistan were capable of finishing either first, last or something in between. Coach Javed Miandad resigned just before the tournament. Still haunted and taunted by cricketing politics at home and the match-fixing allegations, Wasim Akram's side oozed enough variety and talent to win the World Cup if his players could keep their minds solely on cricket. The captain, reinstated after having been sacked or resigning from the position three times previously, was at about the same stage of his career as Imran Khan had been in 1992. His influence might have been just as significant.

Any pace-bowling line-up that boasted Akram, supported by Waqar Younis and the emerging Shoaib Akhtar, could conceivably cut a swathe through opposing top orders. The cold might not suit Mushtaq Ahmed's leg spin, but it would be less of a concern to the off spin of the talented and developing Saqlain Mushtaq.

Shahid Afridi, still not yet 20, offered the possibility of Bothamesque all-round feats. Saeed Anwar's class as a left-handed opening batsmen had been evident in all forms of cricket in every corner of the globe on all wickets. His run-making contributions could almost be taken for granted. Not so those of the lethargic looking Inzamam-ul-Haq. No-one could forget his semi-

final winning innings in New Zealand in 1992. In the ensuing years his mobility might have been compromised, but his power and his size had increased to a corresponding degree.

The gloom that had descended over West Indian cricket after their tour of South Africa was partially lifted by their demonstration of fighting qualities against Australia in the Caribbean. That they were still an unknown quantity could be attributed to a perceived lack of depth. The batting totally revolved around Brian Lara during the Test series against Australia and it was hard to see the West Indies putting together match-winning scores without plenty of runs from the flawed genius from Trinidad. Carl Hooper had retired at just the wrong time in regard to this tournament and Shivnarine Chanderpaul might have found it difficult to attain top form after a long lay-off with a shoulder injury.

Injury might also be a problem for the West Indian attack if the aging muscles of Courtney Walsh and Curtly Ambrose failed to cope with the intensity of a World Cup likely to be played in hamstring-snapping temperatures. The tall pace-bowling pair had lost some speed as they reached their mid-thirties, yet their skill and accuracy were to be marvelled at. With the new white, high-seamed Dukes ball in their hand Walsh and Ambrose were as big a threat to batsmen as they had ever been.

New Zealand's record in World Cups is more than respectable considering their overall standing on the international cricketing stage. It was always within their capacity to spring some surprises and reach at least the semi-final stage of the tournament. Their young captain, Stephen Fleming, and coach, the Australian Steve Rixon, had given New Zealand cricket some purpose and a measure of home success in the late 1990s.

Like South Africa they boasted a couple of genuine all-rounders. Chris Cairns on his day was an explosive proposition and possible match winner. The re-emergence of Dion Nash added quality to both the Kiwi bowling and lower order batting. Two of the dibbly dobblers of Martin Crowe's 1992 side remained. Chris Harris and Gavin Larsen might well have been suited to the greentops provided at Chelmsford, Cardiff and Southampton.

Craig McMillan had displayed attributes of a top-class batsman in his short international career while Fleming himself would be hungry for runs following a lay-off with a groin injury in the months prior to the competition. Hanging over his side was the shadow of a recent thrashing at the hands of South Africa and some consistency problems at the top of the batting order. However, New Zealand remained a country not to be underestimated.

Such is the style and charisma of the Indian batting line-up that most cricket fans hoped that the team would acquit itself well in the 1999 World Cup. They more than anyone might offer batting approaching a carnival with Sachin Tendulkar, the world number one in the eyes of most, as the chief attraction.

The record of Mohammad Azharuddin's team outside India had been poor and it was thought they might also struggle in English conditions, as they had done in 1996. Rahul Dravid, Ajay Jadeja and Saurav Ganguly as support for Tendulkar and the charming Azharuddin suggested potential run feasting. If that occurred Javagal Srinath, Venkatesh Prasad and Anil Kumble, the 10 out of 10 man, had enough skill to give their millions of fanatical followers an exciting ride through May and June 1999.

Zimbabwe arrived in England with just three victories in their previous four World Cups. Indications were that this disappointing return would be improved upon in 1999. Recent Test victories over India and Pakistan indicated a side growing in self-confidence and self-belief. In addition, the men in the red and green had reached the final of the one-day tournament in Sharjah and in late 1996 had beaten England 3–0 in a limited-overs series in Zimbabwe. They had gained full status some years before, now at last they were competing with their opponents at every turn and earning full respect from the world's best players. They started the 1999 World Cup as no more unlikely winners than Sri Lanka had been in 1996.

Alistair Campbell, at 26 equal with Stephen Fleming as the youngest captain in the tourna- ment, led a team with plenty to prove and a real chance to prove it. The efforts of the Flower brothers, Andy and Grant, and of Campbell himself had often given Zimbabwe enough runs to be competitive in limited-overs matches. That ability had been boosted by the recruitment of Murray Goodwin, a Zimbabwe-born Australian product who had moved from Sheffield Shield cricket to international class with deceptive ease and no shortage of runs.

Heath Streak was a highly rated paceman with an impressive record for his country. At times much of his bowling support had been inadequate with the exception of Paul Strang's excellent leg breaks. In the previous months Streak's burden had been reduced. Henry Olonga, despite bursts of inaccuracy, had matured as a bowler without compromising his exceptional speed. Neil Johnson's record as a county bowler in England in 1997 was nothing startling, but in his first Test he claimed perhaps the most prized scalp in the world in Tendulkar. Having returned from South Africa he, like Goodwin, slotted into the team as if a spot had been waiting for him all his life.

Bangladesh should have been viewing the 1999 World Cup in the same way that Sri Lanka did the 1979 tournament and Zimbabwe the competition of 1987. It was to be seen as another stepping stone towards full Test status for a nation whose entire population of 123 million seemed to be cricket fans. They had already played their fair share of Limited-Over Internationals.

Their captain, Aminul Islam, was rated as their best batsman leading in to the tournament, while Akram Khan had also scored some handy runs at the top level. As with most teams taking their first tentative steps at the top level, finding bowlers capable of restricting and dismissing the world's best batsmen was a problem. Mohammad Rafique and Hasibul Hussain had claimed the highest percentage of early wickets, but this was an area team coach Gordon Green- idge must have thought of as possibly inadequate in such unfamiliar surroundings.

Kenya were in a similar position to Bangla- desh. The 1999 World Cup presented them with an opportunity to mix it with the big boys in the hope of increasing their status and recognition. They took to England eight of the players who had participated in the 1996 tournament when to the surprise of everyone they knocked over the West Indies. One of the heroes of that win, Maurice Odumbe, was back although he had handed over the captaincy to Asif Karim, Kenya's leading wicket-taker. Steve Tikolo and Kennedy Otieno had already accumulated enough runs against quality opposition to be confident of their chances of handling anything their Group A opponents could send down.

It is a bit of a surprise to anyone living outside the British Isles that the weather could be tolerable enough to even contemplate cricket in Scotland, let alone put together a side to compete in the World Cup. Gavin Hamilton had originally been in the English squad and he was rated as an extremely promising all-rounder on the English county circuit. James Brinkley was favoured to take the new ball. He was a much

travelled player, having been contracted to both Worcestershire and Essex after having grown up in Australia. His birth certificate was what counted on this occasion. Seventeen-year-old John Blain, another signed up for county cricket, was expected to be his side's fastest bowler.

As the rain tumbled down on the county grounds around England during the first two weeks of May the term 'warm-up matches' looked to be inappropriate. Players barely had the chance to get the newness out of their uniforms, so regular were the interruptions. In five weeks time, on the evening of 20 June, one captain amongst the 12 photographed posing with the cherished trophy would be holding it aloft at Lord's. His side would be 300,000 US dollars richer and he and his team would be the darlings of the cricketing world. That was if the rain did not muck things up. The rain rules had been altered again. Mr Duckworth and Mr Lewis would be called upon in the event of the need for a recalculation.

FRIDAY 14 MAY 1999
GROUP A: ENGLAND vs SRI LANKA
LORD'S, LONDON: ENGLAND WON BY 8 WICKETS

England got the start they wanted to their home campaign with a comfortable victory over the increasingly maligned 1996 champions. The greatest threat to Alec Stewart's team came from persistent showers, but these were always brief enough to cause only short delays or arrived during intervals. Despite the comments over poor pre-match ticket sales there was nothing wrong with this Friday attendance at the home of cricket.

The most controversial change at Lord's over the winter months had been the admission of women to membership of the MCC for the first time. Why that met with resistance and the perching of the world's largest clock radio above the bowler's arm at the Nursery End of the ground did not, cannot be imagined. One kept waiting for the thing to be plugged in and the digital figures to appear on its windows.

Instead, there were big national flags,

fireworks, a speech from British PM Tony Blair and a balloon release in a sort of poor man's Commonwealth Games opening ceremony on the outfield. Finally Alec Stewart and Arjuna Ranatunga, newspaper criticism of him from Shane Warne still ringing in his ears, came out to toss.

That this might be England's day was indicated by Stewart's good fortune at the fall of the coin. He had no hesitation in electing to bowl. The hesitations came a few minutes later when a shower held up the start of the World Cup by a few minutes. Soon Darren Gough opened the tournament with a no-ball to Sanath Jayasuriya but the English opening bowlers then used the Dukes ball to good effect, repeatedly beating the outside edge in helpful conditions.

Sri Lanka had hidden Romesh Kaluwitharana down the order, promoting the experienced Roshan Mahanama back to open. He and

Jayasuriya added 42 until left-armer Alan Mullally, coming on first change, got the ball on line. In his first over the tall fair-haired speedster had Mahanama attempting a pull which steepled over gully. Graeme Hick ran back to take a well-judged catch.

Mahanama and Jayasuriya had used up a lot of the early luck. Marvin Atapattu, Jayasuriya and Aravinda de Silva fell in similar fashion to slips catches. With the bowlers on top Stewart employed three slips. They were not required when Hashan Tillekeratne was caught behind down the leg side from Mark Ealham's first ball. Sri Lanka were in desperate trouble at 5–65. Kaluwitharana and Ranatunga stemmed the decline with a bright stand of 84. The wicket-keeper–batsman dominated the partnership, counterattacking with slashing drives and powerful pulls. One of his six boundaries brought up his fifty in the 32nd over from just 52 balls. Ranatunga joined in when he hit Graeme Hick straight into the pavilion, which was nearly empty. MCC members were protesting at the ECB directive that they had to pay to watch World Cup matches.

Mullally came back to claim Kaluwitharana and after Ranatunga was nicely caught low down in the gully by Nasser Hussain the Sri Lankan batting gradually fell away.

As England batted there was always the fear that showers would alter the direction of the contest and the requirement of the chase. A few heavy clouds dwelt around St John's Wood, but they stayed away from Lord's. Hussain opened with Stewart in place of the injured Nick Knight. He stayed long enough with his captain for 50 runs to be posted before dancing down at Muttiah Muralitharan and being stumped.

Hussain's departure opened the way for Stewart and Hick to compile the partnership that won the match. They put on 125 runs in positive fashion, always keeping well up with the required run rate. Twice Hick skyed the ball only for it to fall between desperate fieldsmen. Otherwise he and Stewart dominated. A front-foot scoop by Hick sent the ball for six into the grandstand crowd at square leg.

Stewart's poor form in limited-overs matches had been coming under scrutiny. His powerful reply was not ended until his side were within 30 of victory. After he had been caught behind off the inside edge from Chaminda Vaas, Hick and Graham Thorpe carried England home with three overs to spare. Hick finished the match with another six, a calmly struck straight drive into the pavilion seats off the expensive Jaya-suriya. Stewart was named Man of the Match.

SRI LANKA

S.T. Jayasuriya c Hick b Mullally		29
R.S. Mahanama c Hick b Mullally		16
M.S. Atapattu c Thorpe b Austin		3
H.P. Tillekeratne c Stewart b Ealham		0
P.A. de Silva c Thorpe b Mullally		0
A. Ranatunga (capt) c Hussain b Ealham		32
R.S. Kaluwitharana (wk) c Stewart b Mullally		57
W.U.J.C. Vaas not out		12
K.E.A. Upashanpha c Thorpe b Hollioake		11
G.P. Wickremasinghe c Stewart b Austin		11
M. Muralitharan b Gough		12
Extras (lb 9, w 9, nb 3)		21
(48.4 overs)		10–204

1/42 2/50 3/63 4/63 5/65 6/149 7/155 8/174 9/190 10/204

Bowling: Gough 8.4-0-50-1; Austin 9-1-25-2; Mullally 10-1-37-4; Ealham 10-0-31-2; Flintoff 2-0-12-0; Hick 3-0-19-0; Hollioake 6-0-21-1

ENGLAND

N. Hussain st Kaluwitharana Muralitharan		14
A.J. Stewart (capt-wk) c Kaluwitharana b Vaas		88
G.A. Hick not out		73
G.P. Thorpe not out		13
Extras (lb 6, w 12, nb 1)		19
(46.5 overs)		2–207

Did not bat: N.H. Fairbrother, A.J. Hollioake, A. Flintoff, M.A. Ealham, I.E. Austin, D. Gough, A.D. Mullally

1/50 2/175

Bowling: Vaas 10-2-27-1; Wickremasinghe 10-0-41-0; Upashanpha 8-0-38-0; Muralitharan 10-0-33-1; Jayasuriya 7.5-0-55-0; de Silva 1-0-7-0

Umpires: R.E. Koertzen, S. Venkataraghavan.

Toss: England. Points: England 2, Sri Lanka 0

SATURDAY 15 MAY 1999
GROUP A: INDIA vs SOUTH AFRICA
COUNTY GROUND, HOVE: SOUTH AFRICA WON BY 4 WICKETS

Down by the seaside at the historic County Ground in Hove, tournament favourites, South Africa won an excellent contest by four wickets with 16 balls to spare.

Umpire Steve Bucknor prepared for his day by the sea by covering his face with sunscreen. It showed a responsible attitude, although it was unnecessary as the weather remained overcast and cold all day. When Venkatesh Prasad fielded at fine leg he let his long-sleeved jumper slip over his hands to keep his fingers warm. Azharuddin, the most experienced one-day cricketer in the world, won the toss and batted on a slow easy wicket. Sachin Tendulkar opened with Saurav Ganguly, the latter resplendent in a light-blue helmet matching his country's uniform. His attire obviously agreed with him because the left-hander got his country away to a great start with a flashing square cut for four off Shaun Pollock from the second ball of the day.

That put the thousands of Indian expatriates in the ground in a good mood, a feeling they retained while Tendulkar and Ganguly tamed the South African new-ball thrust. Tendulkar was eventually the first to go at 67, caught behind dabbing at Lance Klusener

Rahul Dravid and Ganguly kept the Indians on top with a partnership of 130 in 158 balls. They sustained an orthodox approach, concentrating on getting four or five off each over. Ganguly was the more productive partner, punctuating his innings with drives through mid-on and mid wicket and sweet cuts. A lofted drive off Nicky Boje carried for six over long-off. Both batsmen passed 50 and Dravid had faced 75 balls when he was bowled behind his legs swinging at a full-pitched Klusener delivery in the 42nd over.

The Indians reached their final overs with plenty of wickets in hand. However, they failed to take advantage. Ganguly just missed a deserved century when he cut Jacques Kallis wide of gully. He took off for a run only for Jonty Rhodes to elongate himself, grab the ball

one-handed, raise up to his knees and throw to the bowler well before the batsman could make his ground.

It was a brilliant piece of work, only slightly superior to the catch on the cover boundary by Boje who held a well-struck 'inside out' cover drive by Azharuddin. Ajay Jadeja scored at a run per ball until he skyed a pull off Allan Donald whose spells were fast, accurate and economical. South African captain Hansie Cronje had been taking advice from the dressing-room during the Indian innings via a small earpiece, which he was not allowed to use again.

The par for the course total of 253 looked much better when Javagal Srinath sent down a penetrative new-ball spell. He was assisted by the downhill slope at Hove. After Herschelle Gibbs had scored the first boundary for the Proteas with a French cut, Srinath brought the next one back to trap the opener in front of his stumps. Fellow opener Gary Kirsten struggled for 22 deliveries, then edged Srinath onto his stumps.

In a rousing response wicketkeeper Mark Boucher, batting at number 3, pulled two fours off Srinath, then top-edged a six over the wicketkeeper's head from the first ball of the next over. The Indian paceman conceded 25 runs from two overs. Anil Kumble came on in the 12th over. Boucher greeted him with a big straight drive, but was bowled in the same over cutting at a wrong 'un.

After 15 overs South Africa were 3–75. A skyed slog by Daryll Cullinan in Ganguly's first over left them 4–116 with a lot of work to do on a wicket that looked to be losing its pace. Kallis, emerging as a batsman to be ranked with the best, took that work responsibility upon himself and with the assistance of Hansie Cronje and Jonty Rhodes guided his side back into the game. Kallis and his captain put on 64 in just 13 overs. His stand of 47 in seven overs with Rhodes then made South Africa favourites to win. As with Ganguly, a run-out robbed Kallis of his century, but the South African still won the Man of the Match award.

Kallis' dismissal in the 46th over revitalised Indian hopes. Klusener quickly snuffed them out again by hitting three fours while facing just four balls. From the first ball of the 48th over Rhodes clubbed Prasad over mid-off for four, then pushed the next delivery to gully for the single that won the match. One upset Indian spectator who invaded the team group had to be escorted away by police.

INDIA	
S. Ganguly run out	97
S.R. Tendulkar c Boucher b Klusener	28
R. Dravid b Klusener	54
M. Azharuddin (capt) c Boje b Klusener	24
A. Jadeja c Kirsten b Donald	16
R.R. Singh not out	4
N.R. Mongia (wk) not out	5
Extras (b 6, lb 2, w 11, nb 6)	25
(50 overs)	5–253

Did not bat: J. Srinath, A.B. Agarkar, B.K.V. Prasad, A. Kumble

1/67 2/197 3/204 4/235 5/247

Bowling: Pollock 10-0-47-0; Kallis 10-1-43-0; Donald 10-0-34-1; Klusener 10-0-66-3; Boje 5-0-31-0; Cronje 5-0-24-0

SOUTH AFRICA	
H.H. Gibbs lbw Srinath	7
G. Kirsten b Srinath	3
M.V. Boucher (wk) b Kumble	34
J.H. Kallis run out	96
D.J. Cullinan c Singh b Ganguly	19
W.J. Cronje (capt) c Jadeja b Agarkar	27
J.N. Rhodes not out	39
L. Klusener not out	12
Extras (lb 4, w 3, nb 10)	17
(47.2 overs)	6–254

Did not bat: S.M. Pollock, N. Boje, A.A. Donald

1/13 2/22 3/68 4/116 5/180 6/227

Bowling: Srinath 10-0-69-2; Prasad 8.2-0-32-0; Kumble 10-0-44-1; Agarkar 9-0-57-1; Singh 2-0-10-0; Ganguly 4-0-16-1; Tendulkar 4-0-22-0

Umpires: S.A. Bucknor, D.R. Shepherd.

Toss: India. Points: South Africa 2, India 0

SATURDAY 15 MAY 1999
GROUP A: ZIMBABWE vs KENYA
COUNTY GROUND, TAUNTON: ZIMBABWE WON BY 5 WICKETS

Zimbabwe, relishing the chance to go into a match as favourites against a local rival, cruised home with nine overs to spare. Even so, the Kenyans were far from disgraced or disheartened by their performance.

Kenya had to bat first after Alistair Campbell won the toss and sent them in on a wicket that played well throughout. At first he cannot have been happy when Ravindu Shah flayed his opening bowlers. After 13 overs the total was already 62. Shah cracked five boundaries, lifting the drumbeats of the band of Kenyans who had followed their side into Somerset.

Shah and his partner, Kennedy Otieno, were out within two balls of each other. Neil Johnson, coming on as first change, ripped into the middle order. When he bowled Hitesh Modi the Kenyans had lost 4–25 to be 4–87. In the good old days of the first World Cup the Kenyans might have crumbled from there. Not in 1999, though.

Maurice Odumbe held tight for 57 balls while Alpesh Vadher struck a six and five fours while reaching an invaluable half century. Paul Strang broke the 22-over 84-run partnership when he trapped Odumbe lbw. That brought young fast bowler Tom Odoyo to the wicket and he walloped the ball around for a couple of fours and two nice sixes. When he became Johnson's third victim captain Aasif Karim put one over the ropes as well so that Kenya, aided by an extra 29 deliveries and runs from no-balls and wides, finished with a commendable 7–229.

Campbell made his feelings about the performance of his bowlers quite clear: 'Too many loose balls and too many four balls', which is an interesting distinction. His batsmen pleased him, though.

Johnson went straight into business with the bat. He and Grant Flower opened with 81 in 14 very profitable overs. Johnson was severe on the Suji brothers, Martin and Tony, who shared the new ball. He hit seven fours and two sixes in 70 balls. Paul Strang also made good use of the short straight boundaries at Taunton, hitting two of the day's nine sixes. Wides and no-balls haunted the Kenyan attack as they had the Zimbabweans, but a couple of wickets to the

O-Force—Odumbe and Odoyo—reduced their opponents to 4–147.

Andy Flower and Campbell, with over 5000 runs between them in Limited-Over Internationals, were unfazed by the losses and added a further 66 to their combined aggregate. That briskly took Zimbabwe to within a few runs of an obvious victory. Johnson's Man of the Match award was equally clear-cut.

KENYA

K.O. Otieno (wk) c G.W. Flower b Johnson	16
Ravindu Shah c Strang b A. Whittall	37
S.O. Tikolo c A. Flower b Johnson	9
M.O. Odumbe lbw Strang	20
H.S. Modi b Johnson	7
A. Vadher c A.P. Whittall b Strang	54
T.M. Odoyo b Johnson	28
Aasif Karim (capt) not out	19
A. Suji not out	3
Extras (b 2, lb 5, w 25, nb 4)	36
(50 overs)	7–229

Did not bat: M.A. Suji, J. Kamande

1/62 2/64 3/74 4/87 5/171 6/181 7/219

Bowling: Streak 9–1–50–0; Mbangwa 8–0–37–0; Johnson 10–0–42–4; A.P. Whittall 9–0–51–1; G. Whittall 6–0–20–0; Strang 8–0–22–2

ZIMBABWE

N. Johnson c Modi b Odoyo	59
G.W. Flower c Ravindu Shah b Aasif Karim	20
P.A. Strang c A. Suji b Odoyo	29
M.W. Goodwin c Aasif Karim b Odumbe	17
A. Flower (wk) c Tikolo b Odumbe	34
A.D.R. Campbell (capt) not out	33
G.J. Whittall not out	11
Extras (lb 5, w 16, nb 7)	28
(41 overs)	5–231

Did not bat: S.V. Carlisle, A.R. Whittall, H.H. Streak, M. Mbangwa

1/81 2/119 3/123 4/147 5/213

Bowling: M.A. Suji 7–0–47–0; A. Suji 6–1–32–0; Odoyo 9–0–40–2; Kamande 9–0–38–0; Aasif Karim 3–0–30–1; Odumbe 7–1–39–2

Umpires: D.B. Cowie, Javed Akhtar.

Toss: Zimbabwe. Points: Zimbabwe 2, Kenya 0

SUNDAY 16 MAY 1999
GROUP B PAKISTAN vs WEST INDIES
PHOENIX COUNTY GROUND, BRISTOL: PAKISTAN WON BY 27 RUNS

Always providers of a fascinating contest, the West Indies and Pakistan once more turned on a fluctuating cricket match from which the latter eventually triumphed. It was played before a packed house of 8000. Many fans were unable to get tickets which drew people to wonder why the game had not been scheduled at a venue with a larger capacity.

Despite the fact that the three Group A matches had been won by the side going in second and that the weather was grey and overcast, Wasim Akram batted when he won the toss. His openers had to face Courtney Walsh on the pitch that was his own for 14 years and they struggled. In his fourth over Walsh had Shahid

Afridi caught behind and in his next Saeed Anwar, who had earlier been dropped in the slips, was held by Lara at mid-on off a leading edge.

It got worse for the Pakistanis and their thousands of flag-waving fans when Mervyn Dillon bowled Abdur Razzaq between bat and pad on the drive and had Inzamam-ul-Haq top edging a pull to wicketkeeper Ridley Jacobs first ball. Dillon was mixing leg-side wides with unplayable deliveries. Wasim Akram's decision looked sick. Pakistan were 4–42 in the 19th over.

If the West Indies had an extra-quality fast bowler in their line-up they might have finished Pakistan there and then. Alas for the golden years of yore. Ijaz Ahmed and Yousuf Youhana were able to settle in against the support attack and added 60 in 12 overs. Brian Lara recalled Dillon and with the first ball of his second spell he hit Ijaz on the toe right in front.

Yousuf top-edged a slog 33 runs later and at 6–135 Pakistan could still have finished with an inadequate total. It was now, though, that having to use Keith Arthurton, Jimmy Adams and Ricardo Powell as bowlers became costly. Akram and Azhar Mahmood began striking the ball a long way. Between them they smashed 74 in nine overs, including two sixes apiece. Akram hit his off Adams and Powell, Azhar also struck Adams into the crowd and sent a full toss off Ambrose over the ropes at mid-wicket. The part-time bowlers conceded 83 runs in their combined 10 overs. A total of 23 wides and two no-balls added both to Pakistan's total and the balls they could face. Arthurton twisted an ankle in the outfield which would affect his batting later. Pakistan increased their score by 94 in the final 11 overs. The West Indies, so long on top in this match, now had to make 230 to win.

They had to withstand the opening burst of the young man now renowned as the fastest bowler in the world. Shoaib Akhtar excited the Pakistani spectators with his long run-up and extreme pace. He got the adrenalin of the West Indian openers, Ridley Jacobs and Sherwin Campbell, going too. His opening delivery, a short flyer, was hooked for six by Sherwin Campbell. The Bajan was late with the shot and the ball sailed over third man! Jacobs fended off another thunderbolt and it flew from his handle over the wicketkeeper for a first-bounce four.

In his second over, the man tipped to be the first bowler to crack the 100 mph barrier removed Campbell's off stump. Jimmy Adams came in at number 3, unusually for him, supplementing his helmet with a discretionary visor. It worked to the extent that he stayed with Jacobs until 58 runs had been added. Adams was caught at slip off the first ball of the 17th over to become the first of Azhar Mohammad's three victims.

Lara's entrance at 2–72 offered a tantalising prospect, one enhanced by two prompt boundaries through the covers. However, the entertainment lasted a mere nine balls. Abdur Razzaq induced an on drive that skewed off a leading edge to substitute Mushtaq Ahmed at cover point. It was a fatal blow to the chances of his side.

PAKISTAN

Saeed Anwar c Lara b Walsh	10
Shahid Afridi c Jacobs b Walsh	11
Abdur Razzaq b Dillon	7
Ijaz Ahmed lbw Dillon	36
Inzamam-ul-Haq c Jacobs b Dillon	0
Yousuf Youhana c & b Simmons	34
Azhar Mahmood c sub (N.O. Perry) b Ambrose	37
Wasim Akram (capt) b Walsh	43
Moin Khan (wk) not out	11
Saqlain Mushtaq not out	2
Extras (b 1, lb 12, w 23, nb 2)	38
(50 overs)	8–229

Did not bat: Shoaib Akhtar

1/22 2/23 3/42 4/42 5/102 6/135 7/209 8/217

Bowling: Ambrose 10–1–36–1; Walsh 10–3–28–3; Dillon 10–1–29–3; Simmons 10–0–40–1; Arthurton 1–0–10–0; Adams 8–0–57–0; Powell 1–0–16–0

WEST INDIES

S.L. Campbell b Shoaib Akhtar	9
R.D. Jacobs (wk) c Inzamam-ul-Haq b Razzaq	25
J.C. Adams c Inzamam-ul-Haq b Azhar	23
B.C. Lara (capt) c sub (Saqlain Mushtaq) b Abdur Razzaq	11
S. Chanderpaul c Yousuf Youhana b Shoaib Akhtar	77
R.L. Powell c Yousuf Youhana b Saqlain	4
P.V. Simmons c Imran Khan b Azhar Mahmood	5
C.E.L. Ambrose c Imran Khan b Abdur Razzaq	1
K.L.T. Arthurton c Saeed Anwar b Azhar Mahmood	6
M. Dillon run out	6
C.A. Walsh not out	0
Extras (b 1, lb 8, w 20, nb 6)	35
(48.5 overs)	10–202

1/14 2/72 3/84 4/101 5/121 6/141 7/142 8/161 9/195 10/202

Bowling: Wasim Akram 10–3–37–0; Shoaib Akhtar 9.5–1–54–2; Saqlain Mushtaq 9–0–22–1; Azhar Mahmood 10–0–48–3; Abdur Razzaq 10–3–32–3

Umpires: D.B. Hair, D.L. Orchard.

Toss: Pakistan. Points: Pakistan 2, West Indies 0

Shivnarine Chanderpaul fought hard for the rest of the innings to get the West Indies back into the match. If he could have found one decent partner that objective would have been achieved. None was forthcoming. Jacobs became Abdur's second wicket when he was caught at slip driving at a wide ball in the 23rd over. Ricardo Powell and Phil Simmons never got going and only some resilience by Dillon, and Pakistan's

generous quota of wides and a couple of missed chances allowed the total to creep past 200.

Chanderpaul was last out, caught off Shoaib with 28 runs still needed off eight deliveries. The slender, reliable left-hander was still going for the win and his 96-ball innings was by a healthy margin the best of the game. The Man of the Match award, though, went to Azhar Mahmood.

SUNDAY 16 MAY 1999
GROUP B: AUSTRALIA vs SCOTLAND
COUNTY GROUND, WORCESTER: AUSTRALIA WON BY 6 WICKETS

Worcester traditionally hosts the opening fixture to Ashes tours of England. There have been many memorable performances at what is widely regarded as the most beautiful cricket ground in the world. This effort against Scotland, despite the comfortable win, will never be rated among the best by the Aussies at New Road.

To be fair, Steve Waugh's side was on a hiding to nothing against the lowly rated Scots and they certainly came up with a better result than Kim Hughes' side had when they played the Zimbabwean World Cup debutants in the opening round of 1983. The Australians had to contend with a pro-Scottish crowd full of grog, decipherable and indecipherable comments, and weather far better suited to Glasgow than any major Australian centre.

Shane Warne was a special target of the Scottish taunts. The ability of the great leg spinner to tolerate their jibing was diminished by having received a fine and a two-match suspended sentence for his published comments that Sri Lanka would be better off without Arjuna Ranatunga. Warne risked further censure when he gave a single-finger salute to a section of the crowd. However, Ranjan Madugalle took no action.

The cricket action began immediately after Steve Waugh had won the toss and sent Scotland in to bat. Bruce Patterson gave his country a perfect start to their first Limited-Over International when he caressed a half-volley from Damien Fleming through the covers for four.

Patterson and his opening partner, 40-year-old Iain Philip, flattered to deceive with that start as they scratched around for 19 runs in 11 overs. Fleming got his revenge on Patterson, Gilchrist holding a low edge, but he was one of several players to make glaring mistakes in the field. Also, the Australian bowlers had as much trouble keeping the swinging ball on a line that satisfied the umpires as had the other attacks playing that weekend. Adam Dale and Glenn McGrath were the worst culprits, sending down 22 illegal deliveries between them.

Scotland battled to keep their run rate above two an over. Philip was nicely caught in the gully by the Australian captain in the 23rd over, Adam Gilchrist completed a smart stumping when Mike Allingham became too ambitious against Warne, and Michael Bevan flew like a bird to his left to hold Mike Smith at full stretch at mid-on off Shane Lee.

Between those commendable efforts, three catches and three run outs were missed. Fleming misjudged the break on a hit to mid-on and looked a fool as he changed direction too late and the ball ran behind him for four. Gavin Hamilton, a highly rated all-rounder contracted to Yorkshire, and James Brinkley, a fast bowler with connections all over Australia and Great Britain, gave the Scottish total respectability by adding 62 in 10 overs. Even though the pair fell within a couple of balls of each other to Warne in the 47th over, Scotland were able to complete their innings with a far from embarrassing 7–181.

It looked better still when Asim Butt had Gilchrist caught low down at leg gully by Nick Dyer in the sixth over. That was the last real shock and from that point Australia always looked like winning. Mark Waugh was in no mood to encourage Scotland and his was the best innings of the game. He hit five sweetly timed boundaries and his 114-ball knock won him the Man of the Match award. Waugh had a stand of 84 in 21 overs with Ricky Ponting. The Tasmanian was out to the catch of the day by Allingham, a sprinting diving effort, coming in from the square-leg boundary to hold a top-edged pull.

Darren Lehmann underedged his second ball onto his stumps with the score still on 101. Forty runs later, in the 36th over, Mark Waugh chipped a return catch to give Dyer his second wicket.

Then Steve Waugh, who hit seven boundaries, and Bevan saw Australia home with five overs and six wickets to spare.

Steve Waugh, who can match his former captain, Allan Border, for grumpiness, had plenty to complain about after the game. He rated Australia's performance 4 out of 10 and felt dissatisfied at the ground security provided. It was a sensitive issue with the Australian captain after the dangerous pitch invasion and bottle-throwing incidents in the West Indies. On two separate occasions male streakers held up play for several minutes before being removed and after the game the crowd came from all directions. Waugh was none too pleased as his players were subject to some jostling.

SCOTLAND

B.M.W. Patterson c Gilchrist b Fleming	10
I.L. Philip c S.R. Waugh b McGrath	17
M. Allingham st Gilchrist b Warne	3
M.W. Smith c Bevan b Lee	13
G. Salmond (capt) c Gilchrist b S.R. Waugh	31
G.M. Hamilton b Warne	34
J.E. Brinkley c Dale b Warne	23
A.G. Davies (wk) not out	8
J.A.R. Blain not out	3
Extras lb 9, w 22, nb 8)	39
(50 overs)	7–181

Did not bat: Asim Butt, N.R. Dyer

1/19 2/37 3/52 4/87 5/105 6/167 7/169

Bowling: Fleming 9–2–19–1; Dale 10–2–35–0; McGrath 9–0–32–1; Warne 10–0–39–3; Lee 6–1–25–1; Waugh 6–0–22–1

AUSTRALIA

A.C. Gilchrist (wk) c Dyer b Asim Butt	6
M. Waugh c & b Dyer	67
R. Ponting c Allingham b Blain	33
D. Lehmann b Dyer	0
S.R. Waugh (capt) not out	49
M. Bevan not out	11
Extras (lb 3, w 4, nb 9)	16
(44.5 overs)	4–182

Did not bat: S. Lee, S.K. Warne, D.W. Fleming, A.C. Dale, G.D. McGrath

1/17 2/101 3/101 4/141

Bowling: Blain 8–0–35–1; Asim Butt 10–3–21–1; Brinkley 8–0–43–0; Hamilton 8.5–0–37–0; Dyer 10–1–43–2

Umpires: R.S. Dunne, P. Willey.

Toss: Australia. Points: Australia 2, Scotland 0

MONDAY 17 MAY 1999
GROUP B: BANGLADESH vs NEW ZEALAND
COUNTY GROUND, CHELMSFORD: NEW ZEALAND WON BY 6 WICKETS

New Zealand made very short work of Bangladesh at the well-appointed home of Essex County Cricket Club in Chelmsford. The capacity crowd, full of noisy expatriate Bangladeshis down from East London, saw just 70 overs of cricket as the Kiwis strolled to victory.

After Stephen Fleming had won the toss on a cool windy morning and sent Bangladesh in both openers, like-named but unrelated, were back in the pavilion before the end of the third

over. Each fell in identical fashion, trapped lbw by balls from left-armer Geoff Allott that straightened down the line of the stumps.

For the next 10 overs Akram Khan and the captain, Aminul Islam, gave the impression that Bangladesh would recover and build a respectable total. They added 31 before being the first two victims in a startling collapse. Chris Cairns bowled Aminul middle stump then five balls later Gavin Larsen held a caught and bowled from a hard-hit drive by Akram. Cairns and Larsen continued to inflict damage. When Mohammad Rafique was caught plumb in front by Cairns from the first ball he faced Bangladesh was 7–51 in the 21st over and a complete rout was on the cards. Naimur Rahman and Enamul Hoque at least stopped the procession temporarily, and added 34 in the process. The last couple of batsmen continued to fight hard and Hasibul Hussain took 12 off a Chris Harris over, including a swipe for six that landed on the roof of the commentary box. An Allott full toss, possibly an above the waist no-ball, was hit by Hassibul straight to Matthew Horne at mid wicket in the 38th over to end the innings on 116.

New Zealand began their reply before lunch and in the second over Nathan Astle plonked an off-drive off left-armer Manjural straight into the hands of Aminul at mid-off. The Bangladeshi bowlers were able to extract some movement and hit the pads a few times without winning an lbw decision. They had to wait until the 11th over when Craig McMillan, who had just started to hit a few boundaries, completely mistimed a slower ball from Hasibul and was caught at mid wicket.

Further wickets had to follow quickly if the game was to come to life. They didn't. Fleming and Horne put on 45 in 12 overs before the New Zealand captain was caught behind and Horne lasted until his side was just a dozen runs from victory. Roger Twose enlivened the final stages of the match with a huge six over long-on that landed in the back garden of one of the houses in Hayes Close and was lost.

The winning run, scored from the last ball of the 33rd over, heralded yet another energetic invasion. One spectator pilfered a stump. If Steve Waugh had been watching he would have been unimpressed. Gavin Larsen, as accurate as in 1992 if a little more grey-haired, was named Man of the Match.

BANGLADESH	
Shahriar Hossain lbw Allott	0
Mehrab Hossain lbw Allott	2
Akram Khan c & b Larsen	16
Aminul Islam (capt) b Cairns	15
Khaled Mashud (wk) b Larsen	4
Naimur Rahman lbw Larsen	18
Khaled Mahmud c Twose b Cairns	3
Mohammad Rafique lbw Cairns	0
Enamul Hoque b Harris	19
Hasibul Hussain c Horne b Allott	16
Manjural Islam not out	6
Extras (lb 4, w 5, nb 8)	17
(37.4 overs)	10–116

1/0 2/7 3/38 4/38 5/46 6/49 7/51 8/85 9/96 10/116

Bowling: Allott 8.4-0-30-3; Nash 10-1-30-0; Cairns 7-1-19-3; Larsen 10-0-19-3; Harris 2-0-14-1

NEW ZEALAND	
M. Horne lbw Naimur Rahman	35
N. Astle c Aminul Islam b Manjural Islam	4
C. McMillan c Naimur Rahman b Hasibul Hussain	20
S. Fleming (capt) c Khaled Mashud b Mohammad Rafique	16
R. Twose not out	30
C. Cairns not out	7
Extras (lb 1, w 4)	5
(33 overs)	4–117

Did not bat: A.C. Parore (wk), C.Z. Harris, D.J. Nash, G.R. Larsen, G.A. Allott.

1/5 2/33 3/78 4/105

Bowling: Hasibul Hussain 10-2-33-1; Manjural Islam 8-3-23-1; Khaled Mahmud 7-2-12-0; Enamul Hoque 3-0-21-0; Mohammad Rafique 3-0-22-1; Naimur Rahman 2-0-5-1

Umpires: I.D. Robinson, S. Venkataraghavan.

Toss: New Zealand. Points: New Zealand 2, Bangladesh 0

TUESDAY 18 MAY 1999
GROUP A: ENGLAND vs KENYA
St LAWRENCE GROUND, CANTERBURY: ENGLAND WON BY 9 WICKETS

Although Canterbury is a beautiful city and has a lovely cricket ground, it can still be a depressing place when there is rain and it is persistent enough to look like ruining the cricket.

There were showers all morning in the south-east corner of England. They were bad enough to prevent commencement of play and showed no immediate sign of abating. But there is no point in hosting a World Cup tournament if you can't hope for a bit of good fortune with the weather. Eventually the skies cleared enough for England to complete its win over Kenya.

As against Zimbabwe, the Kenyans batted better than they bowled, while England only had to use three batsmen instead of the four they required against Sri Lanka. Nasser Hussain and Graeme Hick were more concerned with the prospect of rain and bad light stopping play than innocuous Kenyan bowling hampered by a wet ball. The match was not completed until 7.52 pm.

Alec Stewart won his second toss and the game was able to get under way 90 minutes late, albeit under a sky that remained grey and threatening. Kennedy Otieno was caught at slip in the fourth over off Ian Austin, cutting too close to his body. Then Ravindu Shah and Steve Tikolo put on 100 for the second wicket in 23 overs.

Tikolo's innings was most impressive. He reached his 50 off 70 balls and hit eight fine boundaries. Darren Gough came back to break the stand, having Shah caught behind off an inside edge. Two overs later he bowled Maurice Odumbe with an inswinging yorker to claim his 100th wicket in Limited-Over Internationals. England took control of the game and never loosened it from that point.

Neil Fairbrother ran out Hitesh Modi at the bowler's end with a throw from short fine leg. Gough picked up two more wickets with inswinging yorkers and Graham Thorpe ended the innings when he ran out Martin Suji in the final over. In the end only the successful continuation of Thomas Odoyo's policy of all-out attack which brought him three fours and a six off Alan Mullally over square leg ensured the efforts of Shah and Tikolo were not wasted.

England's in-form top order were never going to be challenged, but they had to endure more interruptions and for a time feared that the game would have to continue into a second day. According to some, the umpires' decree that the between-innings interval should last an hour was incorrect. At 6 pm rain once more stopped play. Elsewhere in the world that might have spelled the end of the day. England's one climatic advantage over other cricket nations is a lengthy twilight, so an opportunity to re-start presented itself at 6.43.

Stewart had been bowled in the 10th over by a ball that cut back into him. Hick and Hussain then took command of the Kenyan attack. Hussain went to his fifty in 87 balls with seven fours. However, the feature shot of his innings was a pulled six in the 37th over which sent the ball sailing into the top row of a temporary stand beside the ailing lime tree. Hick finished with nine fours in his unbeaten 61, the last of which, a square cut, completed England's win with 11 overs if not much daylight to spare. Tikolo beat Hussain, Hick and Gough for the Man of the Match award.

As with his counterparts at Worcester, the streaker at Canterbury was more than a match for the employed ground security.

KENYA

K. Otieno (wk) c Thorpe b Austin	0
Ravindu Shah c Stewart b Gough	46
S.O. Tikolo c Gough b Ealham	71
M.O. Odumbe b Gough	6
H.S. Modi run out	5
A. Vadher b Croft	6
T. Odoyo not out	34
Aasif Karim (capt) b Ealham	9
A. Suji b Gough	4
Mohammad Sheikh b Gough	7
M.A. Suji run out	0
Extras (b 1, lb 5, w 6, nb 3)	15
(49.4 overs)	10–203

1/7 2/107 3/115 4/130 5/142 6/150 7/181 8/186 9/202 10/203

Bowling: Gough 10–1–34–4; Austin 9.4–0–41–1; Mullally 10–0–41–0; Ealham 10–0–49–2; Croft 10–1–32–1

ENGLAND

N. Hussain not out	88
A.J. Stewart (capt-wk) b Odoyo	23
G.A. Hick not out	61
Extras (b 5, lb 6, w 13, nb 8)	32
(39 overs)	1–204

Did not bat: G.P. Thorpe, N.H. Fairbrother, A. Flintoff, M.A. Ealham, R.D.B. Croft, I.D. Austin, D.G. Gough, A.D. Mullally

1/45

Bowling: M.A. Suji 9–0–46–0; A. Suji 3–0–6–0; Odoyo 10–0–65–1; Aasif Karim 8–0–39–0; Odumbe 6–1–23–0; Mohammad Rafique Sheikh 3–0–14–0

Umpires: K.T. Francis, R.E. Koertzen.

Toss: England. Points: England 2, Kenya 0

WEDNESDAY 19 MAY 1999
GROUP A: SRI LANKA vs SOUTH AFRICA
COUNTY GROUND, NORTHAMPTON: SOUTH AFRICA WON BY 89 RUNS

Sri Lanka's World Cup defence was looking sick after this substantial defeat by South Africa. The reigning champions had some luck with umpiring decisions and at the start of the 49th over of the South African innings looked to have the match under some control.

That was all changed by five exhilarating Lance Klusener hits. His 22-run onslaught was immediately followed by an irresistible spell of fast bowling by Jacques Kallis which swept away the Sri Lankan top order. From that point there was only going to be one winner. It is a measure of South Africa's strength in this type of cricket that their best bowling came from one of their leading batsmen and their match-winning innings was played by a front-line bowler.

Arjuna Ranatunga sent South Africa in on a cool morning at the refurbished Northampton ground. The 7000-capacity venue soon filled up and nobody would have wanted to miss an eventful start. Gary Kirsten drove three consecutive boundaries off Pramodya Wickremasinghe's second over then played on to left-hander Chaminda Vaas from the third ball of the fourth. Two runs later Herschelle Gibbs was given out caught behind driving at a wide ball he did not believe he hit. When Wickremasinghe bowled Mark Boucher through the gate in the next over South Africa were 3–24.

The Northampton wicket was offering assistance to the bowlers so that South Africa had to battle for their runs. It was a fight they continued to lose for quite some time. Kallis fended away from his body and Hansie Cronje called for a second run that was not there. Jayawardene's perfect throw from deep square leg left the Proteas 5–69 in the 21st over.

They had progressed to 6–115 12 overs later when Shaun Pollock drove at Muttiah Muralitharan. He struck the ball sweetly, but straight at Ranatunga fielding in close on the off side. The ball ricocheted off Ranatunga and lobbed up to Muralitharan. The trajectory of the ball off the

bat suggested it had bounced on its way to Ranatunga's ankle, but the Sri Lankans appealed and Steve Dunne referred the matter to third umpire, Ken Palmer. Palmer, an experienced practitioner, viewed the incident from various angles for seven minutes before pronouncing to everyone's surprise that Pollock had been caught and bowled.

Two overs later Daryll Cullinan, whose innings had been the mainstay of the South African effort, lofted Muralitharan down the ground towards long-off. Vaas backed back and judging the ball very well held the catch. His momentum took him back further and as he approached the rope Vaas threw the ball away. If a fielder carries the ball over the rope while completing a catch the shot counts for six. Most believed the Sri Lankan paceman had saved runs by throwing the ball back. Palmer thought he had completed the catch and astonishingly ruled Cullinan out, leaving South Africa 8–122.

A complete capitulation was overcome when Steve Elworthy stayed with Klusener while 44 runs were put on. When Vaas began the 50th over South Africa had worked their way to 9–177. Another 8 to 10 runs would have been valuable. Klusener got those from the first four balls. Anything extra was a bonus. The fifth ball was a waist-high full toss. The big left-hander heaved that over mid wicket for six. Vaas' final ball pitched on a length. Klusener gave himself a little room and swung hard and straight. That ball sailed into the crowd too. It raised Klusener's fifty from 44 balls. The final total was now a competitive 9–199.

The crowd, sitting in welcome sunshine, was buzzing. So too was Kallis when the old 1996 World Cup firm of Sanath Jayasuriya and Romesh Kaluwitharana came out to begin the reply. The objective was a brisk start. However Kallis' bouncy, fast outswingers were nigh on unplayable. His extravagant movement caused Kaluwitharana to swish and miss every ball in his first over. The wicketkeeper–batsman cracked a beautiful pull from the second ball of his next over, but followed that with an edged drive. Cullinan parried the ball before holding it at the second attempt.

Another blow came from the final ball of the same over when the ball jagged into the left-handed Jayasuriya at pace. He guided it into his middle stump which splattered out of the ground. Kallis wasn't finished. Marvin Atapattu also tried to drive, only to inside edge through to Boucher, who dived forward and low to his left to hold an excellent catch. Kallis had three wickets in 11 balls. It could have been four as Klusener had missed a sharp chance off Aravinda de Silva at third slip just before Atapattu's dismissal.

Pollock ensured the chance had little impact when he trapped de Silva in front with an off-cutter in his next over. The little Sri Lankan

walked away shaking his head. He may not have been totally satisfied with Steve Dunne's decision. Nor could he have been happy with his form or that of his team-mates. After being 0–12 Sri Lanka had collapsed to 4–14. And Allan Donald had not yet been needed. As if peeved at missing out on the fun he had Rana-tunga caught behind from his second ball. It was another rearing delivery, Sri Lanka were 5–31 and the show was over. Mahela Jayawardne showed why he is so highly rated with a couple of sumptuous drives and Roshan Mahanama demonstrated the technique that might have been able to handle the new ball more effectively. That allowed the innings to stretch out for another 20 overs before Klusener topped his day with three cheap wickets and a well deserved Man of the Match award.

SOUTH AFRICA

G. Kirsten b Vaas	14
H.H. Gibbs c Kaluwitharana b Wickremasinghe	5
M.V. Boucher (wk) b Wickremasinghe	1
J.H. Kallis c Mahanama b Wickremasinghe	12
D.J. Cullinan c Vaas b Muralitharan	49
W. Cronje (capt) run out	8
J.N. Rhodes c Jayasuriya b Muralitharan	17
S.M. Pollock c & b Muralitharan	2
L. Klusener not out	52
S. Elworthy c Kaluwitharana b Vaas	23
A.A. Donald not out	3
Extras (lb 2, w 7, nb 4)	13
(50 overs)	9–199

1/22 2/24 3/24 4/53 5/69 6/103 7/115 8/122 9/166

Bowling: Wickremasinghe 10-1-45-3; Vaas 10-0-46-2; Jayawardene 10-0-46-0; Muralitharan 10-1-25-3; Chandana 7-0-26-0; Jayasuriya 3-1-9-0

SRI LANKA

S.T. Jayasuriya b Kallis	5
R.S. Kaluwitharana (wk) c Cullinan b Kallis	5
M.S. Atapattu c Boucher b Kallis	1
A. de Silva lbw Pollock	1
R.S. Mahanama lbw Pollock	36
A. Ranatunga (capt) c Boucher b Donald	7
M. Jayawardene c Kallis b Elworthy	22
U.D.U. Chandana c Cullinan b Klusener	9
W.U.J.C. Vaas c Pollock b Klusener	1
P. Wickremasinghe b Klusener	6
M. Muralitharan not out	0
Extras (lb 5, w 10, nb 2)	17
(35.2 overs)	10–110

1/12 2/13 3/14 4/14 5/31 6/66 7/87 8/98 9/110 10/110

Bowling: Pollock 8-3-10-2; Kallis 8-0-26-3; Elworthy 8-1-23-1; Donald 6-1-25-1; Klusener 5.2-1-21-3

Umpires: S. Dunne, S.A. Bucknor.

Toss: Sri Lanka. Points: South Africa 2, Sri Lanka 0

WEDNESDAY 19 MAY 1999
GROUP A: INDIA vs ZIMBABWE
GRACE ROAD, LEICESTER: ZIMBABWE WON BY 3 RUNS

This was a poignant and ultimately heartbreaking game for India. They had to withstand the temporary loss of their best batsmen and all sorts of mistakes in the field, yet still would have won if Henry Olonga had not overcome his own bowling problems and snatched victory for

Zimbabwe. Alistair Campbell's side was elated because this win gave them a real chance of progressing through to the Super Sixes round.

Some members of the Indian team had only found out on the morning of the match that Sachin Tendulkar had flown back to be with his family in India upon hearing the news of his father's sudden death. Both teams lined up for a minute's silence as a mark of respect prior to the start of the game.

There was another good crowd in at Grace Road as the weather continued to be kind, if a little on the cool side, especially for Indians and Zimbabweans. Mohammad Azharuddin won the toss and sent Zimbabwe in. On a firm evenly grassed wicket Javagal Srinath and Venkatesh Prasad responded well to their captain's decision, for several overs keeping the batsmen well under control. Srinath had the left-handed Neil Johnson caught behind in the third over while Grant Flower and number 3, pinch-hitter Paul Strang, were lucky to survive.

That, though, remained the trend of the innings. In addition, the wide and no-ball count mounted and the Zimbabweans took advantage of any loose bowling. Strang was yorked by Ajit Agarkar in the 10th over and when Saurav Ganguly had Murray Goodwin caught in the gully Zimbabwe were 3–87 in the 22nd over. The Flowers combined for a stand of 57. A percentage of the runs actually came off the bat and many of those were unbelievably short singles. Then Campbell and Andy Flower took the total beyond 200 by adding a further 60 in nine overs.

By now the inaccuracy of the Indians was really starting to tell. Anil Kumble was an exception and he picked up the wickets of the Zimbabwean captain and Guy Whittall in quick succession. Nevertheless, by 2.15 pm he and his pace-bowling colleagues had only sent down 276 legal deliveries. This meant that they had to complete their allotment to Zimbabwe, but would receive just 46 overs in return. During the final over another wide from Prasad brought up the half century of extras. The crowd cheered.

The early dismissal of the in-form Ganguly was a further regret for the Indians as they began their pursuit of 253. Eddo Brandes held the opener at fine leg off Johnson. However, Brandes copped some punishment from Rahul Dravid. Heath Streak replaced the expensive veteran and immediately had Dravid cutting to Grant Flower in the gully. When Azharuddin edged the same bowler to his opposite number at first slip India were 3–56 at the end of the ninth over.

Stand-in opener Sadagopan Ramesh and Ajay Jadeja repaired the damage to the extent of an enterprising 99-run partnership in 19 overs. Ramesh pulled Johnson for six. Henry Olonga missed an easy run out then sprayed the ball about in more directions than his dreadlocked hair was pointing. Murray Goodwin just missed holding a skyer in what would have been an early bid for catch of the tournament. Soon after Ramesh was caught at mid-on by the same fieldsman off Grant Flower, whose accuracy was well appreciated by the Man of the Match adjudicator.

Five overs later Streak returned to have an lbw shout upheld. India were 5–174 and six down one run later when Goodwin ran out Agarkar from mid-on. The match was boiling up into a thriller and Nayan Mongia added to the excitement with a quickfire 28. When Srinath hit Paul Strang for six over mid wicket and then repeated the dose to Guy Whittall India needed just another nine runs from two overs with three wickets standing.

On instinct Campbell threw the ball to Olonga. The tearaway responded by having Robin Singh caught at mid-off, then yorked Srinath with his fifth ball to leave India 9–249. Prasad joined Kumble to face the last ball of the penultimate over of the match. It was a full length, Prasad fell across his stumps and was struck on the pads. Up went Olonga, Andy Flower and the entire Zimbabwean nation. Up also, after the briefest of delays, went umpire Peter Willey's left index finger. There was a blur of Zimbabwean red as the players celebrated a real coming-of-age World Cup win.

For India the loss was equally significant. Azharuddin was booed by Indian supporters in the crowd. The *Hindu* newspaper called the loss 'appalling'. Neutrals might have suggested it was 'exciting'. The jostling of Zimbabwean players by invading spectators and the stoning of the team bus after the game were genuinely appalling.

ZIMBABWE		INDIA	
N.C. Johnson c Mongia b Srinath	7	S.C. Ganguly c Brandes b Johnson	9
G.W. Flower c Mongia b Jadeja	45	S. Ramesh c Goodwin b G.W. Flower	55
P.A. Strang b Agarkar	18	R. Dravid c G.W. Flower b Streak	13
M.W. Goodwin c Singh b Ganguly	17	M. Azharuddin (capt) c Campbell b Streak	7
A. Flower (wk) not out	68	A. Jadeja lbw Streak	43
A.D.R. Campbell (capt) st Mongia b Kumble	24	R.R. Singh c Campbell b Olonga	35
G.J. Whittall b Kumble	4	A.B. Agarkar run out	1
S.V. Carlisle b Srinath	1	N.R. Mongia b Whittall	28
H.H. Streak c Mongia b Prasad	14	J. Srinath b Olonga	18
E.A. Brandes c Mongia b Prasad	2	A. Kumble not out	1
H.K. Olonga not out	1	B.K.V. Prasad lbw Olonga	0
Extras (lb 14, w 21, nb 16)	51	Extras (b 1, lb 4, w 24, nb 10)	39
(50 overs)	9–252	(45 overs)	10–249

1/12 2/45 3/87 4/144 5/204 6/211 7/214 8/244 9/250

Bowling: Srinath 10-1-35-2; Prasad 10-1-37-2; Agarkar 9-0-70-1; Ganguly 5-0-22-1; Singh 2-0-11-0; Kumble 10-0-41-2; Jadeja 4-0-22-1

1/13 2/44 3/56 4/155 5/174 6/175 7/219 8/249 9/249 10/249

Bowling: Brandes 3-0-27-0; Johnson 7-0-51-1; Streak 9-0-36-3; Olonga 4-0-22-3; Whittall 4-0-26-1; Strang 8-0-49-0; G.W. Flower 10-0-33-1

Umpires: D.L. Orchard, P. Willey.

Toss: India. Points: Zimbabwe 2, India 0

THURSDAY 20 MAY 1999
GROUP B: AUSTRALIA vs NEW ZEALAND
SOPHIA GARDENS, CARDIFF: NEW ZEALAND WON BY 5 WICKETS

Nothing gives a New Zealander as much pleasure as beating Australia in a sporting contest. Steve Waugh's much vaunted team played lacklustre cricket and were totally out-energised by the committed Kiwis. It put a dampener on later post-match celebrations by Shane Warne and friends who planned to go out and mark the occasion of the overnight birth of his son, Jackson, back in Australia.

There was bright sunshine and blue skies at Sophia Gardens in Cardiff when Steve Waugh won the toss and elected to bat. Those early fears of poor ticket sales were again unjustified as the 10,000-capacity ground was comfortably full at the start of play.

Left-armer Geoff Allott was soon getting some swing and from the first ball of his second over he struck a massive blow. A perfectly pitched inswinger caught Mark Waugh right in front of his stumps and umpire Javed Akhtar had no hesitation.

Adam Gilchrist and Ricky Ponting played tippety run for half a dozen overs before Allott

struck again. Gilchrist's dabbing cut was guided to Nathan Astle at second slip to leave Australia 2–32 in the seventh over and Ponting and Darren Lehmann with some re-building to do. As they did so the skies darkened and at 2–61, after 15 overs, there was a 37-minute interruption for rain.

Upon the resumption Ponting and Lehmann took control. The Tasmanian was dropped by a high-leaping Dion Nash at short mid wicket. He tended to play second fiddle to Lehmann who swatted Chris Harris away a few times. The South Australian brought up his fifty off 65 balls with six fours in the 30th over with another big lofted drive to mid wicket. The partnership of 94 ended an over later when Ponting sliced a drive off Nathan Astle's first over to Chris Harris at backward point.

The belief was that the Australian middle order would capitalise on the sensible batting by Ponting and Lehmann. However it was the New Zealanders who responded at this point. The Australians were never again able to bat with any kind of freedom. Harris had Steve Waugh well caught low down at mid wicket from a cross-bat swipe and then during Harris' last over Lehmann miscued a drive to Astle at cover. Nash following through ran out Shane Lee with a diving throw along the pitch.

Allott came back to shatter Michael Bevan's stumps on the drive and hit Shane Warne's off stump with a ball that moved away. Gavin Larsen had been at his miserly best and Australia had to be content with a non-committal and fairly uninteresting 8–213 from their 50 overs.

The Kiwis hardly got the start they wanted in their reply. Adam Dale's second ball brought him a wicket, Matthew Horne given out caught behind to a ball that went between bat and body. Five overs later Dale's new-ball partner Damien Fleming had Astle slicing a drive to a forward-running Ponting in the gully to leave New Zealand 2–21.

The score had reached 47 when Glenn McGrath ripped a perfect tall man to tall man yorker into Fleming's leg stump. An over later Craig McMillan's poorly fashioned sweep at Warne lobbed the ball to a diving Fleming at mid-on. It was as if world order was restored with New Zealand having difficulty competing against Australia.

Slowly and imperceptibly, Roger Twose and Chris Cairns asserted their dominance over the bowlers. Twose had a lucky break when he hooked a catch to Fleming at fine leg only for Akhtar to call McGrath's delivery a no-ball. The first major sign of a batting revival was a lofted drive by Cairns for six off Warne in the 22nd over. The partnership had started moving and now there was no stopping it. Steve Waugh tried his full hand of bowlers. Bevan's left-arm wrist spin was introduced and Cairns struck him sweetly back over his head for another six. Twose drove and pulled to the boundary on the on side. He reached his fifty from 72 balls with six fours. Cairns' half century was two balls faster and he complemented his three fours with as many sixes.

Even McGrath was punished and the New Zealand win was arriving with a rush when Fleming finally terminated the 148 run fifth-wicket World Cup record-breaking stand. The departure of Cairns caught at long-off caused no panic as Man of the Match Twose belted more boundaries, his 10th, the last, was another mighty pull off Fleming and it completed the Kiwi win with five overs and five wickets to spare.

Mark Waugh nearly lost his cap as the ground security did nothing to control the post-match invasion. His brother needed to put on his thinking cap to restore Australia's form and confidence. New Zealand, according to their captain, had 'hardened up'.

AUSTRALIA

M. Waugh lbw Allott	2
A.C. Gilchrist (wk) c Astle b Allott	14
R.T. Ponting c Harris b Astle	47
D.S. Lehmann c Astle b Harris	76
S.R. Waugh (capt) c Astle b Harris	7
M.G. Bevan b Allott	21
S. Lee run out	2
S.K. Warne b Allott	15
D.W. Fleming not out	8
A.C. Dale not out	3
Extras (lb 10, w 5, nb 3)	18
(50 overs)	8–213

Did not bat: G.D. McGrath

1/7 2/32 3/126 4/149 5/172 6/175 7/192 8/204

Bowling: Allott 10-0-37-4; Nash 8-1-30-0; Cairns 7-0-44-0; Larsen 10-2-26-0; Harris 10-0-50-2; Astle 5-0-16-1

NEW ZEALAND

M.J. Horne c Gilchrist b Dale	5
N.J. Astle c Ponting b Fleming	4
C.D. McMillan c Fleming b Warne	29
S.P. Fleming (capt) b McGrath	9
R.G. Twose not out	80
C.L. Cairns c Dale b Fleming	60
A.C. Parore (wk) not out	10
Extras (lb 2, w 11, nb 4)	17
(45.2 overs)	5–214

Did not bat: C.Z. Harris, D.J. Nash, G.R. Larsen, G.I. Allott

1/5 2/21 3/47 4/49 5/197

Bowling: Fleming 8.2-1-43-2; Dale 5-1-18-1; McGrath 9-0-43-1; Lee 6-0-24-0; Warne 10-1-44-1; S.R. Waugh 4-0-25-0; Bevan 3-0-15-0

Umpires: Javed Akhtar, D.R. Shepherd.

Toss: Australia. Points: New Zealand 2, Australia 0

THURSDAY 20 MAY 1999
GROUP B: PAKISTAN vs SCOTLAND
RIVERSIDE GROUND, CHESTER-LE-STREET: PAKISTAN WON BY 94 RUNS

Scotland, following a fine start, quickly discovered the extent of Pakistan's mercurial ability. They also soon realised that their bowlers had as much trouble as everyone else controlling the much discussed Dukes ball. The India and Zimbabwe match on Wednesday had contained 90 extras. Pakistan and Scotland topped that at Chester-le-Street by six. By the completion of this 11th match of the tournament no batsman had made a century. Mr Extras was easily the most consistent run-maker in the Carnival of Cricket. It remained to been seen who would be the first to crack a ton.

Another venue making its international debut, the Riverside Ground belied its reputation by being bathed in sunshine at the start of play when George Salmond won the toss for Scotland and sent Pakistan in. As had been its habit, the ball started moving around, immediately causing problems for bowlers and batsmen alike. When James Brinkley had Abdur Razzaq lbw in the 26th over Pakistan were teetering a little at 3–55 and half the total was already extras. An over later Gavin Hamilton trapped Salim Malik lbw and it was 4–58.

Inzamam-ul-Haq struggled for 12 in 50 balls before being stumped off Nick Dyer. Scotland had Pakistan 5–92, but that was the end of their fun. Yousuf Youhana and Moin Khan began the fightback with a stand of 103 in 18 overs. When Moin was caught at backward square leg on the sweep, Wasim Akram came in to take advantage of a fading attack. Asim Butt was smacked for two big sixes by the Pakistani captain while Youhana went on to complete a fine unbeaten 81 in 119 balls with six fours. Extras had contributed 59 to Pakistan's 6–261.

Scotland had lost an over through being late after having to send down an extra 48 deliveries. They needed 262 to cause an upset, but by the end of the ninth over half their side were already out for 19. The prospect of the Scottish batsmen coping with Shoaib Akhtar and Akram was a daunting one and they were not up to it.

The rout began with the fourth ball of the innings when Akram bowled Bruce Patterson and did not stop until the Pakistani captain took himself and his fellow spearhead out of the attack. Iain Philip at least got his leg in the way of the ball. Three of the other four top-order

PAKISTAN		
Saeed Anwar c Davies b Asim Butt		6
Shahid Afridi run out		7
Abdur Razzaq lbw Brinkley		12
Inzamam-ul-Haq st Davies b Dyer		12
Salim Malik lbw Hamilton		0
Yousuf Youhana not out		81
Moin Khan (wk) c Brinkley b Hamilton		47
Wasim Akram (capt) not out		37
Extras (b 5, lb 6, w 33, nb 15)		59
(50 overs)		6–261

Did not bat: Saqlain Mushtaq, Shoaib Akhtar, Azhar Mahmood

1/21 2/35 3/55 4/58 5/92 6/195

Bowling: Blain 7-0-49-0; Asim Butt 9-1-55-1; Hamilton 10-1-36-2; Brinkley 10-0-29-1; Dyer 9-0-48-1; Stanger 5-0-33-0

SCOTLAND		
B.M.W. Patterson b Wasim Akram		0
I.L. Philip lbw Shoaib		0
M.J. Smith b Shoaib Akhtar		3
I.M. Stanger b Wasim Akram		3
G. Salmond (capt) c Moin Khan b Shoaib Akhtar		5
G.M. Hamilton b Wasim Akram		76
J.E. Brinkley c Moin Khan b Saqlain		22
A.G. Davies (wk) c sub (Wasti) b Abdur Razzaq		19
J.A.R. Blain lbw Razzaq		0
Asim Butt c Moin Khan b Abdur Razzaq		1
N.R. Dyer not out		1
Extras (b 1, lb 11, w 17, nb 8)		37
(38.5 overs)		10–167

1/1 2/5 3/9 4/16 5/19 6/78 7/139 8/149 9/160 10/167

Bowling: Wasim Akram 7.5-0-23-3; Shoaib Akhtar 6-2-11-3; Azhar Mahmood 7-2-21-0; Abdul Razzaq 10-0-38-3; Saqlain Mushtaq 6-0-46-1; Shahid Afridi 2-0-16-0

Umpires: D.B. Cowie, I.D. Robinson.

Toss: Scotland. Points: Pakistan 2, Scotland 0

batsmen had their stumps blasted.

If Akram had continued with himself and Shoaib, Canada's record World Cup low of 45 might have been threatened. However, against the still testing, but less pacy bowling of Azhar Mahmood, Abdur Razzaq and Saqlain Mushtaq, Gavin Hamilton and to a lesser extent James Brinkley and Alec Davies were able to flourish. Hamilton put on 59 with Brinkley in 16 overs and 61 with Davies in nine overs. He got stuck into Saqlain, hitting the off spinner for two sixes

in one over then raising his fifty from 90 balls.

Davies was caught off a full toss at 139. Hamilton retaliated by clouting his third six off Shahid Afridi. It was all good fun and cheered the Scottish section of the crowd, but it meant nothing in terms of the result. When Akram bowled the tiring Yorkshire all-rounder Pakistan had won by 94 runs and Yousuf Youhana was named Man of the Match. Despite the demolition of the Scottish top order, Akram warned that Shoaib had not been at full pace.

FRIDAY 21 MAY 1999
GROUP B: WEST INDIES vs BANGLADESH
CASTLE AVENUE, DUBLIN: WEST INDIES WON BY 7 WICKETS

This was one of the West Indies' better performances in Dublin. Once, against Ireland in 1969, they had been bowled out for 25. Here, on a day of freezing wind and showers, they at least had a win. Whether their manager, Clive Lloyd, witnessed their success is unsure. He was so rugged up with blankets he might have been unable to see any play.

The West Indies were helped by the fact that Bangladesh hardly relished the cold either. It would almost have been a let-down if there had been no rain on the day of Dublin's World Cup match. At least what came was early, causing a delay of 45 minutes at the start but no problems after that. The West Indian pacemen, given first use of the wicket by Aminul Islam, got no

response from a slow track, nor was their any evidence of warmth in their joints as they sprayed the ball around adding another 25 to the enormous pool of wides in this tournament.

The majority of Bangladeshi batsmen struggled. They had difficulty scoring at a reasonable run rate. Courtney Walsh conceded a mere 11 runs from his first seven overs. The exception was 20-year-old Mehrab Hossain who batted 43 overs for his accomplished 64. He put on 85 for the fifth wicket with Naimur Rahman, the pair coming together at 4–55. Mehrab brought up his fifty off 112 balls with a single to cover off Phil Simmons in the 38th over. Bangladesh were finally all out for 182 from the second ball of their last over.

BANGLADESH	
Shahriar Hossain c Campbell b Walsh	2
Mehrab Hossain c Chanderpaul b Simmons	64
Akram Khan c Lara b Dillon	4
Aminul Islam (capt) c Jacobs b King	2
Minhajul Abedin c Jacobs b King	5
Naimur Rahman lbw Walsh	45
Khaled Mahmud c Bryan b Walsh	13
Khaled Mashud (wk) b King	4
Enamul Hoque c Lara b Walsh	4
Hasibul Hussain b Bryan	1
Manjural Islam not out	0
Extras (lb 8, w 25, nb 5)	38
(49.2 overs)	10–182

1/8 2/29 3/39 4/55 5/140 6/159 7/167 8/180 9/182 10/182

Bowling: Walsh 10-0-25-4; Dillon 10-0-43-1; Bryan 9.2-0-30-1; King 10-1-30-3; Simmons 10-0-46-1

WEST INDIES	
S.L. Campbell c Manjural Islam b Khaled Mahmud	36
R.D. Jacobs (wk) run out	51
J.C. Adams not out	53
B.C. Lara c Hasibul Hussain b Minhajul Abedin	25
S. Chanderpaul not out	11
Extras (lb 2, w 5)	7
(46.3 overs)	3–183

Did not bat: S.C. Williams, P.V. Simmons, H.R. Bryan, M. Dillon, R.D. King, C.A. Walsh

1/67 2/115 3/150

Bowling: Hasibul Hussain 7-1-28-0; Manjural Islam 7-1-15-0; Khaled Mahmud 8-0-36-1; Enamul Hoque 8-1-31-0; Naimur Rahman 9.3-0-43-0; Minhajul Abedin 7-0-28-1

Umpires: K.T. Francis, D.B. Hair.

Toss: Bangladesh. Points: West Indies 2, Bangladesh 0

Manjurul Islam passed the edge of the West Indian openers, Sherwin Campbell and Ridley Jacobs, a few times with the new ball. Once that danger was past, however, they were able to put together a 67-run stand in 20 overs. Campbell eventually mistimed a pull while Jacobs went on to just complete his half century before going for a single that was never on.

Brian Lara warmed the crowd with a run a ball cameo worth 25, then left it to Shivnarine Chanderpaul and Jimmy Adams, who completed his half century from 82 balls with six fours, to complete the win with 21 balls to spare. Walsh's superb bowling figures won him the Man of the Match award.

SATURDAY 22 MAY 1999
GROUP A: ENGLAND vs SOUTH AFRICA
THE OVAL, LONDON: SOUTH AFRICA WON BY 122 RUNS

The inability of cricket to get soccer off the back pages of English newspapers was exemplified by Alec Stewart's side's failure in their first real test of the tournament. They were badly beaten by South Africa on FA Cup final day. A big win in front of a full house at The Oval against the World Cup favourites might have challenged the news of Manchester United's predictable win. Unfortunately, the cricketers were outclassed by their opponents.

Stewart, on his home ground, had a very bad day. He won the toss, sent South Africa in and watched the backsides of Gary Kirsten and Herschelle Gibbs as they put on an opening stand of 111. Later, things got even worse for the English captain, but he would have wondered how when the total started rattling along at an uncomfortably easy pace.

Gibbs was the main aggressor and very severe on the recalled Angus Fraser. After the 50 had been raised he danced down to the medium pacer and clouted him hard and high over long-on for six into the Mound Stand. Soon after drinks Gibbs and Kirsten brought up only the Protea's second century opening stand in Limited-Over Internationals in the last 18 months.

Then, as if such a stand was an unnatural occurrence, three wickets fell in 14 balls. Mark Ealham picked up the two openers, Gibbs, caught deep on the leg-side by Graeme Hick and Kirsten taken behind off an inside edge. Alan Mullally topped that by ripping a beautiful cut 'im in half ball through Jacques Kallis so that South Africa

were suddenly 3–112 and Stewart's decision did not look so bad.

Mullally was in the midst of another fine spell. Daryll Cullinan got a couple of shots away, then skyed an attempted on-drive to Fraser at mid-off. When Shaun Pollock got a swinging Gough special yorker first ball South Africa were 7–168 with 10 overs still to bat.

Lance Klusener, as he had against Sri Lanka at Northampton, rescued the cause. His ally then was Steve Elworthy. This time it was wicket-keeper Mark Boucher, demoted from number 3 to 9 in the order. Both batted with commonsense through to the end of the innings while adding an unbroken 57. Klusener tried to unleash at Ealham in the 50th over and hit one clout that cleared the boundary at mid-on. He had to be satisfied with 13 off the over which lifted South Africa to 7–225, the type of score their attack looked very capable of defending.

England's apprehension about the task in front of them was fully justified. Kallis with the new ball was again damaging. He completed Stewart's miserable day with a lifting off-cutter that Umpire Venkataraghavan thought would have hit the stumps. The English captain was out first ball and two overs later Nasser Hussain flicked at a ball down the leg side. It would have been a wide except Venkat thought Hussain had made contact on the way through to Boucher and gave him out, too.

England was 2–6 and the game of the round was turning into a mismatch. Graham Thorpe unleashed the shot of the innings off Donald, a flashing square drive. The champion paceman's reply was a vicious inswinger that struck Thorpe so plumb in front of middle stump not even the whingeing English press could find an excuse. Then five runs later, at about the same time Paul Scholes was finishing off Newcastle, Graeme Hick's well-timed pull off Steve Elworthy ended in the hands of Gibbs at mid wicket.

England was 4–44 in the 17th, then 5–45 10 balls later. Donald was on song which meant

Andrew Flintoff was out of his depth, well held at gully from a tame push. There was token resistance from that point, the only real reason for continuing attention being the athleticism of the South African fielding. Rhodes made the waiting worthwhile with a leap, parry, twist, dive and hold catch at gully off a Robert Croft drive. A skyed drive by Fraser off Pollock finished England on 103 after 41 overs. Klusener won a second consecutive Man of the Match award.

SOUTH AFRICA	
G. Kirsten c Stewart b Ealham	45
H.H. Gibbs c Hick b Ealham	60
J.H. Kallis b Mullally	0
D.J. Cullinan c Fraser b Mullally	10
H. Cronje (capt) c Stewart b Flintoff	16
J.N. Rhodes c sub (N.V. Knight) b Gough	18
L. Klusener not out	48
S.M. Pollock b Gough	0
M.V. Boucher (wk) not out	16
Extras (lb 7, w 5)	12
(50 overs)	7–225

Did not bat: S. Elworthy, A.A. Donald

1/111 2/112 3/112 4/127 5/146 6/168 7/168

Bowling: Gough 10–1–33–2; Fraser 10–0–54–0; Mullally 10–1–28–2; Croft 2–0–13–0; Ealham 10–2–48–2; Flintoff 8–0–42–1

ENGLAND	
N. Hussain c Boucher b Kallis	2
A.J. Stewart (capt-wk) lbw Kallis	0
G.A. Hick c Gibbs b Elworthy	21
G.P. Thorpe lbw Donald	14
N.H. Fairbrother lbw Donald	21
A. Flintoff c Rhodes b Donald	0
M.A. Ealham c Cullinan b Donald	5
R.D.B. Croft c Rhodes b Klusener	12
D.G. Gough c Cronje b Elworthy	10
A.R.C. Fraser c Kirsten b Pollock	3
A.D. Mullally not out	1
Extras (lb 4, w 9, nb 1)	14
(41 overs)	10–103

1/2 2/6 3/39 4/44 5/45 6/60 7/78 8/97 9/99 10/103

Bowling: Kallis 8–0–29–2; Pollock 9–3–13–1; Elworthy 10–3–24–2; Donald 8–1–17–4; Klusener 6–0–16–1

Umpires: R.S. Dunne, S. Venkataraghavan.

Toss: England. Points: South Africa 2, England 0

SATURDAY 22 MAY 1999
GROUP A: SRI LANKA vs ZIMBABWE
COUNTY GROUND, WORCESTER: SRI LANKA WON BY 4 WICKETS

Sri Lanka were able to get back on the winning list and modestly revitalise their hopes of staying in the Carnival of Cricket with a solid win over a disappointing Zimbabwe. In a game of few individual highlights the difference in the end was Zimbabwe's greater concession of extras to Sri Lanka than they received in return. It was a very 1999-style result.

Arjuna Ranatunga invited Alistair Campbell to bat after he won the toss. A top-edged pull shot by Neil Johnson held by Pramodya Wickremasinghe off Eric Upashantha in the eighth over got the Sri Lankan cause moving and Wickremasinghe further built up the momentum three overs later when Paul Strang

played a shortish delivery on to his wicket.

Murray Goodwin and Grant Flower were restoring the balance with a 44-run stand when the former West Australian misjudged the power and accuracy of Sanath Jayasuriya's arm when calling for a short single. Three more wickets followed quickly so that Zimbabwe were 6–94 in the 26th over when Guy Whittall drove and edged Muttiah Muralitharan to a juggling Ranatunga at slip.

Andy Flower and Stuart Carlisle had to start over again, which they did effectively for 14 overs and 68 runs before undoing the good work with another unnecessary run out. Off the next ball Flower perished to the reverse sweep, as did

Heath Streak not long after. Chaminda Vaas was again caned during the final over, Eddo Brandes hitting the left-hander out of the ground at long-on as part of the 17-run indulgence.

Sri Lanka had to chase a score similar to the one that proved excessive against South Africa. The attack facing them this time, though, was less hostile. An out-of-form Jayasuriya was soon caught cutting to short third man, but Roshan Mahanama and Marvin Atapattu withstood the threat of the new ball and started to benefit from the inaccuracy of Heath Streak and Neil Johnson. They put on 62 before Whittall yorked Mahanama. When Aravinda de Silva and

Ranatunga were dismissed Sri Lanka's position at 4–108 was not secure. It got better when Atapattu, who reached his fifty off 83 balls with four fours, and Mahela Jayawardene compiled another 42. Then Streak got them both and it was 6–157.

Romesh Kaluwitharana's return to the middle order was vital and, cheered on by a pro-Sri Lankan crowd, he and Vaas with a mixture of sharp singles, authentic strokes, slogs and edges were able to guide their side home with four overs and four wickets to spare. Atapattu was named as Man of the Match.

ZIMBABWE

N.C. Johnson c Wickremasinghe b Upashantha	8
G.W. Flower c Kaluwitharana b Wickremasinghe	42
P.A. Strang b Wickremasinghe	5
M.W. Goodwin run out	21
A. Flower (wk) c Kaluwitharana b Jayasuriya	41
A.D.R. Campbell (capt) c Kaluwitharana b Wickremasinghe	6
G.J. Whittall c Ranatunga b Muralitharan	4
S.V. Carlisle run out	27
H.H. Streak c Atapattu b Muralitharan	10
E.A. Brandes not out	19
H.K. Olonga not out	5
Extras (lb 3, w 6)	9
(50 overs)	9–197

1/21 2/34 3/78 4/81 5/89 6/94 7/162 8/162 9/176

Bowling: Vaas 10–1–47–0; Upashantha 10–1–43–1; Wickremasinghe 10–1–30–3; Jayawardene 1–0–8–0; Muralitharan 10–2–29–2; Jayasuriya 7–0–28–1; De Silva 2–0–9–0

SRI LANKA

S.T. Jayasuriya c Goodwin b Johnson	6
R.S. Mahanama b G.J. Whittall	31
M.S. Atapattu c Campbell b Streak	54
P.A. de Silva c sub (A. Whittall) b G.J. Whittall	6
A. Ranatunga (capt) c & b G.J. Whittall	3
M. Jayawardene lbw Streak	31
R.S. Kaluwitharana (wk) not out	18
W.U.J.C. Vaas not out	17
Extras (lb 6, w 21, nb 5)	32
(46 overs)	6–198

Did not bat: E. Upashantha, G. Wickremasinghe, M. Muralitharan

1/13 2/75 3/93 4/108 5/150 6/157

Bowling: Brandes 8–0–28–0; Johnson 7–1–29–1; Streak 8–1–30–2; G.J. Whittall 10–1–35–3; Olonga 9–0–50–0; G.W. Flower 2–0–10–0; Strang 2–0–10–0

Umpires: S.A. Bucknor, D.R. Shepherd.

Toss: Sri Lanka. Points: Sri Lanka 2, Zimbabwe 0

SUNDAY 23 MAY 1999
GROUP B: AUSTRALIA vs PAKISTAN
HEADINGLEY, LEEDS: PAKISTAN WON BY 10 RUNS

The 16th match of the Carnival of Cricket came the closest in atmosphere and actual play to the theme that had been set down for the 1999 World Cup. A wildly fluctuating game of sheer cricketing exhilaration, it built to a fantastic climax, one from which Wasim Akram's side triumphed to the great delight of a capacity crowd most of whom were Pakistani supporters. Not all the green shirts were inside the ground. Those on the steep rooftops surrounding Headingley were

showing their unstinting devotion to cricket and their country on such a windy day.

Cool May breezes swept across the ground and there was never much sign of a warm sun, yet once again the cricket was unscathed by weather and allowed to go its full distance. It seemed at this point that the god of cricket fixture scheduling was well-pleased by the supplications brought to it by the ECB authorities. May was proving strangely co-operative.

A flat and firm Headingley pitch encouraged Steve Waugh to bowl first when he won the toss. Damien Fleming was soon on target but Saeed Anwar took a liking to the recalled Paul Reiffel. Four exquisite shots and one miscue reached the boundary before a short rising delivery on leg stump was edged by the left-hander through to Adam Gilchrist.

This signalled a period when the Australian bowlers were on top. Wajahatullah Wasti, much to the relief of the commentators, drove the first ball of Glenn McGrath's second over to Steve Waugh in the gully and Ijaz Ahmed almost walked before umpire Peter Willey could give him out lbw to an off-cutter from Fleming. Pakistan were in trouble at 3–46 in the 13th over.

Inzamam-ul-Haq announced his arrival with a clip through square leg and a cut off Fleming, which roused the recently subdued crowd back to their usual level of unrestrained excitement. This, though, was a time for consolidation and Abdur Razzaq knuckled down with his hefty partner. Shane Warne was introduced in the 24th over to a chorus of catcalls and boos.

The greatest threat to breaking the partnership was Inzamam's lumbersome running and selfish calling. Only the fact that Fleming's throw ricocheted from the stumps saved Inzamam when both batsmen were caught at the same end. Inzamam voiced his opinion of his partner's calling.

It was as if this galvanised both into action. The run rate had cruised along under four per over. When Steve Waugh was obliged to bowl himself, Damien Martyn and Darren Lehmann the batsmen went into assault mode. Razzaq, who had reached his fifty off 92 balls, launched the acceleration with a flatly driven six off Warne over long-off. He fell to the same shot off the same bowler, ending an invaluable 118-run stand in 27 overs.

Then the fun began. The punishment of the Australian bowlers was brutal. McGrath was brought back for the 45th over and Inzamam greeted him with a mighty hooked six that landed on the roof of the old players' pavilion. Youhana smashed Martyn over mid wicket for a six and scored at two runs per ball before finding his

quick single call totally ignored by Inzamam. There was humour when Inzamam collapsed mid-pitch to tend a bruised foot while his captain, Wasim Akram, scampered a single. After making 81 in 104 balls the big man had to limp away, but he was safe in the knowledge that his side were on target for a 250-plus total.

Moin Khan completed the wonderful display with three great sixes and two fours in 12 balls. When the Australians, cursing and swearing more frequently every time the ball sailed away into the crowd, could finally retreat into the dressing-room they had conceded 108 runs from their final 10 overs and needed 276 to win.

Australia had a mountain to climb and they started disastrously. Gilchrist played crookedly and late at Akram's third ball and was clean bowled. Shoaib was quick without quite living up to his new reputation and Mark Waugh and Ricky Ponting, after the latter had been badly dropped at slip by Inzamam, were able to keep Australian fans, watching on television through Sunday night into Monday morning, interested with a 91-run partnership in 16 overs.

Then it seemed the challenge was routed. Mark Waugh, dabbing outside the off stump, was brilliantly held by a diving Moin, then Ponting and Darren Lehmann were caught off Saqlain three balls apart, both going for the sweep. Australia were 4–101 in the 20th over and their tournament was at the crossroads.

As he had done in the West Indies, Steve Waugh led the revival of his team. He settled in with Michael Bevan and in 22 overs the New South Welshmen added 113 precious runs. They were positive throughout and played their shots with freedom on a wicket that encouraged them. Bevan swiped Saqlain for six over mid wicket and brought up his fifty in 66 balls.

Akram returned and immediately Bevan was caught off a leading edge. Steve Waugh retaliated by cracking Saqlain for another six, but when Shoaib seared a yorker under his driving bat the assignment was getting difficult. The light was fading and there were five overs left with 38 runs still required. Warne and Reiffel fell during the hectic chase for runs. Then with 10 needed off four balls Akram bowled Martyn. This prompted another tiresome pitch invasion from spectators who cannot count to 10. Stumps, time and light were lost by the time the ground was cleared. Australian number 11, McGrath had no chance and a swinging yorker from Akram sealed the result and prompted another invasion.

Steve Waugh felt his side had fought the good fight this time. He denied reports of a rift between himself and his vice-captain, Warne. Rumours started that Pakistan had tampered with the ball. Inzamam was named Man of the Match.

PAKISTAN

Wajahatullah Wasti c S. Waugh b McGrath	9
Saeed Anwar c Gilchrist b Reiffel	25
Abdur Razzaq c Fleming b Warne	60
Ijaz Ahmed lbw Fleming	0
Inzamam-ul-Haq run out	81
Yousuf Youhana run out	29
Wasim Akram (capt) c Gilchrist b Fleming	13
Moin Khan (wk) not out	31
Azhar Mahmood run out	1
Saqlain Mushtaq not out	0
Extras (b 1, lb 5, w 15, nb 5)	26
(50 overs)	8–275

Did not bat: Shoaib Akhtar

1/32 2/44 3/46 4/164 5/216 6/230 7/262 8/265

Bowling: Fleming 10-3-37-2; Reiffel 10-1-49-1; McGrath 10-1-54-1; Warne 10-0-50-1; S.R. Waugh 6-0-37-0; Martyn 2-0-25-0; Lehmann 2-0-17-0

AUSTRALIA

A.C. Gilchrist b Wasim Akram	0
M. Waugh c Moin Khan b Abdur Razzaq	41
R.T. Ponting c Saeed Anwar b Saqlain Mushtaq	47
D.S. Lehmann c Moin Khan b Saqlain Mushtaq	5
S.R. Waugh (capt) b Shoaib Akhtar	49
M.G. Bevan c Ijaz b Wasim Akram	61
D. Martyn b Wasim Akram	18
S.K. Warne run out	1
P. Reiffel c Wasim Akram b Saqlain Mushtaq	1
D.W. Fleming not out	4
Extras (b 7, lb 10, w 14, nb 7)	38
(49.5 overs)	10–265

1/0 2/91 3/100 4/101 5/214 6/238 7/248 8/251 9/265 10/265

Bowling: Wasim Akram 9.5-1-40-4; Shoaib Akhtar 10-0-46-1; Azhar Mahmood 10-0-61-0; Saqlain Mushtaq 10-1-51-3; Abdur Razzaq 10-0-50-1

Umpires: R.E. Koertzen, P. Willey.

Toss: Australia. Points: Pakistan 2, Australia 0

SUNDAY 23 MAY 1999
GROUP A: INDIA vs KENYA
COUNTY GROUND, BRISTOL: INDIA WON BY 94 RUNS

If Australia and Pakistan fought out the great contest on this Sunday, then it was Sachin Tendulkar way out west in Bristol who offered the dazzling exhibition. Batting with the emotional weight of his father's death, Tendulkar played the innings of the tournament to date, a 101-ball extravaganza that thrilled all who witnessed it, but especially the 8000 Indians who filled the ground in Nevil Road. He came in at number 4 to help him recover from his jet lag. On reaching his fifty and then his hundred, Tendulkar gazed at the sky and mouthed words of dedication.

This was also a day for the statisticians as Tendulkar's third-wicket partnership with Rahul Dravid realised a World Cup record-breaking 237 runs in 29 overs. Dravid could only have been overshadowed by one man this day, and his 104 not out in 109 balls was also a treat.

The pair had come together in the 21st over of the Indian innings after Aasif Karim had won the toss and sent India in. Saurav Ganguly was lbw in the 11th over to Martin Suji and Sandagoppan Ramesh missed out on a big score when he backed up too far with the total on 92. Tendulkar and Dravid concentrated on singles and twos at first, then accelerated against a pedestrian attack. The two went neck and neck until well past their fifties, then Tendulkar surged ahead with lofted drives that peppered the boundary. An off drive off Steve Tikolo brought up Tendulkar's hundred, the first of the competition, in 84 balls.

He then toyed with the Kenyan attack, dabbing, reverse sweeping and occasionally thumping the same attack that had been mauled by the Waugh twins in 1996 for the previous record. Dravid, who had gained little strike, raised his century in the last over, then Tendulkar signed off the innings with a drive over mid wicket for his third six. India's 2–329 was their highest-score ever in the World Cup. Kenya's bowlers in three matches had taken 8–764.

Kenya could hardly follow an act like that. Once again, though, their batsmen did themselves credit. After a slow start when two wickets were lost by the 12th over, Kennedy Otieno and Steve Tikolo put on 118 for the third wicket. Both had shown they were not outclassed at this

level and while some pressure was off they emphasised the point again. Tikolo thumped Debashish Mohanty for a pulled six and followed with a flick for four more.

Once that pair had been removed only big-hitting Tom Odoyo adding a couple more sixes to his catalogue, scored with any proficiency. Kenya were left 94 runs short when the overs ran out. Tendulkar was a clear-cut choice for Man of the Match. He said afterwards, 'I did it for my father and my country. This was a difficult, but special occasion.'

INDIA

S. Ramesh run out	44
S.C. Ganguly lbw, M.A. Suji	13
R. Dravid not out	104
S.R. Tendulkar not out	140
Extras (lb 5, w 21, nb 2)	28
(50 overs)	2–329

Did not bat: M. Azharuddin (capt), A. Jadeja, N.R. Mongia (wk), N. Chopra, A.B. Agarkar, J. Srinath, D.S. Mohanty

1/50 2/92

Bowling: M.A. Suji 10–2–26–1; Angara 7–0–66–0; Odoyo 9–0–59–0; Tikolo 9–1–62–0; Aasif Karim 7–0–52–0; Odumbe 8–0–59–0

KENYA

K.O. Otieno (wk) c Agarkar b Chopra	56
Ravindu Shah c sub (R.R. Singh) b Mohanty	9
S.K. Gupta lbw Mohanty	0
S.O. Tikolo lbw Mohanty	58
M.O. Odumbe c sub (R.R. Singh) b Mohanty	14
T.M. Odoyo b Agarkar	39
Aasif Karim (capt) b Srinath	8
A. Vadher not out	6
M.A. Suji not out	1
Extras (lb 10, w 31, nb 3)	44
(50 overs)	7–235

Did not bat: H.S. Modi, J. Angara

1/29 2/29 3/147 4/165 5/193 6/209 7/233

Bowling: Srinath 10–3–31–1; Agarkar 10–0–35–1; Mohanty 10–0–56–4; Ganguly 9–0–47–0; Chopra 10–2–33–1; Tendulkar 1–0–23–0

Umpires: D.B. Cowie, I.D. Robinson.

Toss: Kenya. Points: India 2, Kenya 0

MONDAY 24 MAY 1999
GROUP B: WEST INDIES vs NEW ZEALAND
COUNTY GROUND, SOUTHAMPTON: WEST INDIES WON BY 7 WICKETS

The West Indian win over New Zealand in a lacklustre affair at Southampton threw the last two promotion spots in Group B wide open. New Zealand's first setback exposed the limitations of their top-order batting.

Once Nathan Astle became the first of Ridley Jacobs' five victims behind the stumps in Curtly Ambrose's opening over, the Kiwi batsmen were already deep in trouble. The experienced pacemen were a difficult proposition with the new ball. Courtney Walsh had Matthew Horne miscuing a pull to mid-on in the fifth

over. When Reon King came on as first change he continued Stephen Fleming's run of outs and had Thursday's hero, Roger Twose, edging to first slip on nought. The Kiwis were 4–31 in the 17th over.

Craig McMillan and Chris Cairns batted out of character as they tried to build a competitive total. Their success was limited. Ambrose had sent down 10 superb overs in one spell and the run rate limped along at just above two per over when McMillan, having received a clunk on the head, edged Phil Simmons behind. It was no better at 6–75 as Cairns hit a catch off the leading edge.

Chris Harris and Adam Parore offered resistance for 10 overs, but it summed up New Zealand's day when the wicketkeeper was caught behind down the leg side off Mervyn Dillon. Big Merv picked up two more wickets as the Kiwi innings stuttered along until the first ball of the 49th over, when Harris holed out in the deep.

The West Indies needed just 157 to win and they took nearly 45 overs to get them. Jacobs batted throughout the innings, maintaining his excellent form since coming into the West Indian team in South Africa. He lost a becalmed Sherwin Campbell to a Dion Nash off-cutter and

Jimmy Adams to a fine delivery from Geoff Allott.

Lara came in at 2–49 and, in the spirit of the game, was more restrained than usual. He did, however, strike the sweetest shot of the day when a straight drive off Gavin Larsen carried for six. With Jacobs, Lara took his side to within 36 runs of victory. This was a very important result for the West Indies and they were well pleased to obtain such an emphatic win. Some cynics suggested that as their loss jeopardised Australia's chances, the New Zealanders weren't too disappointed. Jacobs, who batted for 131 balls and hit eight fours and a six while making an unbeaten 80, was named Man of the Match.

NEW ZEALAND

M.J. Horne c Lara b Walsh		2
N.J. Astle c Jacobs b Ambrose		2
C.D. McMillan c Jacobs b Simmons		32
S.P. Fleming (capt) c Jacobs b King		0
R.G. Twose c Williams b King		0
C.L. Cairns c Lara b Dillon		23
A.C. Parore (wk) c Jacobs b Dillon		23
C.Z. Harris c Campbell b Dillon		30
D.J. Nash c Williams b Dillon		1
G.R. Larsen c Jacobs b Simmons		14
G.A. Allott not out		0
Extras (lb 6, w 17, nb 6)		29
(48.1 overs)		10–156

1/2 2/13 3/22 4/31 5/59 6/75 7/125 8/130 9/155 10/156

Bowling: Walsh 10–1–23–1; Ambrose 10–0–19–1; King 10–1–29–2; Simmons 9–2–33–2; Dillon 9.1–0–46–4

WEST INDIES

S.L. Campbell lbw Nash		8
R.D. Jacobs (wk) not out		80
J.C. Adams c Parore b Allott		3
B.C. Lara (capt) c Nash b Harris		36
S.C. Williams not out		14
Extras (lb 4, w 5, nb 8)		17
(44.2 overs)		3–158

Did not bat: S. Chanderpaul, P.V. Simmons, C.E.L. Ambrose, M. Dillon, R.D. King, C.A. Walsh

1/29 2/49 3/121

Bowling: Allott 10–2–39–1; Nash 10–2–25–1; Cairns 9.2–1–42–0; Larsen 7–1–29–0; Harris 8–2–19–1

Umpires: Javed Akhtar, S. Venkataraghavan.

Toss: West Indies. Points: West Indies 2, New Zealand 0

MONDAY 24 MAY 1999
GROUP B: SCOTLAND vs BANGLADESH
RAEBURN PLACE, EDINBURGH: BANGLADESH WON BY 22 RUNS

This almost novelty encounter was never going to turn the tide of the 1999 World Cup, but it was a splendid cricket match. The innings of both teams followed a pattern of top-order collapse followed by recovery. Bangladesh collapsed a little more spectacularly, however they also fought back better, a sign that they just had the edge in depth of talent.

The eventual 22-run defeat was a bitter disappointment to George Salmond's Scottish team. This was their best chance for a win, especially as all went well for Scotland during the first

dozen overs after Salmond won the toss and inserted the Bangladeshis.

The wind was wicked, the pitch bumpy and John Blain and Asim Butt, while still sending down their share of wides, were a handful for the batsmen with the new ball. When Faruk Ahmed played on to give Blain his fourth wicket, Bangladesh were 5–26.

The first stage of the Bangladeshi fightback was led by Naimur Rahman, ably assisted by Minhajul Abedin. They put on 69 in 19 overs. It still looked insufficient when Rahman was caught at mid-on off James Brinkley and Khaled Mahmud was caught low at mid wicket off spinner Nick Dyer. That left Bangladesh in the seemingly hopeless position of 7–96 at the end of the 31st over.

Fortunately Abedin was still at the crease and well settled. He batted through the innings with Enamul Hoque, Hasibul Hussain and Manjural Islam, almost doubling the total in the last 19 overs. Without resorting to fireworks, Abedin reached his invaluable fifty in the 46th over, then hit two boundaries off Brinkley to crown his innings in the 48th.

Scotland now had their work cut out. They had conceded 39 wides and no-balls and had been penalised an over for their late finish. Nor was 185 a straightforward target on a wicket still favouring the bowlers. Two lbw decisions and a caught behind accounted for Scotland's first three batsmen by the middle of the sixth over with only eight runs on board. An excellent catch at backward point by Faruk Ahmed sent Salmond on his way and when Ian Stanger became the third lbw victim the home side were 5–49 and fading fast.

Gavin Hamilton was the remaining hope and he responded brilliantly. He hit hard and well and raced to his fifty in 62 balls. Hamilton celebrated that milestone by sweeping Rahman for the only six of the match, but his dismissal soon after was a tragedy for Scotland. A straight drive by Alec Davies was deflected by the bowler Manjural onto the stumps with Hamilton out of his ground backing up. Even though Davies kept up the fight, Scotland were battling from the moment of Hamilton's dismissal. Abedin was named Man of the Match.

BANGLADESH

Khaled Mashud (wk) c Philip b Blain	0
Mehrab Hossain c Dyer b Asim Butt	3
Faruk Ahmed b Blain	7
Aminul Islam (capt) lbw Blain	0
Akram Khan c Philip b Asim Butt	0
Minhajul Abedin not out	68
Naimur Rahman c Stanger b Brinkley	36
Khaled Mahmud c Salmond b Dyer	0
Enamul Hoque c Philip Dyer	19
Hasibul Hussain c & b Blain	6
Manjural Islam not out	2
Extras (lb 5, w 28, nb 11)	44
(50 overs)	9–185

1/6 2/12 3/13 4/24 5/26 6/95 7/96 8/133 9/164

Bowling: Blain 10-1-37-4; Asim Butt 9-1-24-2; Hamilton 10-3-25-0; Brinkley 10-0-45-1; Stanger 4-0-23-0; Dyer 7-1-26-2

SCOTLAND

B.M.W. Patterson lbw Hassibul Hussain	0
I.L. Philip lbw Manjural Islam	3
M.J. Smith c Khaled Mashud b Hasibul Hussain	1
I.M. Stanger lbw Minhajul Abedin	10
G. Salmond (capt) c Faruk Ahmed b Manjural Islam	19
G.M. Hamilton run out	63
J.E. Brinkley c Hasibul Hussain b Khaled Mahmud	5
A.G. Davies (wk) c Manjural Islam b Khaled Mahmed	32
J.A.R. Blain run out	9
Asim Butt c Aminul Islam b Enamul Hoque	1
N.R. Dyer not out	0
Extras (lb 1, w 13, nb 6)	20
(46.2 overs)	10–163

1/0 2/8 3/8 4/37 5/49 6/83 7/138 8/158 9/163 10/163

Bowling: Hasibul Hussain 8-1-26-2; Manjural Islam 9-2-27-2; Khaled Mahmud 9-2-27-2; Minhajul Abedin 3-0-12-1; Naimur Rahman 10-0-41-0; Enamul Hoque 7.2-0-23-1

Umpires: K.T. Francis, D.L. Orchard.

Toss: Scotland. Points: Bangladesh 2, Scotland 0

TUESDAY 25 MAY 1999
GROUP A: ENGLAND vs ZIMBABWE
TRENT BRIDGE, NOTTINGHAM: ENGLAND WON BY 7 WICKETS

Sent in to bat on a cloudy, swing-inducing Nottingham morning, Zimbabwe were unable to set England a worthwhile total. Their defeat was never in doubt in a match described by *Daily Telegraph* correspondent Michael Henderson as 'wretched stuff'.

The winning of the toss by Alec Stewart was crucial, clouds having swept in after a sunny morning. There was no sudden Zimbabwean collapse, just a gradual demise and no sign that the innings would go up a gear. All the English bowlers were difficult to attack. Angus Fraser swung the ball in and Alan Mullally got it to go both ways. Darren Gough took the first wicket, then Mullally removed pinch-hitter Paul Strang before he hit anything at all. He also had Murray Goodwin caught low at slip to make the score 3–47 in the 18th over.

Grant Flower, Alistair Campbell and Guy Whittall fought hard without being able to play their strokes with any freedom. Extras accumulated as effectively as did runs off the bat. Mullally bouncing and moving the ball off a good length, was untouchable. Only Andrew Flintoff and Adam Hollioake conceded runs at anything like a regular rate. Zimbabwe had two wickets in hand at the end of 50 overs, but with the sun back they did not have nearly enough runs.

There was just a sniff of a turnaround when Stewart clipped a catch off Neil Johnson to Murray Goodwin at mid wicket in the ninth over

and three overs later Graeme Hick wafted outside his off stump at 'Pommie' Mbangwa. That made England 2–36, which was hardly better than Zimbabwe had been at the same time. There was nothing in the Zimbabwean attack to really trouble Nasser Hussain or Graham Thorpe and once they got going the result was never in doubt.

For a time the pair, who have shared some important partnerships in Test cricket, traded boundary for boundary. Then the left-handed Thorpe scooted away as he brought up his fifty in 59 balls. Finally, after a stand of 123 in 22 overs, Thorpe was caught at slip slashing at Mbangwa. England required just nine from there and Hussain and Neil Fairbrother took five overs to get them. Perhaps they were trying to preserve their averages, or maybe they wanted to sedate the crowd for the end of the match. If it was the latter they failed, for when Hussain drove Strang to extra cover the hordes came charging on yet again. Mullally, championing the bowler's cause, won the Man of the Match award ahead of Hussain and Thorpe.

ZIMBABWE	
N.C. Johnson b Gough	6
G.W. Flower c Thorpe b Ealham	35
P.A. Strang c Hick b Mullally	0
M.W. Goodwin c Thorpe b Mullally	4
A. Flower (wk) run out	10
A.D.R. Campbell (capt) c Stewart b Fraser	24
G.J. Whittall lbw Ealham	28
S.V. Carlisle c Fraser b Gough	14
H.H. Streak not out	11
H.K. Olonga not out	1
Extras (lb 16, w 17, nb 1)	34
(50 overs)	8–167

Did not bat: M. Mbangwa

1/21 2/29 3/47 4/79 5/86 6/124 7/141 8/159

Bowling: Gough 10-2-24-2; Fraser 10-0-27-1; Mullally 10-4-16-2; Ealham 10-1-35-2; Flintoff 3-0-14-0; Hollioake 7-0-35-0

ENGLAND	
N. Hussain not out	57
A.J. Stewart (capt-wk) c Goodwin b Johnson	12
G.A. Hick c A. Flower b Mbangwa	4
G.P. Thorpe c Campbell b Mbangwa	62
N.H. Fairbrother not out	7
Extras (lb 3, w 16, nb 7)	26
(38.3 overs)	3–168

Did not bat: A. Flintoff, A.J. Hollioake, M.A. Ealham, D.G. Gough, A.R.C. Fraser, A.D. Mullally

1/21 2/36 3/159

Bowling: Johnson 7-2-20-1; Streak 8-0-37-0; Mbangwa 7-1-28-2; G.J. Whittall 4-0-23-0; Olonga 3-0-27-0; Strang 9.3-1-30-0

Umpires: S.A. Bucknor, D.B. Hair.

Toss: England. Points: England 2, Zimbabwe 0

WEDNESDAY 26 MAY 1999
GROUP A: INDIA vs SRI LANKA
COUNTY GROUND, TAUNTON: INDIA WON BY 157 RUNS

It was as if the batting of Sachin Tendulkar and Rahul Dravid against Kenya had been the warm-

up. At Taunton two Indian batsmen turned it on again as Saurav Ganguly and Dravid broke all sorts of records en route to a complete demolition of Sri Lanka's chances of progressing to the second round of the tournament.

Sunday's had been an emotional game, as millions admired and felt for the grieving Tendulkar. However, this 318-run partnership between Ganguly and Dravid was a celebration of pure classical batsmanship. Without mentioning a shot, the list of records achieved by the pair is exciting enough: India's highest score in a Limited-Over International (LOI), the second-highest innings total in an LOI, and Ganguly's 183 was the highest score by an Indian in a LOI, the second-highest in the World Cup and the fourth-highest by any country. Their second-wicket partnership was the best for any wicket in LOI.

The two came together when the Sri Lankans had their tails up, Chaminda Vaas had bowled Sadagopan Ramesh in the day's opening over with a superb delivery. The left-arm paceman tasted no more success, and nor did his teammates for another 45 overs. This was sweet revenge for India. They had been beaten by Sri Lanka in the riot-ruined World Cup semi-final of 1996 and in August 1997 suffered the humiliation of conceding 6–952 in the Colombo Test.

On a beautiful batting wicket the right- and left-handed combination played scarcely a stroke that was not straight out of the textbook until a position of strength had been established. The bowling of the Sri Lankan seamers was wayward and allowed Dravid the opportunity to unleash a series of gorgeous front-foot drives.

Arjuna Ranatunga had elected to bowl after winning the toss. The decision just about exploded in his face. After 25 overs, the two batsmen became a little more expansive in their shot selection. Dravid had gone to his half century in 43 balls with 10 fours; Ganguly took 68 balls and hit six fours.

Later, footwork and grace counted for little as the pair became dissatisfied with fours and looked to strike sixes instead. Ganguly came into his own in the second half of the stand. His century was reached in 119 balls, a slightly slower rate than Dravid who took just 102 balls. Dravid's effort of scoring consecutive World Cup centuries has only been equalled by Mark Waugh in 1996. Those landmarks opened the way for even faster run scoring as 128 were added in the final 10 overs. Ganguly's beautiful glance brought up the 200 in the 35th over, then Dravid struck an inside-out six over cover off Muralitharan.

In the 45th over Ganguly smashed three fours off Upashantha to raise the 300 partnership, then bettered it next ball with a dancing straight six

INDIA	
S. Ramesh b Vaas	5
S.C. Ganguly c sub (V.D.V. Chandana)	
b Wickremasinghe	183
R. Dravid (wk) run out	145
S.R. Tendulkar b Jayasuriya	2
A. Jadeja c & b Wickremasinghe	5
R.R. Singh c de Silva b Wickremasinghe	0
M. Azharuddin (capt) not out	11
J. Srinath not out	1
Extras (lb 3, w 12, nb 6)	21
(50 overs)	6–373

Did not bat: J. Srinath, D.S. Mohanty, B.K.V. Prasad

1/6 2/324 3/344 4/349 5/349 6/372

Vaas 10-0-84-1; Upashantha 10-0-80-0; Wickremasinghe 10-0-65-3; Muralitharan 10-0-60-0; Jayawardene 3-0-21-0; Jayasuriya 3-0-37-1; de Silva 4-0-23-0

SRI LANKA	
S.T. Jayasuriya run out	3
R.S. Kaluwitharana lbw Srinath	7
M.S. Atapattu lbw Mohanty	29
P.A. de Silva lbw Singh	56
M. Jayawardene lbw Kumble	4
A. Ranatunga b Singh	42
R.S. Mahanama run out	32
W.U.J.C. Vaas c Ramesh b Singh	1
E. Upashantha c Azharuddin b Singh	5
P. Wickremasinghe not out	2
M. Muralitharan c Tendulkar b Singh	4
Extras (b 4, lb 12, w 8, nb 7)	31
(42.3 overs)	10–216

1/5 2/23 3/74 4/79 5/147 6/181 7/187 8/203 9/204 10/216

Bowling: Srinath 7-0-33-1; Prasad 8-0-41-0; Mohanty 5-0-31-1; Kumble 8-0-27-1; Ganguly 5-0-37-0; Singh 9.3-0-31-5

Umpires: D.R. Shepherd, R.S. Dunne.

Toss: Sri Lanka. Points: India 2, Sri Lanka 0

to register his own 150. Finally, in the next over, Dravid failed to beat Muralitharan's throw from long-off. A few wickets fell in the frenzied final overs, but the throngs of singing, dancing and chanting Indians were satisfied that 6–373 was a fair effort.

Sri Lanka were never in the hunt. From the first ball of the third over Sanath Jayasuriya pushed to the on side and called for a quick single. The bowler Javagal Srinath picked up the ball in his follow-through, pivoted, threw and scored a direct hit, running out the hero of 1996 by 10 centimetres. There was a return to form from Aravinda de Silva. Ranatunga and Roshan Mahanama keep the traffic from being totally one way. Robin Singh worked his way through the second half of the order, a skyed slog by Muralitharan ending proceedings with 7.3 overs to play. Ganguly won the toss from Dravid and was named Man of the Match.

WEDNESDAY 26 MAY 1999
GROUP A: KENYA vs SOUTH AFRICA
V.R.A. GROUND, AMSTELVEEN: SOUTH AFRICA WON BY 7 WICKETS

World Cup cricket went below sea level for the first time in an exercise that could be considered a success. The Dutch weather was an improvement on what had been available in Britain. The cricket unfortunately after the first hour was predictable.

South Africa outclassed the Kenyans without ever appearing to be at their absolute best. Only a few sixes at the end by Daryll Cullinan lifted the adrenalin level of the spectators. It hinted at being more than that when Kennedy Otieno and Ravindu Shah were opening the game with some choice shots off Shaun Pollock and in particular Jacques Kallis. They rattled up 66 in 15 overs. Shah looked in great form cracking Kallis through the covers and punishing Allan Donald in the 17th over.

By then Steve Elworthy had already broken the opening stand and with Donald quickly exacting revenge on Shah, the innings quickly began to totter. The runs dried up and Lance Klusener stepped in to make a mess of the middle and lower order. When he bowled Joe Angara, Kenya had lost 10–86 and had been dismissed with five and a half overs to spare.

Herschelle Gibbs and Gary Kirsten got the South African reply away to a bright start. Gibbs lifted Aasif Karim over long-on for six and 55 runs were up by the end of the 11th over when Tom Odoyo had Gibbs lbw playing across the

KENYA	
K.O. Otieno (wk) lbw Elworthy	26
Ravindu Shah c Boucher b Donald	50
S.K. Gupta b Elworthy	1
S.O. Tikolo c Cronje b Klusner	10
M.O. Odumbe b Donald	7
A. Vadher c & b Klusener	2
T.M. Odoyo lbw Klusener	0
Aasif Karim (capt) lbw Cronje	22
Mohammad Sheikh b Klusener	8
M.A. Suji not out	6
J.O. Angara b Klusener	6
Extras (lb 5, w 7, nb 2)	14
(44.3 overs)	10–152

1/66 2/80 3/82 4/91 5/104 6/104 7/107 8/138 9/140 10/152

Bowling: Pollock 8-1-22-0; Kallis 8-0-37-0; Donald 8-1-42-2; Elworthy 10-2-20-2; Klusener 8.3-3-21-5; Cronje 2-0-5-1

SOUTH AFRICA	
G. Kirsten b Odumbe	27
H.H. Gibbs lbw Odoyo	38
M.V. Boucher (wk) c Mohammad Sheikh b Angara	3
J.H. Kallis not out	44
D.J. Cullinan not out	35
Extras (b 4, w 1, nb 1)	6
(41 overs)	3–153

Did not bat: J.N. Rhodes, L. Klusener, S.M. Pollock, W.J. Cronje (capt), S. Elworthy, A.A. Donald

1/55 2/58 3/86

Bowling: Suji 6-0-18-0; Aasif Karim 7-0-43-0; Angara 8-1-34-1; Odoyo 9-3-18-1; Mohammad Rafique Sheikh 4-0-21-0; Odumbe 7-1-15-1

Umpires: D.B. Cowie, P. Willey.

Toss: South Africa. Points: South Africa 2, Kenya 0

line. As it did against England, the dismissal of Gibbs slowed the South African rate of progress. Mark Boucher, back at number 3, made no impression and Gary Kirsten fell foul of his own impatience. There was still no real pressure.

Kallis and Cullinan took their time easing the Proteas to their fourth win, putting on 67 in 18 overs with a mixture of the sedate and the belligerent. Klusener was able to add to his rapidly growing Man of the Match collection.

THURSDAY 27 MAY 1999
GROUP B: AUSTRALIA vs BANGLADESH
RIVERSIDE GROUND, CHESTER-LE-STREET: AUSTRALIA WON BY 7 WICKETS

On a day when it was easy to believe the sun always shone in Durham, it was also easy to believe Australia were still a powerful force in this World Cup tournament. The impeccable weather at Chester-le-Street encouraged an impressive batting display by the Australians. Providing they defeated the West Indies, it would keep them in contention for promotion to the Super Six mini-tournament. Chasing a modest total of 178, they rattled along at nine per over allowing all the Bangladeshis in attendance the opportunity to beat the rush-hour traffic on the A1 motorway back to East London.

When Australia were in the field after Steve Waugh sent Bangladesh in they had one ear on relayed scores from Leicester, where the West Indies were decimating Scotland. There was no sign of the Australian bowlers doing anything like the same job on Aminul Islam's team. The Bangladeshis never got away on the Australians. Nor did they seem likely to be bowled out in 50 overs.

For 21 overs, Mehrab Hossain looked a batsman well within his class, striking seven fine boundaries before slicing Tom Moody to backward point. That shot gave Ricky Ponting his third catch in the same position out of four dismissals, the best of the three was a forward-diving effort that got rid of Faruk Ahmed. He also held Naimur Rahman there off Tom Moody. The captain of West Australia and Worcester had been brought in as an extra seamer after the fifth-bowler debacle at Leeds. Moody came on as first change after Glenn McGrath had picked up two wickets. His splendid spell suggested the change should have been made long before.

When Shane Warne had an lbw shout upheld

against Akram Khan, Bangladesh were 6–99 and there was the possibility of complete collapse. The Australian bowling, though, was tidy rather than penetrative. Minhajul Abedin, the hero of Edinburgh, was once more able to hold the second half of the order together and he went on to complete an accomplished half century with six boundaries.

Australia returned to the dressing-room needing 179 to win in the knowledge that the West Indies had already completed their day's work. Steve Waugh asked for a special effort from his batsmen, setting them a target of winning in 30 overs. They got there in 20.

Adam Gilchrist turned around his earlier poor form. After taking a couple of overs to settle in he clouted the ball through and over the field on both sides of the wicket. One straight drive tested the speed of umpire Steve Bucknor's reactions. His evasive skills were just good enough to maintain his manhood. The wicketkeeper–batsman raced to his half century in 34 balls and when he was stumped dancing down at Minhajul he had hit 12 fours and lifted Australia to 98 in the 12th over. Mark Waugh, who had supported Gilchrist so well must have liked what he saw for the next over he too danced out of his crease and was stumped.

Brendan Julian, promoted to boost the scoring further, hit two boundaries before becoming the second wicket for left-arm spinner Enamul Hoque. Tom Moody had been lifted up the order, too. His pinch-hitting lasted 29 balls. That was enough for him to make the fastest 50 ever in the World Cup. Moody hit six fours and two sixes to win the match for his country from the second-last ball of the 20th over. The winning hit was his second six, a massive blow that cleared mid wicket. Moody's efforts easily won him the Man of the Match award. Like Ganguly the day before, Moody's record meant that another of Kapil Dev's feats at Tunbridge Wells in 1983 had been put in to second place.

BANGLADESH	
Khaled Mahmud lbw McGrath	6
Mehrab Hossain c Ponting b Moody	42
Faruk Ahmed c Ponting b McGrath	9
Naimur Rahman c Ponting b Moody	2
Aminul Islam (capt) b Fleming	13
Minhajul Abedin not out	53
Akram Khan lbw Warne	0
Khaled Mashud (wk) lbw Moody	17
Enamul Hoque not out	17
Extras (b 2, w 10, nb 7)	19
(50 overs)	7–178

Did not bat: Hasibul Hussain, Manjural Islam

1/10 2/39 3/47 4/72 5/91 6/99 7/143

Bowling: McGrath 10-0-44-2; Fleming 10-0-45-1; Moody 10-4-25-3; Julian 10-1-44-0; Warne 10-2-18-1

AUSTRALIA	
M.E. Waugh st Khaled Mashud b Enamul Hoque	33
A.C. Gilchrist (wk) st Khaled Mashud b Minhajul Abedin	63
B.P. Julian b Enamul Hoque	9
T.M. Moody not out	56
R.T. Ponting not out	18
Extras (w 2)	2
(19.5 overs)	3–181

Did not bat: M.G. Bevan, D.S. Lehmann, S.R. Waugh (capt), S.K. Warne, D.W. Fleming, G.D. McGrath

1/98 2/98 3/111

Bowling: Hasibul Hussain 4-0-24-0; Manjural Islam 3-0-23-0; Khaled Mahmud 2.5-0-39-0; Naimur Rahman 2-0-17-0; Enamul Hoque 5-0-40-2; Minhajul Abedin 3-0-38-1

Umpires: S.A. Bucknor, D.L. Orchard.

Toss: Australia. Points: Australia 2, Bangladesh 0

THURSDAY 27 MAY 1999
GROUP B: SCOTLAND vs WEST INDIES
GRACE ROAD, LEICESTER: WEST INDIES WON BY 8 WICKETS

This match did not take very long. The whole affair was completed in less than 42 overs. The weather was fine at Grace Road and the crowd keen, but the wicket was lively and the Scottish batsmen were no match for the West Indian bowlers.

It surprised many that George Salmond batted when he won the toss. He placed himself at number 4 and by the 15th over was already trying to retrieve a dicey situation with his side on 2–18. Ridley Jacobs had taken a catch each off Curtly Ambrose and Phil Simmons. Ambrose was almost unplayable and Salmond lasted just four balls before becoming the giant Antiguan's second victim. He was also caught behind. Jacobs had four catches and Scotland were a disastrous 4–20.

Worse was to follow. Courtney Walsh came on first change and with his impeccable accuracy and variations was also far too good for the Scottish batsmen. James Brinkley was caught at second slip and two balls later when Alec Davies was given out lbw Scotland were 7–29. The ignominy of finishing with a total lower than Canada's 45 in 1979 was a real possibility. Fortunately Gavin Hamilton was a better player than anyone in that Canadian line-up and by cracking Henderson Bryan for a couple of boundaries he eased that threat.

Asim Butt hit an out-of-context six, but Reon King had almost immediate revenge and when Nick Dyer lamely pushed his second ball to second slip, Hamilton had been left stranded and Scotland were all out for 68.

It took the West Indies just 61 deliveries to get the runs. John Blain struck a couple of retaliatory blows, having Simmons caught at mid-on and trapping Stuart Williams lbw first ball. Shivnarine Chanderpaul was in an aggressive mood and struck the ball cleanly. Brian Lara, attracted to the prospect of a whole afternoon off, began flaying the Scottish bowlers upon his arrival at the crease. He targeted Hamilton, taking 17 off his one over. He lifted the all-rounder for six over mid wicket with perhaps the highest hit of the tournament. The tartans in the crowd had to

find some other entertainment for the afternoon. Walsh was named Man of the Match.

SCOTLAND

M.W. Smith c Jacobs b Simmons	1
M. Allingham c Jacobs b Ambrose	6
I.M. Stanger c Jacobs b Walsh	7
G. Salmond (capt) c Jacobs b Ambrose	1
G.M. Hamilton not out	24
J.G. Williamson c Williams b Bryan	1
J.E. Brinkley c Simmons b Walsh	2
A.G. Davies (wk) lbw Walsh	0
J.A.R. Blain lbw Bryan	3
Asim Butt c Williams b King	11
N.R. Dyer c Williams b King	0
Extras (w 9, nb 3)	12
(31.3 overs)	10–68

1/6 2/18 3/20 4/20 5/25 6/29 7/29 8/47 9/68 10/68

Bowling: Ambrose 10–4–8–2; Simmons 7–1–15–1; Walsh 7–1–7–3; Bryan 6–0–29–2; King 1.3–0–9–2

WEST INDIES

P.V. Simmons c Stanger b Blain	7
S. Chanderpaul not out	30
S.C. Williams lbw Blain	0
B.C. Lara (capt) not out	25
Extras (lb 2, w 4, nb 2)	8
(10.1 overs)	2–70

Did not bat: J.C. Adams, R.D. Jacobs (wk), S.L. Campbell, R.D. King, C.E.L. Ambrose, H.R. Bryan, C.A. Walsh

1/21 2/22

Bowling: Blain 5.1–0–36–2; Asim Butt 4–1–15–0; Hamilton 1–0–17–0

Umpires: Javed Akhtar, I.D. Robinson.

Toss: Scotland. Points: West Indies 2, Scotland 0

FRIDAY 28 MAY 1999
GROUP B: PAKISTAN vs NEW ZEALAND
COUNTY GROUND, DERBY: PAKISTAN WON BY 62 RUNS

The talented and flamboyant Pakistanis, their favouritism rising with each win in the tournament, were too good for New Zealand. The strong winds whistling across the old Racecourse Ground in Derby would have reminded the Kiwis of Wellington, but the crowd was straight out of Karachi and the tide of lime green soon became an irresistible one.

Stephen Fleming won the toss, sent Pakistan in and promptly watched his opening bowlers get flogged for 23 in their opening overs. Afridi hooked Dion Nash for six to his team-mates at the front of the pavilion. The total was already 40 when Geoff Allott recovered his composure enough to have Afridi caught behind. The left-armer followed up by bowling Saeed Anwar behind his legs to make it 2–51. Allott would later bend back Salim Malik's middle stump and have Azhar Mahmood caught. His team-mates, however, made little impression on the Pakistani middle order.

Abdur Razzaq and Ijaz Ahmed began the Pakistani assertion with a 19-over stand worth 76. Both were run out, only one dismissal involved Inzamam-ul-Haq. Ijaz reached his fifty

off 68 balls before being punished for daring to look for a short single when batting with Inzamam. He backed up too far and fell to a direct-hit throw from point by Chris Harris. Inzamam maintained his fine batting form from the previous Sunday against Australia, hitting with power off the front and back foot. There was not the final mayhem of the final 10 overs at Headingley. Nevertheless, Pakistan finished with a comparable total of 8–269.

Shoaib Akhtar ensured it would be plenty. Given the tail wind by his captain, he was genuinely fast and quickly had both Nathan Astle and Matthew Horne edging through to Moin Khan. When Craig McMillan miscued a cover drive off Wasim Akram to mid-on New Zealand were 3–35 in the 11th over and effectively out of it.

The Kiwis' pride and their all-important run rate were preserved well enough by their captain, who added 83 with fellow left-hander Harris in 19 overs. That, unfortunately for New Zealand, came after they had been 6–71, so it had no bearing on the result. Fleming had gone to his fifty in 76 balls, one of his straight drives off

Shoaib being the equal of any shot during the day.

Fleming became Azhar Mahmood's third scalp in the 39th over and Harris succumbed to Saqlain Mushtaq when he top-edged a sweep. Then, sadly, with two balls to go there was another pitch invasion. Those involved displayed a counting ability and maturity lower than the Teletubbies who had the commonsense to stay in their seats. The ground announcer was irate calling them, 'fools' and 'idiots'. Inzamam was voted Man of the Match for the second consecutive game. Those who run between wickets with him do not vote on the matter.

PAKISTAN	
Saeed Anwar b Allott	28
Shahid Afridi c Parore b Allott	17
Abdur Razzaq run out	33
Ijaz Ahmed run out	51
Inzamam-ul-Haq not out	73
Salim Malik b Allott	8
Moin Khan (wk) c McMillan b Astle	19
Wasim Akram (capt) lbw Cairns	1
Azhar Mahmood c Twose b Allott	14
Saqlain Mushtaq not out	0
Extras (b 4, lb 10, w 8, nb 3)	25
(50 overs)	8–269

Did not bat: Shoaib Akhtar

1/40 2/51 3/127 4/163 5/180 6/221 7/226 8/255

Bowling: Nash 10-1-36-0; Allott 10-0-64-4; Larsen 10-0-35-0; Cairns 7-0-46-1; Harris 8-0-47-0; Astle 5-0-27-1

NEW ZEALAND	
M.J. Horne c Moin Khan b Shoaib Akhtar	1
N.J. Astle c Moin Khan b Shoaib Akhtar	0
C.D. McMillan c Salim Malik b Wasim Akram	20
S.P. Fleming (capt) c Wasim Akram	
b Azhar Mahmood	69
R.G. Twose c Inzamam-ul-Haq b Azhar Mahmood	13
C.L. Cairns lbw Azhar	0
A.C. Parore (wk) lbw Azhar	0
C.Z. Harris c Abdur Razzaq	
b Saqlain Mushtaq	42
D.J. Nash not out	21
G.R. Larsen not out	3
Extras (lb 15, w 13, nb 10)	38
(50 overs)	8–207

Did not bat: G.I. Allott

1/2 2/12 3/35 4/70 5/71 6/71 7/154 8/200

Bowling: Wasim Akram 9-0-27-1; Shoaib Akhtar 7-1-31-2; Azhar Mahmood 10-0-38-3; Saqlain Mushtaq 10-1-34-2; Shahid Afridi 6-1-26-0; Abdul Razzaq 8-0-36-0

Umpires: K.T. Francis, R.E. Koertzen.

Toss: New Zealand. Points: Pakistan 2, New Zealand 0

SATURDAY 29 MAY 1999
GROUP A: SOUTH AFRICA vs ZIMBABWE
COUNTY GROUND, CHELMSFORD: ZIMBABWE WON BY 48 RUNS

Here was an upset that no-one saw coming, particularly England who, as it turned out, were more upset about it than anyone else. Zimbabwe controlled the game from the first ball to the last and were deserved winners. The success gave special satisfaction to Alistair Campbell's side. They were now assured of progressing to the Super Sixes stage of the tournament with a real chance of reaching the semi-finals. To achieve all that against their highly credentialled neighbours, and so convincingly, was all the more meritorious.

Alistair Campbell won the toss and batted on a fine morning with no suggestion of devilment in the Chelmsford wicket. Soon Neil Johnson, rediscovering the form he had lost after his Man of the Match performance against Kenya, and Grant Flower were trading in boundaries against the much vaunted Protea attack. The first of three fours off one Kallis over brought up the 50. The pair rattled up 65 in 14 overs before Flower edged Steve Elworthy to Daryll Cullinan at slip.

Murray Goodwin continued the good work with Johnson. The opener cracked Elworthy for another four through the covers to bring him to his half century and by the time Goodwin mistimed a pull off Lance Klusener Zimbabwe were already 2–131. Andy Flower flat-batted Allan Donald back over his head for a marvellous six. Generally, though, the early momentum was lost once Goodwin was out.

Donald terminated Johnson's fine innings when he pulled a short ball to Shaun Pollock on the mid-wicket boundary. Then the South African spearhead won an lbw decision against Campbell first ball with a perfectly pitched yorker. Donald celebrated with more than his usual enthusiasm as this was his 200th wicket in Limited-Over Internationals. When Andy Flower made a suicidal call for a second run to Pollock's arm from the point boundary the Zimbabwean innings could have fallen away. Instead Guy Whittall, who hit Klusener for a straight six, and Stuart Carlisle put together enough runs to leave Zimbabwe with a competitive 6–233.

As the Zimbabwean innings progressed the fine morning had deteriorated and during lunch a heavy shower saturated the ground. It meant South Africa started their reply 25 minutes late. It was immediately apparent the rain had livened the wicket. Johnson's first ball to Gary Kirsten lifted from a length, struck him on the gloves and lobbed to gully where Andy Whittall brought off a diving catch.

Such a start, if unfortunate, was hardly insurmountable and for half a dozen overs Herschelle Gibbs and Mark Boucher gave no hint that anything out of the ordinary was about to happen. Then Boucher ignored the adage, 'never run on a misfield' and left Gibbs stranded. The next over the wicketkeeper was caught off a no-ball, then given out lbw essaying a pull shot at Heath Streak. South Africa were now 3–25, which hinted at serious trouble. The threat quickly intensified. On the same score Jacques Kallis drove at a widish ball and was caught behind. Then Hansie Cronje was yorked by an ecstatic Johnson and when Streak hurried a ball through onto Jonty Rhodes' pads and the Proteas were an astonishing 6–40.

At Edgbaston, as they put up their umbrellas against the incoming rain, the English fans began to squirm. It wasn't time to panic yet, though, as the depth in South African batting ensured the continuation of battle. Pollock and Cullinan added 66, then Pollock stayed with Klusener to put on another 43. The scoring rate was now an issue, as well, and soon after Pollock reached his half century off 78 balls he holed out in the deep off Andy Whittall. Six balls later and Steve Elworthy was gone. That left Klusener to do all the work with Donald.

Klusener had a go at it too, reaching yet another half century and once placing Streak into the crowd near the main scoreboard at mid wicket. Another 49 were needed off three overs when Henry Olonga, the hero of the win at Leicester, had Donald caught by a high-leaping

ZIMBABWE

N.C. Johnson c Pollock b Donald	76
G.W. Flower c Cullinan b Elworthy	19
M.W. Goodwin c Kirsten b Klusener	34
A. Flower (wk) run out	29
A.D.R. Campbell (capt) lbw Donald	0
G.J. Whittall c Cullinan b Donald	20
S.V. Carlisle not out	18
H.H. Streak not out	9
Extras (b 1, lb 15, w 8, nb 4)	28
(50 overs)	6–233

Did not bat: A.R. Whittall, A.G. Huckle, H.K. Olonga

1/65 2/131 3/170 4/175 5/186 6/214

Bowling: Pollock 10–1–39–0; Kallis 6–0–36–0; Donald 10–1–41–3; Elworthy 6–0–32–1; Klusener 9–0–36–1; Cronje 9–0–33–0

SOUTH AFRICA

G. Kirsten c A.R. Whittall b Johnson	0
H.H. Gibbs run out	9
M.V. Boucher (wk) lbw Streak	8
J.H. Kallis c A. Flower b Johnson	0
D.J. Cullinan c & b Whittall	29
H. Cronje (capt) b Johnson	4
J.N. Rhodes lbw Streak	5
S.M. Pollock c Olonga b A.R. Whittall	52
L. Klusener not out	52
S. Elworthy c A. Whittall b Streak	1
A.A. Donald c Streak b Olonga	7
Extras (b 2, lb 1, w 8, nb 7)	18
(47.2 overs)	10–185

1/0 2/24 3/25 4/25 5/34 6/40 7/106 8/149 9/150 10/185

Bowling: Johnson 8–1–27–3; Streak 9–1–35–3; G.J. Whittall 4–0–20–0; Olonga 4.2–0–17–1; Huckle 10–1–35–0; A. Whittall 10–0–41–2; G.W. Flower 2–0–7–0

Umpires: D.R. Shepherd, S. Venkataraghavan.

Toss: Zimbabwe. Points: Zimbabwe 2, South Africa 0

Streak at cover. Zimbabwe attacked their neighbours from the start and reaped the benefit. Their success was at the expense of the loser of the England vs India match. When play was washed out at Edgbaston the game lay in the balance. It would be a tense night for both those teams. Meanwhile Zimbabwe could celebrate a sweet moment in their cricket history. Neil Johnson did so with the added satisfaction of a Man of the Match award.

SATURDAY 29 MAY and SUNDAY 30 MAY 1999
GROUP A: ENGLAND vs INDIA
EDGBASTON, BIRMINGHAM: INDIA WON BY 63 RUNS

This started out as a likely vehicle for England to assert their position in Group A and ended in a sudden-death scramble for the last place for promotion to the Super Sixes. The host nation's nightmare eventually came true as their batsmen failed to cope with the pressure of chasing 233 runs for their World Cup survival.

India by contrast had recovered from the setbacks of their first two losses and in front of thousands of raucous supporters bowled and fielded with the passion of obvious match winners. Those with level heads, like outgoing coach David Lloyd, realistically admitted that, 'When we [England] needed to stand up and be counted we weren't up to it'.

Alec Stewart won his fifth toss and on a bright, clear morning decided to bowl. There was no immediate breakthrough although Saurav Ganguly and Sandgoppan Ramesh had the standard amount of difficulty with the new ball. Thirteen overs of survival and occasional strokes brought 49 runs before the consistent Alan Mullally had Ramesh edging to slip. Ganguly and Rahul Dravid were unable to repeat the dramatics of their Wednesday onslaught against Sri Lanka, but their contribution was important.

When Dravid lofted Mark Ealham to mid-off the Indian innings lost its cornerstone. Ealham had also tied down Sachin Tendulkar enough to cause him to hole out at mid wicket. He and Mohammad Azharuddin both got a start without developing their innings into something really substantial. It was Ajay Jadeja with five good boundaries in 30 balls who got the Indian total up to something that might give England some concern. After 50 overs there was virtually no difference between what India finished with and Zimbabwe's effort at Chelmsford.

Alec Stewart made a flying start to the Carnival of Cricket. Since then his form had been in decline and that trend continued when he drove at the energetic Mohanty, preferred to Venkatesh Prasad with the new ball, and edged the ball into the stomach of the Indian captain at second slip. Not expected to make a big impact on the tournament, India's only Orissian cricketer stunned a nation of 60 million and thrilled 900 million others when he ripped through Graeme Hick's crooked defence with his next legal delivery. England was 2–13 in the fourth over and dark clouds were gathering in more ways than one.

Graham Thorpe, at his best a fantastic counterpuncher, responded with three brilliant cover drives to bring the Indian paceman back to earth. His partner, Nasser Hussain, was nowhere near as confident. He survived a perilously close lbw shout and lobbed a leading edge just out of harm's way before chopping on Ganguly's innocuous looking opening delivery. The skies were closing in by now and everyone soon retreated to the dressing-room. They didn't return, the rain being so persistent that not even Edgbaston's mighty 'Brumbrella' could save the day.

England's Sunday offering was 160 runs with 29.3 overs left to bowl. When the players returned after a delayed start, the sky was still overcast and the temperature chill. In contrast to the buzz of yesterday's full house, this was a near-empty stadium of witnesses to a cricketing execution. It was quickly obvious England were losing their heads. Three overs into the day and

Thorpe was given out lbw to Javagal Srinath bowling around the wicket to the left-hander. One shot by Andrew Flintoff that sent the ball over mid wicket for six deceptively hinted at an English revival. Two balls later he was flummoxed by Anil Kumble and out lbw. The run rate was rising and the wickets were disappearing.

Fairbrother still fought on, but there was nothing left to support his efforts. When he charged Ganguly and swung wildly to be caught behind England were 8–132 and the result inevitable. A bit of bat waving by Darren Gough and

Angus Fraser just prolonged the agony. Twenty-four overs into the day's play Srinath ended England's participation by removing two of Mullally's stumps which released the Indian supporters on their joyous stampede. Ganguly, challenging Lance Klusener as the player of the tournament, secured another Man of Match award. Dave Stewart's World Cup song was now ready to be released in Britain. Any English supporters motivated by it now had no team to support.

INDIA

S.C. Ganguly run out	40
S. Ramesh c Hick b Mullally	20
R. Dravid c Ealham b Flintoff	53
S.R. Tendulkar c Hick b Ealham	22
M. Azharuddin (capt) c Hussain b Ealham	26
A. Jadeja c Fraser b Gough	39
N.R. Mongia (wk) b Mullally	2
J. Srinath b Gough	1
A. Kumble not out	6
B.K.V. Prasad not out	2
Extras (lb 7, w 10, nb 4)	21
(50 overs)	8–232

Did not bat: D. Mohanty

1/49 2/93 3/139 4/174 5/188 6/209 7/210 8/228

Bowling: Gough 10–0–51–2; Fraser 10–2–30–0; Mullally 10–0–54–2; Ealham 10–2–28–2; Flintoff 5–0–28–1; Hollioake 5–0–34–0

ENGLAND

N. Hussain b Ganguly	33
A.J. Stewart (capt-wk) c Azharuddin b Mohanty	2
G.A. Hick b Mohanty	0
G.P. Thorpe lbw Srinath	36
N.H. Fairbrother c Mongia b Ganguly	30
A. Flintoff lbw Kumble	15
A.J. Hollioake lbw Kumble	6
M.A. Ealham c Azharuddin b Ganguly	0
D.G. Gough c Kumble b Prasad	19
A.R.C. Fraser not out	15
A.D. Mullally b Srinath	0
Extras (b 4, lb 3, w 5, nb 1)	13
(45.2 overs)	10–169

1/12 2/13 3/72 4/81 5/118 6/130 7/131 8/132 9/161 10/169

Bowling: Srinath 8.2–3–25–2; Mohanty 10–0–54–2; Prasad 9–1–25–1; Ganguly 8–0–28–3; Kumble 10–1–30–2

Umpires: D.B. Hair, Javed Akhtar.

Toss: England. Points: India 2, England 0

SUNDAY 30 MAY 1999
GROUP B: AUSTRALIA vs WEST INDIES
OLD TRAFFORD, MANCHESTER: AUSTRALIA WON BY 6 WICKETS

Australian satisfaction at turning on their best form of the 1999 World Cup and reaching the Super Sixes was tempered by criticism of their go-slow batting tactics when on the verge of victory. On the streets of Auckland the attempt to keep the West Indies in the picture at the expense of New Zealand was seen as a despicable act, the equivalent of the infamous underarm 'sneak' of 1981.

Steve Waugh and Michael Bevan were trying to lift the West Indian run rate to a point that it would stay superior to New Zealand's. If that occurred the West Indies would also make the Super Sixes and Australia would take in the two points from this match. A New Zealand promotion eliminated those points and enabled the Kiwis to take in the two from the win against Australia at Cardiff. Despite the admission from the coach, Steve Rixon, and other New Zealand officials that their side would have done the same thing given similar circumstances, the Fleet Street response was scathing. The next day it amounted to nothing anyway.

The fault lay with the rules rather than the players. Qualification for the Super Sixes has even made the AFL final eight system seem simple and fair. Those to suffer were the fans packed into Old Trafford. As the majority of them were English, by mid-afternoon they were not in a particularly happy state of mind anyway.

If the Australians were boring, the West Indies were insipid against a rejuvenated Glenn McGrath. They had no answer to his pace and movement as the champion from Narromine exposed flaws in technique and application, much as he had done a few weeks before in the Caribbean.

Like the game at Edgbaston, this clash, even without knowing the result between Scotland and New Zealand, was virtually a sudden-death play-off. McGrath was a threat from his first over after Steve Waugh had won the toss and elected to bowl saying he was 'Looking for moisture' on an overcast Manchester morning.

There were occasional puffs of dust rather than clear signs of dampness. However, the Australian pacemen got the desired response from the wicket. In the fifth over Sherwin Campbell played across a McGrath delivery and a leading edge carried to a diving Mark Waugh at second slip. Next ball Jimmy Adams pushed half forward and was struck on the pad right in front of the middle stump.

The contest between Brian Lara and McGrath might well settle the result and was eagerly anticipated for that reason. The West Indian captain looked solid and cracked Damien Fleming off his hip for the opening boundary of the innings. Then McGrath sent down an unplayable off-cutter that went past Lara's impeccable defensive shot and clipped the top of his off-stump. It was a sublime moment for the Australians who knew they had opened the door to a West Indian batting disaster.

That prospect was avoided for 14 overs as Ridley Jacobs, in no real trouble, and Shivnarine Chanderpaul carried the total to a more respectable 3–64. They took advantage of some loose stuff from Brendan Julian. The introduction of Shane Warne for the 23rd over then completely ruptured the West Indian cause. On his 'ball from hell' ground the leg spinner forced Chanderpaul to chop his third delivery into his stumps. Next over Tom Moody, who sent down another impeccable spell, had Stuart Williams badly mistiming a pull shot to Mark Waugh at mid wicket. It was 6–69 in the 26th over when Phil Simmons played on to Fleming, 7–70 when Curtly Ambrose shuffled in front of the stumps to a Warne leg spinner and 8–71 when Mervyn Dillon did likewise to McGrath. Ridley Jacobs watched his side lose 5–7 in seven overs to effectively non-bat themselves out of the World Cup. The composure of the left-handed wicketkeeper-opening batsman put his team-mates to shame. The last two wickets added another 39 until McGrath came back to abruptly finish the innings. He had 5–14, Warne 3–11 and Jacobs had carried his bat through a completed innings, a rarity in Limited-Over Internationals.

The West Indies were never going to successfully defend 110, yet Ambrose did all within his extensive powers to do so. He quickly had Mark Waugh, pushing out tentatively, caught behind. Adam Gilchrist and Ricky Ponting batted positively for eight overs and 33 runs before Ambrose struck a second time, bowling Gilchrist on the crease between bat and pad. A superb diving left-handed catch in the gully by Adams removed Darren Lehmann and gave the Antiguan his third wicket.

When Ponting hooked Reon King to Chanderpaul at deep square leg Australia were 4–62 in the 20th over, in a worse position than the West Indies had been at the same stage. Ambrose, though, was finished his spell which allowed Bevan and Steve Waugh all the freedom they required. They scored the next 30 runs in brisk time, then the last 19 took 13 overs. It was painful viewing as the certain result stifled all tension. Spectators had paid £40 for a seat at Old Trafford. The Carnival of Cricket was short changing them badly. The torment was finished from the fourth ball of the 41st over and Glenn McGrath was named Man of the Match.

WEST INDIES

S.L. Campbell c M.E. Waugh b McGrath	2
R.D. Jacobs (wk) not out	49
J.C. Adams lbw McGrath	0
B.C. Lara (capt) b McGrath	9
S. Chanderpaul b Warne	16
S.C. Williams c M.E. Waugh b Moody	3
P.V. Simmons b Fleming	1
C.E.L. Ambrose lbw Warne	1
M. Dillon lbw McGrath	0
R.D. King lbw Warne	1
C.A. Walsh b McGrath	6
Extras (lb 3, w 18, nb 1)	22
(46.4 overs)	10–110

1/7 2/7 3/20 4/64 5/67 6/69 7/70 8/71 9/88 10/110

Bowling: McGrath 8.4–3–14–5; Fleming 7–1–12–1; Moody 7–0–16–1; Julian 7–1–36–0; Warne 10–4–11–3; Bevan 7–0–18–0

AUSTRALIA

A.C. Gilchrist (wk) b Ambrose	21
M.E. Waugh c Jacobs b Ambrose	3
R.T. Ponting c Chanderpaul b King	20
D.S. Lehmann c Adams b Ambrose	9
S.R. Waugh (capt) not out	19
M.G. Bevan not out	20
Extras (lb 4, w 7, nb 8)	19
(40.4 overs)	4–111

Did not bat: T.M. Moody, B.P. Julian, S.K. Warne, D.W. Fleming, G.D. McGrath

1/10 2/43 3/53 4/62

Bowling: Ambrose 10–0–31–3; Walsh 10–3–25–0; Dillon 7.4–1–22–0; King 10–2–27–1; Simmons 3–2–2–0

Umpires: R.S. Dunne, K.T. Francis.

Toss: Australia. Points: Australia 2, West Indies 0

SUNDAY 30 MAY 1999

GROUP A: KENYA vs SRI LANKA
COUNTY GROUND, SOUTHAMPTON: SRI LANKA WON BY 45 RUNS

While the cricket world followed the dramas at Edgbaston and Old Trafford in Hampshire, the Sri Lankans and Kenyans were going through the motions like a set of county players might at an end-of-season game at, for example, Southampton.

The game produced plenty of runs but was played out to the emptiest house of the tournament. After the Sri Lankans had been sent in by Aasif Karim, Sanath Jayasuriya finally showed glimpses of the form that had made him a star in 1996. He cut Tom Odoyo for six and dominated the opening stand with Roshan Mahanama before both openers were out within a couple of overs of each other.

Aravinda de Silva failed again before a century stand by Marvin Atapattu and Arjuna Ranatunga put Sri Lanka into a strong position. Four wickets then fell between the 40th and 43rd overs. It took a sprightly 64 partnership in seven overs by Mahela Jayawardene and Chaminda Vaas to give Sri Lanka a powerful total. The Kenyans had been hampered by a wet ball while the Sri Lankans batted and during the break between innings the drizzle became more persistent. It delayed the resumption, which sent lots of spectators home.

When play started again at 4.40 pm it was still cloudy and damp enough to suggest that it would be difficult to finish the match before Monday. That assessment was revised when Kenya slumped to 5–52, Vaas and Jayawardene doing a great deal of damage. However, there was to be no easy escape for the Sri Lankans as Maurice Odumbe and Alpesh Vadher took root and batted for 30 overs. They never looked likely to change the result, but had the satisfaction of going into the World Cup and Limited-Over International record books by putting on 161 for the sixth wicket. It must have annoyed the Sri Lankans, who were getting saturated as the drizzle kept on and on through into the evening. Muralitharan bowled in his cap, understanding that most body heat is lost through the head. Several times umpires Dave Orchard and Peter Willey offered the players the chance to come off. No-one wanted to return the next day so everyone kept going.

Jayasuriya finally bowled Odumbe on the drive in the 48th over. The Kenyan had done enough by that stage to receive the Man of the Match award.

SRI LANKA

S.T. Jayasuriya lbw Odoyo	39
R.S. Mahanama b Odoyo	21
M.S. Atapattu c Otieno b Angara	52
P.A. de Silva c Chudasama b Odoyo	10
A. Ranatunga (capt) run out	50
U.D.U. Chandana c Otieno b Kamande	0
M. Jayawardene c Ravindu Shah b M.A. Suji	45
R.S. Kaluwitharana (wk) c Chudasama b Angara	3
W.U.J.C. Vaas not out	29
G. Wickremasinghe not out	0
Extras (lb 7, w 16, nb 3)	26
(50 overs)	8–275

Did not bat: M. Muralitharan

1/72 2/74 3/87 4/191 5/191 6/199 7/209 8/273

Bowling: M.A. Suji 9–1–58–1; Angara 10–0–50–2; Odoyo 10–2–56–3; Aasif Karim 10–0–35–0; Kamande 9–0–51–1; Odumbe 2–0–18–0

KENYA

K.O. Otieno (wk) lbw Vaas	0
Ravindu Shah c Muralitharan b Jayawardene	12
D.N. Chudasama b Vaas	3
S.O. Tikolo lbw Wickremasinghe	19
Aasif Karim (capt) lbw Jayawardene	4
M.O. Odumbe b Jayasuriya	82
A. Vadher not out	73
T.M. Odoyo not out	16
Extras (b 4, lb 8, w 8, nb 1)	21
(50 overs)	6–230

Did not bat: M.A. Suji, J.O. Angara, J. Kamande

1/0 2/10 3/33 4/36 5/52 6/213

Bowling: Vaas 7–1–26–2; Wickremasinghe 9–1–27–1; Jayawardene 10–0–56–2; Muralitharan 3–0–11–0; Chandana 1–0–13–0; Jayasuriya 10–1–39–1; de Silva 10–0–46–0

Umpires: D.L. Orchard, P. Willey.

Toss: Kenya. Points: Sri Lanka 2, Kenya 0

MONDAY 31 MAY 1999
GROUP B: SCOTLAND vs NEW ZEALAND
RAEBURN PLACE, EDINBURGH: NEW ZEALAND WON BY 6 WICKETS

A vibrant performance by New Zealand over-whelmed Scotland so that the Kiwis were able to oust the West Indies from the last spot of the Group B Super Sixes.

The capacity crowd would have hoped for a better effort from their team which, despite not winning a match, could still have affected the destiny of the 1999 World Cup. Scottish flags were prominent prior to the start of play. However they soon were put away when, after Stephen Fleming had won the toss and inserted Scotland, the home side quickly slumped to 3–12.

Dion Nash made the first breakthrough. It was left-arm paceman Geoff Allott who impressed again, though. He brought one back at Scottish captain George Salmond to win an lbw decision, then moved the ball away to catch the edge of Mike Allingham's bat. For a time Gavin Hamilton, obviously a class above England's token all-rounders, and Ian Stanger restored cricketing parity with a partnership of 54. Once Nathan Astle had Hamilton caught at mid wicket the slump was rejoined and Scotland slipped to 6–68 in the 28th over.

Despite Alec Davies' determination, there was no sign of recovery from there. Chris Harris cleaned up the tail, finished with astonishing figures and two thirds of a hat-trick. By the first ball of the 43rd Scotland was all out for a paltry 121.

The pretty tree-lined ground was lifted by the bright afternoon sun as New Zealand began their pursuit. They had 50 overs to win the match, but only 20.5 overs to tip their run rate above that of the West Indies. And they made the worst possible start. Matthew Hart, a tidy left-arm spinner, had been brought in as an opening batsman to replace the out-of-form Matthew Horne. Hart lasted one ball, bowled behind his legs from a fast full-pitched delivery from John Blain. Batting in a fashion a little alien to their normal approach, the uncertainty showed at the start. Halfway through the third over Astle edged another full Blain delivery through to wicket-keeper Davies to make New Zealand 2–19. Everyone took a breather with New Zealand on 2–30 from five overs at lunch.

After the interval, Roger Twose, who kick-started the Kiwi World Cup campaign with his match-winning innings against Australia, approached his task with gay abandon. He was dropped at short cover from a firm dive, at mid wicket from a skyed pull and fine leg from another top-edged pull shot. The New Zealand innings might have been in some disarray if all the chances had been taken. Instead Twose survived and between mishits made some worthwhile connections. Asim Butt was clubbed over mid wicket for six and other hits travelled to the boundary, some on their intended course, others at a variety of angles.

The former Warwickshire opener dived through the stumps at the bowler's end scrambling for a run. He lost Craig McMillan at 81 and Fleming played on 11 runs later to give the promising Blain his third wicket. Twose reached his fifty off 44 balls. Then he sat back and watched Chris Cairns pick up Hamilton and hit him way over square leg for the six that won the game. That shot took New Zealand into the Super Sixes with three overs to spare. Geoff Allott was named Man of the Match.

SCOTLAND

M.W. Smith c Cairns b Nash	1
M. Allingham c Fleming b Allott	2
G. Salmond (capt) lbw Allott	1
G.M. Hamilton c Allott b Astle	20
I.M. Stanger c Astle b Cairns	27
J.E. Brinkley c Parore b Allott	0
J. Williamson c & b Harris	10
A.G. Davies (wk) c sub (D.L. Vettori) b Harris	24
J.A.R. Blain lbw Harris	0
Asim Butt c Twose b Harris	10
N.R. Dyer not out	2
Extras (b 1, lb 7, w 13, nb 3)	24
(42.1 overs)	10–121

1/2 2/11 3/12 4/66 5/68 6/68 7/100 8/100 9/110 10/121

Bowling: Allott 10–3–15–3; Nash 10–3–16–1; Bulfin 6–0–31–0; Cairns 8–0–26–1; Astle 5–1–18–1; Harris 3.1–0–7–4

NEW ZEALAND

M.N. Hart b Blain	0
N.J. Astle c Davies b Blain	11
C.D. McMillan c & b Hamilton	19
R.G. Twose not out	54
S.P. Fleming (capt) b Blain	7
C.L. Cairns not out	20
Extras (b 1, lb 2, w 5, nb 4)	12
(17.5 overs)	4–123

Did not bat: A.C. Parore (wk), C.Z. Harris, C. Bulfin, D.J. Nash, G.A. Allott

1/0 2/19 3/81 4/92

Bowling: Blain 7–0–53–3; Asim Butt 5–0–33–0; Hamilton 5.5–0–34–1

Umpires: R.E. Koertzen, I.D. Robinson

Toss: New Zealand. Points: New Zealand 2, Scotland 0

MONDAY 31 MAY 1999
GROUP B: BANGLADESH vs PAKISTAN
COUNTY GROUND, NORTHAMPTON: BANGLADESH WON BY 62 RUNS

This was not expected to be a memorable cricket match. Pakistan would finish on top of Group B and Bangladesh fifth, whatever the result. So good had Pakistan's form been that their fifth victory looked a mere formality. The odds on Bangladesh winning were 33–1. Anyone willing to lay out money on them would have done very well out of the day. The two teams played as if their records and positions were reversed and Bangladesh won by 62 runs.

It was a fantastic win for a country working hard to have its application for Test status accepted and the landmark result was achieved on the back of consistent batting and some great bowling by Khaled Mahmud which demolished the Pakistani top order. In Bangladesh the government declared a half-day holiday. The people of the former East Pakistan were especially excited to record a win over the country from whom they had to fight to win independence in 1971.

Wasim Akram sent Bangladesh in. However, neither he nor his highly rated pace bowling partners, Waqar Younis and Shoaib Akhtar, could separate Shahriar Hossain and Mehrab Hossain until the total was 69. As usual, the ball regularly beat the bat. Sometimes it was within close proximity to the edge, often it was a long way. Extras did as well as anyone. That is not to deny the quality or importance of the batting of Akram Khan or Khaled Mahmud. They were two of the seven batsmen who reached double figures and with the contribution of extras a competent 9–223 was reached. Saqlain Mushtaq did most to restrain it from being much more by returning the best-ever figures for a Pakistani in the World Cup.

Pakistan was penalised an over for failing to complete their 300 legal deliveries in the allotted time. Then Shahid Afridi was penalised for not being able to handle Khaled Mahmud's fifth ball. Pakistan were 1–5, then 2–7 when Ijaz Ahmed was bowled by Shafiuddin Ahmed in the next over. Saeed Anwar was run out while batting with none other than Inzamam-ul-Haq. When Salim Malik fell lbw halfway through the 13th over to Khaled Mahmud the favourites were

5–42 and defeat seemed inevitable. Eventually Azhar Mahmood, Wasim Akram, Moin Khan and Saqlain Mushtaq gave the Pakistani total some respectability. Another 63 runs were required from 26 balls when Khaled Mashud's direct-hit throw brought a call from Darrell Hair to the third umpire, David Shepherd, to make a run out decision.

Most Bangladeshi supporters never saw the red light to confirm Saqlain's dismissal. They were already on the ground celebrating the win that their captain Aminul Islam called 'A great achievement'. Khaled Mahmud was named Man of the Match.

BANGLADESH

Shahriar Hossain lbw Saqlain Mushtaq	39
Mehrab Hossain st Moin Khan b Saqlain Mushtaq	9
Akram Khan c Wasim Akram b Waqar Younis	42
Aminul Islam (capt) b Shahid Afridi	15
Naimur Rahman b Waqar Younis	13
Minhajul Abedin c & b Saqlain Mushtaq	14
Khaled Mahmud st Moin b Saqlain Mushtaq	27
Khaled Mashud (wk) not out	15
Mohammad Rafique c Shoaib b Saqlain Mushtaq	6
Neeyamur Rashid lbw Wasim Akram	1
Shafiuddin Ahmed not out	2
Extras (lb 5, w 28, nb 7)	40
(50 overs)	9–223

1/69 2/70 3/120 4/148 5/148 6/187 7/195 8/208 9/212

Bowling: Waqar Younis 9–1–36–2; Shoaib Akhtar 8–0–30–0; Wasim Akram 10–0–35–1; Azhar Mahmood 8–0–56–0; Saqlain Mushtaq 10–1–35–5; Shahid Afridi 5–0–26–1

PAKISTAN

Saeed Anwar run out	9
Shahid Afridi c Mehrab Hossain b Khaled Mahmud	2
Ijaz Ahmed b Shafiuddin Ahmed	0
Inzamam-ul-Haq lbw Khaled Mahmud	7
Salim Malik lbw Khaled Mahmud	5
Azhar Mahmood run out	29
Wasim Akram (capt) c Shahriar Hossain b Minhajul Abedin	29
Moin Khan (wk) c Mehrab Hossain b Naimur Rahman	18
Saqlain Mushtaq run out	21
Waqar Younis b Mohammad Rafique	11
Shoaib Akhtar not out	1
Extras (b 1, lb 6, w 21, nb 1)	29
(44.3 overs)	10–161

1/5 2/7 3/26 4/29 5/42 6/97 7/102 8/124 9/160 10/161

Bowling: Khaled Mahmud 10–2–31–3; Shafiuddin Ahmed 8–0–26–1; Neeyamur Rashid 5–1–20–0; Mohammad Rafique 8–0–28–1; Minhajul Abedin 7–2–29–1; Naimur Rahman 6.3–2–20–1

Umpires: D.B. Hair, D.B. Cowie.

Toss: Pakistan. Points: Bangladesh 2, Pakistan 0

THE SUPER SIXES

Following the preliminary rounds of the 1999 World Cup the first three teams in each group were promoted to the Super Sixes. Their standings were as follows.

GROUP A

	P	W	L	Pts	NR/R
South Africa	5	4	1	8	+0.86
India	5	3	2	6	+1.28
Zimbabwe	5	3	2	6	+0.02
England	5	3	2	6	−0.33
Sri Lanka	5	2	3	4	−0.81
Kenya	5	0	5	0	−1.20

GROUP B

	P	W	L	Pts	NR/R
Pakistan	5	4	1	8	+0.53
Australia	5	3	2	6	+0.73
New Zealand	5	3	2	6	+0.58
West Indies	5	3	2	6	+0.50
Bangladesh	5	2	3	4	−0.54
Scotland	5	0	5	0	−1.93

The actual starting table of the Super Sixes was something else.

	Pts	NR/R
Pakistan	4	0.72
Zimbabwe	4	0.33
South Africa	2	−0.35
New Zealand	2	−0.40
India	−	−0.03
Australia	−	−0.35

FRIDAY 4 JUNE 1999
SUPER SIXES No.1: AUSTRALIA vs INDIA
THE OVAL, LONDON: AUSTRALIA WON BY 77 RUNS

Glenn McGrath, proving he is the better of any batsman in the world, inspired Australia to an emphatic and important 77-run win over India. Three perfect deliveries shattered the Indian top order and ruined any hope they might have entertained of chasing Australia's substantial 6–282.

Early rain promptly cleared south of the Thames into cool breezy conditions. Mohammad Azharuddin showed he had the calling ability to end Steve Waugh's unbelievable run of success with the coin. The historic ground quickly filled as Australia began batting at the invitation of the Indian captain.

The bounce in The Oval wicket encouraged Javagal Srinath to bend his back. He worked up a genuine pace and had the ball thumping into Nayan Mongia's gloves on the rise. Mark Waugh and Adam Gilchrist, despite one wicked blow in the groin, withstood that early threat and then prospered. Waugh signalled a change of attitude when he started advancing on bowlers before they released the ball. An edged drive sailed to the third-man boundary, another was smashed to the rope at cover. In other matches Saurav Ganguly had been a consistent partnership breaker. Waugh greeted him by going down on his knee and flat-batting the ball onto the second level of the Barrington Stand.

A calm tickle around the corner raised his second fifty of the competition in the 19th over from 55 balls. The next milestone would be the 100 opening stand. Gilchrist, however, did not quite get there. Three short of the mark he advanced on Ganguly and his totally mistimed off-drive landed in the hands of Debashish Mohanty at mid-off. Ricky Ponting countered that blow with an audacious drive on the up that also deposited the ball over the rope at long-off to get off the mark.

Ponting and Waugh rattled along at a run per ball for 10 overs until the opener's 99-ball innings ended when a leg-side scoop carried to Venkatesh Prasad at fine leg. Robin Singh made it a double breakthrough in the same over when Ponting chopped the ball onto his stumps.

Australia were 3–158 in the 31st over. Their middle order batted profitably from that point. The runs came in ones and twos as Steve Waugh and Darren Lehmann put on 60 in 11 overs. There was real urgency in the final overs which brought acceleration but also cost wickets. Steve Waugh scooped to mid-on, Lehmann got lost in the middle of the pitch as Ajay Jadeja threw down the stumps and Michael Bevan, after hitting a flat scoop for six over long-off, skyed a short rising ball to the wicketkeeper Nayan Mongia off Prasad in the 50th over. Tom Moody with a couple of imperious drives gave a final boost, 78 having come from the final 10 overs.

The question of whether India might seriously challenge Australia's 282 was quickly settled by McGrath. From the final ball of his opening over his away swinger induced an edge from Sachin Tendulkar's defensive bat and Gilchrist made no mistake. Tendulkar had been prolific in his most recent Limited-Over Internationals against Australia. Then, though, the attacks had been without McGrath. Tendulkar was forced to reduce the size of the label on his bat prior to the match. If the size of his bat had been reduced instead, McGrath's delivery might have missed the edge. From the fifth ball of his next over the paceman repeated the dose to Rahul Dravid. Damien Fleming joined in the demolition with the equally valuable wicket of Saurav Ganguly, who chopped on an inswinger to the left-hander.

When Azharuddin could do nothing except parry the ball to gully off the shoulder of his bat India were 4–17 in the seventh over. McGrath had 3–8 in four brilliant overs. It was exciting stuff except for the thousands of Indians in the crowd. They were spared total humiliation by the spirited batting of Robin Singh and Ajay Jadeja who combined to put on 141 in 30 overs. It was fine batting that saved face and run rate, if not the two points from this match. Both batsman got

stuck into Shane Warne, who had been in doubt for this game with a sore neck and shoulder. One Warne over cost 21 as the ball sailed into the crowd three times.

Australian commentator Bill Lawry was close to tears as two pigeons paid for their lack of cricket knowledge with their lives in two separate incidents. One was crunched out of mid air by a Paul Reiffel throw and another could not avoid a powerful shot by Jadeja. The Indian reached a fine hundred a few balls before a comical run out of Mohanty ended the match with 10 balls remaining. India now faced an almost impossible task to qualify for the semi-finals. Australia had won their first game at The Oval for 22 years. McGrath was named Man of the Match.

AUSTRALIA

M.E. Waugh c Prasad b Singh	83
A.C. Gilchrist (wk) c Mohanty b Ganguly	31
R.T. Ponting b Singh	23
D.S. Lehmann run out	26
S.R. Waugh (capt) c Kumble b Mohanty	36
M.G. Bevan c Mongia b Prasad	22
T.M. Moody not out	26
S.K. Warne not out	0
Extras (lb 14, w 10, nb 11)	35
(50 overs)	6–282

Did not bat: P.R. Reiffel, D.W. Fleming, G.D. McGrath

1/97 2/157 3/158 4/218 5/231 6/275

Bowling: Srinath 10-2-34-0; Mohanty 7-0-47-1; Prasad 10-0-60-1; Kumble 10-0-49-0; Ganguly 5-0-31-1; Singh 7-0-43-2; Tendulkar 1-0-2-0

INDIA

S.C. Ganguly b Fleming	8
S.R. Tendulkar c Gilchrist b McGrath	0
R. Dravid c Gilchrist b McGrath	2
A. Jadeja not out	100
M. Azharuddin (capt) c S.R. Waugh b McGrath	3
R.R. Singh c Reiffel b Moody	75
N.R. Mongia (wk) run out	2
J. Srinath c Gilchrist b S.R. Waugh	0
A. Kumble c Gilchrist b S.R. Waugh	3
B.K.V. Prasad lbw Fleming	2
D.S. Mohanty run out	0
Extras (lb 3, w 4, nb 3)	10
(48.2 overs)	10–205

1/1 2/10 3/12 4/17 5/158 6/181 7/186 8/192 9/204 10/205

Bowling: McGrath 10-1-34-3; Fleming 9-1-33-2; Reiffel 10-1-30-0; Moody 10-0-41-1; M.E. Waugh 1-0-7-0; Warne 6.2-0-49-0; S.R. Waugh 2-0-8-2

Umpires: S.A. Bucknor, P. Willey.

Toss: India. Points: Australia 2, India 0

SATURDAY 5 JUNE 1999
SUPER SIX No.2: PAKISTAN vs SOUTH AFRICA
TRENT BRIDGE, NOTTINGHAM: SOUTH AFRICA WON BY 3 WICKETS

The two best-performed teams in the tournament recovered from the shock of their recent defeats to turn on a riveting contest at Trent Bridge. In the end South Africa won with an over to spare, although the margin was tight enough to suggest the result could easily be reversed if the teams met again, which their positions and

form indicated was quite possible.

South Africa's hero was Lance Klusener whose batting was attaining legendary status. Anyone able to spank Shoaib Akhtar for six has an amazing talent.

Every seat was taken at Trent Bridge, as befitted one of the matches of the competition.

Moin Khan of Pakistan is run out by South
African Mark Boucher during this thrilling
Super Six encounter.   (Allsport/Adrian Murrell)

Glenn McGrath takes the prized wicket of Sachin Tendulkar during the first Super Six match at The Oval. McGrath
took 3—8 in four overs and was named Man of the Match.   (Allsport/Shaun Botterill)

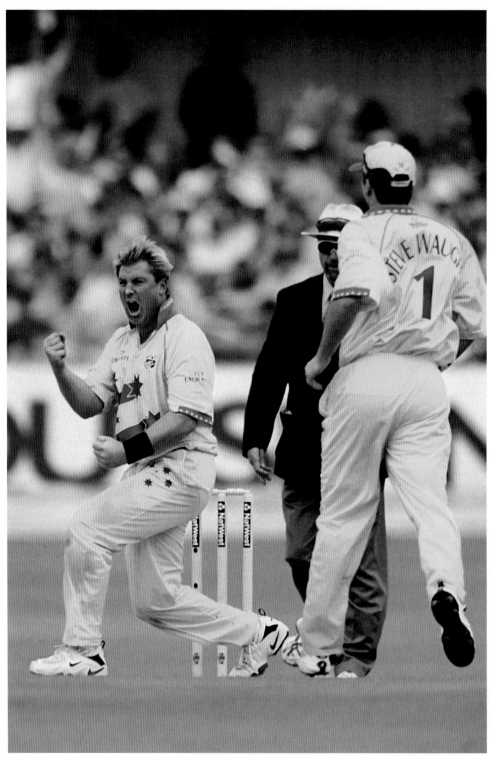

Shane Warne in a celebratory mood during a match against South Africa.   (Allsport/Adrian Murrell)

Steve Waugh in action during the tied semi-
final against South Africa.

It's a tie! (And a victory on Super Six points for Australia, who progress to the final.) (Allsport/Ross Kinnaird)

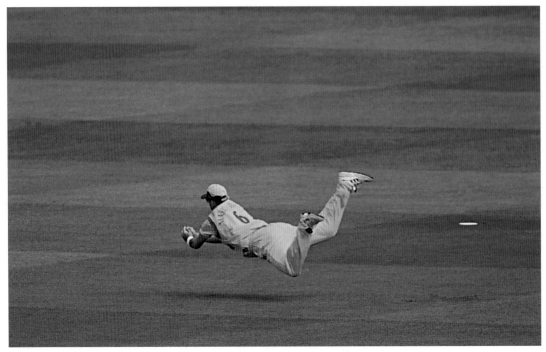

Mark Waugh brilliantly catches Wajahatullah Wasti during the 1999 World Cup final.   (Allsport/Adrian Murrell)

The Australian Team celebrate World Cup supremacy on the balcony at Lord's.   (Allsport/Laurence Griffiths)

Wasim Akram won the toss and batted against a side that had not changed for six matches. As usual, for much of the innings the Pakistanis showed no inclination to take the attack to the bowlers. Saeed Anwar and Wajahatullah Wasti provided a steady start, but like Abdur Razzaq and Ijaz Ahmed could not build upon that. Steve Elworthy was economical and when Inzamam-ul-Haq failed to ground his bat, even though he had lumbered over the line in time to beat Jonty Rhodes' throw, Pakistan were 5–118 in the 36th over and going nowhere.

Moin Khan, supported by Yousuf Youhana, back in the side but soon suffering a recurrence of his hamstring strain, and then Azhar Mahmood, gave the innings some substance. Youhana's runner, Ijaz Ahmed, was run out when Klusener proved an attempted short single was ill-advised.

The last four overs realised another 48 runs as Moin went berserk. He smashed Allan Donald for two fours and clipped him for six behind square leg in the 47th over. In the next over bowled by Shaun Pollock, he hit another four and a six, this time a dancing drive which sailed high over long-off. Moin had completed his half century in 48 balls and although he became the third run-out victim of the innings in the next over, he had given his vaunted bowling attack something to defend.

Allan Donald had consistently clocked 86 mph on the radar gun placed in the ground to measure the pace of the fast bowlers. Shoaib Akhtar set out to top that and by his third ball was well into the nineties. His fifth delivery brought greater reward when Herschelle Gibbs guided a catch to Ijaz in the gully. Hansie Cronje surprisingly promoted himself to number 3 and Shoaib had him jumping as well. The speedster reached 95 mph (153 k/ph) and in his third over Cronje was caught on the third man boundary from a top-edged cut.

Not to be denied, Akram trapped Gary Kirsten lbw not playing a shot and when Azhar Mahmood had Daryll Cullinan caught at cover and Rhodes lbw to an inswinger South Africa were 5–58 and heading for a heavy defeat.

However, the never-say-die attitude of the Proteas has been an obvious attribute since their return to authorised international cricket late in 1991. Jacques Kallis and Pollock showed plenty of that quality in a partnership of 77 in 16 overs. The work was mostly done in smartly taken singles and when Pollock stretched out at Azhar and was caught at slip, the South Africans had just a sniff of their target at 6–135.

Klusener had the form and quality, though, to turn the scent of victory into a very powerful aroma. He and his powerful bat soon drastically reduced the run requirement. Kallis completed an essential fifty in 89 balls with just three fours. Klusener pulled a short Saqlain delivery for six over square leg, then lost Kallis as he top-edged an attempt at a similar shot off the same bowler in the 45th over.

Now Klusener turned the evenly balanced match South Africa's way. Shoaib came roaring in at full steam, determined to break the left-hander's sequence of not outs. Klusener swung hard and a top edge sailed to the boundary at fine leg. He followed that with a mighty hit, rocketing the ball off the bat as fast as it was sent down, over mid wicket for six. This may well have been the shot of the World Cup. When a yorker flew off Klusener's toe through Moin for four leg byes the task had been reduced to 24 runs off 27 balls.

A pull shot off Saqlain for four and a heave over mid wicket for six off Akram by the man of the moment took South Africa to 7–212. Then the silent partner Mark Boucher displayed his wares with a right-hander's six over mid wicket off the suffering Saqlain. The excitement subsided, as did the exhortations of the Pakistani supporters. There was one final flutter as Klusener, never likely to get the runs in singles, skyed another attempted slog at Saqlain. The ball steepled over mid-off. Anwar misjudged the catch which allowed the batsman to complete the two runs needed for the unlikely victory. Trent Bridge had seen a ripper and Lance Klusener had collected four Man of the Match awards in six starts.

PAKISTAN

Saeed Anwar c Boucher b Elworthy	23
Wajahatullah Wasti c Boucher b Donald	17
Abdur Razzaq c Kirsten b Elworthy	30
Ijaz Ahmed c Cullinan b Klusener	23
Inzamam-ul-Haq run out	4
Yousuf Youhana run out	17
Moin Khan (wk) run out	63
Azhar Mahmood not out	15
Wasim Akram (capt) not out	5
Extras (b 4, lb 8, w 11)	23
(50 overs)	7–220

Did not bat: Saqlain Mushtaq, Shoaib Akhtar

1/41 2/58 3/102 4/111 5/118 6/150 7/206

Bowling: Pollock 10–1–42–0; Kallis 10–0–47–0; Donald 10–2–49–1; Elworthy 10–2–23–2; Cronje 1–0–6–0; Klusener 9–0–41–1

SOUTH AFRICA

G. Kirsten lbw Wasim Akram	19
H.H. Gibbs c Ijaz Ahmed b Shoaib Akhtar	0
H. Cronje (capt) c Saqlain b Shoaib Akhtar	4
D.J. Cullinan c Saeed Anwar b Azhar Mahmood	18
J.H. Kallis c Moin Khan b Saqlain Mushtaq	54
J.N. Rhodes lbw Azhar Mahmood	0
S.M. Pollock c Inzamam-ul-Haq b Azhar Mahmood	30
L. Klusener not out	46
M.V. Boucher (wk) not out	12
Extras (lb 11, w 14, nb 13)	38
(49 overs)	7–221

Did not bat: S. Elworthy, A.A. Donald

1/7 2/19 3/39 4/55 5/58 6/135 7/176

Bowling: Wasim Akram 10–0–44–1; Shoaib Akhtar 9–1–51–2; Azhar Mahmood 10–1–24–3; Abdur Razzaq 10–1–40–0; Saqlain Mushtaq 10–0–51–1

Umpires: D.B. Hair, D.R. Shepherd.

Toss: Pakistan. Points: South Africa 2, Pakistan 0

SUNDAY 6 JUNE and MONDAY 7 JUNE 1999
SUPER SIX No.3: NEW ZEALAND vs ZIMBABWE
HEADINGLEY, LEEDS: NO RESULT

The weather finally caught up with the World Cup and ruined a game that was not a spectacle anyway. After an interrupted first day and a blank second, New Zealand and Zimbabwe came away with a point each. For the Kiwis, who believed they would win easily, it was a frustrating time. The Zimbabweans, on the other hand, sneaked a point closer to a surprising semifinal berth.

Between showers on the Sunday, the Zimbabwean batsmen fell away badly during their final overs and set New Zealand a modest 176 for victory. Alistair Campbell had been confident enough to bat when he won the toss and his partnership of 81 for the fourth wicket with Murray Goodwin put his side in a very reasonable position. It was after the second rain interruption that things began to go astray and when Chris Cairns made short work of the tail Zimbabwe had lost 6–39 in 13 overs.

Fearing the worst with the weather Matthew Horne, who had brilliantly run out Grant Flower at the start of the day, and Nathan Astle got the Kiwi reply away to a cracking start. Between them they struck 10 boundaries in nine overs before they fell one after the other to Guy Whittall and Henry Olonga. When Craig McMillan played down the wrong line to Heath Streak and was out lbw the Kiwis were 3–65 and needed a period of consolidation.

It never really got going. Soon, Dave Orchard and Srinivas Venkataraghavan were offering the light to the batsmen. When Stephen Fleming accepted that offer at 7.10 in the evening the game was all over. The next day rain started falling halfway through the morning. Everyone waited until 4.30 pm but to no avail. Geoff Allott's three wickets brought his tally for the tournament up to an impressive 18. In a 'no result', though, there is no Man of the Match award.

ZIMBABWE

N.C. Johnson b Allott	25
G.W. Flower run out	1
M.W. Goodwin c Parore b Harris	57
A. Flower (wk) c McMillan b Allott	0
A.D.R. Campbell (capt) c Nash b Larsen	40
G.J. Whittall c Astle b Allott	21
S.V. Carlisle c McMillan b Astle	2
H.H. Streak b Cairns	4
A.R. Whittall c Astle b Cairns	3
A.G. Huckle c Twose b Cairns	0
H.K. Olonga not out	1
Extras (b 4, lb 11, w 3, nb 3)	21
(49.3 overs)	10–175

1/10 2/35 3/45 4/136 5/148 6/154 7/163 8/174 9/174 10/175

Bowling: Allott 10–1–24–3; Nash 10–2–48–0; Larsen 10–0–27–1; Cairns 6.3–2–24–3; Harris 4–0–12–1; Astle 9–0–25–1

NEW ZEALAND

M.J. Horne lbw Whittall	35
N.J. Astle c Streak b Olonga	20
C.D. McMillan lbw Streak	1
S.P. Fleming (capt) not out	9
R.G. Twose not out	0
Extras (lb 1, nb 4)	5
(15 overs)	3–70

Did not bat: C.L. Cairns, A.C. Parore (wk), C.Z. Harris, G.R. Larsen, D.J. Nash, G.A. Allott

1/58 2/59 3/65

Bowling: Johnson 3–0–21–0; Streak 5–0–25–1; G.J. Whittall 3–0–9–1; Olonga 4–1–14–1

Umpires: D.L. Orchard, S. Venkataraghavan.

Toss: Zimbabwe. Points: Zimbabwe 1, New Zealand 1

TUESDAY 8 JUNE 1999

SUPER SIXES No.4: INDIA vs PAKISTAN
OLD TRAFFORD, MANCHESTER: INDIA WON BY 47 RUNS

India, just clinging on to their World Cup hopes, showed that Pakistan's batting inadequacies were real and could be exploited. If Mohammad Azharuddin's side was relieved to win such a crucial encounter, it was nothing compared to the relief of the Old Trafford authorities that the capacity crowd gave no cause for concern.

Much was made pre-match of the growing tensions between Pakistan and India over disputed territory in Kashmir. The possibility of trouble in a massed gathering of expatriates during a cricket match contested by the two countries led to greatly increased security at the ground. Those fans made a lot of noise, but the only time the security men were conspicuous was near the end of the game when happy Indian fans let off a few fireworks, and then during the after-match invasion.

The cricket itself had few fireworks as batsmen struggled for freedom in a match of major national significance. When India batted after Azharuddin had won the toss Sachin Tendulkar laid the foundation for a strong total with an innings containing some of his best batting of the World Cup. The outfield, sodden from heavy overnight rain, could not stop Tendulkar from striking five fine boundaries. He lost Ramesh at 37, then with Rahul Dravid took the score to 95 in the 21st over.

The importance of the Indian champion's wicket was shown by the fact that once he had been caught at deep mid-off, playing an over-ambitious drive against Azhar Mahmood, the Indian innings lost its punch. Ajay Jadeja did not last long, which forced Dravid and Mohammad Azharuddin onto the defensive. Only two boundaries were struck between the 21st and 45th overs during which time Dravid completed another fifty off 70 balls. He was then caught at cover by a stretching Afridi off Akram.

Azharuddin realised quick runs were needed at the end of the innings. At first he and Robin Singh were all at sea as they tried to lift the run rate through the last overs. Then, suddenly, Singh clouted Saqlain for a big six that nearly landed in Warwick Road railway station. Azharuddin repeated the dose next over to the off spinner, then a bottom-hand clip-chip and a back-foot cover drive both for four off Shoaib

Akhtar raised the Indian captain's 48th fifty in Limited-Over Internationals. Both he and Singh fell in the final rush for runs, leaving India 227 to protect.

Saeed Anwar pulled Javagal Srinath's first ball to the boundary, instigating an early flurry of fours by both openers. They briefly gave the impression that the chase was a straightforward one. Srinath ended that idea when he had Afridi slashing high to Kumble in the gully and, when he changed to the Stretford end, Ijaz Ahmed edging to Azharuddin at second slip. Salim Malik's last World Cup was turning into a personal nightmare and when Anwar drove at Venkatesh Prasad, Azharuddin's low diving slips catch left Pakistan 4–65. Azhar fell cheaply, too. Yousuf Youhana's quality in the middle order was missed and Pakistan were heading for prompt defeat.

Inzamam-ul-Haq, sore fingers and all, held on while Moin Khan engaged in his hitting habit. The in-form wicketkeeper–batsman connected with a swipe off Robin Singh for a six over square leg. The Pakistani supporters chanted for their hero. His aggressive response was a top-edged pull that gave Prasad his third wicket. Abdur Razzaq and big Inzamam kept the game alive for a few more overs. They were unable to reduce the run rate, however, and when Inzamam swung across the line at Prasad the contest finished.

The dismissal of the Pakistani captain, caught on the boundary to give Prasad his fifth wicket, with 48 runs still needed off 27 balls, heralded a fairly wild spectator charge and more fireworks. Only a sensationalist would have called this a riot as exuberance was the main emotion exhibited. The players, including Man of the Match Prasad, were still glad to get off the ground quick smart.

INDIA

S.R. Tendulkar c Saqlain Mushtaq b Azhar Mahmood	45
S. Ramesh b Abdur Razzaq	20
R. Dravid c Shahid Afridi b Wasim Akram	61
A. Jadeja c Inzamam-ul-Haq b Azhar Mahmood	6
M. Azharuddin (capt) c Ijaz Mahmood b Wasim Akram	59
R.R. Singh c Wasim Akram b Shoaib Akhtar	16
N.R. Mongia (wk) not out	6
Extras (b 1, lb 3, w 8, nb 2)	14
(50 overs)	6–227

Did not bat: J. Srinath, A. Kumble, B.K.V. Prasad, D. Mohanty

1/37 2/95 3/107 4/158 5/218 6/227

Bowling: Wasim Akram 10–0–27–2; Shoaib Akhtar 10–0–55–1; Abdur 10–0–40–1; Azhar Mahmood 10–0–34–2; Saqlain Mushtaq 10–0–67–0

PAKISTAN

Saeed Anwar c Azharuddin b Prasad	36
Shahid Afridi c Kumble b Srinath	6
Ijaz Ahmed c Azharuddin b Srinath	11
Salim Malik lbw Prasad	6
Inzamam-ul-Haq lbw Prasad	41
Azhar Mahmood c Mongia b Prasad	10
Moin Khan (wk) c Tendulkar b Prasad	34
Abdur Razzaq b Srinath	11
Wasim Akram (capt) c Kumble b Prasad	12
Saqlain Mushtaq lbw Kumble	0
Shoaib Akhtar not out	0
Extras (lb 11, w 2)	13
(45.3 overs)	10–180

1/19 2/44 3/52 4/65 5/78 6/124 7/146 8/175 9/176 10/180

Bowling: Srinath 8–1–37–3; Mohanty 10–2–31–0; Prasad 9.3–2–27–5; Kumble 10–0–43–2; Singh 8–1–31–0

Umpires: D.R. Shepherd, S.A. Bucknor.

Toss: India Points: India 2, Pakistan 0

WEDNESDAY 9 JUNE 1999
SUPER SIXES No.5: AUSTRALIA vs ZIMBABWE
LORD'S, LONDON: AUSTRALIA WON BY 44 RUNS

At Lord's and the best batting conditions of the World Cup so far, two fine centuries were compiled during a day which realised 562 runs. Yet there was not much tension and, despite the splendid individual efforts of Neil Johnson, never any real likelihood Australia, still on the ascent, would be beaten.

They lost Adam Gilchrist early after Alistair Campbell had won the toss and bowled. Soon, though, the runs were flowing. The advantage of bowling first on the fresh wicket was non-existent. Ricky Ponting was in an aggressive frame of mind. Trying to dominate the opposition, he scored at better than a run per ball. In the 15th over he played an off-cutter from the expensive Henry Olonga onto his stumps. Ponting had, however, set the tone of the innings and opened the way for a great partnership between the Waugh twins. First, Olonga had to get Darren Lehmann out of the way, which he did with the score on 2–97 by banging him on the forefinger of his left-hand, necessitating treatment and X-rays.

Mark Waugh had received little of the strike while batting with Ponting. Now, he and Steve went stroke for stroke, run for run for 25 entertaining overs. After the 100 had been raised in the 18th over Mark Waugh hit Olonga with a trademark on drive for four and in the same over Steve produced a perfect example of his trademark shot, a cracking cover drive off the back foot.

Mark Waugh, who had been dropped at backward point by a leaping Grant Flower early in his innings, smashed a slog straight drive back down the pitch off leg spinner Paul Strang. The only thing that prevented the ball crashing into the boundary was the grille on Steve Waugh's helmet. Fortunately, for future brotherly relations, injury was avoided, but Steve did have to replace his realigned grille.

Both Waughs bent their knees and swiped the spinners, often for four and sometimes for six.

Mark passed 50 for the third time in the tournament in 84 balls, Steve reached the milestone in 54 balls. He hit his second six towards the Tavern side of the ground, then was bowled middle stump attempting to put medium pacer Guy Whittall into St John's Wood Road. The Waugh partnership had been worth 129.

Mark Waugh reached his record-breaking fourth World Cup century just before holing out at deep mid wicket off Johnson. Then Michael Bevan and Tom Moody topped off the innings in a frantic stand of 55. In the final over Australia became the first side apart from India to top 300 runs in an innings in the 1999 World Cup.

Although containing Mark Waugh's fine 104, Australia's batting was a team effort. Zimbabwe's response relied almost totally on Neil Johnson, who batted throughout the innings, topped Mark Waugh's score and pipped him for the Man of the Match award. On the still-perfect batting surface he found a worthy ally in Murray Goodwin with whom he added 114 in 18 overs. Once the number 3 had been caught at deep square leg sweeping at Bevan and Andy Flower was caught behind first ball off Paul Reiffel the Zimbabwean innings lapsed into the realms of interest only for statistical purists. Johnson, who had hammered Shane Warne when the leg spinner was first introduced, completed his century in 118 balls and went on to finish with the second-highest score by a Zimbabwean in the

AUSTRALIA

A.C. Gilchrist (wk) lbw Johnson	10
M.E. Waugh c Goodwin b Johnson	104
R.T. Ponting b Olonga	36
D.S. Lehmann retired hurt	6
S.R. Waugh (capt) b G.J. Whittall	62
M.G. Bevan not out	37
T.M. Moody not out	20
Extras (lb 6, w 13, nb 9)	28
(50 overs)	4–303

Did not bat: S.K. Warne, D.W. Fleming, P.R. Reiffel, G.D. McGrath

1/18 2/74 3/226 4/248 (Lehmann retired hurt at 2–97)

Bowling: Johnson 8-0-43-2; Streak 10-0-50-0; Olonga 7-0-62-1; G.J. Whittall 4-0-24-1; Strang 10-1-47-0; A.R. Whittall 8-1-51-0; G.W. Flower 3-0-20-0

ZIMBABWE

N.C. Johnson not out	132
G.W. Flower lbw McGrath	21
M.W. Goodwin c Moody b Bevan	47
A. Flower (wk) c Gilchrist b Reiffel	0
A.D.R. Campbell (capt) c Fleming b Reiffel	17
G.J. Whittall c M.E. Waugh b Reiffel	0
D.P. Viljoen st Gilchrist b Warne	5
H.H. Streak not out	18
Extras (lb 6, w 13)	19
(50 overs)	6–259

Did not bat: P.A. Strang, A.R. Whittall, H.K. Olonga

1/39 2/153 3/154 4/188 5/189 6/200

Bowling: McGrath 10-1-33-1; Fleming 10-0-46-0; Warne 9-0-55-1; Reiffel 10-0-55-3; Moody 6-0-38-0; Bevan 5-1-26-1

Umpires: D.B. Cowie, R.E. Koertzen.

Toss: Zimbabwe. Points: Australia 2, Zimbabwe 0

World Cup, behind Dave Houghton's unbelievable 141 against New Zealand in 1987.

Paul Reiffel, like Warne, suffered some heavy punishment, but he returned to take three wickets as Zimbabwe finished 44 runs short of their requirement.

THURSDAY 10 JUNE 1999
SUPER SIXES No.6: NEW ZEALAND vs SOUTH AFRICA
EDGBASTON, BIRMINGHAM: SOUTH AFRICA WON BY 74 RUNS

The nightmares of February/March returned to Stephen Fleming's side as they were totally outclassed by an efficient and talented South African unit. The Kiwis did not get a look in, failing to take a wicket for 37 overs and not getting anywhere near the 288 they required for victory. South Africa became the first side to qualify for the semi-finals. New Zealand's position was now quite precarious.

A fine, sunny morning encouraged Hansie Cronje to bat after he won the toss. Edgbaston provides a great atmosphere, but the sprinkling of empty seats suggested the contest had achieved only minor attraction status. Those who attended witnessed an enterprising South African batting display and the openers, Gary Kirsten and Herschelle Gibbs, led from the front with their stand of 176. The left- and right-handed combination complemented each other perfectly. Both had feasted heavily on the same bowlers previously and they had little difficulty on a flat slow surface in doing so again. They paced their stand well, starting quietly then gradually dominating. Kirsten reached his half century first with a pull off Dion Nash. The left-hander's milestone took 79 balls. Gibbs required 76 balls. He had hit just three boundaries by that time, but doubled that with three more in succession off Nash in the 27th over.

Kirsten reached 4000 runs in Limited-Over Internationals, swung Nathan Astle for six over square leg, then offered the easiest of catches to mid wicket off the same bowler with a miscued flick to leg. Lance Klusener, in such outstanding batting form, was sent in to massacre the despondent Kiwi attack. He struck one four then was bowled heaving at Gavin Larsen. Klusener's dismissal gave him a tournament batting average of 210.

When Gibbs became Geoff Allott's World Cup record-breaking 19th victim of the competition, Hansie Cronje and Jacques Kallis indulged

SOUTH AFRICA	
G. Kirsten c Nash b Astle	82
H.H. Gibbs b Allott	91
L. Klusener b Larsen	4
J.H. Kallis not out	53
D.J. Cullinan c & b Cairns	0
H. Cronje (capt) not out	39
Extras (lb 11, w 3, nb 4)	18
(50 overs)	5–287

Did not bat: S.M. Pollock, M.V. Boucher (wk), S. Elworthy, A.A. Donald

1/176 2/187 3/228 4/229 5/283

Bowling: Allott 10–0–42–1; Nash 8–0–44–0; Cairns 7–0–55–1; Larsen 9–0–47–1; Harris 10–0–59–0; Astle 6–0–29–1

NEW ZEALAND	
M.J. Horne c Pollock b Kallis	12
N.J. Astle c Cullinan b Kallis	9
C.D. McMillan c Gibbs b Cronje	23
S.P. Fleming (capt) c Pollock b Cronje	42
R.G. Twose c Cronje b Klusener	35
C.L. Cairns b Klusener	17
A.C. Parore (wk) run out	3
C.Z. Harris not out	27
D.J. Nash b Pollock	9
G.R. Larsen not out	13
Extras (lb 9, w 11, nb 3)	23
(50 overs)	8–213

Did not bat: G.I. Allott

1/20 2/34 3/93 4/107 5/144 6/148 7/171 8/194

Bowling: Pollock 10–1–29–1; Kallis 6–2–15–2; Elworthy 8–0–35–0; Donald 10–0–42–0; Klusener 9–0–46–2; Cronje 7–0–37–2

Umpires: I.D. Robinson, S. Venkataraghavan.

Toss: South Africa. Points: South Africa 2, New Zealand 0

in some Klusener-style hitting that had spectators running in all directions. In five overs the pair hit five sixes between them and rattled up a partnership of 54 in the process. Kallis hit 19 off Chris Harris' 10th over and Cronje pasted Chris Cairns for consecutive sixes.

New Zealand barely offered a shot in reply. Kallis, on way to his second Man of the Match award, had removed both openers by the 12th over and at the halfway stage of the innings the Kiwis had not even brought up three figures. Stephen Fleming, Roger Twose and Chris Harris kept the innings going until its designated conclusion, but they offered little in the way of excitement.

FRIDAY 11 JUNE 1999
SUPER SIXES No.7: PAKISTAN vs ZIMBABWE
THE OVAL, LONDON: PAKISTAN WON BY 148 RUNS

The ease with which Pakistan demolished Zimbabwe quickly put to rest the belief that Wasim Akram's side might be a spent force in the Carnival of Cricket. It did suggest that Zimbabwe's exalted position of likely semi-finalists flattered them. The Pakistanis were now assured of their spot in the final four and their mercurial talent suggested two more wins were well within their capability.

Saqlain Mushtaq grabbed much of the attention when he finished the match with the second ever hat-trick in the World Cup, but it was Saeed Anwar's 103 supported by some effective middle-order hitting that put Pakistan in an unassailable position. At least Zimbabwe, unlike New Zealand the previous day against South Africa, were able to let everyone get away early from Kennington by being dismissed in the 41st over. That they still might make the semi-finals even though their tournament record stood at three and a half wins from eight starts was a reflection on the serious problems with the current points system.

It was an overcast morning at The Oval, the London skyline views from the loftier perches in the ground taking on a grim grey visage. Pakistan, always well supported, were quickly into their stride after Wasim Akram won the toss and batted. Saeed Anwar, despite a few attractive cameos still without a major innings in the tournament, was quickly meting out punishment, and he found an able ally in fellow opener Wajahatullah Wasti. They rattled on 95 at five per over. Then when Wasti was caught at third man off

Guy Whittall and Ijaz Ahmed fell foul of the Pakistanis' inability to judge a run as a batting pair, Inzamam supported Saeed as he continued on his fluent way.

Saeed had a life at 18, dropped at slip by Alistair Campbell, but his 11th boundary, a sumptuous cover drive off Henry Olonga, completed the left-hander's fine century. He was caught soon after, mistiming a pull, and with regular late-order hero Moin Khan missing out for once it was left to Shahid Afridi to provide the crowning fireworks. He hit two sixes, an astonishing hit over cover off Heath Streak and a more orthodox clout off Paul Strang over long-on. Pakistan had 9–271.

Zimbabwe were never in the hunt in the chase for 272. Shoaib Akhtar, bursting to reach 100 mph, got as far as 93 in his opening spell and shattered Grant Flower's stumps in the process. Only Neil Johnson, starting to suffer from his all-round exertions throughout eight big matches, was able to prosper against Pakistan's dynamic attack. He was the sixth batsman out in the 29th over.

Eleven overs later, Saqlain bowled the first ball of his seventh over to Olonga. The paceman stepped forward, heaved, missed and was just unable to beat Moin's glovework with his massive follow through. Next ball Adam Huckle moved out to drive and was beaten by a top-spinner to make it two stumpings in two balls. 'Pommie' Mbangwa, who had been brought into the side as an extra bowler, clearly only had survival on his mind as he faced Saqlain's hat-trick ball.

He played back and across. It was Saqlain's arm ball. Mbangwa was beaten on the outside and struck on his bent back thigh. A thousand Pakistani screaming appeals rent the air, Steve Bucknor nodded his head and slowly raised his finger. Saqlain, the young off-spinning maestro, playing on the ground where he had done so well as Surrey's overseas professional, had joined Chetan Sharma as the only World Cup bowlers to take a hat-trick.

PAKISTAN

Saeed Anwar c A. Flower b Olonga	103
Wajahatullah Wasti c Huckle b G.J. Whittall	40
Ijaz Ahmed run out	5
Inzamam-ul-Haq st, A. Flower b Strang	21
Wasim Akram (capt) lbw Huckle	0
Moin Khan (wk) run out	13
Shahid Afridi c Johnson b Olonga	37
Azhar Mahmood c A. Flower b Streak	2
Abdur Razzaq b Streak	0
Saqlain Mushtaq not out	17
Shoaib Akhtar not out	1
Extras (b 6, lb 3, w 20, nb 3)	32
(50 overs)	9–271

1/95 2/116 3/183 4/194 5/195 6/228 7/231 8/231 9/260

Bowling: Streak 10-0-63-1; Mbangwa 8-0-28-0; G.J. Whittall 8-1-39-1; Olonga 5-0-38-2; Huckle 10-0-43-1; G.W. Flower 2-0-13-0; Strang 7-0-38-1

ZIMBABWE

N.C. Johnson lbw Azhar Mahmood	54
G.W. Flower b Shoaib Akhtar	2
M.W. Goodwin c Afridi b Abdur Razzaq	4
A. Flower (wk) b Abdur Razzaq	4
A.D.R. Campbell (capt) c Wasim Akram b Abdur Razzaq	3
G.J. Whittall c Shahid Afridi b Azhar Mahmood	16
H.H. Streak not out	16
P.A. Strang c Azhar Mahmood b Shoaib Akhtar	5
H.K. Olonga st Moin Khan b Saqlain Mushtaq	5
A. Huckle st Moin b Saqlain Mushtaq	0
M. Mbangwa lbw Saqlain	0
Extras (lb 3, w 7, nb 4)	14
(40.3 overs)	10–123

1/12 2/28 3/46 4/50 5/83 6/95 7/110 8/123 9/123 10/123

Bowling: Wasim Akram 6-1-23-0; Shoaib Akhtar 7-1-22-2; Abdul Razzaq 9-1-25-3; Saqlain Mushtaq 6.3-1-16-3; Shahid Afridi 4-0-20-0; Azhar Mahmood 8-1-14-2

Umpires: S.A. Bucknor, D.L. Orchard.

Toss: Pakistan. Points: Pakistan 2, Zimbabwe 0

SATURDAY 12 JUNE 1999
SUPER SIXES No.8: INDIA vs NEW ZEALAND
TRENT BRIDGE, NOTTINGHAM: NEW ZEALAND WON BY 5 WICKETS

There was unconfined Kiwi joy at their team's win over India and promotion to the semi-finals of the 1999 World Cup. What is more they achieved it by outbatting the batting side of the tournament.

They had to chase a competitive total and re-launch the innings after a late-afternoon rain interruption before reaching their target of 252 with just 10 balls to spare. Win or lose, India were saying their farewells at Nottingham. Neutrals would miss their sensational strokeplay, but inconsistencies had dogged them and disappointed their passionate supporters.

After Mohammad Azharuddin won the toss he decided to bat. He was another making cricketing farewells this day. His prize opener Sachin Tendulkar got a couple of early shots away, then missed a full and straight in-slanting delivery from Dion Nash. Rahul Dravid also prospered, but only briefly, Stephen Fleming holding a hot gully chance. When Saurav Ganguly's slow display was ended by a Geoff Allott leg-stump yorker Ajay Jadeja, supported by his captain and Robin Singh, had to be at their best to ensure the innings went its distance and reached a satisfactory conclusion of 6–251.

Jadeja's 90-ball attacking display was Man of the Match material until Matthew Horne and Roger Twose proved his equal in value to their side. Their 83-run stand quelled the uncertainty of New Zealand being 3–90 in the 22nd over. Horne had been run out by substitute Nikhil Chopra when rain stopped play for 75 minutes at 4–194. That emptied most of the ground. The Indian fans had been told by the PA announcer they were making too much noise, anyway. Perhaps the neighbours complained.

New Zealand soon lost Chris Cairns when play restarted, and the threat of Kiwi jitters still existed. Their previous totals in the tournament had not been higher than 220. Roger Twose was joined by Adam Parore with 35 needed off five overs. He had hardly batted in the Carnival of Cricket. Now he hit five fours in 14 balls,

including three in four balls off Javagal Srinath in the 48th over to take New Zealand to the brink of victory. When Man of the Match, Twose, swung Anil Kumble away to the rope at square leg next over Steve Rixon's boys had struck a blow for the solid work ethic and confirmed a treasured semi-final berth.

INDIA	
S.R. Tendulkar b Nash	16
S.C. Ganguly b Allott	29
R. Dravid c Fleming b Cairns	29
A. Jadeja c Parore b Cairns	76
M. Azharuddin (capt) c Parore b Larsen	30
R.R. Singh run out	27
J. Srinath not out	6
N.R. Mongia (wk) not out	3
Extras (b 4, lb 8, w 13, nb 10)	35
(50 overs)	6-251

Did not bat: A. Kumble, B.K.V. Prasad, D.S. Mohanty

1/26 2/71 3/97 4/187 5/241 6/243

Bowling: Allott 10-1-33-1; Nash 10-1-57-1; Cairns 10-0-44-2; Larsen 10-0-40-1; Astle 7-0-49-0; Harris 3-0-16-0

NEW ZEALAND	
M.J. Horne run out	74
N.J. Astle c Dravid b Mohanty	26
C.D. McMillan c Dravid b Srinath	6
S.P. Fleming (capt) c Mongia b Mohanty	15
R.G. Twose not out	60
C.L. Cairns c Kumble b Singh	11
A.C. Parore (wk) not out	26
Extras (b 4, lb 11, w 16, nb 4)	35
(48.2 overs)	5-253

Did not bat: C.Z. Harris, D.J. Nash, G.R. Larsen, G.A. Allott

1/45 2/60 3/90 4/173 5/218

Bowling: Srinath 10-1-49-1; Mohanty 10-0-41-2; Prasad 10-0-44-0; Singh 4-0-27-1; Ganguly 2-0-15-0; Kumble 9.2-0-48-0; Tendulkar 3-0-14-0

Umpires: D.B. Hair, D.R. Shepherd.

Toss: India. Points: New Zealand 2, India 0

SUNDAY 13 JUNE 1999
SUPER SIXES No.9: AUSTRALIA vs SOUTH AFRICA
HEADINGLEY, LEEDS: AUSTRALIA WON BY 5 WICKETS

A few English grumblers suggested after the previous day's largely featureless match at Nottingham that the tent pegs were already being loosened at the Carnival of Cricket, mainly because their own side was now missing from the action. If that were so, Australia and South Africa banged those pegs back into concrete after this last-over cliffhanging masterpiece at Headingley.

For Steve Waugh and his team the mission was clear enough, win or tie and they would progress through to the semi-finals. A loss against the Proteas and they were on their way home, leaving Zimbabwe to take up the position of semi-eminence. In the end the Australian captain had to do the job himself. He had a few helpers but his second century in 266 Limited-Over Internationals showed an inner strength of

determination to succeed well beyond that of ordinary mortals. It even brought a tear to the eye of some hard-edged Aussies.

Tony Greig's pitch report prediction that the Headingley wicket would provide a batsman's match was accurate. There was occasional variation in the bounce. Mostly, however, batsmen hit confidently through the ball. One to take advantage was South African opener Herschelle Gibbs, whose sweet strokes throughout his 44 overs at the crease brought him his country's first 100 of the competition.

South Africa, who went in first after Hansie Cronje won the toss, were without Jacques Kallis, resting strained stomach muscles. His batting was not missed. Later, though, his bowling was. Even when Shane Warne, still hitting the headlines for the wrong reasons, picked up both Daryll Cullinan and Cronje in the 33rd over the Proteas looked likely to get a big total. Cullinan had come in at number 3 after Gary Kirsten had been caught at backward point driving Paul Reiffel. He cracked Tom Moody for six over long-on and added 95 with Gibbs before swinging across the line at his nemesis.

Jonty Rhodes and Gibbs ran like the speed of light between wickets during their seven per over 78-run partnership while Lance Klusener, even though his final over dismissal reduced his tournament batting average again, gave another joyous exhibition of slogging. He began the 50th over of the innings with an enormous drive that sent the ball way into the crowd at long-off. A totally mistimed slice was beautifully held by Shane Warne running backwards at point a few balls later, but by then South Africa had 271 and Australia were up against it.

There was a fateful-looking similarity to this target for Australia and the one they had just failed to reach against Pakistan back on 23 May. The comparison went even further when Steve Elworthy, going around the wicket, got through Adam Gilchrist's concrete-footed defence as easily and nearly as early as Wasim Akram had done three weeks before, almost to the minute. The removal of the wicketkeeper–batsman's stumps left Australia 1–6 and it was 2–20 a few moments later when Mark Waugh and Ricky Ponting failed to coordinate their running, which left 'Junior' Waugh well short of his ground when Nicky Boje's return reached Mark Boucher. In the same over a top-edged hook by Ponting carried all the way over Boucher's head to the sightscreen for six.

Damien Martyn, in the side for Darren Lehmann who still carried an injured finger, made no real impression before badly mistiming a pull. So at 3–48 Australia's World Cup campaign lay close to ruin when the captain strode to the wicket. After a period of consolidation Waugh and Ponting attacked Klusener and quickly blasted Boje out of the attack, the left-arm spinner conceding 17 in one over. Cronje had to fill in the extra overs and he, too, was expensive. Ponting reached his fifty in 88 balls, while Waugh brought up his in 47 balls with a superb cover drive off Shaun Pollock.

It was brilliant batting. However, the need to maintain it was critical as the required run rate remained high. Australians gasped and South Africans cringed when Gibbs tried to throw up the ball before properly controlling an easy catch off Waugh at mid wicket when the Australian captain was 56. Finally Ponting skyed a leg-side shot to end the 126-run stand. Now with Michael Bevan, Waugh pressed on. Elworthy, so damaging early, was creamed for six over mid wicket. The one-knee slog put Waugh on his back and took him from 91 to 97. A more restrained push to mid-on brought up the 100 in 91 balls, the innings of an utter champion.

There was little time for self-congratulation as a run was needed every ball. Bevan had done his part in a stand of 73, but in Cronje's final over his feigned sally only sent an easy catch to Cullinan, leaving a winner impossible to pick.

There were hits and misses and oohs and ahs. In the big crowd the supporters of both countries were hard to distinguish as both were equally nervous and both were draped and painted in green and gold. The final equation came down to eight runs from the final over to be bowled by Shaun Pollock. A scrambled two from the first ball was followed by Tom Moody's back-foot slash that gave the ball just enough oomph to trickle over the point boundary ahead of the diving South African fieldsman. Two more singles and Australia had won. Steve Waugh at last showed some emotion with repeated punchings of the air as he ran the winning single.

There was joy unconfined on the Australian balcony. The captain was also Man of the Match. He said he had a point to prove. Both sides had to go through it all again in just four days at Edgbaston. 'If this was anything to go by it's going to be one hell of a game on Thursday,' said Cronje. He didn't know the half of it.

SOUTH AFRICA

G. Kirsten c Ponting b Reiffel	21
H.H. Gibbs b McGrath	101
D.J. Cullinan b Warne	50
H. Cronje (capt) lbw Warne	0
J.N. Rhodes c M.E. Waugh b Fleming	39
L. Klusener c Warne b Fleming	36
S.M. Pollock b Fleming	3
M.V. Boucher (wk) not out	0
Extras (lb 7, w 8, nb 6)	21
(50 overs)	7–271

Did not bat: N. Boje, S. Elworthy, A.A. Donald

1/45 2/140 3/141 4/219 5/250 6/271 7/271

Bowling: McGrath 10–0–49–1; Fleming 10–0–57–3; Reiffel 9–0–47–1; Moody 8–1–56–0; Warne 10–1–33–2; Bevan 3–0–22–0

AUSTRALIA

M.E. Waugh run out	5
A.C. Gilchrist (wk) b Elworthy	5
R.T. Ponting c Donald b Klusener	69
D.R. Martyn c Boje b Elworthy	11
S.R. Waugh (capt) not out	120
M.G. Bevan c Cullinan b Cronje	27
T.M. Moody not out	15
Extras (lb 6, w 7, nb 7)	20
(49.4 overs)	5–272

Did not bat: S.K. Warne, P.R. Reiffel, D.W. Fleming, G.D. McGrath

1/6 2/20 3/48 4/174 5/247

Bowling: Pollock 9.4–0–45–0; Elworthy 10–1–46–2; Donald 10–0–43–0; Klusener 10–0–53–1; Cronje 7–0–50–1; Boje 3–0–29–0

Umpires: S. Venkataraghavan, P. Willey.

Toss: South Africa. Points: Australia 2, South Africa 0

THE SEMI-FINALS
WEDNESDAY 16 JUNE 1999
FIRST SEMI-FINAL: NEW ZEALAND vs PAKISTAN
OLD TRAFFORD, MANCHESTER: PAKISTAN WON BY 9 WICKETS

This rematch of the Auckland semi-final of 1992 was almost a clash of cricketing ideologies. Steady, hard-working, well-prepared New Zealand against mercurial, talented, controversial, inconsistent Pakistan. And as in the memorable match at Eden Park, the team selected from a population of 120 million proved too good for the one selected from three and a half million.

Wasim Akram's star line-up still managed to confound the critics with a mixed performance by their bowlers, the branch of the game considered to be their strength, and a brilliant one by their top-order batsmen, thought to be the Pakistani weak link. The joy at their team reaching the prestigious final was too much for some lime-green fans to bear and the end of the match was once again interrupted by the overzealous.

No-one doubted that the Kiwis were the underdogs against one of the best-performed teams in the competition and it was the lovely Manchester weather that surprised more than Nathan Astle and Craig McMillan's struggles after Stephen Fleming decided to bat. Astle had his leg stump ripped out by Shoaib Akhtar and McMillan's tentative push at Akram gave a catch behind to Moin Khan.

Matthew Horne hit the ball as sweetly as he had against India. However, Abdur Razzaq's yorker homed in and then neatly removed the opener's middle stump to leave New Zealand a shaky 3–58. Neither of the two left-handers, Roger Twose or Fleming, looked at his absolute best, however they were able to put on 94 with a mixture of edges, good shots and plenty of free offerings from the Pakistanis as the wide and no-ball count mounted.

When the Kiwis reached 3–152 in the 34th over Pakistan were just starting to slip. Inzamam-ul-Haq had had a couple of fielding fluffs on the third-man boundary and Fleming had just hit two fine boundaries. Shoaib went around the wicket and sent down an unplayable inswinging yorker that crashed the leg-stump of the New Zealand captain out of the ground.

The pattern stayed the same for the remainder of the innings. Pakistani misfields, dropped catches, wides and no-balls punctuated by an occasional piece of brilliance. Ijaz Ahmed held a stunning one-handed catch to his right when Twose slashed Abdur to the gully. Chris Harris suffered the indignity and rarity of playing too early at Shoaib's slower ball. Chris Cairns used the lofted cover drive to good effect through the last few overs. As Pakistan had failed to chase India's 227 on the same ground the previous week, New Zealand's final total of 7–241, with extras top score, was quite a respectable one.

Or so it seemed until Saeed Anwar and Wajahatullah Wasti began striking the ball with complete assurance. The New Zealand attack were soon a spent force. With Geoff Allott unable to extend his record for the number of wickets in a World Cup, no real pressure could be exerted on the Pakistani openers. Therefore they blossomed. Anwar showed he was back to his best form and the openers were soon clocking up personal and partnership milestones.

Even as the possibility of a berth in the final receded, New Zealand maintained their enthusiasm in the field. There was little hint of a breakthrough, though. When the score reached 160 Anwar and Wasti broke their country's 24-year-old World Cup first wicket record. At 187 they bettered the overall World Cup record set in 1996 by Gary Kirsten and Andrew Hudson against Holland. A mistimed big hit by Wasti off Cairns finally terminated the partnership on 194 in the 41st over.

Ijaz kept the runs flowing while Anwar concentrated on reaching his second consecutive World Cup century. As the victory loomed the behaviour of certain members of the crowd changed from noisy to intrusive. Repeated interruptions drew out the finale, spoiled the conclusion for the rest of the crowd and the players and drew attention again to the inadequacy of the security arrangements.

The Pakistanis were rightfully joyous at reaching the final and at their 'Rawalpindi Express' being named Man of the Match. However, it was to be wondered how some of them would restrain themselves at Sunday's emotive occasion at Lord's.

NEW ZEALAND

M.J. Horne b Abdur Razzaq	35
N.J. Astle b Shoaib Akhtar	3
C.D. McMillan c Moin Khan b Wasim Akram	3
S.P. Fleming (capt) b Shoaib Akhtar	41
R.G. Twose c Ijaz Ahmed b Abdur Razzaq	46
C.L. Cairns not out	44
C.Z. Harris b Shoaib Akhtar	16
A.C. Parore (wk) b Wasim Akram	0
D.J. Nash not out	6
Extras (b 4, lb 14, w 17, nb 12)	47
(50 overs)	7–241

Did not bat: G.R. Larsen, G.A. Allott

1/20 2/38 3/58 4/152 5/176 6/209 7/211

Bowling: Wasim Akram 10-0-45-2; Shoaib Akhtar 10-0-55-3; Abdur Razzaq 8-0-28-2; Saqlain Mushtaq 8-0-36-0; Azhar Mahmood 9-0-32-0; Shahid Afridi 5-0-27-0

PAKISTAN

Saeed Anwar not out	113
Wajahatullah Wasti c Fleming b Cairns	84
Ijaz Ahmed not out	28
Extras (lb 3, w 7, nb 7)	17
(47.3 overs)	1–242

Did not bat: Inzamam-ul-Haq, Abdur Razzaq, Shahid Afridi, Moin Khan (wk), Wasim Akram (capt), Azhar Mahmood, Saqlain Mushtaq, Shoaib Akhtar

1/194

Bowling: Allott 9-0-41-0; Nash 5-0-34-0; Larsen 10-0-40-0; Cairns 8-0-33-1; Harris 6-0-31-0; Astle 7.3-0-41-0; McMillan 2-0-19-0

Umpires: D.B. Hair, P. Willey.

Toss: New Zealand

THURSDAY 17 JUNE 1999

SECOND SEMI-FINAL: AUSTRALIA vs SOUTH AFRICA
EDGBASTON, BIRMINGHAM: MATCH TIED

Nothing, not even the extraordinary match at Leeds a couple of days before, could prepare anyone for a finish like this. In scenes of complete cricketing madness, the semi-final between Australia and South Africa resulted in the World Cup's first tie.

As Australia had finished higher than South Africa in the Super Six table the result was as good as a win for Australia and a loss for South Africa. As such, one nation was joyous, another heartbroken. No limited-overs cricket match anywhere on the globe at any time can have matched the excruciating excitement of this game at Edgbaston where brilliance and heroism were mixed in equal doses with comic tragedy. People danced and sang in front of their televisions and winter heaters at 3.30 am in Australia as if they too had been on the terraces in the Hollies Stand. Against the odds, Steve Waugh's side had won five and tied one of the seven matches they had to take on the trot to win the World Cup.

The tournament favourites were now going home, shaking their heads and wondering how they could have missed out on the final. The feeling was that with Jacques Kallis back in the side and on the rebound after the thrilling loss at Leeds, South Africa might just have the edge this time.

That seemed clear-cut when the South African pacemen did their work on the Australian top order. Hansie Cronje had won the toss and sent the Australians in to bat. Shaun Pollock responded with a lifting delivery in the first over which cut back and brushed Mark Waugh's retreating gloves on the way through to Mark Boucher.

Even though the ground was only three-quarters full at this stage on a cool and cloudy morning, many fans being caught up in a good old-fashioned Birmingham traffic jam outside the ground, the atmosphere inside Edgbaston was already electric, this being the only cricket ground in England to give the feel of a stadium. Ricky Ponting's response after a couple of assessment overs captured the atmosphere perfectly when he hooked Steve Elworthy for six and followed it with another hook for four. Adam Gilchrist, a noted aggressor still out of form, concentrated on defence until he let loose at Elworthy, too, and plonked him over the rope at long-on with nothing more than a short-arm jab.

Ponting's habit throughout the World Cup was to play short, brilliant innings. Only at Leeds had he gone on to complete a half century. Here he greeted Allan Donald's introduction for the 14th over with a bent-kneed cover drive on the rise which slapped a catch straight to Gary Kirsten. Suitably inspired, later in the same over Donald got one to lift and cut away enough to make Darren Lehmann's return to the side an unprofitable one. That was 3–58 and just 10 runs later Gilchrist's slice to Donald off Kallis at third man left Australia in deep trouble.

Steve Waugh had to do it all over again. He and Michael Bevan concentrated so hard on defence that just six runs came in nine overs. Waugh survived a run-out scare by a whisker and then, finally, with Elworthy back in the attack for the 32nd over, hit two boundaries, one either side of the wicket. The Australian captain followed that by twice lofting Klusener straight, once for four, once for six. This was a champion batting like a millionaire and showing a mental strength the equal of any man ever to play the game. His fifty, completed with a great cover drive off Pollock, kept Australia in the match. Just as quickly Pollock turned it back the Protea's way in the 40th over having Waugh caught behind on the dab and Tom Moody lbw third ball to a sharp offcutter. Big Tom was so plumb umpire Venkataraghavan's finger almost beat the appeal.

Shane Warne slogged and sliced a few and Bevan pushed here and there to add 49 before Donald and Pollock ended the innings in a flash. They shared nine victims for the innings. Four wickets fell for six in the final two overs and Australia had to be satisfied with that same undistinguished total they had made in their defeat at the hands of New Zealand back in Cardiff, 213.

On a beautiful English summer's afternoon, the full ground a picture, Herschelle Gibbs and Gary Kirsten opened with a confidence which suggested 214 was a formality. Gibbs was in especially commanding form, and 48 had been raised in 12 overs when Steve Waugh introduced Shane Warne. His second ball shattered any Protean complacency at a stroke. A fizzing leg break drifted inside Gibbs' defensive push, then bit back outside it to clip the top of the off stump. 'Ball from hell two' was the call, and there was little difference in its lethal potency and impact on a game from the 1993 version. Warne screamed at his team-mates, 'Come on!' charging their adrenalin while knowing he had to keep a hold on his own emotions. In his next over the leg spinner induced an ugly slog from Kirsten and rattled the stumps again. When Hansie Cronje was given out second ball caught at slip to a yorker-length delivery South Africa had slumped to 3–53.

It was 4–61 when Daryll Cullinan fell foul of an accurate Bevan throw and his own tardy running. Like Steve Waugh and Bevan for Australia, so now did Kallis and Jonty Rhodes have to rebuild the South African cause. Their 84-run effort did just that, but the consumption of 20 overs, Warne hardly conceding a run, ensured the finish would be a tight one. When Paul Reiffel ended the partnership Warne was brought back as the requirement crept up to nine per over.

The 45th over signalled the start of the madness. Kallis was dropped at deep mid-off by Reiffel. Pollock responded with clouts for six and four, then Kallis, who had changed his bat prior to this over, was caught at short cover by Steve Waugh. Damien Fleming was recalled for the 46th over. Klusener greeted him with a smack to mid wicket for four, then from the fifth ball Pollock played on a yorker as he backed away to drive.

Mark Boucher was troubled by the pressure. He struggled to give Klusener the strike and three dot balls in a row in the 48th over increased the pressure even more, if that was possible. Klusener, at last given the chance to swing at a couple, sliced an off drive over point for four and hoisted a ball to mid wicket for two, Moody opting against the attempt at a catch and saving the four instead.

Eighteen were needed from 12 balls as McGrath began the 49th over. Boucher lost his middle stump to the second ball, backing away and never looking like coping with the situation. A gloved single to Elworthy gave Klusener the strike, but next ball the effort to keep him there meant a risky two and Reiffel's throw to the bowler's end was spot-on. The agony was extended by repeated third-umpire replays to ensure McGrath's hand had not broken the stumps.

Nine for 198 left South Africa needing 16 off eight balls, seemingly out of even Klusener's league. Relieved to have made retribution for dropping Kallis, Reiffel might have thought so, too, but only for a moment. McGrath's second-last delivery was a full toss. Klusener struck it baseball style. It flew flat and straight to Reiffel at long-on. There was a suggestion that the shot had been mistimed, but when it struck Reiffel's upstretched hands he was flung back and the ball forced its way through and over the rope behind the fallen and crestfallen paceman for six. Steve Waugh chewed and cursed. Klusener took an easy single from McGrath's final delivery.

Fleming, who had bowled Courtney Walsh to give Australia a five-run victory in the 1996 semi-final, had nine runs to play with this time. Two balls later it was one. He had gone around the wicket and bowled a full length. Klusener creamed both balls for four, one to cover point, the other extra cover. Thrilling, awesome shots, both.

Now, surely the match was won. There were four balls left and the scores were tied, although South Africa actually had to defeat Australia as they had finished lower in the Super Six table. Fleming went over the wicket. Klusener mistimed a pull to the third ball. Lehmann charged in. Donald backed up too far! There was an underarm throw and a reprieve as the ball shaved the stumps with the big South African paceman well out of his ground.

The fourth ball was a fuller delivery which Klusener mistimed again. The ball rolled up the wicket and Klusener ran. Donald was watching the ball and stayed in his crease. Mark Waugh's backhand flick went to Fleming who rolled it to Gilchrist. Donald dropped his bat and realised far too late that he must run. It is a token. He is not in the picture when the Australian wicketkeeper removes a stump and charges in to join his ecstatic team-mates.

There is astonishment, bewilderment, heartbreak and uncontrolled joy, but thankfully no invasion. Australia dance off Edgbaston together in celebration. Cronje and his team are shattered. 'The best cricket game I've ever played,' says Steve Waugh. Cronje is gracious, but his face tells the story of the greatest disappointment of his career. Shane Warne is named Man of the Match.

AUSTRALIA		
A.C. Gilchrist (wk) c Donald b Kallis		20
M.E. Waugh c Boucher b Pollock		0
R.T. Ponting c Kirsten b Donald		37
D.S. Lehmann c Boucher b Donald		1
S.R. Waugh (capt) c Boucher b Pollock		56
M.G. Bevan c Boucher b Pollock		65
T.M. Moody lbw Pollock		0
S.K. Warne c Cronje b Pollock		18
P. Reiffel b Donald		0
D.W. Fleming b Donald		0
G.D. McGrath not out		0
Extras (b 1, lb 6, w 3, nb 6)		16
(49.2 overs)		10–213

1/3 2/54 3/58 4/68 5/158 6/158 7/207 8/207 9/207 10/213

Bowling: Pollock 9.2–1–36–5; Elworthy 10–0–59–0; Kallis 10–2–27–1; Donald 10–1–32–4; Klusener 9–1–50–0; Cronje 1–0–2–0

SOUTH AFRICA		
G. Kirsten b Warne		18
H.H. Gibbs b Warne		30
D.J. Cullinan run out		6
W.J. Cronje (capt) c M.E. Waugh b Warne		0
J.H. Kallis c S.R. Waugh b Warne		53
J.N. Rhodes b Reiffel		43
S.M. Pollock b Fleming		20
L. Klusener not out		31
M.V. Boucher (wk) b McGrath		5
S. Elworthy run out		1
A.A. Donald run out		0
Extras (lb 1, w 5)		6
(49.4 overs)		10–213

1/48 2/53 3/53 4/61 5/145 6/175 7/183 8/196 9/198 10/213

Bowling: McGrath 10–0–51–1; Fleming 8.4–1–40–1; Reiffel 8–0–28–1; Warne 10–4–29–4; M.E. Waugh 8–0–37–0; Moody 5–0–27–0

Umpires: D.R. Shepherd, S. Venkataraghavan.

Toss: South Africa

SUNDAY 20 JUNE 1999
WORLD CUP FINAL
AUSTRALIA vs PAKISTAN
LORD'S, LONDON: AUSTRALIA WON BY 8 WICKETS

Australia, widely regarded as the strongest Test side in the world, added the title as the best Limited-Overs team with a clinical demolition of Pakistan in the most one-sided of all World Cup finals. It was a margin of superiority no-one could have expected, as Australia was brilliant and Pakistan very, very ordinary.

The game thrilled all Australians and maybe a few Indians, but no-one else. In the great cities of Pakistan, like Lahore and Karachi, there was disappointment beyond the scope of a mere cricket match. The national shame manifested itself in burning effigies of Wasim Akram and tomato-bespattered giant screens which had been erected to watch the final. The Pakistani captain suggested he was going to Mecca after the humiliating defeat for divine guidance and prayer. An article in an Australian paper suggested the Pakistan Prime Minister had told Akram he would be better off not coming home if his team did not win the World Cup, anyway. That team, full of inexperienced if talented cricketers, failed miserably to cope with Australia's aggression and expertise. They had reached the final on merit, but on the big day were second-best by a long way.

Neutrals could only admire the great play of the Australians. There was precious little else to excite them or justify the money they had spent to attend the event. Ringside seats were expensive and the fight was over after five one-sided rounds. The decision? A knockout. It was a big let-down after the two wonderful games between Australia and South Africa. As the South Africa vs Pakistan and Australia vs Pakistan matches had also been close and provided plenty of thrills and spills earlier in the competition, the expectation was that the final would do the same.

What turned out to be an anti-climax began the same way with an early-morning shower delaying the start by half an hour. It dampened the sense of anticipation for a time, even though there was a real buzz outside Lord's as fans desperately sought a stray ticket or some sort of elevated vantage point on the buildings around St John's Wood.

Soon enough the skies cleared and the covers were removed. Both squads were introduced to the Duke of Edinburgh and announced teams unchanged from their semi-final victories. The removal of the covers revealed a flat and very hard wicket. Wasim Akram called correctly at the toss and elected to bat. Steve Waugh said he would have done the same as he too believed chasing a substantial total would be difficult, given the pressure of the occasion. However, the Australian captain also said he was not unhappy to lose the toss.

Thirty minutes after the originally scheduled start time umpires Steve Bucknor and Dave Shepherd, given the ultimate honour for their profession, shook hands as they walked onto the now sun-bathed turf signalling that the World Cup final was about to get under way. They were followed by Steve Waugh, proudly leading his Australians onto a cricket ground where they have rarely been beaten. Saeed Anwar took strike to Glenn McGrath, who opened the bowling from the Pavilion End.

After safely negotiating McGrath's two opening deliveries, which showed how much bounce was in the wicket, Saeed cracked the third for four to the Mound Stand boundary at point. Damien Fleming shared the new ball from the Nursery End and he too got the ball to hit Adam Gilchrist's gloves while still on the rise. There was also some movement for the Victorian, but his early control was poor and Saeed took a toll in his second over. He clipped the ball off his legs down the Lord's slope then off the back foot through the covers for a second four.

Twenty-one from four overs indicated a satisfactory start for Pakistan, but Saeed's partner, Wajahatullah Wasti, was far from settled. He tried to guide McGrath's fourth delivery from his third over wide of slips only to lose control of

the shot as the ball lifted. It flew in the air to where third slip should have been. Mark Waugh at second slip took off in a fashion that would not have disgraced Superman and, still horizontal, held a stunning two-handed catch.

That was a setback for Pakistan. When Saeed, who had just stopped the game for several minutes to change the grip on his bat, hit a drive onto his leg, thence onto the stumps from the first ball of Fleming's next over they were 2–21 and showing bad signs. McGrath was pinpoint in his accuracy and after the opening over boundary conceded just another two runs in five overs. Ijaz Ahmed and Abdur Razzaq held firm and looked to score more freely when McGrath and Fleming were relieved by Paul Reiffel and Tom Moody.

Reiffel's second ball beat Gilchrist down the leg side and hurried away for four wides. Ijaz pulled Moody for four, then cracked Reiffel through the covers to raise the Pakistani 50. Nine runs later Abdur overdid the turn of aggression when his attempted hit for six over long-off off Reiffel went straight to McGrath. To the utter amazement of everyone, including the batsman and fieldsman, McGrath dropped the absolute sitter. Steve Waugh cursed and chewed harder on his gum.

Fortunately for McGrath the young Pakistani all-rounder failed to take advantage of the let-off and holed out to cover, giving a low catch to Steve Waugh off Moody. Pakistan were 3–68 in the 20th over. Shane Warne replaced Moody at the Nursery End and Steve Waugh crowded the new batsman Inzamam-ul-Haq. There was no second-ball miracle this time. However, in his next over Warne beat Ijaz with a big spinner then bowled him with one that hurried through his back-foot defence.

Moin Khan had been Pakistan's most consistent batsman in the 1999 World Cup and he started in positive fashion. Warne, though, was in irrepressible form and a lunging defensive push by the wicketkeeper batsman was edged through to Gilchrist. The first ball of the 28th over had given the leg spinner his 200th Limited-Over International wicket and left Pakistan precariously placed at 5–91.

There was no evidence that they would be

able to stem the tide of Australian dominance, either. When Inzamam was unluckily given out caught behind, pushing out at Reiffel, the slide continued. The last recognised batsman was gone. The all-rounders Shahid Afridi, Azhar Mahmood and Wasim Akram were not able to show the brilliance they were capable of, succumbing to a combination of the pressure of the final and Australia's ongoing excellence. Afridi was lbw sweeping, Azhar well caught and bowled driving to Moody's shins, and after one big six to his 'scoring corner' at wide mid-on, the captain holed out at mid wicket trying to repeat the shot. Warne had 202 wickets in Limited-Over Internationals.

When Ricky Ponting dived to his right and held a stunning one-handed catch at third slip to remove Saqlain Mushtaq off McGrath the Pakistani innings had come to an abrupt conclusion at the 39-over mark. Last man Shoaib Akhtar had got lost in the pavilion trying to find his way to the middle. His plight was symbolic of what had happened to his team. Extras boosted by a few strays from Fleming and Reiffel, was top score. The Australians through their efficiency, had made up the 30 minutes lost to the rain so that everyone could have their lunch at the originally scheduled time. They also needed just 133 to win the World Cup.

So confident were they in Australia that during the lunch break on the network telecasting the match thoughts were already turning to how well the Australians would go at Wimbledon in 1999. There was a brief scare when Gilchrist skyed a hook off Shoaib's first ball. Rather than discourage him, though, the bouncy Lord's wicket reminded Gilchrist of the WACA at home and he took 13 runs off Akrams's second over, following an off drive for four with a slashing cut over point.

Some throws went astray, Mark Waugh clipped Shoaib in the air just out of the reach of square leg for four. The Pakistani heads dropped and their fans went quiet. Even the old gentleman in the beard, who had lit up some games like a Pakistani version of Antigua's Gravy, couldn't make an impact. Gilchrist slashed Shoaib over slips to the Compton/Edrich Stand for six, then drove the next ball to the pavilion for four more.

Akram rang in the bowling changes, but it made not the slightest difference. The 50 was raised from the first ball of the eighth over then Gilchrist cut and pulled Azhar and Abdur for a succession of boundaries, the best of which landed one bounce into the New Grandstand and raised his fifty in 33 balls with eight fours and a six. Something finally worked for the Pakistani captain when Gilchrist smashed Saqlain's first ball straight to Inzamam at mid-off. The big man's fingers stung but he held the catch. Gilchrist in a matter of minutes had killed off any lingering thoughts that the Pakistani bowlers might make up for their batting shortcomings.

Ponting joined Mark Waugh. The requirement was 58 runs off 40 overs with nine wickets standing. It was hardly imposing and Ponting was soon into the spirit of the day by taking 14 off a Shoaib over, then raising the 100 in just the 15th over with a dancing on drive for four off Saqlain. David Shepherd hardly bothered with his traditional jig when the scoreboard read 1–111, although Ponting did offer a big edge to Moin off Akram one run later.

Mark Waugh went serenely on, clocking up 1000 World Cup runs in the process to join Javed Miandad, Viv Richards and Sachin Tendulkar. He timed a couple more on drives, then sat back as Darren Lehmann cracked the first ball of the 21st over to the cover boundary to complete Australia's ridiculously easy victory. Security had cleared a pointless ground invasion a few balls before and, prepared for the finish, were able to give the players a reasonably clear passage to the pavilion at the end of the game. Waugh and Lehmann grabbed a couple of stumps each, so the Pakistanis even missed out on the souvenirs. In the crowd inflated toy kangaroos were bouncing around everywhere. The stewards were setting up the presentation area and it was just after 4.30 pm.

The restrained, mostly disappointed crowd gave acknowledgment to the champions who danced and waved on the pavilion balcony. The Australians were in the Lord's away dressing-room, an Australian cricketer's version of Earl's Court. Shane Warne, whose four wickets in the final gave him a World Cup record equalling 20 wickets for the tournament, was named Man of the Match and then hinted at possible retirement. Australian Prime Minister, John Howard, stopped short of declaring a national holiday in celebration of the win. A big cricket fan, he said the nation was allowed to sit up late and watch the game on television, which was extremely generous of him. His Foreign Minister, Alexander Downer, on his way home after a failed attempt to free two Australians in Yugoslavia, might have been the envy of his boss as he watched the match from the Long Room.

At 9.30 pm the Australians, joined by friends like Michael Slater, Justin Langer, Mark Taylor and Ian Healy, were still celebrating. They gathered on the wicket and with Ponting hoisted upon their shoulders sang one more rendition of 'Under the Southern Cross I Stand'. When they returned home there would be tickertape parades and civic receptions, but this moment belonged just to the players.

South African all-rounder Lance Klusener got the car as the player of the World Cup. He would have swapped it for a spot in that evening singing group.

PAKISTAN

Saeed Anwar b Fleming	15
Wajahatullah Wasti c M.E. Waugh b McGrath	1
Abdur Razzaq c S.R. Waugh b Moody	17
Ijaz Ahmed b Warne	22
Inzamam-ul-Haq c Gilchrist b Reiffel	15
Moin Khan (wk) c Gilchrist b Warne	6
Shahid Afridi lbw Warne	13
Azhar Mahmood c & b Moody	8
Wasim Akram (capt) c S.R. Waugh b Warne	8
Saqlain Mushtaq c Ponting b McGrath	0
Shoaib Akhtar not out	2
Extras (lb 10, w 13, nb 2)	25
(39 overs)	10–132

1/21 2/21 3/68 4/77 5/91 6/104 7/113 8/129 9/129 10/132

Bowling: McGrath 9–3–13–2; Fleming 6–0–30–1; Reiffel 10–1–29–1; Moody 5–0–17–2; Warne 9–1–33–4

AUSTRALIA

M.E. Waugh not out	37
A.C. Gilchrist (wk) c Inzamam-ul-Haq b Saqlain Mushtaq	54
R.T. Ponting c Moin Khan b Wasim Akram	24
D.S. Lehmann not out	13
Extras (lb 1, w 1, nb 3)	5
(20.1 overs)	2–133

Did not bat: S.R. Waugh, M.G. Bevan, T.M. Moody, S.K. Warne, P. Reiffel, D.W. Fleming, G.D. McGrath

1/75 2/112

Bowling: Wasim Akram 8–1–41–1; Shoaib Akhtar 4–0–37–0; Abdur Razzaq 2–0–13–0; Azhar Mahmood 2–0–20–0; Saqlain Mushtaq 4.1–0–21–1

Umpires: D.R. Shepherd, S.A. Bucknor.

Toss: Pakistan

POST-MORTEM

Steve Waugh, even now only offering a half-grin, said it was the best win by an Australian side he had ever been in. There had been a few. He was the only survivor of the eleven that had surprised the cricketing world with their first World Cup triumph in 1987, although Tom Moody had also been in that squad.

Now Australia joined the West Indies as the only nations with two trophies in their cabinet. If the 1987 win had been something of a bolt from the blue, no-one was shocked by this result. Australia had started the final as slight favourites. Maligned at the start of the tournament and needing to speak a few home truths within their ranks, the Australians had peaked at the right time and completely vindicated the controversial policies of their selectors in separating the Australian Test and Limited-Overs International teams.

The 1999 World Cup had its ups and downs. The early elimination of England was a disappointment and the crowd invasions were tiresome and threatened danger. In the end, though, the weather held, the crowds were excellent and the Carnival of Cricket could be considered a worthy success. Certainly the eminence of the World Cup in limited-overs cricket went from strength to strength.

Statistics:

Cricket's World Cup 1975–1999

1975

Leading Run Scorers

	Player	Runs	Highest Score	Average
1.	G.M. Turner (NZ)	333	171*	166.50
2.	D.L. Amiss (Eng)	243	137	60.75
3.	Majid J. Khan (Pak)	209	84	69.66
4.	K.W.R. Fletcher (Eng)	207	131	69.00
5.	A. Turner (Aus)	201	101	40.20
6.	A.I. Kallicharran (WI)	197	78	49.25
7.	R. Edwards (Aus)	166	80	55.33
8.	C.H. Lloyd (WI)	158	102	52.66
9.	Zaheer Abbas (Pak)	136	97	45.33
10.	G.S. Chappell (Aus)	129	50	25.80

Individual Batting Performances

	Player	Score	
1.	G.M. Turner (NZ)	171*	vs East Africa
2.	D.L. Amiss (Eng)	137	vs India
3.	K.W.R. Fletcher (Eng)	131	vs New Zealand
4.	G.M. Turner (NZ)	114*	vs India
5.	C.H. Lloyd (WI)	102	vs Australia (final)
6.	A. Turner (Aus)	101	vs Sri Lanka
7.	Zaheer Abbas (Pak)	97	vs Sri Lanka
8.	D.L. Amiss (Eng)	88	vs East Africa
9.	Majid Khan (Pak)	84	vs Sri Lanka
10.	R. Edwards (Aus)	80*	vs Pakistan

Team Batting Performances

	Team	Score	
1.	England	4–334	vs India
2.	Pakistan	6–330	vs Sri Lanka
3.	Australia	5–328	vs Sri Lanka
4.	New Zealand	5–309	vs East Africa
5.	West Indies	8–291	vs Australia (final)
6.	England	5–290	vs East Africa
7.	Australia	7–278	vs Pakistan
8.	Sri Lanka	4–276	vs Australia
9.	Australia	10–274	vs West Indies (final)
10.	West Indies	9–267	vs Pakistan

Leading Wicket Takers

	Player	Wickets	Average	Best Bowling
1.	G.J. Gilmour (Aus)	11	5.63	6–14
2.	B.D. Julien (WI)	10	17.70	4–20
3.	K.D. Boyce (WI)	10	18.50	4–50
4.	D.R. Hadlee (NZ)	8	20.25	3–21
5.	A.M.E. Roberts (WI)	8	20.62	3–39
6.	D.K. Lillee (Aus)	8	27.87	5–34
7.	C.M. Old (Eng)	7	12.28	3–29
8.	J.A. Snow (Eng)	6	10.83	4–11
9.	A.W. Greig (Eng)	6	14.83	4–45
10.	Abid Ali (Ind)	6	19.16	2–22

Individual Bowling Performances

	Player	Analysis	
1.	G.J. Gilmour (Aus)	6–14	vs England
2.	D.K. Lillee (Aus)	5–34	vs Pakistan
3.	G.J. Gilmour (Aus)	5–48	vs West Indies
4.	B.D. Julien (WI)	4–20	vs Sri Lanka
5.	A.W. Greig (Eng)	4–45	vs New Zealand
6.	Sarfraz Nawaz (Pak)	4–44	vs West Indies
7.	J.A. Snow (Eng)	4–11	vs East Africa
8.	K.D. Boyce (WI)	4–50	vs Australia (final)
9.	B.D. Julien (WI)	4–27	vs New Zealand (semi-final)
10.	Imran Khan (Pak)	3–15	vs Sri Lanka
11.	Madan Lal (Ind)	3–15	vs East Africa

1979

Leading Run Scorers

	Player	Runs	Highest Score	Average
1.	C.G. Greenidge (WI)	253	106*	84.34
2.	I.V.A. Richards (WI)	217	128*	108.50
3.	G.A. Gooch (Eng)	210	71	52.50
4.	G.M. Turner (NZ)	176	83*	58.67
5.	J.G. Wright (NZ)	166	69	41.50
6.	J.M. Brearley (Eng)	161	64	32.20
7.	Majid J. Khan (Pak)	150	81	37.50

8.	Zaheer Abbas (Pak)	148	93	37.00	
9.	D.L. Haynes (WI)	144	65	36.00	
10.	A.M.J. Hilditch (Aus)	143	72	47.67	

Individual Batting Performances

	Player	Score	
1.	I.V.A. Richards (WI)	138*	vs England (final)
2.	C.G. Greenidge (WI)	106*	vs India
3.	Zaheer Abbas (Pak)	93	vs West Indies (semi-final)
4.	C.L. King (WI)	86	vs England (final)
5.	B.A. Edgar (NZ)	84*	vs India
6.	G.M. Turner (NZ)	83*	vs Sri Lanka
7.	Majid J. Khan (Pak)	81	vs West Indies (semi-final)
8.	G.R. Viswanath (Ind)	75	vs West Indies
9.	C.H. Lloyd (WI)	73*	vs New Zealand
10.	C.G. Greenidge (WI)	73	vs Pakistan (semi-final)

Team Batting Performances

	Team	Score	
1.	West Indies	6-293	vs Pakistan (semi-final)
2.	Pakistan	7-286	vs Australia
3.	West Indies	9-286	vs England (final)
4.	Pakistan	10-250	vs West Indies (semi-final)
5.	West Indies	7-244	vs New Zealand
6.	Sri Lanka	5-238	vs India
7.	England	8-221	vs New Zealand (semi-final)
8.	New Zealand	9-212	vs England (semi-final)
9.	New Zealand	9-212	vs West Indies
10.	Australia	10-197	vs Pakistan

Leading Wicket Takers

	Player	Wickets	Average	Best Bowling
1.	M. Hendrick (Eng)	10	14.90	4-15
2.	B.J. McKechnie (NZ)	9	15.67	3-24
3.	C.M. Old (Eng)	9	17.44	4-8
4.	Asif Iqbal (Pak)	9	17.44	4-56
5.	M.A. Holding (WI)	8	13.25	4-33
6.	Sikander Bakht (Pak)	8	13.50	3-32
7.	C.E.H. Croft (WI)	8	17.50	3-29
8.	J. Garner (WI)	8	21.50	5-38
9.	R.D.G. Willis (Eng)	7	15.57	4-11
10.	Majid J. Khan (Pak)	7	16.71	3-27

Individual Bowling Performances

	Player	Analysis	
1.	A.G. Hurst (Aus)	5-21	vs Canada
2.	J. Garner (WI)	5-38	vs England (final)
3.	C.M. Old (Eng)	4-8	vs Canada
4.	R.D.G. Willis (Eng)	4-11	vs Canada
5.	M. Hendrick (Eng)	4-15	vs Pakistan
6.	M.A. Holding (WI)	4-33	vs India
7.	Asif Iqbal (Pak)	4-56	vs West Indies (semi-final)
8.	B.J. McKechnie (NZ)	3-24	vs India
9.	B.J. McKechnie (NZ)	3-25	vs Sri Lanka
10.	Sarfraz Nawaz (Pak)	3-26	vs Canada

1983

Leading Run Scorers

	Player	Runs	Highest Score	Average
1.	D.I. Gower (Eng)	384	138	76.80
2.	I.V. A. Richards (WI)	367	119	73.40
3.	G.W. Flower (Eng)	360	81*	72.00
4.	Zaheer Abbas (Pak)	313	103*	62.60
5.	Kapil Dev (Ind)	303	175*	60.60
6.	Imran Khan (Pak)	283	102*	70.75
7.	A.J. Lamb (Eng)	278	102	69.50
8.	H.A. Gomes (WI)	258	78	64.50
9.	G.C. Greenidge (WI)	250	105*	41.66
10.	D.L. Haynes (WI)	240	88*	34.28
11.	Yashpal Sharma (Ind)	240	89	34.28

Individual Batting Performances

	Player	Score	
1.	Kapil Dev (Ind)	175*	vs Zimbabwe
2.	D.I. Gower (Eng)	130	vs Sri Lanka
3.	I.V.A. Richards (WI)	119	vs India
4.	T.M. Chappell (Aus)	110	vs India
5.	C.G. Greenidge (WI)	105*	vs Zimbabwe
6.	Zaheer Abbas (Pak)	103*	vs New Zealand
7.	Imran Khan (Pak)	102*	vs Sri Lanka
8.	A.J. Lamb (Eng)	102	vs New Zealand
9.	M.D. Crowe (NZ)	97	vs England
10.	I.V.A. Richards	95*	vs Australia

Team Batting Performances

	Team	Score	
1.	Pakistan	5-338	vs Sri Lanka
2.	England	9-333	vs Sri Lanka
3.	England	6-322	vs New Zealand
4.	Australia	9-320	vs India
5.	Sri Lanka	9-288	vs Pakistan
6.	Sri Lanka	10-286	vs England
7.	West Indies	9-282	vs India
8.	West Indies	9-276	vs Australia
9.	Australia	6-273	vs West Indies
10.	Australia	7-272	vs Zimbabwe

Leading Wicket Takers

	Player	Wickets	Average	Best Bowling
1.	R.M.H. Binny (Ind)	18	18.66	4–29
2.	A.L.F. de Mel (SL)	17	15.59	5–32
3.	Madan Lal (Ind)	17	17.76	4–20
4.	R.J. Hadlee (NZ)	14	12.86	5–25
5.	V.J. Marks (Eng)	13	18.92	5–39
6.	M.D. Marshall (WI)	12	14.58	3–28
7.	M. A. Holding (WI)	12	19.58	3–40
8.	Kapil Dev (Ind)	12	20.41	5–43
9.	R.G.D. Willis (Eng)	11	18.73	4–41
10.	A.M.E. Roberts (WI)	11	21.63	3–32

Individual Bowling Performances

	Player	Analysis	
1.	W.W. Davis (WI)	7–51	vs Australia
2.	K.H. Macleay (Aus)	6–39	vs India
3.	R.J. Hadlee (NZ)	5–25	vs Sri Lanka
4.	A.L.F. de Mel (SL)	5–32	vs Pakistan
5.	A.L.F. de Mel (SL)	5–32	vs New Zealand
6.	V.J. Marks (Eng)	5–39	vs Sri Lanka
7.	Kapil Dev (Ind)	5–43	vs Australia
8.	Abdul Qadir (Pak)	5–44	vs Sri Lanka
9.	S. Madan Lal (Ind)	4–20	vs Australia
10.	Abdul Qadir (Pak)	4–21	vs New Zealand

1987

Leading Run Scorers

	Player	Runs	Highest Score	Average
1.	G.A. Gooch (Eng)	471	115	58.88
2.	D.C. Boon (Aus)	447	93	55.88
3.	G.R. Marsh (Aus)	428	126*	61.14
4.	I.V.A. Richards (WI)	391	181	65.17
5.	M.W. Gatting (Eng)	354	60	50.57
6.	Rameez Raja (Pak)	349	113	49.86
7.	Salim Malik (Pak)	323	100	53.83
8.	D.M. Jones (Aus)	314	58*	44.86
9.	S.M. Gavaskar (Ind)	300	103*	50.00
10.	A.J. Lamb (Eng)	299	76	59.80

Individual Batting Performances

	Player	Score	
1.	I.V.A. Richards (WI)	181	vs Sri Lanka
2.	D.L. Houghton (Zim)	141	vs New Zealand
3.	G.R. Marsh (Aus)	126*	vs New Zealand
4.	G.A. Gooch (Eng)	115	vs India (semi-final)
5.	Rameez Raja (Pak)	113	vs England
6.	R.B. Richardson (WI)	110	vs Pakistan
7.	G.R. Marsh (Aus)	110	vs India
8.	D.L. Haynes (WI)	105	vs Sri Lanka
9.	S.M. Gavaskar (Ind)	103*	vs New Zealand
10.	Javed Miandad (Pak)	103	vs Sri Lanka

Team Batting Performances

	Team	Score	
1.	West Indies	4–360	vs Sri Lanka
2.	India	7–297	vs Sri Lanka
3.	England	4–296	vs Sri Lanka
4.	India	6–289	vs Australia
5.	Australia	6–270	vs India
6.	England	5–269	vs West Indies
7.	India	10–269	vs Australia
8.	Pakistan	6–267	vs Sri Lanka
9.	Australia	8–267	vs Pakistan (semi-final)
10.	Australia	5–266	vs Zimbabwe

Leading Wicket Takers

	Player	Wickets	Average	Best Bowling
1.	C.J. McDermott (Aus)	18	18.94	5–44
2.	Imran Khan (Pak)	17	13.06	4–37
3.	B.P. Patterson (WI)	14	18.07	3–31
4.	Maninder Singh (Ind)	14	20.00	3–21
5.	E.E. Hemmings (Eng)	13	21.08	4–52
6.	Abdul Qadir (Pak)	12	20.17	4–31
7.	P.A.J. DeFreitas (Eng)	12	23.58	3–28
8.	S.R. Waugh (Aus)	11	26.18	2–36
9.	J.R. Ratnayake (SL)	10	31.30	3–41
10.	C.A. Walsh (WI)	9	25.44	4–40

Individual Bowling Performances

	Player	Analysis	
1.	C.J. McDermott (Aus)	5–44	vs Pakistan (semi-final)
2.	M. Prabhakar (Ind)	4–19	vs New Zealand
3.	Abdul Qadir (Pak)	4–31	vs England
4.	Imran Khan (Pak)	4–37	vs England
5.	Imran Khan (Pak)	4–37	vs West Indies
6.	S.P. O'Donnell (Aus)	4–39	vs Zimbabwe
7.	C.A. Walsh (WI)	4–40	vs Pakistan
8.	E.E. Hemmings (Eng)	4–52	vs India
9.	C.J. McDermott (Aus)	4–56	vs India
10.	M. Azharuddin (Ind)	3–19	vs Australia

1992

Leading Run Scorers

	Player	Runs	Highest Score	Average
1.	M.D. Crowe (NZ)	456	100*	114.00
2.	Javed Miandad (Pak)	437	89	62.43
3.	P.N. Kirsten (SA)	410	90	68.33

4.	D.C. Boon (Aus)	368	100	52.57
5.	Rameez Raja (Pak)	349	119*	58.17
6.	B.C. Lara (WI)	333	88	47.57
7.	M. Azharuddin (Ind)	332	93	47.43
8.	Aamir Sohail (Pak)	326	114	32.60
9.	A.H. Jones (NZ)	322	78	46.00
10.	M.J. Greatbatch (NZ)	313	73	44.71
11.	K.C. Wessels (SA)	313	85	44.71

Individual Batting Performances

	Player	Score	
1.	Rameez Raja (Pak)	119*	vs New Zealand
2.	A. Flower (Zim)	115*	vs Sri Lanka
3.	Aamir Sohail (Pak)	114	vs Zimbabwe
4.	P.V. Simmons (WI)	110	vs Sri Lanka
5.	Rameez Raja (Pak)	102*	vs West Indies
6.	M.D. Crowe (NZ)	100*	vs Australia
7.	D.C. Boon (Aus)	100	vs New Zealand
8.	D.C. Boon (Aus)	100	vs West Indies
9.	D.L. Haynes (WI)	93*	vs Pakistan
10.	M. Azharuddin (Ind)	93	vs Australia

Team Batting Performances

	Team	Score	
1.	Sri Lanka	7-313	vs Zimbabwe
2.	Zimbabwe	4-312	vs Sri Lanka
3.	England	6-280	vs Sri Lanka
4.	West Indies	8-268	vs Sri Lanka
5.	Australia	6-265	vs Zimbabwe
6.	Pakistan	6-264	vs New Zealand (semi-final)
7.	West Indies	8-264	vs Zimbabwe
8.	New Zealand	7-262	vs Pakistan
9.	Pakistan	4-254	vs Zimbabwe
10.	England	6-252	vs South Africa (semi-final)

Leading Wicket Takers

	Player	Wickets	Average	Best Bowling
1.	Wasim Akram (Pak)	18	18.78	4-32
2.	I.T. Botham (Eng)	16	19.13	4-31
3.	Mushtaq Ahmed (Pak)	16	19.44	3-41
4.	C.Z. Harris (NZ)	16	21.38	3-15
5.	E.A. Brandes (Zim)	14	25.36	4-21
6.	A.A.A. Donald (SA)	13	25.31	3-34
7.	M. Prabhakar (Ind)	12	20.42	3-41
8.	A.C. Cummins (WI)	12	20.50	4-33
9.	W. Watson (NZ)	12	25.80	3-37
10.	B.M. McMillan (SA)	11	27.82	3-30

Individual Bowling Performances

	Player	Analysis	
1.	M.W. Pringle (SA)	4-11	vs West Indies
2.	E.A. Brandes (Zim)	4-21	vs England
3.	C.C. Lewis (Eng)	4-30	vs Sri Lanka

4.	I.T. Botham (Eng)	4-31		vs Australia
5.	Wasim Akram (Pak)	4-32		vs New Zealand
6.	A.C. Cummins (WI)	4-33		vs India
7.	M.R. Whitney (Aus)	4-34		vs West Indies
8.	U.C. Hathurusinghe (SL)	4-57		vs West Indies
9.	D.R. Pringle (Eng)	3-8		vs Pakistan
10.	C.Z. Harris (NZ)	3-15		vs Zimbabwe

1996

Leading Run Scorers

	Player	Runs	Highest Score	Average
1.	S.R. Tendulkar (Ind)	523	137	87.17
2.	M.E. Waugh (Aus)	484	130	80.67
3.	P.A. de Silva (SL)	448	145	89.60
4.	G. Kirsten (SA)	391	188*	78.20
5.	Saeed Anwar (Pak)	329	83*	82.25
6.	A.P. Gurusinha (SL)	307	87	51.17
7.	W.J. Cronje (SA)	276	78	55.20
8.	A.C. Hudson (SA)	275	161	68.75
9.	Aamir Sohail (Pak)	272	111	45.33
10.	B.C. Lara (WI)	269	111	53.80

Individual Batting Performances

	Player	Score	
1.	G. Kirsten (SA)	188*	vs UAE
2.	A.C. Hudson (SA)	161	vs Holland
3.	P.A. de Silva (SL)	145	vs Kenya
4.	S.R. Tendulkar (Ind)	137	vs Sri Lanka
5.	M.E. Waugh (Aus)	130	vs Kenya
6.	C.Z. Harris (NZ)	130	vs Australia
7.	S.R. Tendulkar (Ind)	127*	vs Kenya
8.	M.E. Waugh (Aus)	126	vs India
9.	Aamir Sohail (Pak)	111	vs South Africa
10.	B.C. Lara (WI)	111	vs South Africa

Team Batting Performances

	Team	Score	
1.	Sri Lanka	5-398	vs Kenya
2.	South Africa	3-328	vs Holland
3.	South Africa	2-321	vs UAE
4.	New Zealand	8-307	vs Holland
5.	Australia	7-304	vs Kenya
6.	Australia	4-289	vs New Zealand
7.	India	8-287	vs Pakistan
8.	New Zealand	9-286	vs Australia
9.	Pakistan	5-281	vs New Zealand
10.	England	4-279	vs Holland

Leading Wicket Takers

	Player	Wickets	Average	Best Bowling
1.	A.R. Kumble (Ind)	15	18.73	3-29
2.	Waqar Younis (Pak)	13	19.46	4-26

3.	P.A. Strang (Zim)	12	16.00	5–21
4.	R.A. Harper (WI)	12	18.25	4–47
5.	D.W. Fleming (Aus)	12	18.42	5–36
6.	S.K. Warne (Aus)	12	21.92	4–34
7.	C.E.L. Ambrose (WI)	10	17.00	3–28
8.	Mushtaq Ahmed (Pak)	10	23.80	3–16
9.	R.W. Ali (KEN)	9	21.11	3–17
10.	A.A.A. Donald (SA)	8	15.75	3–21

Individual Bowling Performances

	Player	Analysis	
1.	P.A. Strang (Zim)	5–21	vs Kenya
2.	Shaukat Dukanwala (UAE)	5–29	vs Holland
3.	D.W. Fleming (Aus)	5–36	vs India
4.	Waqar Younis (Pak)	4–26	vs Holland
5.	S.K. Warne (Aus)	4–34	vs Zimbabwe
6.	S.K. Warne (Aus)	4–36	vs West Indies (semi-final)
7.	P.A. Strang (Zim)	4–40	vs West Indies
8.	R.A. Harper (WI)	4–47	vs South Africa
9.	B. M. McMillan (SA)	3–11	vs UAE
10.	S.T. Jayasuriya (SL)	3–12	vs India (semi-final)

1999

Leading Run Scorers

	Player	Runs	Highest Score	Average
1.	R.S. Dravid (Ind)	461	145	65.85
2.	S.R. Waugh (Aus)	398	120*	79.60
3.	S.C. Ganguly (Ind)	379	183	54.14
4.	M.E. Waugh (Aus)	375	104	41.66
5.	Saeed Anwar (Pak)	368	113*	40.88
6.	N.C. Johnson (Zim)	367	132*	52.42
7.	R.T. Ponting (Aus)	354	69	39.33
8.	H.H.H. Gibbs (SA)	341	101	37.88
9.	R.G. Twose (NZ)	318	80*	79.50
10.	J.H. Kallis (SA)	312	96	52.00

Individual Batting Performances

	Player	Score	
1.	S.C. Ganguly (Ind)	183	vs Sri Lanka
2.	R.S. Dravid (Ind)	145	vs Sri Lanka
3.	S.R. Tendulkar (Ind)	140*	vs Kenya
4.	N.C. Johnson (Zim)	132*	vs Australia
5.	S.R. Waugh (Aus)	120*	vs South Africa
6.	Saeed Anwar (Pak)	113*	vs New Zealand (semi-final)
7.	R.S. Dravid (Ind)	104*	vs Kenya
8.	M.E. Waugh (Aus)	104	vs Zimbabwe
9.	Saeed Anwar (Pak)	103	vs Zimbabwe
10.	H.H.H. Gibbs (SA)	101	vs Australia

Team Batting Performances

	Team	Score	
1.	India	6–373	vs Sri Lanka
2.	India	2–329	vs Kenya
3.	Australia	4–303	vs Zimbabwe
4.	South Africa	5–287	vs New Zealand
5.	Australia	6–282	vs India
6.	Pakistan	8–275	vs Australia
7.	Sri Lanka	8–275	vs Kenya
8.	Australia	5–272	vs South Africa
9.	South Africa	7–271	vs Australia
10.	Pakistan	9–271	vs Zimbabwe

Leading Wicket Takers

	Player	Wickets	Average	Best Bowling
1.	G.I. Allot (NZ)	20	16.25	4–37
2.	S.K. Warne (Aus)	20	18.05	4–29
3.	G.D. McGrath (Aus)	18	20.38	5–14
4.	L. Klusener (SA)	17	20.58	5–21
5.	Saqlain Mushtaq (Pak)	17	22.29	5–35
6.	A.A.A. Donald (SA)	16	20.31	4–17
7.	Shoaib Akhtar (Pak)	16	24.50	3–11
8.	Wasim Akram (Pak)	15	22.80	4–40
9.	D.W. Fleming (Aus)	14	25.85	3–57
10.	Abdur Razzaq (Pak)	13	23.15	3–24

Individual Bowling Performances

	Player	Analysis	
1.	G.D. McGrath (Aus)	5–14	vs West Indies
2.	L. Klusener (SA)	5–21	vs Kenya
3.	B.K.B.K.V. Prasad (Ind)	5–27	vs Pakistan
4.	R.R. Singh (Ind)	5–31	vs Sri Lanka
5.	Saqlain Mushtaq (Pak)	5–35	vs Bangladesh
6.	C.Z. Harris (NZ)	4–7	vs Scotland
7.	A.A.A. Donald (SA)	4–17	vs England
8.	C.A. Walsh (WI)	4–25	vs Bangladesh
9.	S.K. Warne (Aus)	4–29	vs South Africa (semi-final)
10.	S.K. Warne (Aus)	4–33	vs Pakistan (final)

World Cup Records

Individual Batting Performances

	Player	Score		Year
1.	G. Kirsten (SA)	188*	vs UAE	1996
2.	S.C. Ganguly (Ind)	183	vs Sri Lanka	1999
3.	I.V.A. Richards (WI)	181	vs Sri Lanka	1987
4.	Kapil Dev (Ind)	175*	vs Zimbabwe	1983
5.	G.M. Turner (NZ)	171*	vs East Afica	1975
6.	A.C. Hudson (SA)	161	vs Holland	1996
7.	P.A. de Silva (SL)	145	vs Kenya	1996
8.	R.S. Dravid (Ind)	145	vs Sri Lanka	1999
9.	D.L. Houghton (Zim)	142	vs New Zealand	1987
10.	S.R. Tendulkar (Ind)	140*	vs Kenya	1999

Individual Bowling Performances

	Player	Analysis		Year
1.	W.W. Davis (WI)	7–51	vs Australia	1983
2.	G.J. Gilmour (Aus)	6–14	vs England (semi-final)	1975
3.	K.H. Macleay (Aus)	6–39	vs India	1983
4.	G.D. McGrath (Aus)	5–14	vs West Indies	1999
5.	L. Klusener (SA)	5–21	vs Kenya	1999
6.	A.G. Hurst (Aus)	5–21	vs Canada	1979
7.	P.A. Strang (Zim)	5–21	vs Kenya	1996
8.	R.J. Hadlee (NZ)	5–25	vs Sri Lanka	1983
9.	B.K.B.K.V. Prasad (Ind)	5–27	vs Pakistan	1999
10.	S. Dukanwala (UAE)	5–29	vs Holland	1996

Records for all World Cups 1975–1999

Highest Team Totals

	Team	Score		Year
1.	Sri Lanka	5–398	vs Kenya	1996
2.	India	6–373	vs Sri Lanka	1999
3.	West Indies	4–360	vs Sri Lanka	1987
4.	Pakistan	5–338	vs Sri Lanka	1983
5.	England	4–334	vs India	1975

Lowest Team Totals

	Team	Score		Year
1.	Canada	45	vs England	1979
2.	Scotland	68	vs West Indies	1999
3.	Pakistan	74	vs England	1992
4.	Sri Lanka	86	vs West Indies	1975
5.	England	93	vs Australia	1975

Highest Run Scorers

	Player	Runs	Matches
1.	Javed Miandad (Pak)	1083	33
2.	S.R. Tendulkar (Ind)	1059	22
3.	I.V.A. Richards (WI)	1013	23
4.	S.R. Waugh (Aus)	978	32
5.	A. Ranatunga (SL)	969	30
6.	M.E. Waugh (Aus)	967	21
7.	G.A. Gooch (Eng)	897	21
8.	M.D. Crowe (NZ)	880	21
9.	D.L. Haynes (WI)	854	25
10.	M. Azharuddin (Ind)	826	30

Highest Wicket Takers

	Player	Wickets	Matches
1.	Wasim Akram (Pak)	42	31
2.	A.A.A. Donald (SA)	37	22
3.	Imran Khan (Pak)	34	26
4.	I.T. Botham (Eng)	30	22
5.	C.Z. Harris (NZ)	30	22
6.	P.A.J. DeFreitas (Eng)	29	22
7.	J. Srinath (Ind)	28	23
8.	Kapil Dev (Ind)	26	26
9.	C.A. Walsh (WI)	27	17
10.	C.J. McDermott (Aus)	27	17

Highest Partnerships for Each Wicket

1.	194	Saeed Anwar, Wajahatullah Wasti	Pak v. NZ	1999
2.	318	S.C. Ganguly, R.S. Dravid	Ind v. SL	1999
3.	237*	R.S. Dravid, S.R. Tendulkar	Ind v. Ken	1999
4.	168	L.K. Germon, C.Z. Harris	NZ v. Aus	1996
5.	148	R.G. Twose, C.L. Cairns	NZ v. Aus	1999
6.	161	M.O. Odumbe, A.V. Vadher	Ken v. SL	1999
7.	82	S.P Fleming, C.Z. Harris	NZ v. Pak	1999
8.	117	D.L. Houghton, I.P. Butchart	Zim v. NZ	1987
9.	126*	Kapil Dev, S.M.H. Kirmani	Ind v. Zim	1983
10.	71	A.M.E. Roberts, J. Garner	WI v. Ind	1983

Leading Fielders (excluding wicketkeepers)

	Player	Catches	Matches
1.	A. Kumble (Ind)	13	14
2.	C.H Lloyd (WI)	12	17
3.	C.L. Cairns (NZ)	12	19
4.	G.A. Hick (Eng)	12	20
5.	D.L. Haynes (WI)	12	25

Leading Wicketkeepers

	Player	Dismissals	Matches
1.	Moin Khan (Pak)	29	19
2.	Wasim Bari (Pak)	22	14
3.	I.A. Healy (Aus)	21	14
4.	J. Dujon (WI)	20	14
5.	R.W. Marsh (Aus)	18	11

BIBLIOGRAPHY

Books

Geoff Armstrong and Mark Gately, *The People's Game*, Ironbark, Sydney 1994
Trevor Bailey (ed.), *World of Cricket 1980*, Queen Anne Press, London 1980
Simon Barnes, Phil Edmonds *A Singular Man*, Kingswood Press, London 1986
Scyld Berry, *A Cricket Odyssey*, Pavilion Books, London 1988
Dickie Bird, *That's Out!*, Arthur Barker, London 1985
Henry Blofeld, *My Dear Old Thing*, Stanley Paul, London 1988
Allan Border, *An Autobiography*, Methuen, Sydney 1986
Mihir Bose, *All in a Day*, Robin Clark, London 1983
—— *A History of Indian Cricket*, Andre Deutsch, London 1990
Ian Botham, *Botham: My Biography*, Collins Willow, London 1994
Mike Brearley, *The Art of Captaincy*, Hodder and Stoughton, London 1985
Ian Chappell, *Chappelli: The Cutting Edge*, Swan Publishing, Perth 1992
Denis Compton, *Compton On Cricketers Past and Present*, Cassell, London 1980
John Crace, *Wasim and Waqar: Imran's Inheritors*, Boxtree, London 1992
Martin Crowe, *Out on a Limb*, Reed, Auckland 1995
Mike Denness, *I Declare*, Arthur Barker, London 1977
Kapil Dev, *By God's Decree*, Harper and Row, Sydney 1985
—— *Kapil, The Autobiography of Kapil Dev*, Sidgwick and Jackson, London 1987
Bill Frindall and Victor H. Isaacs, *The Wisden Book of One Day International Cricket 1971–1985*, John Wisden & Co., London 1985
Mike Gatting, *Leading From the Front*, Queen Anne Press, London 1988
Graham Gooch and Frank Keating, *My Autobiography*, Collins Willow, London 1995
Gordon Greenidge, *The Man in the Middle*, David and Charles, Newton Abbot 1980
Edward Griffiths, *Kepler: The Biography*, Pelham Books, London 1994
Chris Harte, *A History of Australian Cricket*, Andre Deutsch, London 1993
Gideon Haigh, *The Cricket War*, Text, Melbourne 1993
Eddie Hemmings, *Coming of Age*, Stanley Paul, London 1991
Graeme Hick, *My Early Life*, Macmillan, London 1991
Derek Hodgson (ed.), *Cricket World Cup 83*, Unwin Paperbacks, London 1983
David Hookes, *Hookesy*, ABC Books, Sydney 1993
Imran Khan, *Imran*, Pelham Books, London 1983
—— *All Round View*, Chatto and Windus, London 1988
Martin Johnson and Henry Blofeld, *The Independent World Cup Cricket '87*, The Kingswood Press, London 1987
Jim Laker, *One Day Cricket*, Batsford, London 1977
Allan Lamb and Peter Smith, *Lamb's Tales*, George Allen and Unwin, London 1985

David Lemmon (ed.), *Pelham Cricket Year—First Edition*, Pelham Books, London 1979
David Lemmon, *Great One-Day Matches*, Pelham Books, London 1982
—— *Benson and Hedges Cricket Year*, Pelham Books, London 1983
Tony Lewis, *A Summer of Cricket*, Pelham Cricket, London 1976
Clive Lloyd, *Living For Cricket*, Stanley Paul, London 1980
Trevor McDonald, *Clive Lloyd, Granada*, London 1985
Mike Marqusee, *War Minus the Shooting*, William Heinemann, London 1996
Rod Marsh, *Gloves Sweat and Tears*, Penguin Books, Melbourne 1984
Malcolm Marshall, *Marshall Arts*, Queen Anne Press, London 1987
Bob Simpson, *The Reasons Why*, Harper Sports, Sydney 1996
Patrick Smith (ed.), *The Age World Cup Cricket, 1992*, Five Mile Press, Melbourne 1992
Ivo Tennant, *Imran Khan*, H.F. and G. Witherby, London 1994
Steve Waugh, *Steve Waugh's World Cup Diary*, Harper Sports, Sydney 1996

Newspapers, Journals and Periodicals

Cricketer, World Cup Special, 1975
Daily Telegraph
The Cricketer, July and August 1975, August 1983, November and December 1987, April and May 1992, March and April 1996
The Times
Wisden Cricket Monthly, July and August 1979, August 1983, December 1987, April and May 1992, March and April 1996

Yearbooks

The ABC Australian Cricket Almanac, 1992
The Australian Cricket Almanac, 1996
Wisden Cricketer's Almanack, 1976, 1980, 1984, 1988, 1993, 1997

Internet

Crick Info—The Home of Cricket on the Internet

Index

347

349